A HISTORY OF

Why did the Anatolians remain illiterate for so long, although surrounded by people using script? Why and how did they eventually adopt the cuneiform writing system and why did they still invent a second, hieroglyphic script of their own? What did and didn't they write down and what role did Hittite literature, the oldest known literature in any Indo-European language, play? These and many other questions on scribal culture are addressed in this first, comprehensive book on writing, reading, script usage, and literacy in the Hittite kingdom (ca. 1650–1200 BC). It describes the rise and fall of literacy and literature in Hittite Anatolia in the wider context of its political, economic, and intellectual history.

THEO VAN DEN HOUT is Arthur and Joann Rasmussen Professor of Hittite and Anatolian Languages in the Department of Near Eastern Languages and Civilizations at The Oriental Institute of the University of Chicago. He is the Chief Editor of the Chicago Hittite Dictionary project, corresponding member of the Royal Dutch Academy of Arts and Sciences, a 2016 Guggenheim Fellow, Senior Fellow at the Institute for the Study of the Ancient World in New York, and the author of various books.

A HISTORY OF HITTITE LITERACY

Writing and Reading in Late Bronze-Age Anatolia (1650–1200 BC)

THEO VAN DEN HOUT

University of Chicago

CAMBRIDGE
UNIVERSITY PRESS

CAMBRIDGE
UNIVERSITY PRESS

University Printing House, Cambridge CB2 8BS, United Kingdom

One Liberty Plaza, 20th Floor, New York, NY 10006, USA

477 Williamstown Road, Port Melbourne, VIC 3207, Australia

314-321, 3rd Floor, Plot 3, Splendor Forum, Jasola District Centre, New Delhi - 110025, India

103 Penang Road, #05-06/07, Visioncrest Commercial, Singapore 238467

Cambridge University Press is part of the University of Cambridge.

It furthers the University's mission by disseminating knowledge in the pursuit of education, learning and research at the highest international levels of excellence.

www.cambridge.org
Information on this title: www.cambridge.org/9781108816496
DOI: 10.1017/9781108860161

First published 2020
First paperback edition 2022

A catalogue record for this publication is available from the British Library

ISBN 978-1-108-49488-5 Hardback
ISBN 978-1-108-81649-6 Paperback

voor Charlotte, Philip en Julia

Contents

List of Figures — *page* xi
List of Tables — xv
Preface and Acknowledgments — xvii
Map — xxi
Timeline and Hittite Kings — xxii
Sigla and Abbreviations — xxiv

1. Introduction — 1
   1.1. Anatolia and Literacy — 1
   1.2. Defining the Hittites — 6
   1.3. A Note on the Hittite Economy — 9
   1.4. Modern Hittite Scholarship and Our Sources — 11
   1.5. The Nature of Our Evidence and How We Use It — 13
   1.6. Doing Things with Tablets — 17
   1.7. A Note on Chronology and Dating — 20
   1.8. Some Final Remarks — 21
2. Writing and Literacy among the Anatolians in the Old Assyrian Period — 24
   2.1. The Beginnings of Writing in Anatolia — 24
   2.2. Anitta and the First Unified Anatolian Kingdom — 27
   2.3. Central Anatolia: An Illiterate Society in the Old Assyrian Period — 34
3. From Kanesh to Hattusa — 38
   3.1. The End of Anitta and the Rise of Hattusa — 38
   3.2. The Origins of the Hittite Cuneiform — 39
   3.3. The Case for a Syrian Origin — 44
   3.4. A Closer Look at the Alalah Ductus — 47
   3.5. Conclusion — 50
   3.6. Appendix: A Brief Introduction to Hittite Cuneiform — 51

4. First Writing in Hattusa 57
4.1. From Mursili I to Telipinu 57
4.2. First Writing in Hattusa 58
4.3. The Allure of Akkadian 63

5. Literacy and Literature in the Old Kingdom until 1500 BC 70
5.1. Hatti-Land after Telipinu 70
5.2. Literacy and Literature of the Old Kingdom 71
5.3. Looking for Writing in the Old Kingdom 73
5.4. Scribes in the Old Kingdom 77
5.5. Evidence for Record Management 81
5.6. The Character of the Earliest Hittite Compositions 83
5.7. The Hittite Laws 87
5.8. Law and Orality 92
5.9. The Corpus of Old Hittite Cult Rituals 94
5.10. Socio-Economic, Legal, and Bookkeeping Texts? 97
5.11. The Early Hittite Kingdom as an Oral and Aural Society 98

6. The Emergence of Writing in Hittite 101
6.1. The Second Half of the Sixteenth Century BC as an Anatolian Renaissance 101
6.2. Adapting to Hittite 103
6.3. The Charters and the Introduction of Writing in Hittite 110
6.4. A Hittite Literature in the Vernacular 113

7. A Second Script 120
7.1. The Anatolian Hieroglyphs 120
7.2. The Iconographic Repertoire and its Development 121
7.3. The Anatolian Hieroglyphs as a Writing System 129
7.4. Conclusion 133
7.5. Appendix: A Brief Introduction to Anatolian Hieroglyphs 134

8. The New Kingdom Cuneiform Corpus 139
8.1. The New Kingdom Period 139
8.2. The Cuneiform Corpus 142
8.3. Historical Prose and Related Texts Using the Past 144
8.4. Treaties, Instructions, Letters, and Depositions 148
8.5. Religious Texts 152
8.6. Scholarly Texts 157
8.7. Bookkeeping and Socio-Economic and Legal Administration 165
8.8. Cuneiform Text Corpora from Central Anatolia Outside Hattusa 169
8.9. Conclusion 171

9. The New Kingdom Hieroglyphic Corpus 173
9.1. Writing for the World 173
9.2. Seals 173

9.3. Inscriptions Erected in the Public Sphere 174
9.4. Graffiti and Small Inscriptions on Objects 176
9.5. Conclusion 179

10. The Wooden Writing Boards 184
10.1. Problems and Evidence 184
10.2. GIŠ.ḪUR 188
10.3. (GIŠ.ḪUR)*ḫatiwi(ya)-* 195
10.4. GIŠ(.ḪUR)*k/gaštarḫait/da* 196
10.5. (GIŠ(.ḪUR))GUL-*zattar* 197
10.6. (GIŠ)*k/gurt/da-* 204
10.7. (GIŠ.ḪUR)*parzaki(š)* 206
10.8. GIŠ.ḪUR*tuppi?* 206
10.9. GIŠ*LĒʾU* 207
10.10. Conclusion on the Words So Far Discussed 209
10.11. Other Evidence for Wooden Tablets 211

11. The Seal Impressions of the Westbau and Building D, and the Wooden Tablets 218
11.1. The Collections of Seal Impressions in Hattusa 218
11.2. The Bullae and the Wooden Tablets: Previous Interpretations 222
11.3. Problems with the Traditional View 225
11.4. An Alternative Interpretation 227
11.5. Conclusion 232

12. In the Hittite Chancellery and Tablet Collections 234
12.1. The Reign of Mursili II 234
12.2. The Hittite Cuneiform Corpus from an Institutional Perspective 236
12.3. Writing: Drafting New Documents 244
12.4. Writing: Copying and Editing 246
12.5. The Editing Process 249
12.6. Writing: Other Types of Documents 256
12.7. Reading 259
12.8. Record Management 263
12.9. Tablet Storage in Hattusa: Can We Detect a System? 265
12.10. Appendix: The Editors at Work 276

13. Scribes and Scholars 287
13.1. The Last Hundred Years 287
13.2. Who Were the Scribes? 292
13.3. Scribes and Wood-Scribes 294
13.4. The Societal Status of Scribes 297
13.5. Scribes and Seal Owners 301
13.6. Scribes Elsewhere in the Cuneiform Corpus 305
13.7. Elite Scribes 305
13.8. Chief Scribes 311

13.9. Apprentices 313
13.10. The Scribal Organization 315
13.11. The Average Scribe 319
13.12. Scholars at the Hittite Court 322
13.13. The *scriba doctus* 325
13.14. The Tablet Inventories as Scholarly Corpora 331
13.15. Memorization as Part of Scholarly Life? 337

14. Excursus: Scribes on Seals? The Hieroglyphic Sign L.326 341
14.1. Introduction 341
14.2. An Alternative Hypothesis 356
14.3. The Shape of L.326 and L.326t 369
14.4. Conclusions 371

15. The End and Looking Back 375
15.1. The Vanishing of the Hittite Kingdom 375
15.2. Looking Back 377

Bibliography 381
Index Locorum 419
General Index 424

Figures

2.1	Small tablet with Anitta's name (obv. 1) from Alişar Höyük (from Gelb 1935: Pl. I).	*page* 29
3.1	Old Assyrian tablet (from Veenhof 2003 Fig. 4; courtesy K.R. Veenhof).	41
3.2	Letter of Hattusili I to Tunip-Tessub (obv., from Salvini 1994; courtesy M. Salvini).	43
4.1	Inscription on ax of King Ammuna (from Salvini 1993: 85; courtesy M. Salvini).	60
4.2	Charter of King Hantili II (from Rüster 1993:66) as if "folded out" along the lower edge (*u. Rd.*).	62
6.1	Tombstone at Chicago's Graceland Cemetery (photo author).	104
6.2	Sequence of signs in KBo 22.1 obv. 13 (drawing author).	107
7.1	Relief at Fraktin portraying King Hattusili III (ca. 1267–1240 BC; photo courtesy JoAnn Scurlock) libating before a deity (left) with an altar between them. The king is identified by the "caption" to the left of his head. The sign closest to his head is MAGNUS.REX with the REX sign being identical to the pointed helmet the king himself is wearing.	121
7.2a and b	Seals from Konya-Karahöyük (a from Alp 1994:173 Abb. 59, and b from Alp 1994: 220 Abb. 171).	123
7.3	Hattusili seal impression (from Boehmer/Güterbock 1987: 39 Abb. 25c; copyright Archive of the Boğazköy Expedition, Deutsches Archäologisches Institut Berlin).	125
7.4	Seal impression of Tuthaliya I (from Otten 2000: Abb. 23).	126
7.5	Seal impression with Satanduhepa found at Maşat Höyük (from Alp 1991: Abb. 2).	128

8.1 Livermodel 59/k = KBo 7.7 (from de Vos 2013; copyright Akademie der Wissenschaften und der Literatur, Mainz). 161
9.1 Hieroglyphic signs L.24 (LIS) and L.344 (CONTRACTUS). 174
9.2 Drawing of a lion (KUB 28.4; copyright Staatliche Museen zu Berlin – Vorderasiatisches Museum, Foto: BoFN 00924). 178
9.3 Drawing of a god(?) (KUB 20.76; copyright Staatliche Museen zu Berlin – Vorderasiatisches Museum, Foto: BoFN 00814). 179
9.4 Drawing of two heads (KUB 38.3; copyright Staatliche Museen zu Berlin – Vorderasiatisches Museum, Foto: BoFN 00993). 179
9.5 Hieroglyphic signs on tablet KBo 13.62 (with cuneiform upside down!; copyright Akademie der Wissenschaften und der Literatur, Mainz). 180
9.6 Bulla with various hieroglyphs drawn on its side (from Güterbock 1942: Tafel VIII 238). 180
10.1 Line drawing of Ulu Burun wooden diptych (drawing Netia Piercy apud Payton 1991: 102 Fig. 2; copyright British Institute at Ankara). The diagonal scratches in the wood served to make the wax adhere better to the wooden surface. 186
10.2a-c Modern replica of a Roman tabula (photos author). 187
10.3 Some possible styli found at Boğazköy (from Boehmer 1972: Pl. xli nos. 1208–1209; copyright Archive of the Boğazköy Expedition, Deutsches Archäologisches Institut Berlin). 212
10.4 Seal SBo 2.130 with the cursive *ma*-sign (ና but facing right) on top (from Güterbock 1942: 72). 213
10.5 Public scribe, Istanbul 1928 (from *National Geographic* January 1929). 215
11.1 Position of the *Westbau* on the slope (from Herbordt 2005: 9; copyright Archive of the Boğazköy Expedition, Deutsches Archäologisches Institut Berlin). 219
11.2 Location of the sealings ("Siegel") found in Bldg. D (from Bittel 1950–1951; copyright Archive of the Boğazköy Expedition, Deutsches Archäologisches Institut Berlin). 221

12.1 KUB 14.13 column i end (from KUB 14 Pl. 31 [Berlin 1926]). 247
12.2 Seal of Taprammi on KUB 25.32 columns iii (left half) and iv (copyright Staatliche Museen zu Berlin – Vorderasiatisches Museum, Foto: BoFN 01748). 253
12.3 Stela base (BOĞAZKÖY 1), Istanbul Archaeological Museum (photo author). 254
12.4 Map of Boğazköy-Hattusa (copyright Archive of the Boğazköy Expedition, Deutsches Archäologisches Institut Berlin). 267
12.5 Map of buildings on Büyükkale with added numbers of fragments found there (after Bittel 1983: 106). 271
12.6 KUB 25.1 obv. columns i-iii (upper half; copyright Staatliche Museen zu Berlin – Vorderasiatisches Museum, Foto: BoFN 01759). 278
12.7 KUB 2.5 obv. columns i-iii (copyright Staatliche Museen zu Berlin – Vorderasiatisches Museum, Foto: BoFN 00005). 280
13.1 KBo 39.43 iv (copyright Akademie der Wissenschaften und der Literatur, Mainz). 326
13.2 KUB 46.34 (copyright Staatliche Museen zu Berlin – Vorderasiatisches Museum, Foto: BoFN 02151). 327
13.3 KUB 4.38 (from KUB 4 Pl. 20 [Berlin 1922]). 329
14.1 Seal impression SBo 1.91 (from Güterbock 1940: 70). 343
14.2 Seal impression on RS 17.28 (from Schaeffer 1956: 51). 344
14.3 Seal impression from Lower City 3 (USt. 3), Beran 1967:29 (no. 125) w. Pl.10. (from Boehmer & Güterbock 1987: 53; copyright Archive of the Boğazköy Expedition, Deutsches Archäologisches Institut Berlin). 345
14.4a Seal ring impression of Sauskawalwi (Herbordt 2005: Pl. 30 No. 382b; copyright Archive of the Boğazköy Expedition, Deutsches Archäologisches Institut Berlin). 347
14.4b Seal ring impression of Tuwarsa (Herbordt 2005: Pl. 37 No. 476b; copyright Archive of the Boğazköy Expedition, Deutsches Archäologisches Institut Berlin). 347

14.5	Sickle blade found at Hattusa (from Bittel 1937: Abb. 9; copyright Archive of the Boğazköy Expedition, Deutsches Archäologisches Institut Berlin).	352
14.6	DEUS.L.326t on KINIK bowl (from Hawkins 1993: 715 Fig. 1).	354
14.7	Seal from Tarsus (from Goldman 1956: Pl. 402 [photo], 406 [drawing]).	355
14.8	Anatolian hieroglyphic signs depicting thrones (L.298 and 294, respectively).	356
14.9	Dresden seal (from Boehmer & Güterbock 1987: no. 151 Pl. XVI; copyright Archive of the Boğazköy Expedition, Deutsches Archäologisches Institut Berlin) with L.326-seat at 11 o'clock.	357
14.10	Hittite seal (from Boehmer & Güterbock 1987: no. 151 Pl. XVI ; copyright Archive of the Boğazköy Expedition, Deutsches Archäologisches Institut Berlin) with seat at 12 o'clock.	358
14.11	Chairs and seats in Salonen 1963: Pl. 23.	369
14.12	Chairs and seats in Salonen 1963: Pl. 25.	369
14.13	Paleography of L.326 and L.326t (drawing author).	370

Tables

3.1 Comparison of some Old Babylonian signs with their older Hittite counterparts *page* 40
3.2 Traditional model of Hittite paleographic stages 46
3.3 Some diagnostic signs as used in dating Hittite texts 46
3.4 Some Babylonian standard signs compared to their Hittite counterparts 47
3.5 Some Babylonian standard signs compared to the same ones in texts from Alalah VII 48
3.6 Percentages for the relative frequency of the Hittite "older" and "later" sign shapes in texts from Alalah VII 48
3.7 Hittite cuneiform vowel signs 52
3.8 Hittite cuneiform consonant+vowel signs 53
3.9 Hittite cuneiform vowel+consonant signs 54
3.10 Hittite cuneiform consonant+vowel+consonant signs 54
3.11 Sumerograms and logograms 55
4.1 Originals from the Old Kingdom 1650–1400 BC 60
4.2 Compositions datable to Old Kingdom Hittite kings regardless of the date or language of the manuscript 68
5.1 Names of earliest datable scribes 78
5.2 Names of scribes datable to mid- and later fifteenth century 79
5.3 Scribes attributable to the period 1500–1350 BC 80
6.1 List of *wa*-signs with subscript 108
6.2 Comparison of Akkadian and Hittite lexical material in the charters 112
6.3 Distribution of genres and the number of manuscripts in Old Script tablets 117
7.1 Reading direction of Anatolian hieroglyphic signs 135
7.2 Second millenium Anatolian hieroglyphic syllabary: vowels 135
7.3 Second millenium Anatolian hieroglyphic syllabary: consonant + vowel 136

7.4 Second millenium Anatolian hieroglyphic syllabary: some signs, transcriptions, and meanings 137
8.1 Hittite lists and bookkeeping texts 165
10.1 Attested forms for GIŠ(.ḪUR)k/*gaštarḫait/da* 196
10.2 Attested forms for GUL-*zattar* 198
10.3 Attested forms for GIŠ*kurta-* 204
12.1 Genres in Hittite literature as short- vs. long-term records 239
12.2 Possible editing stages 255
12.3 Number of text fragment finds in the StT1, HaH, and on Bk. A 269
12.4 Number of text fragment finds in buildings on Bk., and in Temples other than Temple 1 (numbers from the Konkordanz) 270
13.1 Hierarchy of people mentioned in the Maşat Höyük letters. 298
13.2 Most frequently encountered non-royal titles on seal impressions 302
13.3 Names of scribes also attested on seal impressions. 303
13.4 Scribes mentioned in witness lists in KBo 4.10, Bo 86/299, and KUB 26.43 306
13.5 Chief Scribes and Chief Wood-scribes in the thirteenth century BC 312
13.6 Apprentice scribes attested in colophons 314
13.7 Hierarchy of named scribes 318
13.8 Archaic or archaic-looking cuneiform signs in Hittite colophons 330
13.9 Archaic or archaic-looking signs outside colophons 331
14.1 Elements in the so-called "scribal signatures" 363
14.2 Seal impressions with L.326 at Emar 372
14.3 Seal impressions with L.326 at Ugarit 374

Preface and Acknowledgments

The beginnings of this book go back to June, 1995. On the first two days of that month the members of the *Oosters Genootschap in Nederland* (Oriental Society in the Netherlands) convened in Leiden at their annual *Huishoudelijk Congres* to read and hear a great variety of papers. Those of us belonging to the ancient Near Eastern section reflected on the topic *Tekst als Geschiedenis* (Text as History). The organizer of this particular gathering, Sumerologist Herman Vanstiphout, asked me to contribute on the Hittites, the dominating power in ancient Anatolia (modern Turkey) between ca. 1650 and 1200 BC. I had always had an interest in questions of the function of texts in society and the practical and graphic aspects of clay tablets with their cuneiform script, but I had not yet done any systematic research in that direction. The invitation to this conference provided the ideal incentive to start doing so. For the first time I stepped back and tried to oversee the corpus of Hittite texts as a whole, asking why they had been written down, why in many cases the Hittites had themselves held on to them for sometimes considerable time, and why in other cases they had not.

The *Oosters Genootschap* usually did not publish the proceedings of their annual meetings and eventually I submitted a version of my paper for the memorial volume for Fiorella Imparati (2002). Since then I have explored various aspects of text history in a range of articles and talks but over time the thought of a comprehensive monograph developed. It was not until my first sabbatical in 2011–2012 that I was able to make a start on the present book. Resuming duties as chair of the department of Near Eastern Languages and Civilizations at Chicago in the fall of 2012 prevented me from finishing it and I had to put the project aside until my next leave. This came in 2016–2017 when a Fellowship from the John Simon Guggenheim Memorial Foundation enabled me to fundamentally revise what I had written earlier and to complete the manuscript. The forced break between the two leaves proved enormously beneficial. As books go, they do not leave you alone. Although unable to spend any significant time on it, it never left my mind, I kept reading around the topic and continued jotting down thoughts and making notes. By the time the summer of 2016 came around I had changed my mind on a number of issues.

Intending to present an overview and a coherent picture of the function of writing in early historic Anatolia and in the Hittite Kingdom for a non-specialized readership I have had to rehash several topics that I already wrote about previously. In the earlier chapters the Hittitological reader may recognize much that sounds familiar – and I ask for their indulgence – but most of what comes after (Chapters 7–15) is new. But I also hope to attract a wider readership of colleagues working on other parts of the ancient Middle East or of the world, for that matter, as well as people interested in questions of literacy and scripts in general.

I thank the University of Chicago for providing an environment that stimulates profound research. The Humanities Division under then Dean Martha Roth granted me the two leaves, without which this book would never have seen the light of day. For my second leave, Courtney Guerra expertly guided me through the process of applications for fellowships and I had the good fortune to be awarded one by the John Simon Guggenheim Memorial Foundation, to which I will be eternally grateful. For my Guggenheim leave I rented a carrel at the Joseph Regenstein Library at Chicago where I would retreat every morning away from phone and email and would just sit down and write.

I am deeply indebted to Willemijn Waal and Mark Weeden, who read an earlier version of the manuscript. Michele Cammarosano, Thalia Lysen, Seth Richardson, and Cambridge University Press' two anonymous reviewers likewise gave me invaluable feedback. The Oriental Institute always has been an enormously stimulating environment where the answer to many of one's questions is never further than a few doors or a floor away. I am very grateful to its directors Gil Stein and Chris Woods for their support as well as to all my colleagues on whose doors I have often knocked. Without exception, they went out of their way to answer my queries and I always left their offices enriched. I want to especially mention Bob Biggs, Petra Goedegebuure, Rebecca Hasselbach, Janet Johnson, Kate Morgan, James Osborne, Dennis Pardee, Susanne Paulus, Hervé Reculeau, Seth Richardson, Matthew Stolper, Emily Teeter, and Chris Woods. The staff at the Oriental Institute has always been there to help out where needed and never without a smile. I want to mention especially the help of Charissa Johnson and Steven Townshend. The Oriental

Institute's library (strangely known as the Research Archives) rarely let me down and I am indebted to its librarian Foy Scalf for his help on many occasions. I also remember in grateful horror the session with some of the members of Chicago's Society of Fellows where I presented a premature version of my Introduction. The treadmills at the Henry Crown Field House were the source of many ideas when I tried to alleviate the boredom of running by thinking through specific issues relating to my book. And there was always the reward of some good handball games afterwards.

Eric Lindahl and Brian Zimmerle, former preparators at the Oriental Institute, advised me on practical questions concerning clay and the making of tablets, and they even had Willemijn Waal and me do some experiments. Over the years I also received the friendly support of colleagues at this University and from all over the world: Michael Allen, Clifford Ando, James Burgin, Yoram Cohen, Martien Dillo, John "Jay" Ellison, Mark Garrison, Wouter Henkelman, Barbara Jillson, Hakan Karateke, Jörg Klinger, Guido Kryszat, Jake Lauinger, Stefano de Martino, Craig Melchert, Jared Miller, Clelia Mora, Sarah Nooter, Peter Raulwing, Madadh Richey, Mirjo Salvini, Andreas Schachner, Jürgen Seeher, Daniel Schwemer, Ada Taggar-Cohen, Jonathan Taylor, Ben van Gessel, and Gernot Wilhelm. I also want to thank Cambridge University Press and Michael Sharp for accepting my manuscript for publication and guiding me through the process, and Juliet Wilberforce for her meticulous and invaluable editing work.

I am grateful to the Stichting Amstel 218 of the Six Collection in Amsterdam for allowing me to use the Rembrandt van Rijn drawing *Homer reciting Verses* from the so-called *'Pandora', Album Amicorum* for Jan Six from 1652. In the detail shown here on the cover Rembrandt beautifully captures the concentration of the scribe sitting at Homer's feet as he takes down the blind bard's words, encapsulating the oral and the written. The image was not chosen for this reason only. My first archaeology classes as a young student in Amsterdam took me to what was then called the Jan Six Instituut, and in the Classics reading room back then stood the "Six kast", a book shelf in the shape of a Greek temple, once owned by a later Jan Six, the nineteenth century numismatist and Lycian specialist. For other illustrations I am indebted to Gina Coulthard of the British Institute at Ankara, Barbara Helwing of the Staatliche Museen zu Berlin-Vorderasiatisches Museum, Gerfrid Müller and Daniel Schwemer of the Akademie der Wissenschaften und der Literatur,

Mainz, Andreas Schachner of the Deutsches Archäologisches Institut, Istanbul, as well as Mirjo Salvini and Klaas Veenhof.

Finally, I would never have been able to write this book without the never-ending support of my wife Lidwina, the love of my life. I dedicate this book to our children Charlotte, Philip, and Julia for sharing our American adventure.

Late Bronze Age Anatolia

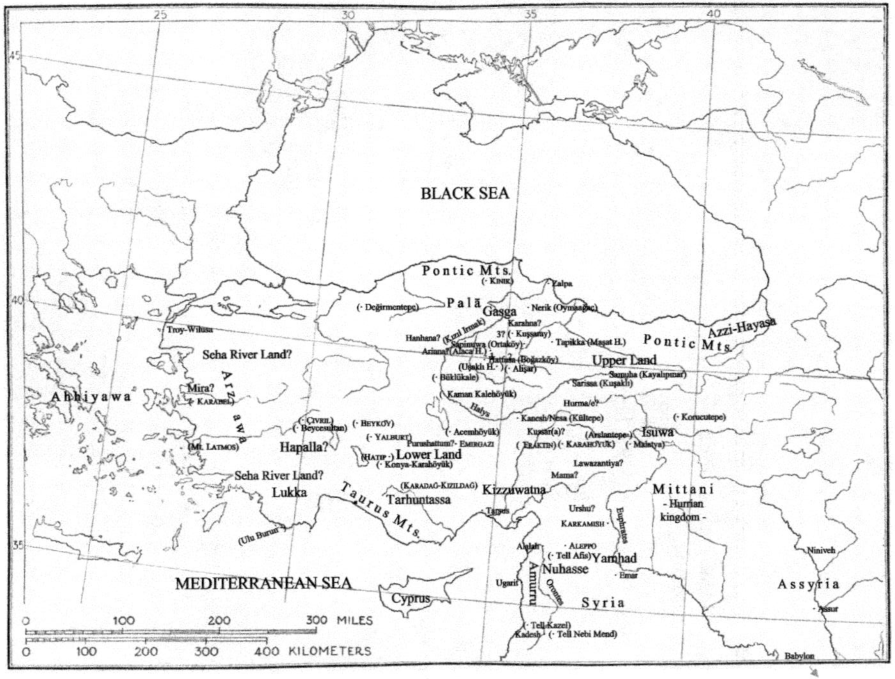

Late Bronze Age Anatolia

Legenda: (Modern Turkish names; H. = Höyük) / ? = uncertain location / 1 = (Eskiyapar), 2 = (Yassı H.), 3 = Katapa / KARABEL: small caps for Hieroglyphic inscription / Arzawa, Pontic Mts., Syria = land, mountain range, or province within or bordering on Hittite kingdom

Timeline and Hittite Kings

Kanesh 2: earliest evidence for presence of Assyrian merchants	ca. 2000	
most Old Assyrian texts written	ca. 1900–1860	
End of Kanesh 2	1835	
Kanesh 1b	1832-ca. 1720	
Anitta	ca. 1750	
Hattusa		
Kings	*reign*	*relation to preceding or other*
Old Kingdom		
Huzziya	ca. 1700(?)	
Labarna		
Hattusili I	ca. 1650	grandson(?)
Mursili I	ca. 1600	grandson
Hantili I		brother-in-law
Zidanta I		son of Mursili I
Ammuna		son
Huzziya I		
Telipinu	ca. 1525	brother-in-law
Alluwamna		son?
Hantili II		son of Alluwamna?
Zidanta II		
Tahurwaili?		
Huzziya II		
Muwatalli I		
New Kingdom		
Tuthaliya I	ca. 1420	
Arnuwanda I		son-in-law
Tuthaliya II		son
(Hattusili II?)		
Tuthaliya III		son(?) Tuthaliya II
Suppiluliuma I	ca. 1350	half-brother?
Arnuwanda II		son

(*cont.*)

Mursili II	ca. 1320–1295	brother
Muwatalli II	ca. 1295–1275	son
Urhitessub/Mursili III	1274–1267	son
Hattusili III	1267-ca. 1240	brother of Muwatalli
Tuthaliya IV	ca. 1240- ca. 1215/1210	
Kuruntiya?		son of Muwatalli II
Arnuwanda III		son of Tuthaliya IV
Suppiluliuma/ Suppiluliyama (II)	ca. 1210–1200	brother

Sigla and Abbreviations

ABoT	Balkan, Kemal (1948), *Ankara Arkeoloji Müzesinde Bulunan Boğazköy Tabletleri* (Istanbul: Millî Eğitim Basımevi).
AlT	Alalah Texts (quoted after Dietrich/Loretz 2004, 2005, 2006).
CAD	Biggs, Robert et al. (1956–2010), *The Assyrian Dictionary of the Oriental Institute of the University of Chicago* (Chicago, IL: The Oriental Institute).
CHD	Güterbock, Hans/Hoffner, Harry/van den Hout, Theo (1979ff.), *The Hittite Dictionary of the Oriental Institute of the University of Chicago* (Chicago, IL: The Oriental Institute).
ChS	*Corpus der hurritischen Sprachdenkmäler, I. Abteilung, Die Texte aus Boğazköy* (Roma 1984ff.).
CLL	H. Craig Melchert 1993, *Cuneiform Luvian Lexicon* (Chapel Hill NC).
CTH	Laroche, Emmanuel (1971), *Catalogue des textes hittites* (Paris: Klincksieck).
HED	Puhvel, Jaan (1984ff.), *Hittite Etymological Dictionary* (Berlin: Walter de Gruyter).
HEG	Tischler, Johann (1977ff.), *Hethitisches etymologisches Glossar* (Innsbruck: Innsbrucker Beiträge zur Sprachwissenschaft).
HKM	Alp, Sedat (1991), *Maşat-Höyük'te Bulunan Çivi Yazılı Hitit Tabletleri/Hethitische Keilschrifttafeln aus Maşat-Höyük* (Ankara: Türk Tarih Kurumu Basımevi).
HW2	Friedrich, Johannes/Kammenhuber, Annelies (1977ff.), *Hethitisches Wörterbuch* (Heidelberg: Winter Verlag).
IBoT	*Istanbul Arkeoloji Müzelerinde Bulunan BoğazköyTabletleri* (Istanbul 1954ff.)

Konkordanz	Košak, Silvin, *Konkordanz der hethitischen Keilschrifttafeln, Online-Datenbank* www.hethport.uni-wuerzburg.de/hetkonk, Hethitologie Portal Mainz, Akademie der Wissenschaften und der Literatur.
KBo	*Keilschrifttexte aus Boghazköi* (Berlin 1916ff.).
KUB	*Keilschrifturkunden aus Boghazköi* (Berlin 1921–1990).
KuSa	Wilhelm, Gernot (1997), *Keilschrifttexte aus Gebäude A* (Rahden/Westf.: Verlag Marie Leidorf).
MSL	B. Landsberger et al., *Materials for the Sumerian Lexicon* (Roma 1937ff.)
RlA	Reallexikon der Assyriologie und Vorderasiatischen Archäologie (Berlin 1928ff.).
TUAT	Kaiser, Otto et al. (eds.), *Texte aus der Umwelt des Alten Testaments* (Gütersloh: Gütersloher Verlagshaus).
VBoT	Goetze, Albrecht (1930), *Verstreute Boğazköy-Texte* (Marburg a.d. Lahn: im Selbstverlag).

Abb.	(German) *Abbildung* ("figure/illustration")
abl.	ablative
acc.	accusative
Akkad.	Akkadian
cat.	catalog
cf.	confer(t), compare
Ch(s).	Chapter(s)
col.	column
com.	common gender
cun.	cuneiform
dat.	dative
DN	Divine Name
dupl(s).	duplicate(s)
ed.	edited
f.	and following page
forthc.	forthcoming
gen.	genitive
GN	Geographical Name
i, ii, etc.	columns on a clay tablet or Roman-numbered pages in the introduction of a book
ibid.	ibidem
instr.	instrumental
Kp.	Kayalıpınar

Kt.	Kültepe
L.#	sign numbers in Laroche 1960
lit.	literature
loc.	locative
n.	note
neut.	neuter gender
nom.	nominative
obv.	obverse
pl.	plural
Pl(s).	Plate(s)
PN	Personal Name
RN	Royal Name
RS	Ras Shamra
rev.	reverse
sg.	singular
Sum.	Sumerian
s.v(v).	sub voce/vocibus
tr.	translation/translated by
unpubl.	unpublished
vel sim.	vel simile/similia ("or similar")
w.	with
* *	text between * * in transcription is written over erasure
*	unattested, reconstructed forms

CHAPTER 1

Introduction

1.1 Anatolia and Literacy

Many biographies like to start at the end of their subject's life. The final moments or days of their hero are presented as the climax of his or her life as if somehow summing it all up. Yet the reader does not know it yet. Her curiosity is piqued and, so the author hopes, she will be eager to read on. The author then turns around and starts at the very beginning, with the hero as a baby and child, with all the excitement still far away but with all the foreboding of the end just told. The hero of this book is literacy, writing and reading, in the Hittite kingdom in ancient Anatolia, or modern-day Turkey, from roughly 1650 to 1200 BC, give or take several years or perhaps even a decade or two. In this case, too, we could begin at the end, but the demise of the kingdom is still shrouded in mystery. Our hero just disappears unseen, it seems. Sometime around 1200 BC, the Hittite state literally vanished into thin air. We think the ruling elite abandoned its central Anatolian capital Hattusa and moved away somewhere south or southeast, but where to exactly? No obvious new capital has been identified as yet. And when did this all take place? Isolated outside references to a Hittite state might extend its life to 1190 or even into the 1180s BC, but nothing compels us to assume that it was still centered at Hattusa. As we will see, the number of written records dating to the very end of the kingdom suggests an earlier rather than later abandonment. After the "fall," Hittite-style great kings pop up here and there, well outside central Anatolia, and may have claimed to carry on or believed they carried on the Hittite kingdom. Central Anatolia, on the other hand, the core of what was once the mighty kingdom, suddenly becomes a *tabula rasa* and stays so until the first Phrygian sources become available some four hundred years later in the eighth century BC.

Besides the inevitable human tragedy that must have accompanied the demise of the Hittite state, and that is invisible to us, another casualty was cuneiform literacy. Although Hittite as a spoken language may have been ailing already for some time, at least its written form and the cuneiform script continued to serve as the official administrative medium until the last king gave up the capital city. But at that fateful moment, both the Hittite language and its cuneiform script became officially extinct. The fate of the other script, the indigenous so-called Anatolian hieroglyphs used by the Hittite kings for inscriptions in Luwian, Hittite's sister-language, was not much better. Although Luwian continued to be spoken and the hieroglyphs kept being written, most inscriptions dating to the early twelfth and eleventh century come from the northern Syro-Mesopotamian area, some 400 km away, and seem to continue a local, rather than formerly Hittite tradition. Also, the Late Bronze Age hieroglyphs' most vital function to write names on seals never returned while former Hittite institutions and artistic expressions suddenly and completely disappear from the kingdom's heartland. What do this sad end of Hittite, its cuneiform script in Central Anatolia, all that it represented, and the narrow survival there of Luwian and the Anatolian hieroglyphs in the Iron Age say about the prime of their lives?[1] For this we need to go back to the very beginning.

Writing ranks among humankind's most important and defining inventions. In history, writing systems were independently created from scratch, that is, without for us discernible outside inspiration from an already literate society, at least four times. The earliest inventions happened in the ancient Middle East, in the land of Sumer in modern-day southern Iraq, somewhere around 3500 BC, and in Egypt, probably around the same time or a little after. The two others were China (ca. 1500 BC) and Mesoamerica (ca. 500 BC). The scripts in these parts of the world arose out of pictograms inspired by their own material cultures, and the gradual evolution into real writing systems usually was a response to the growing administrative, political, and cultural needs of these early complex states. They enabled ruling classes to organize and control labor and trade, and over time writing came to be used also as a means of prestige and propaganda. As rare as these *ex nihilo* creations were, they inspired an endless string of derived scripts and writing systems that continues until the present day. The so-called primary or pristine writing systems of Sumer, Egypt, China, and Mesoamerica were responsible for all or most other scripts in the world. Spreading from its origins in southern Mesopotamia, the Sumerian cuneiform provided most of the Middle East from Iran to Turkey, from the Levantine coast to the Caucasus with

[1] For a rather dark assessment of the aftermath of the Hittite kingdom see Summers 2017.

a script that stayed in use for well over three millennia. Chinese characters became the first script in much of East Asia and still forms part of the Japanese and Korean writing systems, and in the end the very roots of our own alphabet can be traced back to Egyptian hieroglyphs.

The population groups or states that decided to adopt an already existing foreign script for their own internal use went through a fundamentally different process than the four who invented writing. Where the pristine scripts had developed over centuries, either slow and gradual, or in leaps and bounds, dictated by the growing pains of political systems, adoptions could be the result of short-term deliberate decisions. Instead of a slow development one often sees the wholesale introduction of an entire system into a community that had hitherto been illiterate. This does not say that such processes always proceeded quickly, smoothly, and linearly. The development of the originally Phoenician alphabet in the early first millennium BC is a case in point. From about 800 BC onwards we see a sudden proliferation of local alphabetic variants in Asia Minor and further westwards. The two earliest adaptations can be seen right around the turn of the eighth century in Phrygia in Central Anatolia and in the Greek-speaking world with the so far oldest evidence coming from Sicily. Soon the alphabet spread to Lydia, Caria, and Lycia in Western Anatolia. Variants of the Greek alphabet emerged all around the Aegaean. All of these Iron Age alphabets share the innovation of separate signs for vowels but none of these alphabets are identical. With our current evidence it is impossible to come up even with a stemma that neatly explains the neighboring Lydian, Carian, or Lycian alphabets as linear descendants from either the Phrygian or Greek model. Also, all of these alphabets fairly quickly disappeared again in the onslaught, half a millennium later, of Alexander the Great and his immediate successors. Only the Greek Attic-Ionian variant eventually became standardized as *the* Greek alphabet.

One community where we can observe a contained and straightforward development from script adoption and adaptation to continued use by one particular group and one only was that of the early Hittite kingdom. Here there was no spread or diffusion with local variants and hence no standardization of a preferred variant. Around 1650 its early kings imported the cuneiform writing system, as it was used at the time in northern Syria (see Chapter 3), one of the areas that cuneiform had spread to from its Sumerian origins late in the fourth millennium. But why did they wait so long? Even stranger is the fact that already in the period between 2000 and 1725 BC, the Anatolian population had been acquainted with another, simplified cuneiform writing system used by Assyrian merchants, but they did not seem overly interested. When the merchants left the area for good nobody seems to have had the urge to start writing for themselves. Anatolia was politically fragmented and continued its illiterate ways, as it had for ages. Handshake deals and at best impressions of seals formed the backbone of economy and trade.[2]

Anatolia was a harsh country with an "extraordinarily complex" landscape.[3] Not only did huge mountain ranges, rising up to 3000 m in the north, south, east, and west, seal it off from the Mediterranean and neighboring countries, they also created inland pockets where local population groups could develop their own societies with their own social traditions and customs in relative isolation.[4] The Anatolian climate has been described as one "of extremes"[5] with severely cold winters and hot, humid summers. With, moreover, its rivers being unsuited for long-distance transport, travel was difficult enough in the more clement seasons but "virtually impossible" in winter.[6] The resulting social and political fragmentation proved a real challenge to any local chieftains who set their sights on regional domination. There may have been some larger local kingdoms but the first, albeit short-lived, historically attested unified kingdom covering most of Central Anatolia dates to around 1750 BC. But these were not yet complex states. Individual communities continued trading and bartering in small local subsistence economies, as they had done from time immemorial.[7] In these circumstances there was little incentive to either invent or to acquire a writing system.

The second attempt at a Central Anatolian kingdom met with more success. Between 1650 and 1600 BC Labarna, Hattusili I, and Mursili I chose Hattusa as their new power base and soon turned their attention to Syria, gateway to the east as well as to the Mediterranean. It was international diplomacy, contacts with Syrian kings, that convinced them they needed a writing system. Although the Assyrian writing system might still have been remembered by the oldest in society the new kings decided to adopt the very different Syrian cuneiform and to start using it for their own purposes. Writing cuneiform and knowledge of Akkadian

[2] See, for instance, Susan Sherratt 2003: 230 ("people all over the world and throughout history have traded successfully with varying degrees of complexity and sophistication without the need for writing").

[3] Sagona & Zimansky 2009: 1. [4] Schachner 2011a: 33–40 (esp. 36).

[5] Sagona & Zimansky 2009: 1, 5.

[6] Weeden 2014a: 34; see also Hoffner 2009: 18, Alparslan & Doğan-Alparslan 2018: 233.

[7] For the most recent and reliable attempt so far at gauging the population size in Central Anatolia in the Hittite period see Simon 2011a; on a total of 987 settlements he estimates 877 with a population of well under 100.

were prerequisites in the world of politics of the moment. Before long, they adapted the script to write their own language and cuneiform writing became the internal recording standard. But in spite of the Mesopotamian writing conventions that came with the script the Hittite state was selective in what it committed to writing and cuneiform never gained wide acceptance. Existing evidence suggests that writing was only practiced within the circles of the ruling elite and, compared to Mesopotamia, the total volume of written documents remained small. Telling in this respect may be the fact that proper verbs for "writing" or "reading" never developed. The normal Hittite terms are the very generic *iye-* and its derived synonym *aniye-* "to do, make." For "reading" *au(š)-/u-* "to see" was used. The direct object of the "doing" is what one writes, a letter, a literary composition, a ritual etc., and one does so "*on* a tablet" or "*with/using* a tablet."[8] The latter two can overlap but the instrumental "with/using a tablet" is preferred when contrasting a written with an oral message.

In trying to come up with a term for "writing" the Hittites could have compared its characteristic motions to similar looking activities. As we will see (Chapter 6.3), the possibly earliest attested reference to the act of writing used in the Hittite language is *ḫazziye-* "to stab, pierce." This is not an inappropriate way of describing writing if one observes someone applying a stylus to a clay tablet, repeatedly pressing the pointed stylus into the surface. Yet this is only attested twice, the second occurrence stemming from the other end of Hittite history, the late thirteenth century BC, in reference to an iron tablet where the cuneiform signs were probably punched in. Besides the ubiquitous "doing" the only other verb occasionally used is GUL-*š*- or *gulš*- (Chapter 10.5), originally meaning "to make a mark" with something. That "something" could be anything ranging from beer poured in a circle around an object to a sharp instrument to incise signs or figures in a hard surface like metal. These two verbs come close to other languages that often use technical terms for "scratching" or "carving" to express the notion of writing. But the default expression remained "to do/make (a text) on/with a tablet." Like many societies that adopted cuneiform writing, the Hittites did, however, borrow the Mesopotamian word for "tablet," Akkadian *tuppum* becoming Hittite *tuppi*.[9]

8 For the various constructions see van den Hout 2016a.

9 Following Streck 2009: 136–40, I write *tuppum* with a plain *t* instead of emphatic *ṭ*.

What made the Hittites suddenly decide to become literate around the middle of the seventeenth century BC? What was the impetus to start recording the oldest known Indo-European language? What did they use writing for and how did the technology and its use develop over the centuries? What are the reasons to think that writing never caught on in the population at large? Despite this seeming reluctance they developed early on a second script, this time one of their own design, and used it for public display. Why? And what happened to their writing systems when around 1200 BC their kingdom collapsed and vanished? These are the overarching questions I want to answer in this book. Using all available evidence, and only that, as I will explain in more detail below, I have tried to sketch as comprehensive and consistent a picture of writing and reading in Hittite Anatolia as possible. But before embarking on this let us see who these Hittites were.

1.2 Defining the Hittites

The records of the Hittite kingdom reflect the history of Anatolia (nowadays Turkey) from about the mid-eighteenth century BC up to its very end around 1200 BC. The presence of Hittite speakers in Central Anatolia can already be assumed for the turn of the third millennium. Hittite names and those of Luwians, speakers of a language closely related to Hittite, are attested in the records of Assyrian merchants who had settled in Anatolia around 2000 BC. Yet other names point to speakers of the Hattian language in the same area. Hattian is completely unrelated to Hittite and Luwian and remains a so-called linguistic isolate with no immediate connection to any other known language, ancient or modern. Following the sociolinguistic reconstruction by Petra Goedegebuure we can envision the Indo-European Hittites and Luwians settling in Central Anatolia in the course of the third millennium BC.[10] The Luwians largely merged with the already present Hattian population within the bend of the Classical Halys or modern-day Kızıl Irmak River. A bilingual society resulted, in which the Hattian element was culturally dominant, still visible in the early historical period of the Hittite kingdom with its overwhelmingly Hattian pantheon and Hattian names of its kings. The Hittite speakers, meanwhile, inhabited the more eastern parts of Central Anatolia right towards the area where the Halys originates. Around 1750 BC a local king by the name of Anitta established here the center of the first unified Central Anatolian kingdom

[10] Goedegebuure 2008.

including the Luwian-Hattian population groups. Originally, he came with his father from Kussar, probably to be sought in the same general eastern area, and conquered Kanesh or Nesa (modern Kültepe), as it was also known, the center of the Assyrian commercial activities. This town he made his capital. One of his many acts of war was the conquest, subsequent destruction, and cursing of the town of Hattus, as it was called in Hattian, or Hattusa, as Luwian speakers knew it. A few other towns were raided, razed, and perhaps cursed but Anitta seems to have singled out Hattusa for special treatment, sowing cress on its fields in order to avoid immediate resettlement. Although Anitta may have harbored some personal grudge it is more likely that he already sensed the potential of the site as a future power base. Anitta's kingdom was short lived but about a century later that same Hattusa re-emerged as the capital of choice of a new wave of Hittite invaders led by a certain Labarna. This was the beginning of the Hittite kingdom that was to dominate Anatolia for the next almost 500 years.

Somewhat surprisingly perhaps, Labarna and his successors assumed the name of the conquered population and called themselves "men of Hatti" or "men of the land of Hattusa." In doing so they boldly asserted themselves as the new power in the region but at the same time declared their intention to maintain and perhaps even integrate into local conditions. They did not force their own name on the indigenous people. As we will see time and again, this practical attitude towards their new surroundings is perhaps *the* defining characteristic of the Hittite state. It has little to do with altruism and everything to do with a will to survive and cleverly improvising their way to the top. In taking the definitive step towards literacy, however, they chose neither Hattian nor Luwian but held on to their own Indo-European Hittite language, the one they came with, as the official medium of their administration. Even though from now on they wanted to be known as the "men of Hatti," the name from which our modern term "Hittite" derives through the intermediary of the Biblical *Ḥittim* "Hittites," they still called their own language "the language of Nesa (Kanesh)." This is one of the very few explicit holdovers from their roots going back to Anitta and the Hittite kings held on to it for the rest of their history. Since they used the "Nesite" language, that is, Hittite, for internal administrative eyes only, they could do so without political consequences. But, as we will see, they found other means to address the wider and largely Luwian-speaking population. All this was based on practical decisions and they cared little for feelings of nostalgia. For the historical Hittites history started with their rule from Hattusa and there was no "Golden Age" tradition associated with Nesa or any other place or region.[11] With "Hittite" and the "Hittites" I therefore refer to the Central Anatolian kingdom that between ca. 1650 and 1200 BC used the Hittite language as its main internal means of written communication while controlling a population that spoke several other (mostly related) languages and largely continued their own centuries-old customs and traditions. As a consequence, I will also often use the terms "Anatolian" and "Anatolians" for the same people.[12]

To this linguistic diversity of Hittite, Luwian, and Hattian we can add the Palaic language in Northeast Central Anatolia, another branch on the Anatolian branch of Indo-European languages. Also, it is not unlikely that forerunners of the first-millennium Anatolian languages related to Hittite, Luwian, and Palaic, although not yet written, were already spoken during the days of the Hittite kingdom in the western and southern coastal areas. These are the Lydian, Carian, and Lycian languages with inscriptions each in their own distinctive alphabetic scripts from the eighth through fourth century BC. By the beginning of the AD era the Anatolian branch, at least in its written forms, was ultimately extinct. This variety of languages and population groups is not surprising in view of the "extraordinarily complex" landscape with its huge mountain ranges and its climate "of extremes." Anatolia's geography and ecology encouraged social and political fragmentation with pockets of local languages and customs being able to exist in a kind of splendid isolation.[13] Although early Hittite kings liked to boast that they "made the lands the borders of the seas"[14] the truth is that probably only Central Anatolia was ever truly under their direct control. The further one gets away from the center towards the coastal regions in the west and to the mountains separating it from Mesopotamia in the east

[11] Gilan 2015: 195–201.

[12] Hittite culture and society are often described as a kind of melting pot adding a substantial Hurrian element to the mix. From a Central Anatolian standpoint, however, the latter never probably was a substantial ethnic component. The Hurrian wave that we see rising in Hittite history towards the end of the fifteenth century BC was in all likelihood mostly an elite affair that had little impact on the Anatolian population at large. In his article "Toward a Definition of the Term Hittite" Hans Güterbock (1957) drew attention to the various linguistic and cultural elements in the mostly religious Hittite texts and spoke of a "mixed civilization" (1957: 237: "It is the presence of foreign elements that makes us speak of a mixed civilization, and it is their subordination under the Hittite element that justifies the name Hittite for this mixed civilization."). Definitions often amount to an adding up of all linguistic strands we find in the texts (cf. Beckman 2016: 320–1) but by doing so we may overestimate the impact of such cultural influences on the population as a whole. Anatolia may not have been more mixed than most other regions in the ancient Middle East. For a recent discussion of these questions see Gilan 2015: 195–201.

[13] Schachner 2011a: 33–40 (esp. 36).

[14] *n=uš arunaš irḫuš iēt* KUB 3.1 i 16–17 (also i 7, 26; CTH 19, NS), ed. by Hoffmann 1984: 16–17 (in her overall line count: i 8, 17–18, 27).

the more we have to think in terms of spheres of influence instead of domination and direct control.[15] Economically, socially, and religiously these more remote parts were largely independent. The long arm of Hittite power rarely reached there in its full force and Hittite kings may not even have felt the urge to do so. They intervened when they considered their influence imperiled but otherwise contented themselves with control from afar allowing and condoning local conditions and traditions. This practical attitude is aptly illustrated by the Hittite concept of the proverbial "Thousand Gods." Instead of imposing a single centralized pantheon and an accompanying cult, the Hittite kings preferred to induct local gods into an all-encompassing national hall of deities categorized according to a system of Stormgods, Sun deities, Tutelary deities, while at the same time allowing more unique *numina* to be worshiped.

1.3 A Note on the Hittite Economy

The two economic models usually mentioned for ancient Near Eastern societies are the staple finance and the wealth finance systems. In a staple economy it is the state that collects, stores, and controls "subsistence goods such as grains, livestock, and clothing," and it uses them to remunerate people who work for the state.[16] Given the inherent bulkiness of these staples, the efforts in storing them, and the transportation hurdles offered by the Anatolian landscape, a centralized system seems not to be the most obvious option in the Hittite situation. In a wealth economy, the state tries to control the procurement of and trade in raw, precious materials like gold and silver as well as the manufacture of finished products out of them by craftsmen, "provided as part of a labor obligation from the local communities."[17] The state can then use these goods to fund government activities, particularly political services. Because of their being lighter and smaller they are much easier to store and transport. An added bonus is that they are also much less perishable than the usual staple goods.

Although there may not always be an automatic correlation between an area's ecology and its economic system, given the specific character of the Anatolian landscape the Hittite choice for an overall wealth finance model combined with local subsistence economies is exactly what recently scholars have argued for. Of course, wealth and staple finance are not mutually

[15] Glatz 2009. [16] D'Altroy & Earle 1985: 188; see also the various papers collected in Earle 2002.

[17] D'Altroy & Earle 1985: 188; for a full discussion and *Forschungsgeschichte* of ancient world economics see Burgin 2016.

exclusive. On the contrary, they support each other but the question is one of emphasis. The Hittite state clearly cared about and invested in the organization of staples, especially cereals. Agriculture was not without its challenges and cyclical droughts forced the ruling elite to keep a watchful eye on local situations in order to maintain a stable political system. The second part of King Telipinu's proclamation of the late sixteenth century BC documents a network of over ninety storehouses for grain throughout Central Anatolia; the texts from the provincial site of Maşat Höyük attest to the worries in ruling circles about the plundering of grain fields by starving Kaskaeans; on the archaeological side, the silos in Hattusa and provincial centers are an eloquent testament to the Hittite state seeking to guarantee a regular and steady flow of foodstuffs. The recurrent droughts in Anatolia were a potential source of unrest and upheaval among the population. In order to avoid this, the state invested in mobilizing the staples and organizing them at a local level and thus tried to provide for the inevitable lean years. The storage facilities mentioned in the Telipinu text cover the core of Hatti-Land as well as the Upper and Lower Land and bespeak a fine-grained and therefore also highly localized or decentralized system of local networks that together form the Hittite kingdom.[18] Within such a system it is possible to work without written records to a large extent. Also, we need to take into account the fact that the administrative texts from Maşat have so far not been matched by any similar records at other provincial sites. Finally, there is the near-total silence of the Hittite sources on trade.[19]

What might require written administration, on the other hand, is the wealth finance part of the system. This is exactly what our so-called palace storeroom inventories (see Chapter 8.7) are about.[20] Also, the passage from the Instruction of the Temple Personnel quoted extensively later on (see Chapter 10.2) offers the perfect example for the control the palace tried to exert on the distribution of wealth and possible related record keeping:

> If by the palace silver, gold, textiles, (and/or) things of bronze are given to him (i.e., a member of the temple personnel) as a gift, it should be specified: "King so-and-so has given it to him" and it should likewise be recorded how much its weight is. Furthermore, the following should be recorded as well: "They gave it to him at such-and-such festival." Witnesses, too, should be recorded after (it): "When they gave it to him, so-and-so, and so-and-so

18 See Schachner 2017: 230 and the map in Singer 1984: 123.

19 It is interesting to note that the Mycenaean Linear B records are likewise silent on trade relations and trade organization; see Panagiotopoulos 2017: 27–9, for the Hittite situation see Hoffner 2001: 180.

20 For all this see in detail Burgin 2016.

> were present." Furthermore, he shall not leave it in his estate. He must sell it but when he sells it, he shall not sell it in secret! The authorities of Hattusa shall be present and watch. And whatever he sells, they must draw up a document of it and they must seal it in front. When the king comes up to Hattusa, he must show it to the palace, and they shall seal it for him.

Clearly, any gift once given to members of the retaining class was not unconditional. When the beneficiary left the service or died, the gift was not his or hers to do with as they pleased. The state sought to directly control where the object went, and the policy outlined in this passage may be seen as strongly discouraging to "monetize" it in any way. Instead the state itself may have bought it back in exchange for staple goods or with compensation in some other way and no further records were necessary.

1.4 Modern Hittite Scholarship and Our Sources

Whereas the civilizations of the Assyrians and Babylonians in Mesopotamia and that of Egypt never faded from memory, knowledge of the Hittites – at least in a modern western European point of view but not necessarily in that of later Anatolians[21] – was almost fully erased after the collapse of their kingdom around 1200 BC. In the now more than one-hundred-year old "resurrection"[22] of Hittite culture and society that followed the excavations of the early twentieth century AD and the decipherment of the Hittite language in 1915 they have now been restored to their rightful place in the history of the Late Bronze Age in ancient Western Asia or the Middle/Near East, as it is more commonly known. All our sources come from contemporary, that is, Late Bronze Age societies, mostly through archaeological excavations. Impressive material culture ranging from monumental gates and walls down to the tiniest miniature vases has come to light at the ruins of the former capital Hattusa, modern Boğazköy/Boğazkale. Since the early 1970s many provincial towns and centers have added invaluable information to a picture that until then tended to be one-sided coming from the capital only. This book focuses on that part of the material culture that has writing on it and seeks to distill from it something of an intellectual history.

The Hittites first and foremost wrote on clay tablets using the cuneiform script they imported from Syria in the second half of the seventeenth century BC.[23] For special occasions metal tablets in gold, silver, bronze,

[21] On this see Rojas 2019. [22] Güterbock 1995.

[23] For a full and detailed overview of Hittite tablets and their use see Waal 2015. For a brief overview of the general written legacy of the Hittite Kingdom see van den Hout 2011.

and iron were made and there are references to (probably wax-covered) wooden tablets as well. Rarely is the cuneiform script found on objects other than tablets whether clay or metal. Besides Hittite, which was the language of choice for all internal administration, a variety of other languages were recorded in cuneiform on the clay tablets. We have compositions in Akkadian and Sumerian, the "classical" languages of Mesopotamian culture that accompanied the introduction of cuneiform into Anatolia, as well as in Hattian, Luwian and Palaic, and finally Hurrian, the language of the Mittani kingdom of northern Mesopotamia.

Had the Hittites only used the cuneiform script, ready-made and adopted wholesale from Mesopotamia, there would have been little need to define the term "script" or "writing system" here. Our common definition of spoken language recorded graphically (script proper) in a system agreed upon by the group using it would have sufficed.[24] At the same time the Hittites imported cuneiform, however, Anatolia had its own indigenous and local pictographic repertoires of symbols ("hieroglyphs") that by the later fifteenth century BC had developed into a real writing system (Chapter 7). The Hittite elite employed this second script when addressing the population at large. They did so on rock monuments erected in the public sphere as well as through graffiti and seals. Telling for the linguistic demographics of Anatolia at the time is the fact that inscriptions in these hieroglyphs exclusively use the Luwian language. The development of these symbols or pictograms into a writing system happened under the aegis of the Hittite kingdom building on already existing local uses of symbols, likely used for administrative purposes. The earliest hints at the existence of these signs go back to the Old Assyrian Period and perhaps even before that. These attestations usually concern individual pictograms on vases and similar objects and occasionally a couple or even three combined.[25] This was not yet script in the sense of recorded speech, but they did communicate information that could be "read." The symbols were in all likelihood associated with individuals or offices and they delineated their responsibilities. A container with a symbol impressed on it in clay could be identified as belonging to or being the responsibility of a person or office. So, in order to include also these "forms of graphic communication that do not represent language" (at least not necessarily spoken language) or *semasiography* I adopt here the wider definition of

[24] There are many definitions around, cf. for instance Coulmas 1996: 454, 555–6, 560, Daniels & Bright 1996: 3, Rogers 2005: 2–3, Woods 2010: 18–20.

[25] For examples see Waal 2012: 299 Figs. 1–3.

script by Elizabeth Hill Boone as "the communication of relatively specific ideas in a conventional manner by means of permanent, visible marks."[26]

1.5 The Nature of Our Evidence and How We Use It

To date, we have around 30,000 tablets and tablet fragments written in cuneiform and close to seventy hieroglyphic inscriptions from the period of the Hittite kingdom. To these we may add some 5000 seal impressions of kings, queens, and related royalty as well as officials, mostly in the Anatolian hieroglyphs. Along with the non-inscribed sources this material is rich enough to allow us a relatively well-documented and sometimes even surprisingly detailed look into Hittite society. We know the general historical development, the outline of state organization with its religious, judicial, military, and administrative levels.

Inevitably, of course, these sources leave even more unsaid. Most or all excavations have been done at larger sites with big structures highlighting the lives of elites. Besides some relatively isolated hints in our texts, the local population outside those elites remains almost completely invisible. One of the areas most sorely under-documented is that of trade and private enterprise. We do not even have records showing the state and private citizens as partners to an agreement. This absence is all the more surprising since there are so many legal and/or economic records known from neighboring Mesopotamia in the east and the Mycenaean kingdoms in the west. Comparisons with Mesopotamia and other societies prompt the question where such texts are, but they also justify entertaining the possibility that perhaps Hittite society was different in this respect and that such records never existed. I suggest we see these "silences and blanks of the written record"[27] as due to the ancient Anatolians simply not considering such transactions as in need of being written down but the more common assumption in modern scholarship is that such records have not been preserved.

In our urge to round out our picture of Hittite society as much as possible, scholars often resort to the adage "absence of evidence is not evidence of absence." The material was there, we just do not have it any longer. We know the Hittites themselves recycled records, they wrote on perishable materials like wood, and there is the "rude wasting of old time,"[28] things simply turning into dust in the course of the more than

[26] Hill Boone 2004: 313, cf. also Urton 2003: 26–9, and see further Chapter 8.
[27] Bagnall 2011: 4. [28] John Keats, Sonnet no. 4 "On first seeing the Elgin marbles."

three millennia that separate us from the Hittite kingdom. But how far can one go? Writing about the single surviving wooden tablet from the Late Bronze Age, found in the Mediterranean waters just off the Lycian coast near Ulu Burun, Nicholas Postgate, Tao Wang, and Toby Wilkinson assert that it:

> has, or should have, had a disproportionate influence on perceptions of the role of writing in the Eastern Mediterranean in the late 2nd millennium BC, but its discovery is equally significant in a methodological way; a unique survivor of a whole class, it counters the argument 'surely if writing were so prevalent *some evidence* would have survived': before its discovery there was no such evidence, but the great fortune which kept it waterlogged for 3200 years or more has changed this at a stroke.[29]

Actually, there *was* evidence for wooden writing boards all along before the find of the Ulu Burun shipwreck in the form of references to such documents in the clay records. The point is, as we will see (Chapter 10), that the number of such references is very modest and, in my opinion, does not justify wide-ranging conclusions. It is undeniable that evidence has been lost but I think we should be careful not to attribute incidental finds too much influence without checking the total record.

Usually and understandably, we satisfy the urge to fill in the gaps in our view of Hittite history and society by assuming a situation comparable to contemporary neighboring cultures. Debt notes, contracts, adoption, and tax records, census lists, consignment documents, court records, disbursals, land sale documents, memoranda, and similar texts dominate the Mesopotamian written legacy and therefore we like to assume they existed in Hittite Anatolia as well. Mesopotamian scribes started their training with single sign sequences, moving on to so-called lexical lists, and ended with literary compositions in Sumerian and Akkadian and therefore we like to assume the same training sequence for Hittite Anatolia. But for neither case is there any compelling evidence. In this tendency to level out the various ancient Near Eastern societies we run the risk of denying societies the chance to be unique or simply themselves.[30]

In his 2014 book on *Writing and the Ancient State* Haicheng Wang discusses the problems in comparing ancient cultures with very different sets of evidence:

[29] Postgate et al. 1995: 478 (emphasis by the authors).

[30] Besides the authors quoted here and in the following, cf. for a variety of opinions Diakonoff 1967: 351, Palaima 2001: 154, Houston 2004: 12, Waal 2012: 290, Postgate 2013: 328–30, 370–1.

> Cautious colleagues are understandably reluctant to make conjectures about missing evidence. A few regard it as a methodologically virtuous to proceed as though nothing were missing. . . . [But (12:)] many archaeologists have learned that lesson painfully from discoveries they did not anticipate made soon after the publication of their theories.[31]

It is true that anything I say here on the basis of *existing* evidence may no longer be true tomorrow because of newly found evidence but should that give us carte blanche to conjure up any picture of Hittite society, as we think it should have been? This is not proceeding "as though nothing were missing" but refraining from excessive speculation without proper evidence. This approach is methodologically sounder, it seems to me, and there is no shame in standing corrected later on. Daring to be wrong is what often makes scholarship progress more than just daring to be right. Strangely enough, the option of not worrying too much about missing evidence that we just assume to have been there is considered the more "cautious" one. That way one cannot be blamed for overestimating one's hard evidence or be accused of disciplinary chauvinism and hiding under the Mesopotamian umbrella is always a safe space.

In his book *Ancient Kanesh* Mogens Larsen warns us of such chauvinism. In the so-called Old Assyrian Period that he describes merchants from Assur set up a trading network in Central Anatolia with Kanesh as its nerve center. The over 23,000 records they left behind give us an unparalleled insight into private enterprise and conditions in Anatolia of the first two centuries of the second millennium BC. Larsen concedes how "the[se] texts . . . in many respects stand out as unique, a rich and dense record of a commercial society during a brief span of time." He then continues:

> The absence of similar material from other sites of the same period in the region could easily lead us to the conclusion that the Old Assyrians had created a new and different kind of socio-economic system. In other words, it is tempting to isolate the evidence from Kültepe from its contemporary world, simply because we know so little about it, but it would be foolish to assume that because we do not have such evidence, it did not ever exist. It is essential that we accept the utterly fortuitous nature of the material we have and that we avoid the delicious trap of believing that the texts and archaeology must offer us a coherent, typical and representative picture of the past.[32]

The alternative view would hold that other groups or societies in this period had developed similar economic systems and left similar corpora

[31] Wang 2014: 10, 12. [32] Larsen 2015: 9.

of texts that despite all archaeological activity we have not found yet and that we therefore know nothing about. Why should we not consider the possibility that the confluence of Assyrians and Anatolians at this specific time and area indeed gave rise to a unique combination? It is unclear to me why trusting actually existing evidence means having fallen in a "delicious trap" while others who sometimes make far-reaching assumptions based on non-existing evidence are not held to explain the passing of yet another day that the missing evidence was not found.

We end up with a strange paradox. Where there is evidence available, we are willing to accept any differences with other cultures, as long as they are real and cannot be ignored. The Anatolian and Mesopotamian attitudes, for instance, towards celestial phenomena like eclipses and general adversities in life were fundamentally different as shown by the texts. But where there is little or no evidence, we automatically fill in the picture with what we know from elsewhere. It is like looking at an ancient statue without arms or legs or with a nose missing. When gazing at the face without the nose it is difficult to get around the mutilated face but as soon as you cover the nose from view or block the space where the arms should have been attached to the body they suddenly materialize before your mind's eye and the statue becomes whole again. Our brains immediately restore the bronze or marble body to an assumed original state based on our knowledge of the world around us. Stopping the gaps in our evidence in this way we thus risk creating an Anatolia in the image of Mesopotamia, a kind of "Mesopotamia light," instead of allowing the silence to speak for itself and allowing Hittite society to be its own.

Although the adage "absence of evidence is not evidence of absence" may sometimes be true I hold on to the principle that if we have little or no evidence for something, we should seriously consider the possibility that it was not there in the first place or did not play a role of any importance. Of course, there is always the risk that something can be proven to be untrue by some archaeological find tomorrow but, as long as that is not the case, it is from a scholarly point of view methodologically sounder to try to imagine a world without it. In fact, it is an interesting and exciting challenge to do so: what does the Hittite world look like, if we take the consistent absence of certain categories of evidence seriously? By assuming activities and corresponding records, for which we have no evidence and thus may not have been there, we may not only create an incorrect picture of Hittite society, but we may also distort what we have. If we assume a world of bookkeeping and socio-economic and legal administration as well as of private records, we may reach a kind of false equilibrium where the preserved documents with their almost exclusive focus on the king seem counterbalanced by all these alleged secular records. But if the latter were never there the remaining part of what we do have suddenly appears in an altogether different light.[33]

1.6 Doing Things with Tablets

Following the principle outlined in the previous section my aim in this book is to present as comprehensive an account as possible of writing, reading, and literacy in Hittite Anatolia on the basis of existing evidence. I deliberately use the indefinite article ("*an* account") because this book presents *my* view of the role and history of writing in the Hittite kingdom in the Late Bronze Age, between roughly 1600 and 1200 BC. Understandably, Hittite texts have been mined mostly for their contents rather than considered as archaeological objects themselves. Only recently has Willemijn Waal offered a detailed study of Hittite tablets, their shapes and formats as well as a complete edition of all colophons and scribal signatures thus far published and a discussion of the role they played in Hittite scribal culture and management. Still to be answered are questions about the status of records in Hittite society. For whom were the texts written and why? How much, if anything, are we missing and what was perhaps never written down? How widely was literacy spread and what was the role of orality? Who were the people writing and composing the texts; how were they trained and what was their social status? How and where were the texts kept? How did the tablet collections function? Should we describe them as archives, libraries, or a combination of the two? Or should we reject such labels as too modern? From a diachronic point of view, one can add questions concerning the origins of the script, why, how, and when the Hittites adopted and adapted cuneiform, and, although this is by no means a study in Hittite paleography, how it evolved over the centuries. And also, with the cuneiform firmly established, why did they still develop their own indigenous "hieroglyphic" writing system?

Many of these questions have been inspired by reading works on orality, writing, and reading in other times and cultures. This comparative aspect has been helpful in asking questions I had not thought of asking before, and it has offered possible answers I had not imagined before. Reading

[33] A similar argument is made by Josephine Quinn 2018: xxiii-iv in her book on Phoenician identity: hers is "not . . . so much an argument from silence as an argument *for* silence: a silence that can open up other spaces of investigation. . . . This book is not about the lack of evidence for Phoenician identity; it is about what we can do with that fact" (xxiv, emphasis by Quinn).

around has taught me to keep an open mind and has countered automatic assumptions based on Anatolia as part of "cuneiform culture."

These questions are all the more interesting since Hittite Anatolia has a lot to offer to the study of writing and reading. While we often take literacy for granted and assume that any society will jump at the opportunity to adopt it, the Hittites turn out to have been surprisingly reluctant at first to adopt a script for their own purposes. For probably close to three centuries (ca. 2000–1700 BC) they lived around foreigners using cuneiform regularly but only towards the end of that period did they start using the foreign script. It took almost another century and another source before they adapted another cuneiform variant in a sophisticated and innovative way. Yet going by the evidence we have, literacy seems to have been restricted to the ruling elite and the focus of the entire preserved corpus is squarely on the king and queen. Alongside the cuneiform script used for purely internal and mostly administrative purposes the Hittites developed over the centuries the hieroglyphic system used for seals and large, publicly displayed inscriptions. These inscriptions, however, were written in Luwian, a different but closely related language, suggesting that the majority of the Anatolian population in the kingdom spoke Luwian rather than Hittite. This also explains why Hittite and its cuneiform script disappeared when the kingdom broke down around 1200 BC, while Luwian and the hieroglyphs lived on for another five centuries. These and many other issues are of great interest, as the Hittites were quite different from contemporaneous societies in the ancient Near East.

Most chapters in this book begin with a brief historical setting, intended not only for the less specialized reader but also because the developments in literacy sketched here should be seen as part of the general historical context and development of the Hittite kingdom.[34] The first eight chapters following this Introduction (Chapters 2–9) give a chronological account of the development of writing in Hittite Anatolia. Chapter 2 deals with the first attestations of writing in the Old Assyrian Period starting in the twentieth century BC, Chapters 3 and 4 with the transition from Kanesh, the base of an Assyrian merchant colony in Central Anatolia, to the capital of the Old Hittite kingdom in Hattusa. Between ca. 2000 and 1700 BC these Assyrian merchants set up a network of trading posts, using their own specific cuneiform script and their own Assyrian language for contracts and correspondence. The Assyrians lived among the Hittites with whom they traded and there is ample

[34] Since this book is not a general history of the Hittite kingdom very few bibliographical references are given in these historical summaries and I refer the reader to the excellent work of Bryce 2005.

evidence of intermarriage between the two populations – but despite almost three centuries of close contact the Hittites never seemed eager to use the script they saw the Assyrians using. And when they did, they used the Assyrian language; there is no evidence that the Hittites ever used Assyrian cuneiform to write their own language. When the trading network dissolved around 1720 BC darkness set in until we see the beginning of the Old Hittite kingdom around 1650 BC. By then an entirely new cuneiform variant appears that must have originated in northern Syria, borrowed in the course of military campaigns there by the first Hittite kings. Here too, as evidence suggests, the young kingdom first used Akkadian, the language of writing in Syria. Chapters 5 and 6 explore all evidence for literacy and orality pertaining to the Old Kingdom (ca. 1650–1400 BC): names of scribes, possible references to record management and the character of the earliest datable compositions. In the second half of the sixteenth century we see a shift towards writing in the Hittite language and the gradual abandonment of Akkadian as a medium for internal administration. This prompts a reflection on the steps taken to adapt the Syrian cuneiform variant in order to write in Hittite instead of Akkadian. The origins and development of Anatolia's second script, the hieroglyphs, are discussed in Chapter 7. This chapter looks at the roots and early development of this script, elements of which can already be traced back to the glyptic of the Old Assyrian period. Chapters 8 and 9 then present an overview of Hittite literature in the widest sense ("everything written") in the New Kingdom (ca. 1350–1200 BC) when the shift to writing in Hittite had long since been completed. With the above definition of Hittite in mind, Hittite literature has to be understood here as the administrative records generated by the Hittite state including tablets written in languages other than Hittite as well as the inscriptions in the Anatolian hieroglyphs on stone and on seals.

Chapter 10 forms the first of four more thematic chapters (Chapters 10–13). Because of their far-reaching implications concerning literacy in Anatolia, the first two (Chapters 10–11) focus on the theories surrounding the wooden tablets. These wooden tablets are often adduced as a kind of *deus ex machina* to explain the absence of sources that we would like to see (e.g., bookkeeping, contracts, and legal and socio-economic records in general) but that are not there. An added complication is that some scholars hypothesize that these writing boards were inscribed with hieroglyphs rather than with cuneiform. If this were all true, literacy would have been quite widespread in Anatolia. This chapter makes clear, however, that the evidence for the use of wood as a script carrier, although not denied, is overrated: not a single wooden board has ever been found in Anatolia and the textual references to them in the Hittite clay tablets are decidedly poor. Moreover, the assertion that the hieroglyphic script was used on them is highly speculative and unlikely at that. Chapter 11 deals with the role that the close to 4000 seal impressions found at Hattusa play in this discussion and a new explanation for this fascinating find complex is proposed. After the descriptions of all inscribed material in the preceding chapters it is time in Chapters 12 and 13 to reflect on the workings of the Hittite administration in the royal chancellery (Chapter 11) and its employees, the scribes (Chapter 14). If in the Hittite language doing is writing and seeing is reading, as we saw above, the chancellery was the king's hands and eyes. The scribes there composed and wrote, copied and edited, and maintained a tablet collection that sometimes reached back for two to three hundred years. The drawing up of scenarios for cultic celebrations centering around the king and queen turns out to have involved a painstaking editorial process. Scribes also read to the king and his officials and brought to life the voices of a world sometimes as far away as Babylon or Egypt. Among the anonymous people carrying the title "scribe" there were simple tablet writers, administrators, and keepers of the royal storehouses inside and outside the capital. Besides these we know the names of some seventy-five individuals who call or identify themselves as scribes and who are known from the colophons that we find at the end of many Hittite tablets. It is argued that those named scribes were members of the state's elite. They may have shared basic scribal training with their lower ranking colleagues who may have been responsible for the bulk of anonymous Hittite records, but then went on to more learned tasks of dictating, editing, and collecting (foreign) materials. The book provides an Excursus (Chapter 14) on the Anatolian hieroglyph with the number 326, better known as the SCRIBA-sign. In it I discuss and, in the end, dismiss the evidence for the interpretation of this very frequent sign as "scribe" which would otherwise substantially increase the number of such officials and literate individuals in the later Hittite kingdom. Finally, Chapter 15 tells of the demise of the kingdom around 1200 BC and its aftermath. The latter part of that chapter looks back and presents some final thoughts.

1.7 A Note on Chronology and Dating

In spite of modern dating techniques such as dendrochonology, radiocarbon dating, or dating through astronomical events such as solar and lunar eclipses the chronology of ancient Near Eastern history remains notoriously difficult. This is the reason why almost all dates used in this book are either round (e.g. 1600 BC) or are modified by "around" or "ca." In general, I adhere to the so-called *Middle Chronology*, according to which the Hittite king Mursili I conquered Babylon in 1595 BC.[35] The list of Hittite kings (see Timeline and Hittite Kings) reflects this choice and all related uncertainties and contains only two more exact-looking dates. The accession for Urhitessub/Mursili III in 1274 is based on the date for the battle at Kadesh in Ramses II's fifth year (1275 BC) and the assumption that his father Muwatalli II died soon afterwards. The accession of Hattusili III in 1267 goes back to the latter's remark in his Apology that he complied with Urhitessub's policies for seven years until he decided to oust him.

In the question of the number of kings named Tuthaliya between ca. 1420 and the middle of the fourteenth century BC I count the spouse of Queen Nikalmadi as Tuthaliya I (instead of the usual "I/II") and the one of Queen Asmunikal as Tuthaliya II reserving III for the Tuthaliya who is often referred to as Tuthaliya "junior" or "the younger." Since the grandees swore an oath of allegiance to him, he was regarded as king, however briefly, until he was murdered. This leaves IV for the Tuthaliya at the end of the thirteenth century BC.

Relative dating of Hittite texts used to be thought of as more reliable and a helpful complement in Hittite chronology. Especially if a fragment was identified as showing some form of "Old Script" or "Middle Script" that could be used as an important *terminus ante quem* for the events narrated in the text. The most optimistic views claimed a ca. 50-year precision in dating fragments.[36] Over the past 15 years or so this method has come under increasing scrutiny and a complete overhaul of the system is necessary. Although I will sometimes use labels such as OS and MS (Old Script and Middle Script) this only reflects dates traditionally assigned to texts by other scholars. Until a better system has been designed and agreed upon, when dating cuneiform manuscripts in this book, I prefer to use only two general characterizations for the ductus (ie. the specific form in which a sign is written and the order of strokes that together constitute a sign) of Hittite texts: Old Script (OS) for the period ca. 1650–1400/1350 BC and New Script (NS) for the final century and a half between ca. 1350–1200 BC. Obviously, these dates are artificial and approximate, and the transition between the two was gradual.

1.8 Some Final Remarks

This book is not only intended for a Hittitological audience. It is accessible, I hope, also for a non-specialized readership interested in questions of

[35] Schachner 2011a: 14. [36] E.g., Starke 1985: 27.

literacy and script use in the ancient world. No knowledge of Hittite, any of the other Anatolian or ancient Near Eastern languages, or cuneiform or hieroglyphic writing is presumed. Two Appendices following Chapters 3 and 7 offer brief introductions to both writing systems for those who would like to see in some more detail their principles, range and limitations. All quotes from Hittite and other texts will be given in translation with the original language and all necessary references in the footnotes; unless otherwise noted all translations of Hittite or any other language are my own. For Hittitologists, the references in the footnotes include the so-called CTH-numbers, a standard reference in our field. For a less specialized readership, I briefly characterize the kinds of Hittite texts quoted in terms of genre. The genres in question are all discussed in more detail in Chapter 8. In some cases – and here I have to ask for the indulgence of the non-specialized reader – more technical philological parts were inevitable but Appendices 1, 2, and 3 as well as the Excursus in Chapter 14 can be easily skipped.

All Hittite passages in the footnotes are given in *scriptio continua*, or bound transcription, following the system used in the Chicago Hittite Dictionary. This includes the conventional use of *š* and *ḫ* (vs. simply *s* and *h*). In the main text, however, ancient personal and geographical names are given without any diacritics (e.g., Hattusa instead of Ḫattuša). An *s* can be pronounced as a regular English *s*. The only two specific rules are that the *u* is pronounced as in English *put* and ideally *h* like the German *ch* in *Bach*. In the English-speaking world, however, many people just pronounce *h* at the beginning or in the midle of a word as in English *hat*. We know little about word stress in the Hittite language, so some pronounce the name of the Hittite capital Hattusa as HAT-too-sah, others as hat-TOO-sah. Both are fine.

In his book on *Everyday Writing in the Graeco-Roman East* Roger Bagnall sketches the evolution of the modern debate about literacy in later antiquity. From a maximalist high estimate of literate capacities the pendulum swung to the other extreme of literacy being confined to a small elite in an overwhelmingly oral society. This was followed by "a relatively recent wave of scholarship aiming at a more nuanced understanding of writing and the materials of writing in different contexts."[37] Hittite having been deciphered only in 1915 the discipline we call Hittitology is young compared to classical scholarship and we may still be in the first maximalist phase. Some speculate that writing may have started much earlier than our

[37] Bagnall 2011: 2.

sources, strictly taken, allow for; scribes in general are sometimes credited with a wide knowledge of various languages; allegedly, most officials in the kingdom enjoyed a literate education; and writing in both cuneiform script and Anatolian hieroglyphs may have been much more widely spread both in time and social classes than our limited evidence suggests. Although some may consider the views expressed here on these issues as being on the minimalist end of the spectrum following the methodological principles outlined above, I hope they can be taken as riding a more nuanced wave.

CHAPTER 2

Writing and Literacy among the Anatolians in the Old Assyrian Period

2.1 The Beginnings of Writing in Anatolia

The first question that concerns us in a history of writing and reading in Hittite Anatolia, is when script made its first appearance. But then, once arrived, how successful was it? Did it take the country by storm? Was it imported by and for the Anatolians who immediately started using it? Or was it more accidental with the Anatolians looking on and only gradually grasping its advantages? As we will see, the evidence suggests that the local population was not particularly interested at first and by the time writing had won the hearts of some, the political situation changed, and the whole process had to start over again.

For Anatolia or modern-day Turkey history starts some 4000 years ago. Around the start of the twentieth century BC merchants from Assur in northern Mesopotamia set up a network of close to forty trading posts covering all of Central Anatolia and started recording their daily activities.[1] The center of this commercial network was the city of Kanesh (also known as Nesa, modern-day Kültepe) near the upper reaches of the Kızıl Irmak River. The later Hittite capital Hattusa, some 150 km to its northwest, was among the smaller stations. Anatolia with its rich mineral deposits but not much tin was an attractive market. The Assyrians imported just that, tin, much in demand for the local production of bronze, as well as textiles, mostly in exchange for metals such as silver and copper. These metals, in turn, formed the perfect export product to mineral-poor Mesopotamia. The Assyrian traders negotiated conditions for their commerce with the local Anatolian authorities and settled in the towns and villages. Perhaps their most important business tool was the writing system they used. To date over 23,000 documents have come to light, almost all from Kanesh with occasionally texts from other trading posts as well.[2] Currently, just

[1] Veenhof & Eidem 2008: 131–46, Larsen 2015.
[2] On the numbers at Kanesh cf. Michel 2011: 95, 97.

over ninety texts dating to the Old Assyrian Period are known as having been found at Hattusa.[3] All these records together offer invaluable information on the merchants' commercial dealings, their contacts with the local population as well as with their families and business partners back home. They are written in the Semitic language known as Old Assyrian using a specific variant of the cuneiform script well-known from Mesopotamia. Although writing is attested for some 200 years from around 1950 BC onwards, the overwhelming majority of the texts were written in a two-generation period between ca. 1900 and 1860 BC.[4] To what extent the Assyrians used trained scribes for their businesses is difficult to say but this particular system uses one of the most simplified cuneiform orthographies known[5] and many merchants were certainly both passively and actively literate, that is, able to read and write.[6]

This so-called Old Assyrian Colony Period lasted well into the 1720s with one interruption: around 1835 much of Kanesh was destroyed in what may have been an internal Anatolian military conflict and for about two or three years trade came to a halt. A sudden and dramatic drop in text production had already for unknown reasons set in around the mid-1860s but after 1835 records really reduced to a trickle.[7] Archaeologists call the first period (until 1835) Kanesh 2. Business picked up again after 1832, marking the beginning of a new phase known as Kanesh 1b. But if the significantly lower volume of texts left behind by the Assyrians this time – so far only some 450 – is any indication, it may never have fully recovered and completely came to an end perhaps as late as ca. 1700. After this the site remained inhabited for some time (Kanesh 1a) but there is no more written evidence.

Central Anatolia was not a very fertile place. Strips of land with conditions favorable for agriculture were mixed with scrubby forests and the plateau in general is characterized as semi-arid steppe. Its mountainous character made the creation of a unified state encompassing the plateau and beyond a challenge that was not met until the middle of the eighteenth century BC. Until then Anatolia was a conglomeration of independent, large and small, kingdoms[8] as well as probably more remote tribal communities like those of the Kaskaeans that the later king Mursili II would

3 Konkordanz. 4 Larsen 2015: 65–79.
5 Wilcke 2000: 9–10, Dercksen 2007: 32, Kryszat 2008: 231, Larsen 2015: 56–7.
6 Michel 2011: 111, Larsen 2015: 55–6.
7 See the graph in Larsen 2015: 69 and his commentary on the adjacent pages; see also Kloekhorst 2019: 8.
8 Larsen 2015: 137.

describe in his Annals as "not having the rule of one."[9] Some of these may even have attracted early "international" attention witness legendary accounts from the days of Sargon and Naram-Sin in the twenty-third century BC. Supposedly, they came to the rescue of Akkadian merchants in Purushattum (Purushanda) near modern Konya. The Anatolians sustained themselves as best they could in a diversified agropastoral economy: a combination of agriculture and herding, shielding themselves as much as possible against cyclical droughts, moving whenever necessary, and trading with neighboring communities to fill in the gaps. These ecological hurdles may have been one of the reasons for the local populations to also exploit the rich mineral resources and may have encouraged metallurgical expertise.[10] In turn, the abundant presence of copper may have appealed to the business sense of the Assyrians.

In these circumstances the Assyrians lived for well over two centuries among the natives in Kanesh. In terms of material culture they assimilated successfully,[11] it seems, to local conditions and in the course of time also socially: there is ample evidence of Assyrian-Anatolian marriages and inevitably some level of bilingualism on both sides must have resulted from this.[12] Judging by their names and loanwords in the Assyrian records some or even many locals spoke (the Indo-European languages) Hittite and Luwian, others the unrelated Hattian language, and to the south there may have been also some Hurrian speakers around.[13] Given their long presence in Anatolia and the evidence of close interaction between the Assyrians and the local population it is no surprise that on occasion the local Kaneshites started to adopt the foreign cuneiform script for their own purposes.[14] This probably started late in Kanesh 2 and is especially true of the Kanesh 1b phase but on the whole the volume of native Anatolian writing remains small.[15] All evidence, however, shows that they did so using the Assyrian language: no documents from this period have ever been identified as being written in any of the other languages around, whether Hittite, Luwian, Hattian, or Hurrian. The only traces of languages other than Assyrian are the several Akkadianized loanwords from Hittite-Luwian while Anatolian authorship is sometimes betrayed by, for instance, mistakes against Assyrian grammar that

[9] INA [URU]*Gašga* UL ŠA I-EN *tapariyaš ēšta* KBo 3.4 iii 74–5 (Annals of Mursili II, CTH 61, NS), ed. by Grélois 1988: 68, 85 (in his overall line count 77–8).

[10] For a detailed description of Anatolian ecology and the resulting political economy see Burgin 2016 with extensive literature.

[11] Larsen 2015: 244.

[12] See most recently Michel 2011: 111, Larsen 2015: 50, 77, 211–12, 249–52.

[13] Veenhof 2008: 18.

[14] Veenhof 1982, Dercksen 2002: 36, 2004: 137, Kryszat 2008: 235, Michel 2011, Waal 2012.

[15] Michel 2011: 94, 95, 102, 105, Waal 2012: 289.

can most easily be explained from an Anatolian (Indo-European) grammatical point of view.[16] There is also the unequivocal evidence of two letters exchanged between local kings using the Assyrian script and language. One is the letter, found in the palace at Kanesh Ib, sent by Anumherbi, king of Mama, just across the Antitaurus mountains towards Syria, addressed to Warshama, king of Kanesh in the first half of the eighteenth century BC.[17] The text deals with a diplomatic conflict between the two rulers after the violation of Anumherbi's territory by a vassal king of Warshama and has nothing to do with Assyrian commercial affairs.[18] The other is a text, found in Boğazköy in 2018, written by Wiusti to the king of Harsamna (Harsaman) about trade in iron.[19] Wiusti must be the same name as Piusti, king of Hattus, known from the Anitta Text (see §2.2). Both documents suggest that local kings recognized the advantages of a script for long-distance communication and at least occasionally adopted the Old Assyrian writing system and language to correspond with one another.

2.2 Anitta and the First Unified Anatolian Kingdom

It was not until around 1750 BC, during the Kanesh Ib period, that a local warrior by the name of Anitta following in the footsteps of his father Pithana for the first time successfully combined several of the smaller Central Anatolian polities into a unified kingdom. Originally coming with his father from the town of Kussar, probably further to the east, he conquered Kanesh and then chose it as his power base. From there he made himself a kingdom stretching from the Pontic Mountains in the north to the region immediately south of the Kızıl Irmak. One of the other Anatolian kings, the ruler of Purushattum, acknowledged him as a peer and welcomed him to the company of Anatolian kings.[20] In Anitta's own words, one of his exploits was the destruction and cursing of what would later become the Hittite capital Hattusa:

> Whoever becomes king after me and resettles Hattusa, may the Stormgod of Heaven be-*head* him![21]

[16] Dercksen 2007, Kryszat 2008: 234–6, Michel 2011: 107–8, Waal 2012: 289, Kloekhorst 2019: 9. The mistakes in question may also have been made by second- or third-generation Assyrians who, having grown up in Anatolia, might have lost the intricacies of their (grand)parents' grammar.

[17] According to Michel 2011: 109–10, Anumherbi had probably used an Assyrian scribe but Guido Kryszat (personal communication) thinks the text was not written by a native speaker of Akkadian.

[18] Ed. by Balkan 1957. [19] KBo 71.81. [20] Dercksen 2010.

[21] *kuiš ammel āppan* LUGAL-*uš kīšar*[*i*] *nu* URU*Ḫattušan āppa ašāš*[*i*] *n*=*an nepišaš* dIM-*aš ḫazziē*[*ttu*] KBo 3.22 rev. 49–51 (The Anitta Text, CTH 1, OS), ed. by Neu 1974: 12–3. My translation ("*Hatt-* . . . be-*head*")

Anitta's rule is on record for using both the Old Assyrian cuneiform and the language for internal purposes. We have a small tablet probably issued by him and mentioning him as king[22] (Fig. 2.1) and in Kanesh a spearhead was found with the simple inscription: "Palace of Anitta, King."[23] As it stands, it reads as administrative more than anything else, almost as if it were a return address in case the object got lost.[24] In fact, it is a typical example of early, highly object-related script usage marking one's possession.[25]

We do not know for certain what language Anitta's mother tongue was, but a good case can be made for a strong Indo-European element in the population of Kanesh.[26] Anitta, moreover, is the author of an account of his conquests ("The Anitta Text") preserved in Hittite containing the above curse.[27] In it, he narrates his exploits starting from the capture of Kanesh along with his father up to the founding of his kingdom encompassing most of Central Anatolia. The text has not come down to us in a contemporary copy but only as copies from the later tablet collections at Hattusa. The oldest was probably written down somewhere between 1650 and 1400, all others stem from the thirteenth century BC. The text, as we have it, is a compilation consisting of two or three original parts. Anitta concludes the first section as follows:

> "These words [. . .] on/with(?) a tablet at my gate. Let [n]obody in the future destroy th[is tablet]! Whoever destroy[s] it [shall b]e [Nes]a's enemy!"[28]

tries in an admittedly somewhat primitive way to convey something of the pun between the name of the capital Hattusa and the punishment by piercing or stabbing, which in Hitt. is *ḫatt-*.

22 Gelb 1935: text no. 1, pp. 19–21 w. Pl. I; cf. also text no. 49.

23 Larsen 2015: 37.

24 A diplomatic gift, which should have been addressed *to* Anitta and would probably have mentioned the person bestowing it seems unlikely for this object. Neither does it seem to be a dedication, as claimed by Sagona & Zimansky 2009: 250 because one would expect the name of the dedicatee.

25 Thomas 1992: 56–61, Sanders 2009: 55 (for the arrow points of Zakar-Baal), Andrén 1998: 161 ("'Speaking' objects are typical of nascent literacy; they bear reflexive inscriptions such as 'I am a comb' or 'This is a plane'"), Lurie 2011: 68, 74, Woolf 2009: 60.

26 Alp 1997, Carruba 2003: 73, Larsen 2015: 138 ("Most of the people of Kanesh spoke Hittite"), Yakubovich 2010: 1–2.

27 See the edition by Neu 1974 and especially his remarks 132–5; for Pithana and Anitta as Hattians see Popko 1995: 56–7 and, more cautiously, 2008: 47.

28 *kē udd*[*ār*? (*tuppiya*)]*z*? INA KÁ.GAL⸗IA x[. . .] URRAM ŠER[AM] *kī* [*tuppi l*]*ē kuiški ḫul*[(*lezzi*)] *kuiš⸗at ḫulle*[*zzi*] ^{U}[^{RU}*Nēš*]*aš* ^{LÚ}KÚR⸗ŠU *ē*[*štu*] KBo 3.22 obv. 33–5 (The Anitta Text, CTH 1, OS) w. dupl. KUB 36.98a 4–5 (NS), for an edition of this text see Neu 1974: 12–13, for the text as a genuine Hittite composition 132–5; for different translations see Hoffner 1997: 183 ("[I have copied] these [words] from the tablet(s) in my gate") and Carruba 2003: 31 ("Diese Worte sollt ihr aus der Tafel an meinem Tor verkünden"). Whether the tablet mentioned was ever publicly displayed on the city gate is of no importance in this context, cf. Carruba 2003: 112 for more recent literature, and Archi 2015a.

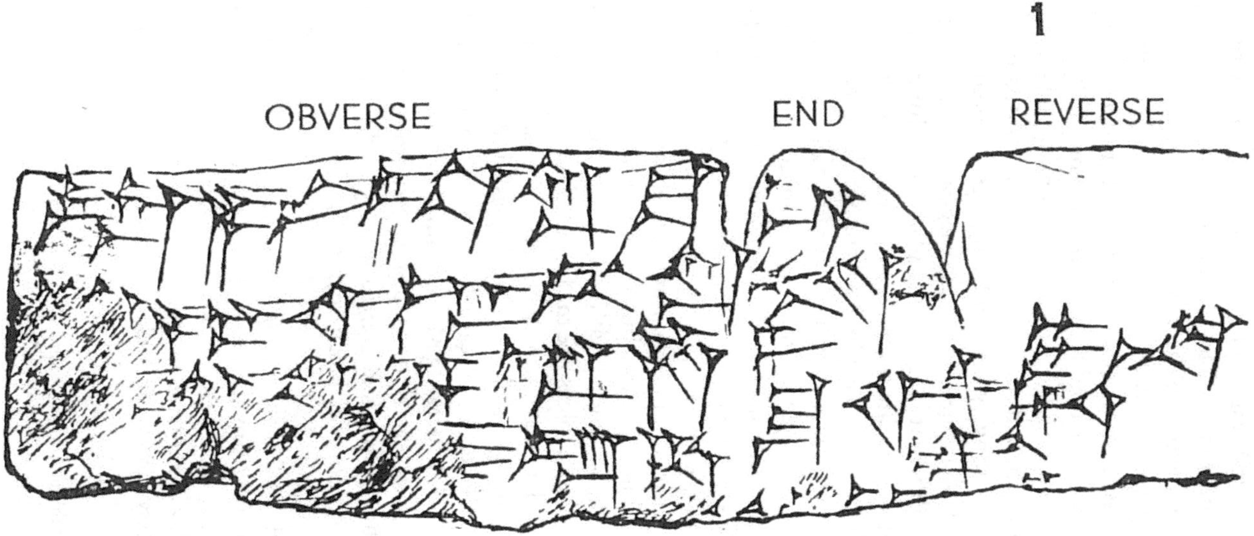

Fig. 2.1 Small tablet with Anitta's name (obv. 1) from Alişar Höyük (from Gelb 1935:Pl. I).

Even though the verb is lost it is clear that the first part of the text, including the curse ("*this* tablet"), was kept or displayed in some written form in or near a city gate in Kanesh. The obvious question is: in what language and what script? And why? To the latter question we will turn at the end of this chapter, but let us first consider the language and script. In the past scholars have observed that the grammar of the Hittite text shows no signs of Assyrian influence and might therefore have originally been composed in Hittite.[29] Although possible, this would be unique: all known records from the Old Assyrian period produced in Anatolia by Anatolians use both the Old Assyrian writing system and language. Typologically speaking, this is normal and what one expects: a society adopting a script from another society with a different language usually starts writing in the language of the other society. There are several reasons for this. First of all, it is not easy to write one's own language in a system not designed to do so.[30] The two languages may well have very different phonological systems (as Indo-European Hittite-Luwian and Semitic Assyrian do in this case) and time is needed to figure out how to express one's own language efficiently and in a way that is understandable to all those participating in the new technology. Using a new script to write the vernacular often takes considerable time experimenting. Also, foreign scribes need time to master the host language while the new, but previously illiterate, local scribes have to learn the writing technique, with all its fine motor skills, and script. Sometimes tradition plays a role: since the first local scribes learn the script along with the foreign language, it may not only be easier or more convenient but perhaps also prestigious and a sign of (quasi-)learnedness to use the other language.[31] In the ancient Near East we see it happening in the case of Sumerian in Akkadian-speaking Mesopotamia, and in the use of the Assyrian dialect in the earliest inscriptions from Urartu from the reign of Sarduri I (ca. 840–820 BC) before they started writing in the Urartean language itself.[32] In similar fashion, the Japanese initially wrote in Chinese and the Romans in Greek.[33]

A final element in all this, is that writing and recording may have been important for the Assyrians to maintain their own identity. The Assyrian presence in Anatolia has been described in anthropological terms as a so-called *trade diaspora*. In such a system it is essential to commercial success for the guest community (the Assyrians) to uphold their own identity, materially

[29] Neu 1974: 132. [30] For more on this process see Chapter 6. [31] Andrén 1998: 147.
[32] Wilhelm 1986: 99, Salvini 1995a: 36–8; more in general see Yakubovich 2015: 49–50.
[33] Feeney 2016: 22–3, 132–3, 173–5.

and socially, as far and as long as possible. While the Assyrians no doubt had to make concessions on a material level (they could hardly move their entire household to Anatolia) and seem to have done so to a large extent, not only their language but also simply using script must have set them off quite effectively from the locals and they may have wanted to keep it that way.[34] The local population may not have been that keen initially to start using the cuneiform script for their own purposes and the Assyrians may not have been eager to share it. But then, was the Old Assyrian cuneiform the only script around and available to Anitta? If so, the choice of the first Hittite dynasty at Hattusa, some three generations later, for a totally different type of cuneiform is very surprising. It suggests a complete break in tradition and a state of illiteracy for Labarna and his descendants, as if they were unfamiliar with the Assyrian script. Had they known it wouldn't they have continued using it? Alternatively, could Anitta already have known and used the cuneiform variant current in Syria at the time, which is considered the forerunner of the later Hittite cuneiform?

It has indeed been suggested that perhaps the Old Assyrian and Syrian cuneiform variants had been used at Kanesh side by side: in his dealings with the merchants, Anitta (or more likely his scribe or scribes) might have used the Assyrian writing system and written in the Assyrian language, and for internal purposes the Syrian one *in Hittite*.[35] The latter is important because usually a society importing a script from another group that speaks and writes a different language, needs some time to figure out how to write their own language in the new script (see Chapter 6). The assumption, then, that Anitta's administration already comfortably wrote in Hittite for internal purposes, would push back the introduction of the Syrian cuneiform by some time. Did this already happen under Anitta's father in the town of Kussar? And if so, from where did the Anatolians get it? The reason this possibility is entertained goes back to two tablets found at Kanesh Ib written not in the Old Assyrian cuneiform but in a Syrian ductus and in a Syrian-influenced Old Babylonian dialect.[36] Both were exchanged between persons bearing Hurrian names, some of them known from the Alalah VII texts.[37] In all likelihood the documents were sent from Syria and

[34] On the trade diaspora model see Stein 2008, for the language as a distinctive element 34; for a critique see Larsen 2015: 149–50.

[35] Güterbock 1983: 24–5; if the correspondence between Anumherbi of Mama and Warshama of Kanesh (see §2.1) is considered internal, then that already speaks against this distinction.

[36] Hecker 1992 and 1995 for Kt k/k 4, and Michel 2010 for Kt 90/k 360; cf. also Weeden 2011a: 63.

[37] The linguistic identity of the sender's name of Kt 90/k 360 (Zi?/Ha?-an, see Michel 2010: 72–76) remains unclear.

therefore not written in Anatolia nor do they allow us to draw any conclusions on the familiarity with this kind of cuneiform script among either the Assyrians or Anatolians at Kanesh. The texts only reflect the Hurrian milieu of northern Syria and their business contacts with Anatolia and it is no surprise two Hurrians would write each other in the script (Syrian) and language (Old Babylonian) familiar to them. The presence of these two texts at Kanesh hardly suffices as a credible source for the later Hittite cuneiform nor are they enough to justify assuming that Anitta's text was written in this rather than the Old Assyrian ductus.

The possibility of a separate and older writing tradition *in Hittite* and in the familiar Hittite ductus has been tentatively raised again after a recent mineralogical analysis of a group of fifty clay tablets found at Hattusa, among which the Old Hittite (OH) exemplar of the Anitta Text.[38] The so-called portable X-Ray Fluorescence analysis places almost all tested Hattusa tablets within a coherent group made of so-called "Hattusa fabric." A few tablets, however, show a different clay composition, suggesting a different place of manufacture and writing of the text in question. The Old Kingdom tablet of the Urshu Text (see Chapter 4.3), for instance, shows petrographic affinities with the Upper-Euphrates area, and the thirteenth century BC Tawagalawa Letter was written on clay coming from the Anatolian west coast. For both texts these results are very valuable but not surprising. In this company, the OH tablet of the Anitta Text, KBo 3.22, is described as "probably Hattusa fabric."[39] The authors do not make clear what the implications of the addition of "probably" are: does the clay still come from Hattusa or not? Did the source of the clay used for this tablet come from Hattusa but removed at some distance from the capital, and is this distance a few hundred meters, some kilometers, or several dozens of kilometers? As the authors state in the article, "clay selection for the production of cuneiform tablets ... was not always consistent."[40] Yet they ask, "is it possible to think of an older Hittite writing tradition starting in a different place may be in Kuššara, the hometown of Hattušili [I]?"[41] Kussar is usually located somewhere east of Kanesh, at roughly 150–200 km from Hattusa.[42] Can that still qualify as Hattusa fabric? For comparison, among the Hattusa tablets tested, there are two Old Assyrian texts. One could be a local product, the other is probably a letter originating from somewhere else. Both apparently show a very different clay composition that places them at quite some distance from the Anitta Text and the

38 Goren et al. 2011. 39 Goren et al. 2011: 687. 40 Goren et al. 2011: 685.
41 Goren et al. 2011: 693. 42 Barjamovic 2011: 143–150.

Hattusa tablets.[43] Without any further explanation, then, this seems like a weak foundation for a far-reaching hypothesis. Again, not only would early Anatolian kings have acquired writing skills before settling in Hattusa, they would already have made the step from writing in Akkadian to writing in Hittite and the typical Hittite cuneiform would already have developed from its Syrian origins (see Chapter 3).

Finally, as another argument in favor of an exposure to Syrian cuneiform writing that Anitta might have used to write his *res gestae* and for a resulting borrowing by the Anatolians, some scholars have referred to the "mountain road of Pithana" mentioned in an edict from Ugarit issued by the later king Mursili II (last quarter of the fourteenth century BC) concerning border affairs.[44] The mountain pass, so the thinking goes, would have taken its name from an alleged military campaign into Syria by Anitta's father, Pithana. Erich Neu presented this reference with all due caution as a possible hint at a folk tradition that once this Pithana had traveled there and thus could have been the conduit for the North Syrian cuneiform variant.[45] The attestation, however, of later namesakes of Pithana and the total absence of any internal records in the Syrian cuneiform make this interpretation of the passage very tentative. Moreover, if the Syrian writing system had been known to the Anatolians to the extent that at some point they consciously preferred the Syrian variant over the Assyrian, the overwhelming presence of the latter and its relative simplicity make it almost necessary to assume that the Syrian system had already been known to them before the Assyrians immigrated with their writing system:[46] only cultural conservatism could have induced the local population to stick with the Syrian cuneiform variant and prefer it over the Assyrian. In the current state of our evidence that seems too much of a stretch. In view of the ca. 450 Assyrian tablets (as opposed to the more than 23,000 from Kanesh 2) known thus far from Kanesh 1b and all we know of the close Anatolian-Assyrian interaction, there is no reason to assume that at this late stage the local Anatolian population would have shown any great interest in the Syrian ductus.

43 Goren et al. 2011: 687 (description), 694 Fig. 6.

44 RS 17.62 + 17.237, see Lackenbacher 2002: 134–5 w. lit.

45 Neu 1974: 135; see also Weeden 2011a: 62–3 w. n. 283. Mark Weeden kindly alerted me to another possible reference to a "servant of Pithana" found as far east as Tell Rimah (west of Mosul) published by Lacambre & Nahm 2015; even if this were Anitta's father (which remains uncertain) it does not necessarily imply that he had been at Tell Rimah himself.

46 Thus Gamkrelidze 2008: 171.

2.3 Central Anatolia: An Illiterate Society in the Old Assyrian Period

All in all, the Anatolians of the Old Assyrian period do not seem to have been that eager to bring writing into their daily lives. As opposed to the situation in the later Hittite kingdom that started around 1650 BC at Hattusa, both the local population living among the Assyrians, and members of the ruling class must have been exposed quite regularly to them writing and doing their business. For centuries if not millennia they had sustained themselves in their ecologically fragmented societies in ways that demanded no written records. Although occasionally already attested for Kanesh 2 native Anatolian literacy seems to have taken off mostly after the destruction that marks the caesura between Kanesh 2 and 1b. It was towards the end of the Assyrian period that the local Anatolian population and ruling elite started to show interest in writing but neither the volume nor the character of Anatolian writing shows an active engagement that permeated their daily existence. The situation is almost paradoxical: it was not until the Assyrian presence had dropped significantly that the native population started using their writing system and language to put in writing several types of agreements that before then they must have concluded orally. But perhaps it is not that much of a paradox if in the context of the trade diaspora with a significantly reduced Assyrian population their hold on the script had perforce loosened.

In the present state of our evidence I consider it unlikely that we can take the two documents found at Kanesh 1b in the Syrian ductus as vestiges of an otherwise hidden or lost world of native writing in an attempt to "save" the Anatolians in the Old Assyrian period from illiteracy. As we will see, the Anatolian hieroglyphs cannot help us either. The earliest individual hieroglyphic signs that later turn up as part of that writing system do not predate the Old Kingdom[47] and we have to wait until about 1400 BC for their first attestation as a fully-fledged script. And, finally, the petrographic analysis of the OH exemplar of the Anitta Text does not seem to justify the speculation of a pre-Hattusa Hittite writing tradition. As a consequence, everything points to a situation where Anatolia under Anitta may have been on the verge of further implementing the Old Assyrian writing system but when Anitta's kingdom broke down and the Assyrians had left, the incentive and inspiration were gone.[48] Anatolians had finally started using

47 See Chapter 7.

48 Cf. the question in Kryszat 2008: 237 ("the most pressing question is why they abandoned it after the end of the Assyrian presence in Anatolia").

the Assyrian cuneiform either because it was fashionable or prestigious, but there may never have been a real need or at least not a need that persisted after the demise of Anitta's kingdom and the Assyrian trading network.[49] Nor did they ever get beyond the first stage of writing in the foreign language. With the Assyrians gone and Anatolia embarking again on a period of economic stagnation and sinking back into their former status of independent city states they may have had other worries and writing disappeared from their daily lives.

In spite of their exposure to writing the native population at Kanesh thus chose to remain illiterate during most of the Old Assyrian Period and when they finally may have been ready to adopt their writing system, the political situation made the choice for them. In the history of writing this is nothing unusual. The Aztecs and Mixtecs of Central Mexico were well aware of Mayan society and their script but it never prompted them to adopt it or to start their own.[50] The tenth century AD Rus were selective in their written contacts with the Byzantine Empire, complying with what was required of them but did not apply any such administrative measures to their own society.[51] If a society runs well without script as "language recorded graphically"[52] the urge to adopt it is often weak or even resisted.[53] Literacy needs a reason: "for literacy to take root in a society it has to have meaning, it needs to have obvious and valuable uses, to be 'relevant' or empowering in some way; and it needs to be in a language that is actually used by the people learning to read."[54] This case can be and has been made for Central Anatolian society in the Old Assyrian Period as well. Neither for Kanesh 2 nor for 1b is there any evidence for a local administrative system at the state level using, for instance, seals.[55] Yet the Old Assyrian documents make it clear there was "a highly structured administration in which each economic sector was represented."[56] It was the local merchants

49 Cf. Spooner & Hanaway 2012: 57 writing about medieval Middle-Eastern societies: "Although writing was within the intellectual reach of all, it attached to only certain positions in the society; if you did not occupy one of those positions, being able to write was not only of no use to you, it was of no interest."

50 Hill Boone 2004: 313, 315. 51 Franklin 2002: 165, 170–1. 52 Hill Boone 2004: 313.

53 Franklin 2002: 7.

54 Thomas 2009: 13, see also McKitterick 1989: 1, and Susan Sherratt 2003: 229 ("[Writing] is not something that people automatically embrace just because they have become aware of the possibility and have encountered the technology. The conditions have to be right. In other words, an appropriate cultural context is needed in which writing can be put to some perceptibly useful purpose").

55 Dercksen 2002, 38 ("Das vermutliche Fehlen einer eigenen Schrift und eigener Siegel bedeutet, dass die einheimische Palastorganisation bis dahin wahrscheinlich sehr gut ohne sie auskam"), 39.

56 Michel 2011: 112.

inspired by their Assyrian colleagues who in Kanesh 2 adopted the cylinder seal albeit with their own indigenous iconography. This was followed by a renewed popularity of the typical Anatolian stamp seal during Kanesh 1b. Such seal impressions have also been unearthed at Acemhöyük, Konya-Karahöyük, and Alişar Höyük in levels roughly contemporaneous with Kanesh 1b. For earlier periods the evidence for administration of some kind in Central Anatolia is extremely scarce. A few stamp seals with geometric designs roughly dating to the Early or Middle Bronze Age have been found at Hattusa.[57] Further east, but still considered Anatolia, the situation is better. Seal-based organization had been in use already during the Middle Chalcolithic at Değirmentepe (ca. 4500 BC)[58] and in the late Chalcolithic (3500–3000 BC) and Early Bronze Age (third millenium BC) at Hacınebi and Arslantepe.[59] Especially the latter site provides a prime example of a detailed and sophisticated bookkeeping system without the need for a script. All this is to show that Anatolian societies were perfectly content with their own ways to administer and conduct transactions and saw no need to upgrade their systems by a wholesale adoption of the Assyrian cuneiform.

Returning to the question of the language and script of Anitta's *res gestae*, in the end the evidence at hand only seems to allow for Anitta having had the first part of his text written in the Old Assyrian language and cuneiform.[60] Witness the tablet, the spearhead, and his text at the gate, all proudly mentioning his name, he had started to discover the power of writing and even if the local Anatolians showed little interest, he wanted to show this off for everybody to see. The step to full implementation of writing was still far away, however, let alone to start writing in Hittite. There is no reason to assume that the existence of the composition excludes a "sudden and total interruption in writing" between Anitta's demise and the rise of the Old Hittite kingdom under Labarna and his successors.[61] Rather, the lore that arose around the founder of the very first Hittite kingdom inspired stories that were kept alive orally in Hittite, which in the end resulted in the text, as it has come down to us in its entirety. Alfonso Archi's observation that the Anitta Text's "literary form excludes its having been transmitted orally as it lacks the necessary narrative tone"[62] does not say that the text could not have been memorized, all the more so since the text goes back to two or three fairly short originally distinct narratives

57 Boehmer & Güterbock 1987: 17 w. Pl. I 1–3.
58 Sagona & Zimansky 2009: 127.
59 Sagona & Zimansky 2009: 146, 155–62 w. lit.
60 Thus also Archi 2015b: 5.
61 Thus Archi 2015b: 6.
62 Archi 2015b: 6.

combined in the Old Kingdom. And who are we to judge how accurately the Hittite version reflects the originals? Also, Anitta and the Old Kingdom were only separated by about three generations.[63] The resulting stories served to give the recently established kingdom some historical depth and legitimacy and were no doubt considered to have pedagogical value as well. The Old Kingdom compilation and redaction was to live on for several centuries in the Hittite state that was to emerge in the city Anitta once cursed.

[63] Carruba 2003: 79–81.

CHAPTER 3

From Kanesh to Hattusa

3.1 The End of Anitta and the Rise of Hattusa

Before we tackle the question of the origin of the Hittite cuneiform we should briefly return to Anatolia's earliest history. Anitta's kingdom and the Assyrian presence at Kanesh both came to an end at roughly the same time but what brought it about is unknown. Although their causes may have been different their roughly simultaneous collapse may not be a coincidence. For Kanesh Ib it is possible that after such a long time the Assyrians were no longer able to maintain their own identity, which was an essential part of their business success. The Anatolians may have started taking over, and trade diluted to the point where it was no longer cost effective for the Assyrians.[1] Because of the lack of records from the subsequent level Kanesh Ia as well as the rest of Anatolia and a gap of about 75 years until Hittite sources start flowing, the intervening years remain largely in the dark. It is not until around 1650 BC that Hattusa re-emerges from Anitta's curse, this time as the capital of a new Hittite kingdom under a Labarna, its eponymous king Hattusili I, and his successor Mursili I. Whether they came from Kanesh or from the still unlocated town of Kussar, the original home of Pithana and Anitta, to which also Hattusili I traced his roots, remains presently unclear. Later Hittite texts suggest that in this transitional period rivalries between several city-states flared up again in the aftermath of Anitta's kingdom, among them Hattusa and Zalpa on the Black Sea coast.[2]

Whatever happened, around the middle of the seventeenth century BC, the first Hittite kings were finally able to transcend the geographical and ecological limitations of their environment.[3] The result was that from around 1650 BC onwards the Hittite kingdom was firmly settled at Hattusa and grew out into an established international power. Our main

[1] Stein 2008: 32. [2] Forlanini 2010, Barjamovic et al. 2012: 43–52, Kloekhorst 2019: 246–68.
[3] Schachner 2017: 220.

source for the Old Hittite Period, the historical introduction to the Proclamation of the later king Telipinu (ca. 1520 BC), describes Labarna as a successful commander conquering several towns in southern Anatolia. According to later tradition he may also have ventured into the country of Arzawa in the west near the Aegaean. His conquests may have served Hattusili I as a stepping-stone for his own campaigns to the northwest but above all those into southeast Anatolia and northern Syria. Being the political and cultural center of the ancient Near East, Mesopotamia attracted all surrounding powers and Syria, as the natural gateway to the Mediterranean and the Aegaean on the Levantine coast, was where they converged. The early kings' initial achievements in the east culminated in Hattusili's conquest of the city of Alalah on the Orontes River but they turned to naught when he had to direct his attention to Arzawa in the west. This gave the Hurrians in the east the opportunity to retaliate. Hattusili, however, struck back with another Syrian campaign and even crossed the Euphrates likening himself to the great Sargon of Akkad.

Meanwhile, Hattusili I had to deal with serious trouble at home. His first appointed successor, the son of his sister, utterly disappointed him and Hattusili therefore deprived him of his status as crown prince. One of his own sons, Huzziya, and a daughter both rebelled and were sent away in exile. In the end Hattusili picked Mursili, his grandson, as heir to the throne. In spite of his remarkable military accomplishments we know relatively little about this Mursili I. He must have been quite young when appointed and was perhaps temporarily guided by a regent. Mursili completed Hattusili's work in Syria by taking Halpa (Aleppo), the most important stronghold and center of the kingdom of Yamhad. He even led his army on a raid against Babylon, some 800 kilometers southeast along the Euphrates. The once famous city was pillaged and left to the Kassites. This extraordinary feat meant little in geo-political terms for the Hittites and is difficult to explain other than being a raid for prestige and loot, but the Syrian conquests at least brought the Hittites the cuneiform script that became their state's foremost administrative medium.

3.2 The Origins of the Hittite Cuneiform

The family of cuneiform writing knows many branches and has a rich ancestry. Extending over more than the first three millennia BC many variants can be distinguished, each having its own characteristic development, changing over time and varying depending on region, and each driven by historical circumstances, expediency, and fashion. Tracking the pedigree of the Hittite variant, as we see it used from the mid-seventeenth century onwards, it is clear that the Old Assyrian cuneiform was not part of its parentage. On the one hand, the departure of the Assyrians – by then two or three generations back – seems to have put a definitive end to the use of their language and their specific cuneiform variety. On the other, we have to take into account that Labarna, as we saw, came from one of the lesser regional settlements, Kussar. Given the very low numbers of Assyrian records found at sites other than Kanesh (compare the ca. ninety tablets known from Hattusa, Chapter 2.1), the exposure to and familiarity with cuneiform by the local populations there must have been modest, to say the least. Whereas we know that the Assyrian script had started to penetrate Anitta's administration, around seventy-five years later, Labarna and his descendants may have had an only vague familiarity with it, if at all. Moreover, early on they turned their political attention to Syria, where another variety of Akkadian was spoken, and another variety of cuneiform was practiced.

The Old Assyrian variety is one of the simpler cuneiform systems with a syllabary of about one hundred signs, a characteristic right slant, and ruled lines (Fig. 3.1).

What we call the typical later Hittite cuneiform has its general place in the Old Babylonian branch of the family used by the dynasty of the famous king Hammurabi. The borrowing cannot have been direct, however. The classic Old Babylonian cursive uses a number of sign shapes that do not match their earliest Hittite counterparts as shown in Table 3.1.

Also, several Hittite spelling characteristics like the lack of distinction between voiced (e.g., *b, d*) and voiceless (e.g., *p, t*) consonants are alien to Old Babylonian and can only be explained from the much older (twenty-third to twenty-second century BC) Old Akkadian language phase. In

Table 3.1 *Comparison of some Old Babylonian signs with their older Hittite counterparts*

sign value	*Babylonian standard*	*Hittite "older"*
AL		
AZ/UK		
IK		
LI		
QA		
SAR		

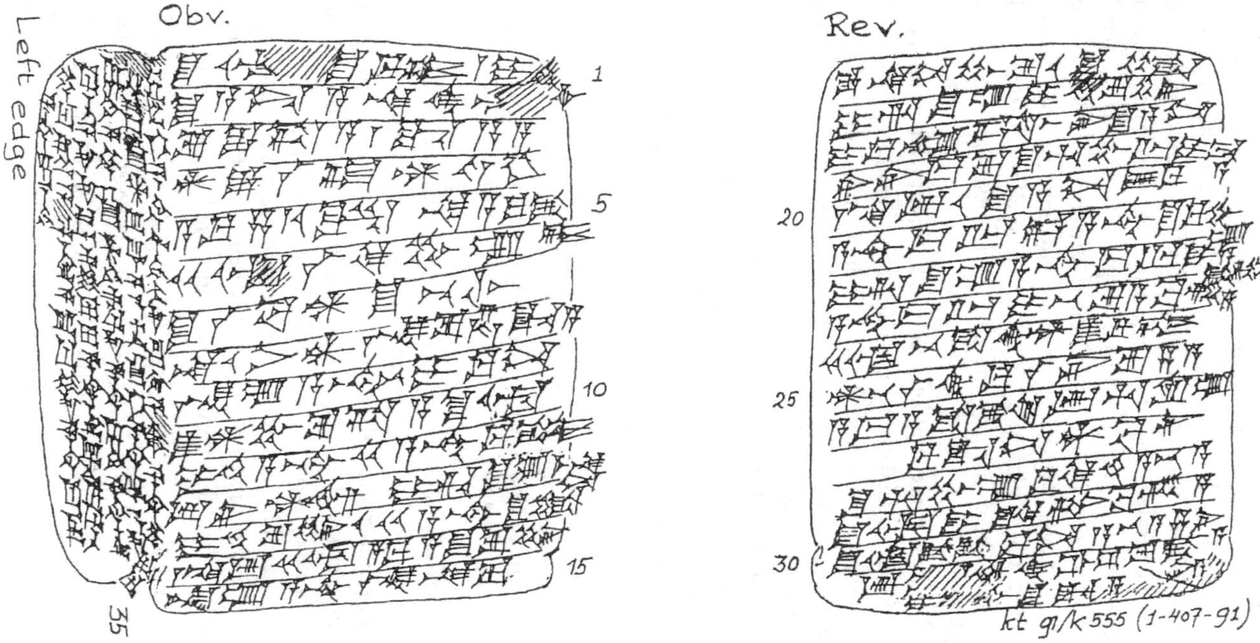

Fig. 3.1 Old Assyrian tablet (from Veenhof 2003 Fig. 4; courtesy K.R. Veenhof).

order to solve these problems scholars already early on looked towards Syria as a possible conduit for this writing tradition to the west.[4] In the period of Kanesh 1b the powerful kingdom of Yamhad ruled Syria from its capital Aleppo with many satellites around it, among which the town of Alalah. Buried as it is under the modern city of Aleppo, the capital itself has yielded no texts but excavations at Alalah produced ample records and scholars' suspicions were confirmed when in 1953 Donald Wiseman published the texts from the Alalah Level VII dating to the eighteenth to seventeenth century BC. For the most part the sign shapes, spelling norms, and grammar can be explained as part of the Old Akkadian and Old Babylonian tradition.

Among the Alalah texts there are likely to be documents that originated in Aleppo and were sent to Alalah. Also, some scribes working there will have been trained in the capital before being stationed at Alalah and so the script and writing system can be considered representative of the kingdom of Yamhad. As to its status of conduit, we know the Hittites were there: when the Hittite king Hattusili I (ca. 1650 BC) had secured his own Anatolian kingdom he immediately looked eastwards. Syria and its fertile plains were the gateway to the then civilized world, Mesopotamia, as well as to the Mediterranean and anything that lay beyond. In his Annals Hattusili describes the *res gestae* of his second year as follows:

> In the following year I went to Alalah and destroyed it. Next, I went to (the town of) Warsuwa, and from Warsuwa I went to (the town of) Ikakali. From Ikakali I went to (the town of) Tashiniya. I destroyed these lands, while taking their goods and filling my palace with goods.[5]

Not only was he there, we even have evidence that he corresponded with local kings. One of them was Tunip-Tessub, also known as Tuniya, ruler of Tikunani. Although not located with certainty, Tikunani is to be sought in the same general northern Syrian area. It is probably there and from illicit excavations that a cache of tablets was found, among them a letter by a certain Labarna (Fig. 3.2). The letter has been dated to Hattusili but in light of recent suggestions to redate some other early documents from Hattusili to his predecessor Labarna, this dating has been called into question as

[4] For a detailed *Forschungsgeschichte* of these matters see van den Hout 2009a; more recently see Wilhelm 2010a and Weeden 2011a: 42–80.

[5] MU.IM.MA-*anni=ma* INA URU*Alalḫa pā⸢un⸣ n=an ḫarninkun* EGIR-*anda*[*=m*]*a* INA URU*Waršuwa pāun* URU*Waršuwaz=ma* INA URU*Ikakali pāun* URU*Ikakalaz=ma* INA URU*Tašḫiniya pāun nu kē* KUR.KUR.MEŠ *ḫarninkun āššu=ma=šši šarā daḫḫun nu* É-*er=mit āššauīt šarā šunnaḫḫun* KBo 10.2 i 15–21 (Annals of Hattusili I, CTH 4, NS), ed. by de Martino 2003: 34–7.

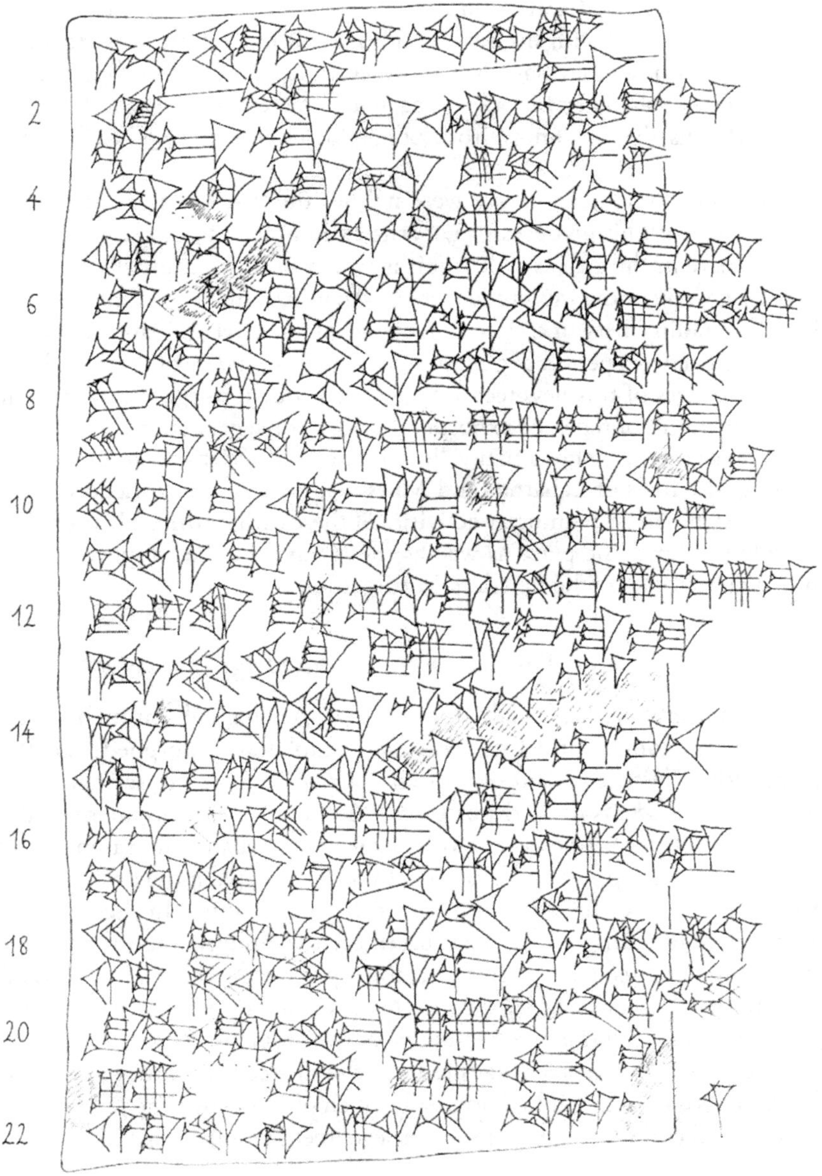

Fig. 3.2 Letter of Hattusili I to Tunip-Tessub (obv., from Salvini 1994; courtesy M. Salvini).

well.[6] The letter is, of course, in Akkadian: if the sender wanted to make himself understood with his Syrian addressee, it made little sense to write in Hittite. Also, he may have wanted to come across as a cultured person, versed in more than just his own vernacular. The text is written in the local Syrian ductus that we know from other documents and especially from Alalah.[7]

Hattusili's Syrian campaigns were neither the first nor the last Hittite ones there. Both his predecessor Labarna and immediate successor Mursili I were active in the area as well. Yet it is Hattusili I who is usually credited as the one reintroducing cuneiform in Anatolia after the demise of the Assyrian trading network. The borrowing of the Syrian script, however, may have needed a period of gestation, of becoming aware of the usefulness and advantages of this new technology for their own purposes. As such, it can be the result of repeated exposure during a concentrated period of time and whoever it was who actually "hired" the first Syrians to do his scribal bidding, the roles of Labarna[8] and Mursili should be acknowledged, too. Whatever the case, the military activities of these earliest three Hittite kings provide the time, the place as well as the motive for the adoption of the Syrian cuneiform by the fledgling Hittite kingdom.

3.3 The Case for a Syrian Origin

While northern Syria is usually identified as the channel, through which the Old Babylonian cuneiform reached Anatolia and morphed into the characteristic Hittite variant, it is often done with some unease. The main reason for this seems to be the assumption of a linear development of the Hittite cuneiform script as well as an alleged discrepancy in a number of sign shapes that supposedly resist this. In order to explain the problem, we need to go back to the 1970s and 80s of the past century. In these years a rigid system of dating Hittite texts based on a seemingly smooth development of the ductus of signs as well as the aspect of the tablets was worked out and widely accepted.[9] The cornerstone of this system was a historical fragment – the "Zukrasi Text" after one of the protagonists in it – found at Boğazköy in 1952 in a layer that predated the thirteenth century BC. Since the events recounted in it had originally taken place in the time of Hattusili I it was declared an original from the seventeenth century BC. The piece

[6] Weeden 2011a: 76.

[7] For a paleographic analysis see Salvini 1994; for further remarks see Weeden 2011a: 70–6, van den Hout 2012a, see also Payne 2015: 16 w. lit.

[8] Forlanini 2010: 118–9.

[9] For the terms "ductus" and "aspect" see van den Hout 2012a: 152–3.

showed certain traits that had been observed before on other fragments that had been unearthed in later strata from the thirteenth century. Now these, too, could be recognized as genuinely Old Hittite. Apparently, the Hittites sometimes stored older tablets for several centuries. The assumption, however, that the Zukrasi Text was a virtually contemporaneous account was exactly that, an assumption not supported by any evidence. Yet it became the keystone of a paleographic construct that soon overshadowed its own foundation witness the fact that many years later the text was officially listed as of uncertain date: "old?/middle? script."[10] By definition, historical accounts are written after the fact but how long after? One year, 100 years, more? The archaeological context of the fragment was only identified as pre-thirteenth century and nothing helped to narrow this down. The assumption that the Zukrasi Text was a scribal product of the days of Hattusili I had yet another implication. Since the fragment was written in Hittite (as opposed to Akkadian) some scholars now believed that the Hittites therefore had been writing in their own language since at least about 1650 BC. Assuming a necessary learning curve that comes with the adoption of any foreign writing system this in turn meant that the borrowing of the Syrian ductus should have happened some time or well before Labarna or Hattusili.[11] The two Syrian ductus tablets found in Kanesh 1b (see Chapter 2.2), as some have suggested recently, would nicely fit this picture. According to that theory, the Syrian cuneiform was already around in the Old Assyrian period, probably still used to write Akkadian, and three generations later the Hittite kings used it for their own language.[12] The inevitable experimentation phase would be hidden in between.

Taking all those now re-dated "old" texts together and comparing them with all the later ones, a set of characteristics was identified that made up what was then called "Old Script." Moving forward, a history of Hittite cuneiform in three subsequent stages was posited (Table 3.2).

Looking at how cuneiform signs changed shape over the course of history enabled scholars to date manuscripts, that is, when a particular fragment had been written. While the changes from OS to MS were supposed to be fairly subtle, the real contrast comes in the second half of the fourteenth century with new sign shapes typical of NS. Those assigned to OS and MS are usually labeled "old" or "older" vs. "late" or "later" for those of the NS period (Table 3.3).

10 "ah.?/mh.?", see Konkordanz (accessed June, 2017) under KBo 7.14 or 29/k; Maciej Popko 2005 was the first to express doubt about the Old Hittite dating of this text's ductus and aspect.
11 Klinger 1998: 374, Wilhelm 2010a: 257 (referring to an earlier publication), Gates 2017: 194–5.
12 See Devecchi 2005: 25 and more explicit Weeden 2011a: 24, 57, 63 w. n. 289, 71–4, 371, 382.

Table 3.2 *Traditional model of Hittite paleographic stages*

Old Script (OS)	1650–1500 BC
Middle Script (MS)	1500–1350 BC
New Script (NS)	1350–1200 BC

Table 3.3 *Some diagnostic signs as used in dating Hittite texts*

Cuneiform sign	OS	MS	NS
AK			
AZ/UK			
DA			
E			
HA			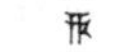
IK			
IT			
LI	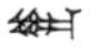		
QA			
SAR			

However, some of the most diagnostic OS and MS signs in this system do not match their Old Babylonian counterpart (Table 3.4).

In all these cases the Babylonian forms that were assumed to be the source for the script adopted in the Old Kingdom correspond to the Hittite NS shapes that were not supposed to be attested before the end of the fourteenth century BC! If the Hittite ductus ultimately arose out of the Old Babylonian cursive, then it should have used those shapes from the outset. This led to speculations that the Hittite cuneiform went back to a variant that was clearly older than the one used in northern Syria in the days of Labarna and his two successors,[13] and older, too, than the ductus of the two Syrian tablets found at Kültepe (see Chapter 2) that also show so-called later signs.[14] But it remains unclear when and where the Hittites would have borrowed this. Also, why did Hittite OS – with a few exceptions – overwhelmingly rely on

[13] Klinger 1998: 371, 374.

[14] Cf., for instance, the signs KÙ, QA in Kt 90/k 360; for the other tablet Kt k/k 4 see Chapter 2 n. 32.

Table 3.4 *Some Babylonian standard signs compared to their Hittite counterparts*

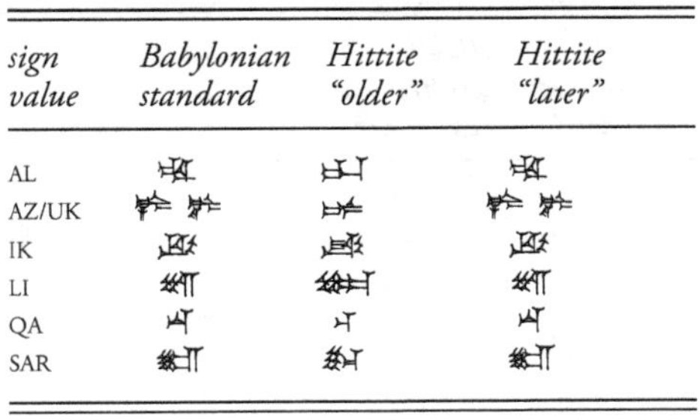

sign value	*Babylonian standard*	*Hittite "older"*	*Hittite "later"*
AL			
AZ/UK			
IK			
LI			
QA			
SAR			

these older forms? And how do we explain these exceptions? The answer to these questions can be found in Alalah in northern Syria.

3.4 A Closer Look at the Alalah Ductus

The military activities in Syria by Labarna, Hattusili I, and Mursili I provide the time, place, and motive for the records found at Alalah to be a fitting candidate for being the source of the later Hittite ductus. All the more so, because the Alalah ductus shows a mix of sign shapes that satisfactorily explains why the "older" variants are so typical of OS.[15]

The Syrian cuneiform for which Alalah is representative ultimately came from Babylon but shows the typical traits of a peripheral area that is no longer subject to the standardizing pressures of its source. In the early centuries of the second millennium Syrian scribes developed certain variant sign forms that were distinctly non-Babylonian (Table 3.5).

As the table (3.5) shows, the newly developed and most frequently used variants at Alalah are the same as the standard "old(er)" (or OS) Hittite forms. The new variant shapes at Alalah even became the most popular appearing on average in 75 percent of the cases.

With the exception of the sign EN, and to a certain extent SAR, the scale clearly tips in favor of the "older" shapes. Most of the more frequent signs in Alalah show some kind of simplification: one or more strokes or wedges less (AL, AK/UZ, QA, SAR) or a turn of the wrist or tablet less while writing (IK). It is nothing surprising that in their adoption of the Old Babylonian

[15] For a full analysis of the Alalah VII ductus compared to the later Hittite see van den Hout 2012a.

Table 3.5 *Some Babylonian standard signs compared to the same ones in texts from Alalah VII*

sign value	*Babylonian standard*	*Alalah less frequent (ca. 25 percent)*	*Alalah most frequent (ca. 75 percent)*
AL			
AZ/UK			
IK			
LI			
QA			
SAR			

Table 3.6 *Percentages for the relative frequency of the Hittite "older" and "later" sign shapes in texts from Alalah VII*

sign value	*"older" percent*	*"later" percent*
AL	69.2	30.8
AZ/UK	87.5	12.5
EN	25	75
IK	68.8	31.2
LI	94	6
QA	64.7	35.3
SAR	50	50
TAR	82.3	17.7
UN	80	20

script out of a "natural inclination to maximize speed and economy in writing" the scribes at Alalah developed their own kind of cursive or shorthand by simplifying frequently used signs, as long as confusion with other signs was avoided.[16] The relative frequency of the variants means that in a situation of borrowing, the more frequent shapes are the ones most likely to be adopted. This brings the Alalah corpus and Hittite OS much closer together.[17] It is exactly this mix of sign forms that makes it

[16] Salomon 2012: 121, 122–3.

[17] This explains the alleged discrepancy between the two groups of signs as compared in Wilhelm 2010a: 260 Fig. 3.

possible to see the Alalah VII ductus as *the* source of the Hittite cuneiform. It also explains the occasional early appearance of some of the "later" sign forms in Hattusa. Both scripts show a combination of shapes for certain signs, one of them decidedly more frequent. The only difference between the Alalah and Hattusa ductus is that the less frequent ones at Alalah appear even less frequently in Hattusa. In a genuine Syrian development, the more cursive shapes started from a minority position until they finally reached the point where the original Babylonian signs were reduced to a 25 percent share. By the time we encounter the Hittite variant in the sixteenth century BC we see that share reduced even further. The Anatolian scribes simply continued and speeded up the process of cursivization their Alalah colleagues had gone through earlier. The first generation of Anatolian scribes around 1650 BC, born into a state of illiteracy since the departure of the Assyrians some three generations before, saw itself confronted with some 300 signs to memorize. In such a situation, needless variants soon lose their charm.

In his study of Hittite logograms Mark Weeden raises the objection that there are many sign forms used at Alalah that we do not see in Hattusa.[18] He lists seventeen signs with variants that we do not encounter in the Hittite texts. But that we do not see the entire inventory of Alalah VII signs and all their variant shapes is hardly surprising: while adopting a script from elsewhere, a society also adapts it, tweaking the system, and certain original nuances can be lost in transition. More compelling would be evidence for the opposite, that is, variants used in the oldest texts at Hattusa wholly unknown from the Alalah corpus. Here the only sign Weeden mentions is Ù (), which, as he himself admits, is known at Alalah but only in its reading for the goddess Ištar (^{d}IŠTAR).[19] Both signs, very much alike, are attested at Hattusa and share at least seven or eight variants between them.[20] All this, therefore, is hardly probative against an Alalah or more general Syrian origin. As Weeden himself states "surrounding cuneiform cultures were using all manner of sign-forms contemporaneously"[21] and it is the traditional view of what constitutes Hittite OS with its strict set of sign shapes that is surprising and leads him, understandably, to conclude that "the scribal school of Hattusa was either extremely small, or very disciplined and conservative."[22] Small the group almost certainly was, as we will also see in Chapter 13, but instead of

[18] Weeden 2011a: 65–70, similarly Wilhelm 2010a: 259. [19] Weeden 2011a: 69.

[20] Variants HZL 265 (Ù)/6, 11–6, 19?, 21 can be found back in basically identical shape in HZL 263 (IŠTAR)/2–4, 6, 8, 9, 12, 16?.

[21] Weeden 2011a: 45. [22] Weeden 2011a: 70, see also 45.

conservative I would rather call them efficient and no-nonsense, streamlining the adopted script ever more, as adoptees are wont to do. The reduction in sign shapes at Hattusa is as evident as it is unsurprising.[23] What *is* surprising is how the scribes of the New Hittite kingdom starting in the fourteenth century BC reversed this process. As we saw above, the "later" sign shapes (that corresponded to the Old Babylonian cursive) were already present in the Old Kingdom but relatively rarely used or largely dormant. When the scribes reinstated some of the original Old Babylonian sign shapes at the expense of the original and typical Syrian ones, they were responsible for a distinctly non-linear development. Future research will have to show whether the introduction of these sign shapes was a relatively simultaneous and one-time event or whether they came into being at different "speeds" and spread over a long time.[24]

3.5 Conclusion

The above facts and considerations strongly suggest that the cuneiform variant that developed into the one we call Hittite found its way into Anatolia in the second half of the seventeenth century BC in the wake of the Syrian campaigns of the first three Hittite kings, Labarna, Hattusili I, and Mursili I. The cuneiform of Alalah VII is the only one that can explain the specific traits of the later Hittite system, especially the curious mix of "older" and "newer" sign shapes. In the course of their military expansion the early kings adopted the Syrian script out of necessity to communicate with their peers and perhaps because the cachet of using writing added prestige to their kingdom on the rise.

The cuneiform script as found in the Labarna Letter or the Syrian tablet from Kültepe fits this picture. With very few and small exceptions the sign shapes of both are very close to the Alalah VII ones. As far as the exceptions are concerned, we have to keep in mind that the Syrian tablets predate the Labarna-Hattusili era by at least two generations and the Labarna Letter was likely written by a local Syrian scribe hired by the Hittite king.[25] With the simplifications that come with the usual process of adoption and adaptation, as we will see them in Chapter 6 as well, the road from there to the later typical Hittite ductus was a fairly straight one.[26]

23 For more on this see Chapter 6.

24 See on this the excellent article by Weeden 2016b.

25 For a palaeographic comparison of the Labarna Letter and the Syrian letter (kt. k/k 4) found at Kültepe see Salvini 1994.

26 It is not quite clear what Wilhelm 2010a: 257 means by "specific" when he writes that "the signs [in one of the two Syrian letters] have hardly anything specific in common with the Old Hittite Script."

The absence so far of any inner-Anatolian and non-Old Assyrian written records datable before them is not only consistent with the view proposed here but this documentary void combined with the clear and consistent choice of the Syrian over the Old Assyrian cuneiform is a powerful argument in favor of an extended period, in which Central Anatolia was cut off from literate traditions. This period may have lasted up to at least two generations (ca. 1700–1650 BC), the time between the definitive end of Old Assyrian presence with their commercial recording practices at Kanesh and the new beginning of the Hittite king Labarna I and his successors. The settling of the new Hittite dynasty at Hattusa meant a significant political break for the local Luwian-Hattian society there. It does not, however, necessarily mean an overall cultural break. They all were Anatolians after all.[27]

3.6 Appendix: A Brief Introduction to Hittite Cuneiform

The standard sign inventory for the Hittite cuneiform script (Rüster & Neu 1989), comprises 375 entries, or 375 different signs. Some 180 can be found in this Appendix, grouped in five tables. Tables 3.7–3.11 contain the most common signs with a syllabic sound value, used to write Hittite; Akkadian texts from Hattusa are usually written with the same signs. These signs either represent just a vowel (e.g., *a*, Table 3.7), or a combination of consonant + vowel (e.g., *pa*, Table 3.8), vowel + consonant (e.g., *ap*, Table 3.9), or consonant + vowel + consonant (e.g., *pap*, Table 3.10). Only one cuneiform variant shape per sign is given here, usually the older one. The occasional accent over a vowel (e.g., *pé/í*or *zé*) or number in subscript (e.g., *kit*$_9$) serves to distinguish the exact sign used on a tablet in case of so-called *homophony* (i.e., the existence of more than one sign with the same sound value): the unmarked transliteration (e.g., *pe* without accent or index number) is "*pe*-one," *pé* is "*pe*-two," *pè* is "*pe*-three," *pe*$_4$ is "*pe*-four," etc. *Polyphony* (i.e., one sign with different sign values: e.g., *pa/ḫat, ut/pir, kal/dan*) also occurs. On the whole, compared to cuneiform writing systems in Mesopotamia, the extent of both homophony and polyphony in Hittite cuneiform was minimal.

He is likewise pessimistic about the Labarna Letter: "The sign forms do not lead to the Old Hittite inventory of sign forms." Although for the most part identical, the few that slightly deviate are fully explainable by the scribe having been a locally hired craftsman.

27 Gates 2017 pleads in favor of significant continuity (in glyptics and texts, 192–6) between the Old Assyrian period and the Old Hittite state while also acknowledging clear breaks in, for instance, architecture or pantheon (196–200).

Table 3.11 lists the most common logograms or *Sumerograms*, single signs that stand for an entire word or concept. One can compare our numerals: the single shape <6> stands for "six" but will be read differently depending on the reader's/text's language. In Dutch it will be read as "zes," in Turkish "altı," etc. As cross-references (>) make clear, many of the logograms also have syllabic (Hittite) values that have already occurred in Tables 3.7–3.10. In addition, several among the logograms can also be used as *determinatives*, signs that mark a word as belonging to a certain class (men, women, deities, animals, things made of wood, metals, stone, geographical names and entities, etc.).

3.6.1 Vowels

The Hittite cuneiform distinguishes five different vowels, two of which are transliterated by *u*. However, the vowel signs <u> and <ú> are generally kept strictly apart pointing to a different quality, possibly /o/ and /u/ vel sim., respectively.

Table 3.7 *Hittite cuneiform vowel signs*

a 𒀀	e 𒂊	i 𒄿	u 𒌋	ú 𒌑

3.6.2 Consonant + Vowel Signs

Table 3.8 offers a full and systematic inventory of all consonants followed by at least four of the above vowels (CV). All possible slots are filled (e.g., *ta, te, ti, tu*). The distinction between and <ú> could be made here, too, by combining <Cu> signs with a so-called *plene-written* or <ú> (e.g., <pu-ú> for /pu/ or <pu-u> for /po/). A distinction between /e/ and /i/ was available for some signs (e.g., <te> vs. <ti>), in others one sign stood for both (e.g., <pé/í>). However, <Ce/i> signs could be disambiguated by adding a plene-written <e> or (e.g., <pé-e> for /pe/, <pí-i> for /pi/). This does not say that, for instance, <te> could not occasionally have a /ti/ reading. It does (<ti$_7$>), but this is rare and usually occurs in rendering Akkadian words only, where Akkadian grammar demands it. Consonants are given in the following order: labials, dentals, dorsals, laryngeals, nasals, liquids, sibilants, and the glides w, and y. The specially created signs consisting of the cuneiform sign <wa> with subscript vowels, probably rendering some /f/- like sound (see Chapter 6.2), are not listed here because they are not used in writing Hittite.

Table 3.8 *Hittite cuneiform consonants+vowel signs*

C*a*		C*e*		C*i*		C*e/i*		C*u*	
pa	𒉺					pé/pí	𒁉	pu	𒁍
ba	𒁀								
ta	𒋫	te	𒋼	ti	𒋾			tu	𒌅
da	𒁕					de/di	𒁲	du	𒁺
ka	𒅗					ke/ki	𒆠	ku	𒆪
ga	𒂵					ge/gi	𒄀	gu	𒄖
ḫa	𒄩	ḫé	𒃶	ḫi	𒄭			ḫu	𒄷
ma	𒈠	me	𒈨	mi	𒈪			mu	𒈬
na	𒈾	ne	𒉈	ni	𒉌			nu	𒉡
la	𒆷					le/li	𒇷	lu	𒇻
ra	𒊏					re/ri	𒊑	ru	𒊒
ša	𒊭	še	𒊺	ši	𒅆			šu	𒋗
za	𒍝	zé	𒍢	zi	𒍣			zu	𒍪
wa	𒉿					we/i$_5$	𒃾		
ya	𒅀								

3.6.3 Vowel + Consonant

Table 3.9 offers a full and systematic inventory of all consonants preceded by at least four of the above vowels (VC). Just as with the CV signs under Table 3.8, through plene-written vowels, signs of the structure <uC> and <e/iC> could be disambiguated. Consonants are given in the following order: labials, dentals, dorsals, laryngeals, nasals, liquids, sibilants; note that in VC signs ending in a labial, dental, or dorsal, there is no distinction between the quality of the stops (e.g., depending on the context, the sign 𒀜 can be transliterated as *at* or *ad*); this is indicated here by writing aP, aT, aK, respectively.

3.6.4 Consonant + Vowel + Consonant

In general, Consonant+Vowel+Consonant (CVC) signs are less frequent and show less system than V, CV, and VC signs. In some cases, CVC signs have variant readings (e.g., the CVC sign <ḫat> doubles as <pa> or the sign <kal> can also be read <dan>). With cross-references in case of polyphony (i.e., one sign with different sign values), Table 3.10 contains a selection of the more common CVC signs.

Table 3.9 *Hittite cuneiform vowel+consonant signs*

*a*C		*e*C		*i*C		*e/i*C		*u*C	
aP						e/iP		uP	
aT						e/iT		uT	
aK						e/iK		uK	
a/e/i/uḫ									
am						e/im		um	
an		en		in				un	
al		el		il				ul	
ar						e/ir		ur	
aš		eš		iš				uš	
az						e/iz		uz	

Table 3.10 *Hittite cuneiform consonant+vowel+consonant signs*

CAC		pár	> maš	nir	
bal		pát		pir	> ut
dan		rat		piš	> kir
gal		šal		šir	
ḫal		šar		tén	
ḫar		taḫ		tim	
ḫaš		ták			
ḫat	> pa	tal	> ri	CuC	
kap		tap		gul	
kal	> dan	tar	> ḫaš	ḫul	
kam		tàš		ḫup	
kán				ḫur	> ḫar
kaš	> pé/í	Ce/iC		kum	
kat		kir		kur	
lam		kiš		lum	
maḫ		kit$_9$	> kat	mur	> ḫar
mar		lim	> ši	pur	
maš		liš		šum	
nam		miš		šur	

3.6.5 Sumerograms and Logograms

Table 3.11 lists 100 of the most common Sumerograms or logograms. According to Hittitological convention they are transliterated in capitals.

Table 3.11 Sumerograms and logograms

reading	sign	meaning	reading	sign	meaning
ALAM		statue	KI	> ki	earth
AMA		mother	KUR	> kur	land
AMAR		lamb	KÚR		enemy
AN	> an	heaven	KUŠ		leather, skin
ANŠE		equid	LÀL		honey
ARAD/ÌR		servant, slave	LÚ		man
BABBAR	> ud	white	LUGAL		king
BANŠUR		table	ME	> me	100
DAG	> tàk	throne, dais	MÈ		battle
DAM		wife, spouse	MEŠ		(forms plur.)
DANNA		mile	MU	> mu	year
DI	>di	court case	MUḪALDIM	> mu	cook
DINGIR	>an	deity	MUN		salt
DÙ		to make	MUNUS	> šal	woman
DUB		tablet	MUNUS.LUGAL		queen
DUG		container	MUŠEN	> ḫu	bird
DUMU		son, child	NA$_4$		stone
É		house	NIN		sister
EGIR		behind, after	NINDA		bread
EME		tongue	NUMUN		seed
EN	> en	lord	PÚ		spring
ÉRIN		troops	SAG		head
EZEN$_4$		festival	SANGA		priest
GABA		breast	SAR	> šar	plant
GADA	> kat	textile, linen	SÍG		wool
GAL	> gal	big; cup	SIG$_5$		good
GAM		down, below	SIPA		shepherd
GAŠAN		lady	SÌR		song
GEŠTIN	> we/i5	wine	SISKUR		ritual
GEŠTUG	> wa	ear	ŠÀ		heart, inside
GIBIL		new	ŠAḪ		pig
GIDIM		deceased	ŠE	> še	cereal
GIDRU	> pa	sceptre	ŠEŠ		brother
GIG		illness	ŠU	> šu	hand
GIGIR		vehicle	TU$_7$		stew, pot
GÍR		knife	TUKU		angry, anger
GÌR		foot	TUKUL	> ku	tool, weapon
GIŠ	> e/iz	wood	TUR	> dumu	small
GU$_4$		bovine	Ù		dream
GÙB	> kap	bad, evil	UD	> ud	day
GUŠKIN		gold	UDU	> lu	sheep

Table 3.11 (*cont.*)

ḪI.A	> ḫi and a	(forms plur.)	UGU	𒌋𒅗	above, over
Ì	> ni	oil	UN	> un	human being
ÍD	𒀀𒇉	river	URU	𒌷	settlement
IG	> ik	door	URUDU	𒍐	copper
IGI	> ši	eye	ÚŠ	> pát	death
INIM	> ka	affair, word	UTU	> ud	sun deity
KARAŠ	𒆠𒆗𒁁	army	UZU	𒍜	meat, flesh
KASKAL	𒆜	road, trip	ZAG	𒍠	right; border
KAŠ	> pé/í	beer	ZI	> zi	soul

As indicated by the cross-references, some signs also have a syllabic value (e.g., syllabic *ḫu* besides Sumerographic MUŠEN), others are only used as logograms (e.g., DUMU); some signs have more than one Sumerian reading (e.g., DUMU/TUR). The choice between all these readings depends solely on the context.

CHAPTER 4

First Writing in Hattusa

4.1 From Mursili I to Telipinu

Mursili I's extraordinary march on Babylon and subsequent sacking of Hammurabi's famous city in 1595 BC literally brought him everlasting fame, as I write these lines more than 3500 years after the fact. Yet he also paid the ultimate price, his life. His campaign must have kept him away from home for at least two or three years in a row. The resulting power vacuum in the capital Hattusa gave free rein to ambitions and intrigues among those left behind. When he finally returned Mursili was murdered by his own son Zidanta and his brother-in-law Hantili. Although Hantili reportedly showed feelings of remorse, it did not keep him from ascending the throne as the next king. Probably fearing he might be passed over for kingship at Hantili's death Zidanta thereupon murdered Hantili's son Piseni along with his sons and servants and seized the throne. Zidanta, in turn, was killed by his own son Ammuna. Ammuna's reign is described as disastrous on several counts: he was unable to check a rebellion and alleged setbacks in agriculture and animal husbandry suggest general hardships. Yet he seems to have died of natural causes and was eventually succeeded by Huzzija whose filiation is not given. For reasons unknown this Huzziya feared his brother-in-law Telipinu and planned to kill both him and his wife. Telipinu found out just in time and not only avoided an early end but even managed to dethrone Huzziya. In a welcome break with tradition Telipinu did not kill Huzziya in revenge but just banished him and his five brothers from the capital. In doing so he hoped to put an end once and for all to the chain of killings which had kept the dynasty in its grip for four generations now: "They did evil to me but I [will not do] evil to them."[1] In his so-called "Proclamation" or "Edict" Telipinu laid down new rules for succession, hoping to avoid any further inner-dynastic strife.

[1] *apē=wa=mu idalu iēr ug=a=war=uš* ḪUL-*lu* [UL *iyami*], KBo 3.1 ii 15 (Telipinu Edict, CTH 19, NS), ed. by Hoffmann 1984: 28–9.

They were meant to be a decisive break with a previous system, in which the son of the king's sister traditionally was the heir to the throne. In a society that otherwise seems largely to have operated along patrilinear principles this custom had come under increasing pressure.[2] In another break with tradition Telipinu's Proclamation was one of the last texts to be composed in both Hittite and Akkadian. From now on internal records were to be written in Hittite only.

4.2 First Writing in Hattusa

We saw (Chapter 3) that there is no evidence for an adoption of the Syrian type of cuneiform or for the existence of any Hittite-language texts before Labarna and the start of the Old Hittite kingdom in Hattusa around 1650 BC. But what about the period of the Old Hittite kingdom itself? In the history of writing it is normal that societies that adopt a foreign writing system start writing in the language that comes with the system. This was certainly true of the Anatolians of the nineteenth century BC when they started slowly adopting the Old Assyrian cuneiform for their own purposes and did so using the Assyrian language. Did this typologically normal process repeat itself around 1650 BC when the Hittites learned to use the Syrian cuneiform? The answer to this question depends on the dating of the texts that belong to this period because of kings or historical events mentioned in them. We have compositions that are set in the time period 1650–1400 BC written in Akkadian, in Hittite, and we also have some Akkadian-Hittite bilingual texts. Unfortunately, the traditional system for the dating of Hittite texts has run into problems that make it particularly difficult to date texts with any precision. Recently, Maciej Popko[3] and Jared Miller[4] have shown that certain texts labeled OS can only have been written after 1500, which traditionally marked the end of the OS period. Both scholars therefore proposed to redefine the OS and MS periods. Popko advocated a three-tiered MS period with the first tier basically overlapping with OS, the second tier starting with King Muwatalli I (ca. 1430/1420) and the third around 1400.[5] We see a similarly short MS phase in Miller's proposal. In doing so both authors have basically given up on a meaningful paleographic distinction within the period 1650–1400 BC and one wonders about the reality of the next paleographic

[2] Sürenhagen 1998, Forlanini 2010 w. lit.; this is the so-called *avuncular* system. However, it should be noted that this is by no means the view advocated by all Hittitologists. Others argue that the Hittite succession system had always been patrilineal and that Telipinu was simply re-stating old rules.

[3] Popko 2005 [2006] and 2007. [4] Miller 2004: 463 n. 773. [5] Popko 2005 [2006]: 11–12.

phase that does not last much longer than 25 to 50 years at the most. Meanwhile detailed observations on several more individual signs have cast even more doubt on what had been presented as chronological developments.[6] The result is that for the present we can no longer safely rely on sign forms and their variants to fine-tune the date of an individual manuscript within the Old Kingdom.

Linguistically we may be able to distinguish three phases of development: texts from the period between Tuthaliya I and Suppiluliuma I (ca. 1420–1325 BC) show clear differences vis-à-vis the compositions from the reigns of Labarna, Hattusili I, and Mursili I through Telipinu (ca. 1650–1500).[7] Other linguistic changes can be observed in texts from the time of Mursili II onwards (ca. 1325–1200 BC). In Hittite political history, however, we have largely given up on distinguishing three stages (Old, Middle, and New Kingdom) and nowadays scholars generally work with a dichotomy into the Old Kingdom (ca. 1650–1400) and the Empire Period or New Kingdom (ca. 1400–1200) and we would do well – at least for the time being – to adopt a similar system for Hittite paleography.

In order to establish a reliable new paleography for dating tablets and fragments we should at first rely only on documents that were written when issued and can be dated with certainty. Such originals, as they are called in diplomatic terms,[8] are, for instance, tablets that bear the seal of a Hittite king. The seal guarantees that the document was drawn up and issued during the king's lifetime and it gives us a fairly exact chronological time frame. Similarly, we may count unique documents like letters and some graffiti as originals as well. Once we have established a true chronology of sign shapes on the basis of such originals, we can start filling it in with sign shapes from other texts that are by themselves not datable. Such a new paleography is not the purpose of this book but making a list of originals for the period up to 1400 can help us in other ways (Table 4.1).[9]

6 Wilhelm 2010b: 628–9, Rüster & Wilhelm 2012: 59–78, Weeden 2011a: 44 n. 192, 46 n. 206.

7 Hittite-language documents from the period between Telipinu and Tuthaliya I are rare and uncertain in their dating. For the typical traits of the Middle Hittite language vis-à-vis Old and New Hittite see Melchert 2008.

8 For the terminology used see Duranti 1998: 49 and see Chapter 10.2.

9 In van den Hout 2009a and 2009b I still included the treaty of the Hittite king Tahurwaili with Eheya of Kizzuwatna in this list. Otten 1971b had assumed that a clay sealing of this king once formed part of the clay tablet containing the treaty text. Now Rüster & Wilhelm 2012: 34 have raised doubts about this saying the sealing might as well have been part of another charter by this king. In this case it would be charter no. 92 but the treaty fragment would no longer count as a sealed document. I have therefore taken it off the list.

Table 4.1 *Originals from the Old Kingdom 1650–1400* BC

date	*found in Hattusa*	*unprovenanced*
middle/later seventeenth century		letter of Labarna to Tunip-Tessub of Tikunani
ca. 1550		ax of Ammuna
ca. 1520–ca. 1400	91 charters	
ca. 1420	sword of Tuthaliya I	

Fig. 4.1 Inscription on ax of King Ammuna (Salvini 1993: 85; courtesy M. Salvini).

The first item, the letter sent by Labarna to Tunip-Tessub of Tikunani in northern Syria, was already mentioned above (Chapter 3) as part of the evidence that these earliest kings did use writing. The script of the document, however, is the Syrian ductus, not the Hittite cuneiform. All other texts on the list show the familiar Hittite script (or contain no elements that patently contradict this). The oldest of these is the ceremonial ax of king Ammuna (ca. 1550 BC) (Fig. 4.1). The most artfully crafted of such weapons is the elaborate ax found at the Turkish village of Sarkışla[10] and a similar exemplar is portrayed in the warrior relief at the King's Gate at Hattusa. While the Sarkışla ax is uninscribed, the much more prosaically looking one of Ammuna carries the following curse in Akkadian:

> Tabarna, Ammuna, Great King: whoever violates (his) just word will die[11]

As can be seen, the personal name Labarna had by now become a title, written either as labarna or tabarna, and would stay in use until the end of the kingdom around 1200. The curse uttered by Ammuna here returns with some variations in the corpus of ninety-one charters or so-called *Landschenkungsurkunden* (LSU) that come next on our list.[12] They all

[10] Bittel 1976. [11] *tabarna Ammuna* LUGAL.GAL *ša išar* INIM *ušpaḫu* BA.ÚŠ, ed. by Salvini 1993.

[12] I use charter here as defined in Horsman et al. 2003:vi n. 2: "A charter is a document, usually sealed, granting specific rights, setting forth aims and principals, embodying formal agreements, authorizing special privileges or exemptions." For a comprehensive edition of all known charters see Rüster & Wilhelm 2012, for the term *Landschenkungsurkunden* see 35; for the formula here and its variants see Rüster & Wilhelm 2012: 36–7.

share a particular thick and pillow-shaped format with a royal seal impressed on the obverse, on either side of which the text was written. Apart from a large group of anonymous so-called tabarna seals because they only mention the king's title tabarna, others contain the name of the king. From at least Telipinu onwards (see Table 4.2) they are attested for every king until Arnuwanda I (ca. 1400 BC) except for his father Tuthaliya I (ca. 1420 BC). Most of these texts record the granting of property or individuals, mostly by the Hittite king. The deeds use a set formula ("The Great King has taken and given to so-and-so as a gift. In the future nobody shall sue so-and-so over it. The Tabarna's words are made of iron, they are not to be rejected, not to be broken. Whoever changes them, his head shall be cut off.") and end with a list of human witnesses and the name of the scribe who wrote the document ("This tablet so-and-so, scribe, has recorded in town so-and-so in the presence of [the following people]"). Apart from the fact that the general sentiment of Ammuna's curse on his ax recurs here ("Whoever changes them, his head shall be cut off") it returns *verbatim* in the seal legend, which is always found on the middle of the obverse of these charters (Fig. 4.2).

Interestingly enough, the first part of the formula and the vindication clause (LUGAL.GAL *iššima ana* PN *ana* NÍG.BA-*šu iddin* "The Great King has taken and given to so-and-so as a gift" and *urram šēram* . . . *lā iraggum* "In the future nobody shall sue so-and-so over it") are attested in almost identical form first and only at Alalah VII, thus providing another link between northern Syria and the later Hittite tradition, although with a Hittite twist.[13] Although originally dated to Telipinu and his successors, scholarship in the early 1970s shifted the oldest of these records to the reigns of Labarna or Hattusili I.[14] Recently, however, Gernot Wilhelm has convincingly shown on prosopographical grounds that some early anonymous charters and the first ones that carry the seals of Telipinu's immediate successors Alluwamna and Hantili II share witnesses and scribes and thus belong closely together in chronological terms. A date for the anonymous charters just prior to the reign of these two kings can now be considered proven.[15] The first king therefore who might be the anonymous tabarna is Telipinu himself. With due caution Wilhelm does not exclude

[13] Riemschneider 1958: 331 w. n. 38, 330–4, referring to ATT 41 = 20.06, but for the use of the Akkad. verb *našûm* for Hitt. *šarā da-* "to take (up)" instead of the Alalah expression *eli* PN *išû* "to have a claim against someone" see Rüster & Wilhelm 2012: 36, 73 n. 42.

[14] See the discussion in Carruba 1993 w. lit.

[15] Wilhelm 2005a, Rüster & Wilhelm 2012: 38–9, 51.

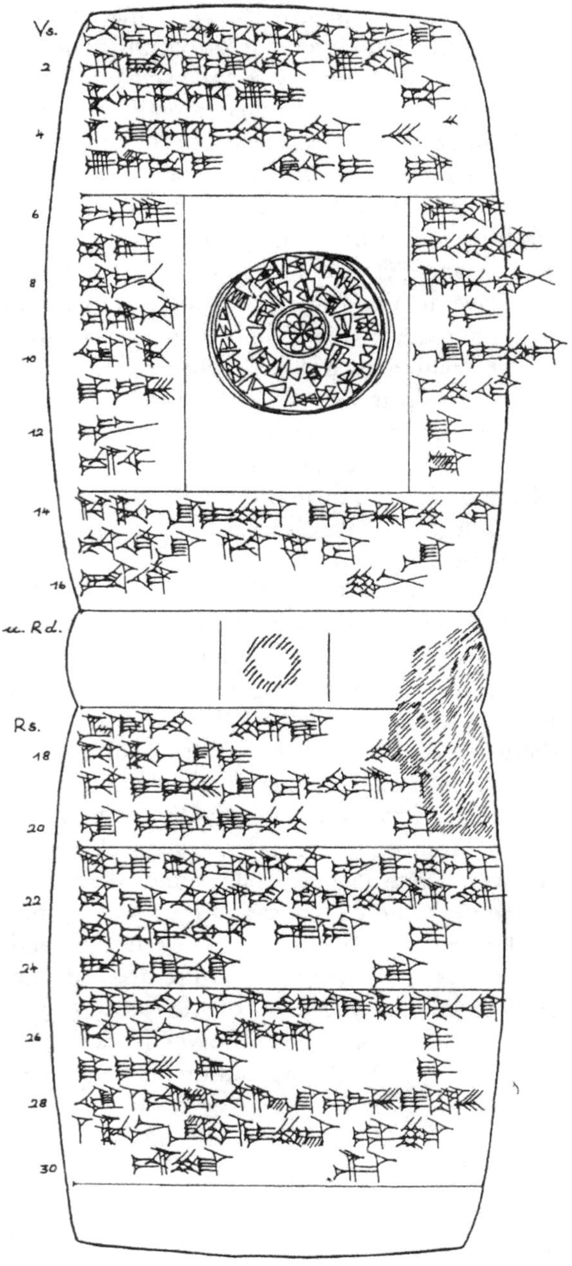

Fig. 4.2 Charter of King Hantili II (Rüster 1993: 66) as if "folded out" along the lower edge (*u. Rd.*).

the possibility that his immediate predecessor Huzziya might also have issued such charters, but there is something to be said for Klaus Kaspar Riemschneider's logic that Telipinu started with these grants and therefore did not need to mention his name: *le tabarna c'est moi*. It was only when his successors continued this policy that they needed to distinguish themselves and started adding their names.[16]

Finally, there is the graffito on a sword of Tuthaliya I, commemorating his victory in western Anatolia:

> When Tuthaliya, Great King, had destroyed the land of Aššuwa, he dedicated these swords to the Stormgod, his lord[17]

Originally one of a pair ("these swords"), it was probably part of the spoils of his battle against enemy forces in western Anatolia. One of the two weapons is still missing, but this one was found just outside the walls of Boğazköy and is likely to stem from a temple dedicated to the Stormgod in the city.

4.3 The Allure of Akkadian

These are all the documents that we can date with certainty to specific reigns within the Old Kingdom. Hattusili's letter to Tunip-Tessub is a diplomatic instrument that had to be written in the international *lingua franca*, Akkadian. But what about the charters and the graffiti? They are internal records whether legal (charters) or ceremonial (the ax and the sword) and written in the typical Hittite cuneiform. Although not denying their status as originals Alfonso Archi has objected that none of them are "suited for determining the written language in use at Ḫattuša."[18] Hattusili I hired a local Syrian to write the letter to Tunip-Tessub, the sword and the ax may have been inspired by "objects pillaged from Syrian cities," and the treaties with Kizzuwatna were in Akkadian because of Syrian influence in the region. The charters, finally, are "based on Syrian models" and continued being used simply out of tradition. Some of this is true. Hattusili's letter and the treaties

16 Riemschneider 1958: 326.

17 *inūma* ^{m}*Dutḫaliya* LUGAL.GAL KUR ^{URU}*Aššuwa uḫalliq* GÍR.HI.A *annūtim ana* ^{d}IŠKUR *bēlišu ušeli*; see Ertekin & Ediz 1993, Ünal 1993. Usually, the weapon is seen as a piece of booty and thus of an Aegean type, but the discussion continues, see Taracha 2003 w. further lit. and most recently Genz 2017.

18 Archi 2010: 39.

had to be in Akkadian, not because of any influence but simply to be understood by their addressees. But the Syrian parallel invoked for the sword and ax remains unsubstantiated. As for the charters, one might say that the charters were framed in Akkadian because it was traditional to do so but the formula ("The Great King has taken and given to so-and-so as a gift. In the future nobody shall sue so-and-so over it") is attested only once there and with a small variation among the numerous juridical texts from Alalah.[19] Moreover, when land grants began to be issued towards the final quarter of the sixteenth century BC there can hardly have been any tradition, as far as we can tell. There certainly was not if we follow Riemschneider's reasoning that it was Telipinu who started it. On the other hand, it is easy to imagine Telipinu's scribes coming across this formula, as it had been part of northern Syrian legal practice, in their search for formal language to give these new documents the necessary *gravitas*. They adapted it, using also partly indigenous phrasing, as shown by Gernot Wilhelm, but in Akkadian guise.[20] They did not need to but chose to do so. The part of the formula forbidding anyone to take the matter to court is known in its Hittite version from later treaties, a thirteenth century BC land grant or bequest, and even from the royal Hittite funerary ritual. When these documents were written Akkadian had long since given way to Hittite. Compare, for instance, the following passage from the Bronze Tablet treaty of Tuthaliya IV with Kuruntiya of Tarhuntassa from the 1230s BC:

> What I, My Majesty, have given Kuruntiya, king of Tarhuntassa, the borders that I set for him, nobody shall take them away in the future from the descendants of Kuruntiya. The king shall not take it away, give it to his son (or) give it to any offspring and nobody shall sue him over it![21]

The most important point to take away here, however, is that even though each individual piece of evidence may not be wholly compelling by itself their cumulative weight is undeniable. What is more, there is not a single

19 See n. 13. 20 Rüster & Wilhelm 2012: 36, 73 n. 42.

21 *nu* ^{d}UTU-*ŠI* *kuit* ANA ^{md}LAMMA LUGAL KUR $^{\mathrm{URU\,d}}$U-*tašša peḫḫun* ZAG.ḪI.A-*iš⸗ši kuiēš teḫḫun n⸗aš⸗kan zilatiya* ANA NUMUN ^{md}LAMMA *arḫa lē kuiški dāi* LUGAL-*uš⸗at⸗za lē dāi* ANA DUMU-*ŠU⸗at lē pāi damēdani⸗at warwalani lē kuedanikki pāi ḫannari⸗ya⸗šši⸗ššan lē kuiški*, Bronze Tablet iv 21–5 (Treaty w. Kuruntiya of Tarhuntassa, Tuth. IV), ed. by Otten 1988: 26–7; see also KBo 4.10 rev. 21–4 (Treaty w. Ulmitessub of Tarhuntassa, CTH 106, NS), ed. by van den Hout 1995: 46–7, for the royal funerary ritual see the same formula on days 8–9 i 18–19, ii 2, day 10 iv 1–2, days 12–14 i 34–5, ed. by Kassian et al. 2002: 378, 384, 462, 482, 746.

text in Hittite that can be identified as an original in the diplomatic sense from that period in the same way as the ones listed above (Table 4.1). This is simply all the evidence, as we have it.

For the ceremonial use of both script and Akkadian on Ammuna's ax and Tuthaliya I's swords prestige, tradition, and an emotional force that writing can have probably go hand in hand. Mesopotamia had this cosmopolitan allure and the Akkadian language was its manifestation. Just as a Latin inscription still lends a monument, building, or coat of arms a flavor of prestige, an Akkadian motto reinforced the Hittite Great King's international standing. Like the figure on the so-called King's Gate in Boğazköy, Ammuna probably carried his ax around as a symbol of power and it may have been displayed at official functions. Of course, few people would have been able to read it, not only because they were illiterate but simply because no one would have been allowed to come up close enough to see there was even writing on it. Legibility was not its purpose but Ammuna may have felt that having the curse written down would render it stronger and more effective.[22] As to Tuthaliya's swords, by his reign in the last third of the fifteenth century BC the switch to Hittite as the official written language of the empire had already been made and there was no need to use Akkadian. He had won a victory in western Anatolia over a coalition of people for whom Mesopotamia was but a far cry. When a few years later these same western Anatolians tried to correspond with Egypt they urged them to write in Hittite, the closest they came to knowing an "international" language. Tuthaliya, moreover, dedicated the swords to the Hittite Stormgod, probably in his temple in Hattusa. But perhaps the temple held other such votive gifts from former kings written in Akkadian like Ammuna's ax. This may have inspired Tuthaliya to do the same and he was not the last. Hittite power would always have a soft spot for Akkadian, as shown by the one area where it continued to be used: seal glyptics. Every king from Mursili II (ca. 1325–1295 BC) to Tuthaliya IV (ca. 1240–1220 BC) used some Akkadian phraseology on their seals: *kīnu* "true, reliable, just" (Mursili II), *narām* DN "beloved of the god . . . " (Mursili II, Muwatalli II, Urhitessub, Hattusili III), *qarrādu* "hero" (Tuthaliya IV), *šar kiššati* "king of the world, kosmokrator" (Tuthaliya IV). They were surely aware of that tradition and contemporary politics

[22] Thomas 1992: 80–1; see also Lurie 2011: 28–33 on what he calls the "alegible" value of inscriptions.

and the vicissitudes of relations with Mesopotamia certainly played a role in keeping it alive.[23]

Before we move on one other text should be added, even though it is not as securely dated as the ones mentioned thus far. This is the extensive and lively account of the Hittite general Sanda of his botched siege of the town of Urshu in northern Syria.[24] The text contains his report but has often been interpreted as a piece of historiography and been singled out for its humor and sarcasm. Although likely not written there but in Syria, the tablet was found in Hattusa and is written in Akkadian in the Syrian ductus.[25] The text shows "numerous Hitticisms"[26] but as an internal Hittite document there is no need for it to be written in Akkadian. Those same influences from Hittite betray a Hittite author with quite excellent knowledge of Akkadian, which at this early point in the first or first two generations of Anatolian adoption of cuneiform taught by Syrian scribes is not surprising.[27] Since Hattusili mentions Urshu in his Annals as one of the cities that he conquers, the event and text usually have been ascribed to him but recently Forlanini has proposed to date at least the event itself to his predecessor Labarna.[28] Since there is no seal or otherwise anything that guarantees its status as an original it cannot be included among the above texts. However, because of the Syrian ductus, its likely manufacture in Syria, and the dating of the events narrated in it to the first Hittite kings, *communis opinio* holds that it is a contemporary document. Finally, the composition is also noteworthy because it contains some Hittite words and even an entire phrase of what is allegedly a war song:

> The sons of Lariya (and) Lariya are marching (singing the song of the war god Zababa): "As helmet wearing(?) puppies we have pissed(?) on the threshing floor with *laḫnali*"[29]

Unfortunately, the sentence does not make much sense to us, but its Hittite-language status is beyond doubt. Whether dated to Labarna or Hattusili, if this is indeed a contemporary document, I follow Aharon Kempinski's suggestion that this may well be the first and oldest Hittite

[23] Cf. Herbordt et al. 2011: 60 w. lit.
[24] Kempinski 1983, Beckman 1995a; see also the discussion by Gilan 2015: 278–95.
[25] Weeden 2016b: 162 w. lit., see also Chapter 2.2. [26] Beckman 1995a: 27.
[27] See also Archi 2010: 40–1 w. lit. [28] Forlanini 2010: 118–19.
[29] DUMU.MEŠ *Lariya* ᵐ*Lariyaš ḫuškiwanteš* . . . KISLAḪ *laḫnit šeḫuwen* UR.TUR *kurziwaneš* KBo I.11 rev.! 14–15 (Urshu Text, CTH 7), ed. by Beckman 1995a: 25–6.

written product (and therefore also Indo-European) sentence on record after the isolated Anatolian loanwords of the Old Assyrian texts.[30] As such it counts as an early attempt at writing the vernacular. Why the scribe did this remains difficult to say.

Both in the case of the early charters and graffiti like on Ammuna's ax it is far more likely that Akkadian was written because at that moment it was the main written language according to the principle we saw earlier: a society that adopts a script from another society with another language will usually start writing in the other language. If the Hittites had acquired the Syrian cuneiform around 1700 BC or earlier and the period of writing in Akkadian had already passed, there would have been little need for Telipinu to compose the new genre of charters in a language other than Hittite.

The role of Akkadian in the earliest Hittite texts becomes even clearer when we extend our view to include all texts we can assign to Old Kingdom Hittite kings regardless of the date or language of the manuscript, that is, not looking for legally authentic originals but simply for historical arguments that allow us to ascribe a composition to a specific king. If we contrast these texts with the contemporary originals, we get the picture as seen in Table 4.2.

The third column (*compositions attributable to*) gives the evidence we have, selected on contents only: the records in question, written in Hittite ("Hitt."), Akkadian ("Akk."), or both in case of a bilingual text, mention a king as the author of the composition or contain historical information that allows us to attribute it to that king. However, these documents are either thirteenth century copies or are written in older script (including the traditional MS) that we cannot date with any more precision. The fourth and fifth columns (*contemporary records*) mention the kings for whom we have the above-mentioned authentic originals, either in the Syrian ductus (column four) or in the Hittite cuneiform variant (column five).

All documents listed are internal except for Labarna's Letter. The mix of Hittite and Akkadian in the third column shows no reasonable ratio for the choice of language, whereas all the securely datable originals are in Akkadian until the reign of Arnuwanda I. He and his queen issued what is the last known charter, the so-called land

30 Kempinksi 1983: 33 n. 20; given the likelihood of the written Hittite version of the Anitta Text as stemming from the Old Kingdom at the earliest, the Hittite sentence in the Urshu text may indeed be older.

Table 4.2 *Compositions datable to Old Kingdom Hittite kings regardless of the date or language of the manuscript*

1	2	3	4	5
		compositions attributable to[31]	*contemporary records in Syrian cuneiform*	*contemporary records in Hitt. cuneiform*
Hittite kings				
Labarna	ca. 1650		**x** (Akk.)[32]	
Hattusili I	ca. 1630	**x** (Hitt./Akk.)[33]		
Mursili I	ca. 1600	**x** (Hitt./Akk.)[34]		
Hantili I		**x?** (Hitt.)[35]		
Zidanta I				
Ammuna		**x** (Hitt.)[36]		**x** (Akk.)[37]
Huzziya I				(**x?** (Akk.))[38]
Telipinu	ca. 1500	**x** (Hitt./Akk.)[39]		**x** (Akk.)[40]
Alluwamna				**x** (Akk.)
Hantili II				**x** (Akk.)
Zidanta II		**x** (Akk.)[41]		**x** (Akk.)
Tahurwaili				**x** (Akk.)[42]
Huzziya II				**x** (Akk.)
Muwatalli I				**x** (Akk.)
Tuthaliya I	ca. 1425	**x** (Hitt.)[43]		**x** (Akk.)[44]
Arnuwanda I	ca. 1400	**x** (Hitt.)[45]		**x** (Hitt.-Akk.)[46]

grant to Kuwatalla, a temple "servant," on whom they bestow large portions of land and real estate.[47] Here tradition definitely played an important role: the familiar granting formula is there in Akkadian, but the descriptions of things granted and framed by the formula are

[31] References are given to the entries in CTH; for the most recent information see the *Konkordanz.*
[32] This is the letter to Tunip-Teššub, which can also be ascribed to Hattusili I.
[33] = CTH 4, 5, 6, 14, 15. [34] = CTH 12, 13. [35] = CTH 10.1, 11? [36] = CTH 18.
[37] This is the ax published by Salvini 1993.
[38] Only if any of the anonymous charters can be ascribed to him: see Wilhelm 2005a: 276, Rüster & Wilhelm 2012: 51.
[39] = CTH 19, 20, 22.
[40] This and the following entries in this column up to and including Muwatalli I refer to the charters issued and sealed by these kings (see CTH 221–2).
[41] = CTH 25.
[42] This a land grant of Tahurwaili, for the alleged sealed copy of the treaty of Tahurwaili with Eheya of Kizzuwatna, see above n. 136. For Tahurwaili's position after Zidanta II see Rüster & Wilhelm 2012: 57.
[43] For a list of possible Hittite texts to be ascribed to this king see Klengel 1999: 104–7.
[44] This is the sword of Tuthaliya for which see above.
[45] For a list of possible Hittite texts to be ascribed to this king see Klengel 1999: 116–20.
[46] = CTH 223, the charter for the priestess Kuwattalla.
[47] Ed. by Rüster & Wilhelm 2012: 231–9 (No. 91).

all in Hittite. This is also the last known internal Hittite document written in Akkadian that contains a significant Akkadian portion. From now on everything was written in the Hittite language. As we already briefly saw and will see in more detail, by the end of the fifteenth century BC the switch to Hittite had been completed.

So far, our discussion has largely dealt with shapes and forms and general writing practices, but they also raise the question of the state of Hittite literacy during the Old Kingdom until the late fifteenth century BC. How literate was Hittite society after the introduction of the Syrian script, and can we determine when they started to write in their own language? These questions will be dealt with in the next chapter.

CHAPTER 5

Literacy and Literature in the Old Kingdom until 1500 BC

5.1 Hatti-Land after Telipinu

The kingdom Mursili I left to his successors does not seem to have suffered too much from the internal upheavals following his death. Continuing control over the inner core of Hatti-Land is confirmed by the last part of Telipinu's Proclamation. There he set up the country's agricultural and fiscal system and the names of several towns and districts listed comprise the area of the Halys basin as well as the Upper and Lower Land. The Syrian conquests, on the other hand, and control over Kizzuwatna were in all likelihood lost. Judging by the parity treaty Telipinu concluded with its king Isputahsu, Kizzuwatna must have regained its independence. In line with the spirit of the Proclamation the treaty signals a new attitude on the side of the Hittites. If possible, the power of diplomacy and the written word came to be preferred over that of blunt military force and domination. The threat of the sword in combination with the written word proved a more potent weapon. After the decline following Mursili's murder, the second half of the sixteenth century BC culminating in Telipinu's reign marks a period of restoration. As we will see, there was a surge of new settlements in Central Anatolia and the capital Hattusa expanded to twice its size. Telipinu's Proclamation, the first "codification" of the Hittite Laws dating back to the same period, and a series of large land grants to members of the ruling elite are all to be seen as important building blocks in this process.

Yet for all the promise of Telipinu's ideals and the spirit of his Proclamation the at most three generations (ca. 1500–1425 BC) following him are characterized by a rapid succession of six kings and at least two of them seem to have come to power through usurpation. If we consider the texts we have as representative of what was generally produced, production stagnated, and even dropped. Almost all contemporary documents are further charters and continuing treaties with Kizzuwatna.[1] The treaties were designed to keep this strategically important region, gateway to Syria and the Hurrian lands, open for Hittite armies and to let Kizzuwatna serve as a buffer against possible invasions. Although this is a poorly documented and chaotic period, later offering lists for deceased kings help us in establishing the sequence of the six rulers. Telipinu was succeeded by Alluwamna and the latter's son Hantili (II). For the reigns of both Alluwamna and Hantili there are indications that Hatti-Land suffered from enemy invasions and uprisings. Most notable was the loss of the cult city of Nerik to the Gasgaean tribes from the Pontic region on the Black Sea coast. At some point there must have been a king named Tahurwaili, but he does not figure in the royal offering lists and his relation to those before and after him remains unknown.[2] After Zidanta (II), to be dated around 1450 BC, comes another Huzziya (II) who is almost exclusively known from land grants but his death at the hand of a usurper, his own Chief of the Royal Bodyguard Muwatalli (I), is preserved in a small historical fragment. As is the case with Tahurwaili, Muwatalli is not mentioned in the offering lists either. He was killed by two high officials, one of whom probably was the father of the next king Tuthaliya I who is usually regarded as the founder of what some call the Hittite Empire.

5.2 Literacy and Literature of the Old Kingdom

Whereas in popular opinion and older scholarship literacy is often regarded as an obvious and self-evident sign of civilization and sophistication, the threshold of history, in scholarly literature it has long since come off its pedestal.[3] It has been accepted that kingdoms and empires can exist and even thrive without writing or without much writing and use of a script is no prerequisite for a complex state. Orality and literacy are far from being mutually exclusive and coexist until our modern day although literacy is likely to change over time the character and extent of oral components in a society.[4] One can no longer meaningfully speak of logo- or syllabographic vs. alphabetic societies. The nature of a writing system has little or no relation to literacy levels. The Hittite case shows how ancient societies

[1] Beckman 1999: 11–13.
[2] Wilhelm 2009: 227–8 n. 15, Rüster & Wilhelm 2012: 57 (after Zidanta II); see the Timeline and List of Kings on p. xxii–xxiii.
[3] For earlier views see Goody & Watt 1963, Goody 1986; for an overview of Goody's relevant works see Thomas 1992: 129, see also Ong 1982.
[4] Ong 1982: 9, Schoeler 2009: passim, Thomas 1992: 4–5, van der Toorn 2007: 218.

could be slow in accepting literacy and once a society made the switch, it was not necessarily the reason for prosperity or a rise to power.[5] As Simon Franklin puts it: "Societies do not change because they introduce writing; they introduce writing because they change."[6] It is also useful to make a distinction between first introduction of script and its further diffusion.[7] Even as writing becomes more established it can for a long time continue its main role as *aide-mémoire* supporting orality as the main channel of communication.[8] Writing will also long remain the realm of distinct and often small groups of people.[9] "General" literacy as we know it is a very recent phenomenon and even then it is often overstated: from antiquity to the present day many forms of literacy have to be distinguished, from barely being able to write one's name to full and active literacy.[10]

All of the above elements have to be kept in mind when assessing the situation in Anatolia of the first centuries of the second millennium BC. The return from incipient literacy during the Old Assyrian period to illiteracy before the start of the Old Kingdom around 1650 BC explains why a completely new cuneiform variant could take hold in Anatolia after the Syrian campaigns of Labarna, Hattusili I, and Mursili I and the latter's Mesopotamian adventure all the way to Babylon in 1595 BC. With them, Anatolia put the days of rivaling city-states forever behind her. From now on until its collapse around 1200 BC there would always be a Hittite state. In times of political upheaval, it might lose its claims to territories outside of Anatolia but hardly ever more than that. Hattusili and Mursili definitively raised Anatolia to the next level and onto the stage of international, that is, Near Eastern world order. The Hittites were there to stay. The Labarna Letter to Tunip-Tessub is immediate and tangible evidence of the international relations that came with this newly claimed status. As we will see, the same is true internally of Hattusili's Annals originally inscribed on a gold statue (see p. 73), and his Testament recorded on a tablet shows that he was well aware of the value and power of writing. His words could now be heard and heeded when he was not physically present, whether during his lifetime or after his death. And writing was there to stay as well, even if

5 See, for instance, Sanders 2004: 38–9 with n. 39, 2009: 44, Blair 2010: 46–7.

6 Franklin 2002: 7, similarly Cooper 2004: 94 ("writing [is not] . . . an obligatory marker for complex societies or civilizations. Rather, writing is a response"), Baines 2007: 62, Spooner & Hanaway 2012: 58.

7 I am avoiding the adjective "general" (diffusion) since that was never realized in the ancient Near East and is a vague term anyhow.

8 Ong 1982: 9.

9 For terms like protoliterate and oligoliterate see Goody & Watt 1963: 313 w. n. 22.

10 Sanders 2009: 45, Thomas 2009.

after Mursili the Hittites lost most of what he and his predecessors had won in the east. The sixteenth century turns out to have been the formative period of the Hittite cuneiform, culminating with Telipinu towards the end of that same century. The script had by then reached the typical form we call "Hittite cuneiform" and was to remain on the whole remarkably stable until its disappearance around 1200 BC.

5.3 Looking for Writing in the Old Kingdom

In trying to gauge the extent of literacy and writing in the Old Kingdom until the end of the sixteenth century BC, we already looked at the originals and compositions that can generally be dated to that period in Chapter 4. Another way is to search for references to writing in the wider corpus of texts that can be attributed to Old Kingdom kings on the basis of their contents. References to tablets and scribes in Old Hittite compositions are rare.[11] The oldest reference probably comes from Hattusili's bilingual (Akkadian-Hittite) Annals where he lists his *res gestae* and the booty he brought home. Towards the end of the text he says:

> and I made myself this statue of gold of(?) myself.[12]

With "this" (*kī*) he implies that the text we are reading was inscribed on or very near a statue he erected.[13]

The oldest mention of a tablet is found in another text of his, known as his Political Testament and addressed to his grandson Mursili I on his

[11] In KBo 7.14 obv. 16 (CTH 14, Konk. "ah.?/mh.?" ed. by de Martino 2003: 112–13), one of the fragments concerning the Syrian campaigns of Hattusili I, tablets (*TUP-PA-*⌜*A-TI*⌝) are mentioned but they were sent by Haluti, a non-Hittite general, to the king of Hassu and thus are not relevant to the point discussed here (for the reading Haluti instead of Zaluti see most recently Soysal 2005: 143). I also omit here the disputed reference to a scribe or scribes in the NS version of the Zalpa Text, usually ascribed to Mursili I (thus, for instance, Otten 1973: 62, and Klinger 1996: 117–23; see, however, differently Sürenhagen 1998: 83 n. 39, and Beal 2003: 21–4): *tupalān kuēl* SAG.DU-*i* x[KBo 3.38 obv. 25 (Zalpa Text, CTH 3, NS), ed. by Otten 1973: 8–9, with commentary 41. It remains very doubtful if we are really dealing with scribes here; see Chapter 15.4.4.

[12] *nu*=*za kī* ALAM=*IA ŠA* KÙ.GI *iyanun* KBo 10.2 iii 21 (Annals of Hattusili I, CTH 4, NS), ed. by de Martino 2003: 68–9; see also Haas 2006: 33, 40.

[13] The Akkadian version KBo 10.1 rev. 14 does not have a matching demonstrative (*ù* ALAM *ša* KÙ.GI *īpuš*=*ma* "and I made a statue of gold"), see Devecchi 2005: 54–5 (for *īpuš* as "I made" instead of "he made" see Devecchi 80). Nor does it have anything resembling the particle -*za* or the Akkadian suffixed possessive pronoun -*IA* Beckman 2006: 221 translates "this golden statue of myself", de Martino 2003: 69 has more neutrally "questa mia statua." Was the statue indeed supposed to be of him, the king, or did Hattusili simply want to emphasize that it was he who had it made and erected ("questa mia statua")? For the "numerous signs alien to the ductus of the rest of the tablet" on the rev. as possibly having "crept in from the original that the inscription was written on" see Weeden 2011a: 76.

deathbed and recorded in the presence of the immediate family and the country's leaders:

> I have given you my advice and this [tabl]et they shall read before you every month.[14]

The composition is preserved in both Akkadian and Hittite but only in a late, that is, thirteenth century BC copy. If indeed the text was originally written in Akkadian – and in Akkadian only at this time – do we then suppose the young Mursili to have known and understood that language? And was it read to him by one of the native Syrian scribes or one of their first-generation Hittite-Akkadian bilingual descendants? The presence of the latter would be unsurprising, in fact, it is what we expect to have happened in these early days of the kingdom when the writing technology was transmitted to a first native Hittite generation. But to assume this kind of knowledge in Mursili would be too self-serving to be believable. There are enough parallels, however, for such bilingual individuals to be able to switch back and forth between two languages. Using the original Akkadian document such a scribe could thus have read a Hittite version to Mursili. As Michael Clanchy showed for medieval England, clerks could easily move between Latin, French, and English:[15]

> A statement made in court in English or French, for example, might be written down in Latin, or conversely a Latin charter might be read out in English or French. Men like Abbot Samson evidently interchanged languages effortlessly, using whichever one was appropriate for the occasion. . . . A royal message to a sheriff in the thirteenth century might have been spoken by the king in French, written out in Latin, and then read to the recipient in English.

A tablet is also mentioned in a fragmentary historical text in NS that refers to Hattusili I and Mursili I as well as to building activities and which must have been composed by one of their Old Kingdom successors, possibly Hantili I:

> [. . .] in just [that wa]y o[n] a tablet [. . . these(?) w]ords.[16]

As others have already said, the tablet referred to may well have been a publicly displayed document just like the text on or near the statue of

[14] *uddār⸗met⸗ta peḫḫun nu kī [tupp]i* ITU*-mi* ITU*-mi peran⸗tet ḫalzeššandu* KUB 1.16 iii 56–7 (Testament of Hattusili I, CTH 6, NS), ed. by Sommer & Falkenstein 1974: 14–15.

[15] Clanchy 1993: 206.

[16] *[apeniš]an⸗pat tuppi[a(-)* . . .]/[. . . *ud]dār* KBo 3.57 iii 19–20 (Annals(?) of Hantili I(?), CTH 11, NS), ed. by de Martino 2003: 200–1; see also Klinger 2006: 6–7.

Hattusili I that we just saw.[17] Another early but, unfortunately, fragmentarily preserved passage stems from a historical composition by Ammuna, the same king to whom we ascribe the ax (see Chapter 4). He does not use *tuppi-* "text, tablet" but GIŠ.ḪUR "document, original":

> [When] I had sat down [on] my father's [thron]e, I governe[d] my country. [On . . .] I [be]stowed (saying): 'You (pl.) shall govern [. . .].' It was in that year[18] that I [t]ook/[s]eized [. . .] and I read my document(?) [. . .] I [. . . -]ed and many a chariot I turned against chariot.[19]

Several scenarios are possible but given the meanings of GIŠ.ḪUR[20] and the verb "bestowed" might Ammuna reference here some investiture or charter-like document? Apparently, some people were given the power to govern part of the kingdom. Did they abuse that power and did the king after checking the original document decide to march against the abusers? The composition as a whole and especially the lines just quoted ("in that year") recall the annalistic structure of Hattusili's Annals and Ammuna may have been imitating or trying to emulate his predecessor. Whether he, too, ever committed the text to stone or metal for public display is unknown but with Hattusili's Annals in mind this is certainly possible.

A use of writing similar to Hattusili's Testament can be found in a passage in Telipinu's Proclamation. Here he formulates rules for royal succession in an attempt to avoid the bloodshed that so characterized the generations that ruled before him. He calls upon his audience to put an end to the chain of murders that took place in the royal family and then continues as follows:

> Furthermore, whoever becomes king and seeks evil for (his) brother (and) sister, you shall be his family council and you must tell him forthright: "Read this record of bloodshed on the tablet (saying): 'In the past bloodshed had become frequent in Hattusa and the gods took revenge on the royal family.'"[21]

[17] Houwink ten Cate 1984: 64, del Monte 1993: 9. Note also KBo 3.57 iii 1 (Annals(?) of Hantili I(?), CTH 11, NS) the verb *IŠṬUR* "he wrote."

[18] For the translation of *apiya* MU.KAM-*ti* (instead of *apedani* MU.KAM-*ti*) s. P. Goedegebuure, forthc.

[19]
8. [*mān=šan* ANA ^{GIŠ}GU.Z]A ABI=IA *ēšḫaḫati n=apa utni=mit ma*[(*niyaḫḫ*)]*aḫḫ*[*ati*]
9. [*ḫ*]*enkun šumeš maniyaḫḫeškketten nu ap*[(*iya=pat* M)]U.KAM-*ti*
10. [*ē*]*ppun* GIŠ.HUR=*mitt=a ūḫḫun nu=šša*[(*n*)]
11. [-]*un* ANA ^{GIŠ}GIGIR=*ia=kan* ^{GIŠ}GIGIR *mekka*[(*n neḫḫu*)*n*]

KUB 36.98b rev. 8–11 (Annals(?) of Ammuna, CTH 18, NS), w. dupls. KUB 26.71 obv. 21–24 (NS), and KBo 3.59: 1–3 (NS), ed. by de Martino 1999: 73–5.

[20] For this see in detail Chapter 11.2.

[21] *namma kuiš=a* LUGAL-*uš kišari nu* ŠEŠ-*aš* NIN-*aš idālu šanaḫzi šumešš=a pankuš=ši<š> nu=šši karši tetten kī=wa ēšnaš uttar tuppiaz au karū=wa ēšḫar* ^{URU}*Ḫattuši makkešta nu=war=at=apa* DINGIR.MEŠ-*iš*

Telipinu is clearly referring to an internal document that he supposes to be available or retrievable in the future. In fact, as has been convincingly suggested[22], he may be referring to his own Proclamation where he has already twice said the same thing albeit in slightly different wording:

> Bloodshed of the royal family has become widespread (... and the Men-of-the-Gods, too, are saying:) "Bloodshed has become widespread now in Hattusa"[23]

From the reign of Telipinu also stems his treaty with Isputahsu, king of Kizzuwatna, where in one of the fragments of the Hittite version we encounter DUB.BA.MEŠ=*IA* "my tablets" in otherwise broken context.[24]

Finally, we need to mention two small tablets, KBo 22.1 and KBo 18.151. KBo 22.1 is written in Hittite and cannot be dated historically but all scholars agree it must be old given the tablet's shape and unexpected spellings in the text.[25] The anonymous author berates his addressees for their behavior towards the have-nots in society, here exemplified by the "carriers," and refers to a written document that his father left them:

> When my father calls (you) to meetings, he investigates your reprehensible behavior, not (that of) your carriers (saying): "Right now each of you is oppressing your carriers!" You are each giving the king causes for anger.
>
> (He says:) "Both you and he are a ^{GIŠ}TUKUL(-man, i.e., tax paying people)." When my father lets you go to your home, just as he is writing to you, has he not inscribed a tablet for you, officials, (saying): "You will now each go to your land?" Aren't you going to investigate a poor man's bloodshed?[26]

If the early date for this tablet is correct this is probably the oldest occurrence for the act of writing: the verb *ḫazziye-* means "to pierce, stab" and seems an appropriate way of describing the motion with which cuneiform signs are created by sticking a stylus into the clay. At the same

šallai ḫaššannai dāer KBo 3.1+ ii 46–9 (Telipinu Edict, CTH 19, NS), ed. by Hoffmann 1984: 34–5. For *-apa* in "rechtlichem Kontext" (here "*re*-venge") see Rieken 2004: 248–9.

22 Cancik 1976: 64–5, see also Gilan 2015: 164.

23 *nu šallaš=pat haššannaš ēšḫar pangariyattati* (...) *kāša=wa* ^{URU}*Ḫattuši ēšḫar pangariyattati* KBo 3.1+ ii 31 and 33 (Telipinu Edict, CTH 19, NS), ed. by Hoffmann 1984: 30–1. For the verbs *makkešš-* and *pangariya-* s. CHD s.vv.

24 KBo 19.37: 6 (Treaty w. Isputahsu, CTH 21, NS).

25 Waal 2015: 23 w. n. 78 where she notes the similar-looking shape of the tablet for KBo 18.151.

26 *mān* ABI *tuliyaš ḫalzai nu=šmaš gullakkuwan šaḫzi natta* $^{\text{LÚ.MEŠ}}$NAŠIṢIDIDI=KUNU *kāša=tta=wa* $^{\text{LÚ.MEŠ}}$NAŠIṢIDIDI=KUNU *dameškatteni ta* LUGAL-*i kardimiyattuš piškatteni* § *zikk=a=wa* ^{GIŠ}TUKUL *apašš=a* ^{GIŠ}TUKUL *mān=šmaš* ABI *parna=šma tarnai nu=šmaš mānḫanda ḫatreškezzi natta=šmaš* $^{\text{LÚMEŠ.}}$DUGUD *tuppi ḫazzian ḫarzi kāša=tta=wa utniya paitteni nu* ŠA LÚ MAŠ.EN.KAK *ēšḫar=šet natta šanḫišketteni* KBo 22.1: 16–25 (Instruction, CTH 272, OS), ed. by Archi 1979: 45–8; see also Gilan 2015: 107–10.

time, the use of this verb for "writing" is extremely rare. It only occurs once more in the late thirteenth century but then for inscribing an iron tablet.[27]

The other text, KBo 18.151[28], is likewise written in Hittite but its date has been disputed. Some have argued for an Old Hittite date, others thought it showed "Middle Script," so that it would date to the fifteenth century BC in traditional terms. Its ductus, however, shows some features that seem to come straight from Alalah VII and it has the same tablet shape as KBo 22.1.[29] The text records an oracle investigation with an extremely simple syntax and spellings that are often unique or highly unusual.

With these scant references to writing for the roughly 150-year period up to the end of the sixteenth century BC we seem to have exhausted our Old Kingdom sources. The character of the compositions referred to is either monumental (Hattusili's and possibly Ammuna's Annals and the Hantili I passage), that of an *aide-mémoire* (Hattusili's advice for his grandson on his deathbed and Telipinu's own Proclamation) or possibly administrative (Ammuna's GIŠ.ḪUR unless this was monumental as well). In their Political Testament and Proclamation Hattusili and Telipinu wanted to ensure that their wishes would be honored after their deaths. None of the texts justify the claim of a society where writing plays an active, let alone an essential role in the administration of the kingdom with a bustling chancellery.[30]

5.4 Scribes in the Old Kingdom

This impression of only incipient literacy is confirmed when we try to identify scribes prior to the reign of Telipinu. We know there must have been because of the documents that we just passed in review but, again, with an active chancellery occasionally or even regularly producing records both in Hittite and Akkadian that has already passed the initial learning stages of early literacy, we would have expected to know the names of some scribes before the start of the charters in the late sixteenth century. All colophons that have been identified as written in OS according to the traditional dating system are anonymous.[31] Even starting with

[27] See Chapter 1. [28] Soysal 2000. [29] van den Hout 2012a: 166 w. lit.
[30] See for instance de Martino 2016: 365–6. [31] van den Hout 2009b: 80–1.

Table 5.1 *Names of earliest datable scribes*

name	*texts*
Askaliya	1
Hutarli	11, 12, 17
Inar	3
Ispunnuma	22, 26[32]
Zuwa	14

Telipinu the number of scribes known to us by name is quite small although percentage-wise perhaps not that much smaller than that of scribes in named colophons of the New Kingdom period. Only eight names are preserved until shortly after 1400 BC.

The charters (ca. 1525–1400 BC) provide us with the earliest datable names of scribes (Table 5.1).[33]

Except for nr. 26, which was written by Ispunnuma under Alluwamna, all show the so-called anonymous tabarna seals that we date to Telipinu (or his predecessor).[34] Ispunnuma may therefore have been the most junior of the group. I have added Inar who is identified as DUB.SAR.GIŠ É^{URU}*Ḫatti* ^{URU}*Šariššai*^{KI} "clerk of the house of Hatti in Sarissa" as the beneficiary of the charter.[35] The name of the actual scribe of the deed is broken away and it remains uncertain whether a wood-scribe was a real scribe (see Chapter 13) or rather an administrator but there is no reason to doubt these clerks' literate capabilities.[36] Later charters provide us with the following scribal names of the mid- and later fifteenth century BC (in chronological order) (Table 5.2).

[32] In both cases the title DUB.SAR has been restored but the position at the end of the list of witnesses supports their identification as scribes.

[33] All text numbers refer to those in Rüster & Wilhelm 2012. Intriguing is the mention of Pirwa, an otherwise unknown scribe (LÚ DUB.SAR), in some fragments of the Disappearing Deity myths: see Otten 1942: 63–4, Pecchioli Daddi & Polvani 1990: 92 w. n. 13, and van den Hout 2003–2005b: 576a and 2009b: 81 n. 64 (the last three publications incorrectly refer to him as wood-scribe). Although the fragments in question are all in NS, the general antiquity of these myths (see however also Popko 2007: 580) makes it possible to think of a scribe from the Old Kingdom.

[34] Wilhelm 2005a, Rüster & Wilhelm 2012: 49–54.

[35] Nr. 3 obv. 25–6, ed. by Rüster & Wilhelm 2012: 92–7.

[36] van den Hout 2010. Since nr. 3 belongs to the earliest datable charters this Inar must be someone other than the scribe Inar who was responsible for KBo 5.7 (p. 79).

Table 5.2 *Names of scribes datable to mid- and later fifteenth century* BC

name	*texts*
Hanikuili	28, 29, 30 (all Hantili II, middle(?) of fifteenth century[37])
Zuzzu	41 (Huzziya II, later fifteenth century[38])
Warsiya	45–48 (Huzziya II?, Muwatalli I[39])
Inar	91 (Arnuwanda I, ca. 1400[40])
Suppiluliuma	91 (idem)

Just as in the case of Inar above, I have added Suppiluliuma, the DUB.SAR.GIŠ *ŠA* É^{LÚ}MUḪALDIM "wood-scribe/clerk of the kitchen" appearing as a real estate owner in Charter nr. 91.[41]

The above eight names – or ten if we add the two clerks – are all attested as scribes of charters. Unfortunately, they are also the only written documents that we can date with certainty in the period between Telipinu and Tuthaliya I/Arnuwanda I towards the end of the fifteenth century. As the record shows, these years saw continued use of writing but there is very little beyond the charters. One possible case is that of Hanikuili, writer of the three land grants just listed; his name is preserved in two colophons written in an older ductus. One of them appears at the end of a so-called prism, a tablet in the shape of a polygonal cylinder, containing the legend – in Akkadian – of Naram-Sin, famous king of Akkad. Hanikuili identifies himself as follows:

> Hand of Hanikuili, scribe, son of Anu-šar-ilāni, scribe, interpreter(?).[42]

In the subsequent lines he styles himself as the servant of a whole series of Mesopotamian deities and as the "beloved of Hebat (and) [. . .]." With Gary Beckman[43] we can trace this family of scribes starting with Anu-šar-ilāni down to the end of the thirteenth century BC ending with another Hanikuili, who

37 Rüster & Wilhelm 2012: 54. 38 Rüster & Wilhelm 2012: 56.

39 Rüster & Wilhelm 2012: 56. 40 Rüster & Wilhelm 2012: 57.

41 Nr. 91 obv. 8, 26, rev. 19. Herbordt 2005: 15 mentions Muwa as a fifteenth century scribe on the only non-royal sealing from that period in the Nişantepe corpus; however, his name is not attested in any cuneiform records mentioning scribes and the interpretation of his title as scribe rests on the hieroglyphic sign L.326, for which see Chapter 14.

42 ŠU ^{m}*Hanikuili* DUB.SAR DUMU ^{d}*Anu*-LUGAL.DINGIR.MEŠ [D]UB.SAR ⌜BAL⌝ KBo 19.99 Seite b: 1–2 (Legend of Naram-Sin, CTH 819, OS); for the reading BAL (instead of BAL.BI) and its translation "interpreter" see Beckman 1983b: 103–4 w. n. 37, HZL 4, and Weeden 2011a: 168–9; for different interpretations see Gordin 2015: 108 w. lit.

43 Beckman 1983b: 103–6. The other colophon concerns KBo 31.48 (Lawsuit(?), CTH 825, palaeographic date undetermined), for which see Rüster 1993: 69–70 w. n. 21 (referred to as unpubl. 1371/u). The fragment preserves the colophon only (in Akkadian!) stating that it dealt with a lawsuit ([DUB.X.K]AM *ŠA DINI*[*M* . . .]).

wrote one of the best-preserved manuscripts of the Hittite laws. As suggested by Jared Miller[47] there is no reason not to equate the Hanikuili of the charters with the one from the two colophons and not to date these last two to the middle of the fifteenth century BC. What is even more interesting is the Semitic name of Hanikuili's father and his (i.e., Hanikuili's) given "profession" as "interpreter." It is unlikely to think of him as a descendant of the early families of scribes coming from Syria for whom – at least initially – writing in Akkadian was the natural thing and whose children and grandchildren grew up bilingually in Hattusa and assumed the logical role of conduits for all things Mesopotamian. By ca. 1450 BC that early period of borrowing lay already some 150 to 200 years back. Instead, Hanikuili's father may have been a recent arrival hired to work as a Mesopotamian specialist for diplomatic and related scribal services in the royal chancellery.

Finally, a small group of cuneiform scribes who cannot be assigned to a specific king, were probably active in the general period between 1500 and 1350 (Table 5.3).

Table 5.3 *Scribes attributable to the period 1500–1350 BC*

name	*texts*
AMAR-ti (Hubiti?)	KUB 32.19 + iv 49, KBo 22.129a rev. 10[44]
Askaliya	Bo 2004/1: 31[45]
Kukkuwa	KUB 34.45 + KBo 16.63 obv. 11
NU.^{GIŠ}KIRI$_6$	KUB 32.19 + iv 50(?)[46]
ŠUKUR-anza	KBo 15.10 iv 3

The composition on the tablet written by ŠUKUR-anza dates to the reign of Tuthaliya I (ca. 1425 BC) but at present we are unable to determine whether this is a contemporaneous exemplar or a copy of several decades later.[48] Note that among all the scribes mentioned thus far there is not a single one that is called "chief scribe" (GAL DUB.SAR(.MEŠ)) or "chief wood-scribe" (GAL DUB.SAR GIŠ). As Marco Marizza has observed, that

44 Mascheroni 1984: 157.

45 Mentioned by Wilhelm 2005a: 274, and 2005b: 77. According to him this would probably be another scribe than the one who wrote Charter nr. 1 listed above.

46 Waal 2015: 558 ("uncertain if it is the scribe").

47 Miller 2004: 37–8. After an analysis of the handwriting of the prism and the two charters Rüster & Wilhelm 2012: 71–2 see no objection to equate the two Hanikuilis either.

48 For a list of scribes who were active around 1375 BC and whom we can identify through the texts found at Maşat Höyük see Beckman 1995b: 33, van den Hout 2007a, and Chapter 13.4.

position is not attested in cuneiform sources until ca. 1375 in the Maşat Höyük corpus, to which we will turn in Chapter 13.8.[49]

5.5 Evidence for Record Management

One of the hallmarks of a full-blown administration is a developed apparatus to manage its constant and, in "a kind of feedback loop,"[50] often increasing flow of records. Regular recycling practices and archival storage and retrieval systems are two of the pillars necessary to keep everything under control. Colophons play an important role in retrieval of documents.[51] They function as *sigla* or as kind of "call numbers" identifying what kind of text one is dealing with, what its position is in a longer chain of documents, and they could be combined for easy identification with small labels that lay on or were attached to a shelf or some container like a basket or a chest. Colophons also sometimes give the name of the scribe who wrote the tablet (see Chapter 13.2). We already saw that no names of scribes are known prior to the end of the sixteenth century BC and for almost a century after Telipinu's reign evidence for scribes is almost exclusively restricted to their presence in the list of witnesses at the end of the charters. The concluding formula (in Akkadian, of course) runs as follows:

> This tablet in town X in the presence of (the witnesses) PN_1, PN_2 etc. PN, scribe, wrote.[52]

The formulation already shows that the scribe mentioned here was not necessarily a witness himself.[53] In at least one, admittedly late, case his name is separated from them by a paragraph line.[54] But there is an additional argument in the form of the bullae that were attached to the records. As we saw, charters stand out among the Hittite texts with their characteristic thick pillow-like shape, their big round edges (see Chapter 4 w. Fig. 4.2) and the royal seal that was impressed in a square frame, with the text wrapped around. In the middle of the lower edge (seen from the obverse) a hole can be observed sometimes with impressions of cords.[55] These, we assume, once held bullae, small lumps of clay, with the seals of the witnesses impressed on them. While the king validated the charters with his big seal impressed on the tablet itself,

[49] Marizza 2010: 42. For the legendary(?) scribe Pirwa in one of the Disappearing Deity myths see n. 32.
[50] Lurie 2011: 119. [51] On this see Waal 2015: 155.
[52] *tuppam anniām ina* [URU]GN *ana pāni* PN_1/PN2 etc. PN [LÚ]DUB.SAR *išṭur*.
[53] Thus already implied by Rüster & Wilhelm 2012: 37 ("Nennung der Zeugen und des Schreibers"), differently Gordin 2015: 50 ("the list of witnesses, of which the scribe was customarily the last to be named").
[54] KBo 5.7 rev. 55 = Charter nr. 91, ed. by Rüster & Wilhelm 2012: 238–9.
[55] Güterbock 1980: 53 w. n. 22.

the usually four or five witnesses listed with their professions at the end expressed their consent by impressing their seals on the attached bullae. Normally it is impossible to make out how many cords were originally inserted but a fortunate accident in the early 1930s made them visible. One day the young Hans Güterbock inadvertently dropped one such tablet, VAT 7436 = Charter nr. 41[56], which then neatly broke into two halves separating obverse and reverse like the halves of a sandwich.[57] This exposed the core of the tablet and the imprint of the cords. The shock of breaking so ancient a tablet prevented Güterbock at the time from carefully studying the inside and counting the cords' imprints. The tablet was quickly repaired but a later X-ray revealed there had been five of them. This coincides exactly with the number of witnesses on this charter excluding the scribe.[58] The scribe's name is therefore better seen as part of the so-called protocol and eschatocol, more specifically the latter[59]: the administrative context of the action of the document (the granting of land and property), where it was drawn up ("in town x"), when (the royal seal indicates under whose reign), who were present (the witnesses), and the circumstances concerning the drafting of the document. In the legal act, however, the scribe has no stake, that is, he stands *super partes* and "was independent from either contracting party."[60] He is a craftsman hired to do the job of recording. As such, the closing formula serves no record management ends, nor should it be regarded as a colophon. Moreover, as we will see later (Chapter 11), the charters were probably not filed as legal acts of the past but later generations may have had other reasons to hold on to them.

56 Ed. by Rüster & Wilhelm 2012: 186–9.

57 Güterbock 1997: 27–30; for a reconstruction of the process of making the tablet, impressing the royal seal, attaching the bullae, and inscribing the tablet see Herbordt 2005: 27–8.

58 Güterbock 1997: 30 cautiously refrains from this conclusion and keeps the possibility open that a combination of witnesses, beneficiary and/or scribe got to attach their seal. Whether the role of the scribe mentioned in lists of witnesses in Mesopotamia was the same as the other individuals mentioned in these lists remains to be seen. The fact that in most areas of the ancient Near East scribes featured mostly last in lists may point to a different status; cf. Petschow 1956: 11–12 Anm. 28 (writing about the Neo-Babylonian period: "Schreiber ... sind zumeist ... nicht zu den Vertragbeteiligten gehörende Personen, hauptsächlich wohl berufsmäßige Schreiber"), Ponchia 2009: 132–5 (writing about the Neo-Assyrian period (132–3): "his role seems to have been that of a super partes, who was independent from either contracting party"), Postgate 2013: 402 (writing about the Middle-Babylonian period: "Ugaritic practice [in non-royal acts (tvdh)] is largely comparable with legal documentation from Mesopotamia: the documents have witnesses, of whom the final one may be the scribe").

59 See Duranti 1998: 142 ("The first, termed *protocol*, contains the administrative context of the action (i.e., indication of the persons involved, time and place, and subject) and initial formulae; ... ; the third, termed *eschatocol*, contains the documentation context of the action (i.e., enunciation of the means of validation, indication of the responsibilities for documentation of the act" (italics Duranti)).

60 Ponchia 2009: 133.

In accordance with this, colophons of non-juridical documents that were identified as written in OS only mention the topic or title of the composition and/or its place in a series but not the scribe's identity. There was no need for a proto- and/or eschatocol here. Adding their names to such documents as part of general record management procedures seems to be a later phenomenon (see Chapter 13.2) starting towards the New Kingdom. The so-called prism (i.e., a four- or six-sided tablet[61]) written by Hanikuili, dated to shortly before the Empire (mid-fifteenth century BC) with its atypically elaborate colophon may not have served record management purposes either. Instead it may have been a showpiece or perhaps literally a masterpiece. Hanikuili's name in the other "colophon" mentioned earlier[62] appears in a legal document and may have been part of the eschatocol similar to that of the charters.

We can be brief about other possible hints at record management and thus signs of an active chancellery that needs to control its "paper" trail. Mostly from the days of the New Kingdom we have tablet inventories (also known as shelf lists or catalogs), that is, tablets listing tablets. To these we will have to come back in more detail in Chapter 13. These inventories make mention of numerous so-called *Sammeltafeln*, that is, tablets comprising more than one composition. Several of these have been preserved. We have tablets, for instance, that contain a number of different rituals or some historical records. They can be seen as genuine dossiers[63] and therefore likewise as activities typical of an institutional collection. Neither for the inventories nor for the *Sammeltafeln* do we have clear pre-Telipinu examples, however.

5.6 The Character of the Earliest Hittite Compositions

What one gains from these references to writing in the Old Kingdom texts is the impression of a young kingdom eager to make its presence felt and having only relatively recently discovered the role writing can play to stay in power and to further its ambitions. But the evidence presented thus far is mostly important for what it does not show. Few are the references to writing and none that point to a chancellery generating and receiving records in the context of the state's administration and neither do we know any scribes by name before the late sixteenth century BC. We should also approach the question from the more positive angle of what *is* there: what kinds of texts can we assign to the Old Kingdom until the New

[61] See Waal 2015: 25. [62] See n. 42. [63] For *Sammeltafeln* see Hutter 2011.

Kingdom or Empire starts with Tuthaliya I shortly before 1400 BC and what do they tell us about the spread of literacy? In many early literate societies, royal accounts and public inscriptions, including laws, are the oldest and first coherent prose after the stage of graffiti and ownership markings.[64] One could say much the same for Mesopotamia after the earliest administrative texts, lexical lists, and *kudurrus* (which resemble land deeds comparable to the Hittite charters).[65]

A look at the compositions datable to the period in question shows a similar trend. What we see are mostly accounts of kingly achievements and royal edicts.[66] They are mostly monumental (see Chapter 4) and serve as *aide-mémoire* at the same time and as such they set the next logical step in ownership marking. After visibly claiming possession of a weapon or some other prestigious and precious object by putting one's name on it, now deeds and decisions are put on record for posterity as belonging to somebody and nobody else. Looking again at the list of compositions at the end of Chapter 4, this is obviously the case for Hattusili's Annals (CTH 4) inscribed on (or near) his golden statue, his Edict and Testament (CTH 5–6), the fragments dealing with some of Mursili's campaigns in Anatolia and against the Hurrians (CTH 12–13), the historical narratives ascribed to Hantili(?) (CTH 10–11) and Ammuna (CTH 18), and of course Telipinu's own Proclamation (CTH 19) and the two historical fragments on his campaigns (CTH 20). Some compositions are too poorly preserved to assign them a specific king, but they seem to belong in the same category (CTH 14, 16–17). As laid out by Amir Gilan in his study of Old Hittite historical literature, what all previously mentioned texts – with the exception of the oracle report KBo 18.151 – have in common, is a strong didactic tone, the lesson being to respect the king's word.[67] At the same time many of the texts may have appealed to a sense of common identity and of pride in the achievements of the young kingdom.

Two compositions deserve special mention because the events recounted in them are usually considered to belong to the pre-Telipinu era even though they cannot be assigned a specific ruler: the so-called Palace Chronicles (CTH 8–9) and the Zalpa Tale (CTH 3). Both have been dated to the earliest days of the Hittite kingdom and in both texts the protagonists are anonymous: a father of the king and the king himself. Although heavily debated most scholars have identified Hattusili I as the

[64] See, for instance, Thomas 1992: 56–73, Sanders 2009: 113–20, 160–2.

[65] Postgate 1992: 66–70 w. Fig. 3: 13; for more detail and a more recent overview of the oldest cuneiform evidence see Sallaberger & Schrakamp 2015: 53–65.

[66] For an overview see Hoffner 1980: 289–308.

[67] Gilan 2015: 98 et passim.

"father of the king" and his successor Mursili I as the "king"[68] and author of the texts but recently it has been proposed to shift this relation up by a generation: Labarna I as the father and Hattusili as the author.[69] Like Hattusili's Annals and similar compositions the Zalpa Tale, too, is an account of the conquest by an unnamed Hittite king of a town called Zalpa.[70] As such it falls in the category of *res gestae* but it stands out for the etiological tale, with which it opens. It tells of a queen of Kanesh who gave birth to thirty sons at once. Horrified she disposes of them by putting them in the river in baskets caulked with a kind of pitch or oily substance so as at least not to drown them. The river carries them downstream to Zalpa where they are rescued and raised. Next, the queen bears thirty daughters and these she keeps. Years later the return of the sons to Kanesh in search of their mother brings about a first reunification of the two cities. The protagonist-king of the second part of the text now wants to forcibly repeat this with his army. The elements in the introductory tale bring to mind other Near Eastern, Biblical and Greco-Roman parallels, and the style and archaic linguistic character of this part suggest an old and oral folk tradition.

That same oral character can be claimed for what are usually called the Palace Chronicles. On the face of it, they form a collection of "anecdotes," as they also have been labeled, but they are neither chronicles[71] nor does "anecdotes" adequately describe the function of the text. According to Gilan the royal banquet scene at the end shows the actual setting. Over dinner and drinks stories are told not just for entertainment but, again, with obvious didactic and moralistic intent.[72] Subject matter is the reprehensible behavior of government officials who invariably come to a bad end, sometimes after a severe case of poetic justice, as illustrated by the following gruesome episode:

> In the country of Arzawiya Nunnu was ruler of the town of Hurma and silver (and) gold that he encountered he did not bring but took to his house. The ruler of Huntara denounced him. The father of the king sent. They brought him up but instead of him he sent Sarmassu, but he was not going yet. The father of the king sent a Man-of-the-Gold-Spear. They took Sarmassu and Nunnu away to Mount Tahaya and they harnessed them like oxen and they arrested a relative of Nunnu's and slaughtered him before Sarmassu's and Nunnu's eyes. When it dawned the father of the king called

[68] Hoffner 1980: 291, Dardano 1997: 10–11, Archi 2010: 42, Gilan 2015: 130–1.
[69] Beal 2003, Forlanini 2010: 118–19, see also Weeden 2011a: 62.
[70] For the most recent analysis and ed. see Gilan 2015: 179–213.
[71] Hoffner 1980: 303.
[72] Gilan 2015: 127–35 (especially 132).

> out: "Who took these away? Why aren't their clothes and belts stained with blood?" Thus, the guards: "Their clothes are turned outside in." They turned the clothes inside out and the king saw the blood. Thus Sarmassu: "My Majesty, I'm not yet going, not yet seeing!" Thus, the king: "Go and have this seared into (your) heart!"[73]

I have deliberately kept the translation as simple and literal as possible to bring out the specific prose style of this composition. The sentences are short with a simple syntax and practically no subordination.[74] There is a single relative sentence ("silver (and) gold *that* he encountered") and one temporal conjunction ("*When* it dawned"). Several pronouns are ambiguous as to their referents and we need some imagination to make sense of the situation that unfolds here. Modern translators use a lot of "i.e.s" or parenthetical clarifications to help the reader understand their interpretation. All this is typical of early writing that is often "under-marked" for its referents, very implicit and compressed, and heavily relying on the information supposed to be known to its audience. It is also typical of an oral style. It resembles a conversation where both parties share knowledge of the situation and not everything needs to be made explicit.[75] Moreover, in a public presentation the written version could be embellished and added on to as far as deemed necessary. Writing is still very much secondary here to the primary oral delivery.[76] As writing takes on a more prominent role in societies and finally reaches a higher degree of authority than an individual's orally presented memory, it will also gain in explicitness. The fact, finally, that not a single fragment of an Akkadian-language version of either the Zalpa Tale or the Palace Chronicles has come to light thus far as opposed to several Hittite copies is fully congruent with their pragmatic and oral origins.

[73] KUR Arzawiya ^{m}*Nunnu* LÚ ^{URU}*Ḫūrma ēšt*[*a*] KÙ.BABBAR*=i*[a GUŠK]IN [*n*]*atta udai kuit wemiezzi apašš=a* [*par*]*na=šša pittaizzi š=an* LÚ ^{URU}*Ḫuntarā išiaḫḫiš* ABI LUGAL *I*[*ŠP*] *UR š=an šarā uwater pedi=šši=ma* ^{m}*Šarmaššun ḫatraet paizzi=ma=aš nāwi* ABI LUGAL LÚ ŠUKUR.GUŠKIN *IŠPUR* ^{m}*Šarmāššun* ^{m}*Nunnunn=a* $^{ḪUR.SAG}$*Taḫayai peḫuter n=uš* GU_4*-li turer* ^{m}*Nunnušš=a* ^{LÚ}*kaina*(*n*)*=ššan ēpper š=an* ^{m}*Šarmāššuwi* ^{m}*Nunnuwi=ia šakuwaš=šma<š> ḫuēkta* § *mān luktat nu* ABI LUGAL *ḫalzaiš kūš arḫa kuiš peḫutet* TÚG*=*ŠUNU ^{TÚG}*išḫial=šemett=a kuit natta ešḫa*[*š*]*kanta* UMMA LÚ.MEŠ *MEŠEDI šekunuš=šmet anda nēan n*[*u*] TÚG.ḪI.A*-uš arḫa naier nu ēšḫar* LUGAL*-uš aušta* UMMA <^{m}>*Šarmaššu* ^{d}UTU*=met paimi nāwi ūḫḫi nāwi* UMMA LUGAL*=MA īt ki=ma=z kar!da šišta* KBo 3.34 i 11–23 ("Palace Chronicles", CTH 8, NS) w. dupls., ed. by Dardano 1997: 32–5.

[74] Dardano 2011: 68 ("Der Stil . . . ist besonders nüchtern und schmucklos."), cf. also Archi 2010: 43 on KBo 22.1 and a ritual like KBo 17.1.

[75] See Coulmas 2013: 11–14 on restricted vs. elaborated code.

[76] Cf. Archi 2005: 26, Thomas 1992: 90–1, Schoeler 2009: 54, Watson & Horowitz 2011: 146–7 (they use the term "under-marked").

The main argument to date the Palace Chronicles to Labarna or Hattusili are some personal names that they and a few documents dated to their reigns have in common.[77] Among the latter are some of the anonymous charters that we saw earlier. These identifications are based on not much more than the fact that the names are the same and are attested in these old texts, not on any further identifying descriptions that provide evidence that we are indeed dealing with the same individuals. The compelling re-dating of the charters by Wilhelm to Telipinu or at least to the second half of the sixteenth century BC has shown how careful we ought to be with such arguments.[78] The strong naming traditions in Anatolia render this line of reasoning unreliable. For the charters this meant a dating down from the second half of the seventeenth century to the later sixteenth century BC but for the Chronicles, all or some of them might as well reach back to times older than those of Labarna. Some of the names in question (Hani, Huzziya, Nunnu) are, for instance, also attested in texts of the Old Assyrian Period.[79] Finally, Paola Dardano, the most recent editor of the Chronicles, has suggested not without plausibility that the expression "father of the king," attested both in the Zalpa Tale and the Chronicles (and the Laws, as we will see shortly), may have been a rhetorical device rather than a historical figure likewise harking back to "the olden days" and lending a certain authority to royal decision making.[80] But what was the goal of this collection of anecdotes?

5.7 The Hittite Laws

The use of examples from daily life to make a point – sometimes of almost comical quality to us – is typical of Old Hittite literature, as we already saw, and can be found also in Hattusili's Political Testament.[81] The Chronicles have been compared to the Urshu Text mentioned in Chapter 4.3 because of its humorous and sarcastic tone and to some isolated later instances of examples inserted in instructions and treaties.[82] Dardano has convincingly described their character as "giuridico-sentenziale" with a pedagogical goal.[83] This makes them typical of another genre of early literate cultures:

77 Cf. Dardano 1997: 10 fns. 32 and 33. 78 Wilhelm 2005a, Rüster & Wilhelm 2012: 38–9.

79 For Nunnu see already: no. 897, for Hani cf. OIP 27 1: 3; r/k 15: 5, 7 (written *Ḫa-ni*), for Huzziya cf. a/k 906: 21(d), BIN 6, 140: 7; CTMMA 96: 15, KTH 18: 26 (written *Hu-zi-a*, *Hu-zi-áš*) (courtesy J. G. Dercksen, Old Assyrian Personal Names, unpubl. ms. Leiden 1991).

80 Dardano 1997: 8–11, cf. similarly Weeden 2011a: 77 n. 357.

81 Hoffner 1980: 300–2, Gilan 2015: 66–98. 82 Dardano 1997: 7–9.

83 Dardano 1997: 10, see also her remarks 4 and Dardano 2011: 64 w. lit., 75 ("eine erzieherische Funktion"), 77 ("Erziehung der Untertanen"). For the banquet scene at the end of the composition

laws.[84] In their oral form laws are originally often disguised as brief stories or anecdotes that exemplify all kinds of undesirable behavior and are much easier to remember than abstract jurisprudence.[85] These short anecdotes could therefore be seen as forerunners of the Hittite law collection that had its roots in such a collection of admonitory tales.

The Hittite Laws, as we have them, show an overall very consistent structure ("If [*takku*] somebody does [present tense] such-and-such, then he/she shall [present tense] . . . ") probably abstracted from concrete cases in the past. Their casuistic origins may still be observed in a series of stipulations (§§48–56) that deviate from the regular and usual structure. The paragraphs in question deal with taxes and people who are exempt from paying them. Two among them still maintain their original anecdotal character and are followed by a third, continuing the topic. The first two are phrased in the past tense and even the "father of the king" of the Zalpa Tale and the Palace Chronicles puts in an appearance. The third is in the present-future tense.

> §54 Once upon a time the *manda*-troops, the troops of Sala[86], the troops of Tamalkiya, the troops of Hatra, the troops of Zalpa, the troops of Tashiniya, the troops of Hemuwa (all towns), the bowmen, the carpenters, charioteers, and their *karuhali*-men did not render *luzzi*-service (and) did not do corvée.
>
> §55 When tax paying Hittite citizens came (and) bow[ed] to the father of the king they said: 'Nobody pays us wages and they refuse us (saying): "You are taxpayers."' The father of the king [issued a] su[mmons] for a meeting and instructed them (saying): 'Go, you shall do just as your peers!'
>
> §56 In that fortification (i.e., Hattusa) none of the copper smith(s) shall be exempt from joining a royal expedition (or) harvesting vineyards. Gardeners shall perform *luzzi*-service in every same (project) as well.[87]

see Dardano 2011: 77. Dardano describes the "Schreiberschulen" as the transmitters of cultural memory but although this may be true of the New Kingdom period it is questionable for the early Old Kingdom.

[84] Ong 1982: 35, 137, 144, Thomas 1992: 65–6, Franklin 2002: 156–60, Sanders 2009: 162–4.

[85] McKitterick 1989: 37–8. [86] I follow Collins 1987 in taking Sala and Tamalkiya as place names.

[87] §54 *karū* ÉRIN.MEŠ *MANDA* ÉRIN.MEŠ Šāla ÉRIN.MEŠ *Tamalkiya* ÉRIN.MEŠ ^{URU}*Ḫa*[(*trā*)] ÉRIN.MEŠ ^{URU}Zalpa ÉRIN.MEŠ ^{URU}*Tašhiniya* ÉRIN.MEŠ ^{URU}*Ḫemuwa* LÚ.MEŠ ^{GIŠ}PAN ^{L}[($^{\text{Ú.MEŠ}}$NAGAR GIŠ-ṢI)] $^{\text{LÚ.MEŠ}}$KUŠ$_7$ Ù$^{\text{LÚ.MEŠ}}$*karuḫaleš=šmešš=a luzzi natta karpe*[*r*] *šaḫḫan natta īššer*

§55 [(*m*)]*ān* DUMU.MEŠ ^{URU}*Ḫatti* LÚ.MEŠ *ILKI uēr* ANA ABI LUGAL *aruwā* [*nzi*] ⸢*nu tar*⸣*šikanzi kūšan=*naš=za* natta kuiški iē*[(*zzi*)] *nu=wa=nnaš=za mimmanzi* LÚ.MEŠ *ILKI=wa šumeš nu* ABI LUGAL [(*tuliya ḫal*)*zaiš*] *n=uš anda šittariet ītten māḫhanda areš=š m*[(*eš*)] *šumešš=a apeniššan ište*[(*n*)]

§56 *edì* BÀD-*ni* LUGAL-*aš* KASKAL-*š=a takšuanzi* ^{GIŠ}KIRI$_6$.GEŠTIN-*aš tuḫḫušuanzi* ⸢ŠA⸣ [(^{LÚ}URUD)]U.NAGAR *natta kuiški arauaš* LÚ.MEŠ NU.^{GIŠ}KIRI$_6$ *ḫūmanti=ia=pat luzzi* [(*karp-*)] *ianzi* KBo 6.2 + KBo 22.62 iii 12–22 (Laws, CTH 291, OS) w. dupls. KBo 6.3 iii 19–25 (NS), KBo 6.6 i 19–32 (NS), ed. by Hoffner 1997a: 65–8; reading *tuliya ḫal*[*zaiš*] (§55) with Mora 1983, for the reading of *edi* in §56 see p. 90–1.

The gist of the first two paragraphs probably is that the troops of §54 got paid for work they performed since they were exempt from rendering their taxes to the state in the form of certain services. Regular taxpayers thereupon appealed to the father of the king complaining they were always told that they were supposed to render their services as part of the taxes they owed and hence were to receive no pay.

Overall, the Laws reveal an explicit chronological layering in that several paragraphs contrast an earlier stage (*karū* "formerly, in the past") with the current situation (*kinuna* "but now"). Because the oldest manuscripts are written in OS and the "father of the king" is mentioned several scholars, with the Zalpa Text and Palace Chronicles in mind, have identified Hattusili I (= father of the king) as responsible for the earliest, not preserved set of laws reflected in the *karū*-clauses, and Mursili I (= the king, although not mentioned in the Laws) as the author of the actual attested *kinuna*-clauses.[88] This would leave about one generation to come from one version to the other. As we saw, however, this dating based on personal names proved invalid for the Chronicles and so they are for the Laws as well. The most recent editor of the Hittite Laws, Harry Hoffner, argued for Telipinu as the king who issued the *kinuna*-stage of the Laws while maintaining an early date to Labarna or Hattusili for the *karū*-version.[89] He did so not only because the changes in the Laws are in line with the spirit of his Proclamation with its new rules and organizational changes but at the very end of the Proclamation there are two law-like paragraphs added on, one on homicide and one concerning sorcery within the royal family in Hattusa. The extra two clauses are not present in the standard Law collection and the one on homicide may even be seen as filling "a notable omission" in the Laws.[90] Hoffner therefore hypothesized that "[i]f the main version of the law corpus was introduced during the reign of Telipinu, it is possible that premeditated homicide (murder) was omitted because it was already described in the Telipinu Proclamation."[91] This would mean the Law collection was put together after the Proclamation. On the other hand, the Laws come across as a collection with a deliberate internal organization, not just because it is a collection in the first place, but the 200 paragraphs are also thematically grouped. Its nature as a collection suggests a striving for comprehensiveness and it would seem strange that the redactors would not have included that one paragraph filling a gap because it was already written down somewhere else.

88 Singer 2001: 288 w. lit., to which can be added Forlanini 2010: 130.
89 Hoffner 1995: 214, 1997a: 230. 90 Hoffner 1995: 214, see also 215. 91 Hoffner 1995: 215.

By the same token, one might claim that the extra stipulation in Telipinu's Proclamation was an addendum to the Laws rather than the Laws an addendum to the Proclamation. The fact that the Laws are the most frequently copied text ensemble in all of Hittite literature and Telipinu's two clauses were never incorporated could even be taken to mean that in Telipinu's reign the collection had already reached a fixed, one would almost be tempted to say, canonical form. The many later copies show only minor changes, mostly just modernizing the language but not revising the Laws' wording or intent nor adding to it.[92]

This prompts an essential question: can we put the stages reflected in the Laws on some kind of a timeline? In order to answer this question, we can look at style and language. Let us look at style first. If the Palace Chronicles with their "anecdotes" and the Laws have a common past, that is, the anecdotes are what the Laws ultimately evolved out of and if the Palace Chronicles go back at least to the days of Labarna if not earlier, as we considered above, can we say the same about the Laws? And at the other end, when did they reach their "final" *kinuna*-form? Starting with the first question, if the Laws originated as anecdotal tales by way of mnemonic device to transmit a body of practical oral jurisprudence, their origins can go back further than the early days of the first kings. Although that is impossible to prove on the basis of the texts at our disposal a promising analysis by Billie Jean Collins of §54 gives us at least something of a *terminus ad quem* for this specific paragraph.[93] She has observed that the towns mentioned there (Sala, Tamalkiya, Hatra, Zalpa, Tashiniya, Hemuwa) were not centers of Hittite power in Anatolia but were located on the eastern Euphrates front. They were strategic places in the buffer zone with Syria during the campaigns of Labarna, Hattusili, and Mursili. This also explains their tax-exempt status. In the war effort all forces were needed, and taxes should not (yet) be imposed on them. Another interesting argument concerns the Hittite word that starts §56 and that has caused interpreters considerable difficulty. Reading *e-di*! "that, yonder" instead of *e-ki* "ice" Petra Goedegebuure argues that, if one accepts the emendation and if the "Hittite citizens" are still addressed here, Hattusa is referred to as "that fortress over there." This would imply that Hattusa would be mentioned as just some town among others and was not yet the capital from

[92] Only in the thirteenth century BC do we find a significantly altered version of §§1–49, the so-called Parallel Text.

[93] Collins 1987.

where the law was decreed. This could only have been said under Labarna at the very earliest.[94]

If the style and historical specificity of §§54–56 is typical of legal formulation in the days of Labarna or earlier then it seems unlikely to ascribe the rest of the collection of the Hittite Laws with their radically different structure to him, Hattusili, or Mursili. The level of abstraction and legal sophistication is clearly more developed in all other paragraphs than in the anomalous §§54–56 that hew stylistically close to the Palace Chronicles. If, following Hoffner, we date the most recent recension of the Laws, as marked by the adverb *kinuna* "but now" to the second half of the sixteenth century BC, there may be just enough time to allow for the new format to develop. The Hittite Laws and their possible anecdotal forerunners may thus be the result of a tradition that stretches back at least to the days of Labarna in the first half of the seventeenth century and, that came to a close in the second half of the sixteenth century BC.

The second argument for stratification of texts from the Old Kingdom comes from the language of these documents. This is a problematic area for two reasons. Firstly, most of the compositions datable to specific kings have come down to us only in later, that is, mostly thirteenth century BC manuscripts. Although they certainly retain archaic linguistic features, we can also see how they were consciously or unconsciously modernized over the centuries in spelling, morphology, and syntax. Secondly, even if they are written in what is called OS, we could still be dealing with a fifteenth century copy of an originally Hattusili I-era composition prior to 1600 BC. However, in an important article on Old Hittite coordinating conjunctions ("and, but" *vel sim.*) Elisabeth Rieken has shown that nevertheless a linguistic stratigraphy can be observed within the corpus of Old Kingdom texts.[95] The oldest layer is visible in (the OS manuscripts of) compositions like the Zalpa Tale (CTH 2–3), the Palace Chronicles (CTH 8–9) and some fragments that probably go back to the days of the Syrian campaigns. A more recent layer is represented in the Laws and the corpus of Old Hittite "rituals" (see §5.9). All other Old Kingdom compositions are late copies, with which linguistically little can be done. But the contrast we saw in style between documents of the second half of the seventeenth

[94] Goedegebuure 2002–2003: 10 n. 24, 2014: 113 n. 112; Hitt. *edi* is the dative-locative of a distal demonstrative pronoun "yonder." Like Goedegebuure others in the past have read with a minimal emendation *e-di*!, the cuneiform signs KI and DI differing only in one horizontal wedge more (KI 𒆠) or less (DI 𒁲), but did not realize the consequences of the reading.

[95] Rieken 2000.

century and those of the later sixteenth century BC is thus matched by a linguistic one.

5.8 Law and Orality

Laws mean nothing if not disseminated. So how do we imagine the Law collection functioning in the Old Kingdom? First of all, it's important to realize that in contrast to many ancient Law Codes like that of Hammurabi there is no Hittite king to lay claim to them, no introduction with lofty principles. In view of the increased "ownership marking" that we saw earlier (§5.6) the anonymity is striking and seems more in line with Telipinu than the days of Hattusili I. There is also no evidence for the laws ever having been publicly displayed like Hammurabi's famous stela.[96] The Hittite collection starts *in medias res* and ends as abruptly as it began. The anonymity may seem a typical Hittite trait: in spite of their quite unparalleled tablet collection Hittite rulers never seem to have prided themselves in having amassed or started it, as is, for instance, the case with Assurbanipal's library and most such collections in the ancient Near East or the Greco-Roman world.[97] No Hittite king boasts of being literate, being a sage, or speaking more than one language. Although perhaps not representative of all Hittite kings, Mursili II is as modest about his military achievements in his Annals as a monarch can reasonably be. Hittite kings seem less prone to self-aggrandizement than many of their peers. On the other hand, the Laws do not seem to have been meant to be universally applicable throughout the realm. Just as seems to have been the case with the toleration of local religious customs and panthea as well as local economies, the ruling elite also allowed room for local jurisdiction differing from that of the state laws:

> Furthermore, the post and town commanders (and) the elders shall properly adjudicate law cases and resolve them. And just as in the past in the provinces, norms were set regarding crimes, if in a town they used to put them (i.e., the perpetrators) to death, let them put them to death, while if in a town they used to expel them, let them expel them.[98]

[96] Bryce 2002: 34. [97] Cf. Casson 2001: 8.

[98] *namma auriyaš* EN-*aš* ^{LÚ}MAŠKIM.URU$^{KI!}$ LÚ.MEŠ ŠU.GI *DINĀTIM* SIG$_5$-*in ḫaššikandu nu=ššan katta arnuškandu karūiliyaz=ia* ⸢*ma*⸣*ḫḫan* KUR.KUR=*kan anda ḫurkilaš išḫiūl iyan kuedani=aš=kan* URU-*ri kuašker n=aš=kan kuwaškandu kuedani=ma=aš=kan* URU-*ri arha parḫišker n=aš=kan arha parḫiškandu* KUB 13.2 iii 9–14 (Instruction for Provincial Governors, CTH 261, NS), ed. by Pecchioli Daddi 2003: 146–9, Miller 2013: 228–9.

The writing down and codification of the Laws may have been intended as a unifying element. The section on price tariffs certainly seems aimed at setting a certain economic standardization although it is unclear for how large an area. On the whole, however, the collection may have had ideological goals rather than real-life consequences on the ground.

Also, in the way they are phrased the individual clauses of the Laws still show some of the compression and implicitness, the same "undermarking"[99] that some of the other early compositions do. The most important point, however, may be that, just as in the case of the Palace Chronicles, among all the dozens of manuscripts of the Laws not a single fragment in Akkadian has ever been identified. When the early kings of the seventeenth century BC ordered things written down it was natural to have it done in Akkadian, as the scribes employed had learned it that way and were not yet fluent in Hittite. Perhaps they even cultivated it to a certain extent. If the Laws had been codified around the time of Labarna we might have expected some portions of it in Akkadian just as we have Akkadian parts of Hattusili's Testament and Annals. There also circulated an Akkadian version of Telipinu's Proclamation. Therefore, writing them down in Hittite only must have been a conscious decision. Unless there was a steady and substantial stream of immigrants, active Akkadian-language skills may well have been on the wane by then.[100] Also, Akkadian being the realm of the early scribal profession, having the Laws drawn up in Hittite and Hittite alone may also have given the king a feeling of more direct control of its contents. In new genres like edicts, annals, and land grants, compositions that owed their existence to the introduction of the cuneiform script, Akkadian was still the way to go and their audience may have been limited to ruling circles. The Laws on the other hand had a long oral and aural history and were, at least theoretically, meant for the population at large, as shown for instance by the parties involved in the §§54–56. An Akkadian version did not make much sense, so a corner was turned, and it may have been the beginning of the end of Akkadian as a written language for internal purposes. Who the king was under whose aegis this step was taken, Telipinu or one of his immediate predecessors, is impossible to tell at this moment but the political situation was ready for a change like this in the second half of the sixteenth century BC, as we will see.

99 See §5.6.

100 In a similar way knowledge of Arabic declined starting in the tenth century AD Iran and lead to a rise of writing in Persian: see Hanaway 2012: 114–20.

Finally, the fact that there is no reference to a monumental version of the Laws comparable to Hammurabi's stela underscores the low-communicative status of Hittite cuneiform writing. It was meant for purely internal purposes. The statue of Hattusili I and perhaps a few other instances of inscribed monuments (see Chapter 3 and 5.2) belong to the earliest days of writing in the Hittite kingdom. They were due to Mesopotamian influence and the practice was discontinued when the immediate link with Mesopotamia was severed in the aftermath of Mursili's murder and Anatolia was once more thrown back unto itself. By the time of Telipinu it opened up again but now a new feeling of cultural independence manifested itself that created its own forms of expression and claimed to no longer need foreign examples.

5.9 The Corpus of Old Hittite Cult Rituals

In Hittite studies the word "ritual" is usually reserved for compositions that describe the actions undertaken by a priest or priestess dealing with a specific, mostly somatic or mental, problem or set of problems with magic as his or her major tool. The party for whom a ritual is carried out is normally an anonymous "ritual patron" (EN or *BĒL* SISKUR/SÍSKUR) or group of patrons. The corpus that we refer to as the Old Hittite Rituals[101], however, contains only few such texts and those that can be called rituals in this sense have the royal family as their patrons.[102] The overwhelming majority of these texts fall in the category of festival scenarios that make up the Hittite cult calendar and that are true cult rituals in the sense that they prescribe the movements and utterances of all participants in the event. The corpus was put together on paleographic criteria and contains no historical references that make it possible to ascribe any of the compositions to a specific reign. Only four personal names are attested overall, and they do not help in pinning down any of the compositions, in which they occur.[103] In light of the extended range of OS the only element that at least provides a *terminus ante quem* of ca. 1400 BC is the ductus shared by all the fragments. The cultic behavior described in the texts is of the kind that gets handed down generation after generation and develops over centuries if not longer. Such folk traditions including etiological tales and hymnic parts[104] will have been transmitted by acting them out time and again accompanied by oral commentary. This is wonderfully illustrated by the

[101] Neu 1980 and 1983. [102] Neu 1980 Text nos. 1–9. [103] For the PNs see Neu 1983: 353.
[104] For the hymnic parts see Wilhelm 1994a: 60–1.

two versions of the Illuyanka myth, so-called after the snake or dragon that initially defeats the Stormgod. The text itself mentions that the two tales were part of the *purulli*-festival associated with the cult center of Nerik. In both cases the Stormgod needs human help to finally overcome the monster. Although transmitted only in NS manuscripts the language betrays older origins. The first version runs as follows:

> §1 When the Stormgod and Illuyanka engaged in battle in (the town of) Kiskilussa, Illuyanka defeated the Stormgod.
>
> §2 And the Stormgod implored all the gods: "Join me!" So Inar organized a feast.
>
> §3 She arranged everything amply: vessels of wine, vessels of *marnuwan*-drink, vessels of [*wa*]*lhi*-drink, and in the vessels she prepared an abundance.
>
> §4 Inar went to (the town of) Ziggaratta and encountered Hupasiya, a mortal.
>
> §5 Thus (said) Inar to Hupasiya: "Right now, I'm doing all these things and you must help me."
>
> §6 Thus (said) Hupasiya to Inar: "If I can sleep with you, I'll come, and do as you wish." So, she slept with him.
>
> §7 Inar [b]rought Hupas[iya] along, hid him, and dressed herself up. She called Illuyanka from his lair: "Right now I'm organizing a feast: come eat (and) drink!"
>
> §8 Illuyanka surfaced with [his children]. They ate (and) drank. They dr[ank] from all vessels so that they became drunk.
>
> §9 They could no longer get into the(ir) lair and Hupasiya came and tied Illuyanka up with ropes.
>
> §10 The Stormgod came and killed Illuya[nk]a and the gods were with him.
>
> §11 Inar built a house on a rock, in (the town of) Tarukka and settled Hupasiya in the house. Inar ordered (as follows): "When I go into the field, don't look out the window. If you look out, you will see your wife (and) children."
>
> §12 When twenty days had gone by, he glanced out the wi[ndow] and [saw his] wife (and) his children.
>
> §13 [W]hen Inar returned from the field, he began to whine: "Let me go [b]ack home!"[105]

105 *mān* ^{d}IM-*aš* ^{muš}*Illuyankašš=a* INA ^{URU}*Kiškilušša arga tiyēr nu=za* ^{MUŠ}*Illuyankaš* ^{d}IM-*an* [(*taru*)]*ḫta* § ^{d}IM≪-*aš*≫-*tašš=a* DINGIR.MEŠ-*naš ḫūma*[*nd*]*uš mūgait anda=m(u)=apa tīy*[*a*]*tten nu=za* ^{d}*Inaraš* EZEN$_4$-*an iēt* § *nu ḫuman mekki ḫandait* GEŠTIN-*aš* ^{DUG}*palḫi marnuwandaš* ^{DUG}*palḫi* [*wa*]*lḫiyaš* ^{DUG}*palḫi* [*nu* ^{DU}]^{G}*palḫaš a*[*n*(*d*)]*an iyāda i*[*ē*]*t* § *nu* ^{d}[(*Inara*)*š* INA ^{URU}Z]*iggaratta pait nu* ^{m}*Ḫūpašiyan* LÚ.U$_{19}$.LU *wemit* § UMMA ^{d}*Inar* ^{m}*Ḫūpašiya kāša=wa ki=ya ki=ya uttar iyami nu=wa=mu=ššan ziqq=a ḫarapḫut* § UMMA ^{m}*Ḫūpašiya* ANA ^{d}*Inar mā=wa katti=ti šešm*[*i n*]*u=wa uwami kardiaš=taš iyami* [*n=aš* (*katt*)]*i=ši šešta* § *nu* ^{d}*Inaraš* ^{m}*Ḫūpaš*[*iyan p*]*ēḫutet n=an mūnnāit* ^{d}*Inaraššaz unuttat n=ašta* ^{muš}*Illuyank-*

After two more fragmentarily preserved paragraphs the text returns to Nerik and its festival celebrations. If this story – actually, two stories in one, one about the dragon and the other about Hupasiya's ordeal or human weakness – is supposed to entertain it does not do a very effective job. In fact, it seems as if everything that could make it exciting or suspenseful has deliberately been taken out. There are no adjectives, no epithets, no descriptions of backgrounds or surroundings, no cliffhangers. It is a list of bullet points together forming the bare-bones elements of the story. Reading it out loud takes just over two minutes. The second version seems to be even shorter. The paragraphs are mostly used to set the story (§1 Kiskilussa), give a change of location (§4 Ziggaratta, §11 Tarukka) or time (§12 twenty days later), and to convey what's being said (§§2, 5–7, 11, 13). As such, the text almost resembles the title cards of silent movies accompanying dramatic actions and moving the narrative forward while giving the audience essential information that is less easy to act out. The Hittite versions make sense only as a basic script or *aide-mémoire* for what must have been a much more dramatic enactment full of sounds (including gasps from the audience when the son of the Stormgod asks his father to kill him and he does!), gestures, and lively action, now and then interrupted by a narrator.[106] Other mythical tales likewise still preserve some of that original dramatic character.[107]

The cultural setting of these compositions is strongly Hattian both geographically and in divine names: Old Hittite religion was dominated by Hattian deities.[108] It is usually assumed that Hattian was still a spoken language in the days of the Old Kingdom and it may have continued being spoken for some time after as well.[109] The institutional memory, on which such traditions rely, is often purely oral and there is no evidence for an indigenous written Hattian tradition.[110] It seems safe to assume that this

[an] ḫantešnaz šarā kallišta kāša=wa EZEN$_4$*-an iyami nu=wa adanna akuwanna eḫu* § *n=ašta* ^{muš}*Illuyankaš* QADU [DUMU.MEŠ=ŠU] *šarā uēr nu=za eter ekue[r (n=)]ašta* ^{DUG}*palḫan ḫūmandan ek-[uer] [(n=)]e=za ninkēr* § *[(n=)]e namma ḫattešnaš kattanda nūmān pānzi* ^{m}*Ḫūpašiyašš[(a uit)] nu* ^{MUŠ}*Illuyankan išḫima[(nta)] kalēliēt* § ^{d}IM*-aš uit nu=kan* ^{MUŠ}*Illuy[(ankan)] kuenta* DINGIR.MEŠ*-š=a katti=šši ešer* § *nu=z=(š)[(an)]* ^{d}*Inaraš* $^{\text{NA4}}$*peruni [(šer)]* É*-er wetet* INA KUR ^{URU}*Tā[(rukki)] nu* ^{m}*Ḫūpašiyan andan* É*[(-ri)] ašašta n=an* ^{d}*Inaraš watarnaḫḫiškezzi mā=wa gi[(mra)] paimi zigg=a=war=ašta* ^{GIŠ}*luttan[(za)] arḫa lē autt[(i)] mā=war=ašta arḫa=ma autti nu=wa=za* DAM=KA DUMU.MEŠ=KA *autt-[i]* § *mān* UD.20.KAM *pait apāš=a* ^{GIŠ}*lut[tanza] arḫa šuwaīt nu* DAM=ZU DUMU.MEŠ*[=ŠU aušta]* §*[(m)]ān* ^{d}*Inarašš=a gimraz* EGIR*[(-pa u)]it apašš=a wešgauan dāiš [(ā)]ppa=wa=mu* É*-na tarna* KBo 3.7 i-ii 5–9 and KUB 17.6 i w. further dupls., ed. by Beckman 1982: 12–14, 18–19, Rieken et al. (ed.), hethiter.net/: CTH 321 (INTR 2010-11-23).

106 See Haas 2006: 97, who went in the same direction.

107 Bryce 2002: 211–13, van den Hout 1991.

108 Haas 1994: 618–20, Popko 1995: 67–8.

109 Goedegebuure 2008.

110 Differently Soysal 2004: 12–14.

corpus had an already long history behind it when it was finally written down. Nevertheless, as mentioned before, according to Rieken these texts reflect, linguistically, a later stage of development than that of the Zalpa Tale or Palace Chronicles. The fact that, again, there is no evidence for any Akkadian versions probably has to do with the purely local and oral tradition of these texts. Moreover, the local Anatolian cultic and magic jargon of their lexicon may have been alien to the Syrian scribes who brought in an Akkadian vocabulary that was much more socio-economically oriented. We will see the same thing happening in the charters in Chapter 6.3. All this suggests that the decision to start recording cult ritual scenarios was made relatively late and paradoxically the incorporation of non-Hittite material may even have been instrumental in the step to start writing Hittite, as we will see in the next chapter (6).

5.10 Socio-Economic, Legal, and Bookkeeping Texts?

The oldest two genres in Mesopotamian literature are socio-economic, legal, and bookkeeping records and the so-called lexical lists. The latter form a typical Mesopotamian genre that only later found its way into Anatolia with the import of Mesopotamian learned culture. The former category of secular administrative records, on the other hand, seems entirely lacking, except for the charters. There are several possible reasons for this. The Hittite tablet collections are fairly unique in the history of the ancient Near East both in their time span and documentary variety, and the Hittites stand out for their record management prowess. Archaeology makes it clear that when the empire broke up around 1200 BC the tablet storage facilities in the capital contained holdings that were up to over 300 years old. This was not because they had forgotten about them but because they deliberately and systematically held on to them. But as every self-respecting administration regularly appraises its collections and throws out those documents that are no longer deemed of use, the Hittites, too, continuously recycled. It is no coincidence then that – apart from the occasional exception that proves the rule – the administrative records that we do have usually date to the most recent period before the end of a site's occupation. The same is true for Hittite Anatolia, as we will see later (see Chapter 8). But does that mean that we should suppose the existence of written administrative records with the bookkeeping of the Old Kingdom on a par with the Mesopotamian situation where at first, we seem to have such records almost exclusively? I think this is unlikely, among other things, because of the history of writing in both places. There is a fundamental difference in the earliest uses of script in societies that invent writing and those that adopt it from others. The cuneiform writing system originated in Mesopotamia and it evolved there over the millennia out of an original bookkeeping system. Bookkeeping was its very *raison d'être*. From there it spread to other genres. There was no similar gradual evolution in Anatolia but a conscious decision to adopt whole cloth a ready-made writing system they had observed others using and of which they decided that it would be good for them to start using it as well. As we saw, they followed the usual path of societies adopting a script from others going from simple graffiti, ownership marking, monumental inscriptions, to edicts, laws, and so forth, but there may well have been no need for writing in the way they conducted their economic life. Again, we go back to the principle that there must be a reason and a function for literacy and internal bookkeeping may not have been one of them. What was needed at this early stage of the Hittite kingdom was prestige and that was what the cuneiform writing system offered them. As opposed to the new political life, their economic habits remained largely unaffected.

Also, one may want to invoke here the principle of "if there is little or nothing left, there may not have been much to begin with." In light of the almost complete absence of evidence thus far for a native Central Anatolian administrative system in the form of sealings in the Old Assyrian period, as we know it from eastern Anatolia from earlier times, it has in my opinion correctly been surmised that the local economy probably did well without.[111] In a fully oral society with small, localized subsistence economies this is nothing surprising. In the Kanesh 1b period the Anatolian stamp seal developed but even then, there is little evidence that a broadly used bookkeeping system grew out of that and was continued into the Old Hittite kingdom. The first tangible evidence for such administrative records belonging to the Hittite state dates to shortly after 1400 BC and it is no doubt safe to say that something like it can be projected back into the fifteenth century. But how much further back we can go, remains unclear.

5.11 The Early Hittite Kingdom as an Oral and Aural Society

With no evidence that the Anatolians ever appropriated the Syrian script during the Old Assyrian period, the earliest exposure to this kind of cuneiform likely took place in the context of the Syrian campaigns that must have started around the middle of the seventeenth century BC.

111 Dercksen 2002: 38.

Scribes from northern Syria were brought in and put to work, first perhaps for diplomatic purposes (compare the Labarna Letter) but soon for incidental internal recording as well. Initially, these internal assignments seem to have been largely of a monumental kind (statues and the like, compare Hattusili's Annals) and in support of oral delivery of the king's words (compare Hattusili's Testament). Judging by the scarcity of compositions between the early days of Labarna, Hattusili, and Mursili of the seventeenth century and those of the middle of the sixteenth century the volume of scribal activity was probably low and mostly still in the hands of Syrian scribes.[112] What was written down was not only in Akkadian but in many instances also partly relied on Mesopotamian examples. In a detailed study Elena Devecchi has shown that the Annals of Hattusili were written up by somebody whose mother tongue and cultural background was Akkadian.[113] This fits the situation of a king employing a foreign scribe telling him what to write and dictating an annalistic frame but leaving the scribe otherwise to fill in the details and to shape the composition as he saw fit since he, after all, was the expert, the craftsman "hired" to do the job. The real impetus for the Syrian ductus to develop into the typical and not so very different Hittite variant of the cuneiform script probably came with the decision in the second half of the sixteenth century to shift from writing internal records in Akkadian to writing them in Hittite and Hittite only.

There surely was some early experimenting to write Hittite, as we can see in the Urshu Text (see Chapter 4.3 and above 5.7) with what may actually be the earliest recorded Hittite sentence, and the occasional Hittite-only document. Texts like the "instruction" known as KBo 22.1, or the oracle report KBo 18.151 may be products of such trial and error, perhaps stemming from the first half of the sixteenth century. But there can be little doubt that even in ruling circles oral communication continued to be the norm and certainly outside the capital the spoken word still carried more authority than the written for a long time. A clear example of this can be seen in KBo 22.1. The addressees are local officials, representing the central authority. They are chastised for alleged abuses of power against the less fortunate in society and reference is made to "the words of my father," recalling the "father of the king" that we saw in the Palace Chronicles and the Laws:

> Is that how you obeyed my father's words? If you don't know, is there no group of elders here to tell you my father's words?[114]

[112] Cf. de Martino 2016b: 365–6. [113] Devecchi 2005: 28–9, 113–27.

[114] *kiššan* *AWĀT* ABI=IA *paḫšanutten takku šumeš natta šaktēni kāni* LU.ŠU.GI-*ešša* NU.GÁL *nu=šmaš memai* AWAT ABI=IA KBo 22.1: 4–6 (Instruction, CTH 272, OS), ed. by Archi 1979: 45–6.

Only later on in the text (KBo 22.1: 23) does the writer mention that the father had issued a written document, which may or may not refer to "my father's words." But by invoking first a group of older people to tell them what the father had said in the past the writer appeals to the memory of the oldest in society as the ultimate source. Whether the original record is still there or not, is not the point. If they still have it, there may be nobody who can read it, either because they were illiterate, because it was in Akkadian, or because the written word did not yet enjoy that kind of authority but those who were there when it was read out to them will remember.

The collection of the Hittite Laws may have given a first real impetus for writing directly and exclusively in Hittite on a more systematic scale. With all due caution the latter could go back to ca. 1550 BC or in the decades immediately following. This may have given rise to a more frequent recording of Hittite compositions, either ones that thus far had been exclusively orally transmitted (Anitta Text, Zalpa Tale, Palace Chronicles and others) or ones that existed in Akkadian-only versions (Hattusili I's Annals and Testament). Not surprisingly the former retained their more archaic quality, both stylistically and linguistically, whereas the latter, being translated (and copied even later), display a more contemporaneous quality. What they have in common, however, is that all could be seen as foundational texts, providing the fledgling Hittite state with a glorious past and identity. The group of people who in the seventeenth century BC resettled Hattusa and started calling themselves "men of Hatti" after the local population, created a new kingdom in search of a new identity. A script of their own not only provided a means of communication with Akkadian-speaking powers in the east but also one to bolster the unity that they wished to forge within Anatolia. When after the political slump following the murder of Mursili I the kingdom was ready to reassert itself in the course of the later sixteenth century the script was adapted to write their own language and to incorporate Hattian and Palaic texts. The Old Hittite "ritual" corpus is likely to be a product of this period. The early kingdom thus used script to record for eternity foundational texts with a clear didactic intention and with an eye on self-preservation in a formerly fragmented country.

The corpus of Old Hittite compositions as sketched above became possible after the transition from writing in Akkadian to writing in Hittite had been made. Before we describe the surge of Hittite literature, as it manifests itself from the fourteenth century onwards, we should look closer at this transition. Can we be more specific about the how and why? We will turn to these questions in Chapter 6.

CHAPTER 6

The Emergence of Writing in Hittite

6.1 The Second Half of the Sixteenth Century BC as an Anatolian Renaissance

The choice of the Syrian cuneiform variant, very different than the Old Assyrian one, under the Old Kingdom kings Labarna, Hattusili I, and Mursili I forces us to assume that after the collapse of the Assyrian trading network, for the duration of about two or three generations, Anatolia returned to a state of illiteracy. All active knowledge of the former writing system must have been lost. But with the new regime the state shifted back, gradually at first and still clinging to the Akkadian language but by the mid-sixteenth century BC Hittite kings now embraced writing wholeheartedly. Overall, the years between ca. 1550 and 1500 BC are increasingly emerging as a period of pivotal changes on many levels. This is the time in which the capital Hattusa undergoes massive changes with the incorporation of the so-called *Oberstadt* or Upper City doubling its territory southwards.[1] Huge grain silos and ponds for water management appear.[2] Buildings are constructed near Sarıkale in the western *Oberstadt* and in the eastern part the first temples (Temples 2–5) are erected. Together these structures evince a "masterplan" as opposed to the gradual add-on style visible in the older Lower City (*Unterstadt*). The walls and fortifications surrounding all this new activity and definitively incorporating the southern extension into the city as a whole are likely to go back to the same period.[3] The principle of city planning has been observed also in new settlements that start appearing in these same years in the Hittite heartland. Hittite towns like Sarissa (Turk. Kuşaklı) and probably also Sapinuwa (Turk. Ortaköy) and Nerik (Turk. Oymağaaç) were founded in the later sixteenth century and their rise cannot be separated from the reforms decreed by

[1] Schachner 2011a: 76, 85–92, 2011b: 87–93, 2017: 230, Schachner apud Schachner & Seeher 2016: 100.

[2] For the ponds as part of the capital's water management see Wittenberg 2017 ("the South Ponds were built in the middle of the 16th century").

[3] Schachner 2011b: 90–2.

Telipinu in his Proclamation or the large group of early land donations that began being issued in that same period. The observed general increase in settlements in central Anatolia in the transitional phase from the Old Kingdom to the empire probably reflects a population growth that both prompted and benefited from Telipinu's policies.[4] Hittite art of this period witnesses the emergence of relief vases with their cultic scenes. As argued by Andreas Schachner, the spread of their iconographic program is characteristic of a shared and centralized attempt at establishing a "clearly defined canon."[5] Likewise, Ulf-Dietrich Schoop observes "a set of changes" in Anatolian ceramics taking place in the sixteenth century BC.[6]

The link between development, growth, and spread of writing and literacy on the one hand and state formation on the other is evident. In many cultures script usage is an unmistakable corollary of an increasing socio-economic complexity. This is true both of the societies that invented scripts from scratch (Mesopotamia, China, Mesoamerica, and Egypt)[7] and those that adopted them from others.[8] Just as in the second half of the seventeenth century Labarna, Hattusili, and Mursili introduced the Syrian cuneiform as part of their ambitions to put the Hittite state on the map, the expansion of the uses of writing and the subsequent development of the typical Hittite cuneiform signals a renewed assertiveness in Telipinu's time. Whereas writing served relatively simple and limited means under the first three kings, now it served more sophisticated ends. Writing and the prestige it commanded enabled Telipinu to conclude the treaty with Kizzuwatna. The written instructions as left behind in his Proclamation made it possible – or so he hoped – to exert an influence that lasted beyond his lifetime. The charters served him to build a strong network of individuals who now owed him their undivided loyalty, all this with the consent of his grandees whose seals were attached. This network also comprised a more fine-grained web of close to a hundred storehouses throughout central Anatolia managed by the AGRIGS or storeroom officials with direct links to the capital Hattusa.[9] A program of ruralization of central Anatolia strengthened the center while reinforcing the stability of local communal subsistence and protecting it against enemy incursions and cyclical

[4] Simon 2011a: 29. For demographic change as an important factor underlying social changes such as the adoption of writing and the spread of literacy see Spooner & Hanaway 2012: 56.

[5] Schachner 2012: 136, Strupler 2012. [6] Schoop 2009: 156, see also Mielke 2017.

[7] Larsen 1988: 184, 187, Visicato 2000: 235, Baines 2004: 166, Cooper 2004: 72, 92, Houston 2004: 352, Wang 2014 passim.

[8] See for instance Thomas 1992: 65–6, Woolf 2009: 48.

[9] Singer 1984b; for a map showing the distribution of the settlements in the core of Hatti-Land, and the Upper and Lower Land see there p. 123.

droughts.[10] At the same time these measures shielded the kingdom from inner unrest. Even if not universally enforced, the codification of the Laws suggests an intention to put the country on an equal footing[11], handing clear rules to local authorities but also allowing them the necessary leeway to use their own judgment. The tariff section (§§176–186) in the Laws tries to regulate a countrywide system of prices for services and commodities and thus to set up a uniform economic system. This attempt at centralization was not based on military enforcement, however. Telipinu was the king who declined to kill his – as he put it – would-be assassins, he was the one who concluded a treaty with Isputahsu, king of Kizzuwatna. This was power based on the partial self-determination of the various and very different parts of central Anatolia knowing full well that in the specific and often harsh conditions of its land this was the only way to create a common Hittite identity and the only guarantee for lasting power. He forged a unity by accepting local religious traditions and bringing them home to Hattusa as part of the "thousand gods." The Old Hittite Ritual corpus includes not only Hattian but also Palaic and Luwian cults. That does not necessarily mean that Hittite religion was "a vast amalgam of numerous substrata, be they Hattian, Luwian, Hurrian, Palaic or Mesopotamian" but first and foremost an expression of Hittite royal *Realpolitik*.

Many of these changes were now phrased in Hittite as the official language of the kingdom. The decision to start writing Hittite directly and exclusively was part of an "imperial" policy. The pride of their new power and renewed international stature demanded a language of their own with a literature of their own. Of course, we should be careful not to pin all this on Telipinu. Most of these things were probably the result of relatively gradual developments that had started already under Ammuna, but it is clear that Telipinu was a central figure in these developments and that many of them came to a head in his reign.

6.2 Adapting to Hittite

In Chicago's Graceland Cemetery, just steps away from the tombstone of Ludwig Mies van der Rohe, there is a simple grave marker for a man who died in 1984 (Fig. 6.1). The stone only bears his name and dates and inbetween there is the following text:

[10] Glatz 2009, Burgin 2016. [11] Postgate 1984: 13.

Fig. 6.1 Tombstone at Chicago's Graceland Cemetery (photo author).

ονε φοοτ ιν φαεριελανδ

After some initial confusion, as you ready yourself for a Greek inscription, you realize that it is English written in the Greek alphabet: one foot in faerieland. It is a simple letter by letter substitution from the English to the Greek by someone literate in both scripts. He was not listening and trying to render the English sounds of, for instance, "one" ([wʌn]) in Greek, which might have yielded something like Ϝαν or ουαν. In the one case where the two alphabets coincided historically (or also graphically, had he chosen to write in capitals), viz. the *y* in fairyland, as it is usually written, and the ypsilon <υ> (capital <Y>), the "archaic or poetic/literary"[12] spelling with *ie* was chosen to achieve maximum clarity in obscurity: φαερυλανδ would have looked too weird. The deceased is cheating but at the same time having some fun with his passers-by. The situation the Hittites saw themselves confronted with was very different.

[12] The *New Oxford American Dictionary* (Oxford, New York 2005) s.v. on the spelling *faerie*(-) vs. *fairy*(-).

Adapting a foreign writing system to your own language can be a complicated task. If you are new to the writing technology, you not only have to learn the necessary fine motor skills, but it is also an intellectual challenge. You have to start thinking about language, about *your* language in a different way, listening to sounds, distinguishing units of speech, and thinking in terms of texts. If the script comes from a neighboring society with a closely related language, chances are that the latter's phonological system maps nicely on to that of your language. But when the source language belongs to another linguistic family with a different phonological system your task is much more difficult.[13] This was the case with Hittites trying to write their Indo-European language with the script that was more suited to record Semitic Akkadian. For example, the Akkadian cuneiform system of the second millennium distinguished between voiced and voiceless consonants, e.g. /d/ vs. /t/ in the signs DA vs. TA. For the Hittite language this opposition seems to have been of little importance and the writing system often uses both signs indiscriminately: whether *a-da-an-zi* or *a-ta-an-zi*, both words mean "they eat." Instead the creators of the new Hittite system introduced an entirely new opposition of single vs. double written consonants, probably to express a distinction between short vs. long consonants (compare in English the geminated long [k:] in "bookkeeping" vs. the single short [k] in "beekeeping")[14]: *a-da-an-na* or *a-ta-an-na* with a single written dental means something other than the double dentals *at-ta-an-na* or *ad-da-an-na*. The latter stands for *attann=a* "and the father" (sg. acc.), the former expresses *adanna* "to eat." Compare also the demonstrative pronoun *apa-* "that one" vs. the adverb *appa* "behind, after." Almost from the very beginning this principle is systematically applied in the Hittite texts. In this way Hittite scribes modified the Akkadian system in order to express something that was important to them and not provided by the source.

Another difference between the Akkadian and Hittite writing systems is the extent of so-called polyvalence or polyphony: in Akkadian a cuneiform sign frequently has multiple and often quite different sound values that have historically evolved. Compare, for instance, the sign UD (HZL 316), which can also be read as U, PIR, TAM, BABBAR, or UTU. In the Hittite system this phenomenon is on the whole very much restricted: not having shared that gradual development and out of what Mark Weeden has called

13 van den Hout 2017.

14 For other opinions see van den Hout 2009a: 28 w. lit.; the example of English "bookkeeping" comes from Daniels 2018: 59.

"its antipathy to polyvalence"[15] the Hittite system did away with almost all of these extra values and developed a highly significant reduction of polyphony as compared to the Akkadian writing system.[16]

Simplification can also be seen in the standardization of certain sign forms that can cause confusion. Take for instance the cuneiform signs

 (ŠA, HZL 158) and  (TA, HZL 160).

With rare exceptions[17] the two are kept strictly separate in the Hittite texts with one small inscribed vertical wedge for ŠA and two for TA. In the Akkadian texts of Alalah VII, on the other hand, TA can be written with no verticals, with one, or with two while ŠA can be found with no verticals or one.[18] Sometimes the same shape stands for ŠA in one line and for TA in the next. Also, we find variants of ŠA with three or four horizontals. It is up to the reader on the basis of the context to determine which sound value applies and how it should be read. For a practiced reader, grown up in the system and the language it records, this hardly poses a problem. A literate native speaker of English will not hesitate for a moment in choosing the correct pronunciation for the word *bough* as either [bō] or [bou] depending on the context or in pronouncing correctly the sentence "I take it you already know / of touch and bough and cough and dough."[19] But for foreigners learning English as a second language it requires years of training to make the same correct choices in a fraction of a second without stumbling. It is not surprising, therefore, that foreign users who are new to a system do away with what they perceive as confusing inconsistencies and want to create a maximum of clarity. It is only in some of the oldest Hittite texts that we occasionally see ŠA and TA without verticals.[20]

Another area of simplification has to do with the aspect of the script. Mesopotamian cuneiform *doesnotgenerallyusespacestoseparatewords*, nor does the Syrian type. This results in a generally dense and massive impression of a block of text. Dense writing and small word spaces are often mentioned as typical of the oldest Hittite tablets.[21] However, words are generally separated by a small space already in the oldest texts and over time this space can become more pronounced.[22] On tablets and fragments written in the Old Hittite period (ca. 1600–1400 BC) word spaces are usually small, and often mostly exist in the sense that within a word, a sign comes right up to or is even slightly overlapped by the immediately

[15] Weeden 2011a: 383 (see also 382). [16] Thus already Forrer 1922b: 6.
[17] For an example of ŠA where TA should have been written see Rüster 1988: 302.
[18] van den Hout 2012a: 160. [19] Quoted from Wolf 2007: 121. [20] van den Hout 2012a: 166.
[21] Neu 1980, xiv–v. [22] See already Forrer 1922b: 4.

Fig. 6.2 Sequence of signs in KBo 22.1 obv. 13 (drawing author).

following sign. This is avoided when the sign is at the end of a word. This often results in a seemingly larger or longer shape for the final sign of a word, something rarely mentioned in the scholarly literature. If, for instance, a word ends in a horizontal wedge, that wedge usually looks longer and more drawn out than when written in the middle of a sequence of signs.[23] What really seems to be the case, however, is that *within a word* the sign was initially written with the same length, but the final part of the wedge was immediately overlapped by the following sign. Compare the shape of the twice occurring sign AŠ ⊢ in KBo 22.1 obv. 13 (Fig. 6.2), the Old Hittite instruction text that mentions the "father of the king."[24] The first of the two between *-wa-* and *-ša-* seems shorter than the second one following *-ša-*.

But what happened is that *ša* was partially written over the first AŠ-sign while the word space before the numeral 50 allows it its full length.[25] The same may be true for the seemingly more pronounced and right-leaning written final vertical wedge of a word.[26] There, too, an immediately following wedge normally obscures the clear shape and space that a final vertical creates.

Finally, already in the oldest Hittite texts we see an entirely new series of signs (HZL 318–326) created for a sound (+ vowel) that was unknown to Akkadian and that is usually described as a kind of /f/. Using the sign WA (Akkadian PI) and adding small subscript vowel signs (/a, e, i, u/), new shapes for /fa, fe, fi, fu/ were created (Table 6.1): wa_{a}, we_{e}, wi_{i}, $wu_{u/ú}$.

The interesting thing is that the sound in question was also foreign to the Hittite phonological system and must have been especially designed in the Old Kingdom for the writing down of Hattian and Palaic texts.[27] Three observations can be made here. First of all, the creation of this series

[23] I remember Prof. Güterbock mentioning this in the late 1980s in Chicago. [24] Chapter 6.3.
[25] Note the ŠA sign without inscribed vertical.
[26] Neu 1980, xiv ("leicht nach rechts hin schräge Neigung der Köpfe senkrechter Keile").
[27] It was later also used for Hurrian; see Wegner 2007: 44–5, Giorgieri 2000: 183.

Table 6.1 *List of* wa*-signs with subscript*

wa+a = wa_{a}	
wa+e = we_{e}	
wa+i = wi_{i}	
wa+u/ú = $\text{wu}_{\text{u/ú}}$	

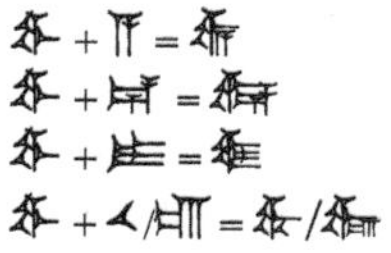

shows a conscious effort to adapt the borrowed script to a specific phonological system.[28] Secondly, it illustrates the principle observed elsewhere[29] that such new signs are usually created on the basis of the borrowed script; they are not free inventions without any relation to – in this case – the borrowed cuneiform. But third and above all, it shows an early use of writing for cultic and ideological purposes. As we saw earlier, incorporating the local cults was already part of Hittite imperial policy of the second half of the sixteenth century BC. The Old Hittite Ritual corpus attests to a conscious effort at recording local festivals *in their own language*.[30]

The above changes in polyvalency, sign variation, and word space could perhaps be viewed as gradual and incremental developments over an extended period of time were it not for the fact that all are in evidence from the beginning of writing in Hittite. Some of them, such as word space, became more pronounced over time but the phenomenon was already there. The four new signs with the subscripts, however, form such a small and coherent subsystem that it must have been deliberately created as a whole to solve a specific problem. This is a solution that an intelligent person could come up with on an afternoon: it does not need a long time to develop. The same is most likely true for the spelling system with the single vs. double consonants: it is a consistently and consciously applied rule affecting the entire system that some individual must have designed. They show a sharp ear that comes with a metalinguistic awareness that only an already literate person acquires.[31]

This is true also of the introduction of word space, which constitutes a deliberate break with the Mesopotamian and, more specifically, the Syrian tradition.[32] Recognizing words, that is, nouns, adjectives, verbs,

[28] Popova 2014: 686. [29] de Voogt 2012: 3.

[30] Weeden 2011a: 3 ("a remarkably conscious approach to the writing of foreign languages").

[31] Wolf 2016: 58–9.

[32] It is true that the Assyrian merchants in Anatolia in their very simplified cuneiform variant sometimes also practiced word separation by using small vertical half-wedges (Hecker 1968: 12) but apart

etc. as discrete entities may not look like much of an achievement to people in literate societies but in those not used to written language linguists have observed great variation from individual to individual in the segmentation of such units.[33] Moreover, Hittite is a language with many so-called *clitics*: small, usually monosyllabic grammatical elements that in spoken speech carry no stress or accent themselves and therefore cannot stand alone but always need another accented word to "lean" on. Very often they are combined into strings and they are usually found attached to the first word of a sentence. Compare the Hittite sequence *maḫḫanmawaduzakan*: on the accent-bearing conjunction *maḫḫan* "when" or "how" five particles are hung (*=ma=wa=du=za=kan*), each with a distinct function and conveying important information to the reader for the rest of the sentence. In the same way Spanish *tráemelo* "bring it to me!" contains the accent-bearing verb (*tráe-* "bring!") followed by a string of two short pronouns (*-me* "to me," *-lo* "it"). The Hittite adapters must have been aware of the status of *=ma=wa=du=za=kan* as distinct morphemes, as they can each occur in different combinations, but they clearly recognized the resulting string together with its "head" *maḫḫan* as a single accentual unit and decided to bring that out by writing it all together (*maḫḫanmawaduzakan*) while separating it from the following word. This principle, too, was very uniformly applied from the beginning of our evidence. This too suggests that the group of scribes that worked out the system, by which they were going to write Hittite, was small[34] and that they did so in a short span of time. It may even have been the idea of a single individual who passed his model on to the first group of Hittite scribes.

Such a conscious and therefore relatively quick adaptation of an imported script is something we see more often in other writing systems around the world. Once the idea of writing has taken root in a society and the need for a script is accepted, a foreign system is borrowed wholesale: a set of sign shapes and a set of sign values. And once the step to writing one's own language is made, a set of modifications and systemic reconfigurations[35] is agreed upon and added relatively quickly, either by a group of people or by a single individual. For examples one can look at the various adoptions and adaptations of the Phoenician alphabet by the Phrygians, the Greeks, and other groups in Anatolia. What is striking in the Hittite case is the economy with which this happened.[36] I quoted Mark

from the fact that the Hittites did not opt for that particular solution we saw there is no evidence for any continuation of Assyrian writing practices from the Old Assyrian period into the Old Kingdom.

[33] Coulmas 2013: 50–1. [34] Cf. Weeden 2011a: 45, 70, as quoted in Chapter 4 w. n. 31.

[35] For the term see Salomon 2012: 132. [36] Weeden 2011a: 3, 382.

Weeden for the "antipathy to polyvalence" in the Hittite writing system but it was perhaps not so much an abhorrence of this particular phenomenon as the natural lack of respect by a total newcomer who is not burdened by tradition and who approaches the new writing system with a fresh look and who is willing to do away with anything that is considered non-essential. The relatively short time span, in which this usually happens, allows us to ask whether we can date these innovations in the Hittite case. It would not make much sense to design rules for how to write Hittite if you are not going to put them into practice, that is, if you continue to write Akkadian only. I therefore assume that the development of those rules did not precede the start of writing in Hittite by much. The incentive to create the above outlined modifications must have been the urge to write in Hittite: "The moment of invention, the standardization and thereby the introduction of a writing system are dependent on the immediate use of the script."[37] The invention of the rules by which to write Hittite may be added then to the changes that mark the second half of the sixteenth century BC as a watershed moment.

The question that has not been answered yet is what set off the decision to switch to Hittite and to transform the Syrian cuneiform in such a way that Hittite could be written with it? First of all, as already mentioned in Chapter 5.8, active native knowledge of Akkadian may have been rapidly disappearing. This in turn led to a problem when the scope of written documents widened. Formulas like the ones on Ammuna's ax and the charters could be endlessly repeated but technical terms, as they were needed, for instance, to describe properties and domains in the charters, many of which may have been specific to the Anatolian landscape, were another matter. The same problem, finally, presented itself when expanding into other genres. The new imperial ideology simply demanded its own language.

6.3 The Charters and the Introduction of Writing in Hittite

"Up until the time of Muwattalli I the charters . . . were largely drawn up in Akkadian."[38] This is how Christel Rüster and Gernot Wilhelm describe them in their recent edition. They add that this is not just an Akkadographic way of writing behind which a spoken Hittite version is

[37] de Voogt & Döhla 2012: 55.

[38] Rüster & Wilhelm 2012: 35 ("Die LSU . . . wurden bis in die Zeit Muwattallis I. weitgehend in akkadischer Sprache abgefasst").

hidden but real-life Akkadian that goes beyond the mere formulaic, as shown particularly by Charter nr. 3 (see p. 113). At the same time "Hittite expressions were used already in the oldest documents to describe agricultural situations and occasionally entire paragraphs with topographical information are rendered in Hittite."[39] The use of Hittite may be somewhat more extensive than this description suggests, however. Overall, the distribution of Hittite words and forms among the charters is mostly a function of the preservation of the individual text or of the extent to which a text has much more than just the Akkadian formula. Of text nr. 10, for instance, only a fragment of the middle section of the document is preserved with quite a few Hittite topographical terms and nothing of the legal formula that frames a regular charter. Nr. 17 on the other hand has only the standard Akkadian ending of the text left and therefore contains no Hittite. The so-called İnandık Charter (nr. 1) is almost perfectly preserved but hardly goes beyond the Akkadian legal phraseology and thus does not show a single Hittite word other than the title tabarna. Nevertheless, a comparison of the lexical material in the charters illustrates the different roles of both languages in these documents (Table 6.2).

Whereas the differences in most categories are either language specific (Hittite has no prepositions but rather works with adverbs and/or postpositions, Akkadian has no particles like Hittite *-kan* etc.) or simply inconsequential the contrast between nouns and adjectives is telling. Seven Akkadian nouns and adjectives come from the legal formulas (*awilum* "human being," *awatum* "word, affair," *bēlum* "lord," *irdum* "servant," *šērum* "morning," *tuppum* "tablet," *urrum* "day") with twenty-five added from the descriptive parts of the charters (*aššutum* "marriage," *dīšum* "spring," *ēdēnûm* "individual," *ḫalqum* "lost," *īnu* "spring, well," *iṣum* "wood," *kūṣu* "winter," *mārum* "son," *mušēniqtum* "wetnurse," *qaqqarum* "field," *rîtum* "meadow," *rupšu* "width," *sīḫu* (a tree), *šapiltum* "remainder," *šumu* "name," *šupe'ultum* "exchange," *warkānum* "later, afterwards," LÚ.UDU-*ru* "shepherd"). All seventy-seven Hittite nouns and adjectives occur in the parts that circumscribe the fields, properties, and individuals that the records are all about. Being lists, these descriptions contain very few verbs whereas the Akkadian formula alone contains eight verbs. Had the charters been better preserved or if more were to be found, the gap between Akkadian and Hittite nouns and adjectives would probably only widen.

39 Rüster & Wilhelm 2012: 35 ("zur Beschreibung von Gegebenheiten der Agrarlandschaft wurden . . . schon in den ältesten Urkunden hethitische Ausdrücke verwendet, und vereinzelt sind ganze Absätze mit topographischen Informationen in hethitischer Sprache abgefasst").

Table 6.2 *Comparison of Akkadian and Hittite lexical material in the charters*

Akkadian							
nouns/adj.	verbs	prepositions	adverbs	pronouns	conjunctions	numerals	loans
32	16	9	7	4	2	2	2
Hittite							
nouns/adj.	verbs	particles	adverbs	pronouns	conjunctions	numerals	
77	5	1	9	2	4	1	

Note: Only lexemes were counted, not individual attestations: there are thirty-two different Akkadian nouns and adjectives as opposed to seventy-seven Hittite ones, etc. The numbers are based on texts nrs. 1–90 in Rüster & Wilhelm 2012. The deviating and most recent Charter nr. 91 (Arnuwanda I and Asmunikkal to the priestess Kuwattalla) is not included because it would have distorted the picture too much in the Hittite direction. Among the nouns were also counted those written Sumerographically with Akkadian or Hittite phonetic complements. Pure Sumerograms, however, are not included since they could be read either in Akkadian or Hittite. For specific references see the Akkadian and Hittite glossaries in Rüster & Wilhelm 2012: 245–54, 262–4. Included in the Hittite word count are GU$_4$-*laš* 15: 48, GÙB-*laz* 40: 35, 39, ÍD-*aš* 39 obv. 4, KASKAL-*ši/-za* 39 obv. 7, rev. 3, (-)*wa-al-d*[*a-* 39 obv. 9, URU?-*i*]*a-aš* 7 rev. 5; except for (-)*wa-al-d*[*a-* no acephalous attestations were counted. As numerals only those with clear phonetic complements were counted; the one Hitt. numeral is 30-*li* 3 rev. 7. Akkadian *-ma* is included under conjunctions.

Charter nr. 3, singled out by Rüster & Wilhelm for showing live Akkadian language skills, may indeed be the product of a Syrian native or a bilingual speaker. It is therefore all the more unfortunate that the name of the scribe has been lost. But the considerable number of Hittite words particularly for several kinds of fields, properties, trees, plants, and related terms that must have been used because they did not know the Akkadian equivalent pleads for scribes who lived in Anatolia and knew more Hittite than Akkadian and knew how to write Hittite. The spelling of the words is, moreover, usually quite consistent in cases where more than one attestation is known and also in view of later standard Hittite writing habits. Interesting in this context are the two Akkadianized Hittite loanwords: ^{GIŠ}*gipeššaranu* "cubit" and *uriannūtum* "office of the *urianni*-official." The latter loan is entirely understandable, as this may have been a typical Anatolian office with no Syro-Mesopotamian counterpart. But one assumes that a native Akkadian speaker would have known the Akkadian word *ammatum* "cubit." The mix of Akkadian and Hittite in the corpus of charters thus shows how the need to describe a world, for which the Akkadian lexicon available to both the author-scribes and their audience simply did not suffice, played a role in the emergence of writing in Hittite.

6.4 A Hittite Literature in the Vernacular

In Chapter 5 stylistic, historical, and linguistic arguments pointed towards the Zalpa Tale about the queen of Kanesh giving birth to first thirty sons and then thirty daughters having a date in the reigns of Labarna I and Hattusili I. The fairy tale was used as a preamble to an account of the historical campaign against the city of Zalpa by these early kings. The motif of *Kinderaussetzung*, however, well known from other tales with Moses, Romulus and Remus, or Cyrus as the *dramatis personae*, lends it an almost universal quality with a time depth way beyond the days of the earliest Hittite kings. It must have been around in oral form long before them. That the Hittites used this motif to create a tale set in their own history and combined it with a contemporary event is in itself not that surprising. What is important is that it was written down.[40]

In a recent book, *Beyond Greek*, Denis Feeney sketches the birth of Latin literature out of Greek forerunners. The earliest known Roman authors still wrote Greek, then translations into Latin followed and eventually the step was made to compose new literary works in their own Latin language.

[40] The point was already made in general by Güterbock 1964: 110.

Although we may think that sounds very normal and self-evident, it is not. As Feeney points out most other ancient literate civilizations never developed their own written literature. They may have had rich oral traditions, but they did not play any role in the written records of these societies. As Feeney writes about Roman literature: "It had never happened before or anywhere else in the Mediterranean that one culture should set out to take over the prototypical literary forms of Hellas in order to create its vernacular equivalent, and for a parallel of any substance we have to wait until the Late Middle Ages, when the Latin forms became in their turn one of the new interactive catalysts for the emerging European vernacular literatures."[41] Indeed, we know of no written Persian literature from the days of Cyrus, Darius, or Xerxes: "Written language was not part of the inherited sense of identity for Persian speakers."[42] The same is true for Parthian, Carthaginian, and Etruscan societies who were likewise exposed to and absorbed Greek culture. Neither do we have Phrygian literature. Creating one's own written corpus of literature is by no means a natural corollary of a literate society. I would contend, however, that Hittite society starting from Mesopotamian examples did create "its vernacular equivalent." Starting with Hattusili I's Annals – with clear influences from the Mesopotamian literary tradition[43] – with among others its allusion to the Legend of Sargon of Akkad, Hittite literature moved on, not only to record the Zalpa Tale and all the other Old Kingdom texts that we have seen but eventually produced the unique historiography of Mursili II. And if we take literature in the wider sense of German *Schrifttum*, anything written, we can say that the Hittite written legacy contains a number of genres unique for its time.

In the process towards creating one's own literature Feeney also draws attention to what he calls the "foreignizing" and "domesticating" strategies in translating and adapting imported literary material. For example, the section of the Hurrian-Hittite bilingual known as the "Song of Release" holds on to all the foreign names and settings. No effort is made to make the Hurrian Stormgod Teshub, Megi, the king of Ebla, or geographical names like Ikinkali any less exotic to a Hittite audience. The Zalpa Tale, on the other hand, is firmly located in central Anatolia. The decision not to "domesticate" the Song of Release may have had different reasons. Perhaps its exotic character appealed to the intended audience and the names were deliberately left in place. Or was it just a piece with very limited (only scholarly?) circulation? No duplicates to any of the manuscripts have been

[41] Feeney 2016: 5. [42] Feeney 2016: 197 (quoting C. Tuplin). [43] Devecchi 2005: 113–27.

identified. An interesting case in this context is another fairy-tale-like composition, the Story of Appu. Unlike the Song of Release, it exists in several manuscripts, all written in the thirteenth century BC but the language clearly betrays an older stage that can go back to the sixteenth century. Like the Zalpa Tale the story bears the hallmarks of fairy-tales and folklore and might therefore be much older. This is how it begins:

> There once was a town named Sudul. It lies in the land of Lulluwai on the border of the sea and in it lives a man named Appu. In the land he is wealthy: he owns cattle and sheep, lots of them.[44]

In spite of all his wealth, however, Appu seems unable to sire children. Eventually, with the help of the Sundeity, his wife bears him two sons whom he names "Bad" and "Good." After Appu's death Bad persuades Good to split up and his argument is that everything and everyone lives apart. Just as mountains sit separately and rivers flow separately, the gods each have their own abode as well:

> The Sungod lives in Sippar, the Moongod lives in Kuzina, the Stormgod lives in Kummiya, Ishtar lives in Niniveh, Nanaya lives in Kissina, while Babylon is the home of Marduk.[45]

Several scholars have tried to track down the roots of this story and it has usually been included among the myths of Hurrian origin. The names of Appu, Sudul or Lulluwai have been rejected as not containing any linguistic clues but the list of deities and their cities hints at Mesopotamian origins. Itamar Singer, however, noted that the cities Kuzina and Kissina are otherwise wholly unknown, which makes such an origin suspicious. He also rightly asked "If the author were anonymous, would we classify Romeo and Juliet or the Merchant of Venice as 'Italian literature in English translation', just because the plot is set in Italian cities and the heroes have Italian names?"[46] He then quickly reassured his readers that he did "not intend to underestimate the debt of Hittite literature to the Mesopotamian and eastern Hurrian heritage" but wanted to leave room

[44] [U]RU-*aš* ŠUM-*an*=*šet* ^{UR}[^{U}*Š*]*udul* ^{URU}*Lulluwayaš*=*š*[*a*]*n* KUR-*e aruni* ZAG=*ši ēšzi nu*=*k*[*a*]*n šer* LÚ-*aš* ^{m}*Appu* ŠUM-*an*=*šet* KUR-*e*=*kan ištarna apāš ḫappinanza* G[U.Ḫ]I.A-*uš*=*šiš* UDU-*uš mek*[*k*]*iš* KUB 24.8 i 7–12 (Tale of Appu, CTH 260, NS), ed. by Siegelová 1971: 4–5.

[45] [^{d}UT]U-*uš*=*za* ^{URU}ZIMBIR.ME-*an ēš*[*zi*] [^{d}]SÎN-*aš*=*ma*=*za* ^{URU}*Kuzinan ēš*[*zi*] [^{d}]U-*aš*=*za* ^{URU}*Kummiyan ēš*[*zi*] ^{d}IŠTAR-*iš*=*ma*=*za* ^{URU}*Nenuwan ēš*[*zi*] ^{d}*Nanayaš*=*ma*=*za* ^{URU}*Kiššinan* [*ēšzi*] [^{UR}]^{U}KÁ.DINGIR.RA-*an*=*ma*=*za* ^{d}AMAR.UTU-*aš ē*[*šzi*] KUB 24.8 iv 13–18 (Tale of Appu, CTH 260, NS), ed. by Siegelová 1971: 12–13.

[46] Singer 1995: 126; for the most recent identification of the story "as part of the Hurrian literary tradition including some Mesopotamian themes" and an attempt to locate the geographical names see Taş & Adalı 2016.

for "original Hittite compositions with 'foreign flavor.'"[47] Given the universal folklore character of the Appu story I would hesitate to call it a Hittite original but I do think the names of Appu, Sudul, and Lulluwai rang a bell with a Hittite audience. Any Hittite speaker could associate Appu as a pun on the word *appuzzi-* "fat" just as we can refer to food as "rich." Sudul could be understood as the action noun to the verb *šudae-* "to seal/close a filled container" and Lulluwai must have reminded any audience of *luluwae-* (with single *-l-*) "to thrive, prosper." The point is not whether a word *appu-* or an action noun *šudul* existed or whether we have an attestation for the verb *luluwae-* or its derivatives written with double *-ll-* to match the name of the alleged country: Cinderella is not called Cinders, but everybody gets it. A Hittite audience thus might have enjoyed the opening lines of the Appu story as:

> There once was a town named Fulton. It lies in the land of Prosperia on the border of the sea and in it lives a man named Mr. Rich. In the land he is wealthy: he owns cattle and sheep, lots of them.

But why then the Mesopotamian gods? Was this the Hittite author snobbishly showing off his familiarity with Mesopotamian culture? Or was it in a Feeney-an sense "part of a wider developing imperial self-consciousness, in which Rome is a newly crucial center for a long-standing habit of cultural exchange," where we should read Hatti instead of Rome? Or is it coincidence that the list comes from brother Bad? Is he portrayed as dumb for matching gods with made-up cities? Is this Hittite humor at work?

If we take a wider look at Hittite written works generally datable to the Old Kingdom the focus of its earliest vernacular literature becomes clear. Table 6.3 is based on those texts that are classified as being written in Old Script.[48] Even though the texts and fragments preserved in this script type cannot be dated with any certainty within the larger period of ca. 1600–1400 BC, we can use it as a general indicator of what was considered worth recording in the Old Kingdom and holding on to by subsequent generations.

The overall picture with its overwhelming presence of over 150 cult-related compositions (everything under the heading of cult administration and festival/cult ritual including those in Hattian, Palaic, Luwian, and

[47] Singer 1995: 128.

[48] As indicated and classified as "ah." (*althethitisch*) in the *Konkordanz* (accessed June 2017); for one exception see the following footnote. Adding the texts identified as "ah.?" does not alter the picture in any significant way.

Table 6.3 *Distribution of genres and the number of manuscripts in Old Script tablets*

genre	CTH	#	*genre*	CTH	#
historiography	1	1		631	4
	2	1		635	4
	3	1		641	1
	8	1		643	1
	9	1		645	2
	39	6		647	5
	215	1		649	8
treaty	21	1		662	1
charter[49]	222	91		665	5
list	238	1		668	6
list	239	1		669	1
instruction/decree	272	1		670	46
law	291	2		676	1
	292	1		677	3
myth	323	1		678	1
	336	2	(Hattian)	731	1
	370	1		733	5
ritual	412	1		734	2
	414	1		735	9
	416	3		736	2
	438	1		738	1
	457	2		742	1
	470	3		744	9
omen	545	1		745	18
	547	3	(Palaic)	752	3
	560	1		754	1

Hurrian) will remain basically the same in the New Kingdom. What changes is that later Hittite kings developed a real taste for written agreements, not only in the form of treaties between external partners and the Hittite state, like Telipinu's treaty with Kizzuwatna, but also with internal groups and parties. What are called "instructions" in the above table are in essence sworn-upon rules of conduct for a variety of professional groups ranging from princes to city mayors to courtiers. But, as the table shows, these treaties and agreements were an expansion of elements already present in the Old Kingdom. The only genre that is not represented above is

49 With a single exception (the so-called İnandık Text = Rüster & Wilhelm 2012: nr. 1, which is labeled "ah.?") all charters are listed on the *Konkordanz* (accessed June 2017) as written in Middle Script ("mh.") even though at least nrs. 2–20 all date to roughly the same period.

Table 6.3 (*cont.*)

genre	CTH	#	*genre*	CTH	#
cult administration	523	2	(Luwian)	772	1
	530	1	(Hurrian)	774	3
festival/cult ritual	627	8	"benedictions"	820	1
			unknown	832	12

Note: The historiographic texts stem from the reigns of Labarna I through Mursili I (CTH 1–9), Telipinu (CTH 21) and some fragments that cannot be further specified (CTH 39 and 215); the treaty is the one concluded between Telipinu with Isputahsu from Kizzuwatna (CTH 21); the charters are those of Telipinu or his predecessor; the instruction is the tablet KBo 22.1 (CTH 272) already discussed. All compositions from the myths and mythological fragments onwards (CTH 323–820) concentrate on the religion and cult of central Anatolia, usually with a heavy Hattian cultural presence. Some of the texts include actual Hattian passages (CTH 731–745), others contain Palaic (CTH 752, 754), or Luwian (CTH 665, 772) language material. Including the Akkadian-Hittite bilingual omina (CTH 545, 547, 560) and the three Hurrian omina (CTH 774) the corpus shows a clear interest in collecting central Anatolian cults and cult practices with also an occasional eye on foreign material. Note that apart from the two lists of unknown purpose (CTH 238, 239) there is no bookkeeping or – besides the charters – no socio-economic/legal administration in the narrow sense preserved.

correspondence both between state officials including the king and between the king and his international peers in Egypt, Babylon, Assur, and elsewhere. This, too, had been there already with the Labarna letter to Tunip-Tessub and may have been one of the decisive factors in adopting writing but it really took off in the New Kingdom, as we will see.

In spite of a possible temporary political relapse during the fifteenth century under Telipinu's direct successors the advances in integrating writing into the fabric of the Hittite state and its administration must have taken further hold. It remains enigmatic why, except for some continued treaties with Kizzuwatna and more charters, practically no internal records can be identified until Tuthaliya I ascended the Hittite throne around 1425 BC. By then the role of Akkadian was restricted to international diplomatic documents, some seal inscriptions, and scholarship while Hittite "literature" took off. It is only then that we can regard Hittite society as truly literate according to the definition of Michael Macdonald,[50] a:

[50] Macdonald 2005: 49; for this use of "non-literate" see also Thomas 1992: 74.

literate society . . . [is] one in which reading and writing have become essential to its functioning, either throughout the society . . . or in certain vital aspects, such as the bureaucracy, economic and commercial activities, or religious life. Thus . . . a society can be literate, because it uses the written word in some of its vital functions, even when the vast majority of its members cannot read or write.

CHAPTER 7

A Second Script

7.1 The Anatolian Hieroglyphs

"Why if you are already familiar with cuneiform invent a script like Hieroglyphic?"[1] One of the fascinating aspects about writing in second-millennium Anatolia is that it not only adopted the cuneiform script from Mesopotamia but also developed a script of its own. It has been dubbed "hieroglyphic" even though it has nothing to do with the Egyptian script. The term simply acknowledges its pictorial character (Fig. 7.1): many sign shapes depict people, animals, trees, and plants or parts of them as well as objects from daily life ranging from bowls to buildings to celestial bodies. The first secure evidence for these hieroglyphs as a writing system with a full and more or less systematic grid of sound values dates to shortly after 1400 BC but they lasted much longer than the cuneiform, which disappeared around 1200 BC along with the collapse of the Hittite New Kingdom. The latest inscriptions in the Anatolian hieroglyphs from the northern Syrian area date to around 700 BC. The New Kingdom sources (until 1200 BC), use, and function will be discussed in the following chapters about writing and reading in that period but since the roots of the hieroglyphic script reach back to the Old Kingdom and possibly beyond, we have to address those first.

Like the Hittite cuneiform writing system, the second-millennium Anatolian hieroglyphic sign inventory shows a combination of some forty-five signs with a syllabic sound value and several hundreds of logograms; for a brief introduction to the Anatolian hieroglyphs see the Appendix (7.5) to this chapter. In current scholarship, logograms are transcribed into capitalized Latin words.

Since the second-millennium hieroglyphic sources are part and parcel of Anatolian-Hittite culture and society, the script was at first referred to as "Hittite" hieroglyphs until it became clear that the inscriptions that go

[1] Hawkins 2003: 169.

Fig. 7.1 Relief at Fraktin portraying on the right King Hattusili III (ca. 1267–1240 BC; photo courtesy JoAnn Scurlock) libating before a deity (left) with an altar between them. The king is identified by the "caption" to the left of his head. The sign closest to his head is MAGNUS.REX with the REX sign being identical to the pointed helmet the king himself is wearing.

beyond mere names and titles were invariably written in the Luwian language. This led to an increasing use of the terms Luwian Hieroglyphs and hieroglyphic Luwian for the language. Recognizing, finally, that this writing system evolved out of a mixed Hittite–Luwian linguistic environment Ilya Yakubovich has suggested we speak of Anatolian hieroglyphs.[2]

7.2 The Iconographic Repertoire and its Development

When discussing the roots of or influences on the Anatolian hieroglyphs it is important to distinguish between the general iconography of the glyphs and the actual later writing system that used them and grew out of them. There are good reasons to believe that the script developed out of indigenous Anatolian pictographic repertoires. Scholars like David Hawkins, Clelia Mora, Alice Mouton, and Willemijn Waal have each pointed to

[2] Yakubovich 2008: 28.

designs on seals or on ceramics dated as early as the late third millennium and/or the early centuries of the second millennium that show certain resemblances with the later hieroglyphic script. Mora lists some hieroglyphic-like symbols on seals from Beycesultan in western Anatolia[3], Hawkins and Waal have done the same for three separate design combinations from Kanesh.[4] Alice Mouton has drawn attention to characteristically Anatolian symbols, prominent in the Kanesh 2 seals, like the deer, hare, bull, double-headed eagle, thunderbolt and *lituus*[5] that later became part of the hieroglyphic inventory of logo- and syllabograms.[6] These designs appear on early Hittite seals of the seventeenth through fifteenth century BC as symbols of prosperity and power, perhaps to invoke divine presence or support, or perhaps as early signs with a tentative syllabic value trying to spell out the seal owner's name. One can see these shapes as gradually folding into a nascent writing system. At Kanesh 2 the cylinder seals made it possible to combine several of the above-mentioned iconographic components into elaborate scenes. It is possible and perhaps even likely that the choice of elements and their arrangement within the horizontal plane of the cylinder seal could be personalized and might have contained hints as to a seal owner's family, name, or geographical origins. As such they could be recognized, associated with, and "read" as belonging to a specific individual. These earliest symbols or signs thus attest to an urge to mark things as one's own, using the world around them as inspirations for the various designs that we encounter. They may have functioned within local administrative systems, in which certain individuals each had their own symbol or set of symbols – like a monogram or a logo – that were traceable to them and them only and that were used to authorize specific actions. Claiming that they were "used to convey messages already from the end of the third/beginning of the second millennium onwards," as Waal writes,[7] can only be true in the most basic sense that a symbol or set of symbols indicated that individual X was responsible for the object bearing his seal. There is no evidence, however, that these designs were writing in the sense of representing speech, let alone that they might "have been used to record economic and administrative documents."[8] Such early systems of communicating through pictograms are known as *semasiography*.[9]

[3] Mora 1987: 333, 350 nr. 3.3 ("fine III millennio-inizio II"), see also 3.9; see also Mora 1991: 1 w. n. 2.
[4] Hawkins 2011a, Waal 2012: 298–301; see also Archi 2015a: 24 and most recently and positively Poetto 2018 [2019].
[5] On the *lituus* see Vorys Canby 2002.
[6] Mouton 2002.
[7] Waal 2012: 311, see also 302, 312.
[8] Waal 2012: 307.
[9] Hill Boone 2004.

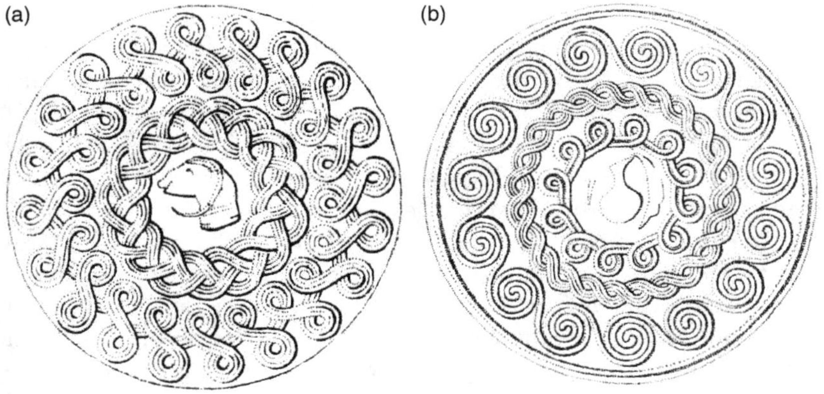

Fig. 7.2 a and b Seals from Konya-Karahöyük (a from Alp 1994: 173 Abb. 59, and b from Alp 1994: 220 Abb. 171).

The same is true of what may be seen as the next chronological phase in our evidence for the Anatolian hieroglyphs, namely, the seal impressions from Konya-Karahöyük (Fig. 7.2).[10] This corpus of about 700 impressions mostly on pieces of clay that sealed ceramic jars or other, sometimes wooden, objects, is dated to the later Old Assyrian period, perhaps contemporaneous with Kanesh Ib or later.[11] There are both cylinder and stamp seals. A large number – over 300 impressions – are found on crescent-shaped objects of unknown function. There are also a number of generally circular applications on pithoi.[12] Finally, mention should be made of a few pottery marks either carved in or impressed on ceramic containers before being fired.[13] The designs on the crescent-shaped objects form a group by themselves: they range from a simple dash (-) to Roman-numeral-like signs (I, II, III), plus signs (+), circles, and semi-circles.[14] Especially the large group of sealings on jars point to a system, in which people took responsibility for the proper handling of goods and their distribution. The scenes on the cylinder and stamp seals show a general similarity with those of Kanesh and other Central Anatolian sites.

The stamp seals mostly have a single design (Fig. 7.2a) surrounded by guilloches or similar patterns. We see the double-headed eagle, bulls, deer,

[10] Alp 1968; for their dating see p. 269–70.
[11] For the possibility of a later date see Weeden 2018: 70.
[12] Alp 1968: nos. 45, 46, 48, 52–4 in the sign list on pp. 287–301.
[13] Those that are "impressed on" ("abgedrückt auf") jars are Alp 1968: nos. 49, 69 in the sign list on pp. 287–301; the carved ones ("eingeritzt") are nos. 29, 50, 59b–c, 60b.
[14] For Late Bronze Age pot marks see Glatz 2012.

hares etc. Given that they appear mostly on their own makes their being part of a writing system where signs have a sound value decidedly less likely but that does not mean that these symbols could not refer to specific individuals or to responsibility-bearing parts of the administration. Sedat Alp who published this material admitted that most of the designs had only symbolic value: people would know which design to associate with what person or entity. He did, however, also state that there were "script signs" (*Schriftzeichen*) among them. Apart from his sometimes subjective-seeming choice of what constitutes a (de)sign[15] (the elements just mentioned like the double-headed eagle etc. are not selected in the corpus of eighty-nine different designs as cataloged[16]) this can only mean there are at best shapes that look like or may even be identical with later signs in the Anatolian hieroglyphic writing system but especially with such a pictorial or semasiographic script[17] that does not say they are already "Schriftzeichen" with a sound value.

Firm, that is, datable evidence for the transition from a *semasiographic* system with symbols to one with sound values is hard to find at Hattusa before the fifteenth century BC. What we find there is a quite disparate corpus of seals and sealings dated mostly on stylistic and sometimes on archaeological grounds to the seventeenth through fifteenth century BC.[18] The earlier material comes from the level known as Lower City 4 (Unterstadt (USt.) 4), which covers the Old Assyrian *kārum Hattuš* period and continues well into the seventeenth century. The seals found *in situ* show a uniform iconography: animals (deer, single- or double-headed eagle, bird(s) with prey), and a few geometric designs and one with a rosette.[19] There are no attestations yet of the later so frequent symbols VITA (), BONUS (Δ) or of the so-called SCRIBA sign (see Chapter 14). The next phase, Lower City 3 (USt. 3), ranging from about the second half of the seventeenth century to ca. 1400 BC, shows the first examples of these symbols with sometimes other hieroglyphic-like signs. In her analysis of this material, Clelia Mora largely denies this corpus the label of script.[20] She suggests an interpretation similar to that of the Konya-Karahöyük corpus with the

15 The criterion for inclusion in the list of Alp 1968: 287–301 is often unclear. It is not clear to me, for instance, why the crescent and circle on cat. no. 249 (Alp 1968: 231) or cat. no. 326 (Alp 1968: 249) are singled out as a "sign" (Alp 1968: 291) but not the animal and rosette on the respective seals. The same crescent and circle are not catalogued among the signs for cat. nos. 26–7 (Alp 1968: 165–6). Also, the dividing elements on the cylinder seals are included as signs in Alp's list.

16 Alp 1968: 287–301. 17 For the latter term see Chapter 1.

18 For the material see Güterbock 1940, 1942, Beran 1967, Boehmer & Güterbock 1987.

19 For a listing see Boehmer & Güterbock 1987: 33 w. n. 14.

20 Mora 1991: 22; Yakubovich 2008: 11 n. 6.

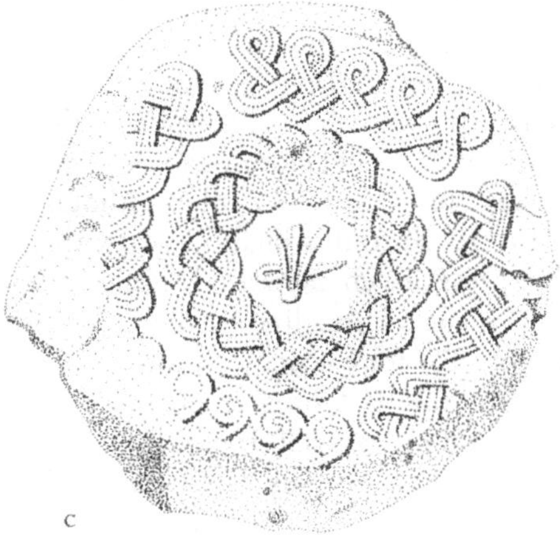

Fig. 7.3 Hattusili seal impression (from Boehmer & Güterbock 1987: 39 Abb. 25c; copyright Archive of the Boğazköy Expedition, Deutsches Archäologisches Institut Berlin).

designs serving as symbols or emblems, probably traceable to individuals or their offices within an administrative system. The oldest of them contain a single or at best two or three signs or hieroglyph-like signs and they are often combined with one or a combination of symbols for prosperity or wellbeing (VITA, BONUS) or status (SCRIBA). Where the rare sequence of two or three signs can be read by assigning them their later sound values occasionally a possible name results but in these cases, we are dealing with seals that may stem from the fifteenth century. Among this material is a seal impression (Fig. 7.3), for which Boehmer and Güterbock, because of its guilloches, suggest an Old Kingdom date (i.e., before 1500 BC in their dating system)[21] but stratified seals from Kuşaklı and Büklükale show that such guilloches were certainly still en vogue in the fifteenth and fourteenth century BC.[22] The impression bears the later familiar ligature 𔗔 to be read

[21] Thus Boehmer & Güterbock 1987: 36 w. Abb. 25c on p. 39 contra Alp 1968: 282–3 (w. lit.) who wanted to date it to the Old Assyrian Period. Most explicitly Boehmer & Güterbock 1987: 43 date the seal to the second half of the seventeenth or sixteenth century BC. It was found out of context in the fill of a Phrygian-era wall. For this reason, Yakubovich 2008: 12–13 n. 11 prefers to regard this seal "as the late imitation of the Old Kingdom artistic style." Since there is no real evidence otherwise for such imitations, I would still regard it as a genuine Old Kingdom piece on stylistic grounds. Note, moreover, the publication of a very similar example not known at the time of Yakubovich's article in Dinçol & Dinçol 2008: Tafel 1 no. 8, found in Temple 26. On guilloches as a help in dating seals see also Weeden 2018.

[22] Rieken 2015: 218 (Kuşaklı), Weeden 2016a: 95–97, 99 (Büklükale), and 2018: 69–70, see also Hawkins 2003: 166–7.

HATTI/HATTUSA x *li* for the name Hattusili.[23] The HATTI/HATTUSA-part () is a logogram of unknown origin standing for the country (Hatti) and/or capital city (Hattusa) but the piercing "dagger" sign () in the background seems to already have its syllabic value *li* while at the same time adding a visual pun: the Hittite verb for "to pierce, stab" is *ḫatt-*.[24] The combination shows that syllabic values had begun to develop, although it remains difficult to pin down the exact period from which the seal impression stems.

Besides the seal impressions characterized by the guilloches surrounding the central field, as in the Hattusili seal, there are also exemplars with a broad outer band of miniature scenes of, for instance, offerings and/or hieroglyphic signs and symbols. Compared to the outer band (sometimes there is a narrower second ring as well) the actual center of the seal is small and encompasses some of the symbols (VITA etc.) and hieroglyphs.[25]

All in all, the Hattusili seal is hard to date precisely within the Old Hittite period. The probably earliest securely datable seal impression with a clear sound value is the seal of a Tuthaliya (see Fig. 7.4).[26] The cuneiform

Fig. 7.4 Seal impression of Tuthaliya I (from Otten 2000: Abb. 23).

23 For the reading see Hawkins 1992: 55; the "x" in the transcription indicates that the sign is a ligature or combination of two signs.

24 The pun was already old, witness the text of Anitta where in his famous curse over the ruins of Hattusa he says (rev. 49–51): "Whoever becomes king after me and resettles *Hatt*usa, may the Stormgod of Heaven *ḫatt-* him!"; see already Chapter 2 w. n. 21.

25 For a succinct sketch of the development see Herbordt 2005: 45–6 w. illustrations, and Weeden 2018.

26 Otten 2000.

rings give the king's genealogy making it more than likely that this is Tuthaliya I who reigned in the last quarter of the fifteenth century BC. The center has his title Great King () on the left and his name written on the right with a ligature of the logograms for mountain and god ( + ), representing the "divine mountain" he was named after, plus a single syllabogram () beneath it for the beginning of his name: DEUS.MONS *tu*.

We may be on slightly firmer ground with two sixteenth century BC seal impressions found in Central Anatolia, from Eskiyapar and Büklükale, that Mark Weeden writes about. Here, too, we have sealings with two signs that with their later readings result in possible names.[27] Weeden thinks it "quite possible and even likely" that we are dealing with real script here.[28] The same applies to some recently found graffiti on a wall at Kayalıpınar. The stratigraphy of the building dates the signs to the period between the early seventeenth century and prior to 1400 BC.[29] Taken together, these sealings from the sixteenth to fifteenth century and the graffiti might thus be indicative of a nascent writing system that with certainty only surfaces as a more or less fully-fledged system in our material around 1400 BC.[30]

The first really datable attestation, finally, of the Anatolian hieroglyphs as a real writing system with a full inventory of syllabic signs remains the seal impression of the Hittite king Tuthaliya II and his queen Satanduhepa (Fig. 7.5).[31] His name is written on the right half of the seal in the same way as on the seal of his grandfather. In the left half we see the queen's name. Starting from the left we first see the title Great Queen ( ; facing right on this seal impression) and then down the very center of the sealing follows the queen's name, fully spelled out as *sà-tà-tu-ha-pa* = Sata(n)tuhapa.[32] The design of the seal suggests that the carver started putting in her name first,

[27] Weeden 2016a: 87–90. [28] Weeden 2016a: 90. [29] Müller-Karpe 2017: 73–7.

[30] Sometimes the seal of the Kizzuwatnean king Isputahsu who concluded the treaty with Telipinu and can thus be dated to ca. 1520–1500 BC has been adduced as the oldest specimen of Anatolian Hieroglyphic writing. It shows in the center the logograms for King and Stormgod (Tarhunt). This can be read as "king ruling by the authority of the Storm-god," as Yakubovich 2008: 11 does, or even as "king of Tarhuntassa," as suggested by Houwink ten Cate 1992: 250, but in either case we are still dealing with pure logograms. Finally, the inscription on a silver bowl now in Ankara and mentioning a Tuthaliya should be referred to here. Initially, identification with Tuthaliya I (ca. 1420 BC) was considered (Hawkins 1996 [1997]) but since then most scholars prefer to date the inscription to a much later date in the Hittite Empire; see Payne 2015: 84–98 w. lit.

[31] Yakubovich 2008: 12, 13, focusing very much on the first evidence of the hieroglyphs writing Luwian, sees this seal as still part of a "rudimentary writing system" (12) and "not yet . . . capable of rendering complex messages" (13). This stands in contrast to Waal 2012, who assumes a fully-fledged writing system already operating early in the second millennium.

[32] Nasals followed by consonants (Satanduhepa) are never expressed in the Hieroglyphic script.

Fig. 7.5 Seal impression with Satanduhepa found at Maşat Höyük (from Alp 1991: Abb. 2).

followed by her title amply spaced in the left half and finally squeezing in the title and name of her husband in the still available but reduced space on the right. This center position of the queen is no coincidence: the bottom of the center field bears from left to right three cuneiform signs TI MUNUS.LUGAL "long live the queen!" Even though appearing next to her husband, this was her seal, as confirmed by what remains (between 3 and 5 o'clock) of the legend in the cuneiform ring surrounding the center field: [N]A$_4$.KIŠIB MUNUS.LUGAL.GA[L. The impression can be dated fairly precisely to around 1375 BC on a combination of dendrochronological and philological arguments.[33] Within a generation may have followed the so-called SÜDBURG inscription at Hattusa's acropolis Büyükkale. Although originally ascribed to the last known Hittite king Suppiluliyama (also known as Suppiluliuma II, ca. 1200 BC) there seems to be a growing consensus to see Suppiluliuma I (ca. 1350 BC) as the responsible king.[34] Compared to hieroglyphic inscriptions of the thirteenth century it is highly logographic but at the same time adds more than twenty sound values to the five visible on the Satanduhepa impression.[35]

Soon after, numerous other seal legends with personal names follow and the oldest securely datable and likewise very logographically written inscription (ALEPPO 1) on stone dates to around or shortly after 1300 BC.

[33] van den Hout 2008a: 397–8. [34] Payne 2015: 78–84 w. lit., Klinger 2015: 101–6.

[35] a, á, i/ia, ta, ti, pa, pu, ka, ku, ma, mi, na, ni, nú, ha, hi, sa, sa$_5$, za/i, la, lu, wa/i, tara/i.

In combination with the seals of Hattusili and Tuthaliya I, the legend for Satanduhepa shows that by reasonable extrapolation the Anatolian hieroglyphic writing system must have existed by 1400 BC[36] and probably evolved in the course of the fifteenth century BC at the latest.[37]

7.3 The Anatolian Hieroglyphs as a Writing System

With the Satanduhepa seal we have definitively reached the stage where we can speak of the hieroglyphs as a writing system. While there is consensus that the Anatolian hieroglyphs in their design were a genuine local creation "within an Anatolian cultural and artistic milieu"[38] there is less agreement on how they became part of the writing system that was so important next to the cuneiform. As David Hawkins points out, we should distinguish between model and inspiration.[39] For either of the two we can look to Egypt, the Aegean, or Anatolia itself in the form of its already established cuneiform script. Direct Egyptian influence on the creation of the Anatolian hieroglyphs seems unlikely. The first reports of Hittite–Egyptian contact go back to the period when pharaohs like Thutmoses III (mid-fifteenth century BC) and Amenhotep II (late fifteenth century BC) campaigned in Syria and the largely hostile relations do not provide the ideal climate for borrowing by or cultural impact on the ruling elite pushing the hieroglyphic script. More importantly, however, the workings of the Egyptian writing system are very different while pictographic origins of a script are near universal. Chronologically, the Anatolian hieroglyphs were probably already developing as a script by then.[40] One very direct loan has been suggested for the sign  transcribed as VITA "life" based on its alleged resemblance to the Egyptian *ankh* symbol. Besides the question whether this is correct – would not the Anatolians have been able to come up with a symbol of their own for such a basic and important concept? – a single logographic sign does not constitute enough evidence to make the Egyptian script the example the hieroglyphic writing system was modeled after.[41]

The chances, on the other hand, of a link with Aegean scripts such as the Cretan hieroglyphs, Linear A, or B, are more promising. It is at least striking that the only deciphered one of the three, Linear B, shares the

[36] See also Rieken 2015: 219. [37] See likewise Mora 1994: 212. [38] Hawkins 1986: 373–4.

[39] Hawkins 2003: 168; discussing the ideas of Günther Neumann Hawkins uses the German terms *Vorbild* and *Anreger* respectively, the latter expressing the concept of encouragement or inspiration.

[40] Mora 1991: 25 considers such contacts very probable but Mora 1994: 214, is more reserved.

[41] In a forthcoming publication James Burgin convincingly shows that the VITA-sign is better interpreted as an allograph or stylized variant of the double-headed eagle symbol.

almost exclusive (C)V-structure of the Anatolian signs.[42] Since the Cretan hieroglyphs are in evidence from ca. 1900 BC David Hawkins suggested already in 1986 that the direction of influence would have been from the Aegean to Anatolia.[43] In that case the Anatolian west coast, that is, Arzawa seemed the most likely point of contact. At almost the same moment (1987) Rainer Boehmer and Hans Güterbock, assuming the VITA-sign as identical with the Egyptian *ankh* and pointing at other Egyptian signs and influences in the glyptic of Alalakh VII, favored Cilicia (the classical name of ancient Kizzuwatna) because of its being at the crossroads to Syria where there was a strong Egyptian presence.[44] Both Arzawa and Cilicia were traditionally seen as Luwian-speaking and thus considered to fit the strong Luwian connection that the script later displayed in the thirteenth century BC. In the end, though, wherever the point of transmission was, Hawkins settled in 1986 for both the hieroglyphic script and Linear B being "ultimately dependent on an external model, i.e. Egyptian Hieroglyphic." The reason for this was "the unsuitability of both the Linear B and Anatolian syllabaries for writing the Indo-European languages Greek and Hittite."[45] Both languages show various clusters of consonants like, for instance, in the word for "hand" *istra/i-*. In a writing system with only V and CV/ CVC(V) signs this had to be spelled with at least three signs: *i-sa-tara/i-*. In such a writing the first two *a*-vowels (*-sa-ta-*) were not pronounced and are thus purely graphic. In his 2003 contribution Hawkins still mentions the early Cretan connection with its "visible Egyptian cultural influence" but otherwise no longer commits himself to either Arzawa or Cilicia.[46] In the end hard evidence for all this is difficult to come by and, as briefly mentioned above, Yakubovich has shown that besides syllabic sound values clearly derived from Luwian words there are also those that presuppose a Hittite origin (e.g., IIII *mi* from Hitt. *miu-* "four" vs. Luw. *mawa-* "id."). Recently, Elisabeth Rieken has added important evidence that the development of the Anatolian hieroglyphic script could only have happened in the context of a mixed Hittite–Luwian-speaking Hittite kingdom.[47]

In Yakubovich's view the moment he wants to label the Anatolian hieroglyphs a writing system is strongly contingent on the recognition of Luwian as *the* language of the inscriptions and he therefore dates that stage to "the last Hittite rulers" of the thirteenth century BC.[48] If the SÜDBURG inscription mentioned earlier indeed stems from the mid-fourteenth

[42] Hawkins 1986: 374, Waal 2012: 304–5 w. lit. [43] Hawkins 1986: 374, 2003: 168.
[44] Boehmer & Güterbock 1987: 40. [45] Hawkins 1986: 374. [46] Hawkins 2003: 168–9.
[47] Rieken 2015. [48] Yakubovich 2008: 32.

century that stage has to move up by two generations or so. Moreover, there is no reason to assume the step to writing Luwian as decisive in the development of the Anatolian hieroglyphs into a writing system. Instead it seems to have been the urge to write names of all kinds that drove the attribution of sound values to signs.[49] This in turn went hand in hand with the growth of the royal dynasty and the administrative apparatus. As several scholars have convincingly argued, it is the seal glyptics that form the roots of the script that would later generate the longer inscriptions. The specific origins of signs carved in stone seals and the resulting high relief when pressed into clay determined the look of the signs. The small circular field the signs had to be carved in led to their vertical staggering, and the antithetic arrangement within the field, as in the Satanduhepa seal (Fig. 7.5), was favorable to the boustrophedic reading direction.[50] That is, the possibility to use all signs including all non-symmetric ones whether facing right or left was not an innovation[51] but an original feature that came in handy and was maintained. Many scripts, among them early alphabets, exploit the so-called *mirror invariance* of signs that proves so natural to beginning and some dyslexic readers: "an ingenious adaptation in the visual system which allows the brain to understand that an object is the same from every direction."[52] Whether we see a chair from the side, the front, or upside down we still recognize it as a chair. It can, therefore, be a hurdle for early readers to learn that and <d> or <p> and <q> are different letters representing different phonemes. In the process of Anatolian hieroglyphs acquiring sound values we see none of the one-time deliberate and systematic innovations that we saw in Hittite cuneiform in Chapter 6.2: nothing like the single vs. double writing of stops to express a phonological opposition, no creation of internally systematic series like the wa_a etc. signs, or the consistent application of word space. The absence of such developments suggests a much more gradual evolution of the hieroglyphs from symbols or logograms to signs with a specific sound value. With the definitive step to writing Hittite in cuneiform around the middle of the sixteenth century BC and this probably more gradual development of the Anatolian hieroglyphs with a fully-fledged sign inventory already developed in the fifteenth century, the two writing systems are not that far apart.

Some scholars have claimed a role for the Hittite cuneiform in the genesis of the hieroglyphic writing system on the basic assumption that

[49] Hawkins 1986: 374. [50] Rieken 2015: 223–7; see also Seeher 2009, Marazzi 2010.
[51] Payne 2015: 21. [52] Wolf 2016: 53; see also in more detail Dehaene 2009: 284–99.

cuneiform scribes must have worked side by side with their hieroglyphic colleagues.[53] The differences between the two systems are significant, however. Not only the consistent V/CV structure of the hieroglyphic syllabary, but also the lack of word space in the Hittite kingdom inscriptions, the boustrophedic reading direction and the vertical arrangement of signs within a register set it firmly apart from the Hittite cuneiform. It has even been argued that there may be a likely instance where the Hittite cuneiform might have undergone influence from the hieroglyphs: one sound value that the Hittite cuneiform added to its inventory is *wi*$_5$ derived through so-called acrophony from the Sumerogram GEŠTIN "wine," which was *wiyana-* in Hittite. In the hieroglyphic script we see the same development: the logogram for "vine" (VITIS ᵞ) can also be read syllabically as *wí*. This reading is already attested in the last quarter of the fourteenth century BC in the name of Mursili II's wife Gassulawiya and probably earlier.[54] Acrophony not being a familiar phenomenon in Hittite cuneiform (which had borrowed the cuneiform script whole cloth) but very much so in the Anatolian hieroglyphic system, the direction of influence here would likely have gone from hieroglyphic to cuneiform.[55] Although possible this is hardly compelling given the near-universal phenomenon of acrophony. The fundamental differences between the two writing systems suggest that they developed rather independently and once in place either moved in quite different circles or that their users simply did not care about the differences or even deliberately kept them in place. As so many writing systems past and present in the world show, obstacles of spelling or consistency perceived by others often mean little to the people using them. Finally, instances where the two writing systems occur side by side on the same medium are exceedingly rare and it does not help that the hieroglyphs on the cuneiform tablet KBo 13.62 (Fig. 9.4) are written upside down vis-à-vis the cuneiform.[56]

53 Payne 2015: 65–6, 68 (quoting Morpurgo Davies 1986: 61), assumes direct contact between scribes of cuneiform and hieroglyphs in Hittite Anatolia and therefore influence from the former on the latter and mentions "viele strukturelle Parallelen in beiden Schriften" (68) but gives no particulars.

54 SBo 1.37 and 104; the earlier examples come from Kaman-Kalehöyük, for which see Weeden 2016a: 97.

55 Weeden 2011a: 375, Waal 2012: 303.

56 Seven such instances are known; for a list see Waal 2017: 297. The fact that the hieroglyphic inscription on KBo 13.62 is upside down in relation to the cuneiform makes it in my opinion unlikely that we are dealing here with a second scribe working on the tablet, as suggested by Gordin 2015: 34. Rather it is indicative of the writer of the graffito being unrelated to the work on the tablet (thus also Waal 2017: 299) or perhaps even not being that familiar with cuneiform and not knowing how to hold a tablet. For a bulla with ornamental(?) cuneiform on the mantle see Güterbock 1942: 3 w. Pl. VIII.

7.4 Conclusion

However diverse and sometimes meager our evidence is, it does suggest a gradual evolution of the Anatolian hieroglyphs out of a variety of local semasiographic systems.[57] The three corpora from Kanesh, Konya-Karahöyük, and Hattusa as well as more isolated examples[58] do not form a coherent whole whether archaeologically or iconographically. What they have in common is that they are part of a wider Anatolian use of pictographic symbols, likely to have expressed identities within local bureaucracies, as it may have been used already in the fourth millennium at Arslantepe in eastern Anatolia.[59] It was only the founding and continued growth of the Hittite kingdom at Hattusa that spurred the development of its designs into a real writing system without much evidence for influence from its cuneiform counterpart. It is because of these power relations that the Hattusa repertoire won out over whatever local ones existed. In terms of roots, therefore, as Philippa Steele recently suggested, one might think not only of the pictograms but also of the later writing system as an indigenous, *ab initio* creation.[60]

The Anatolian hieroglyphic signs were inspired by and reflect the same life and surrounding world. Once people had seen the king with his characteristic pointed crown () on his travels through the country or had been pointed out the sign for Great King () on royal inscriptions, they knew who was their monarch. The effect is what reading researchers call logographic reading: it is when children recognize "the golden arches [and] know this symbol stands for McDonald's." It does not mean that they know it is the letter M and can read it in any other word. "What is happening is a simple paired associate of a visual symbol and a known concept."[61] This built-in capacity made the script the perfect carrier to forge a sense of shared identity, to create a semblance of an Anatolian unity in diversity that was so important to Telipinu and other Old Kingdom kings.[62] It shows the power of *semasiographic* over phonetic systems. "Because their messages are not processed through auditory and verbal channels but are cognitively accessed through sight, recognition is both more immediate and free from any constraints of language; one can grasp the meaning of a shape . . . without knowing its name."[63] It was its alegible quality that made it an effective carrier of the unifying efforts of the ruling elite. As such, Yakubovich's "nationalistic self-expression" may have some truth to it. Not so much in a modern understanding of nationalist and isolationist politics as in

57 As suggested also by Yakubovich 2008, Waal 2012 and Payne 2015: 66–7.
58 See Boehmer & Güterbock 1987: 33–58. 59 Frangipane et al. 2007. 60 Steele 2019: 40.
61 For both quotes and the concept of logographic reading see Wolf 2016: 50–1.
62 Payne 2012: 13. 63 Hill Boone 2004: 317–18.

the sense of an awareness that their self-preservation as a state required an incorporation and acceptance of local cultures and traditions, or in one word, identities.[64] In similar fashion the creation of a series of cuneiform signs for a sound /f/ that was neither part of the north Syrian nor of the Hittite phoneme inventory (Chapter 6.2) made it possible to record local Hattian and Palaic cult rituals and include them in the capital's tablet collections. It is this politics that may be the answer to David Hawkins' question that I quoted at the very beginning of this chapter: "Why if you are already familiar with cuneiform invent a script like Hieroglyphic?"

The cuneiform with its Hittite language became and remained the official medium of the realm and enabled it to communicate with its peers to the east and thus gave the kingdom a cosmopolitan air belonging to the "cuneiform world" but in internal terms it was restricted to the small group of the ruling elite and their retainers. The Anatolian hieroglyphs, on the other hand, reflecting the Anatolian world and, existing in various parts of Central Anatolia, could be expected to transcend whatever local ethnicities and languages existed. Judging by the evidence we have their purpose was monumental in the microform of seal glyptics that eventually generated the larger inscriptions of the publicly displayed inscriptions of the fourteenth (if the SÜDBURG inscription indeed belongs to Suppiluliuma I) and thirteenth century BC. The wider appeal of the script was especially helpful in its earlier highly logographic stages, when there was not yet a fixed relationship between script and language (Luwian). Signs symbolizing not only notions like goodness, prosperity, or power but also kingship, god, country etc. were instilled in Central Anatolian society from early on and remained understandable for all parties to the very end, even when the bond with Luwian had become inseparable.

7.5 Appendix: A Brief Introduction to Anatolian Hieroglyphs

The Anatolian hieroglyphic script only has signs for vowels (1) and consonant + vowel (2). The standard sign list still is Laroche 1960 with a total of 497 entries, covering also all Iron Age (first millennium) attestations; since then the inventory has grown to well over 500 signs (see Payne 2010b: 194–5 with 524; for recent sign lists see Bolatti-Guzzo et al. 1998: 3–124, Hawkins 2000: 23–34; see also Payne 2015: 29–31, 35–41). With forty-five signs, Tables 7.2 and 7.3 constitute the basic second-millennium syllabary. In addition, there are

[64] Cf. Sanders 2009: 55–7; for a similar argument for the "creation and continued use of distinctive Cypriot writing systems" as opposed to cuneiform, or the Aramaic or Greek alphabets see Steele 2019: 199–201, 243.

Table 7.1 *Reading direction of Anatolian hieroglyphic signs*

a	d	g
b	e	h
c	f	i

≫ reading direction

hundreds of logograms, a selection of which is given in Table 7.4. All signs (unless symmetric in shape) are given in *dextroverse* direction (reading from left to right); if an inscription has more than one line the reading direction changes with each subsequent line (so-called *boustrophedic* arrangement). Usually, within a line, signs are stacked vertically from top to bottom, two or three at a time. see Table 7.1.

7.5.1 *Vowels*

The Anatolian hieroglyphs distinguish three different vowel qualities, /a, i, u/ (Table 7.2); there is no separate sign that we transliterate with /e/. The <á> sign is only used word-initially and possibly represents a glottal stop /ʔ/ rather than a vowel.

Table 7.2 *Second millenium Anatolian hieroglyphic syllabary: vowels*

a		i		u	
á					

7.5.2 *Consonant + Vowel*

The signs are given in Table 7.3 in the following order: labials, dentals, dorsals, laryngeals, nasals, liquids, sibilants, and the glides w, and y. Three vowel qualities are possible but not all signs have the full series. The sign <ra/i> only occurs in ligature with any of the other signs. At the end three special combinations with <ra/i> are added. For the occasional accent (e.g., *tá* or *sà*) or index number (sa_5) see the Appendix to Chapter 3; missing entries (e.g., *sá*, sa_4) have thus far only been recognized in the later Iron Age inscriptions and are therefore not included here.

Table 7.3 *Second millenium Anatolian hieroglyphic syllabary: consonant + vowel*

Ca		Ci		Cu	
pa		pi		pu	
ta		ti		tu	
da (tá)					
tà					
ta_x					
ka		ki		ku	
kwa/i					
ha		hi		hu	
hwa/i					
ma		mi		mu	
na		ni		nu	
		ní		nú	
la		li		lu	
la/i					
lá/í					
+ ra/i	+ \			ru	
sa		si		su	
sà					
sa_5					
za/i				zu	
				zú	
ya	> i				
wa/i		wi			
ara/i					
kar(a/i)					
tara/i					

7.5.3 Logograms

Logograms are transcribed into Latin and capitalized (Table 7.4). These signs either directly denote the object they depict like PORTA "gate," or they can cover a wider range like MANUS characterizing all kinds of manual

Table 7.4 *Second millenium Anatolian hieroglyphic syllabary: some signs, transcriptions, and meanings*

hieroglyph	transcription	meaning	hieroglyph	transcription	meaning
	REX	"king"		MANUS	"hand"
	MAGNUS.REX	"Great King"		CURRUS	"chariot, vehicle"
	DEUS	"god"		FUSUS	"spindle"
	DOMUS	"house"		AMPLECTI	"embrace, love"
	DEUS.DOMUS	"temple"		PORTA	"gate"
	ASINUS	"donkey, mule"		MALUS	"evil, bad"
	BOS	"ox, bovine"		VITA	"life"
	REGIO	"country"		LONGUS	"long; measure"
	FILIUS	"son"		CAPERE + SCALPRUM	"inscribe, carve"
	FILIA	"daughter"		CERVUS	"deer"
	AURIGA	"charioteer"		SCALPRUM	"stonemason's tool"

actions or labor. Several signs also double as syllabic signs (e.g., BOS and *u*). Signs can express abstract notions like MALUS "evil, bad" or VITA "life." They can be combined to form new words like DEUS.DOMUS "god + house" = "temple." Sometimes they are recognizable like CURRUS with its two wheels or the pointed crown or helmet in REX, *pars pro toto* symbolizing the king or royal power (see Fig. 7.1). Oftentimes their origin is unknown to us like the hook and three dots for "evil, bad."

CHAPTER 8

The New Kingdom Cuneiform Corpus

8.1 The New Kingdom Period

> "When Tuthaliya, Great King, had destroyed the land of Aššuwa, he dedicated these swords to the Stormgod, his lord"[1]

As attested by these words, after the malaise and turbulent years following the death of Telipinu the Hittite kingdom once more asserted itself beyond its narrow borders and started playing a role of importance again in international politics with the rise to power of Tuthaliya I (ca. 1425 BC).[2] He established what we call the New Kingdom or Empire Period that – in spite of another temporary but significant setback in the first half of the fourteenth century – would remain the dominating power in Anatolia until its ultimate collapse around 1200 BC. His marriage to Nikalmadi, probably a Hurrian-speaking princess from Kizzuwatna, ushered in a period of strong Hurrian influence at the royal court. Princes and princesses started bearing Hurrian names and hundreds of Hurrian texts were written and copied so that – until the possible discovery of genuine Mittanian tablet collections – the bulk of our entire Hurrian corpus so far comes from the collections in Hattusa. When Tuthaliya ascended the throne the Hittites no longer had any Syrian possessions and their territory was probably confined to the Halys basin and to the Lower and Upper Land. The captured swords in the quote above (and see already Chapter 4.2–3), one of which has survived, he dedicated to the Stormgod as a token of his gratitude for campaigns in western Anatolia that brought the Hittites in contact with the Mycenaean Greeks under the name of Ahhiya or

[1] For this text see already Chapter 4.

[2] He is often referred to as Tuthaliya I/II because of different text interpretations and resulting theories. The next Tuthaliya is then counted as III with a son Tuthaliya "the younger" or "junior." I will call the first two of these simply Tuthaliya I and II, and since the one called "junior" was actually sworn in he will be Tuthaliya III. For the latest on this and the filiation of Suppiluliuma with ample literature see Taracha 2016.

Ahhiyawa (i.e., the Homeric Achaeans). The Gasgaeans living in the Pontic Mountains in the north invaded Hatti-Land but were forced back and defeated for the time being. Continuing his predecessors' policy through a treaty with the Kizzuwatnean king Sunassura, Tuthaliya secured his southeastern flank, essential for any activities against the rising power of the Hurrian state of Mittani in northern Mesopotamia.[3] Both Isuwa in the upper Euphrates area and Aleppo had already come under Hurrian influence and had defected to Mittani but were successfully brought back into the Hittite fold.

Tuthaliya undertook some of his campaigns with his adoptive son Arnuwanda I as his co-regent. Texts from the latter's reign attest to mounting pressure from the Gasgaeans and the situation dramatically worsened under Arnuwanda's son and successor Tuthaliya II. This Tuthaliya already appears during his father's reign as *tuhkanti*, a title for a prince who is second to the king only. Apart from the Gasgaean threat in the north further aggression from Mittani resulted in the secession of Kizzuwatna to Mittani. The Mittanian king Artatama I allied himself with Pharaoh Thutmoses IV sealing their bond by the marriage of Artatama's daughter to the Pharaoh and at the same time trying to fend off Hittite progress in Syria. Things came to a head for the Hittites when in addition to the Hurrian threat from the east serious and simultaneous attacks were unleashed on the inner core of Hatti-Land from Arzawa in the west and Gasgaeans in the north bringing the kingdom to the verge of collapse. Tuthaliya even saw himself forced to temporarily move the residence eastwards from Hattusa. Both Sapinuwa (modern Ortaköy) and Samuha (modern Kayalıpınar) probably served as temporary residences. Meanwhile, Arzawa penetrated deep into the southeast as far as the western borders of Kizzuwatna. Just like Artatama, the Arzawan king Tarhundaradu approached Egypt offering Amenophis III his daughter in marriage. He did so by sending a letter that was found in the Egyptian tablet collections at Tel el-Amarna. There is no reason to assume that the Arzawan state had ever been literate and since the Hittite kingdom had blocked its easy and direct access to Mesopotamia there was no Akkadian expertise available. So instead of using Akkadian, the diplomatic language of the day, Tarhundaradu resorted to Hittite, the nearest thing to an "international" language he did have access to and urged his addressee to answer him in Hittite.[4] The Gasgaeans meanwhile reportedly even sacked Hattusa forcing the royal family to evacuate the capital. The corpus of

[3] Beckman 1999: 17–26. [4] Haas apud Moran 1992: 101–3.

almost one hundred letters found at the small site of modern Maşat Höyük, ancient Tapikka, illustrates the Hittite nervousness vis-à-vis the Gasgaean danger.

Having already started campaigning as a general for his father, Suppiluliuma I is largely credited for turning around this disastrous situation towards 1350 BC. Yet somehow Suppiluliuma was not Tuthaliya II's first choice as a successor. That was another (adopted?) son usually referred to as Tuthaliya the Younger or Junior. He seems to have been officially sworn in and can therefore be counted as Tuthaliya III but Suppiluliuma himself seems to have been involved in murdering him. Once alone on the throne Suppiluliuma completed the task of resurrecting the empire. He first chased the Arzawan troops from the Lower Lands and successfully pushed the Gasgaeans back into the Pontic Mountains. More to the northeast he continued the treaty relations his father had established with the people in the area of Azzi-Hayasa towards the Caucasus.[5] In the east and southeast Suppiluliuma exploited the unstable situations that had arisen both in Mittani and Egypt.[6] The death of Amenophis III and the new religious priorities of his successor Amenophis IV, better known as Akhenaten, had derailed Mittanian–Egyptian relations. Suppiluliuma fueled Mittanian internal troubles and seeing this both Assyria and Babylon each closed in, preying on Hurrian territory from their respective sides. This and the loosening Egyptian grip on its Syrian allies gave Suppiluliuma the opportunity to bring almost all of Syria and all lands west of the Euphrates under his control putting the crown on his work by finally conquering the city of Karkamish, a key stronghold in the area. Meanwhile, the Hurrian king Tushratta was murdered and his son Sattiwaza became a Hittite vassal.

At the end of his life Suppiluliuma could look back on an impressive reign and a kingdom defended on its eastern border by a range of vassal states (Azzi-Hayasa, Mittani, and the Syrian territories under Aleppo and Karkamish) and strengthened by a network of diplomatic marriages.[7] Two of his daughters he married off, one to Sattiwaza of Mittani and another to the former king of Arzawa. A sister of his he sent to Hukkana of Hayasa in the northeast of Anatolia. Two sons he left as viceroys in the east: Telipinu in Aleppo and Piyassili (also known as Sarrikusuh) in Karkamish. Finally, he himself married a Babylonian princess, daughter of the Kassite king Burnaburias II. The ultimate success in this policy would have been the marriage of another son, Zannanza, to the widow of the Pharaoh who is by

[5] Beckman 1999: 26–34. [6] Wilhelm 2012. [7] Beckman 1999: 34–54.

some scholars identified as Tutankhamun. She wrote him two letters imploring him to send one of his sons to become her husband and king in Egypt. Suppiluliuma hesitated too long and when he finally conceded and sent Zannanza to Egypt the prince died or was killed. In retaliation Suppiluliuma sent his son Arnuwanda to invade Egyptian territory in Syria. Laden with booty and deportees he returned but an epidemic, which was to last two decades, spread in Hatti-Land. Suppiluliuma died not long afterwards, possibly one of the first victims of the plague, as did his short-lived successor Arnuwanda II. Now it was Mursili II's turn.

8.2 The Cuneiform Corpus

Linguistically the period starting with Tuthaliya I and roughly lasting through the reign of Suppiluliuma I is referred to as Middle Hittite. The sources that start to flow now show a number of subtle but clear changes in the Hittite language vis-à-vis the Old Kingdom texts.[8] These changes must have come about in the course of the fifteenth century BC but because of the absence of securely datable texts in Hittite between Telipinu and Tuthaliya we are unable to track them properly and can only observe them already firmly in place at the end of that same century. After the relative riches of the Old Kingdom with its tales and Palace Chronicles, Hattusili I's Annals and Testament, Telipinu's Edict, and the rituals and laws, our Hittite corpus in the period following Telipinu initially shrinks to just the series of charters and treaties with Kizzuwatna written in Akkadian. But with the coming of Tuthaliya I, towards the end of the fifteenth century BC, the picture changes drastically. The noticeable Hurrian presence in the dynasty is accompanied by a seemingly sudden proliferation of Hurrian text compositions and the simultaneous decline of Hattian influence so prominent during the Old Kingdom. We should keep in mind, however, that we mostly assign the vast corpus of Hurrian texts to the reigns of Tuthaliya I–Arnuwanda I because of the Hurrian dynastic names (for queens, princes, and princesses) that start appearing with them.[9] Such changes hardly ever come that unexpected, though. There is evidence to suggest that Hurrian cultural influence had been building up already before Tuthaliya.[10] His marriage to a Hurrian princess and the subsequent name giving may thus have been a logical continuation of that process rather than a starting point.

[8] Melchert 2008. [9] de Martino 2013. [10] Wilhelm 2010b: 630.

At the dawn of the fourteenth century we see the full range of Hittite literature unfolding and this and the next chapter (9) will pass the New Kingdom period corpus of both cuneiform and hieroglyphic sources from the capital and provincial sites in review. The charters and Palace Chronicles did not outlive the Old Kingdom, at least not in that form. Anecdotes with an educational and warning character continued to be used occasionally within other text genres and, as argued by Elena Devecchi, several treaties and similar texts of the thirteenth century BC are in essence land grants.[11] At the start of the fourteenth century we see in cuneiform script more historiography, more diplomatic texts, and a seemingly ever-expanding corpus of festival or cult scenarios continuing the Old Kingdom cult rituals while the laws continue to be copied and are now joined by deposition records. Some formerly isolated texts or compositions that were only rarely put in writing, it seems, now develop into "popular" genres: instructions, some of which are datable to Tuthaliya I and Arnuwanda I,[12] and hymns and prayers, two of which can be ascribed to them as well.[13] As convincingly argued by Jared Miller, it may not so much be new genres that emerge but the recording of various "administrative" acts that now becomes more common.[14] The kingdom now fully embraces writing.

Especially striking and illustrative of the renewed "global" outlook of the kingdom is the large number of compositions that are either imported or have foreign roots but are adapted to the Hittite situation: horse-training ("hippological") manuals from Mittani, non-Anatolian mythological compositions, omina and lexical lists from Mesopotamia, wisdom literature, and a substantial corpus of rituals from Kizzuwatna in the east as well as from Arzawa in the west. Among the myths and tales, we find the Akkadian, Hurrian, and Hittite versions of the Gilgamesh epic, the Hurrian "Song of Release," the "Theogony" or Kumarbi cycle, and the likewise Hurrian Keššši saga, the latter two mostly in what seem to be adapted Hittite versions. For much of this material Kizzuwatna most likely served as the main conduit. The Hurrian rituals that are linked to the dynasty of Tuthaliya I, however, seem to have been composed in Hattusa

[11] Devecchi 2010: 11–2 w. n. 37, for the *vidimus* (for the term see Chapter 12.6) of the Aleppo treaty with Talmitessub (CTH 75, Mursili II–Muwatalli II) and the Tarhuntassa treaties (CTH 106, Hattusili III and Tuthaliya IV). Of course, there is also the so-called Sahurunuwa-*Urkunde* (CTH 225, Tuthaliya IV), which has always been considered a charter, and Hattusili III's Apology also belongs in this category.

[12] CTH 251, 252, 257, 258, 259, 261; for editions see Miller 2013: 129–53, 168–93, 208–37.

[13] CTH 373, 375; for an edition see Lebrun 1980: 111–20, 132–54, for an English translation see Singer 2002: 31–3, 40–4.

[14] Miller 2011: 196.

and the temporary capital of Sapinuwa. Add to all these the few ephemeral bookkeeping records and we have the collection of around 30,000 preserved fragments of clay tablets now known to us. The tablets they represent were originally housed in a number of tablet storage places in the Hittite capital as well as some of the provincial centers; for an estimate of the total number of tablets present in the capital towards the end of the kingdom see Chapter 12.9. Finally, there are a few more cuneiform inscriptions on metal objects comparable to Ammuna's ax of the Old Kingdom: there is Tuthaliya I's sword mentioned earlier (and see also Chapter 4) as well as a hayfork bearing the inscription "hayfork."[15]

8.3 Historical Prose and Related Texts Using the Past

The combination "historical prose" refers to royal annals and other texts that relate, in the past tense, exploits of kings, their grandees, and subordinates.[16] In most societies such *res gestae* are patently propagandistic and often given to hyperbole. At first sight the intention of some of the relevant Hittite compositions for this genre seems to be the same, judging by the Hittites' own characterization of these texts as *pešnatar* (LÚ-*natar*) literally "manhood, virility," that is, "manly deeds."[17] Yet compared to similar accounts from Mesopotamia or Egypt they often strike us as rather bland and formulaic for the most part. This already applies to Hattusili I's Annals but even more so to the historical writings of the Great Kings of the thirteenth century some three to four hundred years later. Hattusili's Annals were displayed on or near a statue of himself in gold and the last known Hittite king Suppiluliyama (or Suppiluliuma II, ca. 1200 BC) had his conquests hieroglyphically carved in Luwian on the rocky outcrop of Nişantepe in the Upper City of Hattusa. With rare exceptions they offer a dry summation of year after year and conquest after conquest. There is no direct speech to liven things up, no flashbacks, no reports of deliberations, and no king single-handedly slaying his foes. Hattusili I's Testament, on the other hand, shows that already in his time another much more lively

[15] Yalçıklı 2000. The use of lead as a script carrier is uncertain and disputed. Some lead strips with Anatolian hieroglyphs are known from the Neo-Hittite period and generally dated to the eighth century BC. They are mostly economic in character: the ones found at Assur seem to be letters exchanged between merchants (ed. by Hawkins 2000: 533–5, cf. also Giusfredi 2010: 208–33) and those from Kululu (near Kültepe) are straight bookkeeping records (ed. by Hawkins 2000: 503–13, see also Giusfredi 2010: 185–207). The lead strip from KIRŞEHIR is a letter as well but the contents are hard to understand (ed. by Akdoğan & Hawkins 2011, Weeden 2013b and see Giusfredi 2010: 236–9). For a similar looking strip of rolled-up lead from second-millennium Hattusa see §8.7.

[16] For an overview see Hoffner 1980. [17] del Monte 1993: 13–7.

and personal narrative style was possible. This is the style that we also encounter in the so-called Apology of his thirteenth century namesake Hattusili III. The latter composition is in essence a charter of sorts granting large real-estate holdings to the cult of the deity Ishtar and granting it tax-exempt status, but its basic character is buried under such thick layers of historical justification as to become almost unrecognizable. The same could be said of Hattusili I's Testament: this is no more historiography than Hattusili III's Apology or Telipinu's Proclamation. We often refer to these and other texts as historiography because we gratefully use their writings to construct Hittite history. All three compositions make ample use of history to justify their actions, but they are at best what Harry Hoffner has called "history-writing of a very utilitarian sort."[18]

There thus seem to have been at least two distinct prose registers depending on the purpose of the text. The style of the public inscriptions mentioned, which is similar to that of the Annals of Tuthaliya I and Hattusili III, suggests a wider dissemination of these compositions. Hittite texts sometimes contain hints at public readings and perhaps we should suppose a similar use for such propagandistic historical accounts.[19] Their simple syntax may have supported an oral presentation while a public display may have lent it a considerable "alegible"[20] value. The case, on the other hand, for such texts as Hattusili I's Testament and Hattusili III's Apology is clearly different. History is used here in support of a specific cause, which needed arguing and persuading like Hattusili I's appointment of the young Mursili as his heir and successor or the seizure and subsequent granting of large domains by Hattusili III. In these cases, the audience was not the population at large but the royal court and its officials. There may well have been repeated readings of these texts, as shown by the explicit stipulation in the Testament that it should be read out monthly to the young Mursili I, just not to as large an audience. One is reminded also of Suppiluliuma I's order to fetch and solemnly read out loud the old treaty tablet with Egypt concerning the population of Kurustama when he had finally decided to comply with Egypt's request for a son to marry the widow of the deceased Pharaoh. Where Telipinu's Proclamation fits in is hard to say. It certainly uses the past to argue and

[18] Hoffner 1980: 310.

[19] For different views on this see Cancik 1976: 54–5, Hoffner 1980: 325–6, Roszkowska-Mutschler 2002, Polvani 2005, Gilan 2015: 255.

[20] For the term see Lurie 2011: 28–30 et passim; "alegible" describes the impact that the presence of writing can have on people even if they are unable to read it.

defend his changes in the "constitution," but it lacks the unity and sparkle of the two other compositions.

There is one exception to all this and that is the work of Mursili II (ca. 1318–1295 BC). His biography of his father known as the "Deeds of Suppiluliuma I" and the two annalistic works of his own reign, the Ten-Year Annals and the Extensive Annals, are likewise relatively unpropagandistic nor do they seem to have an obviously discernible agenda as, for instance, the works of the two Hattusili's and Telipinu do. Mursili II's style, on the other hand, can at times be quite sophisticated and has even been described in terms of "objective" and "journalistic."[21] The narrative is placed in a larger historical perspective and while there is scant if any attention for battle scenes, for hunting as the sport of kings or grand building enterprises,[22] there is all the more focus on deliberations and movements leading up to military confrontations as well as on their aftermath. There is a clear arc with a prologue and an epilogue, the author refers forward and backward and separate story lines are sometimes interwoven within a single narrative. There are geographical excursuses, discussions on strategy, diplomacy, negotiations, and so forth. Striking is the attention devoted to deliberations that do not result in any actions and the recognition of others contributing to the king's successes.

The sheer length of Mursili's compositions, however, already makes their display as public inscriptions unlikely. Some of his historical writings had a religious dimension as can be seen, for instance, in the epilogue of his Ten-Year Annals: he refers to the Sungoddess of Arinna, his patron deity, as the dedicatee of his work. Having sketched the events and circumstances that led to his rise to kingship at a young age Mursili quotes himself imploring the Sungoddess and then tells the reader what to expect:

> "So, Sungoddess of Arinna, my Lady, stand by me and destroy those surrounding enemy countries before me!" The Sungoddess of Arinna heard my prayer and stood by me. Since I sat down on my father's throne, I did defeat these surrounding enemy countries in ten years and I destroyed them.[23]

Almost four columns and well over 300 lines later Mursili comes full circle in his epilogue:

[21] del Monte 1993: 12, 14. [22] Riemschneider 1962: 110–1, Hoffner 1980: 326–7.

[23] *nu≠wa≠mu* ^{d}UTU ^{URU}*Arinna* GAŠAN≠IA *kattan tiya nu≠wa≠mu≠kan uni araḫzenaš* KUR.KUR LÚ.KÚR *peran kuenni nu≠mu* ^{d}UTU ^{URU}*Arinna memian ištamašta n≠aš≠mu kattan tiyat nu≠za≠kan* *ANA* ^{GIŠ}GU.ZA ABI≠IA *kuwapi ēšḫat nu≠za kē araḫzenaš* KUR.KUR.MEŠ LÚ.KÚR *INA* MU.10.KAM *taruḫḫun n≠at≠kan kuenun* KBo 3.4 i 25–9 (Annals of Mursili II, CTH 61, NS), ed. by Grélois 1988: 55–6, 76.

> Since I sat down on my father's throne, I have already been king for ten years and single-handedly defeated these (i.e., aforementioned) enemy countries in (those) ten years but the enemy countries that the princes and commanders defeated are not included. What the Sungoddess of Arinna further has in store for me, that I will record and deposit (before the deity).[24]

The fact that the "Deeds of Suppiluliuma" was meant to be recorded on bronze tablets[25] may point at a deposition in a temple, just as was done with treaties, and Mursili may have meant it as a prequel to his Annals. The primary purpose of the texts might therefore have been to account for the support of the Sungoddess in achieving his goals. It seems difficult for us to accept, though, that such works would have had no use beyond being deposited in a temple to bear witness of that support. Cynically, one might say that this religious veneer was just that, and that, again, the audience were the immediate elite circles around Mursili who kept him in power. Mursili does twice refer to an audience:

> Now read (lit. "see," second sg. imperative) how the mighty Stormgod, my lord, runs before me, (how) he does not expose me to evil but has exposed me to good.[26]
>
> The city of Ura which was the most advanced post [in the land of] Azzi is located on a place that is hard to reach and whoever hears these tablets (and . . ., let him send (someone) out and check how the city of Ura was [b]uilt!)[27]

[24] *nu=za=kan* ANA ^{GIŠ}GU.ZA *ABI=IA* *kuwapi ēšḫat nu karū* MU.IO.KAM LUGAL-*uiznanun nu=za kē* KUR.KUR LÚ.KÚR *INA* MU.IO.KAM *ammēdaz* ŠU-*az taruḫḫun* DUMU.MEŠ.LUGAL*=ma=za* *BELU*.MEŠ*=ia kue* KUR.KUR LÚ.KÚR *taruḫḫešker n=at=šan* UL *anda parā=ma=mu* ^{d}UTU ^{URU}PÚ-*na* GAŠAN*=IA kuit peškezzi n=at aniyami n=at katta teḫḫi* KBo 3.4 iv 44–8 (Annals of Mursili II, CTH 61, NS), ed. by Grélois 1988: 72, 88; on the translation of the last line see Cancik 1976: 116–7, and Gilan 2005: 365. The understanding that the deposition is meant to be in the temple "before the deity" is supported by a few parallel passages that instead of (*n=at*) *katta teḫḫi* ("(and it/them) I deposited") use the phrase *PĀNI* DINGIR *dai-* ("to put before the deity," cf. Gilan 2005: 365).

[25] DUB.7.KAM N[U.]TIL *ANA tuppi* [Z]ABAR *nāwi* [*a*]*niyan* "Seventh tablet, n[ot] finished; not yet [m]ade into a [br]onze tablet" KBo 5.6 iv 16–18 (Deeds of Suppiluliuma I, CTH 40, NS), ed. by Waal 2015: 215–6.

[26] [*nu=z*]*a kāšma au* ^{d}U NIR.GÁL*=mu* *BELI=IA* *maḫḫan peran ḫūiyanza nu=mu idālaui parā* UL *tarnāi āššaui=ia=mu parā tarnan ḫarzi* KBo 5.8 i 12–14 (Annals of Mursili II, CTH 61, NS), ed. by Götze 1933: 148–9; the use of the verb *auš-/au-/u-* hints at individual reading rather than an adhortation to a scribe to read Mursili's account out loud (*peran ḫalzae-*) before an audience (see Chapter 12.7).

[27] *nu* ^{URU}*Uraš kuiš* URU-*aš* [*ŠA* KUR ^{URU}(*Āzzi* IGI-*ziš*)] *auriš ēšta nu=kan nakkī pēdi* [*aš*(⸢*anza nu ku*⸣*iš kē* *TUPPA*$^{\text{ḪI.A}}$)] ⸢*ištamašzi*⸣ KUB 14.17 iii 21–3 w. dupl. KUB 26.79 i 15–17 (Annals of Mursili II, CTH 61, NS), ed. by Götze 1933: 98–9, cf. Cancik 1976: 54, and Gilan 2005: 364. Another second person singular (twice) can be found in KUB 19.37 ii 31–32 (CTH 61, NS; ed. by Götze 1933: 170–1), but this passage as a whole (KUB 19.37 ii 20–34, ed. by Götze 1933: 168–171) with a surprising third person singular for Mursili II himself may have been lifted out of a treaty-like document and therefore may have no bearing on the issue of dissemination discussed here.

Whereas the first passage could be addressed to an individual reader the second points to his works having been read out loud ("whoever *hears* these tablets") at certain occasions. Unfortunately, however, Mursili II's compositions do not seem to have been a step in a longer development with an upward trend: some fragments have been identified as the possible vestiges of an annalistic work by Hattusili III[28] but, as far as preserved, they do not seem to meet the standard set by Mursili.

What we call Hittite historiography is thus a mix of very different compositions sharing the fact that they use the past to prove a point. The objective may be mere propaganda, it may be to acknowledge the debt to the gods in the king's achievements, or to persuade others of the correctness of certain political decisions. When issuing such decrees, like Hattusili I appointing Mursili I as his successor or Telipinu with his new succession rules and administrative reorganization, Hittite kings seem to have had an urge to root them firmly in the past. Although this is not surprising *per se*, the extent to which they did so is. Half of Telipinu's Proclamation is taken up by a historical prologue meant to persuade the reader or listener of the need for and legitimization of his reforms. Hattusili III spends about 95 percent of his Apology on the past. The problem is that whereas the public inscriptions on the one hand and compositions for more restricted audiences on the other (Hattusili I's Testament etc.) have a fairly obvious goal this is much less clear for Mursili II's "Deeds of Suppiluliuma" and his own Annals. The literary sophistication – if we may call it that – seems almost proportionately inverse to the size of the supposed public: the simple or even simplistic style of the publicly displayed inscriptions versus the syntactically far more complex and lively one of the compositions intended for court-internal dissemination only. In Mursili's case this led to some works that come close to true historiography: a recounting of the past on the basis of older written sources and composed as an entity for its own sake and without an at least too obvious agenda.

8.4 Treaties, Instructions, Letters, and Depositions

Treaties, edicts or proclamations, instructions, and loyalty oaths, as well as laws are the official communications of a state with obvious addressees and they are the typical products of a state chancellery. Our distinction between treaties, instructions, and loyalty oaths is a modern one. The Hittite language made no such distinction: they were all agreements termed

[28] Gurney 1997.

išḫiul or, literally, "bond," that is, a binding contract between two parties, usually bound by an oath to the gods. Such a bond could take many, often very different, forms depending on the contracting parties, from the carefully crafted parity treaty with an equal Great King (e.g., Egypt, Babylon) to the completely unilaterally imposed instructions addressed to the Hittite king's underlings. The compositions that go by the name of instructions seem to have been the product mostly of the Tuthaliya I–Arnuwanda I era around 1400 BC and reflect a further institutionalization of writing in an ever more complex bureaucracy. Several kinds of professional groups such as the royal bodyguard, the "mayors" of Hattusa in charge of the capital's security, commanders of border garrisons, or temple personnel are told how to behave in specific situations and to obey the orders laid down in the document. Although these instructions technically do not contain oaths to the gods there can be little doubt that these groups were sworn in. From the same general period we have a ritual describing the swearing-in ceremony of officers in the royal army. Using analogic and contact magic these oaths could be applied to any level of government officials:

> He puts wax and mutton fat in their hands, throws (it) in the flames and says: "Just as this wax dissolves and just as the mutton fat melts, whoever transgresses the divine oath and betrays the [Ki]ng of Hatti, may he dissolve like wax and may he melt like mutton fat!" Then they say: "Let it be so!"[29]

The loyalty oaths[30] have often been referred to as instructions as well: here, too, people are confronted with situations and told how to conduct themselves but this time the addressees are those closest to the king, that is, courtiers and princes and all stipulations are about maintaining the king's privacy and security and every clause ends emphasizing the oath character:

> Or somebody says this: "These things are not laid down (in writing) on this tablet, so they should be allowed for me." Don't let that thing be, whatever conspiracy (it) is! It shall be put under divine oath![31]

29 *n=ašta* GAB.LÀL ^{UZU}Ì.UDU*=ia* *INA QATI=ŠUNU* *dāi n=ašta ḫappina peššiyazzi nu tezzi kī* GAB.LÀL *maḫḫan šalliyaitta* Ì.UDU*=ma=wa* GIM*-an marritta n=ašta kuišša* *NÎŠ* DINGIR*-LIM* *šarriēzzi n=ašta* AN[A LU(GAL KUR ^{U})]^{RU} *Ḫatti appāli dāi n=aš* GAB.LÀL*[-aš i]war šallittaru* ^{UZU}Ì.UDU*=m[a=w]a iwar marriētta<ru> apē=⌜ma⌝ daranzi apāt ēšdu* KBo 6.34 + KUB 48.76 i 41–5 ii 1–4 w. dupl. 797/v: 1–4 (apud Oettinger 1976: 138; Instruction for Army Officers, CTH 427, NS), ed. by Oettinger 1976: 8–9.

30 Thus rather than "instructions" with Starke 1995: 75–6.

31 *našma kī kuiški memai kēdani=wa=kan tuppi kē* INIM.MEŠ *UL* GAR*- ri nu=war=at=mu=kan parā tarnan ēšdu nu apāš memiaš lē ēšzi kuit imma kuit* ^{É}*kukupalatar* GAM *NÎŠ* DINGIR*-LIM* GAR*-ru* KUB 26.1 iv 49–53 (Instruction/Loyalty Oath, CTH 255, NS), ed. by Miller 2013: 306–7.

This is the final paragraph of the text and the king makes one last sweeping statement trying to include in the oath anything that might not have been mentioned on the tablet, on which the instruction text is written. More than just an *aide-mémoire*, the written version of the oath has become a document that can be referenced by both parties to the agreement and establishes record and proof thereof. The oath is administered orally but the written record is an integral part of the process and proof that it has taken place. Writing has taken over memory.

While decrees, edicts, instructions, and loyalty oaths are the official outcome of government actions with a character that is meant to be definitive, the several hundreds of letters that have come down to us form a much more fluid and at the same time rich and intriguing genre detailing daily policy and regular written communication.[32] Apart from the incoming correspondence from foreign courts, in particular the extensive exchange between the Egyptian court of Ramses II and his Hittite addressees Hattusili III and Tuthaliya IV, most letters concern domestic state business between the king and his subordinates.[33] An especially fascinating corpus is that found in the 1970s at Maşat Höyük, in the Hittite days a settlement bordering on Gasgaean territory to the north of Hattusa. The ninety-eight letters found there attest to the considerable nervousness of the Hittites stationed in the town vis-à-vis the local Gasgaeans who, desperate because of ongoing droughts, raided the storehouses and wreaked havoc in the countryside. As I have argued elsewhere, the letters between the Hittite Great King traveling in the area and his commanders and between the army officials among themselves were written around 1375 BC within the span of probably a single year, just before the site was destroyed.[34] It shows how fast communication at government level could travel and at the same time the ephemeral character of the correspondence. The fact that in none of the other provincial sites similar correspondence has turned up underscores the unique and short-term character of the situation: the raids and attacks had created an emergency that required the king's and his officers' immediate presence in the area as well as the briefest of communication lines.

It is no surprise that overall our letters date to the later thirteenth century only and that no copies were made. The only real exception concerning duplicates among the letters is the one from Tuthaliya IV (ca. 1240–1210 BC) to the high Assyrian court official Babu-ahu-idinna, of which fragments of three copies are known.[35] Not only do we have duplicates here, it

[32] Weeden 2014a. [33] Hagenbuchner 1989b, Edel 1994, Hoffner 2009. [34] van den Hout 2008a.
[35] KUB 23.103//92//KUB 40.77 (CTH 178.1, NS), see Hagenbuchner 1989a: 9 n. 17, ed. 1989b: 249–60 w. lit., and Hoffner 2009: 324–7.

is also a Hittite translation of, or draft for, a diplomatic letter that must have been sent in Akkadian. Moreover, two of the three are preserved on so-called *Sammeltafeln*, tablets, on which different but related compositions are brought together as in a dossier.[36] The other letters on the same tablets likewise belong to the correspondence with the Assyrian king. What we have here is part of the "Assur file" kept in the tablet collection of the Hittite chancellery for ready reference in a time of high tension between the two countries.[37] Although in general an ephemeral, short-lived genre, letters could be kept as long as their contents were important, which could have ranged from several days or weeks to years, decades, or even more before being discarded. The latter no doubt explains some of the older letters dating to around 1400 BC found in the late thirteenth century storerooms at Hattusa.[38]

Similarly ephemeral but of a more legal-administrative character are the court depositions. They contain the statements and affidavits of defendants and others involved in lawsuits and were probably used as the necessary records during trials. There they were read out to the king as evidenced by the passage in the Instruction for the Royal Bodyguard quoted earlier (Chapter 5.8). This points to their primary function of *aide-mémoire*, supporting an oral delivery, either when read out loud in their entirety or by individual paragraphs when the king rendered justice. Such a scene is described in the Instruction for the Royal Bodyguard that is probably to be dated around 1400 BC:

> [The bod]y guard who brings the defendants [steps] behind the Man-of-the-Gold-Spear. [When] the king asks for a case the body guar[d picks] it [up] and p[uts] it in the Chief Bodyguard's hand and tells the Chief Bodyguard [what] case [it is] and the Chief Bodyguard [tells the king].
>
> § Then the Chief Bodyguard goes and behind him [walk] two high officia[ls], either the Chief of the Charioteers or the Decurio, and they stand [behind] the Chief Bodyguard and one (person) holds himself on the outside, either a bod[yguard or] some high official. The body guard who

36 Hutter 2011.

37 The phenomenon of the parallel letter in the two-track correspondence with Egypt, which may be used as a duplicate for our modern purposes is, of course, different from that of the ancient duplicate. The two texts KBo 8.16 and KBo 28.54 presented by A. Hagenbuchner 1989a: 9 n. 17, as duplicates, probably also constitute such a parallel pair, see KBo 28: v-vi. The duplicates KUB 8.79//KUB 26.92 (see Hagenbuchner) do not display any features characteristic of letters, as Hagenbuchner herself remarks (1989b: 403). Their being duplicates may even plead against their identification as letters.

38 For these older letters see de Martino 2005.

> bring[s] the defendants runs right back and then steps behind the Man-of-the-Gold-Spear and they pick up the next case.[39]

In some cases, the sloppy handwriting of such depositions can be taken as evidence for recording on the spot. Larger multi-column tablets in a more careful hand were probably compiled on the basis of such records.[40]

With just a few exceptions and despite their official character the above texts have all come down to us without seal impressions. Yet manuscripts of treaties, for instance, speak of sealed copies. Was there something like "state archives" that we have not found yet? As we will see in Chapter 11.2, in spite of some recent assertions to the contrary, the quest for an institution where such officially sealed copies might be expected has not been resolved. Surprisingly few Hittite tablets other than the charters show impressions of seals. Metal tablets deposited in temples that may have had sealed bullae attached to them were probably melted down in antiquity or the ruling elite took them with them when they gave up the capital around 1200 BC. Whatever happened, the material Maria Elena Balza has collected amounts to no more than ten pieces.[41] Some texts coming from Hattusa but found elsewhere[42] suggest that official records destined to go to an addressee may have been sealed but that did not apply as a rule to the copies that stayed behind in the tablet collections (the so-called *exempla*, see Chapter 12.6).

8.5 Religious Texts

In terms of numbers, the vast majority of Hittite documents fall under the category of religious texts, that is, texts that regulated the cultic calendar or

39 [^{LÚ}MEŠ]EDI *kuiš šarkanduš* [*widāezzi*] *n=aš* ANA LÚ.ŠUKUR.GUŠKIN EGIR-*an* [*tīēzzi māḫḫan=ma*] LUGAL-*uš* DĪNAM *wēkzi n=at* ^{LÚ}MEŠED[*I parā karpzi*(?)] *n=at=kan* ANA GAL MEŠEDI *kiššarī d*[*āi n=at kuit*(?)] DĪNU *n=at* ANA GAL MEŠEDI *memai* GAL MEŠEDI*=ma* [LUGAL-*i memai*(?)] § *namma* GAL MEŠEDI *paizzi* EGIR-*ann=a=šši* 2 $^{LÚ.MEŠ}$BEL[UTI *iyanta*] *mān* GAL $^{LÚ.MEŠ}$KUŠ$_7$ *našma* UGULA.10 *n=at* ANA GAL MEŠEDI [EGIR-*an*(?)] *aranta araḫze=ya=z* 1-*aš ḫarzi mān=aš* ^{LÚ}ME[ŠEDI *našma*] BELU *kuiški nu šarkantīuš kuiš* ^{LÚ}MEŠEDI *widāezz*[*i*] *n=aš* EGIR-*pa=pat piddāi n=aš paizzi* ANA LÚ ^{GIŠ}ŠU-KUR.GUŠKIN *tīēzzi n=ašta namma* 1 DĪNAM *parā karpanzi* IBoT 1.36 iii 1–11 (Instruction for the Royal Bodyguard, CTH 262, OS), ed. by Güterbock & van den Hout 1991: 22–5.

40 Werner 1967: 1.

41 Balza 2012 presents (besides the charters) ten sealed tablets from Boğazköy-Hattusa. The piece Bo 69/200 (Balza 2012: 91–2), formerly associated with the treaty tablet KBo 28.108+, has now been suggested to come from a charter, see Chapter 4 n. 9, the treaty of the Hittite king Tahurwaili with Eheya (KBo 28.108). Two other sealed fragments (KBo 28.65 and KBo 28.82) stem from letters in Akkadian and are therefore not necessarily representative of Hittite sealing practices. With its (traces of) cylinder seals KBo 44.7 may be an import rather than a genuine Hattusa product. On the other hand, we may add KBo 62.32, for which see n. 101.

42 van den Hout 2007a: 393 w. n. 34.

otherwise primarily deal with the metaphysical world. The so-called *festival texts* make up about 40 percent of the entire preserved Hittite text corpus and offer scenarios of cultic celebrations of all kinds. As put by Daniel Schwemer:

> The texts have to be understood as records of the management of the cult within the context of a state in which the correct observance of the cult was regarded as one of the essential responsibilities of the king and in which, consequently, the organization and supervision of major cultic events was entrusted to the royal administration and its scribes.[43]

Mostly these events were regularly returning ones like the "Great Festival" held once every six years, or more often those that dotted the annual cultic calendar like spring and fall festivals. In addition, there were, for instance, festivals of "thunder" and celebrations for specific deities that may have been held at particular times during the year. Other such texts may have had a more incidental character surrounding special occasions like the inauguration of a new king or the death of a member of the royal house. All compositions contain a large ritual component and are in German often appropriately called *Festrituale* or *Kultrituale*. The indigenous Anatolian mythological tales could be integral parts of cultic festivities and sometimes their scenario-like structure suggests they were acted out, sung, and recited.[44] The same is true for almost all of the texts in languages other than Hittite. Hattian[45], Palaic[46], and Luwian[47] compositions are usually preserved embedded in Hittite festival scenarios. Palaic and Luwian texts are mostly incantations with mythological inserts and they were part of Hittite cult practices. Especially intriguing are the few lines of Luwian inserted in a litany of deities. They read like catch phrases for longer compositions and some even have an almost epic ring to them:

> [Ne]xt he/she drinks to the Sun Deity of Istanuwa (singing in Luwian): "The [s]torage jars are good (and) deep. Come [d]own from the hump-backed mountains!" . . . Next, he/she drinks to (the deity) Suwasuna (singing in Luwian): "They came home from steep Wilusa."[48]

43 Schwemer 2016: 12. 44 Bryce 2002: 212–13, Alaura 2011: 19–20.

45 For the most recent overview of Hattian studies see Soysal 2004.

46 For the text corpus and interpretation see Carruba 1970 and 1972.

47 For the text corpus see Starke 1985, for the lexicon Melchert 1993; see also Hawkins 2003: 138–9.

48 [EG]IR≈ŠU dUTU URU*Ištanuwa ekuzi≈pat* [*š*]*uwatra wāšu ala waddati*[*t*]*ta* [*z*]*anta ḫuwalpanati ār* § . . . § EGIR≈ŠU d*Šuwašunan ekuzi aḫḫatata alati awenta wilušati* KBo 4.11 rev. 39–41 and 45–6 (Festival from Istanuwa, CTH 772, NS), translit. Starke 1985: 340–1. For the translation of rev. 40–1 see Goedegebuure 2010: 311. In the translation of *aḫḫatata* I follow Yakubovich 2012 (for this particular passage see there p. 329).

As convincingly shown by Birgit Christiansen in a comparison with, among others, the *missale romanum*, the character of these cult texts is that of manuals to be pulled from the shelves of the tablet collections whenever the time neared for one of the cultic celebrations or when the need arose in order to secure a correct performance.[49] The latter would please the gods as ultimate addressees and would as a consequence benefit the king as embodiment of the country's wellbeing. These manuals were written for an audience or readership that was intimately familiar with the Anatolian cultic rites in general and there was no need to explain technical terms. Such cult rituals were logistically complex and could last anywhere from several days to over a month. Just going by institutional memory of how it was done the last time around simply might not suffice and non-compliance risked divine anger. An interesting illustration of local and probably oral traditions, state intervention, and the role writing played can be seen in a text concerning the cult for the Goddess of the Night. Temple personnel had started changing the liturgy, apparently to the dismay of the central administration:

> It happened that the clerks and the temple personnel had started to change them (i.e., the cult regulations) so I, Mursili, Great King, reversed them using a tablet.[50]

The explicit addition of "using a tablet" suggests that the local priesthood had deliberately or inadvertently strayed from tradition, perhaps based on deficient memory of how things were done in the past. King Mursili II then intervened and reinstated the old regulations while having them written down to make sure it did not happen again. It shows, once more, how writing had acquired a status of authority.

The practical character of these festival scenarios is particularly clear for the so-called KI.LAM festival[51] and the Hittite royal funerary ritual.[52] Both compositions comprise several distinct series: a) a basic and comprehensive script for the entire event in terms of time, place, people, their movements and acts, b) a "liturgy" containing mainly the texts to be spoken with brief directions for who is to say what, when, and where, and c) a props or ration list detailing per day or event, the ingredients needed for the festival or

[49] Christiansen 2016.

[50] *n=at* [m]*Murši*-DINGIR-*LIM*-*iš* LUGAL.GAL *tuppiyaz* EGIR-*pa aniyanun* KUB 32.133 i 6–7 (Expansion of the cult of the Deity of the Night, CTH 482, NS), ed. by Miller 2004: 312; for the translation "using a tablet" (differently Miller) see van den Hout 2016a: 430.

[51] Singer 1983: 40–51; for a complete edition see Singer 1984a.

[52] Kassian, Korolëv & Sidel'tsev 2002 for an edition of the entire text ensemble, for the different series see van den Hout 1994: 58–9.

ritual. Besides their prescriptive character many such texts were kept for the long term, sometimes for several centuries, copies were made, and new redactions drawn up to reflect changes in the cult. Retaining older copies created a history that could be checked when things went wrong and would allow going back to earlier procedures if considered beneficial. In essence, these texts are part of the state administration regulating and maintaining the cult as the ultimate duty towards king and state. As we will see in Chapter 12, the meticulous care taken in establishing the texts that prescribed the cult bespeaks their importance to the state apparatus. The Appendix to Chapter 12 serves as a representative sample for what such cult rituals look like.

The Hittite state also kept an eye on cult performances throughout the realm, that were not necessarily part of the state cult and in which the king did not play any role. Given the general attitude to incorporate and support such local religious traditions, regular inspections were carried out. These were laid down in written reports known as cult inventories that commented, for instance, on the way a certain cult was performed or on the state of temple buildings rituals were conducted in. While cult rituals were organized by deities and their liturgies and were constantly updated and edited in accordance with the king's role in the official religion, cult inventories were reports drawn up town by town. These were purely administrative records whose life expired once the next inspection came around or when the changes ordained from the capital on receiving the report had been implemented. As a result, and as opposed to the cult rituals, few duplicates were made and in general the texts therefore count as semi-current records (see Chapter 12.2.2). For the same reason the preserved majority of such texts is late. Some preserved older cult inventories and the Instruction for the Commanders of Border Garrisons, however, evince that this was standard practice and that they must have been an essential tool in keeping up the kingdom.[53]

Hymns and prayers, rituals, oracles, and vows were likewise part of the administration. The self-preservation of the state called for a "holistic" approach to life's adversities and perhaps life in general.[54] There was a clear understanding of what the regular course of life should be. Maintaining the cult calendar with all the festivals, their rituals and acted-out myths was essential to maintain a healthy balance. Every deviation from this course was treated as an imbalance in relations between gods and men. This imbalance was usually regarded as self-inflicted and its cause could be

[53] For all this see Cammarosano 2018. [54] Singer 2002: 2.

recent but might also lie back several generations. The epidemic, for instance, that ravaged Anatolia in the later fourteenth century BC and may have counted Suppiluliuma I and his immediate successor Arnuwanda II among its victims was the subject of a series of prayers by Mursili II. In them he describes how he consulted oracles to uncover the cause of the divine wrath that had brought this disaster upon him. In the end three transgressions were established that all happened during his father's lifetime when Mursili was very little or had not even been born yet.

Oracles, prayers, vows, and rituals were typical ingredients of the Hittite reaction in such situations and Mursili professes himself ready to do anything to stop the plague. The first step in the Hittite mind was always to contact the gods and to try and determine what the cause of the problem was. The means of communications was the oracle. Through several different techniques the gods' opinion could be investigated. The event in question was a clear sign of divine anger, so what deity was angry and why, and how could they appease the divine power again? The answer could be the performance of a ritual, it could be a vow to give, for instance, something valuable once the normal order of things had been restored, a promise to set things straight again or a combination of actions. During the oracle procedures scribes recorded the priest's questions and deity's answers on the spot. Afterwards the "conversation" was entered in what one might call ledgers but once the emergency, for which the oracle had been undertaken, had passed the document was no longer of use and was thrown out. No copies for future reference were necessary and apart from a few exceptions we have later thirteenth century oracle records only.[55] Similarly, the texts we refer to as vows record the royal family's promises to the gods and they could be destroyed as soon as the promises were fulfilled. Again, we seem to have only late thirteenth century vows and no copies are attested.[56]

Prayers, it seems, could accompany the entire process at any time. As opposed to vows, prayers were kept, copied, and compiled.[57] The oldest prayers are clearly dependent on Mesopotamian models. These models

[55] For older oracle texts in the Hittite tablet collections see van den Hout 2001.

[56] For this genre see de Roos 2007, Burgin & van den Hout 2016. The one exception, the so-called Vow of Queen Puduhepa (ed. by Otten & Souček 1965), with its many duplicates is atypical. It contains a long and detailed listing of households with the number of persons, their names, and cattle owned by them. The queen promises to hand over the households to the service of the goddess Ishtar and the list reads like a census record; for an economic interpretation of this text see Burgin 2016: 204–81.

[57] On prayers see Lebrun 1980, Singer 2002, and Haas 2006: 245–71; for the compilation of prayers using older examples specifically see Singer 2002: 13–14 and van den Hout 2007b.

were adapted to the Hittite pantheon and the need of the situation and over time they seem to gain a character of their own. They were filed to serve as models for ad hoc compositions in times of need. This is illustrated by a hymn to the Sungod that we find used in various forms in at least five different prayers.[58] It needs to be stressed, though, that it is often difficult to tell exactly how free Hittite adaptations were if we do not have the immediate forerunners. It has become increasingly clear, for instance, that literary motifs in the Hittite prayer to the Sungod owe more to Mesopotamian forerunners than was hitherto assumed.[59] Hittite originality often only goes as far as the uncovering of the next Mesopotamian parallel.

Finally, dramatic enactments of mythological tales like the popular Disappearing Deity gave voice to the Hittites' worries and anxieties and could help restore a sense of unity in times of distress.[60] According to these tales a god or goddess would now and then withdraw from the world in anger and go into hiding bringing nature and life to a complete standstill and plunging the human world in turmoil. A search for the missing deity is put on and once found he or she is coaxed to return with offerings and gifts so that normal life can resume again.

8.6 Scholarly Texts

The mentioned urge for self-preservation of the state revolved in Anatolia largely around the person of the king. Many a Near Eastern ruler employed literate individuals to collect and maintain a corpus of compositions with wisdom that might benefit him or his immediate family. Hittite kings were no different. As put by Gary Beckman, at their behest "magical rituals . . . were collected from practitioners, resident in various towns throughout the Hittite realm, apparently to make their recommended procedures available to magic specialists attending the royal family, should one of its members suffer from any of the relevant problems."[61] Besides coming from Central Anatolia itself many ritual compositions stem from Arzawa in the west or Kizzuwatna in the southeast. These texts usually start with the name of the ritualist as the "author" of the procedure ("Thus (speaks) Mr./Ms. So-and-so, diviner from . . . "). Were these real persons known to the scribe who

58 Singer 2002, 30–1, 44–5, 49–50. 59 Wilhelm 1994a: 65–6, and Metcalf 2011.
60 Bryce 2002: 211–15, Haas 2006: 103–15.
61 Beckman 2013: 292; similarly, already Oppenheim 1960: 413 ("a reference library geared to the needs of the diviners and those specialized practitioners of magic who were responsible for the spiritual security of kings and important persons").

recorded the text or were they legendary figures? Also, how the actual collecting worked remains unclear. Were there local oral traditions and did Hittite scribes travel the country recording rituals along the way? Did they interview specialists in or from these parts of Anatolia and use their notes to compose the rituals in their names? Or, were there local written traditions that were then brought to Hattusa and copied? Given the absence of any locally found evidence of written culture in either region, the latter option is not very attractive right now.[62]

Along with the necessary ingredients the rituals describe the magical acts to be performed for all kinds of situations that were considered to have disturbed life's equilibrium. These can be physical (e.g., a bodily illness), or psychological problems (e.g., quarrels within the family), or ones that we might describe as psychosomatic (e.g., temporary speech impediment after a traumatic experience), they may have to do with unfortunate events like a murder, witchcraft, the defeat of an army, or with behavior deemed undesirable in Hittite society like homosexuality. Mostly such phenomena were associated with divine reactions to human wrongdoing that had caused an imbalance, a defilement of a person or place, and rituals were a way of restoring the equilibrium and regaining a sense of purity. As we will see (Chapter 13), these compositions were collected, transmitted, and studied by individuals whom we should call *literati* or scholars rather than mere scribes. As argued in Chapter 13, it is in this context that we also need to see the so-called shelf lists (also known as catalogs or tablet inventories[63]). Originally, they were thought of as ancient catalogs of the Hattusa tablet collections, but they probably functioned in the upkeep of knowledge and training of future literati.

Given the likely original therapeutic goal, for which the "magical rituals" were kept, their character must have been prescriptive, at least initially. But over time the wisdom collected in these texts may have been viewed as a form of cultural capital, maintained for its own prestigious sake. As we will see (Chapter 13), there is reason to believe that such texts became the object of memorization practices with the inevitable corruption of manuscripts due to memory lapses. As a result, the texts often seem to make little sense as manuals and their practical status has therefore been called into question and a more scholarly character proposed.[64] The academic or scholarly interest in these rituals does not totally exclude practical application, however. While many of the observed inconsistencies

62 For a full discussion of these questions see Miller 2004: 469–532.

63 For a full edition and discussion of these texts see Dardano 2006.

64 Christiansen 2006: 1–30.

turn out to be the effect of faulty memorization of the texts, evidence of their occasionally real use shows a pick-and-choose approach rather than a wholesale implementation of a single ritual. When, for instance, Mursili II was afflicted by what he describes as (temporary?) aphasia after a traumatic experience, detailed oracle investigations ordered him to conduct a scapegoat ritual that was subsequently conducted on the basis of tablets present in the capital's collections. A series of burnt offerings of birds accompanied the proceedings. The deity ascertained by the oracle as having caused the speech impediment had his main temple in Kizzuwatna and the ritual measures taken bear the hallmarks of Hurro-Kizzuwatnean magic. The resulting composition is a patchwork of historical passages and prescriptive sounding elements inserted from ritual scenarios kept in the tablet collections.[65] The fact that the same Mursili entrusted his ailing youngest son, the future Hattusili III, to the care of the chief scribe Mittanamuwa surely had to do with the latter's presumed familiarity with healing methods both domestic and foreign.[66] Who those scholars were, is a topic we will have to return to in more detail (Chapter 13).

Other compositions that we might range under the rubric of scholarship are the so-called lexical lists, the Sumerian and Akkadian compositions, and omens, all of them obvious imports from the Mesopotamian world. Lexical lists look like glossaries with columns giving Sumerian words and their Akkadian equivalents mostly in thematic groups like trees and wooden objects or animals and plants of different kinds.[67] Sometimes columns with Hurrian and/or Hittite were added. In Mesopotamia lexical lists are considered the staple and essential tool in a scribe's education. Students went from simple signs and sign sequences to more complex compositions. The lexical material from Hattusa belongs to the more difficult and advanced curriculum and is therefore unlikely to have been part of elementary scribal training. According to Niek Veldhuis their purpose was mostly that of reference without much practical educational value.[68] Rather, it "was a learned corpus . . . actively used and studied by highly trained scribes who were part of the power structure of the Hittite capital."[69] Giulia Torri's observation that "the words listed in the lexical lists found at Hattusa are scarcely reflected in the common production of

[65] van den Hout 2004. [66] Similarly, Hoffner 2009: 9.

[67] For a detailed overview of lexical lists in the Hittite tablet collections see Weeden 2011a: 91–131, Veldhuis 2014: 271–9, and Weeden 2017.

[68] Thus apud Weeden 2011a: 129–30; see also Weeden's own remark (2011a: 90) that "the nature of the lexical lists found thus far at Boğazköy is not at all that which we would expect from learner scribes."

[69] Veldhuis 2014: 278.

Hittite texts" underscores this.[70] That Hittite scribes sometimes struggled with the contents of lexical lists is vividly and almost comically illustrated by an entry in a so-called *erimḫuš*-list, where words of associated meaning are brought together in paragraphs. The first two columns give the Sumerian and Akkadian words, the third adds the Hittite equivalents. One such paragraph, for instance, has Sumerian, Akkadian, and Hittite terms for asking and investigating:

Sumerian	**Akkadian**	**Hittite**	
ÈN.TAR	*šâlu*	*punuššūwar*	"to ask"
ÈN.TAR.TAR	*šitâlu*	*punuškeuwar*	"to keep asking"
ÈN.TAR.RI.A	*uṣṣuṣu*	*katta=ššan arnumar*	"to investigate, subject to an investigation(?)"[71]

The same vocabulary has a paragraph with conjunctions but this time the scribe is clearly at a loss in the Akkadian column:

Sumerian	**Akkadian**	**Hittite**	
DU.GAM	mu ma mi	*mān*	"if, when"
LÚ	ḫu ḫa ḫi	*kuit*	"since, given that"
E.ŠE	lu la li	GIM-*an*	"when, as"[72]

Instead of inserting the corresponding Akkadian conjunctions, "in desperation"[73] the scribe inserts elementary sign sequences (mu ma mi etc.) as fillers or placeholders.

Among the Sumerian and Akkadian compositions those in Hittite can be more or less free adaptations of the original like in the case of the (Akkadian) *šar tamhari*, the "king of combat" epic about the exploits of Sargon, the legendary king of the Old Akkadian period. The same is assumed for the Hittite version of the Gilgamesh Epic. Compared to the "Standard Babylonian" twelve-tablet version known from the seventh century BC Neo-Assyrian library of Assurbanipal it reads as a faster paced retelling with special emphasis on parts that were considered more appealing to an Anatolian audience, reducing or leaving out some of the parts that would be more unfamiliar to them.[74] For the Gilgamesh epic the Sumerian version is separated by several centuries from the Hittite one, and the Neo-Assyrian Standard Version is based on a supposed but not preserved redaction of the twelfth century BC. As argued by Jörg Klinger, however,

70 Torri 2012: 130.

71 KBo 1.44 obv. 11–13 (Lexical List, CTH 301, NS), ed. by Güterbock & Civil 1985: 101.

72 KBo 26.20 ii 39–41 (Lexical List, CTH 301, NS), ed. by Güterbock & Civil 1985: 109; see also Klinger 2005: 112–3, Weeden 2011a: 92 n. 424.

73 Weeden 2011a: 92 n. 424.

74 Beckman 2001b: 157.

it may be the Hurrian rather than any Sumerian or Akkadian version that lay at the basis of the Hittite one.[75] As was the case with the prayers and hymns we need to be careful, though, in recognizing Hittite adaptations, as long as we do not have the forerunners.

To the group of scholarly texts also belong omen compendia, long lists of phenomena in daily life and their implications for the future.[76] They comprise, for instance, celestial observations of solar and lunar eclipses, teratological (i.e., relating to monster births and the like), calendrical, and medical omina or those concerning extispicy (e.g., liver models), dreams, or earthquakes. As their editor An de Vos states, with their combination of text and 3-D shape (Fig. 8.1), the liver models are a plausible teaching tool for would-be diviners.[77] All these texts go back to Mesopotamian examples and some have been identified as actual imported tablets. Many exist only in Akkadian, others have been translated into Hittite. Only the celestial omen texts show a certain degree of adaptation to the Hittite situation and there are indications that they were occasionally consulted.[78] The non-celestial ones, however, were almost never copied and show no real Hittite interference. These texts were not actively used among the Hittite elite. The few exceptions show that the reason for collecting them was, at least initially, the same as for the magic rituals mentioned earlier. One never

Fig. 8.1 Livermodel 59/k = KBo 7.7 (from de Vos 2013; copyright Akademie der Wissenschaften und der Literatur, Mainz).

[75] Klinger 2005: 113–23. [76] Riemschneider 2004. [77] de Vos 2013: 108.
[78] van den Hout 2003–2005a: 89 w. lit.

knew when they might come in handy. Also, Anatolian attitudes towards predictions differed fundamentally from those known from Mesopotamia. There, every phenomenon occurring in daily life that was out of the ordinary came with a fixed prediction. Compare the following omen found in Hattusa:

> When on the twentieth day (in the eighth month) the Moon (god) dies (i.e., eclipses): the Great King will die in battle.
>
> When on the twenty-first day the Moon (god) dies: plague in the country of Elam.[79]

The reference to Elam, the kingdom in western Iran, shows how such texts could be rather mechanically translated without adaptation to the local Anatolian situation. In Mesopotamia it made sense to keep long lists of such events and their accompanying predictions. When something occurred, experts consulted these lists and they could either prepare for the prediction to come out or resort to magic rituals to avert a negative result. For the Anatolians, on the other hand, anything negative happening was seen as revealing their own bad behavior at some point in the past but finding out the details was up to them. Through often-painstaking oracle investigations they had to detect what god they had angered, why the deity was angry, and what was needed to restore life's balance.

To the same group of foreign texts, finally, belong the monolingual Sumerian and Akkadian texts.[80] They are mostly hymns, wisdom texts (e.g., parables), incantations and spells, therapeutic rituals, and medical treatises. An interesting example of the latter is an Akkadian medical treatise published as KUB 37.1 with some Hittite and Luwian explanatory glosses. Recently, Federico Giusfredi has offered a new edition and suggested seeing the text as the product of Hittite higher education.[81] Earlier, the text had been interpreted as an exercise of a student on his way to become a professional scribe. Giusfredi raises the level: for him we are dealing with a "student in medicine, possibly looking forward to starting his career as a ^{LÚ}A.ZU [a kind of physician] in Ḫattusa."[82] The scribal hand is a learned albeit at times sloppy and raw one, as observed by Giusfredi. But why not raise it one notch further and see it as a scholar's product? Would a student insert Hittite and Luwian explanations and

79 [(*mān* INA)] UD.20.KAM ^{d}SÎN-*aš aki* LUGAL.GAL *zaḫḫiya aki* § [(*mān* INA)] UD.21.KAM ^{d}SÎN-*aš aki* KUR ELAM.MA ÚŠ-*an* KUB 8.1 iii 15–16 w. dupl. KBo 13.18 right col. 4–5 (Omens, CTH 532, NS), ed. by Riemschneider 2004: 66, 68.

80 CTH 792–819; for these see Klinger 2010 and Schwemer 2013.

81 Giusfredi 2012b.

82 Giusfredi 2012b: 61.

interpolations? We might as well be dealing with a textbook created by a Hittite specialist who knew Akkadian but was not always readily familiar with all the technical terminology. Note in this context also the fragment KBo 13.2 from the Ugu-mu lexical list with "some 250 human body parts as well as physical and physiological conditions."[83] This list comprises a Hittite column and even shows evidence of "scribes at Ḫattuša to synthesize knowledge learned from different sources."[84]

Jörg Klinger characterizes all these collections as heterogenous, incidental, and not indicative of any in-depth study.[85] Just as with the omina, here too we can recognize imports, that is, texts that were written elsewhere and then brought to Hattusa.[86] Besides mistakes and similar indications, the locally produced texts indicate that Hittite scribes quite regularly had a hard time understanding what they were about. The texts were probably collected and studied by the few people who worked with the Mesopotamian omens, epics, lexical lists and the like but because of their relative inaccessibility due to failing linguistic competence on the side of most Hittite scribes they were probably considered less useful and show little or no signs of having been adapted. Speaking of a school context may evoke associations with too much of an institutionalized situation but, as we will see (Chapter 13), there was a small group of what we might call more academically inclined and interested individuals who may have been responsible for the presence of these foreign compositions in the tablet collections. The fact, however, that the hard-core, monolingual Mesopotamian texts of tradition do not figure in the so-called catalogs or tablet lists (see Chapter 13),[87] probably shows that the involvement of these literati with these texts was little systematic and certainly less than deep.

The situation for the numerous Hurrian compositions is different.[88] As we saw, the later fifteenth century BC is characterized by an increase in Hurrian influence noticeable especially in the considerable corpus of monolingual Hurrian texts. There is some Hurrian omen literature from Mesopotamia and there are fragments belonging to the Gilgamesh epic suggesting a Hurrian intermediary for the Hittite version, as mentioned earlier. More genuinely Hurrian seem to be some isolated historical or wisdom literature fragments[89] and myths and epics like the Kumarbi cycle or the Tale of the Hunter Kešši. A relatively recent find is that of

[83] Cohen 2012. [84] Cohen 2012: 12. [85] Klinger 2010: 332. [86] Klinger 2010: 332, 335.
[87] Dardano 2006: 10.
[88] For a brief overview of Hurrian texts found at Boğazköy see Wegner 2007: 31–2 and see especially Campbell 2016 and de Martino 2017; texts are edited in the series ChS.
[89] Wilhelm apud Rieken 2009: 130–5.

a Hurrian–Hittite bilingual with historical and mythological episodes and parables.[90] Their composition may date back to the early sixteenth century BC but when and how exactly it came to Hattusa remains unclear.[91] While these Hurrian compositions seem to be texts of tradition, most are not. By far the largest group is represented by rituals, of which two subgroups show clear contemporary historical links. One is the corpus of so-called *itkaḫi-* and *itkalzi-* ("mouth-washing") rituals dating in their transmitted form to the Hurrian wave of around 1400 BC. Although they may have reached Anatolia in the late fifteenth century BC in the entourage of queen Nikalmadi, wife of Tuthaliya I, most of these rituals center around the (future?) royal couple Tuthaliya II (using his Hurrian name Tasmisarri) and Taduhepa.[92] The other subgroup deals with the composition of the *hisuwa*-festival and stems from the thirteenth century BC. Colophons state that it was queen Puduhepa, spouse of Hattusili III, who gave orders to assemble tablets of this group in Hattusa and to make new copies (see Chapter 13.12) but there is reason to think that this festival was never part of the regular state cult. Puduhepa herself came from Lawazantiya in Kizzuwatna as the daughter of a local priest of Ishtar and had married Hattusili when he was on his way back from the battle of Kadesh in Syria in 1275 BC.

Finally, there are the Hattian texts. As we saw in Chapter 1, following Petra Goedegebuure, we can envision the Indo-European Luwians and Hittites and the Hattians culturally merging and assimilating to a large extent during the (later?) third and earlier second millennium BC. In this process the Hittites largely appropriated the Hattian pantheon and its cult with some of its pertinent lexicon.[93] In what we can call typical Hittite fashion this appropriation also came with the recording of relevant Hattian literature. Mono- and bilingual compositions almost exclusively concern hymns, prayers, rituals, invocations, and myths.[94] With the demise of the Old Kingdom period Hattian religious compositions seem to have lost their prominent position. Hattian may well, however, have remained a living language in the countryside for a longer time but it is impossible to say at this point for just how long.

[90] Neu 1996, Wilhelm 2001. [91] Wilhelm 2001: 82.
[92] Campbell 2016: 296–8, see also Archi 2015b: 9 n. 13.
[93] On the process see Goedegebuure 2008 w. lit. [94] See the overview in Soysal 2004: 16–21.

8.7 Bookkeeping and Socio-Economic and Legal Administration

The biggest difference between the Mesopotamian written legacy and the Hittite text corpus is the dearth of socio-economic texts and legal documents. Whereas the majority of the Hittite compositions, that is, the religious texts, can be characterized as administrative in the sense that everything that had to do with the cult, from hymns and prayers to the logistics of religious rituals, was the purview of the state and that the state had a direct interest in the correct handling of cult practices, economic bookkeeping is almost completely lacking. Economic texts are understood here as accounts of people, goods, and whatever else that played a role in the business the state and private individuals were involved in. With legal documents I mean all contracts and other documented actions, between private individuals or between the latter and the state that were written down, often sealed, witnessed, and filed away. From Mesopotamia we have adoption records, census lists, consignment documents, contracts, court records, debt notes, disbursals, harvest records, land sale documents, memoranda, tax records, etc., hundreds of thousands of them. And if we turn our attention to the west, to the contemporary Mycenean kingdoms, we see economic bookkeeping only. Yet if we list comparable Hittite texts from 400 years of writing Hittite in Anatolia and out of approximately 30,000 texts and fragments this is what we have (Table 8.1):[95]

Table 8.1 *Hittite lists and bookkeeping texts*

65 lists of people and towns or settlements[96]
26 cadastral texts (the so-called *Feldertexte*)[97]
91 charters[98]
264 palace/store room inventories[99]
ca. 25 ration lists (Akkad. *melqitu*)[100]
1 sales document(?)[101]
66 tablet inventories

95 For a detailed listing of all the texts and their paleographic dates see the Konkordanz.

96 CTH 231–8; fifty-eight come from Boğazköy, seven from Maşat Höyük. Lists from Tel Afis, Tikunani, or Ugarit are not included.

97 CTH 239; two lists from Emar are not included.

98 CTH 222.

99 CTH 240–7, 250; two lists from Emar and Tel Afis are not included.

100 CTH 523 and those belonging to the KI.LAM festival (Singer 1984a: 102–19).

101 KBo 62.32; for lit. see KBo 62 *Inhaltsübersicht* vi, to which can be added Waal 2015: 24 (quoted as 2006/9). The fact that the fragment shows traces of cylinder(!) seal impressions makes this a unique find and import needs to be considered.

The lists excavated at Boğazköy and Maşat Höyük enumerate functionaries of the Hittite state, families, men and women, and villages or towns. What these lists were drawn up for is unclear. The cadastral records list fields with exact delineations of land parcels and indications of the amount of seed needed. The seed amounts may have worked as indicators of plot sizes and been used as instruments in determining levels of taxation.[102] In the context of these first two groups of records one should also mention the listing of households including personnel and cattle in the Vow of Puduhepa already mentioned as an outlier among the religious compositions. The charters or land deeds were discussed extensively in Chapters 5–7; for the tablet inventories see Chapter 13.14. The largest group of texts is that of palace or storeroom inventories, a stock taking of objects stored in chests, crates, boxes, bags, and other containers in the royal treasury. The latter term is appropriate because the objects described are invariably luxury items, not goods that went in and out on a daily basis.[103] The majority of these records from Hattusa were uncovered in the storerooms of Temple 1.[104] Two come from recent excavations at Kayalıpınar and Oymaağaç. The latter aptly illustrates storeroom procedures.

> [These] goods are (stored) in one chest. An [inven]tory tablet is included. It (i.e., the chest) is seal[ed] by me.[105]

According to the text in question, received goods were stored in wooden chests (^{GIŠ}*tuppa-*) along with a packing list. Subsequently, the contents of a number of these packing lists were entered into a ledger. In a final act, the chest (not the packing list or ledger, as variants make clear) was sealed.

The only records we have dealing with food and livestock are the ration lists that were part of the cult administration.[106] These texts detail allotments of food and beverages to the various groups of festival participants and may have been part of a redistribution system. Outside the explicit festival context, documents dealing with foodstuffs, beverages, and livestock are extremely rare. KBo 32.134, a fragment of a small label-like tablet, mentions some flour[107] and KBo 18.189 records the delivery of breads to

102 For the texts see Souček 1959a and 1959b, further see Paroussis 1985 and Tjerkstra 1992.

103 See also Mora 2012 and the link she makes with the sealings found at the *Westbau*, for which see Chapter 11.

104 van den Hout 2006: 84–7.

105 [*kī*=]*kan* UNŪTUM I-*edani* ^{GIŠ}*duppa anda* [*ḫati*]*wīš*=*kan* TUPPU *anda* GAR-*ri ammēdaza šiy*[*anza*] OyT 09/1 (Inventory), ed. by van den Hout 2010: 264 w. lit.

106 Singer 1983a: 141–70, and 1984: 102–18.

107 See KBo 32, *Inhaltsübersicht* vi "Lieferungs-Etikett?"

several individuals.[108] Maşat Höyük is better represented with the texts HKM 109, 110, 111, 113, 114 but, as mentioned above (§8.4), the situation there was not a normal one and the fact that similar records have not turned up at other provincial sites supports their exceptional status. One might say that the lists preserved at Boğazköy reflect a situation similar to the one found at Maşat, but that recycling of tablets was simply more systematic there.

The almost complete lack of economic and legal records, as already mentioned for Mesopotamia (adoption records, debt notes, etc.), cannot be explained that way. Evidence of private enterprise is close to zero. Moreover, as we will see in Chapter 12, the charters should probably be taken out of the list because they were kept for altogether different reasons, and the tablet inventories played no role in economic life. Scholars usually explain this surprising state of affairs in two ways. First, any state or institution that maintains a regular or even daily administration of routine matters recycles its ever-increasing records. Documents that are no longer relevant and administratively active can be thrown out to make place for those that still are. We have already seen how court depositions, oracles, vows, and cult inventories were administrative in character. This is confirmed by the fact that as a rule there are no copies or duplicates in these genres and that, besides the occasional exception, they date to the later thirteenth century BC. They were all expendable records that as soon as they had performed their function could be and were discarded. The ones we have represent the last administrative cycle whose regular destruction was prevented by the abandonment of the capital around 1200 BC by the ruling class. The same might thus be true of what economic or legal records have come down to us. Recycling does not explain, however, the total absence of records related to private enterprise, as one might expect them to be reflected in the state's tablet collections. For this, scholars have mostly resorted to the second explanation of writing on perishable materials such as wood or recyclable ones like lead.[109] According to some, the preferred script used in these cases would have been the Anatolian hieroglyphs instead of cuneiform.

The general distribution of long- and short-term records (see Chapter 12) and their dating shows that the Hittites did indeed recycle.

108 Otten 1958: 75 (referring to the text as unp. 228/p) and Siegelová 1986: 360.

109 See recently, for instance, Gilan 2007: 297–8, Payne 2015: 11, 66, 156.

Generally, the short-term records stem from the thirteenth century BC and one might reasonably assume that similar older records were once there but got discarded. But the dates of a significant number of the few texts we have in terms of economic records listed above do not fit the expectation that these documents should all or at least largely be products of the latest phase of the kingdom. For instance, of the sixty-five lists mentioned above fifty-eight come from Boğazköy/Hattusa and nine of those are paleographically older.[110] Among the ration lists or *melqitus* five display Older Script. This means that either recycling of records was not as systematic as we assume, or such lists were perhaps less than regular practice. As far as the assumed routine character of the administration is concerned, some lists arguably had a special one-time purpose instead of being a record of routine behavior. Not only do the storeroom inventories in general deal with luxury goods but, as convincingly shown by James Burgin, the so-called KASKAL-texts among them detail a one-time shipment that in its wealth could rival any consignment known from the courts in Egypt or Mesopotamia.[111] As for the lists of people, as Jana Siegelová has suggested, one of them from Maşat Höyük contains a selection of enemy chieftains as high-value detainees for blinding as a deterring punishment.[112] According to its editor Vladimír Souček the cadastral texts all belong closely together suggesting a one-time creation for the group as a whole.[113] Paleographically they belong in the thirteenth century BC.

The second line of reasoning to account for the absence of socio-economic administration invokes script carriers of perishable material such as wood or lead. We will discuss the philological foundations of the theory of wooden tablets in more detail in Chapter 10, but something can be said already here. Unless in very wet environments, wood does not preserve well in the Anatolian climate, and no such tablet has yet been found in its soil. Lead, on the other hand, sometimes does survive the ages and a single little rolled-up strip is known from Boğazköy. Hans Güterbock, who probably was the first scholar to mention it, suggested that Anatolian hieroglyphs might be inscribed on it but no one has ever been able to identify any and recent opinions as to whether there was ever

110 Konkordanz CTH nos. 231–8. The seventeen texts from Maşat Höyük (HKM 98–114) with their older ductus have not been counted here because they were part of the last year before the destruction of Maşat Level III.

111 Burgin 2016: 98–203.

112 Siegelová 2002; see also Marazzi 2016a who sees blinding as a measure of control of "low-level/unskilled agricultural laborers." The two interpretations are in my opinion not mutually exclusive.

113 Souček 1959b: 386.

any writing on it diverge widely.[114] The premise for this theory, that any complex state needs and has some kind of written economic administration, heavily depends on comparative evidence from, above all, Mesopotamia. The adage is "absence of evidence is not evidence of absence." In Chapter 1, I discussed some general methodological reservations concerning this principle. In this particular case the main question is why Hittite society chose to write exactly these missing records on wood or any other perishable substance when Mesopotamia did not and when they themselves wrote all other documents on clay. Moreover, what little has come down to us in terms of bookkeeping and administration was written on clay. I have already argued that much of that may have been quite unique and everything but routine but what about both the letters and bookkeeping from Maşat Höyük? They are purely ephemeral yet written on clay as well. As explained in Chapter 1, not every complex state necessarily has the kind of written micro-management, as we encounter it in Mesopotamia or in the Mycenean kingdoms, and until evidence to the contrary turns up it is an interesting challenge to try to explain the Hittite state without it.[115]

8.8 Cuneiform Text Corpora from Central Anatolia Outside Hattusa

Apart from some isolated exceptions the tablet collections from Hattusa were our sole source of texts from the Hittite kingdom until the early 1970s. Those exceptions came mostly from satellite settlements at the fringes of the kingdom, like Alalah, Emar, Tarsus, and Ugarit. Recently some have been added from Tell Afis, Tell Kazel, and Tell Nebi Mend.[116] Only two fragments had been unearthed near Hattusa: one at Alaca Höyük,[117] at

[114] See further Giusfredi 2010: 188 n. 370 ("it is now a known fact that the Boğazköy strip is anepigraphic"), Akdoğan & Hawkins 2011: 2 ("Although the inscriptions and signs have not been preserved very well, this strip proves that the Hittites of the imperial period already wrote on lead"), Weeden 2014b: 6 w. n. 26 ("Inspection of photographs . . . leads me to suspect that there may well be hieroglyphic signs written on it"), Payne 2015: 122 ("das Publikationsphoto (. . .) lässt keine weitere Beurteilung dieses Fundstückes zu").

[115] See Palaima 2001: 154 on the Mycenean kingdoms (" . . . I would like to emphasize here modalities of transactions that must lie behind the records we possess, but which the central administration has no need to keep in written records. There must have been, in this still primarily oral culture with a very specialized and narrow form of literacy, considerable reliance on traditional transactional arrangements that may never have been recorded in writing. The continued use of uninscribed sealings or minimally inscribed sealings is best understood in this way").

[116] For more information, including maps and bibliographical references, on each of the sites mentioned in this section see: www.hittiteepigraphs.com.

[117] ABoT 64.

some 25 km distance from Boğazköy, to which after several decades of excavations one piece has been added now[118], and one surface find from Maşat Höyük in 1943. All these documents were either drawn up by Hittite officials living in those places or they were sent from the Hittite capital. Up to the present day the only texts that did not originate within the sphere of the Empire are the two letters found at Tel-el-Amarna (Egyptian Akhetaten) in Egypt.[119] One of them is the letter sent by Tarhunaradu, king of Arzawa during the reign of Amenophis IV, also known as Akhenaten (ca. 1375 BC). The Hittite Empire was on the verge of collapse and the Arzawan king sought to further capitalize on its vulnerability by proposing a marriage alliance with the Amarna Pharaohs. Without access probably to people with enough knowledge of Akkadian to compose a missive in that language, the Arzawans resorted to Hittite. The other document is probably the Egyptian answer, which either was never sent or was kept as a copy of the message that was sent.

Since the 1970s this situation has changed quite drastically. Thirty years after the chance discovery of 1943, archaeologists returned to Maşat Höyük and uncovered in 1973 the corpus mentioned earlier. More recently other collections have come to light. With the exception of Ortaköy boasting three to four thousand fragments, most of these are small collections, with thus far less than a hundred pieces each (Kayalıpınar, Kuşaklı) or just a few incidental text finds (Alaca Höyük, Büklükale, Eskiyapar, Inandık, Kuşsaray, Oymaağaç, Uşaklı Höyük, Yassı Höyük). All are located in Central Anatolia (see map p. xxi). The texts from these sites illustrate the low degree of diffusion of the cuneiform script or, put differently, the high degree of centralization and appropriation of the script imposed by the capital. Without exception the records found at these sites are the products of the same administration, whether they stem from the fifteenth, fourteenth, or thirteenth century BC and all display the familiar Hittite cuneiform.[120] Small groups of administrators and scribes traveled in the service of the kingdom representing the interests of the central government at Hattusa. And it is not just the same type of script that we know so well from the capital that we find time and again but also the same genres.[121] Cult rituals with sometimes direct parallels to versions attested at Hattusa

118 B. Dinçol 2017.

119 A possible third foreign document in Hittite and in Hittite cuneiform might be KUB 26.91, perhaps coming from the court of an Ahhiyawan/Mycenaean king: see Beckman, Bryce & Cline 2011: 134–9.

120 Cf. Weeden 2011c: 117 ("So unified is the script of finds of Hittite texts from outside Boğazköy in central Anatolia, that one might assume a centralised education in writing") and 2016b: 157.

121 See the table in Weeden 2011c: 118.

were clearly exported from there. At Kuşaklı two tablets of an original series of four describe a spring festival to be celebrated when the Hittite king visits the town.[122] Cult inventories of local religious ceremonies and mythological compositions attest to the interest of the capital in local religious traditions. The one tablet dating to the later Level I at Maşat Höyük belongs to the myths about Disappearing Deities with clear parallels to versions known from Hattusa.[123] Letters show administrative–political contacts. Oracle reports evince the same techniques and formulary as used there. Not surprisingly, as the temporary royal residence during the 1370s(?) BC, Sapinuwa/Ortaköy displays the widest range of genres. Its collection reportedly comprises letters, prayers, magic rituals, and festival scenarios as well as several bilingual texts,[124] lexical lists (Sumerian–Akkadian–Hittite),[125] Hittite–Hattian foundation rituals,[126] and some Hittite and Hurrian ritual fragments.[127] Bookkeeping, on the other hand, in the stricter sense of the word as we have a few of them from Maşat Höyük, is rare, confirming that the situation at Hattusa is no anomaly. None of the sites bear any evidence of literacy or a written tradition independent from the central authority at Hattusa. The most unusual complex is still that of Maşat Höyük with its large cache of letters and lists.[128] The uniqueness of this find underscores the emergency situation in which it arose.

8.9 Conclusion

The continued stability of the Hittite cuneiform over the four centuries of its life as well as its limited scope and diffusion throughout Central Anatolia strongly speak in favor of the centralizing force of the Hittite state. The state kept the technology of writing to itself and felt no urge or need to spread its use.[129] The lack of any substantial development over time

[122] KuSa 1 and 2, see Wilhelm 1997: 9–15. [123] Güterbock 1986. [124] Süel 1992 and 1999.
[125] Süel & Soysal 2003. [126] Süel & Soysal 2007 and Soysal & Süel 2016.
[127] Ünal 1998, 45–65, and 2001.
[128] Only one tablet (HKM 116) was assigned to the later Level I, dated to the thirteenth century BC. The main edition of these texts is HKM (hand copies of all 116 pieces of the 1973–1981 excavations) and Alp 1991 (transliteration, translation, commentary, and glossary of the letters HKM 1–96); for HKM 116 see the edition of H.G. Güterbock 1986. For the earlier found fragment published as ABoT 65 see Güterbock 1944: 389–405. The administrative records HKM 98–114 were edited by del Monte 1995; for the one oracle fragment see van den Hout 2001: 425–6.
[129] Baines 2007: 39–43 for centralization as responsible for the initial very slow spread of writing in Egypt during the Old Kingdom (ca 2575–2150) (39: "Writing was a centrally controlled facility in a state that was focused on its chief representative, the king, and became ever more highly centralized in its first few centuries.").

was initially one of the main arguments for modern scholars in thinking that the Hittite corpus in its entirety was the product of just a century or at most a century and a half (i.e., 1350–1200 BC) of scribal work.[130] Even now that it has been recognized that the Hittite tablet collection shows a far greater time depth extending back to perhaps 1600 BC, the paleographic changes observed are relatively slight and concern a limited number of signs only. Had the script seen a widespread use in larger layers of the population one would have expected a greater variety of forms.[131] In this respect the Hittite cuneiform may be compared typologically with that current in the Ur III period (ca 2100–2000 BC): in spite of its tens of thousands of administrative records the Ur III cuneiform was highly institutionalized, showed very little variation or development and was hardly different from the style used in monumental royal inscriptions.[132] Only during the subsequent Old Babylonian period was "writing [...] unleashed from its institutional reins and put to use in a much wider fashion"[133] resulting in all kinds of innovations and variants. Whether such a fate would ever have been in store for the cuneiform script in Anatolia remains pure speculation, obviously, but its basic restriction to the Hittite language as the Kingdom's official medium of internal communication and the simultaneously gradual demise of that language as a living tongue make such a sequel unlikely. Instead, the collapse of the state structure around 1200 BC unleashed Luwian-speaking forces that had been around already for a few centuries and had been addressed by the state in the Anatolian hieroglyphs, to which we will turn now.

[130] van den Hout 2009a: 12–13.

[131] Cf. for the situation in early Rus Franklin 2002: 100 ("Why were the letter forms so stable and limited? To risk a rash generalisation: because writing in Rus was not in much demand in contexts where other types of lettering tend to flourish. Semi-uncial and especially minuscule and its cursive forms tend to flourish where there is a significant demand for writing to be produced quickly and in large quantities, or with greater economy of time or materials: typically, for the production of administrative documents, or in books for private reading and scholarship.").

[132] Veldhuis 2011: 71–3, 2012. [133] Veldhuis 2011: 72.

CHAPTER 9

The New Kingdom Hieroglyphic Corpus

9.1 Writing for the World

In Chapter 8 we saw how the Anatolian hieroglyphic script probably developed gradually over the course of the Old Kingdom receiving a final impetus during the fifteenth century BC, perhaps during the reign of Tuthaliya I, when the Hittite kingdom regained its former power. The Hittite chancellery, as we may call it by now, had at long last shaken the habit of writing Akkadian for internal records and it has been suggested not without reason that if a nationalistic element was instrumental in this the creation of the Anatolian hieroglyphs as the kingdom's very own writing system may be seen in the same light. The cuneiform script was the common daily medium used by the state chancelleries for internal purposes mostly invisible to the population at large. But as soon as they left the confines of daily administration and showed themselves to the outside world either in the micro-monumental form of seal glyptics or the larger publicly displayed stone inscriptions they used the Anatolian hieroglyphs.

9.2 Seals

Judging by the available evidence the hieroglyphic script developed first and foremost through seal inscriptions that became ever more widespread during the fourteenth century and experienced an explosive growth during the thirteenth century BC. They contain names and for the most part logographically expressed titles and are thus not written in any identifiable language. That is, although names and titles may belong to a specific language (e.g., Tuthaliya is a Hattian name, Arnuwanda a Hittite–Luwian one) the seals do not have sentences with inflected verbs, nouns, and adjectives. Names and titles invariably appear in what we call "stem forms." At present the seal corpus comprises some 5000 impressions in clay as well as some of the original seals, with which impressions could be made.

LIS CONTRACTUS

Fig. 9.1 Hieroglyphic signs L.24 (LIS) and L.344 (CONTRACTUS).

The overwhelming majority of impressions come from Hattusa, about 700 come from identifiable places elsewhere or are of unknown provenance. Among the findspots we find all major and minor Central Anatolian Hittite centers represented. Seals and seal impressions have also been found on the fringes of the kingdom: on the west coast in Troy[1], in Tarsus on the southern coast, in Emar, Karkamish, and Ugarit, and as far as Korucutepe east of the Euphrates. Essentially, seals were a legal instrument functioning in a self-contained (in principle) system without the need for accompanying written documents and attesting to the correctness or validity of the objects sealed.[2] Such objects could be written documents where the seal owner vouched for the correctness of the wording and his agreeing to the document (compare the charters) or they could be goods, of which the quality or quantity were guaranteed by the seal owner. This is nicely illustrated by the incorporation of the (admittedly Iron Age) hieroglyph for "seal" ( SIGILLUM with its syllabic sound value *sa_5* acrophonically derived from Luw. *sasa*(*n*)– "seal") in two complex logograms (Fig. 9.1).

In the conventional system of Latin transcriptions, the signs are rendered as LIS "lawsuit" and CONTRACTUS "agreement, contract." The former shows two opposing and unconnected heads (LIS) whereas the stylized profiles (CONTRACTUS) of the latter have the two faces linked as if shaking hands on a successful deal.

9.3 Inscriptions Erected in the Public Sphere

As we saw in Chapter 7, the first attested public inscription is perhaps the so-called SÜDBURG inscription, if its contents are indeed to be ascribed to Suppiluliuma I around the mid-fourteenth century BC. Although a consensus on this dating seems to be building it does not qualify as *communis opinio* yet. The text commemorates the dedication of what it calls a DEUS.VIA+TERRA (literally "god.road+earth" where the + indicates

[1] Hawkins & Easton 1996.

[2] It is interesting to note that scribes never used seals to "sign" a tablet they had written. This goes to show that sealing was in the first place a legal action, not one of mere identification.

a ligature of the last two signs), a kind of chapel-like structure that was possibly seen as an entrance into the Netherworld:

> When (I did such-and-such . . .) in that year I built this sacred portal to the Netherworld.[3]

The "When – " part describes a series of military campaigns Suppiluliuma conducted during the year that the monument was erected. Some of these campaigns took place in the Lukka Lands in southwestern Anatolia, others perhaps in the more northern Pontic region known for their Gasgaean inhabitants. Despite its strongly logographic character there is no doubt that the language is Luwian.

It is not until the first quarter of the thirteenth century BC that we have the first securely dated monumental inscription in stone from either the final years of Mursili II or the reign of Muwatalli II (ca. 1295–1274 BC). This inscription, found at Aleppo, is almost completely logographic but the opening demonstrative *zaya* "this (temple)" pleads for its Luwian linguistic status. Over time the texts become longer and linguistically more explicit and it becomes evident that all are written in Luwian, not in Hittite. This reflects a sociolinguistic development visible already in its incipient stages in the Old Kingdom Hittite cuneiform texts. Luwian and Hittite speaking population groups had lived next to each other in Central Anatolia since at least the beginning of the historical period and Luwian influence on the Hittite language is manifest from the earliest texts onwards.[4] It is possible that the decimation of the Central Anatolian population during the epidemic that started at the end of Suppiluliuma I's reign and continued for two decades into Mursili II's, and the latter's subsequent mass deportation of – according to his own account – at least 80,000 people from western Anatolia, accelerated the process and must have changed the demographics in the center significantly.[5] Even if Mursili II grossly inflated the numbers for propaganda's sake (but see on this Chapter 8.3) it is good to keep in mind that Zsolt Simon puts his most recent estimate of Central Anatolia's population size during the New Kingdom at about 150,000.[6] These actions may have contributed to a shift in Central Anatolia's linguistic balance such that by the mid-thirteenth century BC Hittite was arguably spoken by a minority only or

[3] REL+*ra/i* . . . *zati* DEUS.VIA+TERRA *pati* ANNUS *izi* Südburg §§1a and 18, ed. by Hawkins 1995: 22–3.
[4] Melchert 2005, Rieken 2006, van den Hout 2007c [2006], Yakubovich 2010: 303–416.
[5] van den Hout 2007c: 241; but for criticism see Simon 2011a: 29–30. [6] Simon 2011a: 32.

was even reduced to an administrative language that no longer was anyone's mother tongue.

The group of about eighty hieroglyphic inscriptions from the period of the Hittite Empire mainly consists of building inscriptions, usually dedicatory in nature, and short epigraphs accompanying iconic representations of deities, kings, queens, and princes.[7] Many of these inscriptions have been inscribed on rock surfaces. Some take the form of stelae, others of reliefs as part of an architectural structure. Each king from Muwatalli II up to the last known king Suppiluliyama (II) is represented except for the briefly reigning kings Urhitessub/Mursili III and Arnuwanda III. As stated earlier, we may need to add Suppiluliuma I to the beginning of that list.[8] Prime examples of the building inscriptions are his SÜDBURG monument, the NIŞANTAŞ inscription for the funerary temple for Tuthaliya IV commissioned by his son Suppiluliyama, the waterworks of YALBURT[9], and the EMIRGAZI altars[10], both from Tuthaliya IV. In the rock sanctuary YAZILIKAYA in the immediate proximity of Hattusa short epigraphs serve as captions to the gods and goddesses lined up along the walls of the monument, representing the pantheon of the New Hittite kingdom.[11] To what extent the entire inscribed complex must be dated to Tuhaliya IV because of the three cartouches with his name remains to be seen. The self-representations of royalty found spread over much of Anatolia are often interpreted as boundary markers and/or territorial claims.[12] Geographically, the inscriptions range from the far west on the coast of the Aegean (KARABEL, LATMOS) through Western (ÇIVRIL, BEYKÖY) and Central Anatolia (YALBURT, BOĞAZKÖY) to the south (KARADAĞ, KIZILDAĞ) and southeast (ALEPPO).

9.4 Graffiti and Small Inscriptions on Objects

A small number of graffiti in Anatolian hieroglyphs of personal names accompanied by the sign L. 326 ("SCRIBA") are carved in some of Hattusa's

[7] Note that a few sites have multiple inscriptions: there are, for instance, over twenty BOĞAZKÖY inscriptions and five known by the name of EMIRGAZI. For a listing see Marazzi 1986: 105–20, for the BOĞAZKÖY inscriptions see Hawkins 1995: 121; for editions of most see Meriggi 1975: 259–331, and Hawkins 1995.

[8] Compare in chronological order the inscriptions SÜDBURG (Suppiluliuma I?), ALEPPO I (Mursili I/ Muwatalli II), SIRKELI (Muwatalli II), FRAKTIN (Hattusili III and Puduhepa), BOĞAZKÖY, EMIRGAZI I (A-D)-V, KARAKUYU, YALBURT, YAZILIKAYA (Tuthaliya IV), NIŞANTAŞ (Suppiluliyama).

[9] Poetto 1993, Hawkins 1995, 66–85, Karasu, Poetto & Savaş 2000.

[10] Hawkins 1995, 86–102.

[11] Bittel et al. 1975.

[12] On this see Seeher 2009; for a map see Hawkins 2003: 142–3.

temple walls.[13] Interpreted as advertisements for public scribes they have been one of the arguments in favor of a general need for literacy among the population in the Hittite kingdom; I will discuss the meaning of L.326 in the Excursus in Chapter 14.[14] Besides these public graffiti there are some inscriptions on metal objects like cups (compare the Silver Stag Vessel at the Metropolitan Museum of New York[15] or the Boston Fist[16]), bowls,[17] tools,[18] and weapons[19] but on the whole they are few and often difficult to date. Unfortunately, the provenance and archaeological context of these objects are rarely known.

Apart from the clay bullae with hieroglyphic signs stamped on them and the large inscriptions on stone, the use of Anatolian hieroglyphs directly written, that is, drawn in still moist clay, is positively rare. Hans Güterbock mentioned one bulla with incised signs (Fig. 9.6)[20] and there are a few known instances of hieroglyphs drawn in the surface of a clay tablet (Fig. 9.5).[21] The reason for this scarcity is not very clear. One might argue that for the round shape of many of the signs to be drawn with a stylus ending in a pointed tip clay is not an ideal script carrier. Yet the Linear B script from Greece with its frequently round shapes and sometimes cursive-looking signs was successfully written in clay. Some line drawings on Hittite tablets[22] (Figs. 10.1–3) and the few hieroglyphic signs just mentioned scratched on a bulla show that Anatolian hieroglyphs could successfully be applied to clay as well.

The same can be said, *mutatis mutandis*, of the comparatively less sophisticated character of the script: the restriction of the script to V and CV/CVC(V) signs leads to a significantly higher number of purely graphic vowels than when writing in the Hittite cuneiform (see Chapter 7.2). But this, too, does not prevent the script from expressing anything it wanted to

[13] Dinçol & Dinçol 2002.

[14] Recently (2015) four hieroglyphs painted or smeared on a wall were found at Kayalıpınar; see Müller-Karpe 2017: 73–7, who suggests seeing them as the "spontaneous graffito . . . of a proud architect" even though that part of the wall was very soon covered under piled up earth. The author dates the graffito to the period before 1400 BC and takes them to show "den Alltagsgebrauch der Hieroglyphenschrift bereits in dieser Periode" (77).

[15] van den Hout 2018. [16] Güterbock & Kendall 1995.

[17] Emre & Cınaroğlu 1993 and Hawkins 1993 and 1996 [1997]; for the several dating proposals see Chapter 7 n. 30.

[18] Bittel 1937: 21 w. Abb. 9, Tf. 13.1. [19] Dinçol 1989. [20] Güterbock 1942: no. 238.

[21] KBo 13.62 rev. (CTH 209, NS), see also Chapter 7.3; for a reading of the signs see Rieken apud Torri 2008: 779–80, see also Waal 2017: 297–9. Another example of signs on a clay tablet is Güterbock 1942: no. 239.

[22] Ünal 1989 and Waal 2017; see also already Forrer 1922a: 180 who wondered whether "der Abschreiber [i.e., of KUB 38.3] hier vielleicht seinen diktierenden Vorgesetzten verewigt [hat]."

Fig. 9.2 Drawing of a lion (KUB 28.4; copyright Staatliche Museen zu Berlin – Vorderasiatisches Museum, Foto: BoFN 00924).

Figs. 9.3 and 9.4 Drawing of a god(?) (KUB 20.76, left; copyright Staatliche Museen zu Berlin – Vorderasiatisches Museum, Foto: BoFN 00814) and two heads (KUB 38.3, right; copyright Staatliche Museen zu Berlin – Vorderasiatisches Museum, Foto: BoFN 00993).

and can therefore hardly have been a reason not to use the hieroglyphs on clay.[23] A possible reason might be that cuneiform signs are on average only about 4 mm high (occasionally even smaller) while still remaining perfectly legible making for an efficient use of one's writing space. Also, because they are lined up horizontally one sign next to another there is no need for rulings. This is not true of the hieroglyphic signs that seem to need a certain minimum height to remain legible while the larger signs are roughly twice the size of the cuneiform signs. If we can use the first millennium lead strips from Assur, Kululu, and Kirşehir as a way to imagine what daily records written in Anatolian hieroglyphs looked like, the height of the signs ranges from about 5 mm for the flatter signs (e.g., *la, tu*) to over 1 cm for the larger vertically shaped signs (e.g., REL, NEG, *za, zi, i, ia*, etc.).[24]

9.5 Conclusion

The reason most likely and fitting in view of the available evidence for the choice of script was the difference in language. Hittite with its cuneiform

[23] Inversely, there is no reason to assume that wax was less suitable a vehicle for writing cuneiform, as Seeher 2003: 8 and Weeden 2011b: 611 seem to suggest. My own (limited) experiment with a modern-made wax covered wooden tablet showed that it lends itself as easily to cuneiform as to hieroglyphic writing.

[24] See Chapter 9.

Fig. 9.5 Hieroglyphic signs on tablet KBo 13.62 (with cuneiform upside down!; copyright Akademie der Wissenschaften und der Literatur, Mainz).

Fig. 9.6 Bulla with various hieroglyphs drawn on its side (from Güterbock 1942: Tafel VIII 238).

script was the internal and official language of the kingdom and its ruling class while Luwian and its hieroglyphic script were the state's preferred medium for communication beyond those circles. Because of this the term *diglossia* has been applied to Hittite society, with Hittite being the socially H(igh) and Luwian the L(ow) linguistic variety.[25] While the majority of the population spoke Luwian and its dialects, Hittite was the language spoken and used by the ruling elite and its administration. In or during the thirteenth century BC Hittite may not even have been a real living language any longer but more of an official administrative one, mostly existing in only written form. On a script level one could describe the situation in the Hittite kingdom of the fourteenth and thirteenth century as one of *partial digraphia*.[26] This term is reserved for situations where one language is written in two scripts like the Runic and Latin alphabets for Old Norse or Nāgarī (or Devanāgarī) and (a variant of the) Arabic script for Hindi-Urdu respectively.[27] The choice for one or the other script is usually carefully delineated and may be determined by, for instance, social class, religion, or function of a text. Of course, in Central Anatolia we have two languages, Luwian and Hittite, and two scripts. Seals, however, bear only names and titles, the latter almost always logographically written, and as a consequence language has become neutralized in this domain. For a member of the ruling elite the Anatolian hieroglyphs clearly were the sole choice when ordering a seal. Using them in combination with cuneiform on the seal seems to have been a royal prerogative. Even though in the daily situation of spoken language Luwian may have been the L variety, the specific medium of the seal – and only this, which is why I add the modifying "partial"[28] – asked for hieroglyphs. Whether for aesthetic–artistic or social reasons (because the seal was going to be used beyond the circles the individual normally moved in), or a combination of the two remains to be determined. In the volume on *Biscriptality* Daniel Bunčić calls this *medial digraphia*, that is, the choice of script depending on the medium it is used on.[29]

Apart from the neutral area of seal glyptics the one-on-one relation between script and language is consistent: Anatolian hieroglyphs were

[25] van den Hout 2007c: 241–2, Yakubovich 2010: 416, Bunčić in Bunčić et al. 2016: 80.
[26] For the phenomenon of biscriptality and digraphia generally see Bunčić et al. 2016.
[27] On the "complex relationship between Hindi and Urdu" see C. Brandt in Bunčić et al. 2016: 149–58.
[28] Full digraphia could be used for the few instances where so-called Empire Luwian, normally written in hieroglyphs, appears in cuneiform.
[29] Bunčić in Bunčić et al. 2016: 81; his full characterization of the Anatolian situation is "medial digraphia with diastratic and diaphasic elements." Diastratic refers to social levels (H/L) and diaphasic to text registers; see Bunčić et al. 2016: 57.

never used to write Hittite. Cuneiform, on the other hand, could be and was used to write many different languages. The Hittite tablet collections, produced for the ruling elite by those in their service, present us with cuneiform texts in Hittite, Luwian, Palaic, Hattian, Akkadian, Sumerian, and Hurrian. The resulting restriction of Anatolian hieroglyphs and the Luwian language to public records, then, creates a problem vis-à-vis the wooden tablets, which many scholars assume were used to write hieroglyphs on and might even have been "used . . . for day-to-day administration and private documents."[30] The first to suggest this was probably Hans Güterbock in 1939 and the view is still popular today.[31] Some have claimed that cuneiform was written on them.[32] To be sure, wooden writing boards were used and one could claim that for pure bookkeeping records the language is inconsequential: it is mostly numbers and lists of words denoting objects. Both the cuneiform and hieroglyphic script could list many things in a purely logographic way, as the cuneiform palace inventories (see Chapter 8.7) indeed show. In the following example from one of those inventories all logograms are underlined:

> One large red (reed) container (on) lion feet, tribute; in (it) linen textiles from the land of Amurru; listed on a document. § . . . § One large red (reed) container (on) lion feet, tax from the town of Ankuwa; a number of textiles, listed on a document. Thus (orders) the queen: "When I will put (it/them) in the storehouse, they will record it/them on a tablet."[33]

Hieroglyphically written versions on wood have also been claimed for some of the festival scenarios where wooden tablets were supposedly used in the field since they weighed less. Given the consistent language dichotomy between cuneiform (Hittite) and hieroglyphs (Luwian) one is almost forced to assume that the Hittite scenarios on clay were written or, more appropriately, translated into Luwian when transferred to wooden tablets. It is true that certainly in the thirteenth century BC many administrators working for the government must have been bilingual Luwian–Hittite but switching from one language to another must have a reason other than just

30 Waal 2012: 310.

31 Güterbock 1939: 36, Payne 2008: 118–9, and 2015 passim, Waal 2011; for older lit. see Symington 1991: 115 n. 33.

32 Singer 1983: 40–1, Symington 1991: 115.

33 I ^{GI}PISAN SA$_5$ GAL GÌR UR.MAḪ IGI.DU$_8$.A *ŠA* KUR *Amurri=kan* GAD.ḪI.A *anda IŠTU* GIŠ.ḪUR GUL-*aššan* (. . .) I ^{GI}PISAN SA$_5$ GAL GÌR UR.MAḪ *MANTAT* ^{URU}*Ankuwa* ŠID TÚG *IŠTU* GIŠ.ḪUR GUL-*aššan UMMA* MUNUS.LUGAL GIM-*an=ma=wa* ŠÀ É.$^{\text{NA4}}$KIŠIB *teḫḫi nu=war=at tuppiaz* 𒑱 **anian***zi* IBoT 1.31 obv. 2–3, 12–15 (CTH 241, NS), ed. by Siegelová 1986: 80–3; see also Archi 1973: 215–6, Siegelová 2015: 244; the *Glossenkeil* preceding *anianzi* marks the indentation of the final line of the paragraph.

the material one writes on. The quote from Michael Clanchy's book *From Memory to Written Record*,[34] given above (Chapter 5.3), shows how medieval English clerks could easily shift back and forth between Latin, French, and English but they did so, depending on the audience and the occasion. In the Hittite case we are dealing with internal records where no change of audience seems to be called for. As Craig Melchert pointed out recently, this becomes decidedly unlikely in the case of an Old Hittite cult text, from a period when the hieroglyphic script had not yet developed into the later writing system. The statement in a NS copy of an OS tablet that it was written in accordance with the wooden tablet, would then imply the translation from the Old Hittite original into Luwian on the wooden tablet and back again in the New Kingdom.[35] Moreover, as we just saw, with the hieroglyphs taking up roughly twice as much space as cuneiform, the weight argument loses much of its attraction. Finally, if wooden tablets were used for private documents as well, we are missing out on an entire world of writing and this would have important consequences for our view of literacy levels in Anatolia at large. What arguments have been put forward in favor of the hypothesis that wooden tablets were so widely used and why do some scholars suppose they were inscribed with hieroglyphic script?

[34] Clanchy 1993: 206. [35] Melchert 2018: 592.

CHAPTER 10

The Wooden Writing Boards

10.1 Problems and Evidence

Once dried and securely buried, clay tablets can survive the ages remarkably well, and if baked, as often happened in fires that accompanied or caused the collapse of buildings, cities, or empires, they are virtually indestructible. Evidence, on the other hand, for the deliberate firing of tablets in Hittite times seems to be lacking.[1] As a consequence, our cuneiform sources for the late Bronze Age Hittite kingdom have come down to us almost exclusively on clay. The only exceptions are the treaty tablet issued in bronze by Tuthaliya IV (ca. 1240–1215/1210 BC), and the three graffiti on weapons of Anitta (Chapter 2), Ammuna, and Tuthaliya I (for the latter two see Chapter 4), all from the Old Kingdom. Because of this overwhelming physical evidence of clay as, virtually, the default material for cuneiform records, we tend to understand the Hittite loanword *tuppi* "tablet," via Akkadian *TUPPUM* going back to Sumerian DUB, as "clay tablet." The many self-references in, for example, colophons ("(on) this tablet") or letters ("when this tablet finds you") seem to confirm this. The same goes for the Old Kingdom charters written on clay that call themselves *TUPPUM*. Only once, however, is clay explicitly mentioned as the material for a tablet ("clay of a tablet" *tuppiaš* IM-*an*[2]) when it is used as an ingredient in a therapeutic ritual. But internal references are also found in the Bronze Tablet (*kī TUPPUM* (iii 78) and *TUPPA ANNIĀM* (iv 30) "this tablet"). Moreover, all metal tablets mentioned in our clay records are invariably referred to as either *tuppi* or DUB/*TUPPUM*.[3] The word *tuppi*, therefore, does not presuppose a specific material and denotes first and

[1] For remarks on the possible (non-)baking of tablets by the Hittites see Seeher 2003: 10, Müller-Karpe apud Wilhelm 1997: 6, Forrer 1922a: 177, Weeden 2013a: 21, Waal 2015: 41–3; for Mesopotamia see Charpin 2002: 489–90.

[2] KUB 41.4 ii 2, 17; Haas 2003: 178.

[3] For references to metal tablets see Siegelová 1993–1997a: 117; to this add the *kī TUPPU* KUB 26.43+ rev. 35 and 36 (Sahurunuwa bequest, NH) referring to a future metal tablet.

foremost any script carrier made of whatever material and often any text, record, or document, inscribed on that carrier.[4] Now, just as we have to assume that most metal tablets were at one point or other in history melted down, wooden writing boards, the third category of possible script carriers, did not survive the ages either, due to the climatic conditions on the Anatolian mainland. Are they referred to with *tuppi* as well in our clay tablets? Or were there special words for such records on wood?

Wooden tablets are an issue of some contention in Hittite and Anatolian studies. At the heart of the discussion lie different viewpoints as to how widespread their use was and what script and language were written on them.[5] The majority of scholars who have expressed an opinion on them assume that wooden boards were a relatively common phenomenon in Hittite Anatolia. They claim their existence in order to explain the absence of certain text genres we seem to be missing if we compare the Hittite kingdom with neighboring societies. The texts in question are mostly legal and socio-economic records from the state and private spheres. To my knowledge nobody has ever denied the use of wood as script carriers in Anatolia, but it is fair to say that my position is on the skeptical end of the spectrum of how common they were. Annick Payne has correctly criticized my overly pessimistic view on the short-term durability of wood in Late Bronze Age Anatolia.[6] I had briefly invoked the harsh climate of Central Anatolia with its hot and humid summers and cold winters to argue that wooden boards could only have been used for temporary records. With this, I unfairly denied the Hittites' expertise in maintaining and conserving wooden objects, which they must have had. The assumption, on the other hand, of a wide usage of wooden writing boards and therefore the existence of an equally widespread literacy among the population beyond the ruling class is a serious claim that deserves serious discussion. Since there is no physical evidence and expectations based on comparison with other societies do not in themselves justify such a claim, caution is called for, and what circumstantial evidence there is, should be carefully weighed, which is what I intend to do in this chapter.

In thinking of wooden tablets, we mostly envision diptychs (or polyptychs) with a recessed area filled with a wax-based substance, on or in which the script was applied. The oldest preserved Near Eastern example

[4] Waal 2015: 125; an interesting case is the list of families KBo 16.65 iv 5–9 that mentions in the colophon four times (iv 5–8) *tuppi* GN "*tuppi* of (the town of) GN" and then concludes with DUB.2.KAM *QATI* "Second tablet; finished", ed. by Waal 2015: 244–5. *tuppi* most likely refers here to the *contents* ("list, record/document" vel sim.) of the two tablets at hand.

[5] For the most recent discussion with lit. see Payne 2015: 104–16. [6] Payne 2015: 112–14.

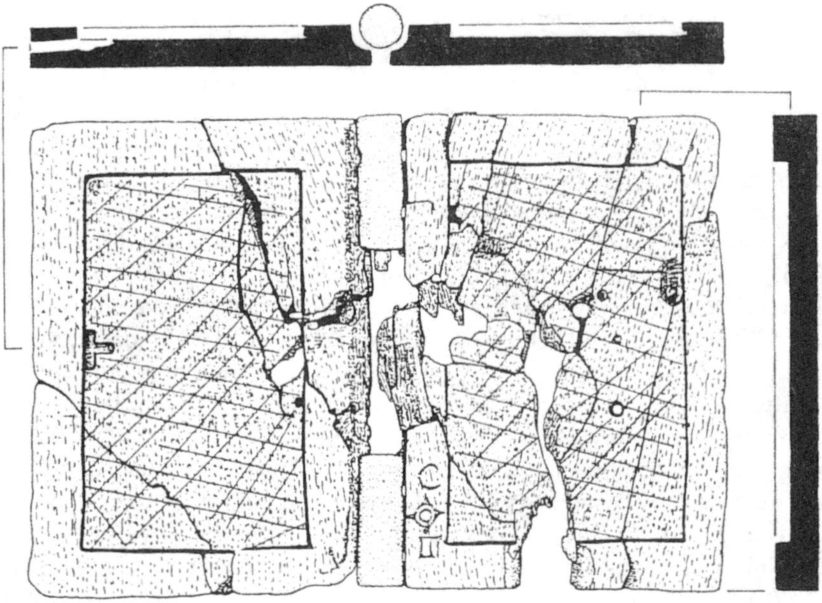

Fig. 10.1 Line drawing of Ulu Burun wooden diptych (drawing Netia Piercy apud Payton 1991: 102 Fig. 2; copyright British Institute at Ankara). The diagonal scratches in the wood served to make the wax adhere better to the wooden surface.

stems from the wreck of a ship that was recovered near Ulu Burun just off the Lycian coast and must have sailed the seas in the fourteenth century BC (Fig. 10.1).[7] Although very small with a ca. 7 × 5 cm inscribable surface it is a prime example of an originally wax-covered wooden tablet. Where the ship and its cargo came from, however, is unknown and the tablet cannot be used therefore as evidence for such script carriers in Hittite Anatolia.[8]

From the Greco-Roman world we also know of flat, whitewashed boards (Lat. *album*)[9] but their existence remains unproven for the ancient Near Eastern cuneiform world (Fig. 10.2). Of course, such flat boards were wholly unsuitable for cuneiform script as being impressed in a soft surface unless one thinks of an artificial two-dimensional imitation of the typical

[7] Payton 1991.

[8] It is not quite clear on what grounds Giusfredi 2012a: 148 assumes that the "cargo of the ship has to be interpreted without doubt as a product of Late Bronze Age Anatolian culture"; see Waal 2011: 21 for possible Aegean connections.

[9] Beal 2008: 11.

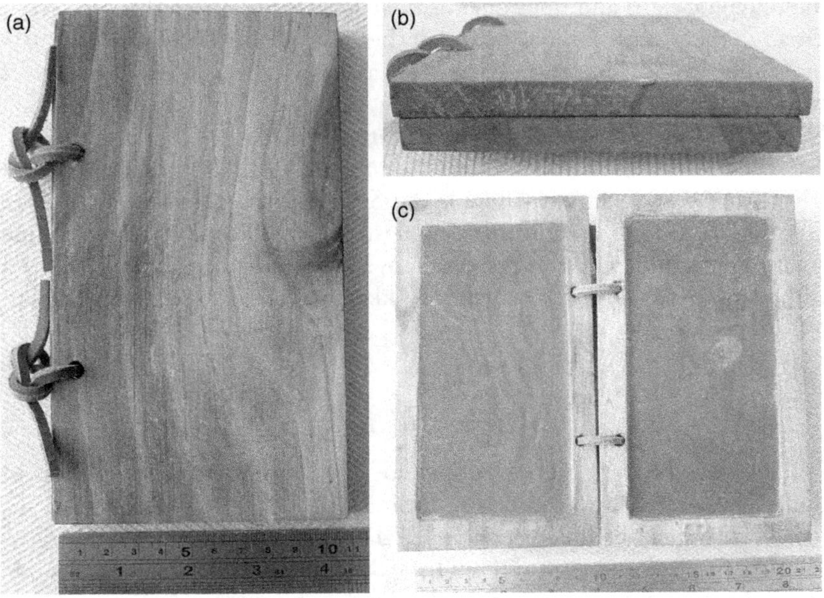

Fig. 10. 2a–c Modern replica of a Roman tabula (photos author).

cuneiform shape in ink.[10] For the Anatolian hieroglyphs this would have been possible, however.

Several arguments have been put forward in favor of the existence of wooden writing boards in the Hittite period. First of all, scholars have pointed to the group of $^{\text{LÚ.MEŠ}}$DUB.SAR.GIŠ "wood (GIŠ) scribes (DUB.SAR)" or "scribes on wood," as they are more commonly rendered; we will look at the "wood-scribes" in more detail in Chapter 13 but suffice it to say for now that the interpretation of the "wood-" part of this designation does not necessarily refer to wood as their primary writing surface. Secondly, the thousands of sealed *bullae* found at different places around the capital and elsewhere in the Hittite lands were allegedly once attached to wooden tablets. As such their existence is taken as a further argument in favor of the wide use of wooden writing boards; we will return to them in Chapter 11. Also, several bronze, pin-like objects with a pointed tip and a flattened end have been interpreted as styli. The pointed end was meant for writing, the flat end for erasing. Obviously, the thin point could only produce

[10] For an instance of an ink-like substance on a Hittite clay fragment see Košak 1988: 147 w. lit.; it is not clear what the ink traces want to convey; Košak speaks in terms of a drawing (*Zeichnung*).

hieroglyphic signs and not cuneiform wedges; for more on this see §10.11. Finally, there are some words that because of the determinative GIŠ preceding it and indicating the object as having been made (largely) of wood, have been adduced as denoting such wooden writing surfaces[11]: Hittite (GIŠ.ḪUR)*ḫatiwi-*, GIŠ(.ḪUR)*k/gaštarḫait/da*, (GIŠ.ḪUR(.ḪI.A))GUL-*zat(t)ar*, (GIŠ(.ḪUR)/GI)*k/gurta-*, (GIŠ.ḪUR)*parzakiš*, (GIŠ.ḪUR)*tuppi*(?), and Akkadian GIŠ*LEʾU*; finally, there is the Sumerogram GIŠ.ḪUR itself (i.e., as a freestanding noun and not as determinative). These we will examine right now starting with the Sumerogram since its frequency and its use as a determinative to all words except for Akkadian GIŠ*LEʾU* makes it central to our discussion.

10.2 GIŠ.ḪUR

In spite of the first sign GIŠ "wood" the combination GIŠ.ḪUR in Sumerian means "drawing, plan, outline, rule," *not* "wooden tablet." In 1973 Gertrud Farber already concluded that from a Sumerian point of view the elements GIŠ and ḪUR did not have their own semantic values, "wood" and "to carve, draw" respectively, but had to be understood as phonetic only.[12] Similarly, Yoram Cohen has recently argued that GIŠ.ḪUR never really was a living Sumerian combination but rather functioned as a pseudo-Sumerogram.[13] In his view both signs have their common Akkadian sign values *iṣ* and *ur*$_5$ standing for an abbreviated Akkadian *iṣur* (*tu*), which is supported by the Akkadian phonetic complement -*TE* in the spelling (*ANA*) GIŠ.ḪUR-*TE* (= *iṣurte*).[14] The latter can mean "drawing" but also "plan, ordinance, decree" derived from the verb *eṣēru* "to draw," not only in the sense of a drawing but also of "drawing up a document."

[11] For earlier discussions on wooden tablets in general and some or all of the terms in particular see Marazzi 1994, Waal 2011, Giusfredi 2012a, Cammarosano 2013: 66 w. n. 11, Gordin 2015: 209–10 w. n. 891.

[12] Farber-Flügge 1973: 182.

[13] He first suggested this at the workshop Hethitische Logogramme, Tagung at the Ludwig-Maximilians-Universität, München, November 14–15, 2014, repeated later in 2017 at the 10th International Congress of Hittitology, Chicago. I am very grateful to Yoram Cohen for sharing with me his written notes on this.

[14] IBoT 2.1 vi 13 (CTH 609, NS). Because of the use of GIŠ.ḪUR as a determinative of GUL-*zattar* Laroche 1963: 246, suggested that the latter might be the Hittite reading of GIŠ.ḪUR. However, given that this combination determines five additional document formats (as discussed in this chapter) this is no longer compelling. Moreover, the agreement both in the neuter (KUB 52.89: 3–4 [CTH 590, NS], see also GIŠ.ḪUR-*mit* "my GIŠ.ḪUR" KUB 36.98 rev. 10 [CTH 18, NS]) and common gender (IBoT 2.131 obv. 21 [CTH 518, NS]) shows that GIŠ.ḪUR had more than one Hittite reading, possibly two or more of the words it could determine.

Both explanations make it clear that GIŠ.ḪUR never denoted a wooden script carrier in Mesopotamian sources.[15]

While scholars like Frank Starke, Massimiliano Marazzi, and Willemijn Waal accept the original meaning of "drawing, draft" as sometimes still present in the Hittite sources, they nevertheless assume an inner-Hittite development to "(wax-covered) wooden tablet."[16] As we will see, however, neither is there evidence for this claim nor for an assumed preliminary character ("draft" vel sim.) of the text written on it. What all attestations do seem to have in common is their official and therefore enforceable character. Thus, GIŠ.ḪUR seems to denote a "document" as defined in diplomatic science: "*evidence* ... produced on a medium ... by means of a writing instrument"[17] or more specifically an "original," that is, a document that the administration knew to be authentic and genuine and "able to produce the consequences wanted by its author."[18] Given that all textual evidence that we have, originated within the Hittite state administration, the attestations for GIŠ.ḪUR point to an official, state-issued, and legally authentic document that could have different formats and functions depending on the situation. It could be a list, an order, legal evidence – sometimes sealed but not always – but the bottom-line was its authoritative status. A good example comes from the Instruction of the Temple Personnel and beautifully illustrates bureaucratic practices:

> If by the palace silver, gold, textiles (and/or) things of bronze are given to him (i.e., a member of the temple personnel) as a gift, it should be specified: "King so-and-so has given it to him" and it should likewise be recorded how much its weight is. Furthermore, the following should be recorded as well: "They gave it to him at such-and-such festival." Witnesses, too, should be recorded after (it): "When they gave it to him, so-and-so and so-and-so were present." Furthermore, he shall not leave it in his estate. He must sell it but when he sells it, he shall not sell it in secret! The authorities of Hattusa shall be present and watch. And whatever he sells, they must draw up a document

[15] I am grateful to my colleague Chris Woods for discussing this question with me.

[16] Starke 1990: 459 ("(Vor-)Zeichnung, Entwurf, Planung"), Marazzi 1994: 153 ("piano, programma" and also "tavoletta (cerata) lignea"; see also his discussion of the term 142–53), 2000: 81, Waal 2011: 25–6, see also Mora 2007: 538, van den Hout 2007d: 341 n. 11, Gordin 2015: 17–20, 209–10 n. 891, 214 n. 911, 236.

[17] Duranti 1998: 41 (emphasis mine); the full definition includes mechanical and/or electronic carriers: "evidence produced on a medium by means of a writing instrument or of an apparatus for fixing data, images and/or voices."

[18] Duranti 1998: 49; for the notions of authenticity and genuineness see 45–8.

> (GIŠ.ḪUR) of it and they must seal it in front. When the king comes up to Hattusa, he must show it to the palace, and they shall seal it for him.[19]

Two official records, both drawn up by the authorities[20], are described here. One is issued when the gift is originally bestowed upon someone by the king and the present instruction prescribes in detail the desired format of the document. The second record is written when the gift has to change owners again, probably when the original beneficiary leaves the temple service. The former "produces evidence" of the original gift, the latter of the enforced sale, probably back to the state. The second, the sale's document, is sealed, and its format reminds one of the charters: a list of goods and properties with a seal on the obverse ("in front").[21] The text does not say whether the document detailing the original gift was sealed but the listing of witnesses makes that likely.

Authoritative in the sense of producing evidence also applies to the document confirming the investiture of Walmu as local vassal on the throne of Wilusa, in western Anatolia. He was expelled and now the Hittite king calls on another one of his vassals in the same area to help reinstate Walmu. To that end he sends his envoy with the original document:

> Kuwalanazidi (i.e., the Hittite envoy) kept the documents (GIŠ.ḪUR.ḪI.A) that [I(?) drew up] for Walmu, and Kuruntiya(?) will now bring them down together with m[y?] son and you must read them. If you, my son, now support the wellbeing of My Majesty I, My Majesty, will trust your good faith. My son, send Walmu off to me and I will reinstate him on the throne in the country of Wilusa.[22]

19 *mān=ma=šši* IŠTU É.[(G)]AL-*LIM AŠŠUM* NÍG.BA=*ŠU* KÙ.BABBAR KÙ.GI TÚG-*TUM UNUT* ZABAR *pianzi n=at lamniyan ēšdu kāš=war=at=ši* LUGAL-*uš paiš* KI.LÁ.BI=*ŠU=ia=a*[(*t*)] *mašiwan n=at iyan=pat ēšdu namma kiššann=a iyan ēšdu kēdani=war=at=ši* ANA EZEN$_4$ SUM-*er kutrūšš=a* EGIR-*an iyanteš ašandu* SUM-*er=wa=at=ši kuwapi nu=wa kāš kāš=a arantat namma=at=za=kan* ŠÀ É-*TI lē=pat dāliyazi parā=pat=za uššaniyaddu uššaniyazi=ma=at=za kuwapi n=at ḫarwaši lē ušniyazi* EN.MEŠ ^{URU}*Ḫatti arantaru nu uškandu nu=za kuit wašiyazi n=at* GIŠ.ḪUR *iyandu n=at=kan peran šiyandu maḫḫan=ma=kan* LUGAL-*uš* ^{URU}*Ḫattuši šarā uizzi n=at* INA É.GAL-*LIM parā ēpdu n=at=ši šiyandu* KUB 13.4 ii 32–44 w. dupl. KUB 13.6 ii 23–35 (Instruction for Temple Personnel, CTH 264, both NS), ed. by Taggar-Cohen 2006: 51–2 (lines 37–49), 75–6, Miller 2013: 255, 393 n. 538. Note also the NÍG.BA LUGAL *tuppi* "royal gift on a tablet" in the Hittite Laws §53.

20 There is nothing to suggest here that such practices existed for private transactions (thus Herbordt 2005: 26, Waal 2011: 27).

21 For another explicit mention of a GIŠ.ḪUR being sealed see KUB 52.89: 3–4 (Vow, CTH 590, NS).

22 *ANA* ^{m}*Walmu=ma kue* GIŠ.ḪU[R.ḪI.A *iyanun*] ⸢*n=at*⸣ ^{m}KARAŠ.ZA *pē ḫarta n=at kāšma* ITTI DUMU=*I*[*A*?] ^{md}LAMMA? *udai n=at au kinun=ma* DUMU-*I*[*A*] *kuwapi* ŠA ^{d}UTU-*ŠI* SIG$_5$-*tar* PAP-*ašti tuēl=za* SILIM-*an* ^{d}UTU-*ŠI ḫāmi nu=mu=kan* DUMU-*IA* ^{m}*Walmun parā nāi n=an* EGIR-*pa INA* KUR *Wiluša* LUGAL-*eznani tiḫḫi* KUB 19.55 rev. 38–42 + KUB 48.90: 6–9 (Milawata Letter, CTH 182, NS), ed. by Hoffner 1982: 131 and 2009: 319.

The documents in question should convince the addressee of the legitimate claim of Walmu to the throne at Wilusa and he should secure safe passage for him to his Hittite overlord who will then bring him back to power. Using written evidence to prove something also means that destroying it can become important. This was apparently a concern, witness the stipulation in an instruction text about state property:

> or somebody has consumed (the contents of) silos while(?) having destroyed incriminating documents.[23]

A likewise legal context is given by the passage from a letter, in which the sender informs his addressee of an attachment in the form of a GIŠ.ḪUR he is sending him:

> Concerning the matter of the lawsuit about Mr. Tarhunmiya's property that I have sent you just now using the (official) document (GIŠ.ḪUR), keep an eye on Tarhunmiya's property![24]

The ablative case (expressed by the Akkadian preposition *IŠTU*) makes it clear that GIŠ.ḪUR describes the vehicle used to convey the information ("I have sent . . . *using* a GIŠ.ḪUR") and the direct object is the matter (*uttar*) of the lawsuit at hand.[25] The term GIŠ.ḪUR here may refer to an itemized list of the property, the official legal record.

An illuminating example for the relation of GIŠ.ḪUR vis-à-vis *tuppi* "tablet" is that of the GIŠ.ḪUR.MEŠ ("official documents containing/detailing requisitions") in the letter of the Hittite queen Puduhepa to Ramses II ("My Brother") concerning the dowry of her daughter:

> (The queen quotes what she wrote in an earlier letter:) "What people, cattle, (and) sheep shall I give to my daughter? I have no grain in my lands! So, the moment (my) envoys meet you, My Brother [must] dis[patch] a rider to me. They (i.e., my envoys) must then bring official documents (GIŠ.ḪUR.MEŠ) to my governors and they shall take away and confiscate the people, and

[23] *našma=kan* ÉSAG.ḪI.A *kuiški šarā adān ḫarzi nu=za* GIŠ.ḪUR.ḪI.A GÙB-*laš=ma ḫarninkan ḫarzi* KUB 13.2 iv 18–19 (Instruction for Provincial Governors, CTH 261, NS), ed. by Pecchioli Daddi 2003: 182–3 ("le registrazioni"), Miller 2013: 234–5 ("wooden writing boards"), tr. McMahon 1997: 225 ("the record tablets"), Gordin 2015: 231 ("ordinances/lists").

[24] *kāša=šmaš* ŠA É [m]*Tarḫunmiya kuit* ŠA DI.ḪI.A *uttar* IŠTU GIŠ.ḪUR *hatrānun nu=ššan* É [m]*Tarḫunmiya* IGI.ḪI.A-*wa ēpten* HKM 60, 4–8 (Letter from Maşat), ed. by Alp 1991: 232–5, Hoffner 2009: 211. Waal 2011: 27 treats this passage and KUB 31.68 obv. 5–6 under the heading of private correspondence but there is nothing to justify that interpretation.

[25] For the syntactic construction see van den Hout 2016a.

> cattle, (and) sheep they have."[26] I have [person]ally sent to th[em (i.e., the governors)] the envoys and the tablets.[27]

The people, cattle, and sheep were part of the expected dowry, but the queen claims she cannot give them due to food shortages. She suggests that Pharaoh tell her how many he expects, and she will then have her officials go to the Hittite provinces to get them there. The GIŠ.ḪUR documents probably contained the sealed ordinance to hand over what the envoys demanded. What makes this passage important is the referral back to the GIŠ.ḪUR.MEŠ by *TUPPA*$^{\text{ḪI?.A}}$. This passage, in fact, confirms that in Hittite, just as in Mesopotamia, the GIŠ in GIŠ.ḪUR did not imply that it was made of wood as mentioned above. Instead it denotes a special kind of document that can be referred back to with the more general term *tuppi*/*TUPPU*. Rather, it refers to the authoritative status of the documents in question: every GIŠ.ḪUR is a *tuppi* but not every *tuppi* a GIŠ.ḪUR. This means that, if GIŠ.ḪUR is not necessarily a wooden tablet, the other script carriers discussed below and determined by GIŠ.ḪUR are not necessarily wooden tablets either.

Similar may be the following passage detailing administrative procedures when storing (luxury) goods in a royal storehouse:

> One large red (reed) container (on) lion feet, tribute; in (it) are linen textiles from the land of Amurru; listed in a(n official) document. § . . . § One large red (reed) container (on) lion feet, tax from the town of Ankuwa; a number of textile(s), listed in a(n official) document. Thus (orders) the queen: "When I will put it in the storehouse, they will record it on a tablet."[28]

What the tablet mentioned at the end refers to is not entirely clear. Is it a new recording of all the objects stored or just a record that the goods had been delivered to the storehouse?

[26] Or with CHD P 177b "and make them into property of the (Egyptian) royal house."

[27] *ANA* DUMU.MUNUS*=wa kuin* NAM.RA.MEŠ GU$_4$.MEŠ UDU.ḪI.A *peškimi nu=wa=mu=kan* ŠÀ KUR.KUR.MEŠ [*ḫal*]*kiš* NU.GÁL *nu=wa=ta kuedani mēḫuni* $^{\text{LÚ.MEŠ}}$*ṬEME anda wemiya*<*n*>*zi nu=wa=mu=kan* ŠEŠ*=IA* ^{LÚ}*PITḪALLI parā* [*nāu*] *ANA* EN.MEŠ KUR-*TI=IA=wa* GIŠ.ḪUR.MEŠ *menaḫḫanda udandu nu=wa* NAM.RA.MEŠ *kuin* [GU]$_4$.MEŠ UDU.ḪI.A *pē ḫarkanzi nu=war=an=kan arḫa daškandu nu=war=an parnawiškandu nu apē*[*daš ammu*]*k=pat* $^{\text{LÚ.MEŠ}}$*ṬEME TUPPA*$^{\text{ḪI?.A}}$(or DUB.BA.A)*=ia AŠPUR* KUB 21.38 obv. 17–20 (Letter Puduhepa to Ramses II, CTH 176, NS), ed. by Edel 1994: 216–19 (vol. I, reading *TUPPA*$^{\text{<ḪI.>A}}$), Hoffner 2009: 283–4 (reading DUB.BA.A), Weeden 2014a: 51–2. The last part of the quote from *nu apē*[*daš* onwards was written between the lines in a much smaller hand and is therefore difficult to read. The distance, however, between the signs BA and A in line 20 seems too large to accommodate A only and a slanted sign(?) is visible in front so that I tentatively read ḪI?.A.

[28] IBoT 1.31 obv. 2–3, 12–15 (Palace inventory, CTH 241, NS), see n. 32.

The only for us perhaps less obvious context is the rather gruesome sounding ritual involving the burial of two live animals:

> Then they [w]rite (the name of) h[is (i.e., the ritual patron for whom the ritual is carried out?)] tribe(?) [using[29] two documents (GIŠ.ḪUR)]. One document (GIŠ.ḪUR) they hang on a sheep, one on a billy go[at]. They hold (them) in the storage pits and bury [them,] [bo]und (lit. held) (and) alive, the sheep in the storage pit of the Sungoddess of the Earth, the billy goat in the storage pit of the Male Gods.[30]

Since only their "tribe(?)" names are written on the device, the documents will have been quite small. They sound like simple tags or labels with the words, either impressed, carved, or written in an ink-like substance depending on their material. However, being meant for the gods and placed in underground storage areas with labels tied on to them sounds like a procedure followed for valuable goods stored in storerooms, which may explain the official format.

A good example of a GIŠ.ḪUR's evidentiary character comes from the bilingual Akkadian–Hittite proverb collection where it is on a par with *išḫiul* "bond, contract, treaty," *tuliya-* "assembly" and finds itself in the company of wisdom and the heart:

> Be quiet and listen: the things that people are confronted with, observe them with wisdom, hold them by contract, know them in (your) heart, investigate them through the assembly, read them from the document (GIŠ.ḪUR), gather them and know them with your [. . . -]s.[31]

Finally, most attestations for GIŠ.ḪUR are found in the formula *ANA* GIŠ.ḪUR⸗*kan ḫandan* in festival colophons like the following:

> Tablet 6, of the Sundeity of the Winter. Not complete. § *ANA* GIŠ.ḪUR⸗*kan ḫandān*[32]

[29] The restoration to the abl.-instr. (*IŠTU*) instead of a dat.-loc. ("on two documents") is warranted by the absence of a sentence particle: see van den Hout 2016a.

[30] *namma lattien⸗š*[*in IŠTU* 2 GIŠ.ḪUR G]UL-*šanzi nu⸗ššan* 1 [(GIŠ.ḪUR)] *ANA* U[(DU)] 1 GIŠ.ḪUR⸗*ma* AN[(A MÁŠ.G)AL *anda ḫ*]*amankanzi nu* ÀRAḪ.ḪI.A *anda appa*[(*nz*)]*i* [*n⸗uš⸗ka*]*n táknaš* ^{d}UTU-*aš* *ANA* ÀRAḪ UDU DINGIR.MEŠ LÚ.MEŠ *ANA* ÀRAḪ MÁŠ.GA[L *app*]*andu<š> ḫuiš*$^{!}$*wanduš anda ḫāriyanzi* KUB 17.18 iii 14–18 w. dupl. KUB 60.161 ii 36–40 (Ritual for Sungoddess of the Earth, CTH 448, both NS), ed. by Taracha 1990: 176–7.

[31] *nu⸗kku karušten nu* GEŠTUG-*ten nu* DUMU.LÚ.U$_{19}$.LU-*li kue* INIM.MEŠ-*ar pean* GAM GAR-*ri n⸗at⸗za⸗kan ḫaddanaza arḫa aušten n⸗at išḫiulaza ḫa*[*r*]*ten n⸗at* ŠÀ-*it šikten n⸗at tuliyaza punušten n⸗at* GIŠ.ḪUR-*za aušten nu anda da<r>upten n⸗at⸗za⸗kan šumēdaza* X[-O.]MEŠ-*za šekten* KBo 12.128 right col. 6–17 (Wisdom Text, CTH 316, NS), ed. by Cohen 2013: 202–3, see also Cohen 2018: 44–5.

[32] DUB.6.KAM *ŠA* ^{d}UTU *KUṢṢI* NU.TI[L] § *ANA* GIŠ.ḪUR⸗*kan ḫandān*, KUB 2.6 vi 1–4 (Festival for Sungoddess of Arinna, CTH 598, NS), ed. by Waal 2015: 407.

> Tablet 1, not complete; of the *nuntariasha*-festival. When the king goes to Arinna for the *nuntariasha*-festival. (blank line) [T]his is a fair copy. [*AN*]*A* GIŠ.ḪUR=*kan ḫandan*[33]
>
> [Tablet x]. Not complete; [of the] regular [K]I.LAM [festival]. [Pre]final draft.[34] (blank line) *ANA* GIŠ.ḪUR=*kan ḫā*(*n*)*da*[*n*]. (blank line) [KASKAL of Pih]awalwa, Wood-scribe (and) [Pal]luwarazidi, Scribe.[35]

Several scholars have taken this to signal that the clay version of the festival was in accordance with a wooden original.[36] Conversely, Willemijn Waal has recently proposed to take the participle *ḫandan* as "matched (to/with a GIŠ.ḪUR)." The phrase would refer to a matching version of the festival scenario written on wood, possibly because they were lighter and thus easier to handle when celebrating outside the capital or in the field.[37] But why would the clay tablet say that it was "in accordance with" the temporary wooden version, made to make things easier at the actual celebration? One would expect the wooden tablet to say that it was faithful in its wording to the (clay) original, not the other way around. If it was meant as an indication of there being a wooden copy for outside use it would have been phrased differently (e.g., *GIŠ.ḪUR Ì.GÁL "there is/exists a wooden tablet"). Waal also keeps open the option that the wooden version might have been of a more administrative character "containing practical information for the performance of the festivals, such as details regarding supplies, offerings, and recitations, etc." This is in line with an earlier suggestion by Massimiliano Marazzi that GIŠ.ḪUR still had its original meaning of "outline, plan": "conformemente al (giusto/originario?) piano/programma."[38] Jürgen Lorenz recently added the important observation that the formula is only attested in festivals that were actually celebrated as opposed to those that were copied and kept in the tablet collections for other reasons.[39] He also shows that the majority of the

33 DUB.I-*PU UL QATI ŠA* EZEN$_4$ *nuntariašḫaš mān* LUGAL-*uš* [URU]*Arinna ANA* EZEN$_4$ *nuntariašḫaš paizzi* § [*k*]*ī parkui TUPPU* [*AN*]*A* GIŠ.ḪUR=*kan ḫandan* KUB 2.9 vi 3–10 (*nuntariyasha*-Festival, CTH 626, NS), ed. by Waal 2015: 427.

34 For this translation see Chapter II.6.

35 [DUB.#.KA]M NU.TIL [*ŠA* EZEN$_4$ K]I.LAM SAG.UŠ [*išta*]*rniyaš* [EGIR-*a*]*n tarnummaš* § [*ANA*] GIŠ.ḪUR=*kan ḫāda*[*n*] § [KASKAL [m]*Piḫ*]*a*-UR.MAḪ DUB.SAR.GIŠ [[m]*Pal*]*luwa*<*ra*>-ZA DUB.SAR KBo 30.15 iv? 1–7 (KI.LAM-Festival, CTH 627, NS), ed. by Waal 2015: 436–7.

36 See Waal 2015: 166 w. n. 503.

37 Waal 2011: 26, 2015: 165–7, see also Schwemer 2012: 48–9 n. 26, 2016: 21–2 ("true to the GIŠ.ḪUR"), Cammarosano 2013: 71 n. 28. The argument of easier handling of wooden vs. clay tablets takes up earlier suggestions by Singer and Starke, for which see Waal ibid.

38 Marazzi 1994: 145–8; see now also Taracha 2017: 10–11, who, however, no longer assumes that a GIŠ.ḪUR would presuppose a wooden tablet.

39 Lorenz 2014: 481.

tablets with this formula in the colophon were found in Building A at the acropolis Büyükkale in Boğazköy. A GIŠ.ḪUR no longer being necessarily a wooden tablet, and the status of Building A being that of a record center for tablets that were no longer administratively active but were kept for future consultation, it makes sense to imagine the originals and officially approved scenarios for the festival celebrations being kept up there. As we will see in Chapter 13, GIŠ.ḪUR is best viewed here as the original in the above-mentioned diplomatic sense, which represented the authoritative copy with the official cult scenario. I will therefore translate *ANA* GIŠ.ḪUR*=kan ḫandan* as "true to/collated against the original."

Finally, interesting in this context is the following passage from the ritual "of sitting down on the throne":

> The wood-scribes have the document of how the [k]ing brings the dail[y] offerings.[40]

The fact that "wood-scribes" occur (only) here in connection with GIŠ.ḪUR has everything to do with their function of administrators or clerks responsible for the royal storehouses and for all provisions needed in cultic celebrations, not because they happen to share the Sumerogram GIŠ; for more on this see Chapter 13.3.

10.3 $^{\text{(GIŠ.ḪUR)}}$*ḫatiwi(ya)-*

The Hittite word *ḫatiwi(ya)-* is usually rendered as "inventory" and appears, for instance, in the colophon of a text known as the Inventory of Mr. Maninni, a list of luxury goods, mostly jewelry.[41] Although elsewhere (about five times) written without any determinative, *ḫatiwi-* occurs twice with GIŠ.ḪUR preceding it without any word space. Unfortunately, the two passages are very fragmentary. One, KBo 42.22 i 7 ($^{\text{GI]Š.ḪUR}}$*ḫa-ti-wi*$_5$*-an-kán*), mentions animal figurines with silver and gold, the other (KUB 38.1 iii 2 $^{\text{GIŠ.ḪUR}}$*ḫa-t[i-*[42]) describes inventories of temples of various towns. There are also a few instances of a derived verb *ḫatiwidai-* "to (make an) inventory,"

40 [L]UGAL-*uš=ma=kan maḫḫan* UD-*til[i] šipanzakizzi nu* GIŠ.ḪUR $^{\text{LÚ.MEŠ}}$DUB.SAR.GIŠ *ḫarkanzi* KUB 10.45 iii 12–14 (Enthronement Ritual, CTH 659, NS), ed. by Kümmel 1967: 46, Mouton 2016: 247, 249.

41 For all attestations, spellings, and references see HW^2 Ḫ s.v.

42 Cammarosano 2018: 312 reads this as ^{GIŠ}*ḪAR-ḪA-TI* "lyre" instead of $^{\text{GIŠ.ḪUR}}$*ḫa-ti[-wi*$_5$*(-)*.

showing an underlying Luwian noun **ḫatiwid-*. Once this verb is preceded by GIŠ (^{GIŠ}*ḫatiwitan* participle "inventoried").[43]

10.4 $^{\text{GIŠ(.ḪUR)}}$*k/gaštarḫait/da*

The word $^{\text{GIŠ(.ḪUR)}}$*k/gaštarḫait/da* is attested in two texts from the thirteenth century BC, one inventorying the cult of the town of Karaḫna, KUB 38.12, and in a vow text (KBo 9.96). All five occurrences come in as many different spellings:

Table 10.1 *Attested forms for* $^{\text{GIŠ(.ḪUR)}}$k/gaštarḫait/da

	KUB 38.12
^{GIŠ}*kaš-tar-ḫa-i-ta*	i 18
$^{\text{GIŠ.ḪUR}}$*kaš-tar-ḫa-i-da*	ii 7
$^{\text{GIŠ.ḪUR}}$*kaš-tar-ḫa-ta*	ii 22
$^{\text{GIŠ.ḪUR}}$*kaš-tar-ḫa-i-ta*	iii 24
	KBo 9.96
$^{\text{GIŠ.ḪUR}}$⸓*ga-aš-tar-ḫa-i-ia-da*	i 5[44]

The last attestation proves that the correct reading is indeed *k/gaš-* (and not **pí-* as the first sign in principle would allow as well).[45] The gloss wedges (⸓) suggest that the word may be Luwian in origin. The one writing with GIŠ instead of GIŠ.ḪUR may be either a scribal mistake or an abbreviation for the latter. The striking instability in spellings points, it seems, to a relative unfamiliarity with the word on the side of the scribe(s), all the more so since they denote morphologically identical forms. The Karaḫna text attestations all occur in the same formula (with one minor variation in the first parentheses): EZEN$_4$.MEŠ(*=ši*) $^{\text{GIŠ.ḪUR}}$*kaštarḫa*(*i*)*t/da tarrauwan*. This has been rendered as "festivals have been established (for it (= *-ši*), i.e., probably the town) according to the *kaštarḫaita*-plan/ *kaštarḫaita*-writing board."[46] While the determinative GIŠ.ḪUR probably refers to its official character the translation "according" is difficult to

[43] HW² emends this on the basis of the two nouns accompanied by GIŠ.ḪUR to GIŠ<.ḪUR> *ḫatiwidai-*.

[44] For a similar case of a *Glossenkeil* in between a determinative and the actual noun cf. $^{\text{LÚ.MEŠ}}$⸓*lapanalli*$^{\text{ḪI.A}}$*-uš* IBoT 2.131 rev. 17 (cf. CHD L s.v.).

[45] Marazzi 1994: 135 n. 13 w. lit.

[46] Thus Tischler HEG T: 154–5 ("(gemäß) dem *gastarhaita*-Plan"), Cammarosano 2013: 66 n. 11.

reconcile with the ending *-a*. Since a Hittite allative ending (*-a*) is no longer likely in the thirteenth century one would either have to assume a (fairly uncommon) Luwian dat.-loc. in *-a* or a nom.-acc. neut. pl. Neither allows for a translation "according to" and only the latter will explain the nom.-acc. neut. sg. of the participle *tarrauwan* (spelled identically *tar-ra-u-wa-an* all four times!) according to the usual rules of Hittite grammar. The Sumerogram EZEN$_4$.MEŠ cannot be subject because of the common gender of the underlying Hittite word.[47] It therefore seems best to take it as dependent on ^GIŠ.ḪUR^*kaštarḫa(i)t/da* or the latter in apposition to EZEN$_4$.MEŠ:

> The festival *kastarhaida*-s (or: the festivals, that is, the *k*.-s) have been established (for it).

KBo 9.96, unfortunately, is fragmentary but again "festivals" are mentioned in the immediate context and ^GIŠ.ḪUR^*kaštarḫa(i)t/da* could be taken as an accusative of respect: [. . .] / ^GIŠ.ḪUR^*gaštarḫaiyada kuiēš* EZEN$_4$.MEŠ x[o]x["As to(?) the *gaštarḫaiyada*-s, that is, the festivals that . . . [. . .]. If indeed a written document, the noun ^GIŠ.ḪUR^*kaštarḫa(i)t/da* could refer to anything like a scenario, script, provisions list, or the like.

10.5 ^(GIŠ(.ḪUR))^GUL-*zattar*

Originally the verb underlying this noun had been taken as a Sumerogram with a phonetic complement (GUL-*š*-) until in 1966 Onofrio Carruba advocated the pure Hittite reading *gulš*- with a noun *gulzattar*.[48] Recently, Willemijn Waal has convincingly proposed to return to the old Sumerographic interpretation GUL-*š/z*- with an underlying but unattested Hittite reading **kuwanzattar*.[49] Ultimately, the exact reading is immaterial for the present purpose of establishing its use and meaning but, following Waal, I will transliterate GUL-*š/z*-.

There are only two attestations for GUL-*zattar* determined by a simple GIŠ, both on the cult inventory from Kayalıpınar; two occurrences show no determinative, all other cases have GIŠ.ḪUR(.ḪI.A). Not knowing the Kayalıpınar examples, Emmanuel Laroche[50] suggested that *gulzattar* (in its

[47] Singer 1983: 45 w. n. 26. [48] Carruba 1966: 34–7.
[49] Waal 2014 and 2019, differently Yakubovich 2013–2014, Melchert 2016; see also Giusfredi 2012a: 147–8.
[50] Laroche 1963: 246; in this he is followed by Starke 1990: 459, Hawkins 2003: 155, Schwemer 2005–2006: 223–4, and Yakubovich 2013–2014: 287 (see also 293), while according to Marazzi 1994: 155–7 the two overlap but are not identical.

Table 10.2 *Attested forms and spellings for* GUL-*zattar*

sg. nom.-acc.	$^{\text{GIŠ.ḪUR}}$GUL-*za-tar*	KBo 31.47 rev.? 7, IBoT 3.101 obv. 4 (]GUL-), Bo 7103: 6[51],
	^{GIŠ}GUL-*za-tar*	Kp 14/95 rev. 4
	$^{\text{GIŠ.ḪUR}}$GUL-*za-at-tar*	KUB 50.6 iii 18
abl.	$^{\text{GIŠ.ḪUR}}$GUL-*za-at-ta-na-az*	KBo 11.1 obv. 41
	$^{\text{GIŠ.Ḫ]UR.ḪI.A}}$⸢GUL-*za-at-ta-na-az-z(=iya)*	KBo 11.1 obv. 21
	$^{\text{GIŠ.ḪUR}}$GUL-*za-at-na-za*	Kp. 15/8+ i 25[52] (only ^{GIŠ})
	$^{\text{GIŠ.ḪUR}}$GUL-*za-da-na-za*	KUB 42.103 iii? 14
pl. nom.-acc.	GUL-*za-tar*$^{\text{ḪI.A}}$	KUB 42.100 i 19
	GUL-*za-at-tar*$^{\text{ḪI.A}}$	KUB 58.7 ii 23[53]
	$^{\text{GIŠ.ḪUR}}$GUL-*za-at-ta-ra*	KUB 50.6 iii 12
	GUL-*za-at-tar-ri*$^{\text{ḪI.A}}$	KBo 55.181: 6
fragm.	$^{\text{GIŠ.ḪUR}}$GUL-*z[a-*	KBo 18.82 obv. 9
here abl.?	$^{\text{GIŠ.ḪUR!?}}$GUL-*za-na-az*	KBo 48.273: 8[54]

alleged full Hittite reading) might be the phonetic reality behind the Sumerogram GIŠ.ḪUR. However, given that the latter determines at least four additional words discussed here this is no longer compelling. Moreover, grammatical agreement both in neuter and common gender[55] shows that GIŠ.ḪUR had more than one Hittite reading, possibly two or more of the words it could determine. Table 10.2 lists the writings attested and known to me (all attestations show NS[56]).

Since in Hittite one would expect the proper inflection of a noun in *-atar* to show an oblique stem in *-ann-* < **-atn-* (gen. sg. *-annaš* etc. with an abl. *-annaz*) the stem *-at(ta)na-/-adana-* has to be explained as Luwian where such assimilation of *-tn-* > *-nn-* did not occur. If interpreted correctly, KBo 48.273: 8 would show the only unambiguous Hittite form. The variation of spellings

[51] apud Otten & Siegelová 1970: 35 n. 4 (but quoted as "7081" in Fuscagni 2007: 159).

[52] apud Cammarosano 2018: 388. [53] On this passage see n. 96.

[54] The tablet has ^{GIŠ}*gul-gul-za-na-az* in unfortunately fragmentary context. A word * ^{GIŠ}*gulgulzana-/gulgulzatar* is otherwise unknown. A scribal error for $^{\text{GIŠ.ḪUR}}$*gulzatar* is imaginable, since both signs GUL and ḪUR start with a Winkelhaken.

[55] For neuter agreement see KUB 52.89: 3–4 (GIŠ.ḪUR *šiyan ēšz[i* "the document is sealed," Vow, CTH 590, NS), for common gender see IBoT 2.131 obv. 21 ($^{\text{ḪUR.SAG}}$*Liḫšaš* GIŠ.ḪUR *siyanteš* ŠA ^{d}*Pirwa ḫarzi* "Mt. Liḫša holds the sealed documents of Pirwa," Cult of Pirwa, CTH 518, NS, ed. by Cammarosano 2018: 262–3).

[56] See also the list of occurrences in CLL: 108.

with double *-tt-* vs. *-t-* and *-d-* within a total of just twelve attestations (KBo 18.82 obv. 9 is too fragmentary) is noteworthy. Just as in the case of $^{\text{GIŠ(.ḪUR)}}$*k/gaštarḫait/da*, in view of the clear majority of attestations that have the determinative GIŠ.ḪUR, the single case with just GIŠ can be either a scribal mistake or an abbreviation.

All well enough preserved attestations for GUL-*zattar* occur in the context of provisions for temples and offerings, revealing a primary administrative nature ("(provisions) list" vel sim.). They are records, that one can check.[57] Compare, for instance, after a list of cereal products, beverages, dairy products, and wool:

> The officials of the storehouse of Hattusa will provide (them, i.e., the items previously listed) (and) th[ey will] copy (*arḫa* GUL-*šan*[*zi*]) them from the old GUL-*zattar*.[58]

Apparently, an older version ("the old GUL-*zattar*") was used as the basis for a new record detailing the most recent expenditures from the royal storehouse. The authoritative nature suggested by the determination of most attestations by GIŠ.ḪUR (although admittedly this particular one only has GIŠ) is confirmed by the use of the compound verb *katta ḫamal/enk-* "to establish, institute"[59] in a cult inventory from Kayalıpınar:

> Concerning the GUL-*zattar* that the decurio of (the town of) Pa-x[. . . issued (?)] just now, he has established the Monthly Festival as follows: . . .[60]

What follows are detailed amounts of animals and foodstuffs. Compare likewise the passage recording oracle investigations:

> Given the fact that the deceased was ascertained in connection with the gods and that his gods have been shut out, will they check the GUL-*zattar* -tablet and will they start [giv]ing them again what His Majesty's father had [establish]ed for them?[61]

[57] Marazzi 1994: 154–7.

[58] LÚ.MEŠ É.GAL ^{URU}*Ḫatti peškanzi annalaz=at=kan* $^{\text{GIŠ.ḪUR}}$GUL-*zadanaza arḫa gulšan*[*zi*] KUB 42.103 obv. iii? 13–14 (Cult of Tessub and Hebat, CTH 698, NS), ed. by van den Hout 2016a: 434.

[59] Cf. HW^2 Ḫ s.v. "festsetzen, festlegen."

[60] *kinun=ma kui*[*t* ^{GI}]^{Š}GUL-*zatar* ^{LÚ}UGULA.10 ^{URU}*Pa*-x[. . .] *nu* $EZEN_4$ ITU.KAM *k*[*i*]*šan katta ḫamak*$^{!}$-*ta* Kp 14/95 rev. 4–5, ed. by Rieken 2014: 46–7, 49.

[61] GIDIM=*ma kuit* ANA DINGIR.MEŠ *šer* SIxSÁ-*at* DINGIR.MEŠ=*ši*=*kan kuit* EGIR-*pa ištappanteš nu* $^{\text{GIŠ.ḪUR}}$GUL-*zattar uwanzi* [*n*]*u*=*šmaš*=*kan* ABI ^{d}UTU-ŠI *kuit* [SISKUR M]E-*iš nu*=*šmaš*=*a*[*t*] EGIR-*pa* [*peš*]*kiuwan ti*[*y*]*anzi* KUB 50.6 iii 16–21 (oracle inquiry, CTH 569, NS), ed. by van den Hout 1998: 184–7, similarly iii 7–15 (p. 184–5).

Ideally one checks things by going back to an official, authoritative, and original document. Muwatalli II mentions a similar checking activity in connection with the cult for the Stormgod of Kummanni:

> And I will do wh[a]t I, My Majesty, will find out now through/from the GUL-*zattar* -tablets.[62]

Earlier, in the discussion of GIŠ.ḪUR, we saw how the latter could be referred to by *tuppi* (*TUPPA*$^{\text{ḪI.A}}$) suggesting that GIŠ.ḪUR was a special kind of *tuppi*. A similar situation can be seen in a cult inventory where we first find *tuppi* and then GUL-*zattar*. Here we would have first the general and then the specific (*TUPPA*$^{\text{ḪI.A}}$⸗ . . . GUL-*zattar*$^{\text{ḪI.A}}$):

> When His Majesty comes [. . .]/ [(for?)] them the tablets, that is, the lists (*vel sim.*)[. . .].[63]

The immediately preceding but, unfortunately, fragmentary context mentions "the Great Festival of the king's trip/campaign."

As we saw, Luwian GUL-*zattar* derives from the verb GUL-*š*- "to draw, mark, carve, incise, engrave."[64] There is, however, no close contextual relation between the two: none of the contexts has GUL-*zattar* as the direct object of a verb that denotes "writing, recording" or the like. In the combination GUL-*zattanaz arḫa* GUL-*š*-[65] an otherwise unspecified record is copied "*from* an old GUL-*zat*(*t*)*ar*." In its most basic meaning GUL-*š*- seems to indicate the act of drawing something, of making a mark using any medium and often doing so with an extended, drawn out motion like painting with a brush or carving something in a hard surface. The medium, with which one draws or marks, can be specified, for instance, when in the Hittite royal funerary ritual after the deceased has been cremated and the bone remains have been gathered they "draw" or "mark" the outline of the deceased with fruit and produce on the extinguished pyre.[66] In other texts

62 ⸢$^{\text{GIŠ.Ḫ}}$]$^{\text{UR.ḪI.A}}$⸣GUL-*zattanazz*[*⸗iy*]*a ku*[*i*]*t* ^{d}UTU-*ŠI kinun wemiškimi n⸗at ēššaḫḫi* KBo 11.1 obv. 21–2 (Prayer, CTH 382, Muwatalli II), ed. by Houwink ten Cate 1967: 106, 115–6; cf. similarly KUB 50.6 iii 18 where the verb *auš*- "to see, read" is used.

63 *kuwapi* ^{d}UTU-*ŠI uizzi* [. . .] / *TUPPA*$^{\text{ḪI.A}}$*⸗ma⸗aš* (or *⸗ma⸗*(*šm*)*aš*?) GUL-*zattar*$^{\text{ḪI.A}}$[. . .] KUB 58.7 ii 22–3 (Cult inventory, CTH 525, NS). The photo shows that GUL-*zattar*$^{\text{ḪI.A}}$[is written over erasure with the first erased sign still recognizable as either A or ZA under GUL and two Winkelhaken under -*at*-(*tar*); for the EZEN$_4$ GAL ŠA KASKAL LUGAL (ibid. 21) see CHD P 71b.

64 On *gulš*- see Starke 1990: 460–4, Marazzi 1994: 138–140, Schwemer 2005–2006: 223–4, Waal 2011: 22–9, 2014: 1016–22, Melchert 2016; for the etymology of *gulš*- as coming from PIE **kwels*- "to dig a furrow", from which Gr. telson "furrow," see Kloekhorst 2008: 492–3, Giusfredi 2012a: 147–8, and Melchert 2016: 357. For an alleged verb **gulziya*- "to give a sign" based on an emended reading GIŠ<.ḪUR>-*ziattari* see Dardano 2006: 80–1 w. lit.

65 See n. 58 KUB 42.103 obv. iii? 14.

66 KUB 30.15+ obv. 21–3, ed. by Kassian et al. 2002: 264–5 ("they decorate").

individuals "draw" a circle(?) around a hearth pouring beer.[67] In the following passage a ritual assemblage is put together and GUL-*š*- seems to indicate the "marking" of certain parts:

> On each single table they place ten soldier breads while they put on top of each two sweet breads made of *šeppit*-grain (and) two sweet breads of porridge. Next, they [p]ut one jug of beer to the right, one jug of beer to the left and one jug of beer in the middle. Next, they mark (GUL-*šanzi*) them with fruit and butter. They insert nine straws (in the jugs) and bind them together with red, blue, and green wool.[68]

At other times it is indicated that the surface is hard (metal, stone) and a meaning like "to engrave" is required. It is these contexts that often imply writing:

> One silver wreath (with) the name of the Mighty Stormgod engraved.[69]

> But whoever does not sell a royal gift on which the king's name has been engraved, . . .[70]

In at least one instance the context, in which the verb is used, can be linked to an existing hieroglyphic inscription carved into stone.[71] The engraving sometimes combines writing and figurative representations:

> The name of the king and animals of the field are engraved.[72]

> A smith cast a cup for fame . . . and he engraved it.[73]

[67] *nu* 1 DUG.KAŠ *ḫupran ḫaššan araḫzanda šiyēššanit* GUL-*ašzi* "(using?) one pitcher of beer he/she draws a circle around the hearth with the beer" KBo 20.34 obv. 11–12 (Prayer, CTH 395, OS), ed. by Kassian 2000: 110–1 ("pours (*lit.* marks)"); cf. similarly KBo 15.25 obv. 30–1, rev. 20–1 (Prayer, CTH 396, OS), ed. by Carruba 1966: 4–5, 6–7, and CHD Š 357b (j).

[68] *nu=ššan kuedaniya* ANA 1 ^{GIŠ}BANŠUR 10 NINDA.ÉRIN.MEŠ *zikkanzi šer=ma=ššan kuwapiya* 2 NINDA.KU$_7$ *šeppitaš* 2 NINDA.KU$_7$ BA.BA.ZA *tianzi namma* 1 DUG KA.GAG ZAG-*az* [1] ^{DUG}KA.GAG GÙB-*az tianzi* 1 DUG KA.GAG=*ma ištarna pidi* [*t*]*ianzi namma=aš* IŠTU INBI Ì.NUN=*ia* GUL-*aššanzi* [0]x 9? ^{GI}A.DA.GUR.ḪI.A *tarnanzi anda=ma=aš* IŠTU SÍG.SA$_5$ [SÍG].ZA.GÌN SÍG ḪAŠARTI *išḫiyanzi* KUB 35.133 i 24–30 (Cult ritual, CTH 665, NS), ed. by Starke 1985: 279.

[69] 1 *KILILU* KÙ.BABBAR ŠUM *ŠA* ^{d}U *GAŠRU=kan andan* GUL-*aššan* KUB 38.1 i 32–3 (Cult inventory, CTH 501, NS), tr. Jakob-Rost 1961: 179, Waal 2011: 23.

[70] *kuiš=ma=za* NÍG.BA LUGAL *UL ḫappirāizzi* ŠUM LUGAL-*kan kuedani* GUL-*šan* KUB 13.4 ii 51–2 (Instruction for temple personnel, CTH 264, NS), ed. by Taggar-Cohen 2006: 52–3, 76.

[71] KBo 12.38, see Waal 2011: 23.

[72] (said of a statue of a god:) *ŠUM ŠA* LUGAL=*kan kimrašš=a ḫūitar andan* GUL-*aššan* KUB 38.3 ii 8–9 (Cult inventory, CTH 502, NS), ed. by Jakob-Rost 1961: 183–4, Waal 2011: 23. An example of this, albeit with the name of an official not the king's, is the KINIK bowl, for which see Emre & Çınaroğlu 1993: 684–703.

[73] *tessummin* ^{LÚ}SIMUG *walliyanni lāḫuš . . . n=an* GUL-*ašta* KBo 32.14 ii 42, 44 (Parable, CTH 789, OS), ed. by Neu 1996: 81.

There are also several instances where GUL-*š*- refers to writing in an administrative context:

> One large red (reed) container (on) lion feet, tribute; in (it) are linen textiles from the land of Amurru; listed (GUL-*aššan*) on a GIŠ.ḪUR. § . . . § One large red (reed) container (on) lion feet, tax from the town of Ankuwa; a number of textiles, listed (GUL-*aššan*) on the GIŠ.ḪUR.[74]

Sometimes the verb GUL-*š*- appears alone and no script carrier is mentioned, as seen in a few passages from the Instruction for the Border Commanders:

> The commander of the border garrison must keep counted and listed (GUL-*aššan*) for himself what the advanced border garrisons are and what enemy roads there are. (. . .) He must count and keep listed (GUL-*aššan*) for himself what border troops he has. (. . .) Then the commander of the border garrison must list (GUL-*ašdu*) the implements of the god and bring it (i.e., the list) to His Majesty. (. . .) What field belongs to a deceased veteran and what unoccupied *pietta*-allotments there are, that must all be listed (GUL-*aššan*) for you(r own administration).[75]

Note how, except for the third clause quoted here about the list of temple inventory that has to be delivered to the Hittite king, all passages underline the personal nature of the bookkeeping by adding the reflexive particle -*za* ("for himself") or the personal pronoun -*tta* ("for you"). This is the commander's own, personal administration. Given the earlier observation that for $^{\text{GIŠ.ḪUR}}$GUL-*zattar* the material of the script carrier is irrelevant, this probably extends to the verb GUL-*š*- as well and there is no reason to assume *a priori* the border commander wrote on wood. In terms of semantic development these diverse meanings seem most easily derived from a general notion "to mark, make a mark(ing)." Its administrative preponderance may go back to tallying practices in daily (economic?) life.[76]

This, finally, raises two more questions: where do the personified Hittite "Fate" deities, the ^{d}GUL-*šeš*, fit in all of this[77] and how does the Old Assyrian *iṣurtum* relate to GIŠ.ḪUR? As to the first question, it is nowhere

[74] See Chapter 9 n. 33.

[75] *ḫantezziēš⸗ma kuēš* MADGALATI *nu* ŠA LÚ.KÚR *kuiēš* KASKAL.ḪI.A *n⸗aš⸗za* BEL MADKALTI *kappūwan ḫardu n⸗aš⸗za* GUL-*aššan ḫardu* (. . .) *auriyaš⸗a⸗šši kuiš* ÉRIN.MEŠ *n⸗an kappūwaeddu n⸗aš⸗za* ⸢GUL⸣-*aššan ḫardu* (. . .) *namma* ŠA DINGIR-LIM UNUTUM *auwariyaš* EN-*aš* GUL-*ašdu n⸗at* MAḪAR ^{d}UTU<-ŠI> *uppau* (. . .) *ḫarkantašš⸗a* LÚ ^{GIŠ}TUKUL *kuiš* A.ŠÀ.ḪI.A *t́annātta⸗ia kue piētta n⸗e⸗tta ḫū[m]an* GUL-*aššan ēštu* KUB 13.2 i 8–10, 13–14, ii 42–3, KUB 31.84 iii 66–7 (Instruction for border commanders, CTH 261, NS), ed. by Pecchioli Daddi 2003: 90–5, 140–1, 166–9, Miller 2013: 220–1, 226–7, 230–3.

[76] For an extensive survey of notched tally sticks and similar tokens attested since 30,000 BC see Henkelman & Folmer 2016.

[77] For attestations see van Gessel 1998: s.v. w. lit., most recently see Melchert 2016 w. lit.

specified how exactly these deities determine an individual's future. The image of deities spinning one's life thread and cutting it through at the end is present in Hittite sources, but it is the goddesses Isdustaya and Papaya, not the GUL-*šeš* who do this, and it is not clear whether they are, for instance, subsumed under the GUL-*šeš*. Together with the Mother goddesses the GUL-*šeš* "create" or "shape"[78] human beings, their "life, health, strength, longevity, happiness" and other life essentials, and determine their end.[79] Were they outlining people's lives, marking the beginning and end as well as life's major milestones in between as if on some kind of record? There can be little doubt that the GUL-*šeš* are something old and indigenously Anatolian, perhaps even Proto-Anatolian in a linguistic sense. Craig Melchert is right that this cannot have been writing in the real sense of the word projected back into some period in the third millennium.[80] But if markings on records like tallying sticks or similar devices existed, it is easy to see how Fate got its name from a verb that meant making a mark or a notch.

The possible existence of some tallying system, in turn, would make it possible to understand why the Assyrian merchants, confronted with an indigenous way of listing debts, chose the noun *iṣurtum* (= Akkad. *uṣurtum* = Sum. GIŠ.ḪUR; note that the Akkadian phonetic complement -*TE* visible in the writing GIŠ.ḪUR-*TE* speaks in favor of the equation) for a listing of debts mostly owed by local Anatolians to the Assyrians.[81] The Assyrian noun derives from the verb *eṣērum* with a range of meanings very comparable to that of *gulš*-.[82] Daniel Schwemer sought to counter the problem that according to *communis opinio* a GUL-*zattar*/GIŠ.ḪUR had to be made of wood while the OAss. *iṣurtum* was a clay object by assuming that GUL-*zattar* originally meant "marking, listing, design." Only secondarily did it become "wooden tablet" because such listings were preferably recorded on writing boards. The first assumption is correct, in my opinion, if understood as an Anatolian way of marking debts by creating a record with an authoritative character. But the second one is no longer necessary: the automatic linkage between GUL-*zattar*/GIŠ.ḪUR and wood as its material is no longer given or even tenable, as we saw.[83] Finally, Schwemer assumed that the Old Assyrian figura etymologica *iṣurtam eṣērum* "to draw up an *iṣurtum*-document"

[78] Bo 3617 i 16–17 w. dupls.; for the text see Otten & Siegelóva 1970, Fuscagni, hethiter.net/: CTH 434.1. The verb used here is *šamnae*- for which see CHD Š s.v.

[79] Haas 1988a: 87–92 for KUB 43.55 ii 11–21.

[80] Melchert 2016: 357–8, Yakubovich 2017a: 534–5.

[81] Schwemer 2005–2006: 223–4.

[82] Veenhof 1995: 314–15.

[83] For Laroche's view that GUL-*zattar* was the Hittite reading behind GIŠ.ḪUR see n. 13.

reflected an originally Anatolian usage of GUL-*zattar* GUL-*š*-.[84] The latter, however, is not attested. The closest we get to this is the expression *arḫa* GIŠ.ḪUR GUL-*zadanaza gulš*- "to copy *from* the GUL-*zattar*-tablet" that we saw earlier. An unspecified document is drawn up (GUL-*š*-) *from* a GUL-*zattar*-tablet and, as a consequence, no inherent relation between the two can be asserted on the basis of this expression.

10.6 (GIŠ)***k/gurt/da-***

The noun (GIŠ)*k/gurt/da-* is well attested and usually determined by a simple GIŠ but once preceded by GIŠ.ḪUR. Where photos are available there is no word space between between GIŠ and *k/gurt/da-* while there is clear word space after GIŠ.ḪUR in IBoT 2.102 (see Table 10.3).[85]

The word has been plausibly linked to GIŠ/GI*kurtali*-, a container of some kind, made out of wood (GIŠ) or reed (GI), so either a box, chest, crate, or basket. Jaan Puhvel has suggested that GIŠ*kurta*- may have been such a container, specifically to store tablets in.[86] The word is sometimes preceded by a royal name and Puhvel quite ingeniously points to the hoard of over 3400 bullae from the so-called *Westbau* in the Upper City as a possible parallel (Chapter 11). Those bullae were stored in chronological order and

Table 10.3 *Attested forms for* GIŠ*kurta-*

sg. nom. com.	GIŠ*kur-ta-aš*	KBo 17.65 + FHG 10 rev. 45
	GIŠ*gur-da-aš*	Bo 3295 iii 7[87]
abl.	*gur-da-za*	KUB 55.48 i 16 (2x; "1")
	[. . .]*gur-da-za*	Bo 3289: 12[88]
	GIŠ*kur-ta-za*	KUB 42.100 i 17, iii 22
	GIŠ*gur-ta-za*	KUB 42.100 iv 10
	[. . . -*t*]*a*!-*za*	KBo 26.181: 4[89]
stem form	GIŠ*gur-ta*	KUB 42.100 iv 34
fragmentary	GIŠ.ḪUR *gur-*⸢*da*⸣[	(KUB 38.19 +)IBoT 2.102 rev. 4

[84] On the Old Assyrian *iṣurtum* see Veenhof 1995 and most recently Waal 2012.

[85] Marazzi 1994: 157–9; since *k/gurta*- is homographic with *gurta*- "fortress" it is, especially in small and fragmentary contexts and when there is no determinative, not always easy to determine with which word one is dealing; cf., for instance, *gur-ta-aš* ABoT 2.292: 6. All attestations listed show NS except for KBo 17.65+, which has OS. KUB 57.91 i 4 (Fragments of cult rituals, CTH 670, NS) 2 GI GUR-DA-A-*an* ZÌ.DA DUR$_5$ x[is to be read 2 GI A!.DA!.GUR!-*an* etc. "two drinking straws (for?) batter(?)" with the signs A.DA.GUR jumbled (see Rüster 1992: 477).

[86] HED K 277. [87] apud Beckman 1983a: 162 n. 386. [88] apud Beckman 1983a: 162.

[89] Thus Cammarosano 2018: 342 (line 38 in total line count).

have been supposed to have sealed wooden tablets, possibly stored in something like boxes or baskets carrying the names of kings from whose reigns the documents stemmed. The ^{GIŠ}*k/gurta*-s, serving as folders or dossiers, could have been marked with the names of kings perhaps with brief indications of what tablets were stacked inside. Compare the following entries from a cult inventory:

> On the *kurta* of Muwatalli twelve monthly festivals (and) one spring festival [have been recorded] but the harvest festival has not been recorded; as to the *gulzatar*-s [in?] the storehouse, the spr[ing] festival has been recorded but [not] the h[arvest] festival.[90]

(. . .)

> On one *gurda* [of PN] and [on] one *gurda* of Muwatalli [. . . ?] a [. . .] has been written . . .[91]

If one thinks that twelve festival names written directly on a box or chest might be a bit too much, one could think of a list or label attached to or accompanying the container. The expression would be shorthand for "(according to the label) on the *kurta* . . . ."[92] In another, unpublished, and unfortunately very fragmentary, cult inventory *gurda-* is mentioned in the context of the É *tuppaš* "the storehouse" (lit. "house of chests/boxes/crates").[93] While the determinative GIŠ likely refers to the material of the objects in question, the GIŠ.ḪUR in IBoT 2.102+, itself not being a material, would seem to clinch the matter – at least for that attestation – in favor of a label or list instead of a container:

> Copied from an old *gurda*-document/record.[94]

Because of its fairly consistent determination by GIŠ this is the only word that together with ^{GIŠ}*LĒ'U* may really denote a wooden writing board.

90 ŠA ^{m}NIR.GÁL ^{GIŠ}*kurtaza* 12 EZEN$_4$ ITU.KAM 1 EZEN$_4$ Ú.BAR$_8$ [DÙ-*an-za*] EZEN$_4$ *zēni=ma* UL DÙ-*anza* [ŠÀ?] É *tuppaš kue gulzatar*$^{\text{HI.A}}$ *nu* EZEN Ú.B[AR$_8$] DÙ-*anza* EZEN$_4$ *zēni=ma* [UL DÙ-*anza*] KUB 42.100 i 17–19 + KBo 26.181: 1–3 (Cult inventory, CTH 673, NS), ed. by Cammarosano 2018: 342–3.

91 (. . .) [. . .] 1 *gurdaza* Ù ŠA ^{m}NIR.GÁL 1 *gurda*[*za*(?) . . .] / [. . .]x-*pí* (erasure) *iyan* . . . KUB 55.48 i 16–17 (Cult inventory, CTH 525, NS), ed. by Groddek 2002: 85, see also Marazzi 1994: 158.

92 When looking at the label on a bottle we, too, can say "this bottle has only 20 calories."

93 Bo 3289: 12' (with the storehouse mentioned in line 9) apud Beckman, StBoT 29: 162.

94 [*k*]*arū*[*i*]*liyaz=at=kan* GIŠ.ḪUR *gurda*[*z* ?] / *arḫa* GUL-*aššanza* x[?] KUB 38.19 rev. 1–2 + IBoT 2.102: 4–5 (Cult inventory, CTH 521, NS), ed. by Starke 1990: 458, van den Hout 2016a: 434; cf. also Giusfredi 2012a: 149 w. lit. In order to make the syntax work Starke emends to GUL-*assan*≪*za*≫ *t*[*eš*], in which case the pronoun *-at* becomes the subject ("they are copied from . . . "). The traces of an alleged *-t*[*e-* seem doubtful on the photos, however.

10.7 (GIŠ.ḪUR)*parzaki(š)*

(GIŠ.ḪUR)*parzaki(š)* is attested twice[95] in two duplicating or overlapping fragments of the thirteenth century BC: once with a *Glossenkeil* ("two small wooden containers, ⸓parzak[*i*-")[96], once without but preceded by GIŠ.ḪUR ("One large wooden container, sealed, without GIŠ.ḪUR*parzakiš*").[97] The inventory of both texts mentions the inthronization of the king and queen and underlines the special character of the objects listed. The lack of word space between GIŠ.ḪUR and *parzakiš* in the latter occurrence pleads in favor of a function as determinative for GIŠ.ḪUR.[98] It has been suggested that *parzaki(š)* might be the word for clay bulla impressed with a seal[99] but there is nothing that specifically points in that direction. One might even say that the statement "sealed without a (sealed clay) bulla" amounts to a *contradictio in terminis*. Given the evidence from Oymaağaç (see Chapter 8.7) that unsealed packing lists were often included with goods within a sealed container such a meaning would seem more appropriate.[100]

10.8 GIŠ.ḪUR*tuppi*?

The two terms GIŠ.ḪUR and *tuppi* appear in immediate juxtaposition in a passage from the Instruction for border commanders:

> If someone brings a lawsuit, sealed, using a GIŠ.ḪUR *tuppi* . . . .[101]

Neither of the two copies, in which these lines are preserved, conclusively either confirm or deny, by the presence or absence of word space between the two elements, that GIŠ.ḪUR functions as a determinative

[95] For both see CHD P s.v.; given the writing with the CVC sign -*kiš* in both cases a neut. *s*-stem can also be considered.

[96] 2 GIŠ*tuppaš* TUR TUR *⸓parzak[iš* KUB 42.22 rt. col. 13 (Palace inventory, CTH 241, NS), ed. by Košak 1982: 50, Siegelová 1986: 42–3.

[97] 1 GIŠ*tuppaš* GAL *KANKU* GIŠ.ḪUR*parzakiš* NU.GÁL KBo 18.179 v 9 (CTH 241, NS), ed. by Košak 1982: 52, Siegelová 1986: 40–1; all read GIŠ.ḪUR as a freestanding Sumerogram.

[98] Košak 1982: 51 does mention that the two are written without spacing but does not consider the possibility of a determinative for GIŠ.ḪUR.

[99] Košak 1982: 51–2, 231, Siegelová 1986: 40–1 w. n. 7, CHD P s.v., Mora 2007: 539.

[100] van den Hout 2010: 264–5.

[101] *mān* DÎNU*=ma kuiš* GIŠ.ḪUR *tuppiaz* (or GIŠ.ḪUR*tuppiaz*?) *šiyan udai* KUB 13.2 iii 21–2 w. dupl. KUB 31.86 iv 6–7 (Instruction for border commanders, CTH 261, NS), ed. by Pecchioli Daddi 2003: 152–3 ("Ma se qualcuno presenta un caso legale convalidato da sigillo su tavoletta di legno o d'argilla"), who quotes several translations that try to do justice to the difficult structure of the sentence, Miller 2013: 228–9 ("If, however, someone brings a law case, with a sealed writing board from a clay tablet"), Gordin 2015: 18 (" . . . sealed by means of an ordinance (GIŠ.ḪUR) (issued) from a tablet (*tuppiaz*)"). Waal 2011: 27 n. 6, hypothesizes that GIŠ.ḪUR *tuppi* "had become a frozen phrase for 'written documents.'"

to *tuppi* (GIŠ.ḪUR*tuppi*), as it does to the several other words. However, the otherwise difficult syntax with the somewhat surprising lack of any case marker on GIŠ.ḪUR or of a conjunction ("using a GIŠ.ḪUR (and?) a clay tablet"?) pleads in favor of a determinative. A direct apposition ("using a GIŠ.ḪUR, (that is) a tablet") is unlikely because one would expect the inverse order ("using a tablet, (that is) a GIŠ.ḪUR") if GIŠ.ḪUR is indeed a special kind of *tuppi*. In light of the preceding words this would not be surprising at all: any kind of special text format can be described as having documentary or evidentiary value by having it determined by GIŠ.ḪUR. The writer of the instruction would simply indicate the importance of the situation if somebody produces written evidence that, moreover, carries the imprint of a seal.

10.9 GIŠ*LĒ'U*

Unlike the words just discussed, in none of its sixteen occurrences (in ten compositions) is the Akkadian GIŠ*LĒ'U* ever determined by GIŠ.ḪUR instead of just GIŠ but like them it is primarily associated with cultic provisions and bookkeeping.[102] Given its Mesopotamian origins and occurrences this is the only word that unequivocally means "wooden tablet" and thus provides evidence for the use of such script carriers in the Hittite kingdom. The two most explicit passages are those from the so-called Aphasia of Mursili and the deposition of Ukkura. At the end of the text that describes the ritual undertaken by Mursili II to heal his speech impediment it says that for the substitute ox and the offerings to the deity they should follow the ritual as described "on the old wooden tablet" (*annallaz IŠTU* GIŠ*LĒ'E*[103]). The verbs used here to describe the actual recording or writing of the texts on the wooden tablet are both *iye-* (lit. "to make, do"), together with *aniye-* "id." the regular *terminus technicus* for writing, and GUL-*š*-. Very similar is the following passage:

[102] (Unless otherwise indicated all in NS:) KBo 4.14 i 25, KBo 18.181 obv. 15, rev. 30, KUB 13.35 + KUB 23.80 i 15, iv 36, KUB 15.34 iv 56 (OS), KUB 22.60 i 17, KUB 42.11 ii 3, KUB 43.50+ rev. 31 w. dupls. KUB 12.31 rev. 19, 21 and KBo 4.2 iv 43, 45, KUB 43.55 v 2, KUB 45.79 rev.? 19, VBoT 114 obv. 3; see the discussion by Marazzi 1994: 140–2, for the use in Mesopotamia see CAD L s.v.; for a GIŠ*LĒ'U* at Alalah VII see Dietrich & Loretz 2006: 121 (43.12 = ATT 882/9), 4 (I am grateful to Jake Lauinger for pointing out to me this attestation): here, too, the clay tablet that mentions the wooden tablet has the text transferred from the wooden board onto the clay tablet.

[103] KUB 43.50 + KUB 12.27 rev. 29, 31 w. dupls. (Aphasia of Mursili II, CTH 486, NS), ed. by Lebrun 1985: 108, 112, van den Hout 2016a: 431. Of course, how old "old" means in this passage is impossible to say.

> Next, they bring the *purullišsiya*-offering. The liturgy(?)[104] of the burnt offering to the Male Cedar Deities is recorded (GUL-*šan*) on a ^{GIŠ}*LĒ'U*.[105]

In the deposition text just mentioned, a man named Ukkura, *decurio* to the queen, defends himself concerning alleged irregularities in the shipping of horses and mules to Babylon. He was sent along with a sealed ^{GIŠ}*LĒ'U*, possibly containing the exact number of animals, but upon return was accused, it seems, of embezzling a number of them. Albeit fragmentary, the following oracle passage, too, may illustrate its administrative character:

> [. . . l]ist [of gods(?) to be] drawn along the paths (lit. of the drawing of the paths) . . .] copie[d from a ^{GIŠ}*LĒ'U*[106]

For a ^{GIŠ}*LĒ'U* as the basis for a clay version containing a ritual ("festival") for celebrating certain deities or providing for them (EZEN$_4$ *ašnuwaš*) compare:

> [Tablet no. #]; finished. Festival of celebrating. [T]hese tablets we copied [f]rom ^{GIŠ}*LĒ'U*-s [a]nd on these tablets [n]ew (ones) were written; of these one is old: (follows the title of a ritual from probably around 1400 BC).[107]

The plural "[T]hese tablets" refers to the series ("[Tablet no. #]") mentioned at the outset, of which the present tablet is the final one ("finished"). The "new (ones)" cannot refer to "[T]hese tablets" on grammatical grounds[108]: the Hittite word for tablet *tuppi* is neuter and not compatible with the common gender *aniyanteš* "were written." Both Marazzi and Waal try to make the wooden tablets the subject of *aniyanteš* resulting in forced translations that do not match the Hittite.[109] Instead, "new/additional (compositions)" must be meant. It is after all a *Sammeltafel*. The first one

[104] Hitt. *uttar* "word, thing, deed" resembles Latin *res* in that it takes its meaning largely from the context. I have chosen "liturgy" here but one could also think more literally of the "words" spoken during the offering rite.

[105] EGIR=ŠU=*ma purullišsiya šipantanzi* [*nu*] *ANA* DINGIR.MEŠ LÚ.MEŠ ^{GIŠ}ERIN-*aš ambaššiyaš uttar IŠTU* ^{GIŠ}*LE'U* GUL-*šan* KUB 15.34 iv 55–57 (CTH 483, OS), ed. by Haas & Wilhelm 1974: 208–9.

[106] [. . . *k*]*ā*[*l*]*utin* [*Š*]*A* KASKAL.MEŠ *ḫuittiy*[*auwaš*? . . .] / [. . . *IŠTU* ^{GIŠ}*L*]*Ē'E a*[*rḫa*] *aniya*[- KUB 45.79 rev.? 18–19 (Kizzuwatnean cult rituals, CTH 500, NS).

[107] [DUB.#.KA]M *QATI* EZEN$_4$ *ašnuwaš* [*k*]*ī*=*ma*=*kan TUPPA*$^{\text{HI.A}}$ *IŠTU* ^{GIŠ}*LĒ'E* [*a*]*rḫa aniyauēn* [*n*]*u*=*kan kītaš ANA TUPPA*$^{\text{HI.A}}$ [*E*]*ŠŠUTI*$^{\text{HI.A}}$ *aniyanteš* [*Š*]À.BA I-*EN karūili* KUB 43.55 v 1–6 (Rituals for the Sungoddess of the Earth, CTH 448, NS), ed. by Haas 1988a: 90, 94, Marazzi 1994: 141, Waal 2015: 327–8.

[108] Thus the translations in Haas 1988a: 94.

[109] Marazzi 1994: 141 ("queste tavolette (d'argilla) le abbiamo redatte sulla base di tavolette di legno (cerate) . . ., le quali perciò si trovano ad essere ricompilate su tali nuove tavolette (di argilla)"), and Waal 2015: 328 ("[T]hese tablets we copied from wooden tablets and on these tablets they are made [a]new").

added is a ritual concerning a dream (or nightmare) of a king named Tuthaliya, the second one a ritual against an attack by a demon.[110]

Unfortunately, too fragmentary to be of much use is the treaty-like text KBo 4.14:

> [. . . and] for him he had already written a [^{GIŠ}*L*]*Ē'U* [. . . and t]hus [he had] sw[orn].[111]

$^{\text{(GIŠ)}}$*LĒ'U* is also attested in two fragmentary inventory texts. Whereas in one text the board may refer to a list of things[112], in the other "2 ^{GIŠ}*LĒ'U*" seem to be part of a long list of luxury items.[113] Since in Akkadian $^{\text{(GIŠ)}}$*LĒ'U* can also be a wooden board or plank without writing[114] that might be the case in the Hittite text here as well.

10.10 Conclusion on the Words So Far Discussed

With GIŠ.ḪUR in the contexts presented above (10.2) as an official document and/or original in terms of "evidence produced on a medium by means of a writing instrument" it could have different formats or functions depending on the situation. Also, in Mesopotamia it never meant "wooden tablet" and in none of the Hittite attestations is there positive evidence that it ever did in Anatolia. As a consequence, neither a GIŠ.ḪUR nor any of the words determined by it were necessarily made of wood. When present, the determinative only indicates that the list, ordinance, or whatever documentary type is referred to by GUL-*zat(t)ar*, *ḫatiwi-*, *k/gaštarhai(a)t/da*, *parzaki*, *k/gurta-*, or even the most general *tuppi*, had evidentiary, that is, authoritative and legal status in that specific context. It is difficult on the basis of the available evidence to make clear distinctions between the terms in question. They were probably technical designations of different kinds of administrative documents, each serving a particular purpose. Only when determined by GIŠ alone (six for *k/gurta-*, one attestation for GUL-*zat(t)ar* and *k/gaštarhai(a)t/da* each, one possibly for *ḫatiwi-* if we include the derived verbal form) are we possibly dealing with wooden writing boards. The only true candidate for "wooden writing board," both on account of

110 Haas 1988a: 86.

111 [. . . *nu*]*=šši karū* [^{GIŠ}*L*]*Ē'U* GUL-*ašta* / [. . . *k*]*išan le*[*k*(-?)] KBo 4.14 i 25–26 (Treaty, CTH 123, NS), ed. by Fuscagni, hethiter.net/: CTH 123.

112 KBo 18.181 obv. 15, rev. 30 (Palace inventory, CTH 243, NS, both times modified by *ipurauaš*, ed. by Siegelová 1986: 372–3, 376–7).

113 KUB 42.11 ii 3 (Palace inventory, CTH 241, NS), ed. by Siegelová 1986: 400–1, cf. Mora 2007: 539.

114 CAD L s.v. *lē'u* a.

its consistent determinative GIŠ and on the basis of its Akkadian usages, is GIŠ*LĒ'U* attested in ten compositions. For comparison, references to metal tablets can be found in six, arguably seven, compositions but nobody has ever claimed they were widely used.[115]

The consequently modest amount of evidence for the use of wooden tablets in the Hittite kingdom suggests a relatively lesser importance for these documents vis-à-vis the clay tablets[116]: even if we leave out the hundreds of colophons written on clay and referring to themselves as Hittite *tuppi* (or Sumerian DUB, Akkadian *TUPPUM*), can one still easily find over a hundred references to what are likely to have been clay tablets in the Hittite sources. The less prominent role these writing boards seem to have played probably has to do with their largely ephemeral and frequently ephemeral–administrative character, something they share with wooden writing boards in most other cultures. The erasable quality of wooden writing surfaces (whether as a whole or just a patch) could have a distinct advantage over clay in an administrative context: once dried a clay tablet is not inscribable again unless totally recycled – losing all data – by immersing it in water again.[117] Another advantage of wooden tablets is their relatively reduced weight compared to clay tablets.[118] The use of clay tablets in the field, especially in the case of the typically Hittite large tablets measuring, for instance, 30 × 20 cm, surely must have been cumbersome and it has been suggested that wooden versions therefore may have been preferred at such occasions.[119] As we shall see (Chapter 12.7), however, in cases where we encounter scribes participating in rituals in a reading role it always is the regular and not the wood-scribe who is reading although the latter is usually assumed to be the one handling wooden tablets. Also, concerning the transport of clay tablets, labor was generally cheap in antiquity and for the ruling regimes easy to come by. Finally, as we saw in Chapter 9, the same composition on a clay tablet may have taken up considerably more space, perhaps up to two wooden tablets of the same size, creating a different kind of problem.

115 Siegelová 1993–1997a, for the seventh attestation see van den Hout 2003: 176.

116 This in contrast to the characterization of the evidence in favor of wooden tablets as "ampiamente attestati" (Marazzi 2000: 80) or a "Fülle" (Payne 2015: 112, cf. also 156); likewise, I do not think there is enough evidence to suppose a widespread use of wooden tablets (thus, for instance, Marazzi 1994: 159, 2007: 465).

117 For the process see Taylor & Cartwright 2011: 310–6 et passim.

118 Based on an experiment carried out at the Oriental Institute in Chicago (with thanks to Erik Lindahl) a clay tablet with an inscribable surface of ca. 10 × 20 cm weighs approximately one kilo heavier than a wax-covered wooden diptych with the same space available for writing.

119 Singer 1983: 42, Starke 1990: 459 n. 1668, Taracha 2000: 165, Waal 2011: 26, Payne 2015: 110.

An interesting question, finally, to briefly ponder here is why four of the five terms discussed show some form of Luwian influence: (GIŠ(.ḪUR))GUL-*zattar*, (GIŠ.ḪUR)*ḫatiwi-*, GIŠ(.ḪUR)*k/gaštarḫait/da*, and (GIŠ.ḪUR)*parzaki(š)*. Three of them show the occasional gloss wedges, GUL-*zattar* is certifiedly Luwian, and when made into a verb *ḫatiwi-* betrayed a Luwian background. The answer may have to be sought in the generally Luwian-speaking demographic character of the Hittite kingdom in the thirteenth century BC (see already Chapter 9.5). If daily administration was largely in the hands of people whose mother tongue was Luwian instead of Hittite, which at that point may not have been more than an administrative language, it would not be surprising that they used technical terms relating to their work from their own vernacular. At the same time the specific and often unstable spellings in GUL-*zattar* and *k/gaštarḫait/da* could point to the lack of standard spelling conventions for Luwian, and thus the cuneiform scribes' relative unease or unfamiliarity in writing their own language.

10.11 Other Evidence for Wooden Tablets

In Hattusa several bronze implements have been found with one pointed and one flattened end (Fig. 10.3). Inspired by later Roman and medieval European examples some scholars have interpreted them as *styli* for wax-covered writing boards.[120] The pointed end, obviously not suited for cuneiform (because not producing the characteristic wedge shape), was intended for incising hieroglyphic signs while the flattened part could erase what had been written previously. Although hard to prove this is certainly possible and perhaps even attractive, although the same objects have been known to be used as surgical instruments elsewhere.[121] Also, we should be careful not to be caught in circular reasoning, arguing for the existence of wax-covered writing boards based on the alleged existence of styli and using the former to justify the interpretation of these objects as styli.

Another line of thinking observes that hieroglyphic signs over time become more abstract, moving away from their pictographic origins, and turning more cursive, that is, simplified or stylized. This is indeed obvious in the Iron Age inscriptions, but some scholars have claimed that the earliest examples of this tendency are already visible in some of the Hittite period seals.[122] Tied in to this is the argument that it was the

120 Payne 2015: 111–2 w. lit. 121 See Rimon 1997: 66 w. fig. 7.

122 On cursivization see Güterbock 1937: 53, 1939: 36, Payne 2008: 119, 2010a: 184, 2015: 45, Waal 2011: 28, Weeden 2018: 61.

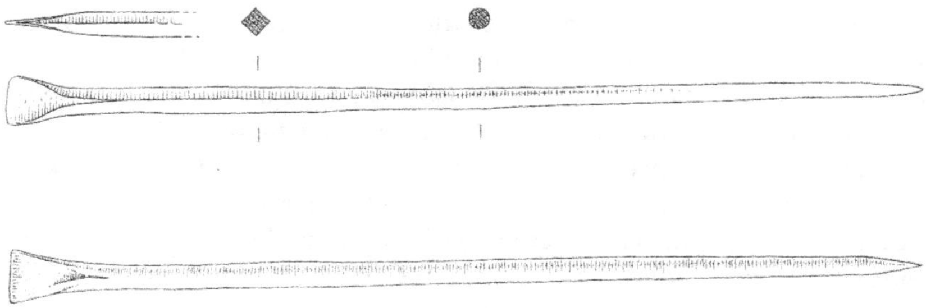

Fig. 10.3 Some possible styli found at Boğazköy (from Boehmer 1972: Pl. xli nos. 1208–1209; copyright Archive of the Boğazköy Expedition, Deutsches Archäologisches Institut Berlin).

cuneiform script that died and vanished along with the Hittite kingdom around 1200 BC while the Anatolian hieroglyphs survived well into the Iron Age and became *the* vehicle for Luwian inscriptions. Both developments would only have been possible, so the reasoning goes, if the hieroglyphic script was widely and frequently enough used. Several scholars therefore postulate a widespread use of the hieroglyphs among not just the kingdom's officials but among the general population as well. The cursivization would point to pen, or brush and ink as writing materials.[123] Very little research has been done on the paleography of hieroglyphic signs and their development within the second millennium and from the second to the first. In his first remark on the subject of "cursive" shapes of the Anatolian hieroglyphs Güterbock gave the seal he would later publish as SBo 2.130 (Fig. 10.4) as his sole example.[124] On this seal impression the only sign that has a stylized form is the MA on top, originally a sheep's head that in its standard second-millennium form already shows an advanced stage of abstraction.[125] David Hawkins mentions the signs *u* and *mu* in their cursive form appearing in second-millennium monumental inscriptions but without giving specific references.[126] What other changes can be

[123] Hawkins 1986: 374, Neumann 1992: 43.

[124] Güterbock 1937: 53 Abb. 31. He then added a bulla (later published as SBo 2.238, see Fig. 10.5) that bears a seal impression on the flat bottom and has additional hieroglyphic signs carved into the sides in order to show that the script was really written instead of just used in seals and monumental inscriptions. Payne 2008: 119 repeats SBo 2.238 as an argument for cursive shapes but Güterbock did not quote them for that purpose nor do they qualify as such. Neumann 1992: 43–4 discusses the stylized form of some first-millennium signs as opposed to their Bronze Age counterparts in terms of "demotivation" (*Demotivierung*), that is, sign shapes losing their motif and pictographic character. The four specific shapes (*pa*, PUGNUS, SCRIBA, *ta*), however, seem to be restricted to Iron Age inscriptions.

[125] For an overview of forms see van den Hout 2009–2011a: 122.

[126] Hawkins 2003: 155.

Fig. 10.4 Seal SBo 2.130 with the cursive *ma*-sign (ᕋ but facing right) on top (from Güterbock 1942: 72).

observed are usually from the second to the first millennium, not within the second millennium itself.[127] If there is a simplification of some signs this may equally well be due to the micro-format of the seal glyptic that allows for less artistic elaboration vis-à-vis the large scale monumental inscriptions and/or to the varying talents of individual seal cutters and the prices they charged for manufacturing a seal.

We should now come back to the hieroglyphic graffiti of personal names accompanied by the sign L.326 ("SCRIBA") in some of Hattuša's temple walls, as mentioned in Chapter 9.4. They have been taken as advertisements for public scribes that people could go to if they needed something written. This would suggest there was a "great" need for scribes offering their services for writing in hieroglyphs and that as a consequence the wealth of written culture was far more extensive than our preserved sources might lead us to think.[128] As we will see (in the Excursus, Chapter 14), the

[127] Payne 2015: 47 ("Die größte entwicklungsgeschichtliche Zäsur stellt der Übergang von der Bronze- zur Eisenzeit dar, bronzezeitliche Inschriften und einige wenige aus der frühen Eisenzeit zeigen distinkte, frühere Zeichenformen."); see also her important first steps towards a paleography of the Anatolian hieroglyphs 44–64 as well as D'Alfonso & Payne 2016.

[128] Dinçol & Dinçol 2002: 210 ("Diese Anzeigen oder Schilder legen nahe, daß es einen großen Bedarf für die öffentlichen Schreiber in der Haupstadt gab und daß das unoffizielle Schrifttum der

interpretation of L. 326 as "scribe" is less certain than hitherto assumed but even if taken as SCRIBA, the fact that there would have been scribes publicly offering their services to write up documents in Anatolian hieroglyphs would show only one thing, namely, that the population at large did *not* have the skills to produce such documents.[129] Nor would it necessarily be true that because of the hieroglyphic sign used to advertise themselves these scribes would write in hieroglyphs (and Luwian). Assuming that the population, almost certainly unfamiliar with cuneiform, might have recognized the L.326 sign, they would thus have known what service was being offered here: writing of an official nature or, simply, the place where an official held his "office hours." Meant for the Hittite administration the documents they provided would most naturally be in cuneiform. An interesting parallel can be seen in the photo (Fig. 10.5) that Ali and Belkıs Dinçol added to their publication of the graffiti. It shows a public scribe who has set up shop on the steps of the Valide Mosque in Istanbul in 1928 right after Kemal Atatürk had introduced the Latin alphabet instead of the Arabic. Behind him, on the steps, a large piece of unfolded paper shows the Latin alphabet in upper and lower case and one step down he keeps his seal cutting implements. Right next to them a sign can be seen that says *imza ve mühürlücü*: "scribe and seal maker."[130] This is his "ad," his shop sign, just like allegedly the graffiti of the Hittite officials on the temple wall, but the sign is written in Arabic script! This was the traditional script that could probably be read or recognized by most educated people in Istanbul at the time but much less the Latin alphabet, which had just been introduced. So, the script he advertised in was different than the script he offered his services in.

Apart from the uncertainty of the alleged SCRIBA sign we should therefore be careful with conclusions concerning the script that was supposedly offered here.

Finally, does the choice of verb for applying script to the surface tell us something? As argued by Willemijn Waal, the verb GUL-*š*- would imply writing hieroglyphs as the preferred script for wooden tablets. As we saw, GUL-*š*- has a wide range of meanings most easily derived from a general "to mark, make a mark(ing)." It is true, as Waal argues, and as we saw above, that some passages with this verb in all likelihood refer to inscriptions in

hethitischen Gesellschaft viel reicher war, als wir von dem materiellen Befund entnehmen können"); cf. similarly Doğan-Alparslan 2007: 247–8, Payne 2008: 118–19, 2010a: 185, 2015: 139–41, Waal 2011: 30.

129 Dinçol & Dinçol 2002: 213.

130 I am grateful to my colleague Prof. Hakan Karateke for reading the inscription for me.

Fig. 10.5 Public scribe, Istanbul 1928 (from *National Geographic* January 1929).

Anatolian hieroglyphs but the text about Mursili II's Aphasia also uses *iye-*, the most general term for writing and recording, in connection with the only certain candidate for wooden tablet, $^{(\text{GIŠ})}$*LĒʾU*. Also, the fact that we happen to have hieroglyphic inscriptions on metal and stone matching some of the attestations for GUL-*š*-[131] says little since we also have ample evidence of cuneiform on metal. Twice only do we find in Hittite texts a term that seems to be specific for cuneiform, *ḫazziye-* "to stab, pierce (with a pointed tool)."[132] It is with certainty attested for an iron tablet of the thirteenth century BC and once in reference to a tablet of unspecified material.[133] We encounter this verb most frequently to describe the slaughtering of animals and the playing of musical instruments, more specifically the plucking of strings. The stabbing- or pricking-like motion adequately expresses both the technique of hitting a punch or chisel in the case of a hard metal tablet and the delicate impression of a stylus in still malleable clay as opposed to the more "drawn out" motion implied by the verb GUL-*š*-. As Heinrich Otten observed for the Bronze Tablet from Hattusa, the signs seem to have been *punched* into the bronze surface with a chisel or similar instrument.[134] Yet, again, the term used in the text for its manufacturing or recording is the general *iye-*.[135] This is not the only way, however, to write cuneiform signs in metal. According to the authors of the publication of the sword of Tuthaliya I the cuneiform inscription "was *cut* into the blade of the sword with a pointed metal chisel."[136] The bronze hayfork mentioned earlier had its cuneiform signs apparently *carved* in with an instrument with a hard pointed tip.[137] This means that, whereas GUL-*š*- and *ḫazziye-* denote different motions or techniques of making marks on a surface, they may not necessarily imply a specific script.[138] Similarly, one can speak in English of "drawing up" a document even though no actual drawing is involved. We also have to keep in mind that the wax-covered tablets from Mesopotamia were with certainty inscribed with cuneiform signs.[139] In the case of the Hittite *decurio* Ukkura who went to Babylon with a document detailing the cargo he brought along, such a document written in Anatolian hieroglyphs would have been of little use to the locals there.[140] I do not think therefore that there is any compelling evidence for the assumption that wooden writing boards were inscribed with the Anatolian hieroglyphs. They may have been occasionally but there is no way of knowing and no evidence that they were.

131 Waal 2011: 23. 132 See Waal 2011: 24 and HW^2 Ḫ s.v., see also Chapter 1.
133 KBo 22.1: 22–3, for which see Chapter 6.3.
134 Otten 1988: 1 (" . . . die Keilschriftzeichen augenscheinlich mit einem meißelähnlichen Gerät in die polierte Oberfläche eingeschlagen worden sind").
135 iv 44, ed. by Otten 1988: 28–9. 136 Ertekin & Ediz 1993: 721 (emphasis mine).
137 Yalçıklı 2000: 115 ("Die Schriftzeichen wurden mit einem spitzen harten Metallstift eingeritzt").
138 Thus already Marazzi 1994: 140. 139 Boehmer 1972: 133, Marazzi 1994: 136–7.
140 Symington 1991: 115.

Within the Hittite administration clay tablets remained the primary and default script carriers with wooden tablets coming in a probably distant second. Clay tablets were the preferred writing surface for all levels of recording, from the most ephemeral (e.g., the Maşat Höyük letters and administrative texts) to the ones intended to be more permanent (e.g., treaties, charters) overlapping with the wooden writing boards only in the first category. Metal tablets occupied the other extreme on the scale of permanence. All three materials were inscribed with cuneiform script although the occasional use of hieroglyphs on wood can be neither excluded nor proven.

CHAPTER 11

The Seal Impressions of the Westbau and Building D, and the Wooden Tablets

11.1 The Collections of Seal Impressions in Hattusa

Under the direction of Peter Neve, German archaeologists uncovered in the years 1990–1991 a hoard of 3402[1] sealed pieces of clay in the northern part of the Upper City (*Oberstadt*) of Boğazköy. The sealings cover the last ca. 150 years of the Hittite kingdom, from about 1350 to the end around 1200 BC. Most of the sealed lumps of clay are teardrop-shaped and are called *bullae* or *cretulae* (German *Tonbullen*). If preserved there is at their narrow, pointed end a small hole visible where originally a cord came out, with which the bulla was attached to the commodity that needed sealing. Besides these bullae there is a much smaller number (430) of more irregularly shaped lumps of clay (German *Tonverschlüsse*) that on their reverse, the non-sealed side, show traces of rope and leather or textile, suggesting that they sealed pouches or bags, that is, the bags were tied shut with pieces of rope and then a piece of clay was pressed on to it and sealed.[2] The sealings overwhelmingly stem from the typical Anatolian round stamp seal. Exceptions are two rectangular stamp seals and impressions from seal rings.

In addition to the bullae and sealed lumps the rooms contained twenty-eight charters, as we saw them in Chapters 4 and 5. Unsealed tablets were apparently never part of this complex and we can therefore say that the defining trait of the objects stored there was their sealed status. This collection was originally kept on an upper story of a building called the *Westbau* (Fig. 11.1). The structure, built on a slope, went down in a fire and the contents of the storerooms collapsed along with the floor into the basement partially spilling unto the slope. The *Westbau*'s function was in

[1] For all details see the edition by Herbordt 2005 and Herbordt et al. 2011. For the total of 3402 see Herbordt 2005: 3 n. 42, 32 n. 261.

[2] For the mechanics of sealing see Herbordt 2005: 25–39; for text references to leather bags see Mora 2006: 539; for textile see Güterbock 1942: 3, Bittel 1950–1951: 169, Herbordt 2005: 34 n. 273; for sealing with clay on wooden surfaces see Alp 1968: 10–2, Müller-Karpe et al. 2009: 191.

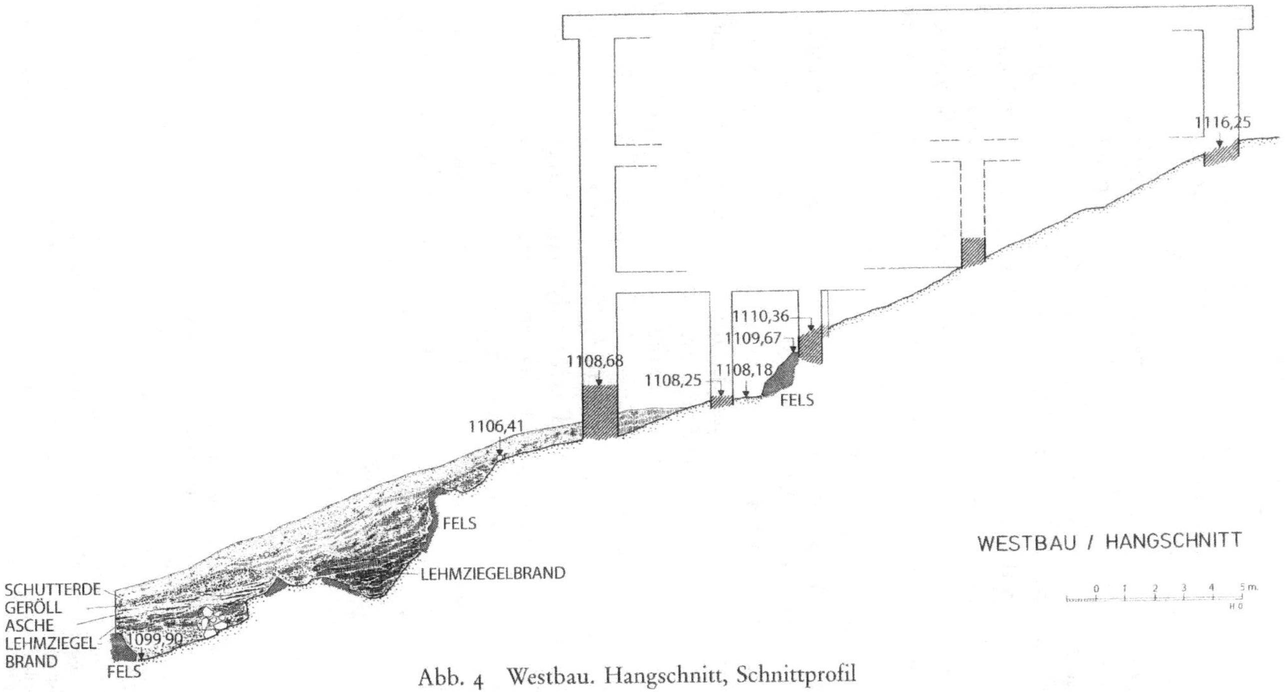

Fig. 11.1 Position of the *Westbau* on the slope (from Herbordt 2005: 9; copyright Archive of the Boğazköy Expedition, Deutsches Archäologisches Institut Berlin).

all likelihood secular in character. Because of a ramp leading to the nearby acropolis a connection to the palace complex has been suggested with probably – in view of the sealings – an administrative function.[3] Finally, it is important to stress that in rooms 1–3 of the *Westbau* the excavators observed an original keeping of the sealings in chronological groups.[4]

The same combination of bullae and charters is known also from elsewhere in Hattusa. In 1936 some 200 bullae and (fragments of) probably fifteen charters were found in a long and narrow room on the west side of Building (Bldg.) D on the acropolis Büyükkale (Fig. 11.2). This collection, too, may originally have been stored on a higher level before collapsing into the basement room and the adjacent area.[5] An even smaller collection of eighty-three bullae and ten charters came to light in Tempel 8 in the Upper City. Some texts other than charters, that is, a few fragments of royal letters and rituals were found here as well, however.

The bullae and charters of Bldg. D and the *Westbau* show a rough chronological distribution. The charters date to the late sixteenth and fifteenth century BC while almost all bullae and clay lumps from the *Westbau* start with the reign of Suppiluliuma I and end in the late thirteenth century BC. Exceptions here are thirteen older impressions probably from around the reign of Tuthaliya I (ca. 1425 BC). Bldg. D probably also had a few older sealings. The situation in Temple 8 is again somewhat different with thirty to thirty-five sealings out of eighty-three that Ali and Belkıs Dinçol dated stylistically to the sixteenth through fourteenth century BC. Including the charters, all tablets there are pre-Suppiluliuma I as well. Finally, Suzanne Herbordt mentions another thirty-seven bullae found in Rooms (Rms.) 27–34 in the storeroom area surrounding Temple 1 in the Lower City (*Unterstadt*) and suggests they were kept in a space over the present Rm. 32. In contrast to Bldg. D, the *Westbau*, and Temple 8, however, no charters (or any tablets, for that matter) were found in combination with these bullae.

[3] Herbordt 2005: 22–3. [4] Herbordt 2005: 9–18.

[5] Bittel 1950–1951: 165–6 maintained that the bullae were kept together in Rm. 1, although at first, he entertained the possibility of their having been kept on a higher floor. However, the majority of the approximately 200 bullae were found in such clear concentration in Rm. 1 that he claims it is hard to imagine they were kept on a higher level. According to the find spot descriptions in the *Konkordanz* only one charter fragment (48/l) was really found inside Rm. 1 although its quadrant q/12 is on the far eastern end of the room. Herbordt 2005: 19, on the other hand, focuses on the bullae that were found strewn beyond Rm. 1 and concludes that the bullae and charters must have been deposited on an upper floor, possibly in a space just over Rm. 1 and adjacent to the audience hall that has been reconstructed for Bldg. D.

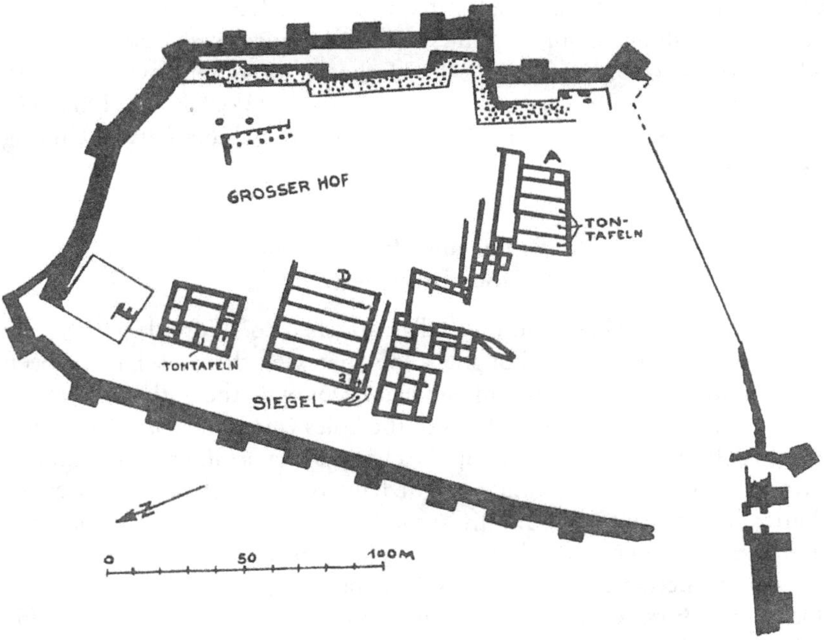

Fig. 11.2 Location of the sealings ("Siegel") found in Bldg. D (from Bittel 1950–1951; copyright Archive of the Boğazköy Expedition, Deutsches Archäologisches Institut Berlin).

The seal impressions provide the names and in most cases titles and/or qualities of the seal owners, usually in Anatolian hieroglyphs. Here, too, the collection from Temple 8 behaves differently in that almost half of the sealings give no profession or quality.[6] The use of cuneiform script on the round stamp seals seems to have been a royal prerogative. In the center field the king or queen's name is written in hieroglyphs while the surrounding rings repeat the name in cuneiform and usually add some genealogy and/or epithets. This restriction was apparently not valid for seal rings where we sometimes find cuneiform also for non-royal individuals. Out of the 3402 pieces from the *Westbau* there are 2062 with royal seal impressions, the remainder belongs to individuals with military, priestly, administrative, or judicial titles. Among the "qualities" are those of princes and courtiers. With only one-eighth in this particular corpus, seals with just names and

[6] van den Hout 2012b: 353.

no titles are relatively rare.[7] All three collections have been published in exemplary fashion: compare Güterbock 1940 (royal seals) and 1942 (all others) for the collection of Bldg. D, Herbordt 2005 (non-royal seals) and Herbordt et al. 2011 (royal seals) for those from the *Westbau*, and Dinçol & Dinçol 2008 for all bullae and clay lumps from the Upper City (including Temple 8).

11.2 The Bullae and the Wooden Tablets: Previous Interpretations

The question is: what were the bullae attached to? Nowadays there are basically two schools of thought. One that sees them as having been attached to texts exclusively and one that keeps open the option of sealings of non-textual goods. On the basis of the holes where the cords were once attached, both in the bullae and in the charters, Hans Güterbock suggested already in 1940 that the bullae might have been attached to charters or charter-like documents.[8] In his second volume of 1942 he added the "remarkable" observation that many bullae looked so evenly fired that he wondered whether the officials had deliberately separated them from their documents or goods and baked them in order to serve as references.[9] He did not specify, however, as references to what. The fact that the documents to which the bullae supposedly had been attached were missing he explained by assuming they were written on wood.

In an influential article of a few years later Kurt Bittel, the director of the Boğazköy excavations that brought to light Bldg. D, followed Güterbock in his interpretation of the wooden tablets but considered the hypothesis of the bullae as deliberately fired and stored references unlikely.[10] Assuming an ever-ongoing stream of goods flowing into the capital over the course of the several centuries that the Hittite kingdom existed one would surely, so Bittel, expect to find more than just the ca. 200 bullae found in Bldg. D.[11] On the other hand, accepting Güterbock's idea of wooden tablets Bittel seems to have been the first scholar to link their supposed existence to the lack of economic and legal (contracts, debt notes etc.) texts, including those

[7] Herbordt 2005: 92. [8] Güterbock 1940: 47.

[9] Güterbock 1942: 3; later Güterbock changed his mind and no longer assumed a deliberate firing of the bullae.

[10] Bittel 1950–1951, cf. similarly Papritz 1959: 30–1.

[11] The later find of the 3402 sealed pieces unknown to Bittel in 1950 does not really remedy his objection. Even if we add up all sealed bullae and clay lumps from the three locations and assume a minimum time span of 150 years (ca. 1350–1200 BC) we still end up with only ca. 25 sealings per year.

involving private individuals: all such texts had apparently been recorded on wood. This has been the prevailing view ever since.[12] In a series of three articles[13] Massimiliano Marazzi follows Bittel and interprets Bldg. D, the *Westbau*, and Temple 8 as "un archivio specializzato di atti amministrativi 'originali.'"[14] He envisages all clay tablets bearing the royal seal in front impressed on the tablet itself, as on the charters, and those of the witnesses appended on cords. The wooden tablets, on the other hand, would have had all seals including that of the king hanging down from them.[15] Marazzi also concludes that in all cases the witnesses' bullae of the preserved clay charters had been separated from them. This assumption is necessary, for none of the names on the bullae found at any of the three locations matches any of the charters' witnesses.[16] Suzanne Herbordt, the editor of all the *Westbau* material, expands Bittel and Marazzi's views to include the seal impressions that once sealed the leather bags. The keepers of the collection apparently grouped various wooden tablets together into dossiers, which were placed into the bags and then sealed.[17]

The reconstruction by Marazzi and Herbordt comes close to answering at least partially Heinrich Otten's question of 1959 where the Hittite "state archives" had been.[18] In spite of all the treaty texts that we have and of all references to their originally sealed status Otten observed that we only seem to have drafts and never the sealed originals. As we already saw (Chapter 8.4), apart from the charters, sealed tablets are extremely rare in the Hittite tablet collections.[19] Whereas Marazzi and Herbordt allow for a certain variety of documents written on the wooden tablets, Itamar Singer has advocated the most restrictive interpretation thus far. In what was probably his last article[20] he claimed that the records once kept in Bldg. D and the *Westbau* comprised charters only and he therefore characterized both buildings as "(crown) land registries," that is, "repositor[ies] for land donation deeds, which were first written on clay tablets and thereafter on wooden tablets." Such deeds were kept "as long as a deed was valid, . . . sometimes for several hundred of years."[21] Although it is true that there is evidence for the Hittite tablet collections holding on to certain records for perhaps reasons of future reference (see Chapters 12 and 13) "state archives" that systematically filed

12 Cf, for instance, later authors like Diakonoff 1967: 351, Beckman 2009: 224, Gilan 2007: 297–8, Bryce 2012b: 226.

13 Marazzi 1994, 2000, and 2007.

14 Marazzi 2000: 86, see also 92, and 2007: 466, 468.

15 Marazzi 2000: 86.

16 Marazzi 2007: 467–8.

17 Herbordt 2005: 39, Herbordt et al. 2011: 29.

18 apud Papritz 1959: 29 n. 57, see also Posner 1972: 35, Güterbock 1980: 53, Mora 2007: 545 n. 49.

19 Balza 2012.

20 See the remark of the editors of Bibliotheca Orientalis at the end of Singer 2013.

21 Singer 2013: 7.

and kept all records that were generated and especially agreements with outside parties, the so-called *external archive* (see Chapter 12.6), was not a typical ancient Near Eastern phenomenon and should not be expected.[22]

The second school of thought is represented by, among others, Clelia Mora. While partially accepting the wooden tablet hypothesis, she more strongly emphasizes the bookkeeping character of the Hittite texts that mention wooden tablets (that is, in the traditional understanding of GIŠ.ḪUR and related words). She establishes an interesting link between the sealings of the *Westbau* and the officials' names on them and the palace storeroom texts (see Chapter 8.7).[23] On the one hand she reconstructs a system, in which incoming goods went through a preliminary registration on wooden tablets and a subsequent definitive phase on clay. These wooden tablets functioned as labels next to the goods and were probably not sealed. Others that were sealed traveled along with the goods as packing lists.[24] On the other hand, in her view, the leather bags may have held commodities rather than tablets and given the links with the palace storeroom texts these commodities were probably luxury goods of the ruling elite who kept charters documenting the real estate they possessed on the shelves as well as their precious objects in the bags and other containers.

In two articles I joined the debate on the functioning of the sealings. In a review of Herbordt's 2005 edition and more pointedly in the proceedings of a workshop held in Pavia in 2009[25] I raised the question of the disconnect between the alleged importance of these documents because of their sealed status and their sometimes centuries-long storage, and their being written on wood. As most authors agree (see §11.3), wooden script carriers are typically used for ephemeral business.[26] Now, with seals of the last known Hittite king Suppiluliuma II of around 1200 BC as the most recent items in the collection and the charters of Telipinu from the end of the sixteenth century BC as the earliest, the total time span amounts to about 400 years. Judging by the earliest seal impressions on the bullae and clay lumps from the reign of Suppiluliuma I (ca. 1350 BC) onwards some of the wooden tablets would have been about 150 years old. If the sealings were indeed attached to wooden writing boards, why did the Hittites around the middle of the fourteenth century decide to shift from using

[22] Charpin 2002: 505. [23] Mora 2007 and 2012; see also Mora 2016.

[24] Mora 2007: 545 also mentions wooden tablets used in cultic ceremonies but these, she assumes, were not sealed and therefore play no role in the interpretation of the collections discussed here.

[25] van den Hout 2007d and 2012c respectively, see also 2012b (= review of Herbordt et al. 2011).

[26] Marazzi 2000: 81, Mora 2007: 538 ("tavolette di legno provvisorie"), 540 ("tavoletta provvisoria, di legno").

clay to wood? Conversely, if not attached to textual records, I reasoned that the bullae most likely had been separated from their commodities. If the bullae and clay lumps had sealed containers with perishable goods, only the most recent ones of those containers, that is, at the moment the elite decided to give up Hattusa as their residence, might have been unopened. Alternatively, if the bullae had sealed non-perishable goods, their containers, too, would be unlikely to have remained unopened for 150 years. In the end, I reluctantly suggested that they might have been used as references of past transactions, as Marcella Frangipane *cum suis* explained the sealings collections at Arslantepe. But then, what good would it do to know in 1200 BC about specific transactions of 150 years earlier?[27]

11.3 Problems with the Traditional View

The most fundamental question that is left unaddressed by almost all scholars who have expressed an opinion on the matter[28] is *why* the Hittite administration made the shift from clay to wood. Only Singer has tried to answer it by pointing to our civilization "using papyrus, parchment and paper for thousands of years to keep its records and oeuvres. When we fill up our libraries and archives . . . we do not necessarily think of the devastating results of a major inflagration. . . . The switch from one technology to another often follows new trends and practicality of usage." Also, he pointed out "important advantages" of wax-covered wooden boards: they could be prepared ahead and recycled. With the latter he probably meant that what had been written could be erased again or an entirely new layer of wax could be applied. Erasure would, however, always leave traces. Also, they were easy for travel and a closed and sealed diptych was "surely less susceptible to erasures or additions than one might think."[29] In short, durability and fear of forgery were not driving factors in the shift from clay to wood and we are left with subjective notions such as trend and practicality. Most of Singer's points are true but, in the end, both carriers have their pluses and minuses. It is undeniable that once made, a clay tablet's inscribability is limited compared to a wooden wax tablet due to the

[27] Cf. also Singer 2013: 7. For the idea of the sealings as references to administrative acts see the ingenious explanation by Frangipane et al. 2007 (and earlier publications); the same explanation has been applied since then on material from Egypt (Smith 1996) and Minoan and Mycenaean hoards (Panagiotopoulos 2014). These collections are seen, however, as covering much shorter time periods, sometimes no longer than just a single administrative cycle, which obviously does not work for the Hittite ones that stretch over a roughly 150-year period.

[28] Marazzi 2007: 466, 468 and Herbordt 2011: 23 acknowledge the shift but make no attempt at explaining it.

[29] Singer 2013: 8.

drying of the clay, but it also requires less effort to make a clay one.[30] A wooden board could be taken from a stash prepared ahead of time and a clay tablet could in most cases be shaped on the spot. Both are recyclable in different ways and, as to journeys, it is debatable how much charters needed to travel. Besides the odd emergency, as may have been the case with Walmu, king of Wilusa (see Chapters 10.2 and 12.6), charters and the like would usually just sit on a shelf, perhaps being checked from time to time until their validity expired. Dried clay tablets can keep forever without maintenance while wooden tablets need to be kept in good shape with oil or wax.[31] As far as the risk of unauthorized changes or forging is concerned, anything can be forged, and forgeries were, as we will see, a recurrent concern. In the case of a wax-covered wooden tablet a word, a phrase or some lines could probably be erased and rewritten or a whole new text could be inscribed on the same tablet but for even the smallest change on a clay tablet the entire document had to be destroyed and replaced. In both cases original seals had to be taken off and probably new ones forged.

The essential question remains what was in Singer's view the ratio behind using wood for charters exclusively while writing everything else on clay? The same question can be asked of the somewhat wider but still restricted range of genres that Marazzi and Herbordt allow in their views. If it was a "trend" or wooden boards were considered so practical, why were they not used for all or many of those other genres we have on clay? The review of words in Chapter 11 that most scholars see as candidates for wooden writing boards showed a mostly basic administrative function for these records. Charters and treaties, however, were not among them. We also know that really important documents such as treaties (including an instruction), occasionally historical accounts, and charters, were transferred to copies in gold, silver, bronze, and iron.[32] We have references to such copies and one bronze tablet, the treaty between the Hittite king Tuthaliya IV and his vassal Kuruntiya, has even survived the ages in pristine condition.[33]

Two additional problems should be mentioned. One is the absence of any bullae that can be convincingly matched with the witnesses on the clay charters of the late sixteenth through fifteenth century BC.[34] Is this a second change in administrative procedures along with the shift from clay to wood, namely from now on to hold on to witnesses' seal impressions as opposed to the practice to dump them in the past? Normally, one would

[30] On recycling of clay tablets see in detail Taylor & Cartwright 2011. [31] Payne 2015: 113–14.
[32] See Chapter 10.11. [33] Otten 1988.
[34] Mora 2012: 66, van den Hout 2012c: 51–2 n. 33, Marazzi 2007: 467.

think that removing the seals would rob a document of its validity.[35] This is what we assume happened to the Bronze Tablet with the treaty of Tuthaliya IV and Kuruntiya in the later thirteenth century BC. Archaeologists found it secondarily buried and stripped of its seals in the Upper City close to the Sphinx Gate. In general, one wonders to what extent the old charters were still in force anyhow in, say, the thirteenth century BC, what with the political, military, and territorial vicissitudes of the Hittite kingdom over the centuries. Places like Hanhana, Katapa, and Tapikka in the Gasgaean region that are among the territories being given away according to the old charters were later lost to the Hittites for shorter or longer periods.

The second is that, if one thinks with Marazzi, Herbordt, and Singer that the wooden tablets were charter-like records or simply charters sealed by the king and a group of witnesses, this only accounts for a small part of the royal seals. Assuming four witnesses to a document[36] the 1365[37] non-royal sealings divided by four could only result in 341 documents, which would still leave 1438 of the 1779[38] royal bullae to account for that must have been used for other documents or purposes. Finally, the fact that there are sites in Anatolia that have produced sealings and bullae, but no written records thus far suggest that the two may not always have to go hand in hand.

11.4 An Alternative Interpretation

The lack, in my opinion, of a convincing explanation of the particular combination of charters, bullae, and clay lumps, and its implications of a shift in administrative procedures (i.e., from clay to wood) forces us to consider alternative ideas. As a point of departure, I take the remarks of Suzanne Herbordt about the so-called double sealings. Herbordt reports thirty-three bullae bearing two different royal seals.[39] She compares this practice to the medieval *contrasigillum*, a kind of two-factor authentication, according to which a second, different seal was applied to a document in order to avoid the risk of fraud and forgery.[40] In the same vein she explains the existence of multiple seals of a single king. In Medieval Europe fear of

[35] Ewald 1914: 239. [36] The actual average on the charters is closer to five.

[37] These are the 1364 pieces with officials' seals as reported in Herbordt 2005: 3 plus the later found stray exemplar of a prince's sealing as reported in Herbordt 2005: 32 n. 261.

[38] Herbordt 2005: 3; one gets slightly different numbers when applying the Table (Abb. 5) in Herbordt et al. 2011: 22 but this does not influence the overall argument.

[39] Herbordt et al. 2011: 28–32.

[40] Herbordt et al. 2011: 41–2. For the medieval practice see in detail Ewald 1914: 89–104.

falsification was a major reason for rulers and authorities to regularly change seals and to have simultaneously multiple seals.[41] In the Hittite kingdom we can see the number of different seals used by kings since Suppiluliuma in the middle of the fourteenth century BC rise steadily to reach a climax under Tuthaliya IV in the late thirteenth century BC with forty-seven! This amounts to roughly two seals per year for his reign. It is entirely possible that some of these were handed out to high officials to seal on his behalf. Herbordt quite convincingly interprets the so-called labarna seals as such administrative seals or *Beamtensiegel*. These are seals without a specific royal name bearing only the title labarna that she convincingly dates to Tuthaliya IV.

The loss of seals and seal fraud were a recurrent phenomenon in the ancient Near East.[42] Model "contracts" concerning the loss of a seal were part of the curriculum of Mesopotamian scribes.[43] The most notorious case for the Hittite kingdom is the arrest of three men at Ugarit for forging a seal of King Mursili II (ca. 1318–1295 BC).[44] The existence of clay seal copies (*tönerne Siegelkopien*), that is, seals that were created by applying fresh clay to an imprint of an already existing impression thereby creating a new "negative" that, in turn, could be used to make identical impressions, has been interpreted as a possible attempt at forgery.[45] Impressions from such seals are usually of much less quality and are slightly smaller than the ones made with the original seals and are thus fairly easy to detect especially if they can be compared to impressions made by the genuine seal.[46] To cut by hand an exact replica of an existing seal in stone or to cast it in metal is virtually impossible and after careful examination even the smallest deviation from the original would give the presenter of the document away as an impostor.

One wonders what procedures were in place to check claims to any rights or goods. That seals were taken seriously in Hattusa and inspected

41 Ewald 1914: 241.

42 Cf., for instance, Steinkeller 1977: 48–9, Hallo 1977, Collon 1987: 116, 119, Bodine 2014 (see following footnote 43).

43 Bodine 2014: 39–40, 123–30, 138–43.

44 RS 16.249, ed. by Nougayrol 1955: 96–8, see Márquez Rowe 2006: 104 ("This incident shows . . . that at least as important as the written word, in the sense of legally effective, was the seal impression on the tablet, a fact that brings us back to the phenomenon of literacy and illiteracy"), 135.

45 Boehmer & Güterbock 1987: 70 and more explicitly Dinçol & Dinçol 2008: 11 w. Lit. ("Erstens kann jeder mit dieser Methode unentgeltlich und sofort beliebig viele Dubletten seines Siegels herstellen, falls das Original verloren gegangen sein sollte oder falls er aus irgendeinem Grund sein Siegel einer anderen Person aushändigen möchte. Zweitens könnten diese Dubletten für illegale Tätigkeiten missbraucht werden").

46 Ewald 1914: 231.

when broken by officials is clear from the procedure of opening a sealed city gate in the morning:

> When he (i.e., the town mayor's son or some other representative) turns the seal at the gate, then whatever Hittite lord or Overseer-of-Thousand or whatever lord is on duty, they must inspect the seal at the gate together.[47]

What exactly did they check? That it had not been broken or tampered with? That it was genuine? But how would they do that? What happened in general if some individual showed up with a sealed document claiming a privilege or entitlement allegedly granted by the current or some past king or high official? If that king or official was still alive and present, they might check directly although the king might not want to be bothered every time this occurred. But if the seal owner was deceased this was impossible. The most certain way to assess the validity of any claim would be to check the authenticity of the seal by comparing it to other, previous seal impressions of the same seal owner. If an imprint of the same seal could not be found the claim could be rejected out of hand or one needed to check back with the seal owner, in case he had started using a new seal. If an identical-looking imprint was identified among the older sealings in the collection the new imprint was to be examined very carefully for any suspicious deviations. The practice of building and maintaining collections of seal impressions in order to detect and prevent seal fraud is therefore well known. Christophe Maneuvrier und Marion Thébault describe such *dèpôts de sceaux de réference* for thirteenth century AD Normandy.[48] But a parallel much closer in time and region to the Hittite kingdom can be found in a letter of a Neo-Assyrian vassal to his lord Sargon II:

> The signet ring (impression on the letter) which he delivered is not made like the signet rings of the king, my lord. I have a thousand signet ring(-sealed letters) of the king, my lord, with me and I have compared it with them – it is not made like the signet ring of the king, my lord! I am herewith sending the signet ring(-sealed letter) to the king, my lord. If it is genuine, let them write

47 *n=ašta maḫḫan* ANA KÁ.GAL $^{\text{NA4}}$KIŠIB *uēḫzi* EGIR=ŠU=*ma kuiš* BĒLU ^{URU}*Ḫatti naššu* ^{LÚ}UGULA *LIM našma kuiš imma* BĒLU *ḫandaīttari* (latter word partly over erasure) *n=ašta* $^{\text{NA4}}$KIŠIB (followed by erasure) ANA KÁ.GAL *takšan* (written over erasure) *katta uwandu* KBo 13.58 ii 21–5 (CTH 257, NS), ed. by Miller 2013: 184–5. It is not immediately clear what "turning" the seal means here. Earlier authors (see Miller 2013: 364 n. 217) have taken it as the breaking of the seal so that the gate can be opened but the explicit "inspect the seal *at* the gate" instead of "the seal *of* the gate" may imply that the representative of the mayor only "turns" it (in case it is a bulla on a cord) facing the higher official (the "Lord") so that he can see it and both can inspect it. Miller renders it as "*he turns to* the seal (of) the gate" (italics Miller).

48 Maneuvrier & Thébault 2011 (I am grateful to Michael Allen, University of Chicago, for this reference).

> a copy of the signet ring(-sealed letter) which I am sending and I will place it with him, so that he may go where the king, my lord, sent him to.[49]

The individual in question, on a mission with a document bearing the seal of Sargon, made a stop at the residence of the vassal showing his credentials. Studying the seal, the vassal became suspicious and before letting the man travel on, he checked the seal impression against previous ones he had apparently kept. Unable to match it with any sealing in his collection he wrote to his king to verify the authenticity of the document. Even though the vassal may be exaggerating when he claims to have checked all "thousand" sealings in his possession the number is interesting in view of the over 3400 pieces in the *Westbau*. This was a minor vassal king, but in the *Westbau* we are dealing with the capital of the Hittite kingdom. The vassal does not explicitly say that he kept the older documents for that purpose, but it is clear that the idea of using them to establish the authenticity of new incoming sealed documents was entirely self-evident.

In light of the above I suggest we see the hoards of seal imprints of the *Westbau* and Bldg. D in the Hittite capital as reference collections. Officials used them in the same way the Neo-Assyrian vassal did. They built up these collections by detaching seals from written documents and/or goods when they had served their initial purpose of validation. The charters found at these locations must therefore have lost their original evidentiary value and were only kept for their royal seals. The witnesses' impressions had been removed marking the invalidation of the document, but the royal seals were still useful in case an old claim was brought forth allegedly in the name of one of the former kings. The chronological groupings, in which they were kept, facilitated searching for the relevant impressions. This means that the question of what the seals were originally attached to is no longer relevant for the interpretation of the *Westbau* and Bldg. D. Of course, it would be very interesting for us to know but due to the Hittite practice of removing and collecting old sealings we are not able to answer that question on the basis of these two find complexes. As collections, they are secondary and do not even deserve the label "archive" although they did serve an important role for the Hittite administration as a tool in their daily work. This proposal also relieves us of the onus to find an explanation for the alleged shift from clay to wood in the Hittite chancellary practices.

A final objection to this interpretation could be the high number of sealed pieces in the *Westbau* and the high number of sealings for certain kings or

[49] Translation Karen Radner 2008: 488. I am most grateful to Mark Garrison and my colleague Susanne Paulus for drawing my attention to this letter.

officials. For Tuthaliya IV, for instance, with his forty-seven different seals we have about 450 sealed pieces. Why could they not have kept just one or two really good impressions instead of storing dozens for a single individual? First of all, it probably does not work that way in a collection maintained and amassed over 150 years. Already after a few decades or so no custodian would know exactly what the state of preservation of each of the individual pieces of the various seal impressions of kings, queens, princes, and officials was, nor are they likely to have taken the time with every incoming sealing to check whether there already was a complete one or not. As officials go, they probably preferred to err on the side of caution and would rather throw another lump of clay on one of the piles than being lectured on the principles of efficient collection keeping. Second and more importantly, the custodians of the collections of the *Westbau* probably faced the same challenges that a modern editor of this material is confronted with. It is rare that a seal's entire surface is pristinely impressed and preserved. Edges frequently do not make it in their entirety onto the bulla and if imprinted on the side of a bulla one usually only gets a sliver of the original seal. Also, when arriving as part of a larger shipment, there is probably no reason to check a sealing and the seal may be ripped off and broken, but it could be used for checking official documents later. In her publication of the bullae, Suzanne Herbordt has meticulously recorded the state of preservation of every sealing and it turns out there are hardly any complete sealings, i.e., ones that show the entire surface of the original seal. Besides many impressions that are completely abraded (*völlig verwittert*), preserved only partially (*nur zur Hälfte/zu einem Drittel erhalten* etc.) or simply not completely preserved (*unvollständig erhalten*) the best two categories are "almost completely" (*fast vollständig*) or even "completely preserved" (*vollständig erhalten*). For the seals of princes and officials the following are listed:

> "almost completely preserved": 14, 45.5, 47.5, 60, 74, 100.1,[50] 113, 128.1–2, 131, 170.1, 177.1, 196.1, 222.3, 239, 307, 333.2, 360, 369, 370.4, 456.2, 376.1, 535, 546.2, 607, 619, 626, 643.3, 645, 667, 671.2, 691, 694. 33 = 2.4 percent (total 1364 sealings)
>
> "completely preserved": 46, 128.3, 172, 376.4, 222.1,[51] 226, 227.2, 382.3, 408, 473, 489.3, 598, 613, 644,[52] 649,[53] 652.1–2, 653.1–2, 685.1, 726. = 21 = 1.5 percent (total 1364 sealings).

50 Herbordt 2005: 130 no. 100.2 does not record the state of preservation.

51 Herbordt 2005: 153 no. 222.1 adds "aber verw(ittert)"; although it is possible that the abrasion happened in the collapse of the *Westbau* or the centuries following, I still include it here.

52 Herbordt 2005: 227 no. 644 adds "aber verw(ittert)"; although it is possible that the abrasion happened in the collapse of the *Westbau* or the centuries following, I still include it here.

53 Herbordt 2005: 228 no. 649 adds "aber verw(ittert)"; although it is possible that the abrasion happened in the collapse of the *Westbau* or the centuries following, I still include it here.

For kings and queens:

> "almost completely preserved": 1.3, 8.1, 27.1, 36.1, 55.6, 68.1, 3–4, 69.1–3, 10, 27, 38, 41, 89.1, 93.1, 94.3, 97.1, 115.22, 134.1–2, 13, 26, 31, 135.1, 5, 12, 16, 21, 138.2–3, 5–6, 17, 21, 141.4, 149.5–6, 19, 31, 35, 150.4, 12, 153.1–3, 155.15, 157.1, 4, 8, 19, 25–26, 159.1, 161.2, 180.1. = 57 = 2.7 percent (total 2095 sealings)
>
> "completely preserved": 55.1, 56.1, 114, 76.46, 77.8, 173.1–2. = 7 = 0.3 percent (total 2095 sealings).

In the majority of cases the ancient officials therefore needed more pieces to check the entire surface of an impression just as the modern editor pieces together a complete or near complete reconstruction of a seal out of numerous fragments. As a consequence, the high number of sealings kept is testament to the seriousness with which the Hittite civil servants approached their task.

11.5 Conclusion

In the end the large number of seal impressions over all from the capital, from Central Anatolia, and from the fringes of the Hittite kingdom somewhat alleviates the absence of socio-economic administration.[54] Their presence attests to the importance of sealing in Hittite administrative practice. If not all bullae and sealings were attached to land registry records, they can have been affixed to other kinds of documents accompanying or attached to goods packed and stored in crates and bags. Hittite administration of goods on a regular and routine basis (as opposed to more unique transactions like seen in the KASKAL-series, see Chapter 8.7) may have proceeded largely through a system of sealings documenting the moment in time and the individual and/or office responsible for the latest state of the commodity and for the subsequent phase marked by the removal of the seal and the possible application of a new one.[55] Much of this can have happened without written documentation, as long as the persons involved knew each other and knew what was going on. We can see this illustrated in the passage about the opening of the city gate at dawn and its implied closing in the evening quoted earlier. The interpretation proposed here for the collection of seal impressions kept at several places in Hattusa shows the importance of the seal and its integrity within the system of the Hittite kingdom. The same explanation may work for similar collections like the ones at

[54] See the map with the distribution of finds of sealings in Anatolia in Mora 2000: 63.
[55] On this system see Fissore 1994.

Acemhöyük or Konya-Karahöyük, and perhaps also at Kaman-Kalehöyük, although the latter must then have been secondarily discarded.[56] This system worked, as long as seals kept their one-to-one relation with the person they represented. This explains the lengths kings went in maintaining that integrity by frequently changing seals. Carrying someone's seal, for instance, could mean being under that person's protection, as we see twice in the contexts of safe-conducts where someone was issued "something sealed" enabling that person to travel unharmed.[57]

With this we have entered the chancelleries of the Hittite kingdom and their *modus operandi*. How should we characterize the Hittite collections and how did they function within the state? These and related questions we will investigate in the following chapters.

[56] For Acemhöyük see Veenhof 1993 and Topçuoğlu 2016: 234–90; for Konya-Karahöyük see Alp 1968: 12–5.

[57] See CHD Š 339.

CHAPTER 12

In the Hittite Chancellery and Tablet Collections

12.1 The Reign of Mursili II

Mursili II ruled for at least twenty-two years and is by any standard the most prolific king from a literary point of view: besides his extensive historical works we have a number of prayers – often of a deeply personal nature – testifying to a strong involvement in many issues.[1] There is the unique account of the rituals performed because of a temporary loss of speech he suffered following a traumatic experience.[2] Finally, he was the driving force behind a series of state treaties, a genre that finds its culmination in his reign. Whether Mursili himself was literate we may never know but he certainly is on record for being aware of and using the power of the written word. Our picture of the Hittite state chancellery as a vital piece of state machinery with historical documents being used and consulted to generate new ones is largely due to him. Works like his Deeds of Suppiluliuma, the biography of his father, the double account of his own reign in the Ten-Year Annals and Extensive Annals could not have been written without access to systematic tablet collections. The perfection of the treaty genre with their historical preambles was possible only through the consultation of already existing sources like earlier pacts and treaties, correspondence, and historical works of his predecessors' reigns. Also, in executing his office as king he used the tablet collections, as becomes clear in his handling of the epidemic that occurred during his reign. From the Hittite point of view this was the gods' revenge for the murder of Tuthaliya III by Suppiluliuma, the latter's breach of a former Hittite–Egyptian treaty when sending two of his generals raiding the Amka territory in Egyptian controlled Syria, and finally for neglected cultic duties. The gods did not readily offer these transgressions as reasons for their punishment. This was for the king to find out by searching his memory and by ordering priests to

[1] Singer 2002: 47–79. [2] van den Hout 2004.

conduct oracle investigations. For Mursili, searching his memory meant searching the institutional memory that was the tablet collection:

> [Then the matte]r [of . . .] started to weigh [on me] again and I made the go[ds' anger the subject of an oracle inquiry(?).] Two [o]ld tablets [I found.] One tablet ab[out an offering to the River Mala: in the past] for [me]r kings [had] brought the offering to the River Mala, but for as long as [people have] d[ied] in Hatti-Land since the days of my father, we had never made [the offering] to the River Mala.
>
> (§) The second tablet is about the town of Kurustamma: how the Stormgod of Hatti brought the people of Kurustamma to Egypt and how the Stormgod of Hatti made a treaty for them with the people of Hatti, (and how) they were then put under under oath by the Stormgod of Hatti. Now that the people of Hatti and Egypt were put under oath by the Stormgod, it happened that the people of Hatti turned away and suddenly broke the divine oath: my father sent troops and chariots and they attacked Egyptian territory, the land of Amqa. And again, he sent them and again they attacked.[3]

Mursili also depended on the collections as a source of, literally, collective wisdom. Over time scribes had accumulated and studied foreign rituals usually aimed at healing individuals or groups from psychological and somatic trauma. So, when his youngest son, the later Hattusili III, turned out to be a sickly child Mursili did not approach a "doctor" but Mittannamuwa, the head of the capital's tablet collections, as the boy's caretaker. He would surely be able to locate the relevant remedies.

Mursili needed all these resources, for at his accession he faced a range of serious problems. First there was the epidemic that would continue to rage for twenty years and cost many lives, among them that of his father and his older brother, Suppiluliuma's first successor. Surrounding peoples sensed the vulnerability that came with the deaths of Mursili's two immediate predecessors and jumped at the opportunity to rise up. Mursili may have been relatively young when coming to the throne and at any rate complained he was seen as inexperienced. Of a more personal nature but not

[3] [. . . *memiy*]*aš namma nakkišta nu* ŠA DIN[GIR.MEŠ . . . *ariyanun*(?) *nu=za k*]*arūila* DUB.2.KAM.ḪI.A *peran u*[*emiyanu*]*n* I *TUPPU* Š[A SISKUR ŠA ^{ID}*Māla karū=m*]*a=wa* SISKUR ŠA ^{ID}*Māla karū*[*ili*]*ēš* LUGAL.MEŠ *ḫinka*[*n ḫarker*] *kuitman=ma IŠTU* UD.KAM-*U*[*M*] *ABI=IA INA* KUR ^{URU}*Ḫatti a*[*kkiškettat nu* SISKUR] *ŠA* ^{ID}*Māla UL k*[*u*]*wapikki iyauē*[*n*] § [(*ŠA*)N(*U TUP*)P] *U=ma ŠA* ^{URU}*Kuruštamma* LÚ.MEŠ ^{URU}*Kuruštamma maḫḫan* [(^{d}U ^{URU}*Ḫa*)]*tti INA* KUR ^{URU}*Mizri pē*[*d*]*aš nu=šmaš* ^{d}IM ^{URU}*Ḫatti maḫḫan* [(*išḫiū*)]I *ANA* LÚ.MEŠ ^{URU}*Ḫatti menaḫḫanda iyat namma=at IŠTU* ^{d}U ^{URU}*Ḫatti li*[*n*]*ganuwanteš nu* LÚ.MEŠ ^{URU}*Ḫatti kuit* LÚ.MEŠ ^{URU}*Mizri=ya IŠTU* ^{d}IM *^{URU}*Ḫatti lin***ganuwanteš ešer nu uēr* LÚ.MEŠ ^{URU}*Ḫatti peran waḫnuēr nu=kan NÎŠ* DINGIR-*LIM* LÚ.MEŠ ^{URU}*Ḫatti ḫūdāk šarriēr nu ABU=IA* ÉRIN.MEŠ ANŠE.KUR.RA.MEŠ *uiyat* **nu* ZAG KUR *Mizri* KUR *Amga walaḫḫer namma=ia uiyat nu namma** *walaḫḫer* KUB 14.8 obv. 8–20 w. dupl. KUB 14.10 ii 1–14, ed. by Goetze 1929: 208f., Rieken et al., hethiter.net/:CTH 378.2 (TX 2017–09-07).

less worrying was the influence his stepmother exerted in the capital. He portrays her as continually invoking the gods, indulging in black magic, squandering his father's estate, and causing the death of his beloved wife Gassulawiya. Although oracle inquiries authorized him to put her to death Mursili sent his stepmother into exile: the epidemic had once more proven that raising your hand against a family member would sooner or later be severely punished.

After fulfilling his religious duties Mursili turned his attention first to the Gasgaeans in the north. Then, on the west coast, Uhhazidi, king of Arzawa, possibly with help from Ahhiyawa, had started to undermine Hittite power and persuaded neighboring kings to join him. In his third and fourth year Mursili defeated the Arzawa coalition and split up Arzawa into three separate appanage kingdoms, Mira, Haballa, and the Seha River-land with treaties for each of its newly minted vassal kings.[4] In the later years of his first decade Mursili was called to the northeast and the most southern part of his kingdom. In Syria the kings of Nuhasse and Kadesh had defected with support of the Egyptian pharaoh Horemheb. The Assyrians seized on the deaths of Mursili's two brothers Piyassili (also known as Sarrikusuh), viceroy at Karkamish, and Telipinu, king in Aleppo, as an opportunity to invade the land east of Karkamish on their side of the Euphrates. Mursili restored Hittite authority in Syria in his ninth year, appointed the sons of Piyassili/Sarrikusuh and Telipinu as viceroys and concluded treaties with Amurru and Ugarit.[5] In the following two years he finally solved the problems with the region known as Azzi-Hayasa in the Caucasus foothills. Here, too, a new treaty set an end to the hostilities. Preferring treaties to militarily enforced loyalty Mursili thus continued his predecessors' policy and refined the state treaty into a fine-tuned instrument of international diplomacy. In order to do so he had to rely on an apparatus of officials well versed in the intricacies of such agreements, with the necessary institutional memory, and able to produce new ones.

12.2 The Hittite Cuneiform Corpus from an Institutional Perspective

The organization that was the Hittite state was responsible for its economic, military, judicial, and religious needs. These different areas culminated and were ultimately combined in the person of the king who was

[4] Beckman 1999: 69–86. [5] Beckman 1999: 59–69.

CEO, commander in chief, chief justice, and high priest. Ideologically, the king embodied the Hittite state to the extent that his fate was synonymous with its wellbeing. The chancellery and its tablet collections both of the capital and its provincial centers served him to run that organization in all its aspects as smoothly and effectively as possible. Each of the four areas (economy, military, judiciary, religion) was essential to the state. Military campaigning was as much the king's task as was taking care of his religious duties, rendering justice at the highest level and keeping the royal storehouses and coffers well filled. Each of these tasks is reflected, sometimes amply, in the preserved corpus of cuneiform texts. To support the king in performing them the administration enabled the king to correspond with his officers in the field, wrote, sent, and received correspondence with his peers in the wider world of the ancient Near East, made sure cultic celebrations were done on time and properly, composed new prayers and hymns, changed existing compositions according to need, took down depositions, etc. All resulting documentation, which is most of what has been described in the Chapter 8, was kept, filed, stored, and after a while appraised, and then either discarded, or kept for the longer term. Most of the preserved Hittite material thus has a clear archival character according to the definition adopted of that term here: the corpus as we have it is the whole of the written documents – including sometimes drawings – officially received or produced by the administrative bodies and officials of the Hittite state, in so far as these documents were intended to remain in the custody of those bodies and officials.[6]

The Hittite corpus is quite unique in the sense that it allows us to follow the written administration of a large state over a period of at least three to four centuries. During that time the Hittite state was basically ruled by a single extended family or close circle of intermarrying families, making for a relatively unparalleled continuity. When the capital was given up around 1200 BC and the kingdom de facto ceased to exist, its administration came to an end. If it continued elsewhere, we have not found it yet. We do not know what happened when the ruling class packed up and left. It is usually assumed they intended to continue their empire somewhere else. It is very well possible that along with their valuables the ruling elite took those records with them, which they considered important. Perhaps it was the most recent records that were still "active," or the metal tablets of treaties deposited in the various temples, so they could identify themselves at foreign courts. Whatever

[6] For a definition of "archive(s)" used here see van den Hout 2005.

happened, they also left thousands of records behind. As we will see shortly, we can divide these into short- and long-term records. The former usually exist in single copies only and would be discarded after a while. The latter often come in multiple copies from different periods and clearly were the kinds of texts the Hittite administration wanted to hang on to. The short-term compositions indeed overwhelmingly date to the thirteenth century BC. On the other hand, rarely can they be ascribed with certainty to the last known king Suppiluliuma II, as one might expect. In fact, as far as we are able to date them, most short-term records were produced under the reigns of Hattusili III or Tuthaliya IV. This is true of many letters, of cult inventories, oracles, and vows. Also, as we saw (Chapter 8.7), several of the few but truly administrative texts show Older Script and are likely to predate the thirteenth century BC. Real bookkeeping does not seem to have been practiced much anyhow. As a consequence, there is a surprising dearth of texts from the reign of Suppiluliuma II, which can mean that his administration quite effectively took most of the records with them or they abandoned the city relatively early and his reign there did not last that long.

The mentioned dichotomy into short- and long-term texts brings to mind the distinction Leo Oppenheim introduced in his ground-breaking book *Ancient Mesopotamia, Portrait of a Dead Civilization* for the Mesopotamian written legacy that spanned some three millennia. He distinguished short-term texts that talk about the "day-to-day activities of the inhabitants of Mesopotamia, from kings down to shepherds," consisting primarily of "records and letters,"[7] and longer term works that he called "literary texts." The former group can be directly compared in function to the short-term Hittite genres but the situatedness of the "literary texts" is of a somewhat different order. For the latter Oppenheim coined the expression "stream of tradition."[8] Only a small part of this literary tradition matched what we would most readily associate with that term, epic tales, fables, and the like, but mostly comprised omens, lexical lists, and medical texts, in short, scholarly compositions. Most of these were "at some early point . . . frozen into a specific wording and an established arrangement of content" and faithfully transmitted in scribal circles for about two millennia.[9] As we will see, the long-term texts from Anatolia are mostly of a more practical nature. Foreign, that is, Sumerian, Akkadian, and Hurrian, compositions like rituals, lexical lists, epic,

[7] Oppenheim 1964: 23.
[8] Oppenheim 1964: 13 but see also the remarks by Radner & Robson 2011: 659–60.
[9] Oppenheim 1964: 18.

mythological, and wisdom texts probably do deserve the label "scholarly" but most others emerged and functioned within a specific practical day-to-day setting that could be either diplomatic–political, judicial, or religious. Apart from perhaps the Law collection (but that was in its written history at least once revised as well) these compositions were hardly frozen but regularly modified and sometimes profoundly changed over the course of their existence in the Hittite tablet collections.

Let us list all genres as usually recognized and group them according to their short- and long-term properties:

Table 12.1 *Genres in Hittite literature as short- vs. long-term records*

Short-term texts:[10]
letters (CTH 151–210)
storeroom inventories and administration (CTH 231–250)
tablet inventories (CTH 276–282)
tablet labels (CTH 283)
court depositions (CTH 293–297)
cult inventories (CTH 501–530)
oracle practice (CTH 561–582)
vows (CTH 583–59 0)
Long-term texts:
historiography, treaties, edicts (CTH 1–147, 211–216)
charters (CTH 221–225)
instructions and loyalty oaths (CTH 251–275)
laws (CTH 291–292)
mythology (Anatolian) (CTH 321–338)
hymns and prayers (CTH 371–389)
festival scenarios (CTH 591–721)
Hattian, Palaic, and Luwian compositions (CTH 725–773)
rituals (CTH 39 0–500)
non-Anatolian imported writings:
omina (CTH 531–560)
Sumerian, Akkadian and Hurrian compositions (CTH 310–316, 774–819)
non-Anatolian myths and epics (CTH 341–370)
hippological texts (CTH 284–287)
lexical lists (CTH 299–309)

[10] The CTH numbers refer to the *Catalogue des textes hittites*, a standard listing of Hittite compositions by genre by Emmanuel Laroche with supplements in Laroche 1972 and 1975. This work has now been replaced by the online *Konkordanz der hethitischen Keilschrifttafeln* (I-LX) by Silvin Košak on the website Hethitologie Portal Mainz at www.orient.uni-wuerzburg.de/hetkonk/.

I follow Willemijn Waal[11] in distinguishing within the above corpus the following four categories or groups[12]:

1. temporary or disposable records
2. semi-current records
3. permanent records
[4. charters.]

12.2.1 Temporary or Disposable Records

Under this heading Waal subsumes letters, small oracle reports, storeroom inventories, and depositions. "They belonged to the first level of administration; they were made on the spot and were of a temporary nature. The tablets can be hastily written and may be of a lesser quality of clay."[13] The smaller size made the documents easier to handle in situations where a letter was quickly dictated, where an inventory had to be drawn up on the spot, as goods were delivered or taken out, or when notes were taken while witnessing an oracle investigation. The resulting records were not meant for long-term storage, if at all, and therefore never show a colophon. The information may have been as short-lived as the items recorded and the record was either soon discarded and/or the data were incorporated in larger and more carefully executed tablets that belong to the semi-current records of group 2. As may be expected, such tablets are rare at Hattusa, but the entire archive found at Maşat Höyük (Level III) should be assigned to this group.

12.2.2 Semi-current Records

In this group we find many of the same genres as in group 1 but now the data of group 1 records have been transferred to more lasting documents

[11] Waal 2015: 173–5.

[12] This replaces my earlier Groups A (texts with duplicates) and B (unica) in van den Hout 2005: 282–3. Waal's grouping deals more adequately with the charters and with compositions like, for instance, the horse-training texts where we have (apart from one small exception) no duplicates but that are not short-term texts either. By relying less on the presence of duplicates and by taking into account formal criteria of the tablets themselves Waal's system allows more flexibility and is more realistic: it does mean that it is sometimes less clear-cut (oracle reports, for instance, appear under both groups 1 and 2, depending on their size and execution: small hastily written oracles that formed the basis for later more carefully written reports fall under group 1 while the later reports belong to group 2) but at the same time it better reflects the daily situation on the ground. It also uses the terminology of the Society of American Archivists (www.archivists.org/glossary) and is therefore rooted in archival science.

[13] Waal 2015: 173.

with a more careful script and layout.[14] In contrast to group 1 these records had something of a shelf life but judging by the fact that we usually do not have such texts preserved from before the mid-thirteenth century BC that life probably did not exceed one or at most two generations and may often have been a lot shorter. Good examples of semi-current records are the larger two-column oracle reports and depositions, or the ledger preserved at Oymaağaç combining several packing lists.[15] Since storage was necessary, records from this group sometimes have a colophon but as observed by Waal they are not as frequent as in the case of the group 3 permanent records and less uniform.[16] The fact that they repeated information from earlier stages in the administrative process or that the information was needed in more than one place simultaneously sometimes leads to the existence of what seem to be duplicates or parallel versions. A case in point may be the oracle ensemble known as CTH 568, of which there existed at least four exemplars. Rather than a "classic" oracle text with all the detailed descriptions of the mantic techniques the text is a list of results that needed to be incorporated in new redactions of at least two of the great state festivals of spring and autumn. It is conceivable that the presence of more versions is connected to the number of festivals affected. Occasionally, duplicates have been identified among other oracle records, but given the complex text tradition they may not always be actual duplicates but rather fragments of a group 1 disposable record that we also find back in a group 2 semi-current record.[17] Similarly, there are some isolated cases of multiple versions among the palace and temple administration, cult and tablet inventories, and vows.[18] It is striking, however, that the compositions in question almost always stand out in their genre for other things, too, besides having one or more duplicates.[19]

12.2.3 Permanent Records

As opposed to the semi-current records that only occasionally exist in more than one version these are the compositions that as a rule have duplicates because they were copied and redacted time and again. The versions we have often include copies from the fifteenth and/or fourteenth century BC

[14] For the economic inventories see Siegelová 1986, for depositions Werner 1967, for the process of oracles from the smallest and most ephemeral pieces to large ledger-like tablets see van den Hout 2001: 433–4.

[15] See Chapter 8.7. [16] Waal 2015: 174. [17] Berman 1982: 124, and van den Hout 1998: 14.

[18] On these see van den Hout 2002: 872–5.

[19] For the Vow of Puduhepa see already Chapter 8 n. 56.

and enable us to witness changes in Hittite language and culture. Given the number of texts of the same genre that do exist in more versions, the occasional lack of a duplicate is easily accounted for through archaeological coincidence. Moreover, not every tablet needs to have a duplicate in order to be considered a permanent record. Some compositions may have been deemed important enough to keep but may never have ranked high on the copying priorities list. The same goes *a fortiori* for the lack of older exemplars. Many thirteenth century copies show in their language that they go back to older compositions but only in a minority of cases do we have physical evidence of them. Either they have been lost over time and did not survive the ages or they were deliberately discarded once a new copy had been made. The reasons for holding on to these compositions were manifold. In the case of state festivals, they supported the complex logistics of the rites and were kept up for future reference preserving institutional memory. The latter is true also for all political texts (treaties, edicts, etc.) that provided the necessary information in matters of national and foreign policy. In these cases, a written record often served as an example for drawing up a new record instead of having to compose from scratch. Treaties and similar texts but also historiography were composed and often compiled after careful consultation of existing records like letters, field reports, previous treaties, and earlier historical prose. At the same time, as much as earlier records helped their composition, they themselves were supposed to provide a source for future consultation. Prayers and hymns, too, were re-used over and over and close reading of many genres among the permanent records can often reveal the seams where older and newer patches were sewn together.[20] In archival terms such older manuscripts can be called *retroacta*: earlier documents relating to the same matter. Such direct practical use may not as a rule apply to most of the rituals and the non-Anatolian material although in the case of rituals, they may well have been kept for their healing potential, as we will see in Chapter 13. In Chapter 8.6, I also quoted academic-like interests of Hittite scholars as responsible for the presence of learned texts from Mesopotamia in the tablet collections. This is not to say, however, that texts from this group were never put to practical use. When Mursili II lost his ability to speak, priests ordered Hurrian-inspired rituals to be carried out. Occasionally Mesopotamian omens were consulted, and their predictions taken seriously. Sometimes Mesopotamian literary topoi turn up in Hittite prayers and literary emulation started already early when the actual

[20] See, for instance, Carruba 1988, van den Hout 1989.

author responsible for Hattusili I's Annals made an allusion to Sargon's Legend.

12.2.4 Charters

We have already discussed these *Landschenkungsurkunden* or charters in previous chapters. Separating them off from the rest of the records is justified on several grounds. First of all, the Hittites did so as well. Charters never formed part of the regular tablet storage facilities at Hattusa as we saw in Chapter 11. They were in some cases kept alongside sealed bullae but never with tablets of the preceding three categories. Secondly, one can see them either as a prime example of permanent records having been filed away since the later sixteenth and fifteenth century BC or as an important tool for the Hittite administration in performing its job. If kept on file as still valid and part of the Hittite "state archives," as some would have it, of around 1200 BC, they would be a stunning testament to the endurance and professionality of the custodians of the tablet collections. The observation, however, that their appended seals had in all likelihood been removed already in antiquity by those same custodians and that thereby they had lost their evidentiary value prompted the view advocated in Chapter 11 that they were only kept for their seal impressions. This reduces their presence in the Hittite capital's collections to a mere diplomatic tool in assessing the authenticity of later claims. But it does not in any way diminish the reputation of the Hittite administrators as *gens ordonnés*, as Emmanuel Laroche once characterized them.[21] We will turn to them now.

As stated earlier, the chancellery and their tablet collections served the king and his retainers in running the state. The people at the chancellery were their hands and eyes: everything that needed written or read went through them. Since all written material that has come down to us originated in the state administration, we have ample evidence of the ruling elite making use of the chancellery in performing its regular tasks. In her book on *Hittite Diplomatics* Willemijn Waal has analyzed the physical remains of these activities in great detail.[22] The various tablet formats, their development, the colophons and scribes named in them, all give us insights into the inner workings of the Hittite administration that

[21] Laroche 1949: 7.
[22] Waal 2015; for the topics of this chapter see especially Waal 2015: 176–89.

will form the topic of this chapter. The next two chapters will deal with its officials and personnel, the scribes.

12.3 Writing: Drafting New Documents

Original documents were drafted on a regular basis. Whether purely administrative like storeroom and cult inventories, oracle reports, or permanent records (see the previous sections), as part of the state administration all were ultimately if mostly not explicitly written in the name of the king. He was the author of the administrative acts that the texts documented in the sense of German *Urheber*. His name or at least his title as author occurs usually only in the permanent records in the formula *UMMA* RN "Thus (speaks) King so-and-so." Charters and other decrees, treaties and instructions, as well as some prayers start this way. The actual author of the text in the sense of German *Aussteller*, however, will often have been some official. This official does not need to have been literate himself since he will often have dictated to a scribe what to write. There are a few colophons of cult rituals that say a text was written down literally "for His Majesty from the mouth." According to the rules of Hittite grammar the dative case in "*for* His Majesty" can be interpreted as indicating possession ("from *His Majesty's* mouth") and the phrase has sometimes been taken as referring to dictation, as in the following example mentioning a scribe named Hattusili:

> Hattusili wrote this text *from His Majesty's mouth*.[23]

Differently but still taking "from the mouth" as dictation, the dative can indicate the beneficiary: "for His Majesty('s benefit)" we wrote these tablets through dictation (by someone else). Less literally, the combination could also mean "at His Majesty's orders." With Waal we have to leave this question unresolved.[24] Unequivocal examples of the king dictating to a scribe do not seem to be extant.

[23] *kī=ma=kan tuppi* ANA ᵈUTU-*ŠI* KAXU-*az parā* *m*GIŠGIDRU.DINGIR-*LIM*-*iš aniyat* KUB 15.31 iv 38–40 (Invocation of the Mother Goddesses and Fate Goddesses, CTH 484, NS), ed. by Gordin 2015: 135, Waal 2015: 185 w. n. 587, 352. In this particular case another scribe, Pihhuniya wrote the actual tablet and with his reference to Hattusili he adds information about the history of the composition. So, when he writes *kī tuppi* lit. "this tablet" he cannot refer to the tablet Pihhuniya has written here but only to the composition, the "text" as a whole. This still leaves open the two possibilities, either Hattusili originally having witten down the text from dictation or having composed it at the king's orders.

[24] Waal 2015: 185; note that the nexus between *ANA* ᵈUTU-*ŠI* and KAXU-*az parā* is interrupted by two noun phrases ("in the town of Zithara at harvest time") in KUB 29.8 iv 38–9.

We do not know for sure whether any of the Hittite kings was actively or passively literate. Did Mursili II at least dictate his Annals or did he simply order one of his officials, perhaps his chief scribe as a kind of ghostwriter, to have them composed? Interesting in this respect but in the end likewise inconclusive are the opening lines of Mursili II's prayer to the god Telipinu:

> The/A scribe will speak [this] text daily in the presence of the God and he will praise [the G]od:
>
> § Telipinu, you are a mighty, powerful god! Mursili, the king, your servant, and the queen, your maidservant have sent me. They sent (me, saying): "Go, invoke, Telipinu, our lord, our patron God!"[25]

The scribe is literally the mouthpiece for the royal couple; they do not go to the temple themselves to pray to Telipinu. They do not even send a priest or some other religious official but a scribe who can read and recite from the tablet and leads the congregation in prayer, as the final sentence before the colophon makes clear:

> and the congregation says "amen!"[26]

Similarly, according to its opening lines, that same Mursili's so-called Second Plague Prayer, is spoken by an anonymous person addressing the gods on behalf of the king. Given the parallel situation of the prayer to Telipinu and the length of the text, this was almost certainly a scribe as well.[27] So, even if not helpful in answering the question of royal literacy, these passages may be revealing in terms of the not so general spread of literacy.

That literate officials had an active hand in drawing up new documents is evident in texts that were not completely composed *ab ovo* but show clear signs of relying on older sources. Seemingly *verbatim* quotes can be found in historiography when, for instance, Mursili II cites from the two letters of the Pharaoh's widow (see Chapter 8.3). A fragment of her actual second letter has been identified among the Boğazköy texts, but its preserved part

[25] [*kī*]*⸗ma⸗kan t*[(*uppi* DUB.SAR *ANA* DINGIR-*LI*)]M *anda* [(UD-*at* U)]D-*at memiškez*[*zi nu* DING(IR-LAM)] *walliškez*[(*zi*)] § [(d*Telip*)]*inuš šarkuš n*[(*akkiš*)] DINGIR-*LIM*-*iš zik uiyat⸗mu* m*Murši*-DINGIR-*LIM* L[(UGAL-*uš tu*)]*ēl* ARAD⸗KA MUNUS.LUGAL-*ašš⸗a tuēl* GÉME⸗*iš* [(*ui*)]*ēr īt⸗wa* d*Telipinun anzel* EN⸗*NI* DINGIR-*LAM ŠA* SAG.DU⸗*NI mugāi* KUB 24.1 + KBo 58.10 i 1–7 w. dupl. KUB 24.2 obv. 1–6 (Prayer to the god Telipinu, CTH 377, both NS), ed. by Kassian & Yakubovich 2007: 428, 432.

[26] *nu pānkuš apāt ēšdu ḫalzāi* KUB 24.1+ iv 18 (Prayer to the god Telipinu, CTH 377, NS), ed. by Kassian & Yakubovich 2007: 432, 434. "Amen!" is my translation of *apāt ēšdu* lit. "let that be!" Note that it is embedded in the *nu pānkuš ... ḫalzāi* clause and has no quotative particle *⸗wa*.

[27] See KUB 14.10 i 2–5, ed. by Goetze 1929: 206–7.

does not figure in the lines that Mursili quotes.[28] Often enough, however, we can identify the sources. The Bronze Tablet treaty of Tuthaliya IV with his cousin Kuruntiya and the probably earlier version of the treaty between Hattusili III(?) and Ulmitessub forms such a pair of interdependent documents.[29] We observe the same procedure in the various stages of recording oracle investigations.[30] Physical evidence of compiling can be seen when a scribe at first leaves a section on his tablet blank, estimating the space he intends to fill later on. Working with one tablet at a time, he prefers to continue before returning to the tablet room to get the source for the part he wants to insert. When he has it, it turns out he miscalculated and towards the end of the insert he has to start writing really small in order to squeeze everything in.[31] Sometimes the insertion never came. In KBo 5.6, one of the manuscripts of the Deeds of Suppiluliuma[32] there are three blank spaces. Two of them appear at the end of columns i and ii and we have no way of telling if text is actually missing. The third one, however, seems to fall *in medias res* (between iii 43 and 44) and can be filled using a duplicate version. The latter shows exactly what part of the text had been left out and when the text of KBo 5.6 picks up again (iii 44) there is an anaphoric pronoun (iii 44 "with *him*"), which in that version makes no sense because its referent was in the missing part. In the colophon the text is marked as non-final because of the remark that it had "not yet been made into a bronze tablet."[33] Were they waiting for the tablet to be completed?

12.4 Writing: Copying and Editing

As was made clear in the previous chapter, the tablet collections in the Hittite capital of the thirteenth century BC comprised older tablets from the sixteenth through fourteenth century BC but above all copies of such older tablets. Given the number of duplicates of Hittite compositions we have, copying was standard procedure in the scribal offices and the reasons for doing so were probably diverse. Tablets suffered from frequent use, they broke or became illegible, or use at different locations demanded

[28] KBo 28.51 (Letter, CTH 170), ed. by Edel 1994: 14–5.
[29] For editions see Otten 1988 and van den Hout 1995 respectively; for a translation see Beckman 1999: 109–23. For similar quotes from older sources see Sürenhagen 1985: 25–6, 32–3.
[30] van den Hout 1998: 10–30, Tognon 2004: 76.
[31] van den Hout 1995: 59; see also the remarks §12.5 on KUB 2.5.
[32] Ed. by Güterbock 1956, del Monte 2008.
[33] *ANA ṬUPPI* [Z]ABAR *nāwi* [*a*]*niyan* KBo 5.6 iv 17–18 (CTH 40, NS), ed. by Waal 2015: 215–16.

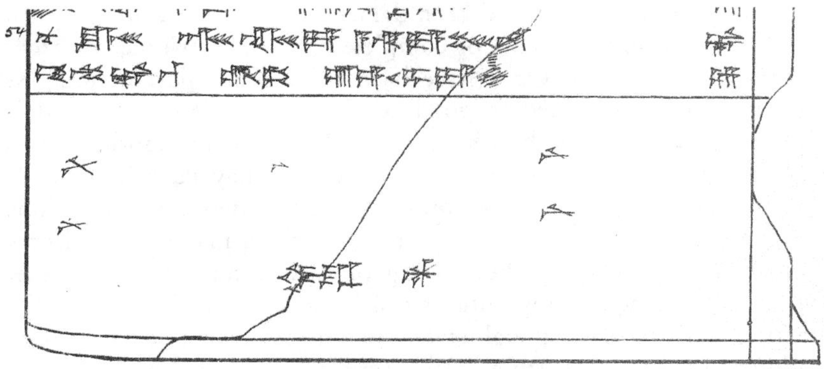

Fig. 12.1 KUB 14.13 column i end (from KUB 14 Pl. 31 [Berlin 1926]).

multiple copies. The damaged state of tablets is at times explicitly referred to in colophons:

> This tablet was damaged. . . . I, Duda, made a new version.[34]

In KUB 14.13 column i (Fig. 12.1) the scribe marked a passage as *ḫarran* "damaged" accompanied by four *cruces* or so-called PAB-signs (𒉽) right there where text should have been written.[35]

There is little information on the specific reasons behind copying activities but sometimes the demand came from above as when Queen Puduhepa ordered to collect tablets of the *hisuwa*-cult ritual from her homeland:

> When Queen Puduhepa called upon Walwazidi, chief scribe, in Hattusa to search for tablets from Kizzuwatna he had these tablets of the *hisuwa*-festival copied on that day.[36]

Understanding "in Hattusa" as the place where Walwazidi had to carry out his search the tablets were already there, and the queen perhaps wanted her own set of the *hisuwa*-cult ritual.[37]

34 *kī* TUPPU *arha ḫarran ēš[ta]* . . . *ūk* ^{m}*Dudaš* EGIR-*pa newaḫḫun* KUB 13.7 iv 3, 6–7 (Instruction, CTH 258, NS), ed. by Gordin 2015: 206, Waal 2015: 251–2.

35 Waal 2015: 82.

36 MUNUS.LUGAL ^{f}*Puduḫepaš=kan kuwapi* ^{m}UR.MAḪ.LÚ-*in* GAL DUB.SAR.MEŠ ^{URU}*Ḫattuši* ANA TUPPA$^{\mathrm{ḪI.A}}$ $^{\mathrm{U[R]U}}$*Kizzuwatna šanḫūwanzi ueriyat n=ašta kē* TUPPA$^{\mathrm{ḪI.A}}$ *Š*[A E]ZEN$_4$ *ḫišuwāš apiya* UD-*at a[rḫ]a aniyat* KBo 15.52 vi 39–45 (*hisuwa*-Cult ritual, CTH 628, NS), ed. by Waal 2015: 441–2.

37 If it was meant to say that he was the Chief Scribe in Hattusa with other (Chief?) Scribes being elsewhere then his search may have reached beyond the capital. The addition "on that day", however, might plead against that.

Copying of tablets that had been damaged indicates an urge to keep a tablet collection up to date or complete but, on the whole, *verbatim* and slavish copying may not have been the most important task. As long as a tablet remained in good condition, the need for an additional copy for use either in Hattusa itself or in another town may have been the main reason. Some copies may have been made as exercises for apprentice scribes but, killing two birds with one stone, it could also be that instead of having them make copies simply for the sake of copying, the making of such extra copies for other locations was a typical apprentice's task. The work could serve both a practical and an educational end. Apprentices may also have been working on dictation from older scribes. In such cases new or improved compositions were the result, as we see in the case of Sipazidi and Zidi:

> Sipazidi made a ne[w] version. (blank space; then on the left edge:) Zidi, the scribe wro[te it].[38]

As was the case in the quote above about Duda, this time the colophon does not say that the source tablet was damaged as a reason for the new tablet. The combination of Sipazidi, responsible for the "renewing," and the actual scribe Zidi suggests that Sipazidi prepared a new redaction of an older text, a scenario for one of the lesser cult rituals, which he then dictated to Zidi.[39] Often it may have been changes in content that prompted a new redaction. Hittite cult practices, for instance, were not so static or canonized over time that scenarios became frozen and could be slavishly copied. Instead they changed over time following the demands of the political situation and/or religious and ideological reforms. In such cases we are no longer dealing with copying in the literal sense of the word but with editing: the act of making changes in an existing text with the intent of improving on its wording in preparation for publication. That such a practice existed is the subject of the next section.

38 ᵐ*Šippa*-LÚ-*iš ne*[*wa*]*ḫḫa*[*š*] (blank space until lower edge, then on left edge:) ᵐLÚ DUB.SAR *IŠṬ*[*UR*] KUB 27.59 iv 22 and left edge (preserved on join piece KBo 45.168; Cult ritual, CTH 691, NS), ed. by Waal 2015: 486–7, Gordin 2015: 204–5; KBo 14.86 iv 14–15 (ed. by Waal 2015: 272, Gordin 2015: 204; Cult for the Stormgod of Kuliwisna, CTH 330, NS) has the same combination but here Zidi adds his father's name (DUMU ᵐNU.ᴳᴵŠKIRI$_6$).

39 On this see more extensively Gordin 2015: 204–8, Waal 2015: 397.

12.5 The Editing Process

Many colophons of cult rituals contain the usual information about the tablet on which it is written: the number of the tablet in a series, whether it is the last one in that series or not, its title, and sometimes also the name of the scribe. Compare for instance:

> Tablet no. 8, of the 3rd day; finished. (Title:) "When the king celebrates the Festival of the Month." (break of one line) Hand of Tarḫundazidi, son of Pidā; he wrote in the presence of Anuwanza.[40]

But it is only in the colophons of these cult scripts that we find an additional set of terms that occur together and seem to have been part of a system:

> ANA GIŠ.ḪUR*=kan ḫandan* "true to/collated against the original"[41]
> *parkui tuppi* "fair copy" (lit. "clean tablet")
> *ištarniyaš appan tarnumaš/appan tarnumaš* "preliminary draft/to be released"[42]
> KASKAL PN$_1$ PN$_2$ "task force of Mr. So-and-so and Mr. So-and-so."

Two representative examples of such extended colophons are:

> Tablet no. 1; not finished; of the festival of haste. (Title:) "When the king goes to Arinna for the festival of haste." § This is a fair copy, true to/collated against the original.[43]

and

> Tablet no. 1; not finished. (Title:) "When the king [goes?] to the temple of the Tutelary Deity." Preliminary [draft; collated against] the original. Task force of Pihaw[alwa, wood-scribe] and Palluwarazidi, [scribe]. Hulla, . . . [. . .]. (Break of one line, then indented:) Hand of (i.e., written by) Hesni, [son? of] Naniy[a].[44]

40 DUB.8.KAM *ŠA* UD.3.KAM *QATI mān=za* LUGAL-*uš* EZEN$_4$ ITU.KAM *iyazi* (break of one line) ŠU ^{md}U.LÚ DUMU ^{m}*Pidā PĀNI* ^{m}*Anuwanza IŠṬUR* KUB 2.13 vi 32–37 (Monthly cult ritual, CTH 591, NS), ed. by Waal 2015: 399–400.

41 For the latter translation see already CHD P 166a, cf. also Hoffner 2009: 11.

42 For *appan tarna-* "to release, authorize" see van den Hout forthcoming.

43 DUB.1-*PU UL QATI ŠA* EZEN$_4$ *nuntaryašḫaš mān* LUGAL-*uš* ^{URU}*Arinna* ANA EZEN$_4$ *nuntaryašḫaš* [*p*]*aizzi* § [*k*]*ī parkui* TUPPU [AN]A GIŠ.ḪUR*=kan ḫandan* KUB 2.9 vi 3–10 (*nuntarriyašḫa*-Cult ritual, CTH 626, NS), ed. by Waal 2015: 427.

44 DUB.1.KAM *UL* [*QATI*] *mān* LUGAL-*uš* [?] *INA* É ^{d}LAMM[A *paizzi*] *ištarniyaš* [*appan tarnumaš*] ANA GIŠ.ḪUR*=ka*[*n ḫandan*] KASKAL ^{m}*Piḫa*-U[R.MAḪ ^{LÚ}DUB.SAR.GIŠ] ^{m}*Palluwara*-LÚ [^{LÚ}DUB.SAR] ^{m}*Ḫulla* LÚ [?] (Break of one line, then indented:) ŠU ^{m}*Ḫešni* [DUMU] ^{m}*Naniy*[*a* . . .] KUB 44.24 vi 4–13 (Cult of the Tutelary Deity, CTH 685, NS), ed. by Waal 2015: 486.

Now, if one compares the various versions we have of a certain cult ritual, the differences are often not just in spelling or of a few words more or less but sometimes they are substantial to the point that we prefer to no longer speak of duplicates but of parallel versions. A case in point are two versions of the third day of the so-called Crocus or AN.TAḪ.ŠUM Festival celebrated at spring time. The tablets in question cover the same rites. The two manuscripts differ in spelling here and there, sometimes one of the two adds a word that the other does not have (A iii 8 *tūwaz* vs. B i 33–37 ø), and once the order of two sentences is inverted (A ii 44–45 [GIŠ.^{d}INANNA GA]L $^{LÚ.MEŠ}$*ḫalliyarieš* [SÌR-*RU* LUGAL-*uš*? *ḫup*]*pari šipanti* vs. B i 13–15 LUGAL-*uš ḫuppari* [*ši*]*ppanti* GIŠ.^{d}INANNA[.GA]L [$^{LÚ.ME}$]^{Š}*ḫalliyariēš* SÌR-*RU*).[45] But as we noticed earlier (§12.4), it will hardly have been such minor deviations that were decisive in preparing a new edition of the text. It must have been actions in the cult proceedings that must have been relevant, and this is where a comparison between these two versions becomes interesting.

The ritual action takes place mostly in the temple of the War God Zababa. The king and queen go through a series of drinking ceremonies to various deities, sometimes it is the king alone who offers a toast to a deity. These rites follow a fairly standard procedure. It usually starts with the coming of the cupbearer (lit. "the man-of-kneeling") who brings the vessels and beverages used in the ceremony and hands them over while going down on one knee as an act of reverence. The king and queen thereupon "drink to the deity" accompanied by music and usually also some singing. This basic pattern can be expanded upon by various rites, often involving breads that the cupbearer also brings in and that the king then breaks.

Five times one of the texts (B = KUB 2.5 i 16–18, ii 6–8, iv 4–6, 14–16, vi 8–10; see Appendix, §12.10), before the cupbearer brings in a bread, adds to the end of a drinking ceremony the sequence "The ALAN.ZU-man speaks. The reciter recites. The *kita*-man calls out."[46] In similar fashion, the other version adds to the cupbearer bringing in the bread the remark that he carries it away again (A = KUB 25.1 ii 46–48, iii 30–33, iv 51–54, v 1–7; see ibid.). Whereas the carrying out of the bread by the cupbearer may be said to simply make explicit something that was considered obvious in B, the oral performances of the three men are a clear addition in B vis-à-vis A.

Not knowing the relation between the two manuscripts it is difficult to assess these differences. Both were written in the thirteenth century BC but which of the two is the older one is impossible to say. Was B a forerunner in

45 All such variations can be found in the critical apparatus in Badalì & Zinko 1994.

46 For the full Hittite versions of both texts see Appendix, §12.10.

the editorial process resulting in A, and were there reasons, logistical, religious, ideological, or otherwise, to deliberately and consistently throw out the sequence involving the ALAN.ZU-man, the reciter, and the *kita*-man? Or does B represent a later stage adding in these participants? Whichever of the two possible scenarios applies, we are dealing with deliberate changes in the cult and we see the editors at work.

In true Hittite fashion such changes were sometimes first put to the gods to gain their approval and to legitimize them in the eyes of all concerned.[47] Once the approval was in, these changes had to be implemented and all existing scripts needed to be revised and updated. This is where the editing comes in. Correct performance of the logistically often very complex rites mattered a lot to the ruling elite and the editing process reflects this. The new version was made on the basis of the existing, now old, script. First, a preliminary draft was made, and the colophon reflected this, as in the previous quote (*ištarniyaš appan tarnumaš*).

The striking regularity with which the *ištarniyaš appan tarnumaš*-formula is always accompanied by KASKAL "task force," and the names of the two exact same officials Palluwarazidi, the scribe, and Pihawalwa, the wood-scribe, suggest that this specific editing stage or at least its formalization may have been an innovation and specific to their cooperation. As we will see in Chapter 13.3, the so-called wood-scribe was a storehouse administrator, and his cooperation with the scribe in charge of the revised edition was probably necessary because of the complex material logistics of the rituals. If we follow Shai Gordin's recent study on scribal circles in the Hittite capital Hattusa in dating the activities of these two men to the reign of Tuthaliya IV (ca. 1240–1210 BC),[48] this in all likelihood means that this king gave special instructions to make new editions of several festivals. The fact that the terms *ANA* GIŠ.ḪUR*=kan ḫandan* and *parkui tuppi* are attested by themselves without the KASKAL-phrase and the two officials, makes it likely that there already had been an editing practice, but it was refined or formalized by Palluwarazidi and Pihawalwa during the reign of Tuthaliya IV. Their absence with these terms also makes sense because it was the *editing* process for which the two officials were responsible. Once the editing had finished their job was done.

In the next stage, a final draft, marked "ready to be released/authorized" (*appan tarnumaš*), could be made. But since the latter phrase is not very often attested it is possible that in most cases the next phase was simply to

47 An example of such an oracle investigation is CTH 568, for which see Houwink ten Cate 1986.
48 Gordin 2015: 2012.

immediately produce the required official document or master copy (GIŠ.ḪUR). As we saw (Chapter 10), such documents could be sealed and there is indeed one cult ritual that carries a carefully impressed seal right on the middle of the reverse of the tablet (Fig. 12.2). Since the text carefully wraps around it, the tablet could have been sealed in advance when the approval had been given or the space where the seal was going to be applied was marked beforehand and the seal impressed afterwards.[49]

The seal imprinted belonged to Taprammi whom we know well from several sources as a high official[50] in the second half of the thirteenth century BC. The most telling of those sources is the hieroglyphic inscription on a stela base found at Boğazköy (Fig. 12.3) mentioning his name and depicting an individual in front of an altar. The inscription identifies Taprammi as the one who commissioned the monument (on this see the Excursus in Chapter 14).

> This stela I, Taprammi, dedicated.[51]

Whether the person portrayed is indeed Taprammi remains uncertain. At least in the thirteenth century, this kind of iconography on stone seems otherwise only known of kings, but that does not say that he could not have had the base and its statue (if that is what the base served for) erected; for such dedicatory inscriptions see the Excursus in Chapter 14.

Once a new master copy or archetype (GIŠ.ḪUR) had been made, copies for actual use "in the field" had to be produced. These could be labeled as *ANA* GIŠ.ḪUR*=kan ḫandan* "true to/collated against the original" or as *parkui tuppi* "fair copy." An overview of fragments and tablets that have the label *parkui tuppi* preserved shows that it does not necessarily mean a neatly written tablet, a display copy, free of errors or corrections. Although some fragments do show a beautifully regular and careful hand[52], others have erasures, cramped or vertical writing in the *intercolumnium* because the

[49] The way in which the sign PÁR (in iii 24 *pár-ši-ia-an-ni-an-zi*) is impressed seems to point at the second option: the beginning of the horizontal wedge seems to disappear in the depression caused by the pressing down of the seal in the clay. If the seal had been impressed before the tablet was inscribed the scribe would probably have started line 24 a bit more to the right.

[50] Note the use of the hieroglyphic qualification L.326, for which see in detail the Excursus in Chapter 14. For a brief overview of the sources known for Taprammi see Hawkins 2002: 225–6, see also Mora 2016: 228.

[51] *zi/a* STELE EGO LEPUS+*RA/I-mi* VERSUS PONERE, BOĞAZKÖY 1, ed. by Hawkins 2002: 226 n. 67; following Hawkins, this translation takes the portrayed individual as the "I" (EGO) of the inscription, which is certainly possible although not compelling. Alternatively, the person and the altar could also be taken as an iconographical unit around which the text is grouped ("This (base vel sim.) Taprammi erected/Taprammi had this (base vel sim.) erected").

[52] E.g. the two rituals KUB 15.42 and KUB 43.58 (both CTH 491, NS and OS, respectively).

Fig. 12.2 Seal of Taprammi on KUB 25.32 columns iii (left half) and iv (copyright Staatliche Museen zu Berlin – Vorderasiatisches Museum, Foto: BoFN 01748).

Fig. 12.3 Stela base (BOĞAZKÖY 1), Istanbul Archaeological Museum (photo author).

writer ran out of space, additions, and slanted lines and paragraphs.[53] This indicates that *parkui* was not so much an aesthetic assessment as a declaration and approval that the copy in question had the most up-to-date and correct version of the ritual described in it. This is indeed what the terms "fair copy" and German *Reinschrift* want to convey: "A fair copy . . . is a neat, or at least legible, copy or transcript of any kind of text, made . . . as an acceptable version of it, deemed fit to be read by others."[54] The *parkui tuppi* can thus be what in diplomatics they call "a copy in the form of original," the highest degree of a copy.[55] Only one document can be the original (= GIŠ.ḪUR) but there can be multiple "copies in the form of original."

As we know, the proper performance of these rituals was important to the Hittites and not doing so could have serious repercussions. Seen in this

[53] E.g. KUB 55.39 i (CTH 591, NS), KUB 58.43 i (CTH 616, NS), KUB 35.16 i-ii and KUB 35.18 i (both CTH 761, NS and OS, respectively).

[54] Beal 2008: 151. [55] Duranti 1998: 49–50.

light it is not surprising that the chancellery had a rigorous system in place to establish and authorize the official scenario. The qualification *parkui tuppi* was important to the authorities. Such a text could be trusted as a guide in the performance of religious rites. This was not necessarily true of the *ištarniyaš appan tarnumaš* tablets, which could represent lesser degrees of perfection and were only leading up to an authorized text. The label itself declares it unfit to serve as a script. Such tablets first had to be checked against the existing older original and editors had to make sure that all relevant changes had been made before they could be approved. The goal was to establish a new "original."

We can thus tentatively establish an editing process in various stages, as maintained in the chancellery of the late thirteenth century BC. If a ritual script was ordered to be changed its most recent original (GIŠ.ḪUR 1) was used as the basis for the changes. Existing copies "in the form of original" (*parkui tuppi* 1) probably had to be taken out of circulation. A pre-final copy (*ištarniyaš appan tarnumaš*) of the desired new version was drawn up under the supervision of two senior scribes, checked against the old original, and if approved, either another copy was submitted for final approval (*appan tarnumaš*) or immediately a new original (GIŠ.ḪUR 2) was made. The newly authorized version then served as the basis for new copies (*parkui tuppi* 2).

Finally, what about texts without a colophon? How many are there and what was their status in the editing process? It is good to remind ourselves that the overwhelming majority of permanent records (see §12.3.3) had a colophon. This is especially true of festival texts, as clearly shown by Willemijn Waal: out of 359 festival texts with enough of the end of the tablet preserved to tell whether the composition had a colophon or not, only twelve, with certainty, had none.[56] It is also interesting to observe that

Table 12.2 *Possible editing stages*

GIŠ.ḪUR (1)	(an earlier) "original/master copy"
parkui tuppi (1)	"copy in the form of original"
ištarniyaš appan tarnumaš	"pre-final draft" (for a new revised version)
appan tarnumaš	"final draft" (pending approval)
GIŠ.ḪUR (2)	(the new revised and authorized) "original/master copy"
parkui tuppi (2)	"copy in the form of original."

[56] Waal 2015: 398–9.

close to seventy of the 347 texts with a colophon contain one or more, if applicable, of the terms discussed above. Many more colophons are too damaged to be sure whether they had them or not. Of the twelve texts with no colophon, five are relatively rare single-column tablets with perhaps "a different status and function than the larger three-columned festival texts."[57] So, even though we are unable to say much about their specific status, the numbers speak for themselves.

12.6 Writing: Other Types of Documents

Within an administration one can distinguish between the internal and external (living) archive. The internal administration produced, for instance, all the scenarios for the cultic celebrations and all related documents. The documents produced are originals that stay in the administration. An outside party interested in such a record can get a copy or extract (*extractus*). Duplicates or parallels of texts known from Hattusa that we find at other Central Anatolian sites might be such extracts or be based on them.[58] A special kind of extract is the *vidimus* (literally "we have seen").[59] Mursili II had at one time concluded a treaty with Talmisarrumma, a king of Aleppo in Syria. As usual, several copies were made. Some may have been deposited in one or more temples in Hattusa, and one was given to Talmisarrumma as the treaty partner. However, the latter copy was stolen whereupon Mursili's successor Muwatalli II issued Talmisarrumma a new copy, an extract from the records kept in the capital, probably one of the earliest documented cases of a *vidimus*:

> My father Mursili made a treaty [tab]let for Talmisarrumma, king of Aleppo, but it was stolen. So, I, the Great King (i.e., Muwatalli II), made [him] a second tablet and I placed my seal on it. In the future nobody shall alter the words of the content of this [tablet]. The word of Tabarna, Great King, is n[o]t to be cast away or to be broken. Whoever will alter (them) shall die! The tablet of the treaty that my father Mursili made for him was written as follows: . . . (follows *verbatim* the wording of the original Mursili document).[60]

[57] Waal 2015: 399.

[58] One thinks, for instance, of the Disappearing Deity myth found at Maşat Höyük (Güterbock 1986) or the cult ritual celebrated in the Spring at Sarissa (Kuşaklı).

[59] Duranti 1998: 52–3 ("'inserts' (or insets), that is, the documents entirely quoted . . . in subsequent original documents in order to renew their effects").

[60] [*tup*]*pa ša rikilti ana* [m]*Talmi*-LUGAL-*ma* LUGAL KUR [URU]*Ḫalap abua* [m]*Murši*[*li*] *epušaššu u tuppa ittaḫbat* LUGAL GAL *tuppa šanama alta*[*ṭaršu*] *ina* [NA]KIŠIB-*ia aknukam attannaššu urram šēram amātū ša pî* [*tuppi*] *annî mamma lā ušpaḫ awāt tabarna* LUGAL GAL *ša l*[*ā*] *nadê ša lā šebēri ša ušpaḫḫu*

Supposing, as was the custom in other cases, copies of the treaty were distributed among a number of temples in Hattusa it is unclear what copy was used to produce the *vidimus*. Was it one of the officially sealed ones – possibly cast in metal – deposited in a temple or one of the clay copies kept in the regular tablet rooms? A similar case is known involving a certain Walmu, local king of Wilusa on the west coast of Anatolia, the site of ancient Troy, during the reign of the Hittite king Tuthaliya IV. Walmu had been deposed, sought refuge with the nearby king of Mira and appealed for help to his Hittite overlord. The latter sent the king of Mira, addressed as "my son," an envoy with documents that proved Walmu's claims to the throne at Wilusa:

> Kuwalanazidi (i.e., a Hittite official) kept the docume[nts] that [I(?) had drawn up] for Walmu and he brings them here now together with m[y?] son . . . . Read them! If now, my son, you guard My Majesty's wellbeing, I, My Majesty, will trust your good will. Send Walmu to me, my son, and I will restore him in kingship in the land of Wilusa. Just as he used to be king of Wilusa, likewis[e] he [shall be] now![61]

Except for the letters most or all short-term records listed in §§12.2.1–2 concern the internal administration and document the daily functioning of the state. But apart from the treaties so do most of the genres under the long-term records. The laws and depositions, the texts that we like to call religious compositions, the foreign and imported texts, they all regulate the judicial, cultic, and scholarly life of the state respectively and usually did not leave the capital.

The external administration, on the other hand, deals with all contacts with parties outside. Outgoing records to those parties, like letters or judicial decisions, are originals that stay with the partner or addressee that receives them, but the external administration can keep one or more copies or *exempla*.[62] Until the 1970s (AD) the literate life of the Hittite state was limited for us to Hattusa. As a consequence, the written products of its external archive were largely unknown to us. A few exceptions like the stray

BA.ÚŠ *u tuppa rikilti ša abu[a]* ᵐ*Muršili epušaššu akanna ša[ṭ]er* KBo 1.6 obv. 3–8 (Treaty, CTH 75), ed. by Weidner 1923: 80–1, tr. Beckman 1999: 93; on the text as a whole see Devecchi 2010.

61 ANA ᵐ*Walmu=ma kue* GIŠ.ḪU[R.ḪI.A *iyanun*(?) *n=at*] ᵐKARAŠ.ZA *pē ḫarta n=at kāšma* ITTI DUMU-x[. . .] . . . *udai n=at au kinun=ma* DUMU=I[A] *kuwapi* ŠA ᵈUTU=ŠI SIG$_5$-*tar* PAP-*ašti tuēl=za* SILIM-*an* ᵈUTU-ŠI *ḫāmi nu=mu=kan* DUMU-IA ᵐ*Walmun parā nāi n=an* EGIR-*pa* INA KUR *Wiluša* LUGAL-*eznani teḫḫi n=aš karū* GIM-*an* LUGAL KUR *Wiluša ēšta kinun=aš* QATAMM[A *ēšdu*] KUB 19.55 rev. 38–42 + KUB 48.90: 6–10 (Milawata Letter, CTH 182, NS), ed. by Hoffner 1982: 131–2 and 2009: 319.

62 The terms internal and external administration used here do not necessarily refer to real-life offices in different buildings or rooms but only describe different activities within an administration.

letter found on Maşat Höyük in 1943 hinted at the existence of a written administration beyond the capital but tablet *collections* were never found. That changed when in 1973 regular excavations started at Maşat and brought to light a corpus of 117 documents. In Chapter 8.8 we looked at the various other sites that have yielded texts since then and saw that all of them are the products of the Hittite kingdom's state administration at large. The letters at Maşat are originals that stayed with the addressee there. They originated from the central administration or its representatives in the field. They show the micro-management and the short lines of communication the chancellery was capable of in case of an emergency. Royal missives could be delivered and answered within days or even hours depending on the proximity of the correspondents and the urgency of the situation. Driven by hunger Gasgaeans had started plundering grain fields of nearby Hittite settlements. Apprised of this by a letter the king orders to start harvesting what they can before the starving looters have taken everything. Such an exchange makes sense only for a situation where messengers are running back and forth within a very short time span.[63]

From Emar on the Euphrates in Syria, to mention one more example, we have two letters dealing with the same case, one sent by the Hittite king from Hattusa and one by his viceroy from Karkamish. A local Emariote priest felt wronged by a Hittite representative and had appealed to his overlord in the Hittite capital. Since Karkamish usually tended to all affairs concerning the southeastern part of the Empire it was involved as well.[64] Having been sent to Emar these documents belong to the local Emar archive only and even if one day an *exemplum* may turn up in the tablet collections of either Hattusa or Karkamish that is where they belong.

Conversely, letters from elsewhere, international correspondence, or letters from sites within the kingdom, addressed to the Hittite king, were originals that became part of the capital's external archive. In Hattusa archaeologists found the rich correspondence coming from Ramses II, his wife, and some of his officials, as well as letters from Assur and Babylon. In these cases, we usually miss what the Hittite king wrote since his letters should be part of the Egyptian, Assyrian, and Babylonian archives respectively. Sometimes, however, the chancellery did keep *exempla* of outgoing letters either in the form of the original drafts or deliberate copies of what was ultimately sent. This is evident in the case of Hittite versions of letters to, for instance, the Assyrian or Egyptian courts that had to be translated into Akkadian, the diplomatic language of the day, before they could be

[63] van den Hout 2007a: 396–7. [64] For these letters see Singer 1999a, Hoffner 2009: 367–72.

sent out. We have, for instance, part of the (Hittite) letter Suppiluliuma I sent to Egypt to protest the murder of his son.

12.7 **Reading**

The purpose of writing is the ability to store information that at some later point in time can be read back. Writing presupposes reading. As we saw in Chapter 6, not being an integral part of the Mesopotamian cuneiform world and having adopted and implemented this writing system deliberately as well as within a restricted period, the Hittites adapted it to their own needs. Using columns and paragraphs already help in structuring a document. An important adaptation was the introduction of word space. Relatively subtle at first, these word spaces became more pronounced over time. Still, a modern observer of a cuneiform text may wonder about the seeming uniformity and undifferentiated massiveness of paragraphs on a tablet. There are no differing font sizes within a text, no capitals, and usually no rulings. A cuneiform text has no punctuation in the form of periods, (semi-)colons, question or exclamation marks. Ancient and modern students, however, soon learned and learn to recognize other signs that structure a sentence or a text. Where we use capitals for proper nouns the cuneiform script uses the so-called *determinatives*, special signs that were normally not read, marking the following word as the name of a person, a deity, or place name. Similarly, there were determinatives for objects made of specific materials (stone, wood, metal), for plants, foodstuffs (meat, cereal products), mountains, springs and wells, and rivers. Where we might use *italics* to signal a foreign word, the ancient Hittite scribe could mark it with a single or double wedge (∡ or ∡∡) to alert the reader.[65] Finally, the Hittite language itself makes it relatively easy to recognize the beginning and end of sentences through grammatical means. Armed with these tools, a literate individual could make sense of a text written by others quite easily.

Indeed, other than preparing documents, reading to the king and his grandees must have been an important task for those working at the chancellery.[66] When the opening formula of letters says: "As follows so-and-so to so-and-so: speak!," the second person singular exhortation "speak!" is usually explained as an invitation to the scribe on the receiving

[65] For these and other reading aides in the Aegaean and the ancient Near Eastern world see Duhoux 2017.
[66] Gordin 2015: 35–9.

end to read the message out loud to the addressee. Although most members of the ruling elite, including the king and queen, may well have been illiterate, this does not necessarily imply that they were. Where it concerns a king or a high official it was probably beneath their dignity to do so. Particularly at a solemn or festive occasion this would not do, as when Suppiluliuma finally consented to send one of his sons to marry Pharaoh's widow, he marked the occasion by having somebody publicly recite a former Hittite–Egyptian treaty:

> [A]nd when the tablet had been read out loud to them, my father spoke to them as follows: "In the [p]ast Hattusa and Egypt [w]ere friends with each other but now this too has [hap]pened between the two of u[s] so that Hatti [and] Egypt will be fri[ends] with each other [for e]ver more!"[67]

They had their personnel to take care of this, just as they would not prepare their own food. A head of state does not drive his or her own car and many a CEO rarely touches a computer.[68] We can also see the king as supreme judge assessing and judging cases in public. Again, of course, he does not read the dossiers himself nor does his immediate assistant, the Chief Bodyguard.

> [The bod]yguard who brings the defendants [steps] behind the Man-of-the-Gold-Spear. [When] the king asks for a case the bodyguar[d picks] it [up] and p[uts] it in the Chief Bodyguard's hand and tells the Chief Bodyguard [what] case [it is] and the Chief Bodyguard [tells the king].[69]

Supposing the "case" being "picked up" refers to a written document, was the simple bodyguard relaying the information for the next case literate or was there a scribe in the background who does not even get mentioned? The passage above from Mursili II's prayer to Telipinu where the royal couple sends a scribe instead of a priest to the temple to read their prayer suggests that literacy was not very widespread beyond scribal circles. This

[67] [n]u=šmaš=kan maḫḫan tuppi peran ḫalzer namma=šm*aš* ABU=IA kiššan IQBI [k]arūiliyaza=wa=kan ^{URU}Ḫattušaš [^{U}]^{RU}Mizrašš=a ištarni=šummi āššiyanteš [e]šer kinun=a=wa=nnaš=kan ki=ia ištarni=šu[mmi ki]šat nu=wa=kan KUR ^{URU}Ḫatti KUR ^{URU}Mizr[i=ia ukt]ūri namma ištarni=šummi aššiy[anteš] KBo 14.12 iv 33–9 (Biography of Suppiluliuma I, CTH 40, NS), ed. by Güterbock 1956: 98.

[68] Cf. also the story of the Dutch Queen Juliana "going shopping downtown [in the 1950s]. She was afraid of the heavy traffic. Lady Roëll had to give her an arm. She loved to walk around like a regular housewife with a purse, to pay for things and receive change. She had no idea what things cost; normally she never had money on her" (" . . . boodschappen deed in de stad. Ze was bang voor het drukke verkeer. Freule Roëll moest haar een arm geven. Ze vond het heerlijk als een gewone huisvrouw met een handtas te lopen en te betalen en geld terug te krijgen. Ze had geen idee wat dingen kostten; ze had normaal nooit geld op zak"), Withuis 2016: 649.

[69] IBoT 1.36 iii 1–5, ed. by Güterbock van den Hout 1991: 22–3 (Instruction for the royal bodyguard, CTH 262, OS), see n. 441.

can also be seen in the following request by the scribe Tarhunmiya around 1375 BC, tacked on to an official missive:

> Read this message well to Pallanna, my lord, and my lady. Then let them send me their greetings back!"[70]

Tarhunmiya was a scribe in the service of the Hittite king who probably grew up or at least had formerly lived in Maşat Höyük. Now that he is writing a letter to an official in that same town, he takes the opportunity to send Pallanna and "my lady" a short note. If, as has been assumed, they were Tarhunmiya's parents,[71] there is no reason for having the message read out to them other than their being illiterate. Requests for reading messages are found in other *Zweitbriefe* or postscripts as well. Other than simply social, as in the example we just saw, they can deal with personal business ("Convey (literally: read out loud) my greetings to Pulli and tell him to send me the ox he promised me"[72] or "My stylus broke. Please, my dear brother, send me a stylus!"[73]) or could be written perhaps even in jest. In an exchange between two officials one complains to the other about a lack of courtesy:

> Given the fact that my messenger came from you (lit. from there (where you are)), why, my dear brother, didn't you send me greetings?
> Now I'm mad at you!

The sender then continues to make a request to send him weapons. In the following postscript the scribe, mockingly or in jest perhaps, echoes the message almost *verbatim* to his colleague scribe:

> My dear brother, why aren't you sending me greetings?[74]

Although it should hardly need confirmation nowadays, such postscripta make it likely that silent reading (or comprehension literacy) was not only

[70] *kī=kan tuppi* PĀNI ^{m}*Pal[l]anna* BELI[=I]A ^{MUNUS}BAD-TĪ=IA SIG$_5$-*in ḫalzai namma=mu* EGIR-*pa aššul ḫatrāndu* HKM 81: 29–32 (Letter, CTH 186, OS), ed. by Alp 1991: 274–5. Pallanna and the "lady" may have been the writer's real parents.

[71] Thus, for instance, Gordin 2015: 36.

[72] PĀNI ^{m}*Pullī=kan ammel aššul ḫalzai* GU$_4$=*ia=wa=mu kuin tet nu=war=an=mu uppi* HKM 22: 12–16 (Letter, CTH 186, OS), ed. by Alp 1991: 156–7; cf. also HKM 21: 20–21 (Letter, CTH 186, OS; ed. HBM 154–5).

[73] GI.É.DUB.BA=*mu=kan ḫarkta nu=mu* ŠEŠ.DÙG.GA=IA GI.É.DUB.BA *uppi* HKM 71 left edge 1–3 (Letter, CTH 186, OS), ed. by Alp 1991: 256–7; on the differing interpretations of this passage see Torri 2012: 129–30.

[74] *ammel [k]uit* ^{LÚ}ṬĒMU *apez uit* ŠEŠ.DÙG.GA=IA=*ma=mu aššul kuwat* UL *ḫatrāeš* § *nu=ddu=za=kan kāša šanza* § . . . §§ DUMU.DÙG.GA=IA=*mu aššul kuwat* UL *ḫatreškiši* HKM 56: 7–12, 26–7 (Letter, CTH 186, OS), ed. by Alp 1991: 224–7.

well within the abilities of regular scribes but also practiced.[75] When reading a message out loud the scribe had to scan forward (the so-called eye-voice span[76]) to make sure where a postscript began: in front of an audience he would not have wanted to be caught in mid-sentence realizing too late that what he had started reading was inappropriate or simply irrelevant. It is unlikely the king and his cabinet members would have appreciated such a sense of humor.

Scribes also provided reading services in cultic rituals. In the so-called AN.TAḪ.ŠUM festival celebrated in the spring, for instance, a scribe reads out a list of gods who receive offerings:

> He/She (i.e., a participant in the ritual) places (certain things?) on the soldier breads and makes the round of all the gods while the scribe reads out [from] a tablet the god[s] to whom he/she has offered sheep.[77]

Although no tablet is mentioned the same happens in the cult ritual for Infernal Deities. In a repeated offering sequence, in which the Head of the Deaf Men, the king, and a palace attendant participate, a scribe each time reads out the name of the deities to whom an offering is made:

> [The Head of the] Deaf Men gives the cup to the king. The king [l]ibates. The Head of the Deaf Men libates in the basket and consecrates (it) over the king. [The scrib]e reads out "Ḫašša," ditto ["Ḫil]ašši." The palace attendant hands the king [one thick br]ead. The king breaks (it). [The scrib]e reads out "Ḫašša", ditto ["Ḫil]ašši." The palace attendant [h]olds out [one thick bread] to the king and places the bread halves on either side [aroun]d the basket.[78]

With minor variations these offerings continue all through the preserved parts of the second, third, and fourth columns with the scribe each time reading the litany of gods. In view of the theory that wooden tablets could

[75] For silent reading in antiquity and in the European Middle Ages see most recently a history of the debate in Johnson 2010: 4–9 and further Carruthers 2008: 212–7, Thomas 1992: 9, Charpin 2008: 55–6, Blair 2010: 82.

[76] Johnson 2010: 8, 29.

[77] ANA NINDA.ÉRIN.MEŠ=*šan šer d*[*ā*]*i nu* DINGIR.MEŠ *ḫūmantiu*[*š*] *kalutitti ḫalz*[*iš*]*ai=ma=aš=kan* ^{LÚ}DUB.SAR *tuppiy*[*az*] UDU.ḪI.A=*kan kue*[*d*]*aš* ANA DINGIR[.MEŠ] *šipanz*[*a*]*š ta* KUB 20.59 v 1–6 (Spring cult ritual, CTH 616, NS), ed. by Gordin 2015: 37 (with slightly different reading and lit.). The preceding context is lost so it is not clear what is put on the soldier breads.

[78] [GA]L Ú.ḪÚB LUGAL-*i* GAL-AM *pāi* LUGAL-*uš* [*ši*]*panti* GAL Ú$^{?}$.ḪÚB=*kan* ŠÀ ^{GIŠ}PISAN [*šip*]*anti ta* LUGAL-*i šer šupiaḫḫi* [^{LÚ}DUB.SA]R *ḫalzāi* ^{d}*Ḫaššaš* KI.MIN [^{d}*Ḫil*]*aššiš* DUMU.É.GAL LUGAL-*i* [1 NINDA.GUR$_4$.R]A *pāi* LUGAL-*uš paršiya* [^{LÚ}DUB.SA]R *ḫalzāi* ^{d}*Ḫaššaš* KI.MIN [^{d}*Ḫil*]*aššiš* DUMU.É.GAL=*kan* LUGAL-*i* [1 NINDA.GUR$_4$.RA *ē*]*pzi nu* ^{GIŠ}PISAN-*li* [*araḫza*]*nda kēz* ½-AM *kēzz=iya* ½-AM *dāi* KUB 20.24 obv. iii 6–15 (Cult ritual, CTH 645, NS). Restorations are based on the further context including the join piece KUB 58.38 and the dupl. KBo 27.40. The "ditto" (KI.MIN) stands for the sequence ^{LÚ}DUB.SAR *ḫalzāi* "the scribe reads out."

have been preferred in the actual ritual performances because of their lesser weight it is interesting to see that in these cases it is always the scribe (LÚDUB.SAR) and never the wood-scribe (LÚDUB.SAR.GIŠ) who is doing the reading.[79]

12.8 Record Management

The ability to read was also a prerequisite for record management in the sense of filing and retrieving tablets in the tablet storerooms. Suppiluliuma I's decision to have the old treaty with Egypt solemnly read out loud implies people were able to find it in the storage rooms. As Waal has convincingly shown, the function of colophons was first and foremost to enable efficient archiving.[80] Apart from such occasions, as with the Egyptian treaty, the Hittite corpus is replete with examples of the use of older documents (*retroacta*) in drafting new ones. But besides serving as sources for new documents to be drafted the collections were also used as an instrument to decide on a policy in certain situations. When faced with an ongoing and unrelenting epidemic Mursili II ordered to scour the collections in an attempt to come up with possible causes of the epidemic:

> Also those [few], that were [lef]t of the ones who offer bread [and wine] to the gods, s[tarted to] die. [Then the matte]r [of . . .] started to weigh [on me] again and I made the go[ds' . . . the subject of an oracle inquiry.] Two [o]ld tablets [I found.] One tablet ab[out an offering to the River Mala: . . .] . . . for[me]r kings [had] brought the offering to the River Mala, but [now], for as long as since the days of my father [people have] d[ied] in Hatti-Land, we had never made [the offering] to the River Mala.[81]

"Old" tablets are regularly referred to in the texts as sources of information. We already briefly referred to the following passage in the text about Mursili II's aphasia:

[79] I am aware of one example only of a chief wood-scribe in what might be a similar role in a festival, in KUB 58.11 obv. 11 (CTH 678, NS; ed. by Haas 1970: 214–15, quoted as unpubl. Bo 2710) but here he is speaking (*memai*) and not reading out loud. Note a few lines earlier (obv. 6) how several officials, among them the chief wood-scribe, speak (*memanzi*) "the words of invocation(?)" (INIM.ḪI.A *talliyauwaš*) "as they know them" (GIM-*an šekkanzi*), which points to reciting memorized words rather than reading from a tablet.

[80] Waal 2015: 179–80.

[81] [*nu=kan š*]A DINGIR.MEŠ=*ia kuieš* LÚ.MEŠ NINDA.GUR$_4$.RA[-*uš* LÚ.MEŠ*išpantuzziyaliuš tēpaweš ašša*]*nteš ešer n=at nakki*[*škettat nu . . . memiya*]*š namma nakkišta nu* ŠA DỊN[GIR.MEŠ . . . *ariyanun nu=za k*]*arūila* DUB.2.KAM *peran w*[*emiyanu*]*n* I *TUPPU* Š[A SISKUR ŠA ID*Māla zilad*]*uwa* SISKUR ŠA ID*Māla karū*[*ili*]*ēš* LUGAL.MEŠ *ḫenka*[*n ḫarkẹr kinun=a*] *kuitman=ma* IŠTU UD.KAM-*UM* ABI=IA INA KUR URU*Ḫatti a*[*kkiškettat nu* SISKUR] ŠA ID*Māla* UL *kuwapikki iyauē*[*n*] KUB 14.8 obv. 6–12 (Second plague prayer Mursili II, CTH 378, NS), ed. by Goetze 1929: 208–9.

> When they bring the substitute ox, just as the ritual of the substitute ox has been written down on the old tablet, just as the regulation is recorded for it and just as for the deity the burnt offering and *keldi*-ritual has been recorded on the old tablet, thus they shall carry it out.[82]

Also, in the cult inventories, the reports checking on the status of the cult, its provisions, and temple buildings throughout the empire, older records were part of the process:

> On the [ol]d tablet(s) we didn't find any festival provisions.[83]

The tablet inventories, lists of tablets with titles of their compositions and with occasionally additional information, mention older tablets as well. The function of these lists has not yet been fully elucidated (see more on them in Chapter 13) but they attest to the presence of older records in the chancellery's holdings and the Hittites' awareness of them.[84]

In a prayer to the Stormgod, King Muwatalli II (c. 1295–1274 BC) vowed to set straight and fulfill cultic requirements in southeast Anatolia that apparently had been neglected for a while:

> "[I will ask] the people who are still there and who were there with my father (and) [my grandfather] and whatever I, My Majesty, will find now in the written records, I will carry out. You, O Stormgod my lord, know [whatever] rites [of the gods] I have not fulfilled. And about each one I will ask a venerable old man and, [as] they remember [(each) single] requirement and report it, just so I will carry it out."[85]

Whether the written records the king refers to are those of the capital Hattusa or local ones we cannot tell but this prayer shows that the memory of the oldest in society was still a resource of some authority and that the cuneiform system may never have extended far beyond the confines of the state administration. This also means that in the absence of written records, if an event lies back by more than three generations there are no longer any

82 *maḫḫan=ma* GU$_4$ *pūḫugarin arnuwanzi nu* ŠA GU$_4$ *pūḫugari* GIM-*an* SISKUR *annalaz* IŠTU ^{GIŠ}LĒU GUL-*aššan išḫiul=ši* GIM-*an iyan* ANA DINGIR-LIM=*ia* SÍSKUR *ambašši keldiya annalaz* IŠTU ^{GIŠ}LĒE GIM-*an iyan n=at* QATAMMA [(*ēššanz*)]*i* KBo 4.2 rev. 41–6 w. dupl. KUB 43.50 + KUB 12.27 rev. 28–32 (Aphasia Mursili II, CTH 486, NS), ed. by Lebrun 1985: 108, 112.

83 [*annal*]*aza=ma tuppiza* EZEN$_4$.MEŠ *ḫaziwi* UL$^{!}$ *kuitki* KAR-*uen* KUB 42.100 iii 26 (Cult inventory, CTH 673, NS), ed. by Hazenbos 2003: 19, 23. For other instances see KUB 42.100 i 22, ii 6, iv 3, 33

84 van den Hout 2005: 283 n. 26, Dardano 2006: 12.

85 *ēšzi=ma kuit* UN.MEŠ-*tar nu at$^{!}$ti=mi ḫ*[*uḫḫi=mi katta*]*n ēšta n=at* [*punušmi* GIŠ.Ḫ]UR.ḪI.A [*gulzattanazz=i*[*y*]*a kuit* ^{d}UTU-ŠI *kinun uemiškemi n=at eššaḫḫi nu=kan š*[A DINGIR.]MEŠ [*kuit š*]*aklāyaš par*[*ā* UL] *arnuan ḫarmi* ^{d}U=[*a*]*t* EN=IA *šakti kuitta=ya šallin* LÚ.ŠU.GI *punuškemi nu=kan* [1-*an*] *šaklāin* EGIR-*and*[*a* GIM-*an*] *šekkanzi n=at memanzi n=at ēššaḫḫi=pat* KBo 11.1 obv. 21–4 (Prayer Muwatalli II, CTH 382, NS), ed. by Houwink ten Cate 1967: 106–7, 115–16; cf. also Schwemer 2012: 49–50.

people to remember them. In the Alaksandu Treaty the same Muwatalli II claims that he knows that his long-ago predecessor Labarna conquered Arzawa and Wilusa but that it is unknown to him under which king they again defected since the matter is long past:

> When in the past Labarna, the father of my fathers, [had defeated and] subjugated all of Arzawa (and) Wilu[ssa], Arzawa later on turned hos[t]ile for that reason. Under what king, however, Wi[l]ussa defected from Hatti-Land, I do not know because the matter is so long ago.[86]

12.9 Tablet Storage in Hattusa: Can We Detect a System?

The ability to retrieve older tablets from storage presupposes a system and raises the question whether the archaeological record reflects anything of the kind. Cuneiform tablets, that is, mostly fragments of tablets, are as much archaeological objects as ceramics, or artifacts made out of metal, wood, stone, or any other materials, or organic remains. The only difference is that tablets are usually inscribed while the other artifacts, except for occasional graffiti and hieroglyphic inscriptions, are not. Essential for the interpretation of all is context. The inventory of a building or room can help identify the structure as palatial or residential, secular or cultic, as a workshop or a throne room, and so on. Alternatively, if the layout of a building points to having had a cultic character, this may inform the interpretation of the objects found inside. Which is why illicitly dug up artifacts lose so much of their value and are robbed of their chance at full interpretation. The same is true of texts. A good illustration of a tablet being instrumental in identifying a building is the case of a prestigious looking structure in the western Upper City of Hattusa. On the basis of its rich inventory it is likely to have been the residence of a member of the local elite. But the find of a letter in that building addressed to the Commander of the Royal Bodyguard led the excavators to narrow its inhabitant down to this particular high officer.[87] Conversely, a small cache of tablets found in Temples 15 and 16 in the Upper City turned the collection, as Heinrich Otten put it, into the “private library of an

86 *karū=za kuwapi* ᵐ*Labarnas* ABI [(ABBA=IA)] KUR ᵁᴿᵁ*Arzawa* KUR ᵁᴿᵁ *Wilu*[*šša*] *ḫūmand*[*a taruḫta n=at=za*] ÌR-*aḫta nu apattan* EGIR-*an*[*d*]*a* ˹KUR˺ ᵁᴿᵁ*Arzawa kuru*[*r*]*iyaḫta* KUR ᵁᴿᵁ *Wi*[*l*]*ušša=ma* ANA KUR ᵁᴿᵁ*Ḫatti kuedani* LUGAL-*i auwan arḫa tīyat nu memīyaš kui*[(*t i*)]*štantanza n=an* UL *šaqqaḫ*[*ḫi*] KUB 21.2 + KUB 48.95 i 3–9 w. dupl. KUB 21.5 i 2–6 (Treaty Muwatalli II, CTH 76, NS), ed. SV 2: 50–1, tr. Beckman 1999: 87; see also Starke 1997a: 473–4 n. 79, and Klinger 2001: 285 n. 37. For the historical setting see Bryce 2003: 46–8.

87 Schachner 2011a: 282–4.

educated man (priest?) or the founding inventory of a temple, likely dedicated to the cult of a Hurrian deity from northern Syria (Tessub of Ebla?)."[88]

But what about a chancellery, an office where scribes and officials worked for the king and his elite, generating, receiving, and filing written records? One would suppose that certain archaeological contexts might point to a building's status as one dedicated to scribal activity. A high concentration of tablet finds might be one obvious clue. Another hint was tentatively identified in Building A on the acropolis Büyükkale (Bk.) in Hattusa. From the very beginning, the large number of tablets found there convinced the archaeologists that it had been a major place of tablet storage. But aside from housing many texts, the rooms of Bk. A are characterized by small stone supports at regular intervals, whether as bases for wooden shelving[89] or as reinforcement for an upper story where the tablets were kept.[90] Hundreds of tablets, let alone if they number in the thousands, represent a huge weight, calling for extra support, just as modern libraries and archives are subject to special building codes. Similar small pillars have been found in buildings Bk. K and H and it has therefore been suggested that these, too, were tablet storage areas.[91] And, finally and theoretically, the nature of the tablets might even make it possible to be more specific and identify a building as, for instance, the foreign office or a scriptorium dedicated to only scholarly writings or religious texts. Or, does the distinction between short- and long-term compositions correspond to differences in find spots and thus actual storage by the Hittites (see §12.2)?

Unfortunately, the situation surrounding the find spots of tablets at Hattusa is fraught with problems. In an oft quoted passage, Ludwig Curtius described his experiences as an archaeologist working in 1907 for Hugo Winckler and Theodor Makridi at Boğazköy. One day, he observed a Kurdish workman going off to Room 11 of the storerooms surrounding Temple 1 in the Lower City where he saw "clearly stacked rows of fully preserved tablets. Just like a countrywoman gathering potatoes from her field, the Kurd quickly wriggled loose as many pieces of them as his basket would hold."[92] Makridi would then carry them over to the tent where Winckler was working. Curtius' description suggests that the tablets were

88 Otten 1984: 375 ("Privatbibliothek eines gebildeten Mannes (Priesters?) oder zum Stiftungsinventar eines Tempels, der dann wohl dem Kult einer hurritischen Gottheit aus Nordsyrien geweiht war (Teššub von Ebla?)").

89 Neve 1982: 106. 90 Bittel & Naumann 1952: 54.

91 Neve 1982: 106, 108, 117, for Bk. H see also Francia 2015.

92 Curtius 1950: 311 ("klar geschichtete Reihen schräg liegender, ganz erhaltener Tontafeln . . ., von denen der Kurde in kurzer Zeit, so, wie eine Bäuerin Kartoffeln aus ihrem Acker klaubt, so viele Stücke loslöste, als in seinem Korbe Platz fanden.").

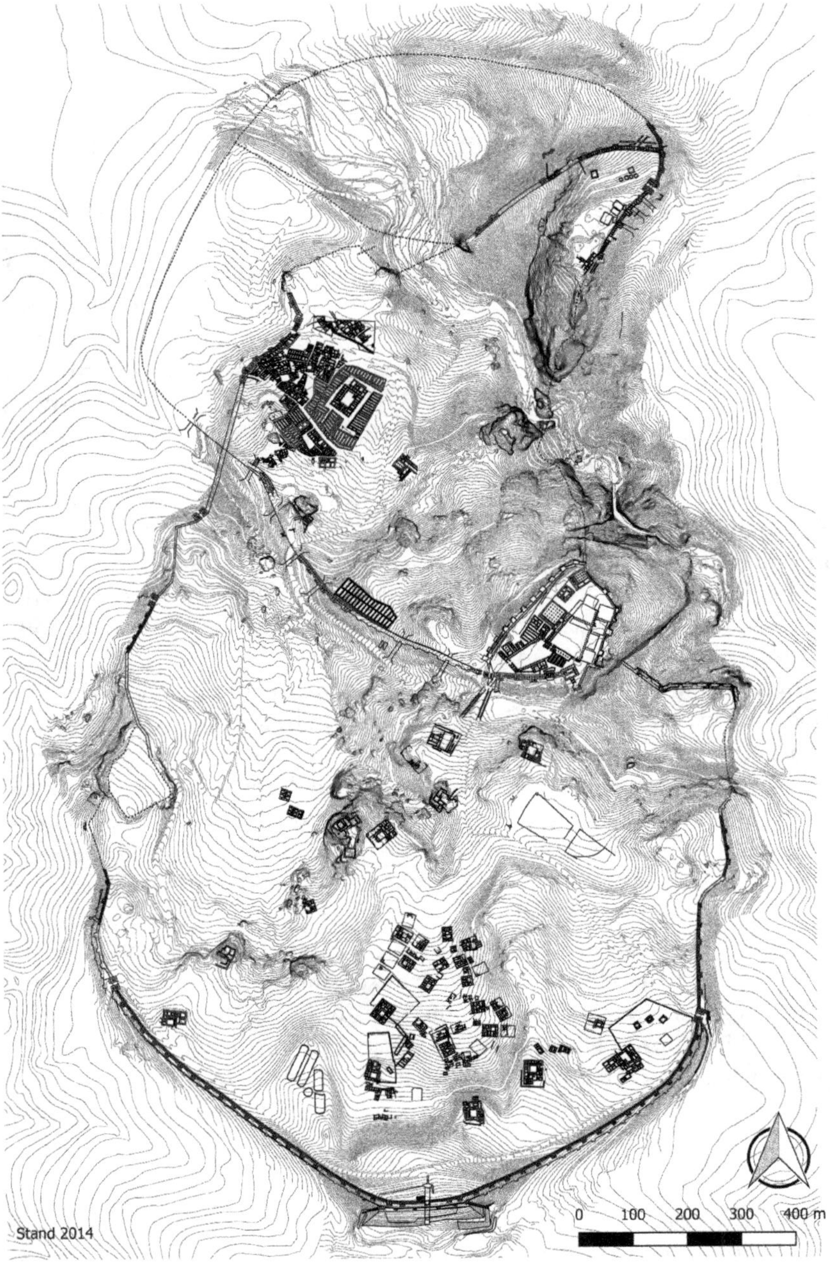

Fig. 12.4 Map of Boğazköy-Hattusa (copyright Archive of the Boğazköy Expedition, Deutsches Archäologisches Institut Berlin).

once kept on shelves that subsequently collapsed while still by and large maintaining their original order. One can only imagine what information modern excavation techniques conserving and recording the exact order of those "clearly stacked rows" might have yielded!

As may be clear from the quote just given, the earliest excavations at Hattusa between 1906 and 1912 by Winckler and Makridi were not conducted to today's standards and often not even to those that some contemporaneous excavations adhered to.[93] Winckler was mostly interested in what the texts said, not so much in what the archaeological context could contribute. To be fair though, Winckler has often been accused of not even recording where the tablets came from, yet it turns out that the find spots *were* recorded – at least in a general kind of way – but that the information was lost not too long afterwards in the Berlin Museum.[94] The excavations that resumed in 1931 – and besides an interruption from 1940 until 1952 continue up to the present day – generally did follow the standards of their day, but the seemingly ideal circumstances, as observed by Curtius in Room 11, almost never repeated themselves. The only comparable situation may have been that of the bullae and charters found at the *Westbau* in the Upper City. As we saw in Chapter 11, even though largely washed down the slope of the structure, archaeologists were able to determine how they were all originally kept in chronological groups.

Besides the lack of archaeological standards in the early years of the Boğazköy excavations, several other reasons can be adduced for this general and unfortunate state of affairs. First of all, as we will see below, there is evidence that discarded tablets were moved and dumped elsewhere, as early as in the Hittite or immediate post-Hittite period. Such dumps were identified at Büyükkaya (Bkaya), the large rock outcrop at the northeastern end of Hattusa, and at the so-called *Ostteich* 2, an artificial water reservoir in the Upper City. As explained by their excavator Jürgen Seeher, this probably happened late in the history of the capital, maybe even "when the 'custodians of the tablets', that is, civil servants and priests, had already left."[95] In the latter case, we would already be in the immediate post-Hittite-kingdom-at-Hattusa period. Secondly, further disruptions happened when over the course of the next few centuries Iron Age population groups took over the site and used Hittite spoils for their buildings.

[93] Miller 2017: 73 w. n. 6.

[94] Alaura 2006: 117; see also the non-random pattern of find spots among the Bo-tablets as detected by Miller 2017: 77–80.

[95] Seeher 2001: viii-ix ("als die 'Hüter der Tontafeln', also die Beamte und Priester, bereits abgezogen waren").

Table 12.3 *Number of text fragment finds in the StT1, HaH, and on Bk. A*

StT1	6808
HaH	1674
Bk. A	4779

Similarly, there is evidence of Galatian, Roman, and Byzantine occupation of parts of what was once the imposing capital of the Hittite kingdom. All of them left their imprint on the city, changing to a larger or lesser extent the Hittite archaeological record.

Understandably, these circumstances have resulted in a recent pessimism about the possibilities of answering any questions about a system in the physical organization and distribution of texts in the capital. To be sure, higher concentrations of tablet finds are discernible in the archaeological record: the Storerooms surrounding Temple 1 (StT1), the *Haus am Hang* or House on the Slope (HaH), and Bk. A all stand out by the sheer numbers of fragments found there (Table 12.3[96]).

One might add the *Westbau* with its combination of over three thousand bullae (and twenty-eight charters). For comparison, Table 12.4 gives the numbers for all other buildings where texts have been found (for Büyükkale see map Fig. 12.5).

The contrast in numbers might plead in favor of the StT1, the HaH, and Bk. A having been original tablet storage areas. Two recent papers on the tablets and fragments found in the first two locations, however, have cast severe doubts on our chances to detect a system.[97] One, for instance, referred to the final report of archaeologist Wulf Schirmer, that all tablet finds associated with the HaH stem from "secondary deposit."[98] They *may* have belonged to the building but that remains uncertain. The two largest text groups there come from an "old excavation dump" and from layers

96 The numbers are taken from the Konkordanz.

97 The papers were delivered by Jörg Klinger (Berlin) on the HaH, and Jared Miller (München) on the StT1 at the colloquium Stand und Perspektiven der Hethitologie. Kolloquium zum Abschluss des Projekts "Hethitische Forschungen," September 7–8, 2015, Akademie der Wissenschaften und der Literatur, Mainz (Germany). Miller's paper is now Miller 2017, Klinger's remains unpublished to my knowledge.

98 Schirmer 1969: 20 ("sämtlich aus sekundärer Lagerung").

Table 12.4 *Number of text fragment finds in buildings on Bk., and in Temples other than Temple 1 (numbers from the Konkordanz)*

Büyükkale	# fragments	Temple	# fragments
B	102	2	5
C	226	3	10
D	809	5	1
E	380	6	5
F	42	7	5
G	144	8	21
H	202	9	3
J	1	10	2
K	493	11	2
L	2	12	52
M	136	15	37
N	61	16	123
		18	4
		19	4
		20	3
		26	4
		30	5

that contained post-Hittite/Phrygian debris. Of the thousands of fragments originating from the StT1, only those from Room 11 might have been originally deposited there but the evidence is weak.[99] The same is true for Bk. E, as analyzed by Silvia Alaura.[100] Erected above the western slope of the acropolis, this was one of the first places where Winckler reported tablet finds, large and "fully preserved" pieces near the top and ever smaller ones going down.[101] Because of this, Winckler and Makridi immediately identified the structure as an "archive."[102] Later on, the Iron Age occupants incorporated the west side of Bk. E and adjacent structures into a casemate wall. Were the numerous fragments unearthed in the rooms on the west side of Bk. E part of the building's original inventory, were they Hittite fill, or Iron Age dump? One of the pieces joins fragments from Bk. C and N, covering a stretch of approximately 150 m, with an additional piece found during the Winckler–Makridi excavations that might have come from

[99] Miller 2017: 80–3. [100] Alaura 1998. [101] Winckler 1907: 12 ("vollkommen erhalten").
[102] For the history of the excavations here see Alaura 1998: 193–9.

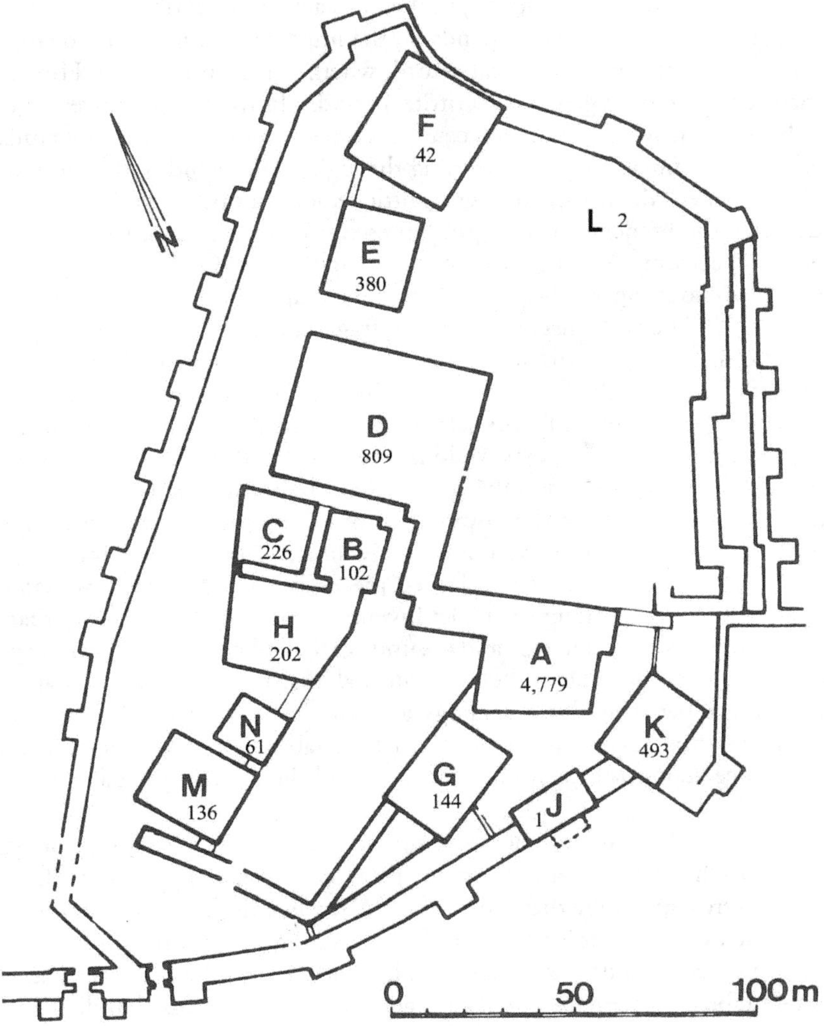

Fig. 12.5 Map of buildings on Büyükkale with added numbers of fragments found there (after Bittel 1983: 106).

anywhere in the Lower City or from the slope towards Bk. E, showing just how confusing the situation is.[103]

[103] 51/g(Bk. E)+403/f(Bk. C)+178/n(Bk. N)+Bo 938.

Any reconstruction of the physical parameters of the scribal administration at Hattusa ultimately depends on the impact we assume later disruptions had on the archaeological record, whether attributed to the Hittites themselves or dating to post-Hittite periods. If we accept far-reaching upheavals due to at least several centuries or even more than two millennia of diverse population groups coming through and inhabiting the grounds of the former Hittite capital, there is little reason for optimism. Emmanuel Laroche, the French Hittitologist, represented the far and pessimistic end of the spectrum. Writing in 1949 on the tablet inventories (see Chapter 13.14), his solution to these problems was simple: "there is but a single library."[104] The wide dispersal of tablet fragments all over the city was the result of later disruptions all ultimately originating from Bk. A. He based his conclusion on the fact that practically all tablet inventories known at the time were found on Büyükkale (mostly in Bk. A) whereas the majority of tablets listed in these texts could be identified with tablets found in the Winckler–Makridi years (1906–1912). Reportedly, the Winckler-excavations were conducted in the Lower City (StT1, the HaH, and on the slope towards Bk. E) exclusively, not on Büyükkale. Also, several fragments found on Büyükkale after 1931 joined pieces stemming from those same early excavations. Taking the tablet inventories as the ancient counterpart of modern library catalogs and assuming they should have been kept together with the tablets they inventoried, Laroche thus saw a serious disconnect between those catalogs and the actual whereabouts of the texts. For this reason, he assumed that all tablets produced at Hattusa were once kept on the acropolis in Bk. A and then got dispersed over the entire city.

On the other end of the spectrum is the often-tacit assumption in modern scholarship to assume that, in the case of larger text finds, fragments were kept where they were found. Or, when dealing with joins with multiple find spots, at least one of them was found in its original locus.[105] This approach results in a capital bustling with many offices, that is, places where tablets, if perhaps not always generated, were at least handled and part of some administrative process. It invokes the image of government employees rushing back and forth between them and – in view of the fact that there is very little system detectable in what kind of records were found where – exchanging records as part of a "paper" trail. It is also suggestive of

[104] Laroche 1949: 23 ("Il n'y a qu'une seule bibliothèque"). Laroche referred to the tablet collection at Hattusa as a "library" rather than an archive.

[105] I have been guilty of this myself: see, for instance, van den Hout 2005 and 2006.

an environment where written records played an important role in the daily business of the state and where literacy was perhaps a relatively normal phenomenon. The question is whether such a picture is realistic in view of what we know about scribes and the total number of tablets we assume to have been present in Hattusa.[106] In a recent and thus far most optimistic estimate, characterized as a "best case scenario," Jared Miller has proposed to assume "at least one tablet in the original archives of Hattusa for every two fragments found."[107] If, in trying to gauge scribal activity, we limit ourselves to the thirteenth century BC, that is, to tablets written in that time period, we then arrive at a total of just over ten thousand tablets for that entire century.[108] This would result in an average tablet production of one hundred per year. Even if we double or triple that number to account for tablets completely lost to us, this still means less than one tablet produced per day. Obviously, massive recycling may have been a common practice (see already Chapter 8.7) and no doubt many tablets have turned to dust irretrievably, but tripling the assumed amount of written production for just the thirteenth century goes some way to compensate for those losses. It is good to remember that, in numbers, short-term and semi-current records (see above §§12.2.1–2) remain significantly behind the permanent ones (§12.2.3). This is, admittedly, a rather crude and artificial way of doing so, but it does not really fit the busy picture of multiple offices and scribes rushing about. It rather seems as if the overall volume of writing may have been relatively modest, which in turn fits the impression of the limits of writing and general literacy, as advocated in this book.

The objections thus raised against a reconstruction of the administrative infrastructure are serious, and the historical reality may have been somewhere in between Laroche's view and those of modern scholars. With the current methods and techniques, we are not able to solve the problems. The existence of joins from different find spots, however, may be of some help in getting a perspective on Laroche's single "library" vs. the existence of multiple offices throughout the City. If indeed, in a massive dispersal, all our fragments originated from Büyükkale or, more specifically, from Bk.

106 Cf. the cautionary words of Taylor & Cartwright 2011: 318: "It is not clear that tablets were used in as great quantities as often assumed. We probably overestimate the time scribes spent actually producing tablets."

107 Miller 2017: 77; for earlier attempts to estimate the total number of tablets in the collections at Hattusa, see already Forrer 1922a: 176, Košak 1995: 174.

108 The Konkordanz currently lists 17,366 fragments written in New Script ("jh."), and 2777 fragments written in Late New Script ("sjh.").

A, then one would expect a fair number of joins between pieces found on Büyükkale and the rest of the city. This is not borne out by the available evidence. There is only a single join listed between Bk. A and the HaH. The join is indirect and there is no certainty that the two pieces indeed once formed part of the same tablet.[109] The same is true for the two joins listed between StT1 and Bk. A.[110] With thus only three possible, indirect joins on a total of 13,261 pieces (= StT1 + HaH + Bk. A) and no evidence for direct ones, it seems highly unlikely that any material moved between Büyükkale and the Lower City. This, then, makes it fair to assume that these two locations at least housed two originally separate places of administration and scribal activity.

To what extent some of the buildings on Büyükkale other than Bk. A housed administrative units with their own tablet storage, is hard to tell. Currently, twelve fragments from Bk. A, out of a total of 4,779 pieces, are listed as joining texts found elsewhere on the acropolis, in the buildings Bk. B, D, E, G, H, K, and N.[111] Together, these latter buildings yielded 2,191 fragments (see Table 12.4). Only twelve joins between them seems like a very modest number, but it does show that there is at least some overlap between Bk. A and the rest of the acropolis. Given the total amounts per building it is more likely that they originated from Bk. A and "radiated" out from there than *vice versa*. Just going by the numbers and its central position along the west edge of the acropolis, Bk. D may be a candidate for a second administrative center on Büyükkale. It shows by far the largest number of text finds in that area (809) and one can see the numbers dropping off to its northeast (Bk. E and F with 386 and 42, respectively) and southwest (Bk. C, H, M, N with 226, 202, 61, and 136, respectively; see Fig. 12.5). Note that Bk. D was also home to the second-largest collection of seal impressions and charters (*Landschenkungsurkunden*) after the *Westbau* (see Chapter 11) and that it has been reconstructed as an audience hall.[112]

Given the low number of joins between all buildings on Büyükkale, it is striking, therefore, that on a total of only seventy-five fragments (that is, about 6.5 percent), five pieces from Büyükkaya are listed as joining fragments from Bk. A, the StT1, or that they join fragments from the Winckler-excavations with unknown find spots. Two of these are indirect,

109 See the Konkordanz under 39/e. 110 See Konkordanz under 310/b and 383/b.

111 See the Konkordanz under 332/b, 645/c, 1253/c, 1523/c, 1600/c, 434/e, 67/k, 171/m, 234/m, 118/n, 348/n, 119/p.

112 Schachner 2011a: 143.

not physically fitting together, but we assume that the fragments once belonged to the same tablet based on similarity of handwriting, aspect, and matching text.[113] However, all such indirect joins ultimately remain uncertain and unverified and I will therefore not consider them here. The remaining three joins are certain, that is, physical and direct joins, like two interlocking pieces of a jigsaw puzzle. They point to at least two different sources: the Lower City, and, possibly, the acropolis, "possibly," because one fragment was found on the west slope of the acropolis, not from its plateau. But it is easier to imagine a fragment from the plateau rolling down and ending up on its slope than coming from, say, the StT1 area and moving up. With a steep cliff and the Budaközü river separating Büyükkaya from both locations, the tablet material must have been transferred there deliberately. As suggested by Jürgen Seeher, the number of inscribed fragments being relatively small and all of them fired or burned,[114] they must have been part of rubble or fill that was collectively moved. Büyükkaya itself shows no traces of destructive fire that could have been responsible for the baking of the tablets,[115] nor is there evidence for primary tablet storage there, and the same fill also contained many other, smaller, objects.[116] Among them was a large sherd from a pithos with markings, as they are exclusively known from the Temple 1 area. With Seeher, therefore, the material probably stemmed from deliberately discarded tablets, after a fire had destroyed one or more tablet storage structures.[117] Evidence for such a conflagration has been observed in the StT1 rooms 10–12.[118] Burned tablets were used as fill for the rebuilding of the storerooms and some of it may have been dumped elsewhere and ended up on Büyükkaya.[119] Whether the StT1 were the original locus for the burned debris is ultimately uncertain but it remains attractive to think of these rooms as a tablet storage area. The strikingly high percentage of joins within the Büyükkaya material with fragments from elsewhere compared with that of joins between other locations is partly explained by the fact that, being dumped, all those fragments by definition came from elsewhere and none were ever kept on Büyükkaya. This does suggest, however, that if all text material found on the acropolis Büyükkale had originally been

[113] Directly joining are 3005/k+132/x (from the west slope of Bk.), 2015/l+Bo 4815+Bo 9717, and 896/z (StT1)(+)Bo 68/11(StT1)+Bo 97/1; indirectly joining are 1335/c(Bk. A)(+)11/f and Bo 97/9(+)Bo 702 (+)Bo 750.

[114] Seeher, personal communication March 8, 2019. [115] Seeher 2018: 84. [116] Seeher 2018: 88.

[117] Seeher 2018: 88. [118] Puchstein 1912: 123–6, Neve 1975: 77, Miller 2017: 80–3.

[119] Thus Seeher, personal communication March 8, 2019.

stored in Bk. A, we should expect a larger number of joins among the fragments found on the acropolis.

We can thus posit, at a minimum, the Lower City and Bk. A as the two main places of administration and accompanying scribal activity during the Hittite kingdom. Furthermore, it seems likely that besides Bk. A some other buildings on the acropolis (Bk. D?) served similar purposes. In addition, we can make a few more observations. First of all, there is no obvious distinction between the Lower City and Büyükkale, as both places held tablets of all genres. Sometimes, a certain genre may be poorly represented in one of the two but that may be a coincidence. There seems to be, however, at least one relevant difference between the text corpora. Silvin Košak has convincingly shown that the holdings of Bk. A contained a significantly higher percentage of older tablets than the collections that came to light in other buildings.[120] This has then led to the description of Bk. A as a "record center," that is, an archive where tablets were brought together and kept that were no longer administratively active or of daily relevance to the current administration.[121] At the same time, it was considered premature to discard and recycle them. Such compositions could still be useful to future administrations, and evidence for use of older documents in the drafting of new ones is very strong, as we saw above. This suggests that the first-line administration took place in the Lower City, right there where the major storerooms were and near the Lower West Gate with a residential and workshop quarter. By its very nature, the acropolis, also often described as the palace complex, was a more restricted area, lending itself to storage of longer-term but no longer very active documents. How much scribal activity that included in the sense of generating documents is difficult to say. But any further details about a possible filing system at either location remain elusive.

12.10 Appendix: The Editors at Work

Ideally, we would have two clear duplicate texts, one either a *parkui tuppi* or carrying the designation ANA GIŠ.ḪUR=*kan ḫandan* and the other *ištarniyaš appan tarnumaš* so that we might compare them and see the kinds of differences between the two. Unfortunately, that is not the case. What we do have, are two versions, already mentioned, of the sixteenth day of the AN.TAḪ.ŠUM cult festival, one labeled ANA GIŠ.ḪUR=*kan ḫandan*

[120] Košak 1995, see also Klinger 2006: 12 (Abb. 1 and 2) vs. 14 (Abb. 3), and Miller 2017: 70.
[121] van den Hout 2008b: 219.

(A = KUB 25.1), the other (B = KUB 2.5), as far as preserved, without any indication of its editorial status[122]:

> Third tablet of the cult ritual of the temple of Zababa of the ANTAḪŠUM; not finished; collated against the original.[123]
>
> Third tablet of the ANTAḪŠUM; not finished.[124]

This Appendix presents the Hittite text and translation of the parts where both manuscripts overlap. B stands for the majority of festival or cult ritual texts with a preserved colophon but without any of the additional terms discussed in the previous chapter. It gives information about what ritual it belongs to, which tablet in the series it is, and it adds the name of the scribe. Even though we do not know the exact relation between the two tablets A and B they cover almost the same text (A has a column and a half of text more at the beginning) and both are the third tablet in an AN.TAḪ.ŠUM series. Comparing these two tablets can at least illustrate the kind of changes that were occasionally made in the cult and which ones found their way into the official and authorized version.

Neither tablet is perfect. In its general aspect, A (Fig. 12.6) looks perfunctory rather than beautiful or written with great care. This is not a scribe trying to produce a masterpiece but an experienced hand working its way through a long text that has to be finished more or less in one go before the tablet gets too dried out to write on. It is a large (ca. 24 × 18.5 cm) tablet, preserved in its full length and width, with three columns on either side, quite typical of such festival manuscripts. It is striking, however, that the usual horizontal line (so-called *Randleiste*) marking the top of the reverse is missing.[125] The *intercolumnia* are somewhat sloppily drawn, the three columns not of equal width, and paragraph lines often very thin and slanting upwards. Three times (vi 7, 8, 28) the scribe has to write vertically upwards into the *intercolumnium*, both side edges are frequently used to accommodate text that did not fit on the obverse or reverse, and there are numerous erasures covering up mistakes (in the transliterated part in the

122 The space available after AN.TA[Ḫ.ŠUM^{SAR} is almost certainly not large enough to accommodate *ištarniyaš appan tarnumaš.*

123 DUB.3.KAM *ŠA* EZEN₄ É ^{d}ZABABA AN.TAḪ.ŠUM^{SAR} *UL QATI ANA* GIŠ.ḪUR=*kan ḫandan* KUB 25.1 vi 43–48, ed. by Waal 2015: 414–5.

124 DUB.3.KAM *ŠA* AN.TA[Ḫ.ŠUM^{SAR} *UL QATI*] KUB 2.5 vi 1–2, ed. by Waal 2015: 414; the hand copy of KUB 2.5 counts the colophon lines separately as lines 1–2 after 18 lines of regular text. The break after AN.TA[Ḫ is large enough to accommodate the above restoration but not for *ANA* GIŠ.ḪUR=*kan ḫandan*.

125 For a discussion of such tablets see Waal 2015: 104–5 and the catalog (among which KUB 25.1) 205–7.

Fig. 12.6 KUB 25.1 obv. columns i-iii (upper half; copyright Staatliche Museen zu Berlin – Vorderasiatisches Museum, Foto: BoFN 01759).

Appendix indicated by *asterisks*). Some additional scribal errors have been left standing (marked by ! or ≪ ≫ in the transcription). On the whole, however, the writing is regular, and the tablet quite densely covered with script.

Text B looks like a more "finished" product, certainly at first sight (Fig. 12.7). This, too, is a large (ca. 26.5 × 21.5 cm) three-columned tablet on both obverse and reverse. The *intercolumnia* are straight and steadily drawn, paragraph lines clear, and usually fairly straight. On the lower edge of the obverse and on the top and bottom (preserved at the end of col. iv) of the reverse we see the usual *Randleiste*. The writing, however, especially in the beginning, is irregular. The first six paragraphs of the text (i 1–18) are set up with an unusual amount of space both interlinear and between words and with extensive erasures, it seems, but lines i 19–24 suddenly become very dense and cramped. As of i 25 the writing is more regular and normal and stays that way throughout the remainder of the tablet. It almost looks as if the entire beginning of the tablet up to line 25 was erased and written again but only after lines 25ff. had already been inscribed. When starting over, the scribe may initially have thought he had ample room but then discovered he had more text and had to squeeze in the remainder in lines 19–24. As of line 25ff. there are some more erasures and the inevitable minor scribal errors.

In general, one can state that A tends to be more explicit than B. The latter manuscript, for instance, with a single exception, consistently (B i 1, 6, ii 1, 19, iii 45–46, vi 16; exception iii 9–10) very briefly describes the coming of the cupbearer as "(the one-)of-kneeling comes" whereas the former always has "The cupbearer-of-kneeling comes" (ii 35–36, iii 41–42, iv 47–48, 55–56, v 8–9, vi 39–40). The same is true for the cupbearer bringing in bread after the drinking ceremony where KUB 25.1 always adds "from outside" (*āškaz*) where KUB 2.5 leaves this unspecified.[126] As we will see in Chapter 14, there are clear indications that magic rituals imported from other parts of Anatolia were memorized and written down again from memory sometimes resulting in random deviations caused by deficient memorization. The consistency of the deviations between the two AN.TAḪ.ŠUM festival tablets, however, makes such an explanation here unlikely.

126 Similarly, when the pieces of bread are put on "the consecrated table" it is the "waiter/table man" who does it in A ii 53 vs. the cupbearer in B i 23; also, in A iii 34–9 the table is twice called "consecrated" vs. only once in B ii 2–17; inbetween the drinking ceremony and the bringing of bread A iii 27–9 adds the consecration of an emptied silver *išqaruḫ*-vessel.

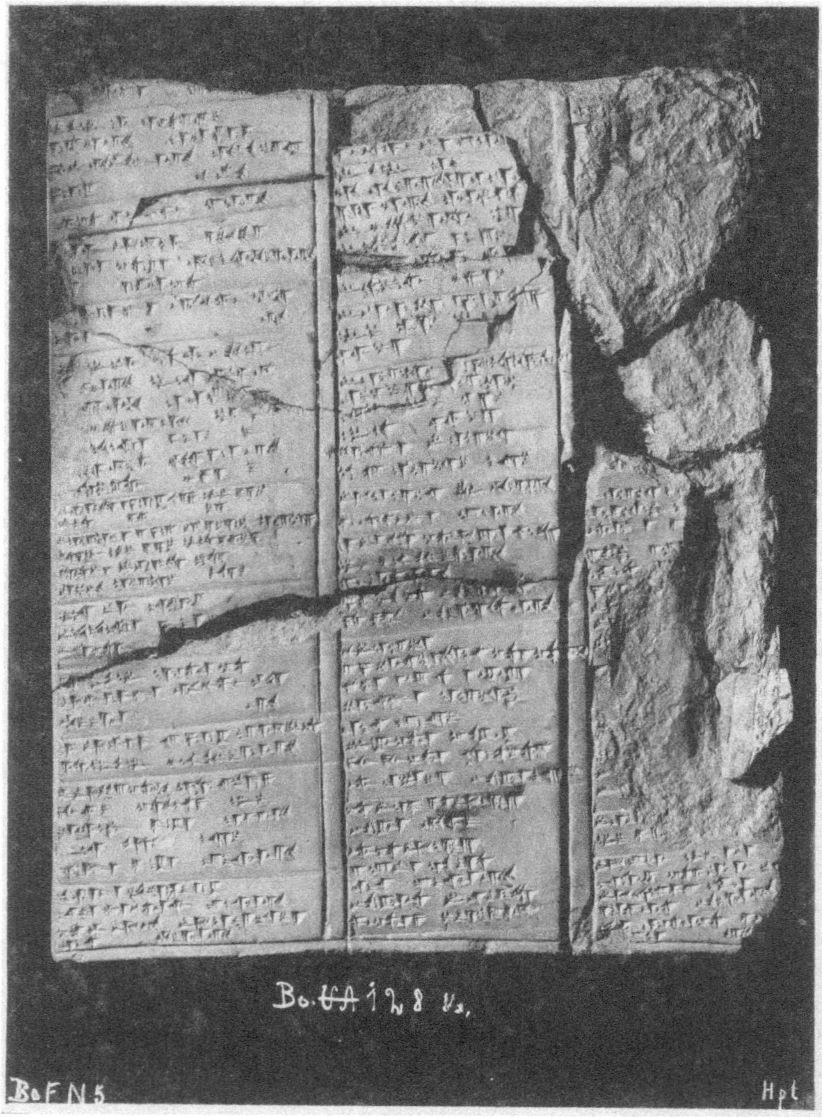

Fig. 12.7 KUB 2.5 obv. columns i-iii (copyright Staatliche Museen zu Berlin – Vorderasiatisches Museum, Foto: BoFN 00005).

A. KUB 25.1 **ii**	**B.** KUB 2.5 **i**
. . . -31 [. . . -]*zi*	1 *parašnauwaš=kan uizzi*
32–34 [LUGAL MUNUS.LUGAL TUŠ-*aš* $^{d/GIŠ}$*Ta*]*urit akuwanzi* [GIŠ.^{d}INANNA.GAL *ḫazzikkanzi*? *U*]*L* SÌR-*RU* [NINDA.GUR$_4$.RA] NU.GÁL	2–5 LUGAL MUNUS.LUGAL TUŠ-*aš* ^{GIŠ}*Taurī akuwanzi* GIŠ.^{d}INANNA.GAL *ḫazzikkanzi UL* SÌR-*RU* NINDA.GUR$_4$.RA NU.GÁL
35–36 *n*[*=ašta paraš*]*nauwaš* ^{LÚ}SAGI.A-*aš ú*[*iz*]*zi*	6 *n=ašta paraš*[*n*]*auwaš uizzi*
37–41 *nu* LÚ[^{GI}]^{Š}GIDRU $^{LÚ.MEŠ}$*UBARU ašeš*[*ša*]*r ḫūman* **šarāt**[**i**]**t**[**tan**]**uwanzi** *ne arantari* *t*[*a*? DUMU.M]EŠ.É.GAL *ginuwaš* [GAD.ḪI.A] *danzi*	7–9 [LÚ] ^{GIŠ}GIDRU $^{LÚ.MEŠ}$*UBARU ašeššar* [*ḫ*]*ūman šarā* **ḫūittiyanzi** [*n*]*e aranta* 10–11 [DUMU.MEŠ?]É.GAL=*kan ginuwaš* GAD.ḪI.A *danzi*
42–45 [LUGAL MUNUS.LUGAL T]UŠ-*aš* ^{d}*Ištanun* [^{d}*Tapp*]*inunn=a*! *akuwanzi* [GIŠ.^{d}INANNA GA]L $^{LÚ.MEŠ}$*ḫalliyarieš* [SÌR-*RU* LUGAL-**uš**? **ḫup**]**pari šipanti**	12–18 LUGAL MUNUS.LUGAL GUB-*aš* ^{d}UTU ^{d}*Tappinū* [*aku*]*wanzi* LUGAL-**uš ḫuppari** [**ši**]**ppanti** GIŠ.^{d}INANNA[.GA]L [$^{LÚ.ME}$]^{Š}*ḫalliyariēš* SÌR-*RU* [LÚ A]LAN.ZU$_9$ **memai** [^{LÚ}**p**]**alwatallaš palwāezzi** ^{LÚ}**kītaš ḫalzāi**
46–48 [^{LÚ}SA]G[I.A]-*aš āškaz* [. . .]*dai* LUGAL-*i pāi* [LUGAL-*uš p*]*arši*[*y*]*a* **n=at**? [**par**]**ā**? **pē**? [**dai**?]	19–20 ^{LÚ}SAGI.A 1 NINDA.GUR$_4$.RA *EMṢA* LUGAL-*i pāi* LUGAL-*uš paršiya*
50–54 [LÚ] ^{GIŠ}BANŠUR[*=kan* x?^{NINDA}? *mitg*]*aimiuš* [*š*]*uppaz* ^{GI}[^{Š}BANŠUR-*a*]*z dāi* [LUG]AL-*i pāi* LUGAL[-*u]š paršiya* [*t*]*=uš=kan* LÚ ^{GIŠ}B[AN]ŠUR *āppa* [*š*]*uppai* ^{GIŠ}BANŠUR-*i dāi*	21–24 LÚ ^{GIŠ}BANŠUR=*kan* 2 NINDA.KU$_7$ *šuppayaz* ^{GIŠ}BANŠUR-*za dāi* LUGAL-*i pāi* LUGAL-*uš paršiya t=uš=kan* ^{LÚ}SAGI.A EGIR-*pa šuppi* ^{GIŠ}BANŠUR-*i dāi*
55–57 LUGAL-*uš* GUB-*aš UŠKEN* LÚ.ALAN.ZU$_9$ *memai* [. . .]	25–27 LUGAL-*uš* GUB-*aš UŠKEN* LÚ.ALAN.ZU$_9$ *memai* ^{LÚ}*kitāš* [*ḫalzāi*]
58–59/60? [. . .]	28–30 *ta* LUGAL MUNUS.LUGAL *ešanta* DUMU.MEŠ.É.GAL=*kan ginuwaš* GAD.ḪI.A *tīyanzi*
iii	
1–3 *nu* 12 NINDA.GUR$_4$.RA ^{URU}*Ari*[*nna*] GAL DUMU.É.GAL LUGAL-*i* MUNUS.LUGAL[?] *tarkummiyaezzi*	31–32 GAL LÚ.MEŠ.É.GAL 12 NINDA.GUR$_4$.RA ^{URU}*Arinna ANA* LUGAL MUNUS.LUGAL *tarkummiyaezzi*
4–10 UGULA $^{LÚ.MEŠ}$MUḪALDIM 3 *TAPAL* ^{GIŠ}*kišdun ḫaššī tapušza* LUGAL-*i* ***tūwaz parā ēpz*[*i*] LUGAL-*uš=šan* **tūwa**[**z**] *QATAM dāi n=at=kan p*[*arā*] *udanz*[*i*] 11- . . . (?) *nu* EGIR=*ŠU taḫtu*[*mmara I*]*ŠTU* É.NA$_4$[.DINGIR-*LIM udanzi*? *ta* UGULA] LÚ.MES ^{GIŠ}B[ANŠUR? . . .]	33–37 UGULA $^{LÚ.MEŠ}$MUḪALDIM 3 *TAPAL* ^{GIŠ}*kišdun ḫaššī tapušza* LUGAL-*i tūwaz parā ēpzi* [LUG]AL-*uš QATAM*** *dāi n=at=kan parā udanzi* 38–41 EGIR=*ŠU=ma taḫtummara IŠTU* É.NA$_4$.DINGIR-*LIM udanzi ta* UGULA $^{LÚ.MEŠ}$MUḪALDIM LÚ.MEŠ ^{GIŠ}BANŠUR=*ia anda tiyanzi*

[break of ca. 9 lines]
[. . .]
24–29 [. . . ^{d}]U ^{URU}*Z*[*ippalan*]*da* [*akuwa*]*nzi* [GIŠ.^{d}IN]ANNA.GAL $^{LÚ.MEŠ}$*ḫalliyarieš* SÌR-*RU* [^{LÚ}]SAGI.A ***išgaruḫi*ya*?*** [K]Ù.BABBAR ***šannapili šer šuppaḫḫi*** §§
30–33 ^{LÚ}SAGI.A ****āšk*az*** 1 NINDA.GUR$_4$.RA *EMṢA* ***udai*** LUGAL-*i pāi* LUGAL-*uš paršiya* ***n=an=kan parā pēdai***
34–39 LÚ ^{GIŠ}BANŠUR *šuppayaz* ^{GIŠ}BANŠUR-*az* 2 ^{NINDA}*mitgaimiuš* LUGAL-*i pāi* LUGAL-*uš paršiya t=uš=kan āppa*** ***šuppai*** ^{GIŠ}BANŠUR-*i dāi*

40 TU$_7$.Ì *tianzi*
41–42 *n=ašta parašnauwaš* ^{LÚ}SAGI.A-***aš*** *uizzi*
43–47 *nu=kan* GAL *MEŠEDI* ***anda paizzi nu*** LUGAL-*i ŠA* LÚ.MEŠ UR.GI$_7$ IGI.DU$_8$.A *tarkummiyaezzi waššuwanti* ^{NINDA}*wagatan* KÙ.BABBAR KÙ.GI *pianna*
48–57 *nu* LÚ ^{GIŠ}BANŠUR 2 ^{NINDA}*tunnaptuš ŠA* 2 *ŠATI* ** ŠÀ.BA 1 BABBAR 1 SA$_5$ *t=uš=kan* ^{GIŠ}BANŠUR-*az anda udai šer=a*≪*ašša*≫*=ššan* GA.KIN.AG *ḫašḫaššan kittari n=aš* ^{GIŠ}AB-*ia peran dāi*
58–61 *nu* LÚ ^{GIŠ}GIDRU *ANA* LÚ.MEŠ E.DÉ.A *peran ḫūwāi n=ašta* LÚ.MEŠ E.DÉ.A 2 SAG.DU GU$_4$ KÙ.BABBAR (**iv**) 1–3 *anda udanzi perann=a* ^{LÚ}SAGI.A *waššanza iyattari*
[. . .]
47–48 *n=ašta parašna*[*uwaš*] ^{LÚ}SAGI.A-*aš u*[*izzi*]
49–50 LUGAL MUNUS.LUGAL TUŠ-*aš* ^{d}*Ḫ*[*ullan*] *akuwanzi* LÚ.MEŠ [GI.GÍD SÌR-*RU*]

ii
[break of 3–4 lines]
1 *parašnawaš=kan uizz*[*i*]
2–8 LUGAL MUNUS.LUGAL TUŠ-*aš* ^{d}U ^{d}U ^{URU}*Zippalan*[*da*] *akuwanzi* GIŠ.^{d}INANNA.GAL ^{LÚ}*ḫalliyariaš* SÌR-*R*[*U*] LÚ.ALAN.ZU$_9$ ***memāi*** ^{LÚ}***palwatallaš palwā*[*ezzi*]** ^{LÚ}***kīdaš ḫalzāi***
9–11 ^{LÚ}SAGI.A 1 NINDA.GUR$_4$.RA *EMṢA* LUGAL-*i pāi* LUGAL-*u*[*š*] *paršiya*

12–17 LÚ ^{GIŠ}BANŠUR*=kan* 2? ^{NINDA}*midda!gamiš* ***šuppayaza*** [^{G}]^{IŠ}BANŠUR-***az dāi*** LUGAL-*i pāi* LUGAL-*uš paršiya t=uš=kan*[127] LÚ ^{GIŠ}BANŠUR EGIR-*pa* ^{GIŠ}BANŠUR!-*i dāi*
18 LÚ.MEŠ ^{GIŠ}BANŠUR TU.Ì *tiyanzi*
19 *parašnauwaš=kan uizzi*

20–24 GAL ^{LÚ}*MEŠEDI ŠA* LÚ.MEŠ UR.GI$_7$ IGI.DU$_8$.LIŠ.A LUGAL-*i tarkummiyaezzi waššūwanzi* ^{NINDA}*wagata piyanna* KÙ.BABBAR KÙ.GI *piyanauwanzi*
25–32 *nu* LÚ ^{GIŠ}BANŠUR 2 ^{NINDA}*tunaptuš ŠA* 2 *ŠATI* ŠÀ.BA! 1-*EN* BABBAR 1-*EN* SA$_5$ *t=uš=kan* ^{GIŠ}BANŠUR-*az anda udāi šerr=a=ššan* GA.KIN.AG *ḫašḫaššan kittari n=aš* ^{GIŠ}**AB-*ia peran dāi*
33–39 *ta* LÚ ^{GIŠ}GIDRU *ANA* LÚ.MEŠ E.DÉ.A *peran ḫūwai n=ašta* LÚ.MEŠ E.DÉ.A 2 SAG.DU GU$_4$ KÙ.BABBAR *anda udanzi perann=a* ^{LÚ}SAGI.LIŠ.A *waššanza iyattari*
[. . .]
iii 45–46 *parašn*[*auwaš=kan*] *uizzi*

iv 1–6 LUGAL MUNUS.LUGAL ^{d}*Ḫu*[*llan*] *akuwanzi* LÚ.MEŠ GI.GÍD SÌR-*RU* LÚ ALAN.ZU$_9$ ***memai*** ^{LÚ}***palwātallaš pal*[*wāezz*]*i*** ^{LÚ}***kītaš ḫalzāi***

[127] From here a horizontal paragraph-like line runs dextroverse through LÚ ^{GIŠ}BANŠUR into the intercolumnium.

51–54 ^{LÚ}SAGI.A ***āšk[az]*** I NINDA.GUR$_4$.RA *udai* LUGAL-*i pāi* LUGAL-*uš p[aršiya]* ***t=ašta parā pē[dai]*** 55–56 *n=ašta parašnauwaš* ^{LÚ}SAGI!.A-*aš uizz[i]*	7–8 ^{LÚ}SAGI.LIŠ.A I NINDA.GUR$_4$.RA *EMṢA* LUGAL-*i pāi* LUGAL-*uš paršiya* 9–10 *parašnauwaš=kan* ^{LÚ}SAGI.LIŠ.A-*aš uizzi*
v 1–7 LUGAL MUNUS.LUGAL TUŠ-*aš* ^{d}*Telipinu**? *akuwanzi* GIŠ.^{d}INANNA.GAL $^{\text{LÚ.MEŠ}}$*ḫalliyarieš* SÌR-*RU* ^{LÚ}SAGI.A *āškaz* NINDA.GUR$_4$.RA *udai* LUGAL-*i pāi* LUGAL-*uš paršiya* ***t=ašta parā pēdai*** * *[128]	11–16 LUGAL MUNUS.LUGAL TUŠ-*aš* ^{d}*Telipinun akuwanzi* GIŠ.^{d}INANNA.GAL $^{\text{LÚ.MEŠ}}$*ḫalliyarieš* SÌR-*RU* LÚALAN.ZU$_9$ ***memai*** **[**^{LÚ}***palwat]allaš palwāezzi*** **[**^{LÚ}***kītaš***] ***ḫalzāi***
8–9 *n=ašta parašnauwaš* * *[129] $^{\text{LÚ.MEŠ!}}$SAGI!.A-*aš uizzi* [. . .]	17–18 [. . .]I? NINDA.GUR$_4$.RA *EMṢA* [LUGAL-*i pāi* LUGAL]-*uš paršiya* [. . .]
45–49 *nu* GAL *MEŠEDI* ^{LÚ}SAGI[.A] ^{TÚG}*šeknu=ššan a[rḫa tarnāi]* ^{LÚ}SAGI.A LUGAL-*i UŠK[EN] t=an* GAL *MEŠEDI namma=pat* ^{TÚG}*šeknu=ššan ēpz[i]* [. . .]	**v** 10–16 *ta* GAL LÚ *MEŠEDI* ^{LÚ}SAGI.LIŠ.A ^{TÚG}*šeknun=šan arḫa tarnāi* ^{LÚ}SAGI.LIŠ.A[?] LUGAL-*i UŠKEN ta* [. . .] *namma=pat* ^{TÚG}*šeknu[n ?] ēpz[i* . . .] ***parā*** [. . .] [. . .]
vi 18–21 *nu* LÚ.MEŠ *^{GIŠ}GIDRU* LÚ.MEŠ *UBARUTIM ašeššarr=a ḫūman šarā tittanuwanzi ne artari*	**vi** 1–2 [. . .] *šarā* ***ḫūit[tiyanzi]*** *ne aran[ta]*
22–24 *n=ašta* 2 DUMU.MEŠ É.GAL *ANA* LU[GAL-*i*? MUNUS.LUG]AL *ginuwa[š]* GAD.ḪI.A *[da]nzi*	3–5 *n=ašta* 2 DUMU.MEŠ É.GAL *ANA* LUGAL-*i* MUNUS.LUGAL *ginuwaš* GAD.ḪI.A *[da]nzi* **?
25–30 LUGAL MUNUS.LUGAL GUB-*aš* *^{d}UTU-*AM** *akuwanzi* $^{\text{LÚ.MEŠ}}$GALA SÌR-*RU* ^{GIŠ}***argami galgaltūri*** *^{GIŠ}***ḫuḫupa*llitt=a ḫazzikanzi palweškanzi=ya***	6–10 LUGAL MUNUS.LUGAL GUB-*aš* ^{d}UTU-*AM akuwanzi* ***walḫanzi=ššan*** $^{\text{LÚ.MEŠ}}$GALA SÌR-*RU* LÚ.ALAN.ZU$_9$ ***memai*** ^{LÚ} ***palwatallaš palwāezzi*** ^{LÚ}***kitaš ḫalzāi***
31–35 ^{LÚ}SAGI.A ***āškaz*** I NINDA.GUR.RA ZÌ.DA ZÍZ **ŠA* 3 *UPNI** * * *udai* LUGAL-*i pāi* LUGAL-*uš paršiya* ***t=ašta parā pēdai***	11–12 ^{LÚ}SAGI.LIŠ.A I NINDA.GUR$_4$.RA *EMṢA* LUGAL-*i pāi* LUGAL-*uš paršiya*
36–40 LÚ ^{GIŠ}BANŠUR-*aš* ^{NINDA}*zippulašni udāi t=a*! ^{GIŠ}AB-*ia peran dāi* *t=ašta parašnauwaš* ^{LÚ}SAGI.A-***aš*** *uizzi*	13–15 LÚ ^{GIŠ}BANŠUR-*aš* ^{NINDA}*zippulaššin udai t=an* ^{GIŠ}AB-*ia peran dāi* 16 *t=ašta parašnauwaš uizzi*

128 The erased traces show the scribe wrote *na-aš-ta*, which is the beginning of the next paragraph.

129 Possibly the scribe started writing $^{\text{LÚ.MEŠ}}$SAGI.A-*aš* but then noticed that this sequence would be too long for this line. So, he erased what he had written and then started a new line.

41–42 *aše*š*šar*=*ma* LÚ *UBARUTIM arantari*=*pat*	17–18 *aše*š*šar*=*ma* LÚ.MEŠ *UBARUTIM arantari*
colophon 43–48 DUB.3.KAM *ŠA* EZEN$_4$ É ^{d}ZABABA AN.TAḪ.ŠUM^{SAR} *UL QATI ANA* GIŠ.ḪUR=*kan ḫandan*	colophon 1–2 DUB.3.KAM *ŠA* AN.TA[Ḫ.ŠUM^{SAR} *UL QATI*]

Translation of A (with B added where deviating):

(A ii 31/B i 1) The (man-)of-kneeling comes.

(A ii 32–34/B i 2–5) Sitting, the king and queen drink to the god Taurit. The great lyre is played. There is no singing. There is no thick bread.

(A ii 35–36/B i 6) The cupbearer-of-kneeling comes. (B: omits "The cupbearer")

(A ii 37–41/B i 7–11) The heralds make the foreigners/foreign guests and the entire assembly rise (B: pull up) and they stand. The palace attendants take the knee cloths.

(A ii 42–45/B i 12–18) Sitting, the king and queen drink to the god Tappinu. The great lyre. The *halliyari*-men sing. The king libates in the *huppar*-vase. (B: Sitting, the king and queen drink to the god Tappinu. The king libates in *the huppar*-vase. The *halliyari*-men sing to the great lyre. The ALAN.ZU-man speaks. The reciter recites. The *kita*-man calls out.)

(A ii 46–48/B i 19–20) The cupbearer takes one sour thick bread from outside. He gives it to the king. The king breaks (it). He/They? carry it forth. (B: The cupbearer takes one sour thick bread from outside. He gives it to the king. The king breaks (it).)

(A ii 50–54/B i 21–24) The waiter takes x *mitgaimi*-breads from the consecrated table. He gives it to the king. The king breaks (them). The waiter places them back on the consecrated table. (B: The cupbearer places them back on the consecrated table.)

(A ii 55–57/B i 25–30) Standing, the king bows. The ALAN.ZU-man speaks. The *kita*-man calls out. (break in A; B continues: The king and queen sit down. The palace attendants place the knee cloths.)

(A iii 1–3/B i 31–32) The chief of the palace attendants informs the king and queen of the twelve thick breads of Arinna.

(A iii 4–10/B i 33–37) The chief cook presents to the king three *kisduns* besides the hearth from afar. The king lays his hand on them from afar. They bring them forth.

(A iii 11- . . . /B i 38–41) Next, they bring *tahtummara* from the Stone House. The chief of the waiters and the waiters take a stand.

(B ii 1) The man-of-kneeling comes.

(A iii 24–29/B ii 2–8) Sitting, the king and queen drink to the Stormgod and the Stormgod of Zippalanda. The *halliyari*-men sing to the great lyre. The cupbearer consecrates the empty silver *isqaruh*-vase. (B: The *halliyari*-men sing to the great lyre. The ALAN.ZU-man speaks. The reciter recites. The *kita*-man calls out.)

(A iii 30–33/B ii 9–11) The cupbearer brings from outside one sour thick bread. He gives (it) to the king. The king breaks (it). He carries it forth. (B: omits the final sentence)

(A iii 34–39/B ii 12–17) The waiter gives from the consecrated table two *mitgaimi*-breads. The king breaks (them). He puts them back on the consecrated table. (B: The waiter takes from the consecrated table two *mitgaimi*-breads. He gives (them) to the king. The king breaks (them). The waiter puts them back on the consecrated table.

(A iii 40/B ii 18) They set down a fat stew. (B: The cooks set down a fat stew.)

(A iii 41–42/B ii 19) The cupbearer-of-kneeling comes. (B: omits "The cupbearer")

(A iii 43–47/B ii 20–24) The Chief of the Bodyguard enters. He announces to the king the contribution to(?) the dog-men (B: omits "enters") to give *wagata*-bread, silver (and) gold to the dressed one. (B: to reward the dressed ones with *wagata*-bread, silver (and) gold)

(A iii 48–57/B ii 25–32) The waiter (takes?) two *tunnaptu*-breads of two *sūtu* weight, one of which is white, one red. He brings them in from the table. On top lies shaved/grated cheese. He places them in front of the window.

(A iii 58-iv 3/B ii 33–39) The herald marches in front of the smiths. The smiths bring in two ox heads of silver and the dressed cupbearer goes in front.

(A iv 47–48/B iii 45–46) The cupbearer-of-kneeling comes. (B: omits "The cupbearer")

(A iv 49–50/B iv 1–6) Sitting, the king and queen drink to Hulla. The GI.GÍD-men sing. (B continues: The ALAN.ZU-man speaks. The reciter recites. The *kita*-man calls out.)

(A iv 51–54/B iv 7–8) The cupbearer brings one thick bread from outside. He gives (it) to the king. The king breaks (it). He brings/They bring (it) forth. (B: The cupbearer gives one sour thick bread to the king. The king breaks (it).)

(A iv 55–56/B iv 9–10) The cupbearer-of-kneeling comes.

(A v 1–7/B iv 11–16) Sitting, the king and queen drink to Telipinu. The *halliyari*-men sing to the great lyre. The cupbearer brings a thick reed from outside. He gives (it) to the king. The king breaks (it). He brings (it) forth. (B: . . . The *halliyari*-men sing to the great lyre. The ALAN. ZU-man speaks. The reciter recites. The *kita*-man calls out.)

(A v 45–49/B v 10–16) The Chief Bodyguard lets go of the cupbearer's robe. The cupbearer bows before the king. The Chief Bodyguard seizes him by the robe again. (B: The Chief Bodyguard seizes him by the robe again. . . . forth . . .)

(A vi 18–21/B vi 1–2) The heralds make the strangers/foreign guests and the entire assembly rise (B: pull up [the entire assembly]) and they(!; A lit. it stands) stand.

(A vi 22–24/B vi 3–5) Two palace attendants take the knee cloths from the king and queen.

(A vi 25–30/B vi 6–10) Standing, the king and queen drink to the Sundeity. The GALA-men sing. They strike the *argami*, *galgalturi*, and *huhupal*(-instruments) and they recite. (B: . . . the Sundeity. They hit (the instruments). The GALA-men sing. The ALAN.ZU-man speaks. The reciter recites. The *kita*-man calls out.)

(A vi 31–35/B vi 11–12) The cupbearer brings from outside one thick bread of three handfuls. He gives (it) to the king. The king breaks (it). He carries it forth. (B: omits the final sentence)

(A vi 36–40/B vi 13–16) The waiter brings a *zippulasni*-bread. He places (it?) in front of the window. The cupbearer-of-kneeling comes. (B: He places it in front of the window. The cupbearer-of-kneeling comes. (B: omits "The cupbearer")

(A vi 41–42/B vi 17–18) The assembly and the foreigner/foreign guests all stand. (B: The assembly and the foreigners/foreign guests all stand.)

(Colophon)

(A vi 43–48) Third tablet of the festival of the Temple of Zababa of the AN.TAH.SUM. Not finished. True to/Collated against the original.

(B vi 1–2) Third tablet of the AN.TAH.SUM.

CHAPTER 13

Scribes and Scholars

13.1 The Last Hundred Years

When around 1295 BC Mursili handed down the crown to his eldest son Muwatalli II the latter not only inherited a kingdom saved from the rebellions that had accompanied Mursili's own accession and strengthened by a network of treaty, family, and marriage relations but also the well-oiled machinery of a state chancellery. As we saw in the previous chapter, Mittannamuwa had occupied the key position of chief scribe and gained the trust of Mursili. It comes as no surprise then that Muwatalli kept him on. When at some later point Muwatalli decided to transfer the capital to the southern town of Tarhuntassa he left the old chief scribe in charge of what was now the former residence and made Mittannamuwa's son Purandamuwa the new chief scribe. This dual appointment is testament to the regard for the family as well as to the importance attached to having a chancellery *cum* tablet collection.

Hattusa had been abandoned before. Almost a century earlier, under threat of Gasgaean invasions, Tuthaliya III had temporarily taken refuge in the town of Sapinuwa. Muwatalli's reasons to move the capital are unclear, however. Some scholars have mentioned the continuing threat posed by the Gasgaeans or the upcoming confrontation with Pharaoh Ramses II at Kadesh in Syria, for which a southern location was considered strategically more advantageous. Alternatively, arguments have been put forward in favor of an above all religiously inspired move to a city wholly dedicated to the cult of a single deity, the Stormgod of Lightning.[1] It is beyond doubt that Muwatalli had chosen him as his patron god who was especially venerated in the south, evident in the name of the city Tarhuntassa, "(city) of the Stormgod." Or, as has been suggested recently, his piety was actually a pretext to win over the Hattusa elite for what was in reality a pragmatic, economically motivated move.[2] Whatever his reasons were, even though left in the capable hands of Mittanamuwa,

[1] Singer 2006. [2] Matessi 2017: 30–1.

Hattusa may never have recovered from this "demotion." What must have been a city of considerable splendor, with its imposing acropolis, over thirty temples, and seven kilometers of impressive walls and bastions, changed. According to the latest archaeological insights this was the moment when many of the temples started being dismantled and transformed into workshops.

With his youngest brother Hattusili as army commander and governor of the Upper Land, Muwatalli II initially focused his attention on the west. The king of Wilusa in the Troad, Alaksandu, called upon Muwatalli to suppress a rebellion in parts of the Arzawa lands.[3] Backed by the king of Ahhiyawa in mainland Greece a certain Piyamaradu had begun to raid Hittite territory and seems to have temporarily chosen Wilusa as his power base. Muwatalli intervened in Seha River-land whose king he deposed probably out of discontent with his behavior regarding Piyamaradu and installed a new king to whom he gave his sister in marriage. Hattusili, meanwhile, as his brother's foremost military commander, kept the Gasgaeans at bay, at which he seems to have been generally successful. Concerning Syria, Muwatalli issued what may be the oldest explicit *vidimus*, a treaty formerly drawn up between his father and the king in Aleppo, Talmisarruma, because the original treaty tablet had gone lost.[4] During Muwatalli II's rule, Egypt had recovered from the instabilities of the Amarna period and under Pharaohs Sety I and Ramses II it was ready to regain its lost influence in Syria. Already during Sety's reign both the land of Amurru under its king Bentesina and the area around Kadesh were probably forced to defect from the Hittites and to return to the alliance with Egypt. As was to be expected, it came to an armed confrontation over this between Hatti and Egypt, from which Sety emerged victorious. Encouraged by these initial successes Ramses II led a vast army a few years later (1275 BC) to Kadesh to meet Muwatalli and his troops, which according to the Pharaoh amounted to some 48,000 men. Among these were Gasgaean contingents under Hattusili's command. Although the confrontation ended in a draw the Hittites could report a victory in the sense that they had fully reached their objectives. The kingdoms of Amurru and Kadesh were once again Hittite.

Due to the transfer of the capital to Tarhuntassa, which has not yet been identified archaeologically, we have relatively few documents for Muwatalli's reign. He must have died soon after the battle of Kadesh and was succeeded by his son Urhitessub, also known as Mursili III. Although one of the young king's first decisions seems to have been to return to Hattusa his reign was cut short after a few years by his uncle Hattusili. He

[3] Beckman 1999: 87–93. [4] Beckman 1999: 93–5; see Chapter 12.7.

blamed his nephew for systematically undermining his power and position until he no longer complied and rose in revolt around 1267 BC. With an army and his vast military experience, he staged a coup and became Hattusili III. Urhitessub was sent into exile in Syria. Due to the tension between them and because of the close ties between Hattusili and the family of Mittannamuwa, Urhitessub had appointed a new chief scribe upon his accession. Mittannamuwa's son Purandamuwa was never heard of again and with the king returning to Hattusa there was no longer need for Mittannamuwa as governor. Now, with Hattusili in power, the family was restored to its old position and Walwazidi, another son of Mittannamuwa, became the next chief scribe.

With the royal house firmly back in Hattusa sources start flowing again. Continuing the now well-established treaty policy of his predecessors as well as all the correspondence leading up to the treaties' conclusion Hattusili kept his chancellery busy. Treaties and similar diplomatic documents were exchanged with Ahhiyawa in mainland Greece, Amurru, Assur, Babylon, Egypt, and Ugarit. As preserved, the dossier of incoming letters from Egypt alone concerning among other things the upcoming treaty of 1259 and the later marriage of a daughter to Ramses II in 1245 consists of 107 pieces.[5] Besides this, Hattusili and his wife Puduhepa were active with prayers and vows, and we already saw how the queen ordered a full set of the *ḫišuwa*-festival from her native Kizzuwatna. Plagued possibly by feelings of guilt or probably just thinking his coup did not earn him the respect he deserved from the local elite and his peers in other state capitals Hattusili felt the urge to justify on clay, time and again, his power grab. Finally, and likewise following a family tradition, Hattusili engaged in annalistic history, of which unfortunately little has been preserved thus far.

Hattusili concluded one treaty with Kuruntiya, a brother of Urhitessub's, whom he had raised and probably adopted at the request of his late brother Muwatalli. In an obvious attempt to counter possible feelings of loyalty on Kuruntiya's side to his biological father and exiled brother, one of Hattusili's first decisions was to install Kuruntiya as viceroy in Tarhuntassa, the former seat of the capital during his father's reign. On the one hand this gave Kuruntiya the third position in the hierarchy of the empire after the *tuhkanti* or "second-in-command"[6] and the Great King himself. On the other, it put him at a comfortable distance from the capital.

[5] Edel 1994.

[6] Sometimes also described as heir presumptive in the sense that a *tuhkanti* might cherish reasonable hopes of one day becoming ruler himself although no guarantee was given.

When Hattusili III eventually died around 1240 BC some unrest or rebellion may have come up but not on a large scale, it seems.[7] Judging by some so-called "instructions," feelings of nervousness and insecurity may have led his son and successor Tuthaliya IV to enforce loyalty on several professional groups such as army generals and his closest aides by way of oaths in much the same way his father had done.[8] An extensive land grant to a part of the royal family may have had the same purpose.[9] Tuthaliya certainly continued his father's policy towards Kuruntiya. In the so far unique Bronze Tablet he renewed the relation, granting him additional rights and privileges.[10] The marriage of another sister of Tuthaliya's to Ramses II shortly after the former's accession as well as continued correspondence with Egypt[11] may be viewed as a token of ongoing friendly relations with Egypt.[12]

Other texts from Tuthaliya IV's reign attest to his active involvement in the political situation in Syria, especially Ugarit and Amurru. The accession of the new Assyrian king Tukulti-Ninurta I led to several military confrontations in that region that did not end well for the Hittites. Tukulti-Ninurta's expansive behavior culminated in the annexation of Babylon near the end of the twenties of the thirteenth century BC. After this, however, he seems to have contented himself with his achievements, no longer bothered the Hittites, and concentrated on building a new capital named after himself. Tuthaliya seems to have been more fortunate in dealing with the island of Alasiya/Cyprus resulting in yet another treaty. In the west he dealt with situations in Seha River-land and Lycia but the most important piece of information available on western Anatolia in this period is the so-called Milawata Letter.[13] It shows Tuthaliya coming to the aid of Walmu, king of Wilusa, usually identified with the site of ancient Troy, who had been driven out of his kingdom. Tuthaliya was able to send him, from the capital's archives, a copy of his original investiture document, possibly another *vidimus* (see Chapter 12.7), so that he could prove his rights to the local throne.

In spite of Tuthaliya's efforts towards his adoptive brother Kuruntiya we have irrefutable evidence for Kuruntiya in the position of Great King.

7 See Otten 1988: 19, 49, Houwink ten Cate 1992: 268 with n. 48 and Klengel 1999: 287.
8 See von Schuler 1957: 8–35 and Starke 1995a.
9 Ed. by Imparati 1974, see also Klengel 1991: 233.
10 Edited by Otten 1988, for an English translation see Beckman 1999: 114–23.
11 For the correspondence and its date see Edel 1994: 257–8 and van den Hout 1984: 89–92.
12 For the marriage see van den Hout 1998: 85 n. 48.
13 See Hoffner 1982 and Hawkins 1998: 18–9.

Several seal impressions of at least three different types[14] and a rock relief in HATIP near modern Konya attest to this.[15] Although other scenarios are possible a not too long interregnum during Tuthaliya's reign through a coup by Kuruntiya still seems the best option.[16] What happened to Kuruntiya afterwards remains unknown but Tuthaliya seems to have reclaimed and ascended the throne in Hattusa a second time before passing on power to his son Arnuwanda III.

Although Tuthaliya is no longer believed to be responsible for shaping the capital Hattusa, as we know it now, he certainly left his imprint on the city in the form of several stelas that bear his name and genealogy in Anatolian hieroglyphs. At least three such monuments are known, and the impressive open-air shrine of Yazılıkaya near Hattusa carries his signature three times. His son and second successor Suppiluliuma II (also known as Suppiluliyama) added to this a memorial temple on top of Nişantepe and there is some evidence that the capital as a whole may have been renamed "Hattusa-Tuthaliya-City."[17] More than any other king, finally, Tuthaliya IV left large hieroglyphic inscriptions in the countryside at EMIRGAZI and YALBURT.[18] Both the text on the EMIRGAZI altars and several depictions of Tuthaliya portray him assuming divine status and honors, fully in line with naming the capital after himself.

How and when Tuthaliya died is unknown, neither at present can it be determined how long his reign lasted. Assuming he came to the throne somewhere around or shortly after 1240 BC[19] it seems not unreasonable to grant him a relatively long reign of twenty years or more because of the fact that he must have lived into the late twenties of the thirteenth century at least. Since no texts can be attributed with any certainty to his son and first successor Arnuwanda III and because of a later report about a possible conspiracy that he fell victim to, the latter is usually given a very brief reign "of only a year or so."[20] In spite of this he is still present with forty-four sealings at the *Westbau* (see Chapter 11). His brother, the last known Hittite ruler in Hattusa, Suppiluliuma II's textual record, is better although still much less extensive than his father's. We have fragments of treaties with Alasiya/Cyprus and Karkamish plus an instruction and a loyalty oath. Alasiya/Cyprus is also mentioned in an account of a sea battle with "the

[14] See van den Hout 1995a: 82 and Neve 1996: 21 Abb. 40–2.
[15] See Dinçol 1998, and Goedegebuure 2012: 432–4.
[16] Bryce 2005: 319–21; see also the important observation by Goedegebuure 2012: 432–4.
[17] See van den Hout 1995b: 572–3 with literature to which can be added Giorgieri & Mora 1996: 71, 75–6, Güterbock 1998: 202; doubts as to this interpretation are expressed by Lombardi 1997: 95–6.
[18] Chapter 9.3. [19] See van den Hout 1984: 90, Singer 1987: 417. [20] Bryce 2005: 327.

enemy from Alasiya." The cuneiform text in question has been linked to the large Luwian hieroglyphic inscription of NIŞANTAŞ in Hattusa's Upper City. On the other hand, the low number of only nine seal impressions for him is surprising. This pales in comparison to the 447 pieces of his father Tuthaliya IV. Given this suddenly diminished corpus of written material and knowing that the Hittite kingdom did not survive long after 1200 bc there is an understandable tendency to interpret all this as signs of impending doom. Even the grandiosity of Tuthaliya's reign and the accompanying nervousness witness the forty-seven different seals he used (Chapter 11.4) can be seen as the typical behavior of a ruler desperately clinging to power, only to come crashing down under his successors.

13.2 Who Were the Scribes?

Of the two main pillars of our knowledge of the ancient Near East, the texts and the uninscribed material heritage, we owe the first to the ancient scribes. From a purely statistical point of view they remain anonymous most of the time: only now and then did a scribe take responsibility for his work and sign a tablet with his name. In Mesopotamia such colophons mark the end of what are called "literary" compositions or texts of the "stream of tradition."[21] Based on them many Assyriological studies have focused on scribal culture and education. An entire curriculum has been reconstructed that young men had to go through, probably from an early age onward, from basic TU-TA-TI exercises to lexical lists to high-level literary works.[22] No wonder the social standing of these men was relatively high: being able to devote their days to the study and production of such academic-like material must have been a relative luxury and almost inevitably an elite occupation. Sometimes such scribes are in our times quite rightly referred to as scholars and *literati*. But what do we know of Hittite scribal training and education? What social class did Hittite scribes belong to? This chapter will deal with these and related questions.

Our main source for Hittite scribes is the corpus of ca. 900 colophons preserved at the end of cuneiform tablets.[23] Usually they give the title (in most cases this is or closely resembles the *incipit*) or nature of the composition on the tablet and whether the composition is complete as is or spread over more tablets. In little over 10 percent of the cases the scribe identifies himself, usually

21 Hunger 1968: 1, Veldhuis 2011: 81, and for the "stream of tradition" see Chapter 12.2.
22 Márquez Rowe 2006: 108–20, Veldhuis 2011: 82–6, 2014 passim.
23 For a full edition of all colophons and a discussion of their characteristics and function see Waal 2015: 139–561, see also Gordin 2015: 39–50.

in the manner ŠU PN "hand of Mr. So-and-so" often with an added genealogy and/or the mention of what may have been a supervisor, for instance:

> Hand of DINGIR.GE$_6$-zidi; he wrote it before Anuwanza, the courtier.[24]

This use of the word "hand" was ultimately borrowed from Mesopotamia. Out of the thirty-nine Old Babylonian colophons collected by Hermann Hunger in his book on *Babylonische und assyrische Kolophone*, ten show the same phraseology, and out of thirty-two Middle Assyrian and Babylonian colophons, thirteen have it.[25] Colophons in general functioned within the classification and filing system of the tablet collections and facilitated the retrieval of documents and records.[26] But what function exactly the scribal signature served is a difficult question that we will have to come back to below.

Because Mesopotamian scribes are mainly attested in literary compositions the focus on these texts as part of their training curriculum is understandable, but we should be careful not to extrapolate too much when speaking of literacy in ancient Near Eastern societies in general. Scribal names do not appear on the tens of thousands of ephemeral administrative and bookkeeping records. All this attention to the world of learning and "higher" culture threatens to overshadow what must have been a work force of average tablet writers and clerks, simple scribal craftsmen working in chancelleries, temples, and all kinds of offices doing the bookkeeping and drawing up of standard documents.[27] Right now they seem almost wholly eclipsed by their more learned and privileged colleagues. Nor does it do justice to several kinds of functional literacy, both active and passive, restricted to specific social and professional situations.[28] Reading general studies on scribal education in the ancient Near East one might get the impression that all scribes, including the Hittite ones, were trained and well versed in the Sumerian and Akkadian literary canon. This seems unlikely: the ancients were modern enough to be aware of what skill needed what training and to get the best return on the inevitable investment in the education necessary for basic literacy skills. Also, scribes are often said to have belonged to the upper strata of their society[29] That may have been true for those *literati* but was it for the scribal rank and file?

The ancients themselves are at least partly to blame for this confusing situation: they use the same term (DUB.SAR) for what might be best

[24] ŠU ^{m}DINGIR.GE-LÚ *PĀNI* ^{m}*Anuwanza* SAG *IŠṬUR* KUB 7.1 iv 15–16 (Prayer, CTH 390, NS), ed. by Waal 2015: 303.

[25] Hunger 1968: 8. [26] Waal 2015: 179–80. [27] Veldhuis 2014: 225, Márquez Rowe 2006: 132.

[28] For Mesopotamia see Veldhuis 2011; cf. also Thomas 2009: 14 et passim on name literacy, commercial literacy, list literacy, and the like.

[29] van den Hout 2009-2011b: 276 w. lit.

described as both scribe and scholar. On the other hand, we should know better. Even though the Hittites, for instance, used a single term (*išḫiul*) for any agreement between two parties, whether it was a parity treaty between two Great Kings or a so-called "instruction" text from the king to a group of his underlings (Chapter 8.4) we make all kinds of fine distinctions depending on the relation between the partners of the agreement. The situation for the title DUB.SAR is much the same. Speaking of scribes only therefore risks misrepresenting past practice and sells both scribes and scholars short. Is the same true for the Anatolian situation and what can we say about the people to whom we owe our Hittite corpus?

13.3 Scribes and Wood-Scribes

The Hittite cuneiform texts make a basic distinction between scribes (DUB.SAR) and wood-scribes (DUB.SAR.GIŠ).[30] *Communis opinio* has it that the "wood" part GIŠ refers to wooden writing boards. An overview of passages where they are mentioned neither confirms nor denies this but points to a predominantly administrative, that is, bookkeeping activity for these wood-scribes:

> The wood-scribes have the document of how the [k]ing brings the dail[y] offerings.[31]

> Thus Ḫuzziya, the wood-scribe: 'I delivered in good condition whatever stuff they gave me that had been sealed. I didn't break the seal, nor did I rip open the chest.'"[32]

> It so happened that the wood-scribes and the temple personnel had started changing the cult provisions and regulations that he had decreed in the temple of the Goddess of the Night. So, I, Muršili, the Great King, laid them down again in writing (lit. with a tablet/with tablets) and when in the future the king ... will come to the temple of the Goddess of the Night of Šamuḫa, let them prepare these cult provisions.[33]

30 For *tupala-* as the alleged reading behind DUB.SAR see the Excursus in Chapter 14.

31 See Chapter 10 n. 40.

32 *UMMA* ^{m}*Ḫuzziya* ^{LÚ}DUB.SAR.GIŠ *UNUTE*^{MEŠ}*=wa=mu kuit kuit šiyān pīēr nu=war=at* SIG$_5$*-in arnunun* $^{\mathrm{NA_4}}$KIŠIB*=wa UL duwarnaḫḫun* ^{GIŠ}PISAN*=ia=wa UL iškallaḫḫun* KUB 13.35 iv 28–31 (Deposition of Ukkura, CTH 293, NS), ed. by Werner 1967: 12–13.

33 *nu=za ḫazziwita išḫiuli*$^{\mathrm{HI.A}}$*=ia kue INA* É.DINGIR.GE$_6$ *kattan ḫamankatta uēr=ma=at=kan* $^{\mathrm{LÚ.MEŠ}}$DUB.SAR.GIŠ LÚ.MEŠ É.DINGIR-*LIM=ia waḫnuškewan dāer n=at* ^{m}*Murši*-DINGIR-*LIM-iš* LUGAL.GAL *tuppiyaz* EGIR-*pa aniyanun nu ziladuwa kuwapi INA* É.DINGIR.GE$_6$ ^{URU}*Šamuḫa mān* LUGAL ... *uezzi nu kē ḫazziwita ēššandu* KUB 32.133 i 4–10 (Expansion of the cult of the Deity of the Night, CTH 482, NS), ed. by van den Hout 2016a: 430; differently Miller 2004: 312, cf. also Waal 2011: 29 n. 7, Cammarosano 2012a: 9 w. n. 11.

> Thus the wood-scribe: "The men of Kattanna [made(?)] a reque[st and] they se[nt(?)] me to record the damage."[34]

Their office, the "house of the wood-scribes," serves as a storehouse and facilities center:

> All things they will provide new and the palace attendant will bring the following from the house of the wood-scribes: . . .[35]
>
> [. . . x min]a(s) (and) thirty shekels of copper, two bronze daggers. § [. . .] . . . silver *magāreš*, [. . . x m]ina(s), their copper [. . . fro]m(?) the house of the wood-scribe.[36]
>
> They will provide all the *ḫāpiya*-men's silver (and) gold decorations from the House of the wood-scribes.[37]

None of the above passages provides unequivocal evidence for the material of the script carriers these wood-scribes used. We saw in Chapter 10 that the term GIŠ.ḪUR does not imply a wooden writing surface and that the evidence for wood as a writing vehicle is modest anyhow. So, what else could the GIŠ in DUB.SAR.GIŠ refer to? First of all, we should recognize that the combination DUB.SAR.GIŠ seems to be an Anatolian innovation: the term is not known from Mesopotamia even though wooden writing boards were used there. It is not clear why the Anatolians saw the need for a separate term if the society from which they adopted their writing practices did not.[38] However one interprets the wood element in the combination DUB.SAR.GIŠ it must be an elliptical expression: GIŠ by itself simply denotes the material *per se* without specification in what form or for what purpose. So, a DUB.SAR.GIŠ can be a "scribe of wood(en tablets)" but another option would be "scribe of wood(en chests)." According to the texts Hittite storerooms were crammed with chests, crates, boxes, and baskets. The two terms used in the administrative texts for such containers are ^{GIŠ}*tuppa-* and the Sumerogram $^{\text{GI/GIŠ}}$PISAN. Judging by the

34 *UMMA* ^{LÚ}DUB.SAR.[GIŠ] LÚ.MEŠ ^{URU}*Kattanna=wa arkuwa*-x[. . . / *nu=w*]*a=mu apēdaš dammešḫaš* [*š*]*arā* GUL-*šūwanzi ui*[*ēr*?] (restoration of GIŠ after line 7) KBo 8.32 obv. 9–12 (Deposition, CTH 295, NS), ed. by Werner 1967: 58–9.

35 *nu ḫūman* GIBIL-*an pianzi* Ù *IŠTU* É $^{\text{LÚ.MEŠ}}$DUB.SAR.GIŠ DUMU.É.GAL *kī pēdāi* (follows list of objects) KUB 25.31 + KBo 55.263 obv. 8–9 (Local cult offerings, CTH 662, NS), ed. by Haas 1988b: 288–9, 290.

36 [. . . MA.N]A? 30 GÍN URUDU 2 GÍR ZABAR § [. . .]x KÙ.BABBAR *magāreššieš* / [. . . M]A.NA URUDU=*ŠUNU* / [. . . *IŠ-T*]*U*? É DUB.SAR.GIŠ KUB 34.89 rev. 2–5 (Ration lists, CTH 677, OS), cf. CHD L-M s.v. *magareš*.

37 *ḫūmandan* $^{\text{LÚ.MEŠ}}$*ḫāpiyan unuwašḫuš=*(*š*)*muš* KÙ.BABBAR-*aš* KÙ.GI-*aš IŠTU* É [(DUB.SA)]R.[(G)]IŠ *pian*[(*zi*)] KBo 10.31 iv 29–34 (KI.LAM Cult ritual, CTH 627, NS), ed. by Singer 1984a: 105.

38 Remember that the Akkad. ^{GIŠ}*LĒ'U* "wooden tablet" is attested in the Alalaḫ Level VII tablets: see Chapter 10 n. 102.

determinatives GIŠ and GI they could be made of wood (GIŠ) or reed (GI) respectively. Together, ^{GIŠ}*tuppa-* and $^{GI/GIŠ}$PISAN belong to the most frequently attested items in the corpus of storeroom inventories.[39] In another text we encounter the $^{LÚ.MEŠ}$DUB.SAR ^{GIŠ}*tuppaš* translated as "storeroom managers" (lit. "scribes of the chest(s)").[40] Storerooms themselves appear as É *tuppaš*, lit. "house of chests."[41] The combination $^{LÚ.MEŠ}$DUB.SAR ^{GIŠ}*tuppaš* might thus be the full version of $^{LÚ.MEŠ}$DUB.SAR ^{GIŠ}/GIŠ. If so, the term would reflect the handling and administration of goods stored in the wooden crates and boxes. It would be entirely comparable to the LÚ.DUB.SAR.GIŠ KARAŠ "wood-scribe of the army/army wood-scribe," that is, such titles define the areas where the scribes work, in short, they are a kind of job description.[42] Without further evidence this matter cannot be decided at present but it does seem clear that wood-scribes were "clerks" in charge of securing and recording goods entering and leaving the storerooms.[43] Their status as clerks makes it understandable that on a total of 205 employees in some otherwise unidentified "workshop" there were more wood-scribes than regular scribes (that is, without the additional GIŠ), if the latter implied working with narrative texts instead of chests, lists, and tables:

> Total: 205 employees (lit. sons) of the workshop of which 18 priests, 29 *katra*-women, 19 scribes of which ten are there but nine have not been given (yet), 33 wood-scribes, 35 diviners, ten Hurrian singers, [. . .][44]

In the capital of an empire like the Hittite one with all its logistic demands in matters political, religious, economic, and judicial, and with goods from taxes and tributes flowing in on a regular basis, many such clerks would have been needed, at any rate probably more than scribes for texts like Mursili II's Annals or even for all the cult rituals. Remember the collaboration between the regular scribe Palluwarazidi and clerk Pihawalwi in the colophons of several festivals that were celebrated across the Hittite annual cult calendar. The clerk played an important role as the manager of goods and foodstuffs needed in the course of

39 Siegelová 1986: 624, 668. 40 Bronze Tablet i 78, ed. by Otten 1988, 15 ("Magazinverwalter").

41 Otten 1988, 40 ("Lagerhaus, Magazin"). See also KBo 26.181: 2, KUB 38.1 iii 1 (É *tup*[-); the É ^{LÚ}*tup-pa-a-aš* (or É LÚ *tup-pa-a-aš*) KUB 13.3 iii 10 (ed. by Miller 2013: 82–3 "of the warehouse") probably also belongs here.

42 For references see van den Hout 2009–2011b: 273–5; for similar subdivisions of the scribal profession in Mesopotamia see Hunger 1968: 9.

43 van den Hout 2010, see also Gordin 2015: 140–1.

44 ŠU.NÍGIN 205 DUMU.ḪI.A É.GIŠ.KIN.TI ŠÀ 18 $^{LÚ.MEŠ}$*šakkuniš* 29 $^{MUNUS.MEŠ}$*katraš* 19 $^{LÚ.MEŠ}$DUB.SAR ŠÀ 10 Ì.GÁL 9=*ma UL* SUM-*er* 33 $^{LÚ.MEŠ}$DUB.SAR GIŠ 33 $^{LÚ.MEŠ}$ḪAL ⸢10⸣ $^{LÚ.MEŠ}$NAR ḪURRI [. . .], KBo 19.28 obv. 1–7 (List of people, CTH 237, NS), ed. by Weeden 2011a: 86.

any cult ritual.[45] But what does the presence of singers, priests, and diviners say about the company scribes and clerks kept?

13.4 The Societal Status of Scribes

Two cuneiform documents may elucidate the general societal status of both kinds of scribe. One is the enumeration of 205 workers in the workshop just quoted, and another comes from a cult inventory listing the workforce of the temple in the town of Karahna:

> Total: 26 *hilammati*-men, of which one anointed priest, one scribe, one wood-scribe, one diviner, two musicians, one table-man, two cupbearers, one spear-man, one gatekeeper, one singer, one reciter, one *arkammiyala*-player, one beer brewer, two bakers, one water carrier, two temple court sweepers, one bird breeder, one potter, one porridge maker. The *hilammati*-men (and) . . . are included in its workshop.[46]

Both lists count the scribes employed by the "workshop" (É.GIŠ.KIN.TI) among priests, diviners, singers, and musicians, but also among bakers, beer brewers, cooks and waiters, spearmen, gatekeepers, water carriers, bird breeders, and potters. They belonged to a large group of retainers, specialists or professionals on whom the state relied heavily for its day-to-day business but who are unlikely to have formed part of the ruling elite.[47] This is true for most ancient and any pre-modern societies where literacy is not yet widespread: "writing is a trade practiced by craftsmen."[48] Also, reading and writing were two quite distinct activities and abilities: "in sixteenth-century England many quite educated people could only read, not write, and it was common to go to a specialist writer, a scrivener or secretary, if you needed something written."[49] A scribe was an *amanuensis* for tasks that were considered mechanical and otherwise beneath somebody from the higher echelons of society.[50]

This picture can be seen reflected in the corpus of letters from Maşat Höyük exchanged between the Great King and his officials or between representatives of the latter group. Individual members maintained a clear

45 Note how this pair does not appear in the colophon of the *ḫišuwa*-festival, which was not part of the traditional cult calendar; see Lorenz 2014: 481.

46 ŠU.NÍGIN 26 $^{\text{LÚ.MEŠ}}$*ḫilammatieš* ŠÀ 1 ^{LÚ}GUDU$_{12}$ 1 ^{LÚ}DUB.SAR 1 ^{LÚ}DUB.SAR GIŠ 1 ^{LÚ}ḪAL 2 ^{LÚ}NAR 1 LÚ ^{GIŠ}BANŠUR 1 ^{LÚ}MUḪALDIM 2 ^{LÚ}SAGI.A 1 LÚ ^{GIŠ}ŠUKUR 1 ^{LÚ}Ì.DUḪ 1 ^{LÚ}GALA 1 ^{LÚ}*palwatallaš* 1 ^{LÚ}*arkammiyalaš* 1 ^{LÚ}KÚRUN.NA 2 ^{LÚ}NINDA.DÙ.DÙ 1 ^{LÚ}A.ÍL.LÁ 2 ^{LÚ}KISAL!(over erasure?).LUḪ 1 LÚ MUŠEN.DÙ 1 ^{LÚ}BAḪAR 1 ^{LÚ}EPIŠ BA.BA.ZA [^{L}]$^{\text{Ú.MEŠ}}$*ḫilammattieš* LÚ.MEŠ GUB-X-ḪA *ŠA* É.GIŠ.KIN.TI*=ši=kan anda* DAB-*anza* KUB 38.12 i 11–18 (Cult inventory, CTH 517, NS), translit. Pecchioli Daddi 1982: 211, tr. Taggar-Cohen 2006: 22, cf. also Weeden 2011a: 88–9 and 2011c: 128–9.

47 Lenski 1966: 62–3 and Fig. 1 on p. 80. 48 Ong 1982: 93. 49 Thomas 1992, 10.

50 Blair 2010: 108–9.

Table 13.1 *Hierarchy of people mentioned in the Maşat Höyük letters*

Piseni	
Hattusili	Himuili
Hulla	Kassu
Pulli	Zilapiya
DINGIR-BELI (Ilumbeli)	DINGIR-LIM.MUL (Ilikakkabu)
DINGIR-LIM-TUKULTI (Ilitukulti)	DUMU.UD.20.KAM (Marešre)
Hasammeli	^{d}IM-BELI (Adadbeli)
Sanda	Surihili
Tarhunmiya	Uzzu[51]

hierarchy by addressing each other as "dear brother" in case of supposed equal status, or as "dear son/father" if the writer felt a difference in standing needed to be expressed. If we arrange the officials according to their own use of these familial appellations, we get the following three-tiered pyramid of persons appearing in these texts (Table 13.1).

With few differences, both Sedat Alp, the editor of the Maşat corpus, and Gary Beckman, identify the majority of officials in this correspondence as scribes. The most restrictive list is that of Alp[52] who considers Hasammeli, DUMU.UD.20.KAM/Marešre, Sanda, Surihili, and Tarhunmiya as scribes working in Hattusa and ^{d}IM-BELI/Adadbeli, Uzzu, and Walwanu in Maşat.[53] Alp explicitly states that Hattusili and Himuili are not scribes. Beckman adds Hattusili whom he suggests might have been the anonymous chief scribe who wrote (or dictated) the letter HKM 72, and DINGIR-LIM.MUL/Ilikakkabu to those working in the capital[54]; that Ilikakkabu and Ilitukulti do not figure in Alp's list may simply be an oversight since Alp does take them in consideration as scribes elsewhere.[55] The reason to view the entire third tier or most of them as scribes is their use of said familial appellations ("my dear brother/son/father") as well as the Akkadian names

[51] For the relation between Piseni and those in the second tier see HKM 18, for those of the second and third tier see HKM 17 (Hasammeli as "servant" of Hulla, Kassu, and Zilapiya). All those in the third tier address each other as "brother." Since Tarhunmiya describes (HKM 62) his relation with Himuili as that of "son" and "father" (note also his self-designation as Himuili's "servant" in HKM 27) I have assigned Himuili and his "brother" Hattusili to the second tier. Note that the same Tarhunmiya calls Walwanu (HKM 56) "son", which might create a further level (cf. Alp 1991: 105).

[52] 1991: 104. [53] For the latter three see Alp 1991: 52–3, 104, and 105 respectively.

[54] Beckman 1995b: 25–6, 33. [55] Alp 1991: 65; he does not commit on Ilumbeli.

for Adadbeli, Ilikakkabu, Ilitukulti, Ilumbeli, Marešre, and perhaps Surihili, something we will discuss further below.[56]

The letter-writers use these forms of address mostly, if not exclusively, in postscripts (German *Zweitbriefe*), sometimes also referred to as "piggyback letters": in many cases the main letter is followed by a second with its own introductory formula ("Thus PN_1 to $PN_{2(,3\ldots)}$, speak!"),[57] often separated by a double paragraph line, and with its own items of business. The interpretation of these follow-up letters as more private exchanges between scribes only who knew who would be on the receiving and reading end goes back to Heinrich Otten.[58] Referring to the usage of such terms among students and teachers in the Old Babylonian school system he saw this as yet another borrowing along with the cuneiform script itself. However, as Albertine Hagenbuchner has correctly observed[59], apart from the fact that some of his examples are ambiguous or could also be explained as exchanges between real family members, these appellations were also used by and for individuals who – at least at the time of writing – were not scribes. Clearly, this custom was followed outside scribal circles as well. Piseni, for instance, a royal emissary and the highest-ranking officer after the Great King, addresses both Kassu, one of the senior military commanders in that area and his subordinate Pulli as "my dear sons."[60] Himuili, the commander of the border province, calls Huilli, some kind of civil authority[61], his "dear brother."[62] In the absence of explicit titles it is thus not compelling to see all those who make use of these expressions as scribes and, as all letters, these follow-up messages could have been dictated to a scribe instead of having been written by those whose voice they pretend to convey. Of the individuals listed by Alp and Beckman only Tarhunmiya is explicitly mentioned as a scribe.[63] Sanda and Uzzu were almost certainly scribes as well since they mention "reading" tablets in the postscripta they exchange[64] but the evidence for Ilikakkabu, Ilitukulti, Marešre, and perhaps Surihili contains nothing that explicitly points to their being scribes. For Adadbeli it is even unlikely given the military matters that he is involved in. Instead, the familial address may be simply that of individuals working for the government conferring among themselves and reflecting in the texts their fraternal status

56 For a full list of these Akkadian-named scribes with attestations see Weeden 2016b: 160.

57 Exceptions seem to be HKM 55: 36 and 72: 34 where the change in addressee is simply marked by *zik/ziga* "you!" and a following PN that is different than the addressee of the preceding words.

58 Otten 1956, Hoffner 2009: 58–9, Weeden 2011c: 123–4.

59 Hagenbuchner 1989a: 12.

60 HKM 18: 22.

61 Thus Beckman 1995b: 33.

62 HKM 56: 2.

63 Thus HKM 12: 4–5, more indirectly in HKM 52; none of the others is identified as such (contra Beckman 1995b: 25).

64 Cf. HKM 21: 22–4 for both. I am grateful for having been able to discuss this point with Michele Cammarosano.

and hierarchical relations. What it does show is that scribes such as Tarhunmiya, Sanda, Uzzu, and perhaps some others are on a lower rung of the societal ladder vis-à-vis officials such as Piseni and Himuili *cum suis*.

But where do the Akkadian names like Adadbeli etc. in the Maşat Höyük letters come from? Seeing them as evidence that "clearly Akkadian as the language of scholarship was flourishing at this small provincial centre"[65] is, I think, not very likely. First of all, the scribal status for these men is uncertain and being the senders instead of addressees at Maşat, none of them – at least at the time these letters were exchanged – was working or residing in Maşat. Secondly, Maşat seems to have been a small border town that temporarily found itself in the line of Gasgaean fire prompting a frantic exchange of letters and requiring the presence of the Hittite king. Along with his most important officers he tried to coordinate military activities in the immediate vicinity and to save what he could. Thirdly, if a lively scholarly culture in the Hittite kingdom at large were the background for such names one would expect even more Akkadian names, either of native Mesopotamians or of "Hittite scribes affecting Babylonian names"[66] in Hattusa, which is not the case. Out of eighteen Mesopotamians (or individuals with Akkadian names) who Gary Beckman mentions as having been in the Hittite kingdom, seven were ambassadors or envoys from either Assur or Babylon, two were women from Mesopotamia married to members of the Hittite royal house, and three were "medical" specialists. In addition, there is one unknown individual, an unidentified group of "men of Assur," and only three are scribes.[67] It is, of course, possible that during the early fourteenth century BC there was a sudden Mesopotamian "revival," perhaps it was briefly à la mode to choose an Akkadian sounding name. As Mark Weeden remarks[68], "the names Ilī-tukultī and Ilī-kakkabu look decidedly odd from the perspective of Akkadian onomastics." That names of a certain ethnicity become fashionable and can take on forms that sound unusual in the culture of origin is a common enough phenomenon. To what extent this went hand in hand with an increased use of Akkadian in Hittite circles is unknown or at least undocumented. The plot thickens when we add the seemingly casual remark at the end of a letter found at Maşat:

> You, Zū, my dear brother, write back to me about the *murta*(-wood) *pabilau*![69]

[65] Weeden 2011c: 127; cf. also Bryce 2002: 63. [66] Weeden 2011c: 127. [67] Beckman 1983b: 108.
[68] Weeden 2016b: 160–1 n. 16.
[69] *zik=mu* ^{m}*Zūš* ŠEŠ DÙG.GA=I[A] ^{GIŠ}*murtanza* EGIR-*pa* PABILAU *hatrā*ˀ*i* HKM 72: 34–6 (Letter, CTH 190, OS), ed. by Alp 1991: 258–9.

Thus far, all scholars have taken *pabilau* as "in Babylonian." As to the reason of the request to write back in Babylonian, Sedat Alp, the original editor, called it an "enigma" and suggested that it might have been to keep the affair a secret.[70] The main letter is addressed by an anonymous chief scribe to Kassu, one of the high-ranking field officers in the area, and he may be the one responsible for the postscript as well, although it is somewhat surprising then that as chief scribe he addresses Zū as his "brother." He passes on to Kassu a message from a certain Tarhunpihanu about wood and stone as bridge-building materials, specifically mentioning *murta*-wood, as needed to finish a particular bridge. Since that same *murta*-wood is the topic of the message to Zū and since, moreover, these final lines do not follow the usual letter formula ("To PN_1, my dear brother, thus PN_2, speak!") this is not a typical postscript. Instead, the letter continues talking about the same topic. Zū, therefore, is more likely another person involved in the bridge building, even though not mentioned in the address lines (1–2) at the opening of the letter. This makes the request to answer "in Babylonian" even more bizarre. And if Akkadian were a normal language of communication between scribes why did the chief scribe not write these lines "in Babylonian" to begin with? No such letters exchanged between two Hittite speakers and/or officers of the Hittite kingdom are known.[71]

How can we further assess the status of Hittite scribes? Apart from the company they kept of beer brewers, potters, and others, two more ways are open to us. On the one hand we can compare the names of scribes in tablet colophons with those of the individuals known from the seal impressions. On the other we can look for those same scribes in the rest of the cuneiform sources.

13.5 Scribes and Seal Owners

In the corpus of seal impressions (see Chapter 11) seal owners very often added titles and distinctive qualities to their name on the seals. Although not all of these titles and qualities can be interpreted with certainty, those that find matches in the cuneiform corpus show them to be leading

70 Alp 1991: 341 ("ein Rätsel"); see also Hoffner 2009: 230–2.

71 Years ago, when reading this letter in class with students, one of them, Ryan Winters (I cite his name with his permission), asked if "in Babylonian" could mean "in cuneiform." Although I do not know of any societies using cuneiform calling their script "Babylonian" it is an intriguing suggestion that, if true, would constitute by implication the first real evidence for the Anatolian hieroglyphs (and thus probably Luwian) as an alternative means of communication between officers of the Kingdom.

Table 13.2 *Most frequently encountered non-royal titles on seal impressions*

hieroglyphic title	*cuneiform title*	*meaning*
PRINCEPS	*tuḫkanti*	(second-in-command after the king)
REX.FILIUS	DUMU.LUGAL	prince (lit. son of the king)
EUNUCHUS	LÚ.SAG	courtier
MAGNUS.VIR	LÚ.GAL	grandee
MAGNUS.HASTARIUS	GAL *MEŠEDI*	chief of the royal bodyguard
MAGNUS(.BONUS$_2$).VITIS	GAL.GEŠTIN	chief military commander
MAGNUS.AURIGA	GAL *KARTAPPU* / LÚ.MEŠ KUŠ$_7$	chief charioteer
MAGNUS.URCEUS	GAL.SAGI(.A)	chief cupbearer
MAGNUS.PASTOR	GAL NA.GAD	(high military title)
MAGNUS.DOMUS.FILIUS	GAL DUMU.MEŠ É.GAL	chief of the palace attendants
AVIS$_2$+MAGNUS	GAL LÚ.MEŠ.MUŠEN.DÙ?	chief augur
MAGNUS.L.135.2	GAL LÚ.MEŠ IGI.MUŠEN?	(idem?)
L.23.DOMINUS	UGULA/GAL *MUBARRÎ?*	(high judicial title)
REGIO.DOMINUS	EN.KUR	governor
URBS.DOMINUS	*ḪAZANNU*	mayor

positions. Compare Table 13.2 of the most frequently encountered non-royal titles on seal impressions and their probable cuneiform counterparts.[72]

Most of the sign combinations are real titles such as the "chiefs" of the various professional groups while others like the *tuḫkanti*, prince, courtier, and grandee indicate more of a status or quality. In her analysis of all titles and professions on the seal impressions found at the *Westbau* in Hattusa, Suzanne Herbordt calculated the portion of the above "chiefs" (leaving out the princes as not being a profession) at 22.2 percent.[73] This finds confirmation in the smaller corpus of sealings from the Upper City temple district by Ali and Belkıs Dinçol that comes out at 22.0 percent for the same titles.[74] The remaining titles are those working under those chiefs but as seal-carrying members of Hittite society their status may still have been considered "elite."

Returning to the scribes, we know some seventy-five individuals by name, that have signed as scribe of a cuneiform tablet.[75] Only eleven of

[72] For details and percentages within the *Westbau* corpus see Herbordt 2005: 92.
[73] Herbordt 2005: 92. [74] Dinçol & Dinçol 2008: 90–6.
[75] See the list in Waal 2015: 553–61, with a total of eighty-eight different names or entries. A few predate the thirteenth century, some are broken and acephalic and, as explicitly noted by Waal, in some cases it is not certain that the name is that of the actual scribe. Another list of ninety-six names can be found in Gordin

Table 13.3 *Names of scribes also attested on seal impressions*

name	*titles/qualifications on seals* (H. = Herbordt 2005, D. = Dinçol & Dinçol 2008, both with catalog number)	*genealogical information given in tablet colophon*
Alalimi	H. 3: PITHOS.VIR.DOMINUS	—
	H. 4–5: EUNUCHUS	
	H. 6: L.326	
	H. 7: URCEUS	
	H. 8–9, 10?[76]: L.326, L.414-DOMINUS	
Kunizidi	H. 178: L.326	—
Luwa	H. 209: –	—
	H. 210–213: L.326 "2"	
	H. 214: CRUX$_2$	
Palla	H. 291: L.326	—
Pihami	H. 298: URCEUS	—
Pihazidi	H. 312–313: –	—
	H. 314–315: URCEUS VIR$_2$	
	H. 316: *hilami*	
Tuwa	H. 470: L.443 VIR$_2$	—
	H. 471: L.326	
Tuwazi	H. 473: AURIGA	—
	H. 485: EUNUCHUS SACERDOS(?)	
Zuwa	H. 68, 539–540: L.326	son of Uza/U.ZA[77]
	H. 536: AURIGA	
	H. 537: CRUX$_2$	
	H. 538: PITHOS VIR$_2$	
	D. 163: SACERDOS	
Zuzzu	H. 549: L.135.2 CRUS(?)	son of Sanda
^{d}U.LÚ (Tarhu(nta)zidi)	D. 202: L.326	son of Pida
	D. 242: SCUTELLA(?)	

their names (Table 13.3) can be matched to a name written in hieroglyphs on seal impressions in roughly the same period (thirteenth century BC).

Each number in the catalogs of Herbordt (e.g., H. 291) and Dinçol & Dinçol (e.g., D. 163) refers to an originally distinct seal. Among the

2015: 96–105, but that includes also "chief scribes, and their family members" (p. 95). All in all, about seventy-five seems a realistic number for attested Hittite cuneiform scribes working in the (mostly second half of the) thirteenth century BC; see also van den Hout 2015: 206 w. n. 11.

76 On this piece the name Alalimi is reportedly followed by two more signs ("*i*(*a*)-*na*(?)" as read by Herbordt 2005: 116) but the reading Alalimi is considered "unlikely" by Hawkins apud Herbordt 2005: 248.

77 On the reading of this name see Gordin 2015: 214 n. 907.

different seals or seal owners listed here and the names from the cuneiform texts it is almost impossible to tell whether we are dealing with the same persons. Sometimes we find more than one title or quality on a single seal. A man named Armanani, for example, (not in the above list because he is not known to have been a scribe according to the cuneiform sources) styles himself on the same seal as "prince" (REX.FILIUS), "military commander" (MAGNUS.VITIS), "country lord of Hatti/Hattusa" (MAGNUS.*HATTI*.DOMINUS), and "L.326 two"; for L.326 see in detail the Excursus in Chapter 14. In cases such as that of Armanani we are evidently dealing with an important individual who held different titles simultaneously or continued to use former titles showing off a distinguished career.[78] But looking at Alalimi, the first person on our list, there is one seal[79] for a person by that name as PITHOS.VIR.DOMINUS (title of uncertain meaning[80]), three seals as EUNUCHUS, two seals as L.326, and one as URCEUS (cupbearer) but never in combination. The possibilities thus include anything from four different functionaries named Alalimi to one Alalimi having used six different seals during a career that centered around four different qualifications and/or professions.[81] Similarly, for Zuwa we have three seals with L.326, one with AURIGA (charioteer, possibly a diplomat or emissary), one with $CRUX_2$ ("?"), one with PITHOS (storeroom related?), and one with SACERDOS (priest). Unless evidence from the cuneiform texts allows us to equate two or more of these not much certainty is to be gained here. The cases with an accumulation of titles and/or qualities on a single seal urge for caution in identifying persons and names too quickly: if there had been only a single Alalimi or Zuwa with four "titles" why did they not combine all of them on one seal just as Armanani did? Of course, theoretically we could be dealing with promotions and job changes but that remains impossible to prove.

The yield of this approach thus seems to be bleak: only few of the named scribes turn up in the glyptic material and if so, identity between seal owner and scribe is rarely certain. For our present purposes, though, it is enough

[78] Cf. the continued use of formerly held titles (Mr. President, Madam Secretary, Governor, Senator) in the United States.

[79] "Seal" means there is proof of an original seal of which there can exist one or more impressions. So, two or more seals with the same title or quality indicate that there were two different original seals with the same title or quality. Whether this means that there were two or more persons with the same name and same title or quality or whether one person had multiple seals during his lifetime can only be decided, if at all, on a case by case basis.

[80] Hawkins apud Herbordt 2005: 305–6.

[81] For a more positive assessment see Gordin 2015: 226, who, however, relies on the interpretation of the hieroglyphic L.326 = SCRIBA, for which see the Excursus in Chapter 14.

to observe that even if a match is found there are no "chiefs" or "heads" among them. As a consequence, in most cases we are left with the scribe's name in the colophons with no additional information.

13.6 Scribes Elsewhere in the Cuneiform Corpus

Moving to the second group, the cuneiform sources other than colophons, the most promising case is again that of Alalimi since he is well attested in the cuneiform material. Cuneiform attestations for Alalimi from the thirteenth century BC include six different titles[82]: chief cupbearer, "overseer-of-1000" (probably a military function), scribe, augur, governor of the land around Kanesh, and merchant. Of these the chief cupbearer and the "overseer-of-1000" are almost certainly the same individual, while Alalimi, the merchant from the town of Ura on the southern coast, doubtless has to be kept separate from all others. Evident overlaps, however, between the scribe, augur, and governor on the one hand, and the cupbearer-commander on the other are lacking. Adding the hieroglyphic material helps to identify the URCEUS with the cupbearer in a most welcome way.[83] There is no obvious match, however, for the PITHOS.VIR.DOMINUS, and since we do not know what a L.414-DOMINUS did[84], that title could be any of the cuneiform six or none. With EUNUCHUS and probably likewise L.326 (see the Excursus in Chapter 14) being qualities rather than professional titles, they could apply to any of the persons. The scribe Alalimi thus remains an isolated figure and the other attestations do not help in raising his profile.

Another person is Palla who is attested as "lord" of the town of Hurme, scribe, and courtier in a single text for which see the next section. The other names listed in Table 13.3 are either only attested as scribes or cannot be further identified with other persons with the same name but with a different title or context.

13.7 Elite Scribes

The difficulty to connect the named scribes with bearers of seals and the observation that there are no chiefs or heads among them might seem not

82 van den Hout 1995: 138–42 w. lit.

83 On the equation of the titles see Hawkins apud Herbordt 2005: 310, see also Herbordt 2002: 59 and 2005: 78–9.

84 Hawkins apud Herbordt 2005: 312; note that this title in combination with Alalimi occurs on a seal impression where the reading Alalami is disputed (see n. 76).

Table 13.4 *Scribes mentioned in witness lists in KBo 4.10, Bo 86/299, and KUB 26.43*

name	*titles/qualities*
Anuwanza	DUB.SAR EN ^{URU}Nerik ^{LÚ}SAG (scribe, Lord of Nerik, courtier)
EN-tarwa	DUB.SAR UGULA É.GAL LÚ.SAG (scribe, royal storeroom overseer?, courtier)[85]
Kammaliya	DUB.SAR GAL $^{LÚ.MEŠ}$MUḪALDIM (scribe, chief of the cooks)
Mahhuzzi	DUB.SAR GAL *MUBARRÎ* (scribe, judicial officer)
Naninzi	LÚ DUB.SAR.MEŠ UGULA *MUBARRÎ* (scribe, judicial officer)
Palla	EN ^{URU}Ḫurme ^{LÚ}DUB.SAR LÚ.SAG (scribe, Lord of Hurme, courtier)
Sipazidi	DUB.SAR (scribe)

to bode well for an elite status of scribes. Yet there are some scribes who clearly were members of the thirteenth century BC kingdom's elite, for which see the list in Table 13.4.[86]

The individuals mentioned in Table 13.4 along with their accompanying titles or positions appear as witnesses at the end of one or more of three documents dating to the second half of the thirteenth century. These are the Treaty with Ulmitessub (KBo 4.10, probably Hattusili III), the Treaty with Kuruntiya of Tarhuntassa (Bo 86/299, Tuthaliya IV), and the so-called Sahurunuwa-Urkunde, a late charter or bequest (KUB 26.43 w. dupls., Tuthaliya IV). All three documents together cover a time span of probably no more than two or at best three decades with some persons like Kammaliya as Chief of the Royal Kitchens, being mentioned in all three and even with the same title. The positions encompass the highest military, diplomatic, administrative-economic, and judicial competencies of the state, those otherwise closest to the king (the *tuḫkanti* or second-in-command, princes, some in-laws), and probably the most important vassal kings (from Karkamish, Tarhuntassa, Seha River-land, Isuwa, Mira, and Amurru) as well as some local governors (the towns of Hurme and Nerik).[87] Obvious religious titles seem to be absent. Prosopographical analysis underscores the elite status of most of those men in that they are in one way or another linked to the ruling dynasty, either directly as sons, cousins, nephews, or as in-laws. As such these three lists form a veritable who-is-who of all the most important male individuals of the Hittite

85 van den Hout 1995: 235. 86 See also Gordin 2015: 229.
87 For synopses of the lists see van den Hout 1995: 76–81.

Empire in the second half of the thirteenth century BC during the reigns of Hattusili III and Tuthaliya IV. As so often, the literal meaning of a title may have little bearing on the real responsibilities. Kammaliya, "Chief of the Cooks," for instance, was in all likelihood not a chef but, being in charge perhaps of the royal kitchens and food supply, he must have had a central function at court. We know from other texts dealing with the ritual purity of the king that from the slaughter of an animal to the end products that reached the king's table the kitchen played an essential role in this aspect of royal life. As most recently argued by David Hawkins the "Chief *MUBARRÎ*" was a legal officer or judge of some kind.[88] With the É.GAL (lit. the big/royal house) referring to the royal storerooms or treasuries spread throughout the kingdom EN-tarwa may have had one of the more important economic jobs in the country.

Serving as witnesses alongside others belonging to the highest echelons of Hittite society, this is indisputable evidence of elevated status of the seven scribes listed. For most of them we do not have tablets that they themselves wrote but all of them have connections to the scribal profession, some unequivocally so, for others the link is more speculative. The two most convincing cases are those of Anuwanza and Sipazidi. Anuwanza is called scribe, Lord (i.e., local ruler, governor) of Nerik, the important cult center to the north of Hattusa, and courtier.[89] Although this is basically all we know about his person he is amply attested as supervisor of at least fifteen scribes in the second half of the thirteenth century BC. Besides these there is one fragment of a tablet that he probably wrote himself.[90] We do not know how long his tenure at Hattusa lasted and how literal we have to take his title as "Lord of Nerik." It should not be excluded that the latter was mostly honorific and may have indicated, for instance, his status as coming from an elite family that had its roots there. According to Giulia Torri Anuwanza may have run his own office or "scribal bureau" in Hattusa, sometimes working on specific assignments and projects with his "team."[91]

Sipazidi is the only one of the witnesses appearing as just DUB.SAR "scribe."[92] Yet he was probably no mere scribe either. Not only do we have no tablets written by him but in three of the five colophons where he is

[88] Hawkins apud Herbordt 2005: 299–300.

[89] van den Hout 1995: 238–42, Torri 2008: 777, 2010a: 388–92, 2011; see Gordin 2015: 166–98 for a reconstruction of Anuwanza's scriptorium and the scribal circles around him.

[90] KBo 45.37 vi 1; for two more possible examples, KBo 59.111: 6 and KBo 40.345 iv 4, see Torri 2011: 137 w. n. 11.

[91] Torri 2011 and Gordin 2015.

[92] van den Hout 1995: 235–8.

mentioned he acts as the person "before" (PĀNI) whom other scribes wrote their tablets. Twice he is the subject of the verb *newaḫḫ-* "to make a new version" in the sense of "collecting sources and preparing the new composition ... [b]ut clearly he did not engage in the menial task of copying/writing the tablets himself"[93]:

> Sipazidi made a ne[w] version. (blank space; then on the left edge:) Zidi, the scribe wro[te it].[94]

Mahhuzzi we encounter in a very similar situation.[95] He is not attested as scribe of a tablet himself either, but he does appear – together with a certain Halwazidi – in a colophon in a supervising capacity to a certain Duda:

> This composition (lit. tablet) wa[s] damaged and before Mahhuzzi and Halwazidi I, Duda, made a new tablet again.[96]

Both Mahhuzzi and Naninzi probably served as chief legal officers and depending on the chronological order of the witness lists, they were each other's successors or predecessors in that function. As scribe and officer of the judiciary, Naninzi could be the same individual as the son of Mittannamuwa, erstwhile chief scribe. Although by some taken as a possible mistake for GAL DUB.SAR.MEŠ "Chief Scribe" his title LÚ DUB.SAR.MEŠ (Bo 86/299 iv 41) is different.[97] Without the Sumerian plural ending MEŠ he would have gone through life as a simple scribe and the preceding LÚ would have been the male determinative (ᴸᵁ́DUB.SAR) but perhaps this was a subtle way of distinguishing himself from the scribal rank and file as "man (LÚ, i.e., overseer but not really chief?) of the scribes"? He cannot have been "Chief Scribe" since his brother(?) Walwazidi already fills that position in the same text (Bo 86/299 iv 40; see §13.8) but it may have implied something more than the average scrivener.

The weakest links are those for Kammaliya and Palla. Someone named Kammaliya is attested as father of a scribe.[98] Since the scribal profession could run in families (although sons were not necessarily trained by their

93 Gordin 2015: 205; whether these two occurrences are enough to make this Sipazidi's specialty (thus Gordin 2015: 166, see also 199–208) remains to be seen.

94 See Chapter 12 n. 38. 95 van den Hout 1995: 225–6, Marizza 2010: 37.

96 *kī* TUPPU *arḫa ḫarran ēš[ta] n=at* ANA PĀNI ᵐ*Maḫḫuzi* U ANA ᵐ*Ḫalwa*-LÚ *ūk* ᵐ*Dudaš* EGIR-*pa newaḫḫun* KUB 13.7 iv 3–7 (Instruction, CTH 258, NS), ed. by Waal 2015: 251–2, Gordin 2015: 206.

97 Otten 1988: 76 declares it a scribal mistake, Hawkins apud Herbordt 2005: 300 adds an exclamation mark to the title.

98 KUB 30.33 iv 14, ed. by Waal 2015: 307–8, cf. van den Hout 1995: 178–9.

fathers[99]) we could be dealing with a similar family here as well and he could be equated with the Kammaliya, scribe and head of the royal kitchens. Palla is known from two of the witness lists as "Lord of (the town of) Hurme" and one of the lists adds the qualifications scribe and courtier. We have two tablets that were written by an actual scribe of the same name, twice does somebody named Palla appear as father of a scribe named Angulli, and once we find a Palla addressed in a postscript to a letter written by another scribe.[100]

Searching for other higher-level scribes beyond the seven individuals just discussed, we can widen the circle to include at least four more scribes from the thirteenth century BC who appear in a formula *ANA PĀNI/PĀNI* PN, lit. "before PN": Angulli, Halwazidi, Muwa, and Zidi.[101] Usually the phrase is explained as describing a supervisory capacity of sorts[102] and these supervisors, too, may not have been average scribes. According to Hunger's book on Mesopotamian colophons, supervisors were not unknown in Mesopotamia but this *ANA PĀNI/PĀNI* as such is not attested in Old and Middle Babylonian or Middle Assyrian colophons.[103] Giulia Torri has suggested that the *ANA PĀNI/PĀNI*-formula was connected to specific projects like the one about the *ḫišuwa*-festival tablets as ordered by Queen Puduhepa. Since the phrase can occur with and without an apprentice status of the actual scribe it does not seem to express a teacher–student relation. Interesting is one possible attestation with the Hittite king:

> One tablet: (there follows a description of what is on the tablet; after a slight interlinear space the text continues:) *PĀNI* His Majesty Tuthaliya [so-and-so] wrote it.[104]

99 van den Hout 2009-2011b: 276, Weeden 2011b: 606, Gordin 2015: 130; Gordin, however, keeps open the option that the very first stage of training, not reflected in our texts by the term GÁB.ZU.ZU "apprentice," might have taken place at home.

100 For details on Palla see van den Hout 1995: 216–25; see further Herbordt 2005: 82, Gordin 2010: 160, 2015: 188–90.

101 Two more names are attested in this formula but are broken, GIŠ-x, and PÚ/TÚL[- and cannot be identified with any one known; for GIŠ-x see Waal 2015: 388–9, Gordin 2015: 60 n. 295, 208.

102 Cf. Torri 2011: 138 and Gordin 2015: 133–6.

103 Hunger 1968: 11; he sees the Mesopotamian counterparts as *Prüfer*, cf. the *diorthotes* or "corrector" of Greco-Roman times, for which see Houston 2009: 255.

104 1 *TUPPU* . . . [*P*]*ĀNI* ^{d}UTU-*ŠI* ^{m}*Tutḫaliya* [. . .] KIN/ SIxSÁ!-*it* KUB 25.23 iv 60, 63–4 (CTH 525, NS), ed. by Waal 2015: 371–2; instead of KIN-*it* Torri 2010b: 325–6 w. n. 39 reads SIxSÁ!-*it* (= *ḫandait* "he prepared") and renders *PĀNI* here as "in the presence of"; Cammarosano 2012b: 112 and Waal also read SIxSÁ-*it*. Both readings are difficult and I have nothing better to offer. More text follows on the left edge of the tablet and at the very end of this addendum follows a PN (^{m}Lila-PÌRIG(-)^{d}Kartait), which has puzzled all editors both in its form and function (second signature of the scribe or was he just the scribe of the addendum?). The combination *PĀNI* ^{d}UTU-*ŠI* also occurs

If this is indeed meant the same way as ANA PĀNI/PĀNI elsewhere in the colophons, then something like "at the behest/orders of" or just a literal "in the presence of" might seem more appropriate than "under the supervision of." Whatever the exact interpretation, a hierarchical relation seems given.

If we take a closer look at the four individuals found in this formula, Angulli may have been the son of Palla, the governor of Hurme and likewise "scribe," as we saw when discussing Palla above. Three tablets bear his name as the actual scribe[105] but three times he appears in a colophon following ANA PĀNI. Since at one point Angulli himself worked "before" Anuwanza, Giulia Torri has suggested that his tenure as scribal manager may have temporarily overlapped with that of Anuwanza and/or that he might have succeeded him in that function.[106] The case of Halwazidi is more complicated.[107] First there is the question of the spelling of the name with *-wa-* next to a variant with *-pa-* (Halpazidi). We know of at least two different individuals with scribal connections by the name Halwazidi/Halpazidi, one perhaps deliberately distinguishing himself from the other by using the *-wa-*variant. Halpazidi appears only as the father of the scribe GUR-sarrumma and has therefore been taken as a scribe himself[108] but that is in itself not compelling. The position of Halwazidi, son of a certain Lupakki, is stronger. He "signed" as scribe of the Bronze Tablet with the treaty of Tuthaliya IV and Kuruntiya and a Halwazidi is twice mentioned as the teacher of other scribes and once alongside Mahhuzzi as the supervisor of the scribe Duda (see p. 308). Again, identity cannot be proven but is attractive. Muwa (written ^{m}A.A) occurs only once as supervisor of the scribe Attanalli and is otherwise unknown.[109] Zidi (written ^{m}LÚ) presents an interesting case. After Anuwanza he is probably the second most frequently attested supervisor with at least five scribes working for him.[110] Although we know next to nothing about him he seems to have been part of the scribal family that with Gary Beckman and others might even reach back all the way to the Old Kingdom and he may have counted Anu-šar-ilāni and Hanikkuili (see Chapter 5.4) among his Old Kingdom ancestors.[111]

in KBo 26.178 iv 7 (likewise Tuthaliya IV, ed. by Waal 2015: 371) with the verb *ḫandae-* "to arrange, establish." Finally, cf. the OS colophon in Bo 2004/1: 31–4 (ANA PĀNI *Labarna*), ed. by Gordin 2015: 134 w. lit.

105 Waal 2015: 554, Gordin 2010: 164, 2015: 189–91. 106 Torri 2011: 138.

107 For all references and details see van den Hout 1995: 186–93, Marizza 2007: 158–61, Gordin 2015: 219–21.

108 Thus van den Hout 1995: 186. 109 Waal 2015: 512–3, Gordin 2015: 222–4.

110 Waal 2015: 557 (under LÚ), Gordin 2015: 179–85.

111 Beckman 1983b: 105–6, Devecchi 2010: 21–4, Gordin 2015: 181.

Finally, we can tentatively include among higher ranking scribes Pihawalwi and Palluwarazidi, wood-scribe and scribe respectively, and overseers of the "task force" (KASKAL?, see Chapter 12.6) appearing at the end of several festival colophons.

13.8 Chief Scribes

As is to be expected, we encounter the title chief scribe (GAL DUB.SAR(.MEŠ), GAL DUB.SAR.GIŠ) much less frequently and relatively late.[112] Gary Beckman has suggested that a certain Hattusili attested as a high official in the Maşat letters and therefore datable to the first quarter of the fourteenth century BC might have been chief scribe, but this must remain conjectural.[113] The most valuable evidence comes again from the lists of witnesses of the two treaties and one charter mentioned in §13.7. They make clear that for most professions there is, as a rule, only a single person mentioned per title. In other words, there could only be one "chief" at any one time. There are two exceptions: the chief royal emissary (GAL *KARTAPPI* lit. chief charioteer), possibly the highest-ranking diplomat, and the highest military title (after the king as commander in chief) of GAL GEŠTIN (lit. chief of the wine) are mentioned with two different individuals in the Bronze Tablet treaty. The latter document is unique in this respect.[114] While one could envisage that from a practical foreign policy perspective more than one person should be able to present himself at foreign courts as the chief diplomat from the Hittite Great King, this is more difficult for the position of GAL.GEŠTIN.[115] For the positions of chief scribe and chief wood-scribe, on the other hand, we have for each title one person per list: Walwazidi and Sahurunuwa are the only chief scribe and chief wood-scribe respectively in all three. This finds confirmation in other cuneiform sources in that we find no evidence to the contrary. Through the cuneiform texts we can follow how one person at a time filled the position of chief scribe over the course of the late fourteenth to thirteenth century BC (Table 13.5).[116]

112 Marizza 2010: 42, see further Chapter 5.4; for detailed information and complete listing of all attestations see Marizza 2010.

113 See Beckman 1995b: 25, more recently see Marizza 2010: 35 and Weeden 2011c: 121 w. n. 34.

114 Marizza 2007: 164–6.

115 The only other title that occurs with more than one person is that of "simple" scribe, DUB.SAR, that accompanies four persons in the Sahurunuwa-charter: the already discussed Anuwanza, Kammaliya, Palla, and Sipazidi. However, we know that there were more scribes simultaneously and the first three each have other, different titles (see Table 13.4) while scribe is Sipazidi's sole title.

116 Thus also Marizza 2010: 42; for an attempt at filling out Table 13.5 with the hieroglyphically attested titles see Marizza 40.

Table 13.5 *Chief Scribes and Chief Wood-Scribes in the thirteenth century* BC

Chief Scribe	*Chief Wood-Scribe*	*Great King*
(Hattusili ?)		(Tuthaliya III/Suppiluliuma)
Mittannamuwa	?	Mursili II
Mittannamuwa	?	Muwatalli II
Purandamuwa	?	Muwatalli II
Zidi?[117]	?	Urhitessub
Walwazidi	Sahurunuwa	Hattusili III
Walwazidi	Sahurunuwa	Tuthaliya IV
?	?	Arnuwanda III
?	[. . .]-sarrumma	Suppiluliyama

As observed by Marco Marizza, the positions of chief scribe and chief wood-scribe appear towards the end rather than at the beginning of the witness lists and assuming a hierarchical structure these positions therefore may not have been the most important.[118] To call their presence as witnesses exceptions based on their personal prestige as royal family members, as Marizza suggests, is hard to corroborate since we have only these lists as evidence. It is, however, fair to say that their specific activities as scholars were less central to the administrative acts (two treaties and a charter) at hand. When the later King Hattusili III was ill as a child it was the chief scribe Mittannamuwa who was asked to take care of him because as a scholar he was supposed to have access to and knowledge of such cures to heal Hattusili. But in the daily business of running the kingdom *literati* were not at the forefront of things. The fact that none of the chief scribes is attested among the seal owners is probably another function of their politically "less central" activities.[119]

For none of the chiefs listed in Table 13.5 do we have tablets that they claim to have written.[120] The *arḫa aniyat* "he copied" in the standard

[117] Marizza 2010: 36 w. lit. and n. 54, Devecchi 2010: 22, Gordin 2015: 161–2, 185; this Zidi (written ^{m}LÚ) occurs in a colophon as father of a scribe NU.^{GIŠ}KIRI$_6$. Another NU.^{GIŠ}KIRI$_6$ mentions ^{m}SAG as his father (KUB 44.61 left edge 4), the latter name attested only there. Could it be that Zidi (^{m}LÚ), father of NU.^{GIŠ}KIRI$_6$ was a courtier (^{LÚ}SAG) and that the text should have read *^{m}LÚ ^{LÚ}SAG (GAL DUB.SAR.MEŠ) but that NU.^{GIŠ}KIRI$_6$ got confused by both LÚ-signs and jumped ahead writing only ^{m}SAG? As far as eunuchs being fathers is concerned, it should be remembered that Anuwanza, scribe and eunuch, reportedly had a son as well (cf. van den Hout 1995: 240).

[118] Marizza 2010: 41.

[119] There are four seal impressions known bearing the name Walwazidi (SBo 2: 99–100, Herbordt 2005: no. 515, see also 83, and Dinçol & Dinçol 2008: no. 260); the final one has the qualification L.326 (for which see the Excursus in Chapter 14).

[120] The same seems to be true for the Mesopotamian *rab tupšarrī*, cf. Hunger 1968: 9.

colophon of the *ḫišuwa*-festival[121] ("When Queen Puduhepa called upon Walwazidi, chief scribe, in Hattusa to search for tablets from Kizzuwatna he *arḫa aniyat* these tablets of the *hisuwa*-festival") must be translated according to the *Caesar pontem fecit* principle: "he *had* them copied (by others)." This is clear from those cases where subsequently a (lower ranking) scribe professes to have done the real job (e.g., "Before Walw[azidi, chief scribe] LAMMA.DINGIR-LIM wrote (it)"[122]). This colophon, on the other hand, seems to show that this title was not a mere honorific for the men involved. The wording seems to indicate that men like Walwazidi truly headed the scribal organization and assumed final responsibility for its products.

13.9 Apprentices

Before we move on to consider the scribal organization as a whole, we should go from one extreme, the chief scribes, to those on the lowest rung of the professional ladder, the trainees or apprentice scribes. Of the ca. seventy-five scribes known by name (see §13.5) thirteen mention their status as "student" (GÁB.ZU.ZU, LÚDUB.SAR TUR "junior scribe," or the rare ŠAGAN.LÁ) and give their teacher's name often adding that of their father and sometimes further ancestors (Table 13.6).[123]

All of the above individuals lived and worked in (the second half of) the thirteenth century BC. First of all, it should be noted how overall very few scribes identify themselves as apprentices given the fact that all scribes must have started out as such. Secondly, it is striking that six or seven out of the thirteen give filiations and that five belong or might well belong to the elite scribal families whom we already encountered several times. Alihhini is a member of the ancient family that may reach back to Anu-šar-ilāni (see Table 13.6) and was the nephew of Zidi who supervised so many scribes. We do not know Ashapala's father Tarhundassu[124] but his grandfather dLAMMA.SUM (Kurunt(iy)apiya) could be the *anduwašalli*-man and scribe mentioned at the end of the list of witnesses of Mursili II's treaty with

[121] See Waal 2015: 440–50. Gordin 2011: 183, 185 tentatively suggests there might have been an original version made by him, from which all others were copied by his scribes.

[122] KBo 15.52 vi 46–7; for the Hittite text see p. 324.

[123] For references see Weeden 2011a: 84–5, Waal 2015: 553–61, and Gordin 2015: 126–9. If one scribe could have more than one teacher it is possible that the [. . . -]sarrumma, apprentice of Halwazidi, is the same individual as [GUR?-]sarrumma, apprentice of Zidi. The names of both the apprentice and teacher are completely broken away in KBo 42.2 iv? 1–2 and are therefore not included in the list.

[124] Tarhundassu is possibly attested on a seal (Dinçol & Dinçol 1988: 90–1) and seal impression (Dinçol & Dinçol 2008: no. 71) but both belong stylistically in the Old Kingdom.

Table 13.6 *Apprentice scribes attested in colophons*

student scribe	*teacher/supervisor*	*genealogical information given in the colophon*
Alihhini	Zuwa, EN GIŠ.KIN.TI (lit. lord of the craft)	son of AN.ŠUR.LÚ, grandson of NU.^{GIŠ}KIRI$_6$
Ashapala	Zidi	son of Tarhuntassu, grandson of ^{d}LAMMA.SUM, <great> grandson/ descendant? of Warsiya[125]
[GUR?-]sarrumma	Zidi	son of Halpazidi, grandson of Zuwanni
Lurma(zidi?[126])	[. . .]	son of Akitessub
NU.^{GIŠ}KIRI$_6$	Hulanabi	son of SAG
Palla	[. . .]	[?]
Pihami	Halwazidi	—
Pihuna[127]	TÚL/PÚ(-)x[	[. . .]
Pikku	NU!.$^{GIŠ!}$KIRI$_6$	— (?)
[. . . -]sarrumma	Halwazidi	—
[. . . -]tessub[128]	MAḪ.DINGIR.MEŠ-na	son of Walwazidi, grandson of Mittannamuwa
DINGIR-ublan [ni?][129]	[. . .]	[?]
[. . .]	Meramuwa, [E]N GIŠ.KIN. TI (lit. lord of the craft)	[probably extensive but very fragmentarily preserved genealogy]

Talmisarrumma of Aleppo (KBo 1.6 rev. 21–22).[130] If the combination DUMU.DUMU-*ŠU* (or DUMU.DUMU<.DUMU>-*ŠU*) ^{m}*Waršiya* in his colophon stands for "descendant of . . . " one could point to Warsiya, the scribe of three Old Kingdom charters, one of which is dated to Muwatalli I (second half fifteenth century BC).[131] For Lurma(zidi) it has been suggested that his father Akitessub might be the same person as the scribe of the scholarly tablet KUB 4.53.[132] Besides being an apprentice-scribe Lurma(zidi) also professes himself in his colophon as "junior physician" (A.ZU TUR); we will encounter him once more (see §13.13) in the company

[125] Or grandson of Tarhuntassu and Warsiya? For the text see Waal 2015: 274–5.
[126] On the reading of the name see Waal 2015: 288 w. n. 824.
[127] Bo 3785 iv 6–7 apud Torri 2012: 129.
[128] Gordin 2015: 64 n. 305, 153, 156–7, restores the name to [Talmi-]tessub based on Talm[i- KBo 35.260 left edge 1 (for the relevant colophons see Waal 2015: 559). However, a join by Francesco Fuscagni apud Everling† & Földi 2015, shows that KBo 35.260 left edge 1 has to be completed to Talm[i-LUG]AL-ma. I see no reason to doubt the join.
[129] So read by Weeden 2011a: 84, followed by Waal 2015: 535 and Gordin 2015: 127.
[130] Thus Devecchi 2010: 20–1 w. n. 86, Gordin 2015: 216.
[131] Gordin 2015: 216, 353. A scribe [Warsi]ya is also restored in KBo 39.272: 8 (cf. KBo 39, p. xvi).
[132] Rutz 2012: 184, Gordin 2015: 139.

of learned men. NU.^{GIŠ}KIRI$_6$, son of "SAG" is likely to belong to the same family.[133] Palla is, again, likely to be the Palla, father of Angulli as well as the Palla, Lord of Hurme and courtier.[134] [... -]tessub was the grandson of Mittannamuwa, the chief scribe under Mursili II and Muwatalli II and governor of Hattusa under the latter. This coincidence of scribal apprentices and influential families suggests that scribes mentioning their teachers as well as often their genealogy belonged to the empire's higher echelons and may not really have been part of the scribal rank and file toiling away in anonymity.[135]

13.10 The Scribal Organization

In his detailed study of *Hittite Scribal Circles* Shai Gordin reconstructs two main scribal groups or schools, working independently of each other and even with "[s]cholarly as well as social tension" between the two.[136] One group is associated with Anuwanza; these are the scribes that are attested as working "under his supervision" (see §13.7). The other is the group around Walwazidi, the Chief Scribe under Hattusili III and Tuthaliya IV, working on *ḫišuwa*-festival texts. Such a reconstruction does not do justice, however, to the difference in titles of Anuwanza and Walwazidi. The latter is amply attested as Chief Scribe whereas Anuwanza, although clearly a scribe overseeing the production of many tablets was not. Important here is the colophon of a tablet containing the description of the twenty-ninth day of the AN.TAḪ.ŠUM festival, KBo 42.28 vi. The scribe Hapatiwalwi, belonging to the Anuwanza group, first mentions him as "supervisor" but then adds another remark:

> [Han]d of Hapatiwalwi [... ? s]on of Tūwattazidi, physician, cour[tier], wr[ote (this tablet)] under the supervision of Anuwanza, courtier, while w[e] wrote each of these tablets in the prese[nce of Walwazidi, son of?] Mittannamuwa, Chief [Scribe].[137]

133 On this NU.^{GIŠ}KIRI$_6$ and the name of his father see n. 117. 134 Torri 2010a: 391–2.

135 van den Hout 2015: 210. 136 Gordin 2015: 238, see also 116, 354–5.

137 [š]U ^{m}*Ḫapati*-UR-MAḪ (one sign erased) [DU]MU ^{m}*Tūwatta*-LÚ LÚ.A.ZU LÚ.SAG *PĀNI* ^{m}*Anuwanza* LÚ.SAG *I*[*ŠṬUR*] *kī̆ma* *TUPPA*$^{ḪI.A}$ *ANA* *PĀN*[*I* ^{m}UR.MAḪ.LÚ DUMU?] ^{m}*Mittannamūwa* GAL.[DUB.SAR.MEŠ] *ānniškeyawe*[*n*] KBo 42.28 vi 3–8 (AN.TAḪ.ŠUM cult ritual, CTH 616, NS), ed. by Gordin 2015: 169–70. Gordin translates "But *we* prepared these tablets ..." (emphasis Gordin), but the rendering of *-ma* with "but" and the stress accorded to the 1. plur. verbal ending are both uncalled for. I take the *-ške*-suffix in *ānniškeyawe*[*n*] in its distributive function referring to all the tablets that together make up the liturgy of the AN.TAḪ.ŠUM festival.

According to Gordin (with a slightly different translation) this last sentence marks "the transfer of coordination of scribal control" from the Walwazidi-group to that of Anuwanza. But this may be reading too much in this passage. Going from top to bottom we have here a micro-hierarchy of chief scribe (whether Walwazidi or Mittannamuwa) > Anuwanza > Hapatiwalwi. Whereas Hapatiwalwi wrote the present tablet (KBo 42.28) bearing this colophon, he puts it with his further remark in the larger context (plural "these tablets") of a wider-ranging project overseen by the chief scribe and carried out by a collective of scribes ("we"). Even though there may have been different offices (*scriptoria*; see Chapter 12.9) with perhaps at times distinct tasks, on a higher level the evidence of apprentices, scribes, "supervisors," and chiefs points at a three- or four-tiered system with a single chief scribe at the top. Unfortunately, the various stages or ranks seem to have been only informally and quite poorly marked. There seems to have been no specific designation to distinguish what we termed "supervisors" from regular scribes other than through the *ANA PĀNI*/*PĀNI*-phrase. Another possible clue at a ranking system are the different modes of address. When writing each other, scribes, like others, use either "my dear father" (*ABU* DÙG.GA=*IA*), "my dear brother" (ŠEŠ. DÙG.GA=*IA*), or "my dear son" (DUMU. DÙG.GA=*IA*), but, as we saw (§13.4), this was not specific to the scribal profession.

On the whole, one wonders why we know so few scribes given the fact that they sometimes did make themselves known in the colophons. Out of 900+ colophons only about 120 of them show a scribal name. If colophons had been part of a system of checks and balances, in which the individual responsible for drawing up the record played a role, we would have expected many more scribes to have "signed" their products. In isolated cases the scribe's name may have had just that function. For instance, a certain Duwazi signed a census-like administrative list and identifies himself as "Man from the town of [. . .]." Here it is likely that the record was written on the spot and it is easy to envisage that the central administration wanted to know who took responsibility for the correctness of the report. If so, Duwazi may technically not even have been the scribe but the local authority answerable to the central government in whose name an anonymous scribe working for or under him drew up the record.[138]

[138] KUB 31.49 left edge (CTH 233, NS), ed. by Waal 2015: 245. Two other colophons show an added provenance for the scribe (KUB 7.20 rev. 6–7, ed. Waal 2015: 347–8, and KBo 12.95 rev. 2–3, ed. by Waal 2015: 536). The first is a ritual, the second preserves only part of the colophon and is therefore unidentified.

So, what purpose did the name of a scribe serve then? As we saw (§13.9), at least six out of thirteen apprentices added their father's name and at least five may arguably have belonged to upper class families. Out of the ca. 120 colophons only ten have with certainty the scribe's name and nothing else.[139] In sixteen there are breaks that would allow for some kind of filiation and/or the mentioning of a supervisor. In the remaining ninety-two cases the colophon contains at least the father's and/or the supervisor's name. If we look at individuals rather than colophons, of the ca. seventy-five scribes known by name we see that twenty-seven mention their fathers while at least fourteen more have breaks in their colophons with room for added filiations. Partially overlapping with those that mention a father, sixty-one colophons give the name of the person "before" (*ANA PĀNI/PĀNI*) whom the scribe worked. With just the scribe's name in less than 10 percent of the named colophons we can thus say that when a scribe did sign his work, he almost always mentioned a father and/or supervisor. Even more striking is the fact that the *ANA PĀNI/PĀNI*-formula "before (PN)" exclusively occurs in named colophons. All scribes must have worked under supervision and if the "supervisor's" identity were to have had administrative relevance one could easily envision anonymous colophons, that is, without the scribe's name but mentioning the "supervisor" under whose responsibility the tablet in question had been written (compare the case of Duwazi above). Yet these are not attested.

It should also be noted that it was not customary among Hittite administrators to use patronyms to distinguish individuals. This poses a real problem for prosopographical research into Hittite administration, which has to rely mostly on circumstantial textual evidence if it wants to equate two or more persons with the same name.[140] The use of genealogies therefore did not come naturally and seems to have been a foreign feature. Just like signing a tablet with your name using the phrase "hand of PN" derived from Mesopotamia[141], the custom to add genealogies to colophons may well have derived from Mesopotamia as well. It was the learned scribes who made themselves known in this way. Whereas only a single out the thirty-nine Old Babylonian colophons collected by Hermann Hunger has a listing of one or more ancestors, the percentage of genealogies among the Middle Assyrian and Babylonian colophons stands at almost 50 percent with fifteen out of thirty-two.[142]

139 Alalimi KBo 22.214 vi 3, DINGIR.GE$_6$-zidi KUB 4.1 iv 41, Hillu KBo 13.106 left edge, AMAR-ti KBo 22.129 rev. 10, Ibizzi KBo 10.47c left edge 1, Kuparabi KBo 5.1 iv 43, SA$_5$-pala KUB 17.28 iv 59, ŠUKUR-anza KBo 15.10 iv 3, Tattiya KBo 1.28 rev. 13, Tatigganna KBo 3.3 iv 14.

140 van den Hout 1995: 2–5.

141 See the beginning of this chapter and Maul 2011: 42–3.

142 Hunger 1968, Maul 2011: 29.

Table 13.7 *Hierarchy of named scribes*

chief scribe
|
"supervisors"
|
named scribes
|
named apprentices

Therefore, returning to the apprentices of whom at least half could be linked to prominent families, it is conceivable that all or most of the scribes signing their name enjoyed some kind of elevated status and may not have belonged to the largely anonymous scribal rank and file responsible for the roughly 800 other colophons and the hundreds of tablets that never had a colophon to begin with.[143] They may have been part of a system or organization of their own with a simple hierarchy (Table 13.7).

Whether the anonymous scribes likewise answered to the chief scribe is impossible to say and I have therefore left them out of Table 13.7. If they were the clerks, as defined at the beginning of this chapter, that is, "wood-scribes," then they had their own chief wood-scribe and may have formed a separate organization. The "wood-scribe of the army/army wood-scribe" whom we saw earlier may simply have served under his army commander. The "supervisors," named scribes, and named apprentices, on the other hand, may have formed a level or "guild" of their own, largely independent of the probably much more extensive group of anonymous tablet writers.

Of course, it is almost impossible to give any numbers for the size of these units without entering into some form of speculation but let us try nevertheless. The list of people employed by the workshop we saw earlier (§13.3) counted "19 scribes and 33 wood-scribes." The record in question is just one snapshot of a single workshop with over fifty scribes in total. There may have been more of such workshops in the capital and smaller numbers of scribes working in the provincial centers as the list of *hilammati*-men from the workshop in Karahna evinces (§13.4). It is tempting to think that these were all scribes of the anonymous kind although this is by no means proven. As for the named scribes we have only the ca. seventy-five names to

143 Cf. Waal 2015: 183 who already considered "a certain pride or vanity" on the part of the scribes who gave their name conscious "of the tradition of which [they] were a part."

work with for the thirteenth century BC. Historically these individuals cover three or at most four generations spanning the last fifty to seventy-five years of the Hittite kingdom. Assuming some names might have been lost to us we can for argument's sake put the total of named scribes at something approaching one hundred, resulting in about twenty-five to thirty of such scribes per generation.

13.11 The Average Scribe

Unfortunately, all this means that we know little of the scribes who seem to have been responsible for the bulk of the texts that have come down to us but who did not make themselves known in a colophon, nor do we know anything of their training. To start with the latter, there have been suggestions to locate a scribal school (the É GIŠ.KIN.TI or "workshop") in the Lower City just south of Temple 1 but that remains unsubstantiated since based on a single (stray?) tablet find there referring to such a workshop.[144] Only once is a local É.DUB.BA.A attested in a letter written to Maşat Höyük (see Chapter 8.8)[145]: unfortunately, it is not clear where exactly the writer and the House were at the moment but not in the capital Hattusa. Is that really enough to postulate a scribal school as an institution as it was known in the Ur III and Old Babylonian Periods?[146] Because of three colophons mentioning "students" (GÁB.ZU.ZU) found in HaH, the so-called House on the Slope (*Haus am Hang*) to the west of Temple 1, Giulia Torri has suggested to see that institution as partly functioning as a school.[147] This may be true if seen in the context of an apprentice system where aspiring scribes were assigned to chancellery offices working and learning alongside more experienced employees. And if the HaH was one of the primary administrative centers it is not surprising to find apprentices there. Other tablets, however, written by "students" were found in building Bk. K on the acropolis and in the storerooms surrounding Temple 1, both places of possible scribal activity as well. Apprenticeships certainly make sense for the mostly anonymous scribal craftsmen[148] but it may also have worked for the initial stages of the scholars-to-be we saw earlier. Given

[144] = KBo 19.28, for which see §13.3 w. n. 44, see also Weeden 2011a: 16, 86–9, 129, 2011b: 605, Gordin 2015: 13–14; for the uncertainty of the identification between the find spot of the tablet and the alleged school see, for instance, Hoffner 2009: 8.

[145] ABoT 65 rev. 8 (CTH 199, OS), ed. by Hoffner 2009: 242–5, see also Weeden 2011c: 120–4.

[146] See Weeden 2011a: 81–3 and 2011c: 119–22 (scribal school at Sapinuwa?); see also the *caveat* about the reality of such an institution in Weeden 2011b: 599.

[147] Torri 2008: 776 w. n. 31. [148] Veldhuis 2011: 83, 85.

the highly standardized use of the Hittite cuneiform script in central Anatolia it is not implausible to assume that both groups shared a common basic training.

In search of scribal trainees, we can point – in terms of products – at best to tablets with more than the average number of mistakes or tablets that show unusual features but otherwise they just blend in with their more advanced colleagues. Counting mistakes and erasures is a dangerous method, however. We may also be dealing with a draft as shown by fragments with such features but otherwise written in what looks like an experienced hand. They may also simply be characteristic of a well-trained and experienced hand, writing quickly.[149] In other cases a large hand may betray a student.[150] Before the writing of tablets, however, comes a long and laborious period of practicing and memorizing all the signs of the cuneiform sign inventory. Anyone who has ever tried to master them knows that it is one thing to be able to passively recognize all the signs but quite another to actively reproduce them. This requires endless practice and rote copying. It is striking that we have not been able to identify a single obvious training exercise[151] with, for instance, simple sequences of signs (e.g., TU-TA-TI), as they are known from Mesopotamia.[152] Even if a few were still to be found among the Hittite ruins we have to assume they had a very efficient recycling process in place, be it for clay tablets or wax-covered writing boards. The first stage of learning isolated signs and perhaps sign sequences[153] was no doubt at some point followed by reproducing more meaningful strings of signs and words gradually increasing to sentences and texts.

There is no evidence to assume that the Mesopotamian "canon" ever played a role in basic scribal training, that is, in the education of the average (mostly) anonymous scribe. A common explanation for the presence of Sumerian, Akkadian, and Hurrian compositions in the Hittite tablet collections is that they were used in the training of scribes based on Mesopotamian models.[154] Often an "extensive education" is assumed.[155]

[149] See, for instance, Siegelová 1986: 137; cf. also Giusfredi 2012b: 60: "writing quickly, paying little attention to the aesthetics of the signs and the layout of the tablet is likelier to be an indication that the text is *not* a scribal exercise or exam" (italics Giusfredi).

[150] Waal 2015: 154. [151] Thus already Otten 1956: 180. [152] See Chapter 8.6.

[153] Cf. the insistence in Roman literate education on writing and memorizing meaningless syllables of all kinds; see Johnson 2010: 27–9.

[154] See e.g. Beckman 1983b: 97–8, 2001a: 86–7, Bryce 2002: 58–60, Lorenz & Rieken 2010, Weeden 2011b: 612, von Dassow 2013: 147–8. Note also the identification of KUB 4.53 as a school tablet by Wilhelm 1994b: 5 n. 28, 73–4, and as a *Sammeltafel* by Rutz 2012.

[155] Cf., for instance, Ünal 1989: 505 ("the Hittite scribes underwent an extensive education. ... As a result of this extraordinary strong education the scribes were versatile and prolific in various fields. First of all as scribes they were able to use at least three languages, namely Hittite, Akkadian and

However, on the one hand this view assumes too much of an equation of scribes and scholars, while, on the other, we lack any information on how scribes were educated in Hatti. It is true that scribes did need some knowledge of Akkadian and Sumerian; without exception every Hittite text contains a number of Sumerian word signs or logograms reflecting the Mesopotamian origins of the script.[156] Some words are even exclusively written with such "Sumerograms" to the extent that we still do not know the reading of the underlying Hittite word. To a lesser extent, we find Akkadian words like the negation UL "not" instead of the rarely spelled out Hittite *natta*. Such Sumero- and Akkadograms are nothing more than isolated words and occasional short phrases that do not require real grammatical knowledge. Neither do we assume that anyone using words and phrases in English like *i.e.*, *et al.*, *quid pro quo*, *sine qua non*, *data*, *etc.* knows Latin. This is confirmed by the texts themselves in the sense that the thirteenth century BC average Hittite scribe often seems to lack even the most basic Akkadian language skills just as modern-day speakers often manhandle Latin expressions. It is, for instance, not exceptional to encounter an Akkadian nominative or accusative after prepositions requiring an oblique case ending or an accusative case to indicate the subject of a clause.[157] As shown by Weeden "a greater amount of awareness for correct Akkadian declension and even gender is observable in Akkadograms from the Old Hittite period"[158] but with the inevitable assimilation of the first generations of Syrians into Anatolian society this familiarity gradually faded. The Sumero- and Akkadograms lend Hittite texts a thin Mesopotamian veneer but we should be careful not to over-interpret this and "think of Ḫatti as a peripheral Mesopotamian culture."[159] Most Sumerian and Akkadian compositions seem to have been the realm of a small circle of scholars at the Hittite court, but they may not have mingled much with their anonymous colleagues. Lexical lists, as we saw in Chapter 8.6, are unlikely to have played a significant role, if any, in standard scribal education. Native Mesopotamians served as specialists in the chancelleries and were probably largely responsible for monolingual Akkadian compositions like international treaties and correspondence. The same was probably true for the corpus of monolingual Hurrian text compositions. Such specialists may have moved in scholarly circles and

Sumerian. Some scribes, especially the chief scribes, might also have studied Hurrian, Luwian, Hattic, Palaic and Hieroglyphic Luwian – in all the famous eight languages of the Hittite capital.").

156 See most recently Beckman 2001a: 86. 157 For an overview see Weeden 2011a: 344–52.

158 Weeden 2011a: 351. 159 Beckman 2001a: 86, 2019: 66.

may have been instrumental in importing tablets from Mesopotamia.[160] This is not to say that Mesopotamian compositions could not at times influence Hittite literary expression: the explicit allusion to Sargon's crossing of the Taurus in Hattusili I's Annals is always referred to in this context. This is, however, a relatively isolated and very early example from the days when Syrian scribes had just been brought to Hattusa. Historical, that is, more scholarly oriented interest may have played a role here, too, in keeping the Mesopotamian epic in the collections.[161]

13.12 Scholars at the Hittite Court

When Muwatalli II moved his residence from Hattusa to the city of Tarhuntassa somewhere in the south he left his chief scribe Mittannamuwa in charge of Hattusa. No reasons for the move are given and for a long time scholars attributed it to the upcoming confrontation with Ramses II at Kadesh (1275 BC) assuming Muwatalli wanted to be closer to the scene where he expected their clash to unfold. Others pointed at the threat to the capital by the Gasgaeans in the north. More recently Itamar Singer rejected those views in favor of an attractive scenario of a religiously inspired move comparable to that of Pharaoh Akhenaten with his new capital Akhetaten at modern el Amarna in Egypt.[162] To his arguments against a perceived danger posed by the Gasgaean tribes one might add that the appointment of a chief scribe without any known military experience might not have been the wisest choice. In the few references to the transfer of the capital nothing is said about the tablet collections. If Muwatalli decided to leave those behind in Hattusa his choice of Mittanamuwa as caretaker of the capital could signal that he still valued them as a resource and intended for the former residence to remain the empire's record depository and did not want them to waste away.[163] He even appointed Mittannamuwa's son Purandamuwa to be his new chief scribe although strictly taken it is unclear where: did Muwatalli intend to take him along to Tarhuntassa to head a new chancellery while Mittanamuwa was to administer both Hattusa and its tablet collections or did he see the latter two tasks as too demanding for one person and was Purandamuwa from now on in charge of Hattusa's collections?[164] Both

160 Also, the find spots of untranslated Sumerian and Akkadian literary works on the acropolis Büyükkale might point to a more dormant existence for these texts instead of a much-used tool in scribal training.

161 Beckman 2001a. 162 Singer 2006. 163 Doğan-Alparslan & Alparslan 2011: 93.

164 van den Hout 2016b.

decisions at any rate confirmed the royal appreciation for Mittanamuwa's family and the importance of the position of chief scribe. The latter is underscored by Urhitessub's subsequent dismissal of Purandamuwa, when he came to the throne. He must have felt the urge to purge the ranks and fill key positions in the kingdom with his own people.[165] Urhitessub's rejection was only temporary, though. As soon as Hattusili came to power he reinstated the family paying back a very personal debt to Mittannamuwa that went back to the latter's earlier days as chief scribe under Mursili II:

> In my father's days I (i.e., Hattusili III) fell seriously ill as a small child. My father entrusted me to the care of Mittannamuwa, the chief scribe and he did his utmost for me and saved me from the illness. Mittannamuwa was a man esteemed by my father and when he had saved me from the illness he honored him for my sake as well.[166]

It is not very likely that Mittannamuwa was entrusted with this risky task because of his organizational skills vis-à-vis the tablet collections and the scribal work force. I would like to think it was on the basis of his status as a learned man, a scholar. To his intellectual skills he probably owed his position in the first place. He must have known his way around the tablet rooms and may even have impressed the king at times by quoting arcane texts from memory (see §13.14). The king probably counted on his special familiarity with those compositions that dealt with the adversities in life, the rituals, prayers, omens, and oracles, all those texts that together made up the holistic approach we saw earlier (Chapter 8.5). The fact that this tradition was carried on by his son Walwazidi who became chief scribe under Hattusili III, and that several sons of Mittannamuwa were scholar–scribes with written products to their names plead in favor of his status as an intellectual. Puduhepa, Hattusili III's queen, put Walwazidi in charge of a project to collect all tablets or compositions from Kizzuwatna, her homeland, dealing with the *hisuwa*-festival. As several colophons to the tablets produced under Walwazidi's supervision put it:

> When Queen Puduhepa called upon Walwazidi, chief scribe, in Hattusa to search for tablets from Kizzuwatna he had these tablets of the *hisuwa*-festival

165 For Zidi (I) as the possible replacement see n. 117.

166 ANA PĀNI ABU=IA=*mu kappin* DUMU-*an* ḪUL-*lu* GIG GIG-*at nu=mu=kan* ABU=IA ANA ᵐ*Mittanna*-A.A GAL DUB.SAR ŠU-*i dāiš n=aš=mu=kan anda dāriyat nu=mu=kan* GIG-*az* TI-*nut* ᵐ*Mittannamūwaš=ma* IŠTU ABI=IA *kaneššanza* UN-*aš ēšta ammukk=a kuwapi* GIG-*az* TI-*nut n=an=kan ammukk=a anda kanešta* KBo 4.12 obv. 5–11 (Decree for Mittannamuwa, CTH 87, NS), ed. by Goetze 1925: 40–1.

> copied. (blank space of ca. four lines) Before Walw[azidi, chief scribe,] LAMMA.DINGIR-*LIM* wrote (it).[167]

This time it was Walwazidi who was trusted to be able to find the texts the queen was looking for. If we understand scholarship loosely as higher learning as opposed to pure handcraft, men like Mittannamuwa and Walwazidi are probably the closest we come to scholars in Hittite society, men who spent their days in the tablet collections, who knew what was there, had a prodigious memory and were sought after as advisors for their wisdom. Either because ordered to, as was the case with the queen, or simply out of their own interest and passion for learning they collected, studied, and worked with foreign compositions like rituals, omens, lexical lists, epic tales, and wisdom literature. They did not do much writing themselves. As we saw, we have no tablets written by chief scribes and for those who served as "supervisors" they are rare. The preferred medium of these officials was probably dictation. Compare the portrait of a man like Thomas Aquinas by Bernardo Gui:

> His memory was extremely rich and retentive: whatever he had once read and grasped he never forgot ... he used to dictate in his cell to three secretaries, and even occasionally to four, on different subjects at the same time.[168]

The chief scribes and "supervisors" may not even have been particularly proficient at writing.[169] An apt illustration of their activity may be the two colophons we saw earlier (§13.7) where the "supervisor" Sipazidi is responsible for the new redaction of a composition while the tablet itself was written by the scribe Zidi. Men like Sipazidi, Mittannamuwa, and Walwazidi probably were ultimately responsible for the presence of foreign compositions in the capital's tablet collections but also for the upkeep and editing of indigenous festivals and such domestic rituals as the royal funerary ritual. They may well also have had a role in formulating treaties and perhaps the historical oeuvre attributed to King Mursili II. But the latter has to remain speculation. What is clear is that, as history shows,

[167] MUNUS.LUGAL ^{f}*Puduḫepaš=kan kuwapi* ^{m}UR.MAḪ.LÚ-*in* GAL DUB.SAR.MEŠ ^{URU}*Ḫattuši* *ANA* *TUPPA*$^{ḪI.A}$ ^{U}[^{R}]^{U}*Kizzuwatna šanḫūwanzi ueriyat n=ašta kē* *TUPPA*$^{ḪI.A}$ *Š*[*A* E]ZEN$_{4}$ *ḫišuwāš apiya* UD-*at a*[*rḫ*]*a aniyat* (blank space of ca. four lines) *PĀNI* ^{m}UR.MA[Ḫ.LÚ GAL DUB.SAR.MEŠ] ^{m}LAMMA.DINGIR-*LIM* *IŠ*[*ṬUR*] KBo 15.52 vi 39–47 (*hisuwa* cult ritual, CTH 628, NS), ed. by Waal 2015: 441. The scribal signature of LAMMA.DINGIR-*LIM* at the very end shows that Walwazidi (^{m}UR.MAḪ.LÚ) did not do the copying himself but "had these tablets copied" by his scribes.

[168] Quoted after Carruthers 2008: 3, see also Blair 2010: 83.

[169] For the notion of illiterate scholars, unable to read or write, in the medieval Arabic world of the eleventh through sixteenth century AD, see Hirschler 2012: 16, 197; for blind scholars see 16–17.

Mursili II's confidence in Mittannamuwa for his infant son Hattusili was not in vain. Occasionally the knowledge gained from learned and, often, foreign tablets could be put to use as can be argued in the case of Mursili's Aphasia (see Chapter 12.1). With Mittanamuwa, Walwazidi, and Sipazidi we are back in the company of the elite scribes. Rather than simple scribes they and most of those who set so much store by their family connections and ancestry may be more appropriately termed scholars.

13.13 The *scriba doctus*

The existence of higher learning in Hattusa has never been doubted but it has mostly been attributed to foreigners and their descendants. In an important article on "Mesopotamians and Mesopotamian Learning at Ḫattuša" Gary Beckman sketched a history of Sumerian and Akkadian compositions in the tablet collections of the capital and listed the names of Assyrians and Babylonians working there. Foreign experts must have regularly stayed and worked in Hattusa.[170] Native speakers of Akkadian were responsible for many of the Akkadian language diplomatic texts like treaties and correspondence. It is not only the grammatically correct Akkadian that separates them from the average Hittite scribe but often times also the foreign (e.g., Middle Assyrian/Babylonian, Assyro-Mittanian) ductus they used.[171] Hurrian speakers composed and wrote many of the Hurrian-only texts, found at Boğazköy, that form such an important part of the Hurrian corpus. But what has been termed a "mixed ductus"[172] (i.e., showing both Hittite and non-Hittite features, linguistically and graphically) may at times betray a native Anatolian scribe able to write a ductus different than the traditional Hittite one.[173] Tablets in this mixed ductus were reserved for Akkadian language texts and they thus show that there were at least some Hittite scribes well versed in that language and its ductus.

How general this capability was among them is difficult to gauge. As Giulia Torri has shown for the cuneiform sign AN and some other sign shapes, Hittite scribes sometimes liked to show off their learnedness by using archaic non-standard and foreign cuneiform signs in regular Hittite-language compositions. Interestingly, they almost only did so in

170 van den Hout 2015: 203 n. 2 for lit., to which should be added Cohen 2012: 12 ("the product of intellectual activities of foreign teachers from Mesopotamia together with the local scribes and practitioners").

171 For these see Wilhelm 1992, Klinger 1998 and 2003, Devecchi 2012, Weeden 2016b.

172 Schwemer 1998: 13–14.

173 Devecchi 2012.

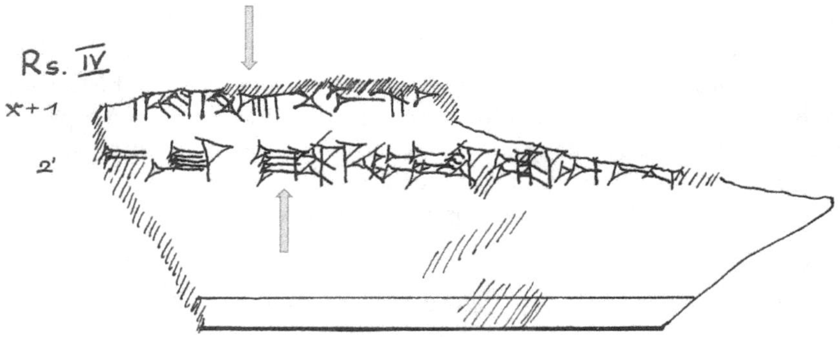

Fig. 13.1 KBo 39.43 iv (copyright Akademie der Wissenschaften und der Literatur, Mainz).

colophons, probably so as not to render the main text illegible and confuse their less learned readers.[174] This practice is also known in Syro-Mesopotamia from the Middle Babylonian period onwards.[175] Another example in Hittite texts is the archaic and unusual shape of the signs AḪ (line 1; normally 𒄴) and ŠA (line 2; normally 𒊭) in the *ḫišuwa*-festival[176] colophon (Fig. 13.1) signed by a grandson of Mittannamuwa.

Or compare the rare but consistent use by Ashapala, the possible descendant of the Old Kingdom scribe Warsiya (see p. 313–4), of the sign ŠÁ (𒃻) instead of ŠA (𒊭) to write the Akkadian preposition *ša* "of" in a colophon only.[177] The knowledge of such sign shapes can only have come from exposure to and study of imported tablets as they have indeed been found in Hattusa.[178] As the scribal counterpart of the classical Roman *poeta doctus* ideal, these scholar–scribes probably reveled in such small displays of learning to be appreciated by the circle of their immediate colleagues only. A review of all 900 odd colophons shows both the limits and extent of such behavior: see Table 13.8 (p. 330).[179]

174 Torri 2010b, see also Lorenz 2013: 165–7, Gordin 2014: 72–4, 2015: 341.

175 Hunger 1968: 4, Veldhuis 2011: 81–2, Weeden 2011b: 601. On such practices of "'old looking' spellings, even intentionally obscure spellings" at Ugarit see also Roche-Hawley & Hawley 2013: 263.

176 Thus Haas & Wegner 1996: 574.

177 KUB 33.120 + KUB 48.97 + KBo 52.10 iv 30–32 (CTH 344, NS), ed. by Waal 2015: 274–5; for the use of the rare Sumerographic combination GÁ.É.A "departure(?)" by Ashapala in the same colophon (line 28) see Corti 2007, and Weeden 2017: 50–5.

178 See for instance, Klinger 2010: 332–5, 2012: 91.

179 Gordin 2015: 338–40 gives a short list of "Unique, Abnormal, or Archaic Sign Forms and Unusual Markings" that is, however, based only on the various scribal circles he distinguishes.

Fig. 13.2 KUB 46.34 (copyright Staatliche Museen zu Berlin – Vorderasiatisches Museum, Foto: BoFN 02151).

Two other instances of this phenomenon mentioned by Torri should be added here (Table 13.9, p. 331) that are not colophons proper but do qualify as scribal interventions. The first one is a manuscript (KUB 14.13) from the Plague Prayers of Mursili II. The tablet lacks a colophon at the end but working on column i the scribe could not read his original and left an open space but for four *cruces* (so-called "PAB"-signs) indicating an illegible passage and the word *ḫarran* "damaged" (see Chapter 12.4 w. Fig. 12.1). The AN sign concluding *ḫarran* (*ḫar-ra*-AN) shows archaic features.

The second fragment, KUB 46.34 (Fig. 13.2), is perhaps the clearest example of what could be a practice tablet.[182] While the reverse is uninscribed the obverse shows the familiar two-column format with a listing of

[180] The colophon says that ^{d}AMAR. ^{d}LAMMA [?] / *ḫandā*[*n ḫarzi*? or *ḫa-an-da-a*[-*it*?] and did so *PĀNI* ^{d}UTU-*ŠI* "before His Majesty." The meaning of the verb *ḫandae-* here is not clear. Torri 2010b: 325–6 w. n. 39 renders it as "prepar[ed?", Waal 2015: 371 offers "establish[ed"; cf. also Cammarosano 2012b: 112. It certainly does not mean "he wrote" it and Waal correctly does not include ^{d}AMAR. ^{d}LAMMA as a scribe in her list on p. 553. The colophon sums up the expenditures for twelve different festivals and the verb could thus refer to the work of putting all the data together on this one tablet. Whether the writing itself was done by ^{d}AMAR. ^{d}LAMMA or some scribe did it for him remains an open question. He is thus far not attested as scribe elsewhere.

[181] Lorenz 2013: 165. [182] Thus Torri 2010b: 323–4.

what seem to be cultic offerings (cf. DN Kantipuitti i 6) with blank spaces in between. Apart from some isolated signs (ii 1: 4/NINDA 2-*an*, ii 3: LI) column ii might be an exercise, practicing – randomly placed – the introductory formula for letters (ii 2: *UMMA* *tutḫali*, ii 4: *UMMA* ᵈUTU-*ŠI-MA*) and a twice begun PN (ii 5: ᵐᵈ ᵐᵈAMAR.UTU.ᵈLAMMA).

All sign variants in the colophons and the latter two texts are those current in Old and/or Middle Babylonian. Only KUB 4.38 (Fig. 13.3), listed in Table 13.8, stands out: the signs in its colophon look like pseudo pre-Old Babylonian monumental script but with almost in every sign additional wedges.[183] The wording of the colophon makes it likely that the fragment is not an import: the *PĀNI* ᵐLÚ (line 6) "before (Mr.) Zidi" is typical of Hittite colophons and not known from Mesopotamia.[184]

As far as the state of preservation of the fragments listed above allows us to judge, in all cases the relevant sign shapes (or function of a sign in the case of ŠÁ for the Akkadian preposition ŠA[185]) were only used in the colophon (or in a clear scribal note in the case of KUB 14.13) and not in the body of the composition itself.[186] The above list is conservative in the sense that more research might identify additional signs or confirm certain tendencies. It is, for instance, my impression that one encounters certain sign variants more often in colophons than elsewhere, even though not exclusively. This might be the case, for instance, for so-called (sometimes heavily) *gunû*-ed variants (i.e., with extra wedges) of signs like DUB, LÚ, and DUMU.[187] One also frequently sees ŠÚ (instead of ŠU) used in the colophons for the Akkadian possessive pronoun *-ŠU* "his." Finally, the Sumerographic combinations GÁxÈ.A and ŠAGAN.LÁ (see Table 13.8), both *hapax legomena*, are in all likelihood also products of scholarly creativity. If the rare use of A.BA for DUB.SAR "scribe" on the seal of Layadagan (see the Excursus in Chapter 14) from Ugarit is seen in the same light that suggests that he, too, was more of a scholar than a simple scribe, which is probable anyhow for someone with such an elaborate seal.

183 Weeden 2011a: 84 ("a very exaggerated 'monumental' script"), Gordin 2014: 72, 2015: 331, Weeden 2016b: 158–9.

184 Hunger 1968: 11.

185 The use of ŠÁ for the Akkadian preposition outside colophons in Hittite texts is quite rare, cf. Lorenz 2013: 167. For one case of syllabic ŠÁ in a Hittite divine name see KUB 52.68 iii 31, 41, cf. Catsanicos 1994: 320 w. lit.

186 Except for KBo 5.11, KUB 10.96, and KUB 44.61 that do not contain any other ŠA signs used as the Akkadian preposition, and KBo 22.214 that does not show any further LI-signs.

187 Cf., for instance, Gordin 2015: 310, 325.

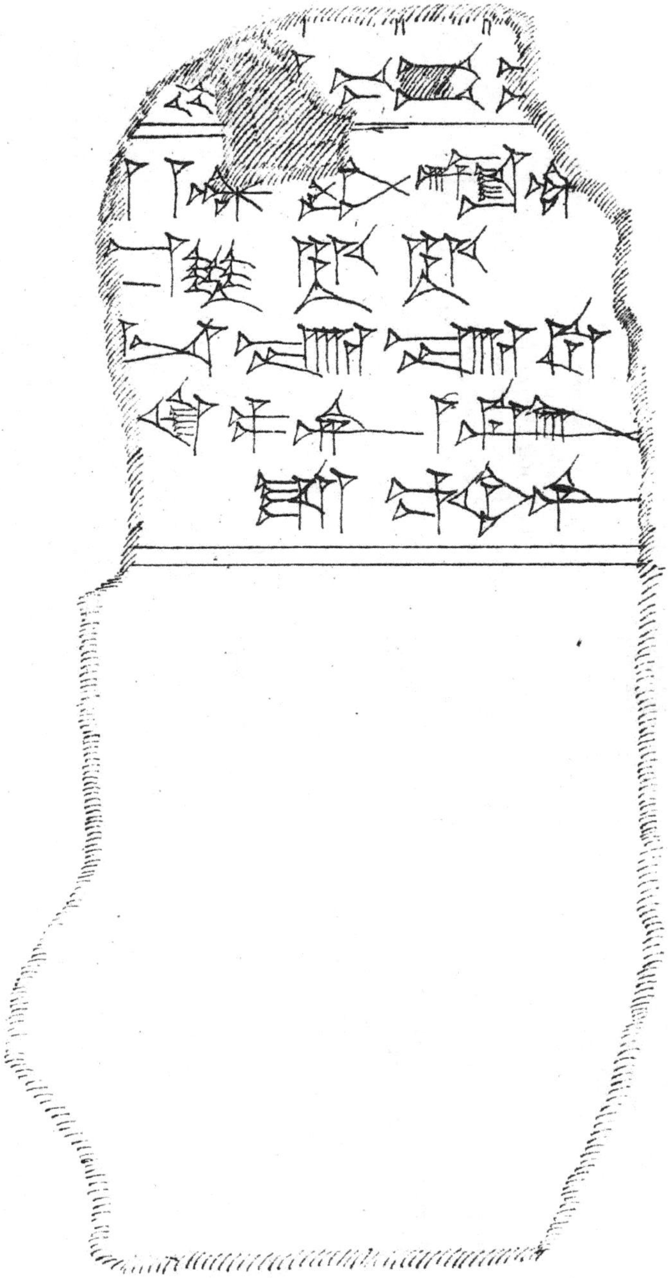

Fig. 13.3 KUB 4.38 (from KUB 4 Pl. 20 [Berlin 1922]).

Table 13.8 *Archaic or archaic-looking cuneiform signs in Hittite colophons*

text	*signs*	*scribal signature (scribe)*	*CTH*	*remarks*
KBo 5.11	ŠÁ (for ŠA) iv 27	+ (Sakkabi, before Angulli)	263	
KBo 11.1	LU rev. 26	+ (Lurma(-zidi), A.ZU TUR)	382	
KBo 22.214	LI vi 3	+ (Alalimi)	620	
KBo 26.178	ḪAR iv 2, LI? iv 3, LUGAL iv 8	+? (^{d}AMAR.^{d}LAMMA[180])	523	by its position in the left margin the archaic LUGAL-sign seems to be a later addition; cf. Torri 2010b: 326, for ḪAR cf. HZL 333.
KBo 34.195	AN rev. 5, 6, ŠIR rev. 5	+ ([PN lost])	700	for the cruciform ŠIR cf. Torri 2010b: 321.
KBo 35.200	AN iv 15, ŠA? iv 15	+ ([PN lost])	479	for the reading ŠA cf. Strauß 2006: 319, Torri 2010b: 322, Waal 2015: 350, Konkordanz suggests "Nananza(?)."
KBo 39.43	AḪ iv 1, ŠA iv 2	+ (Alihhisni)	628	
KUB 4.38	AN 3 (2x), GEŠTIN 3, LA 3, ḪUR 4, ŠÈ 4, ZU 5 (2x), ŠÁ (for ŠA) 5, LÚ 6, IŠ 7	+ (DINGIR/^{d}x-lan[. . .], before Zidi)	819	
KUB 10.96	ŠÁ (for ŠA) 3, 4	+ ([PN lost])		the Sumerographic combination ŠAGAN.LÁ "apprentice" seems to be a *hapax* in Hittite.
KUB 12.31	LI rev. 27	[?]	486	the LI sign occurs here in the king's name Mursili.[181]
KUB 33.120+	ŠÁ (for ŠA) iv 28, 30, 31, 32	+ (Ashapala, before Zidi)	344	on the unique Sumerographic combinations ^{d}A.GILIM, ^{d}KA.ZAL, and GÁXÈ.A cf. Torri 2010b: 318 w. lit., Gordin 2015: 330.
KUB 43.77	DUMU? rev. 3, TI rev. 5	+ (Tummani, before Anuwanza)	828	the reading of the DUMU-sign is not certain, cf. Otten 1971a: 49 n. 105 ("DUMU"), Pecchioli Daddi 1982: 515 ("⌜NUMUN⌝??"), Torri 2010b: 320 ("DUMU") and 2012: 131, Waal 2015: 547 ("DUMU"), Gordin 2014: 73; the sign looks more like a conflation of DUMU and NUMUN than either of the two.
KUB 44.61	ŠÁ (for ŠA) left edge 5	+ (NU.^{GIŠ}KIRI$_{6}$)	461	
VAT 13019b	TI rev. iv 19, DUMU? iv 20, NU iv 20, AN iv 20	+ ([PN lost])	360/?	cf. Torri 2010b: 320 w. lit.
VBoT 24	KU iv 38	+ (Hanikkuili)	393	

Table 13.9 *Archaic or archaic-looking signs outside colophons*

KUB 14.13	AN i 58	(*ḫar-ra-*AN)	378
KUB 46.34	AN ii 5 (3x)	(AN/DINGIR in ^{md} and ^{d}LAMMA)	834

Besides imported texts or Mesopotamian compositions written in Hattusa by foreign specialists, such patently archaic signs occur almost exclusively in *named* colophons, as the list clearly shows. Only in the case of KUB 12.31, one of the manuscripts of the Aphasia of Mursili (II), are we unable to tell whether the colophon contained the scribe's name or not. Moreover, some of these scribes or their families we have encountered before: Alihhisni was a grandson of Mittanamuwa, Ashapala's pedigree may go back to Warsiya, scribe in the days of Muwatalli I (second half of the fifteenth century BC), Tummani was the son of the "supervisor" Anuwanza, NU.^{GIŠ}KIRI$_6$ came from the family of the "supervisor" Zidi, and Hanikkuili could count Anat-šar-ilāni among his ancestors. Is it coincidence that three of the scribes, Ashapala, Lurma(zidi), and NU.^{GIŠ}KIRI$_6$, were also in the group of apprentices? Apart from those cases where a break prevents us from knowing the scribe only two (Alalimi and Sakkabi) are without genealogy. Again, these results seem to confirm the impression that named colophons reflected some special status and were not the prerogative of the average clerk. It seems unlikely that the training that produced these men and that their ability to reproduce these variants was shared by the anonymous scribes responsible for the bulk of the Hittite written legacy.

It is, finally, sobering to see with what little these scribes tried to impress: the most frequent display of learnedness concerns the sign AN, followed closely by the use of ŠÁ for the Akkadian preposition ŠA, and the sign LI. All in all, this is hardly a record betraying intense familiarity with foreign sources. The scribe of KUB 4.38 is the only one going overboard in his attempt to produce something archaic and thus learned but his signs rarely seem quite correct, if that was his intention.

13.14 The Tablet Inventories as Scholarly Corpora

Now that we have identified the presence of a separate class of scribes who, more than just scribal craftsmen or clerks, showed an interest in learning for its own sake, we can look for other expressions of their activity. In Chapter 8.7 we briefly encountered the tablet inventories, also known as catalogs or shelf lists: occasionally lists of certain tablets were drawn up giving the number of tablets comprising a composition (anything from "one tablet" to "eighty tablets"), its title (= mostly the *incipit* or first line, e.g. "Two tablets: 'When the king, queen and princes give substitutes to the Sungoddess of the Earth'"[188]) and whether the composition was complete ("finished/not finished"). Sometimes other information like, for instance, the format (single-column or not single-column), the age of the tablet ("old"), or whether everything was there ("Two tablets: . . . We have not found its first tablet"[189]) is added. Compare the following example:

> Two tablets: "When the king, queen, and princes give substitutes to the Sungoddess of the Earth." Finished. We did not find its first tablet.
>
> One tablet: Text of Annana, woman from Zigazhur. "When I invoke the deity Miyatanzipa." Finished.
>
> One single-column tablet: "When a singer brings a libation in the temple of the deity Inar, breaks thick breads, and prays in Hattian." Finished.
>
> One tablet of the *zinduhi*-women, how they speak in the presence of the king in the temple of the Sun God. Finished.
>
> One single-column tablet: Songs of the men of Istanuwa. Finished.
>
> One tablet of a treaty: When Ispudahsu, king of Kizzuwatna, and Telipinu, the Hittite king, concluded a treaty. Finished.
>
> One single-column tablet: Text of Ammihatna, Tulpiya, and Mati, *purapsi*-priests, of (the land of) Kizzuwatna. "When they detect in the temple, in a holy space, whatever kind of defilement. § This is its ritual. Finished."[190]

As observed by their most recent editor, Paola Dardano, the approximately 430 reasonably preserved entries (out of a total of about 650 in sixty-six manuscripts) concern a selection of genres only, all of them

188 ⌜DUB.2.KAM *mā*⌝*n* LUGAL MUNUS. ⌜LUGAL DUMU.MEŠ.LUGAL*=ia*⌝ *taknaš* ^{d}UTU-*i tarpalliyaš pianzi* QATI KUB 30.42+ iv 9–10 (Tablet inventory, CTH 276, NS), ed. by Dardano 2006: 26–7.

189 *ḫantezzi=ma=šši* TUPPA UL *wemiu*[?]*en* KUB 30.42+ iv 11 (Tablet inventory, CTH 276, NS), ed. by Dardano 2006: 26–7; Laroche, CTH p. 163 transliterated "*ú-e-mi-ú-en*", although there is no *-ú-*, Dardano has the grammatically impossible form "*ú-e-mi-en.*" The form is written at the end of the line with EN in the intercolumnium. There may be a U visible right in between MI and EN, perhaps written after the scribe had impressed the EN-sign.

190 ⌜DUB.2.KAM *mā*⌝*n* LUGAL MUNUS. ⌜LUGAL DUMU.MEŠ.LUGAL*=ia*⌝ *taknaš* ^{d}UTU-*i tarpalliyaš pianzi* QATI *ḫantezzi=ma=šši* TUPPA UL *wemiu*?*en* § DUB.I.KAM INIM ^{f}*Annana* MUNUS $^{\text{<URU>}}$*Zigazḫur mān* ^{d}*Miyatanzipan mugāmi* QATI § I IM.GÍD.DA *mān* ^{LÚ}NAR INA É ^{d}*Inar išpanti* ^{NINDA}*ḫaršauš paršiya ta kiššan mālti ḫattili* QATI § DUB.I.KAM ŠA $^{MUNUS.MEŠ}$*zinduḫiyaš* ANA PĀNI LUGAL INA É ^{d}UTU-*aš* GIM-*an memieškanzi* QATI § I IM.GÍD.DA SÌR.ḪI.A LÚ.MEŠ ^{URU}*Ištanuwa* QATI § DUB.I.KAM *išḫiula*<š> ^{m}*Išpudaḫšuš=za* LUGAL KUR ^{URU}*Kizzuwatna* ^{m}*Telipinušš=a* LUGAL KUR *Ḫatti* GIM-*an išḫiūl iēr* QATI § I IM.GÍD.DA AWĀT ^{m}*Ammiḫatna* ^{m}*Tulpiya* Ù ^{m}*Māti* $^{LÚ.MEŠ}$*purapšiš* ŠA KUR ^{URU}*Kizzuwatna man=kan* INA É.DINGIR-LIM *šuppa pedi kuin imma kuin maršaštarrin umiyanzi* § [*n*]*u kī* SÍSKUR*=ŠU* QATI KUB 30.42+KBo 31.8 iv 9–30 (Tablet inventory, CTH 276, NS), ed. by Laroche 1971, 163–4 (with different line numbers 3–18), Dardano 2006, 26–9, van den Hout 2015: 218.

belonging to the group of what we earlier termed permanent records (compare Chapter 12.2). Imported genres such as rituals and omina as well as festivals form the overwhelming majority.[191] One such list, however, just quoted, cites amid rituals and cult scenarios the state treaty between King Telipinu and his Kizzuwatnean counterpart Isputahsu[192] and another list – unfortunately very fragmentary – contains some legal records and royal edicts or decrees followed by rituals, festivals, and omina.[193] Hymns, prayers, and mythological tales are also represented. Only about eighty entries can be linked to a composition that we actually have.[194] A satisfactory explanation of the function of these inventories within the Hittite tablet collections has been lacking thus far.[195] Dardano convincingly states that these texts are not catalogs in the modern sense but characterizes them as lists that record the "holdings, state of preservation or simply the availability" of *sectors* of the tablet collections at Hattusa.[196] But of what sectors?

The above recognition of a class of scholars seems the proper climate for these texts.[197] Similar documents, often understood as curricular lists, compilations of existing or desired knowledge, are known from Mesopotamia.[198] Compare, for instance, catalogs of Sumerian, mostly literary, compositions whether thought of as curricular lists or inventories.[199] A Neo-Assyrian inventory from the so-called House of the Diviner in Assur carefully identifies titles that were not available at the time.[200] "Library Records" from Nineveh attest to the incorporation of formerly private collections into Assurbanipal's palace library.[201] Some Mesopotamian catalogs contain references to the exact spot where a certain composition or tablet was to be found: "located in the lower (reed) basket."[202] Lists of literary and scholarly works on papyri document the existence of institutional and private

191 Dardano 2006: 1–17.
192 KBo 31.8 + KUB 30.42 iv 21–4 (Tablet inventory, CTH 276, NS), ed. by Dardano 2006: 28–9.
193 KBo 31.1++ I (Tablet inventory, CTH 278, OS), ed. by Dardano 2006: 190–3.
194 Dardano 2006: 5–7.
195 Dardano 2006: 9 in her edition of these texts suggests "sie . . . als Inventare zu betrachten, die sich auf begrenzte Sektoren der Tafelsammlungen beziehen." See also Christiansen 2008: 306 ("in Zusammenhang mit bestimmten Problemstellungen oder Ereignissen angefertigt"), and Gordin 2015: 115–19 (117: "inventories of tablets removed from specific collections").
196 Dardano 2006: 13 ("Die Tafelkataloge sind also mehr als Kataloge Textlisten, die den Bestand, den Konservierungszustand oder einfach die Verfügbarkeit von Sektoren der Tafelsammlungen feststellen sollen"), see also 7 ("sie sind eine Art Inventar von einigen Abteilungen der Tafelsammlungen").
197 van den Hout 2015.
198 van der Toorn 2007: 242–3, Tinney 2011: 582–3, Maul 2011: 38–9.
199 Delnero 2010.
200 Maul 2011: 38–9.
201 Parpola 1983.
202 Delnero 2010: 47; cf. also Houston 2009: 245 n. 37.

collections in Hellenistic and Roman Egypt.[203] All such lists may have served as reference tools much like the *pinakes* in the library of Alexandria: "the entries offered biographical and sophisticated bibliographical information, including title, *incipit*, and number of lines for each work, sorted by literary form or scholarly discipline."[204] In other times and cultures we encounter such inventories as well. Staying in the Middle East, the catalog of the Ashrafiya Library in thirteenth century AD Damascus carefully describes the scholarly collection of the mausoleum for al-Malik al-Ashraf.[205] Besides the title of the various works, the 1707 entries contain information such as the number of volumes, the age, format, and condition of the copies.[206] For the Carolingian period, according to Rosamond McKitterick, such catalogs "should be understood as a dynamic expression of literate and intellectual aspirations."[207] Here, too, like the Telipinu Treaty that was wedged in between a cultic text and a magic ritual, the order of works listed sometimes comes across as odd but may at times "simply reflect the personal, and thus, inevitably, the miscellaneous nature" of a collection.[208] In general "they effectively defined the intellectual framework within which literate skills were to be exercised."[209] Just like the Hittite tablet inventories some Roman exemplars likewise indicate the completeness of works with the added remark *omnia quae extant* "all that are there" or ὅσα εὑρίσκ(εται) "as much as is found."[210]

Our Hittite inventories, too, can be seen as lists of texts collected and maintained by ancient scholars. In that sense they are catalogs and their order might even – although that is impossible to prove or verify – reflect the order they were in on a shelf or in some container. What to us might seem unsystematic may not have been so for the ancient scholar. We usually perfectly find our way in our own personal libraries and they, too, may sometimes show a "system" that is not immediately evident to others.

With Gary Beckman, the initial impetus for collecting foreign texts (mostly rituals and omina) may have been to "make [foreign practitioners'] recommended procedures available to magic specialists attending the royal

203 Otranto 2000; the author mentions (p. xvi) "il catalogo della *biblioteca di Stato* del regno ittita . . . contenente un elenco alfabetico degli autori e delle opere possedute dalla biblioteca" (Otranto's italics) but the alphabetic claim must surely be a misunderstanding.

204 Blair 2010: 16 205 Hirschler 2016. 206 Hirschler 2016: 134. 207 McKitterick 1989: 166.

208 McKitterick 1989: 174, cf. also 171.

209 McKitterick 1989: 210; for lists of Roman libraries and book collections see the fascinating article by Houston 2009, although their function is not as clear (cf. p. 236–7). For "the first monastic book catalogues in the twelfth century" in England see Clanchy 1993: 15–9.

210 Houston 2009: 236–7.

family, should one of its members suffer from any of the relevant problems."[211] We know that Hittite kings and queens occasionally did consult and use such foreign rituals and Mesopotamian omens.[212] This is exactly what Mursili II expected of Mittannamuwa for his sickly son Hattusili. Note also the request by Queen Puduhepa to collect all manuscripts of the *ḫišuwa*-festival of her native Kizzuwatna that we saw earlier. Having collected the original texts scholars compiled the inventories to organize their knowledge and guide their students and successors. Working for the Hittite king, scholars managed and transmitted the collection for the next generation. The collection comprised not only native and foreign rituals or literary works but also some political and diplomatic documents from the past like the Telipinu Treaty with Isputahsu and the list of royal decrees. We know (Chapters 8 and 12) that for the drawing up of new treaties previous versions were consulted and, in many cases, excerpted to compile a new one. We can be sure that this was not a task for the simple scrivener but for those who in consultation with a king's further advisors functioned as doctors, diviners, diplomats, and lawyers all rolled into one.

This role for the tablet inventories is reinforced if we compare the text genres represented in the named colophons with those in the tablet inventories or catalogs. The ca. seventy-five scribes of the named colophons were responsible for about 120 manuscripts. The overwhelming majority (ca. 90 percent) of these consists of texts belonging to the scholarly realm: rituals, cult rituals or festivals, omens, and foreign literature. The remaining ca. 10 percent is made up of some instructions, oracles, prayers, lexical lists, laws, and depositions.[213] But if we compare this list with the tablet inventories the overlap with the inventories is striking. Of the reasonably identifiable 400 entries the overwhelming majority consists of rituals, festivals, and omens, to the point that about only 3 percent fall outside these genres. These consist of four treaties, one possible instruction, two legal records (depositions?), and the seven decree-like texts. The genres and their distribution represented in the inventories are thus a close match of those in the colophons.[214]

211 Thus Beckman 2013: 292, for Mesopotamia cf. already Oppenheim 1960: 413, and much more recently Frahm 2004, Maul 2011: 28, 39–40, Robson 2013: 38 ("a royal collection . . . in order to support royal decision making").

212 See already Chapter 8.6. Cf. the consulting of omina by the Tawananna during Mursili II's reign or the use of a Kizzuwatnean ritual by Mursili II to heal his aphasia; see also van den Hout 1998: 90–2.

213 van den Hout 2015: 206–7.

214 van den Hout 2015: 219.

Finally, it is interesting to consider and compare for a moment the intellectual profile and size of the collection. In a rough estimate Leo Oppenheim set the library of Ashurbanipal at Niniveh at 1200–1500 "tablets" including a "safety margin" of some 600.[215] The core of 700 texts consisted of omens (300), lexical lists (200), Sumerian-Akkadian bilingual incantations and prayers (100) as well as rituals. Epic literature like the Creation story or Gilgamesh cycle was represented with only "35 to 40" tablets. To this he added another 200 to be "inferred with varying degrees of certainty from isolated fragments and other indications, such as catalogs of tablets" plus said safety margin. Even down to the low number for the "literary" compositions in the catalogs of texts the overall character of the Ashurbanipal library is much the same as the Hittite collection. If we are right in seeing in this a reflection of royal interests this illustrates how much the ruling elite cared for its self-preservation, as argued by Beckman for the Hittite corpus and by others for Mesopotamia. This accounts for the apparently low priority of epic literature and similar texts in both the Mesopotamian and Hittite collections. The Hittite collections, moreover, with their overall very modest showing of classical Mesopotamian scholarship like the lexical lists, show an early shift in interest to Anatolian materials betraying an increasingly limited and nationalistic intellectual radius of the royal house. It is possible that the few "literary" entries in the Boğazköy lists and what little there is of Mesopotamian scholarship in the Hittite collections at large reflect the real and personal interests of the Anatolian *literati*.

In his book on the seventh/thirteenth century AD Ashrafīya Library in Damascus Konrad Hirschler usefully compares its holdings of over 2000 "books" with some of the other roughly contemporary libraries. Medieval British collections like those of Norwich Cathedral Priory, Christ Church Cathedral and St. Augustine's Abbey in Canterbury, and St Edmundsbury Cathedral in Bury St. Edmunds all fall in the range between 1600 and just over 2000 works; but "the number of books in medieval monastic libraries typically did not exceed the low to mid-hundreds."[216] It may not be fair to compare the total of about 650 entries coming from sixty-six different manuscripts with these numbers. Strictly taken we also do not know to what extent the catalogs all belonged to a single organization or were products of individual scholarship. A clear majority, on the other hand,

[215] Oppenheim 1960: 412, and see more recently Streck 2010: 52; note that Oppenheim writes of "tablets" where nowadays one might prefer to speak in terms of compositions.
[216] Hirschler 2016: 3.

seem to come from the acropolis,[217] and while just a few may go back to the fifteenth or early fourteenth century BC most were written in the thirteenth century. I think it is unlikely that they were all just isolated lists. The findspot of most fragments on the acropolis, the remarkable coincidence in genres with the colophons of named scribes, and the overall focus of the lists on the same kinds of compositions rather speak in favor of a common element. With these *caveats* in mind the Hittite "archive library"[218] is comparable in size to the European medieval monastic collections, as mentioned by Hirschler, and not too far behind Ashurbanipal's. Also, the few catalogs written in Older Script show how this scholarly interest already started early on.

13.15 Memorization as Part of Scholarly Life?

I mentioned Thomas Aquinas (p. 324) as someone known for his astounding memory. For the Islamic world Konrad Hirschler describes:

> ... the active role of numerous blind teachers who not only taught in subjects as varied as *hadith*, jurisprudence, philology and grammar [which] indicates that recitation from memory still commanded an elevated position in the hierarchies of scholarship. The ability to recite the texts from memory thus remained an indicator of prestige and a crucial element of cultural capital in order to make one's living.[219]

Memorization was also an integral part and key component of literacy training. Reading served to train the memory and the written record served to maintain and expand the memory. As Eleanor Robson writes:

> Scribal and scholarly training depended heavily on memorisation, so that writing was often simply a means of learning by heart and written exercises essentially ephemeral byproducts of that process. Gradually the emphasis shifted, however, from the transmission of knowledge through memory and recitation (with concomitant textual flexibility) towards an increasing dependence on copying out manuscripts (and careful recording of sources) in the first millennium BC.[220]

The shift as described by Robson may be true for first-millennium Mesopotamia, as she claims, but in general the role of memorization vis-à-vis reading in cultures that were largely oral remained of prime

217 Dardano 2006: 4–5. 218 van den Hout 2015: 224. 219 Hirschler 2012: 16–7, cf. also 197.
220 Robson 2013: 40.

importance. This can be seen in the early Islamic parallels given by Hirschler and it remains true for certain oral activities today.[221]

Using a long research tradition in cognitive psychology Paul Delnero has made a convincing case for a range of Sumerian literary compositions as having been written down from memory.[222] He lists variations that typically occur when quoting or writing from memory. These include changes in tense, mood, and number, substitutions of words with (near) synonyms, additions (often connectives or adverbs, sometimes entire sentences), omissions (from small words to entire sections), and substitutions (often of text passages with passages from elsewhere in the same composition), inversions of word combinations or even lines, and numerical errors. Although it cannot be excluded that some of these "flexibilities" might occasionally result from either dictation (through hearing mistakes) or copying from an archetype (certain omissions) they are more convincingly explained by insufficient memorization or memorial transfer, especially when found in combination.

As shown by Hannah Marcuson and me, the same kinds of variation are found in many Hittite manuscripts of magic rituals.[223] This may indicate that also among scholarly circles in Hittite society memorization was a normal practice going hand in hand with written sources as *aide-mémoire*. In pre-modern societies "orality and literacy often not only coexisted but were in many cases mutually dependent."[224] And one can add that that is still the case. In recent scholarship the deviations between individual Hittite manuscripts of a ritual were often attributed to deliberate scribal interventions but such interventions often do not make much sense. Especially if the texts were regarded as prescriptive, as manuals for how to conduct a certain magic procedure, the ancients must have experienced considerable difficulty following the guidelines. Rather these compositions were treated as static documents, as expressions of mostly foreign and perhaps even ancient wisdom to be handled with care and as the proper object of learning. It is instructive in this respect to see whether other text genres show similar deviations. As Marcuson and I showed, the various manuscripts of Mursili II's Ten-Year Annals had no such "mistakes." Variations between the manuscripts concerned almost exclusively small differences in the spelling of words. A cursory overview of variants in several long compositions with a rich manuscript tradition confirms this picture. This does not only apply to historiographical texts like Mursili's

[221] See Macdonald 2005: 69–71. [222] Delnero 2012: 196–8.
[223] Marcuson & van den Hout 2015. [224] Hirschler 2012: 12, cf. also Maul 2011: 47–8.

Annals or Hattusili III's Apology but seems to hold for cultic scenarios like the AN.TAḪ.ŠUM, KI.LAM and *nuntarriyašḫa*-festivals, and prayers like those spoken in connection with the epidemic raging during Mursili II's reign as well.[225] The character of deviations between manuscripts and its implications for how we see the function of texts in the Hittite chancelleries needs more study but this potential difference between magic and cultic rituals can be a fundamental one. The magic rituals were treated as a canon, a body of literature with only limited practical impact. The cultic rituals or festivals, on the other hand, were of prime practical importance as they regulated the ceremonies, in which the king enacted the royal ideology that was the glue that kept the Hittite state together. Moreover, as ideology and politics evolved, so did these texts and regular updates reflecting the changes were required. This was not something to be left to memory but to be closely guarded in a complex redactional system starting with preliminary drafts and culminating in copies "true to the original."[226]

Memorization makes sense only in a professional and educational context where transmission of knowledge took place primarily on an oral and aural level. This context is not scribal but rather one that we would consider scholarly or professional, *in casu* medical. One is reminded of Lurma(zidi) who identified himself as both scribe and "junior physician." With some of the therapeutic rituals dating back to the Old Kingdom, if we are correct in attributing certain variants as at least partially due to memorization, then it would attest again (see already §13.14) to the existence of such a class of persons already in that period.

As we saw earlier, a general training for the average Hittite scribe in Akkadian and Sumerian is unlikely but there are indications that those whom I suppose to have been scholars did have knowledge of Mesopotamian literature. It was they who followed the originally Mesopotamian custom of using the term "hand (of PN)" in signing their tablets, they were the ones adding their ancestors' names to the colophons, and it was them using the archaic and foreign sign shapes and rarest of Sumerograms. With the addition of the tablet inventories and the possible evidence of memorization as an integral part of the scholarly profession a class of Hittite *literati* comes into view that was unknown before. The

[225] For Hattusili III's Apology cf. the listing of variants in Otten 1981: 66–80; for the AN.TAḪ.ŠUM see the critical apparatus of Badalì & Zinko's 1994 edition of the sixteenth day of that festival, likewise Singer's 1983 with his 1984a edition of the KI.LAM festival, and Nakamura 2002 for the *nuntarriyašḫa*-festival. Andrea Trameri came to the same conclusion in his paper at the Tenth International Congress of Hittitology, Chicago, in August 2017.

[226] See Chapter 12.6.

roots of their existence may originally have been wholly practical and grown out of a royal desire for self-protection with whatever means, including foreign ones, but over time these men and women – the so-called Old Women priestesses may have been an important living source of this knowledge – may have developed an interest that led to knowledge for its own sake.

All the strands that make up a scholar's person seem to converge in Lurma(zidi)'s case: an apprentice mentioning his father, displaying his learning (however modestly, see §13.9) in his colophon while at the same time showing off his "medical" training as a student physician, that is, exactly the combination of skills that Mittannamuwa must have had when asked to save the young Hattusili III. The true status of many of these named scribes as scholars rather than scribes may also be the reason why they do not normally turn up among the seal-bearing elite and why we find them towards the end rather than in the beginning of the witness lists of important state documents: the offices mentioned early in this chapter dealt with the more worldly matters of military and civil government whereas the scholars were concerned with those of the mind, which already back then had a relatively limited impact on the daily running of the state.

CHAPTER 14

Excursus
Scribes on Seals? The Hieroglyphic Sign L.326

14.1 Introduction

In the context of the present book the Anatolian hieroglyph that carries the number L.326 in the standard list of signs published in 1960 by Emmanuel Laroche and that we commonly transcribe as (Latin) SCRIBA "scribe" is of potentially great importance. The seal impressions as published by Suzanne Herbordt and Ali and Belkıs Dinçol (see Chapter 11) alone provide us with at least 135 different names of such SCRIBAE living and working in the thirteenth century BC. Because of the overall prominent status of seal owners and the frequent pairing with other titles and qualities scribes have more than once been described as learned people belonging to the highest strata of society. In fact, the sign is the most frequently attested title on seal impressions. For that reason, it was plausibly suggested by modern scholars that all of these persons with their many titles could hardly have been the daily scribes responsible for the festival scenarios, the letters, the laws, and all those other texts that have come down to us. The sign thus came to be regarded as a mark of literacy: in this view many (or even most?) members of the royal elite went through an education that taught them at least basic reading skills that they then proudly displayed on their seals. If so, Hittite high society would be quite unique for its time. Literacy may have been relatively normal among the Old Assyrian merchants and perhaps in other periods in the ancient Near East but never before was it considered so prestigious. Never before did it elicit such showing off of literate capabilities. It seems appropriate, therefore, to review carefully what this interpretation is based on and to propose an alternative explanation.

The Late Bronze Age evidence for the sign L.326 is extensive, albeit somewhat one-sided, for its near-exclusive appearance on seals. In comparison, the material for the Post- or Neo-Hittite period and Iron Age is relatively scarce but more diverse and therefore potentially more telling. In both periods we can distinguish between L.326 by itself () and L.326 with an extended middle straight vertical or "tail" (; henceforth provisionally L.326t if this specific variant is meant). The latter often appears with the slanted so-called *Dorn* (sound value: *ra/i*) attached: L.326t+*RA/I*. In the following I will present the evidence in chronological order.

14.1.1 L.326 in the Hittite Kingdom: Attestations, Problems, and Questions

The sign L.326 is not attested at either Kanesh or Konya-Karahöyük but starts appearing on the seal impressions from Hattusa dated to the mid-seventeenth century BC and then becomes one of the most frequently used symbols of the Hittite kingdom glyptic. Until evidence to the contrary comes to light it can thus be seen as an invention or innovation of the Hattusa-based Old Hittite kingdom. Originally often described as a *Gitterrechteck* ("rectangular lattice frame") in German or *grille* in French, the shape of L.326 is very consistent with a flat top, a straight cross in the center, and an open base. Compare the typical shape of the sign in the center of this Old Hittite kingdom seal impression from Boğazköy (Fig. 14.1).

In 1934, led by the hieroglyphic sign for "throne" L.298 (THRONUS) Piero Meriggi interpreted it as the possible depiction of a seat or throne[1] without a backrest indicating "government" or something equivalent.[2] Without attempting an iconographic interpretation Hans Güterbock thought of a relation to administration or an institution, perhaps the palace.[3] More specifically, Helmuth Bossert saw the sign as the façade of a house with a flat roof, standing for a storeroom and denoting an administrative function.[4] However, in 1956 on the basis of a digraphic cuneiform-hieroglyphic seal impression Emmanuel Laroche proposed the now generally accepted interpretation of "scribe."[5]

When describing the sign Laroche apodictically stated "Le dessin représente une tablette"[6] leaving the reader only the choice between a

[1] Meriggi 1934: 159 ("THRON . . . Unkomplementiert ist das Zeichen auf Siegeln sehr häufig"), 1937: 89 (Nr. 258 THRON), 110 ("trône").

[2] For an example of L.326 with a "backrest" see Dinçol & Dinçol 2008: Tafel 4 no. 36 (in the drawing it is more pronounced than it appears on the photo) who simply identify it as "ein Thron mit Rückenlehne" while mentioning in the commentary (p. 24) another Old Kingdom sealing with the same name (Inara) and the title "SCRIBA"; on chairs in the ancient Near East cf. Symington 1996.

[3] Bittel & Güterbock 1935: 78: "scheint irgendetwas 'Amtliches' zu bezeichnen, sei es einen Beamten, sei es eine Institution; etwa 'Palast'?"

[4] Bossert 1944: 237–44. [5] Laroche 1956a: 147, 1956b: 26–9.

[6] Laroche 1956b: 28; Laroche 1956a: 147 was more careful saying "le dessin conviendrait assez bien à la représentation d'une tablette." Among many others he has been followed by Starke 1990: 463 (adding that it is "zweifellos eine Holztafel"), Symington 1991: 114, Neumann 1992: 29, 1998: 131, Payne 2010a: 183 (showing L.326 with the "tail": "looks like a diptych mounted on a stylus"), Weeden 2011b: 610–1.

Fig. 14.1 Seal impression SBo 1.91 (Güterbock 1940: 70).

clay tablet and a wooden one. This view has never been challenged, it seems, but with its consistently open base and internal cross I do not see how it could depict either.[7] The seal impression, on which Laroche based his identification, is found on a tablet from Ugarit (RS 17.28, Fig. 14.2) dating to the second half of the thirteenth century BC. The document in question deals with the acquisition of a family of servants by the king of Ugarit and one of the witnesses to the sale is a certain Lat-^{d}KUR (Layadagan according to the accompanying hieroglyphic inscription) whom the cuneiform text identifies as the "scribe (^{LÚ}DUB.SAR) of (Mr.) Tilisarrumma," son of the king of Karkamish. His presence is explained by the fact that the family used to be owned by two servants of Tilisarruma. This Lat-^{d}KUR has the seal impressed on the tablet shown in Fig. 14.2.

The seal bears both a three-line (vertical 1–2–3) cuneiform legend and some Anatolian hieroglyphs in the scene depicted between the horizontal guilloche borders. The cuneiform inscription reads: (left 1) $^{\mathrm{NA4}}$KIŠIB (right 2) ^{m}*La-at-*^{d}KUR (3) ZA A.BA "Seal of Lat-^{d}kur, scribe." The writings ZA instead of the usual LÚ ("man, male") and A.BA for the more familiar DUB.SAR ("scribe") are rare and A.BA is a learned late Sumerian logographic

[7] See already van den Hout 2009–2011b: 275.

1 3 2

Fig. 14.2 Seal impression on RS 17.28 (from Schaeffer 1956: 51).

combination that is not attested at Hattusa thus far (see Chapter 13).[8] The scene framed in between $^{\text{NA4}}$KIŠIB and the rest of the inscription shows the Hittite Sun God on the left holding the VITA (*ankh*) sign (☥) on his outstretched hand and the winged sun disk hovering over his head. He faces the familiar bow-shouldering figure in soldierly attire. In front of the latter, from top to bottom, are hieroglyphs spelling out his name *La-ia-tà-ka*. In front of the Sun God, beneath his outstretched arm we recognize the combination L.326-*la*. It is repeated behind the Sun God topped by the triangle read as BONUS. In the bottom left-hand corner, one sees a bird.

In search of a hieroglyphic counterpart for the cuneiform ZA A.BA there are in principle three candidates: BONUS, the bird, and the combination L.326-*la* that Laroche decided on. A variant of the bird glyph is often taken as standing for the profession of augur or diviner.[9] With its complement -*la* the sign L.326 is likely to designate some kind of agent noun, which makes the equation with the A.BA of the cuneiform legend and the DUB.SAR of the witness list at least more attractive than linking it to BONUS. The fact, however, that neither BONUS nor the bird find an obvious match in the

[8] On A.BA at Ugarit see Roche-Hawley & Hawley 2013: 249–50 n. 30.

[9] Herbordt 2005: 97–8, and Hawkins apud Herbordt 2005: 302 (AVIS$_3$+MAGNUS = GAL LÚ.MEŠ.MUŠEN.DÙ?).

cuneiform means that we do not *a priori* have to look for one with L.326-*la* either. As we will see below, other evidence from Ugarit and Emar provides a confusing picture and makes the equation much less compelling.

What is the chronology of the evidence? Recently Mark Weeden has proposed a development of glyptic styles and of the role of hieroglyphic signs on seals before the thirteenth century BC that is based on archaeological evidence rather than stylistic comparisons.[10] According to this improved chronology, the first seals and sealings would date to the late seventeenth and early sixteenth century (1630–1580 BC) with the earliest attestations of L.326 appearing on sealings in Boğazköy from archaeological level *Unterstadt* 3 (Lower City 3) datable to the sixteenth and fifteenth century. They are found alongside the signs that are taken as wishing prosperity (VITA) and wellbeing (BONUS) for the seal owner. As pointed out by Weeden, it is "difficult" to see what a profession like scribe is doing in this company and he suggests that at this moment the symbol rather denotes "something auspicious" like the other ones.[11] A good example is the following impression accompanied by the so-called *signe royal* (center top) and the VITA symbol (left, Fig. 14.3):

Fig. 14.3 Seal impression from Lower City 3 (USt. 3), Beran 1967: 29 (no. 125) w. Pl.10. (drawing from Boehmer & Güterbock 1987: 53 Abb. 38; copyright Archive of the Boğazköy Expedition, Deutsches Archäologisches Institut Berlin).

[10] Weeden 2018; for earlier attempts see Boehmer & Güterbock 1987 and Herbordt 2005: 45–51.
[11] Weeden 2018: 52 n. 1, see also 59.

The emergence of L.326 in the Old Kingdom might be taken to underscore the prestige of the recently, that is, around 1650–1600 BC, acquired writing technique spreading top-down through the ranks of the ruling class. On the other hand, as we saw in Chapters 4 and 5, the volume of writing for these early days of the kingdom seems to have been quite low. Scribes do not appear by name in the written record until about a century later, that is, around 1525 in the reign of Telipinu or his immediate predecessor. From that period may stem the anonymous *tabarna*-impression (see Fig. 14.1) used to seal a jar.[12] It has the usual structure of such seals with a double cuneiform ring (outer ring: ⸢NA$_4$⸣[KIŠIB *t*]*a*-⸢*ba*⸣[-*ar-na* LUGA]L.⸢GAL⸣, inner ring: *ša* ⸢*uš*⸣-*pa-aḫ-ḫu* BA.ÚŠ "S[eal of t]aba[rna], Great [Kin]g; he who violates/changes it dies"). However, where other such seals on the charters have a rosette or a combination of symbols in the center (rosette, VITA, BONUS), this one shows L.326 only. Onofrio Carruba suggested seeing this and two other *tabarna*-seals (one with the "shepherd" sign and the other with simply BONUS) as "Palastsiegel," that is, as a kind of stamp used by the king's officials to "sign" or seal on his behalf.[13]

If L.326 indicates a profession, as has been assumed thus far, why does it occur several times on Old Hittite kingdom seals from *Unterstadt* 3 while other possible titles on sealings from most of that period are relatively rare and often uncertain in their interpretation?[14] In stark contrast, during the thirteenth century L.326 appears so often and with persons of such high rank, already holding multiple offices, that it has been claimed, as we saw, that it was used to boast a degree of literacy rather than stating a profession.[15] And, as has been correctly observed, if it is a profession, how do we then distinguish in this period between a real scribe and a proudly literate person?[16] Seal owners of the Empire Period even go so far in their alleged pride that L.326 becomes a decorative element, filling entire outer rings either on its own or in combination with other elements.[17] As Suzanne

[12] SBo 1.91 = Beran 1967: no. 148.

[13] Carruba 1993: 75, 84; similarly, already Bossert 1944: 241.

[14] Cf. SBo 1.90 = Beran 1967: no. 149 and Beran 1967: no. 126 for PASTOR (in spite of the Latin "shepherd" probably a military title), Beran 1967: no. 134 and Dinçol & Dinçol 2008: no. 10 for URCEUS (cupbearer?), Dinçol & Dinçol 2008: nos. 16 and 25 for HASTARIUS (bodyguard).

[15] For literacy as part of the general skill set of higher officials see Hagenbuchner 1989a: 12, Bryce 2002: 57, Herbordt 2005: 91, 98, van den Hout 2009-2011b: 276; cf. however Weeden 2011b: 606 who seems to take all of them as scribes.

[16] Marizza 2007: 168–9.

[17] cf. SBo 2: nos. 144, 204, 231, Herbordt 2005: nos. 43, 68, 84, 178, 212, 226, 230, 368, 379, 382, 415, 417, 421, 447, 476, 529, 545, 548, 566, 569, 629, 644, 649, 676, 685, 696, 755, 776 (cf. also 775), Dinçol & Dinçol 2008: nos. 78, 156, 205, 206, 314, 318, 337.

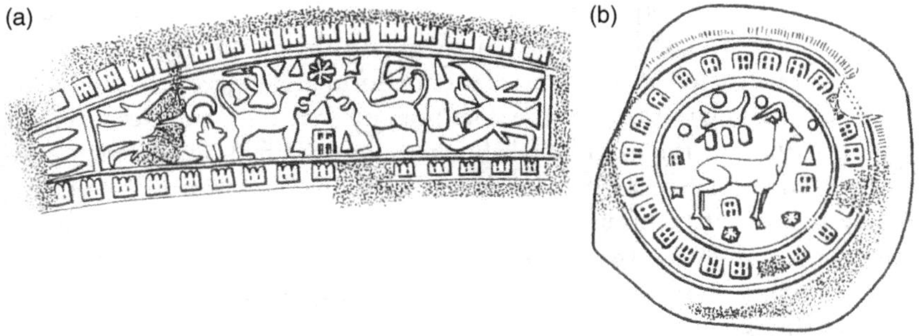

Fig. 14.4a Seal ring impression of Sauskawalwi (Herbordt 2005: Pl. 30 No. 382b, copyright Archive of the Boğazköy Expedition of Deutsches Archäologisches Institut Berlin).
Fig. 14.4b Seal ring impression of Tuwarsa (Herbordt 2005: Pl. 37 No. 476b).

Herbordt observes, the most elaborate and most beautiful impressions from seal rings are those of the alleged scribes.[18] Compare, for instance, the seals of Sauskawalwi (Fig. 14.4a) and Tuwarsa (Fig. 14.4b).[19]

The antithetically arranged design on the signet ring shows at the far ends the double-headed eagle, symbol of power, Sauskawalwi's name consisting of the facing lions and the caprid heads above them, and down the very center from top to bottom a rosette, a triangle (BONUS) and L.326. Right behind the lion on the left there may be the title(?) L.414-DOMINUS+*MI*(?).[20] The sign L.326 then runs along the upper and lower borders of the ring. L.326 is the only "title" ever used in this manner.

How normal is this alleged pride in being literate? In most ancient, medieval, and pre-modern societies literacy was regarded as a craft, just like pottery making or beer brewing. If you need a vase you go to a potter, if you need a written document you hire a scribe.[21] Bureaucratic officials typically belonged to the middle class wedged inbetween the elite on one side and the poor and the peasants on the other.[22] That everybody should be literate, and that illiteracy is something one should be ashamed of, is a modern notion. As a state, the Hittite kingdom adopted writing out of expediency and prestige; every state of importance around them used the technique, so they ultimately had to acquire it as well but that does not mean that every individual needed to be literate.[23] Out of over 400 different names/individuals, overwhelmingly dating to the thirteenth

18 Herbordt 2005: 110. 19 = Herbordt 2005: nr. 382. 20 Herbordt 2005: 105.
21 Ong 1982: 93. 22 Lenski 1966: 62–3, 80.
23 Ong 1982: 93, McKitterick 1989: 28, Woolf 2009: 47.

century BC, in the corpora of seal impressions edited by Herbordt[24] and Dinçol&Dinçol,[25] 135 have L.326 engraved on their seals but only eleven names can be matched with one of a cuneiform scribe (see Chapter 13.5). Moreover, having the same name does not automatically mean that we are dealing with the same individual. For many of the seal owners we know from the cuneiform texts that they belonged to the highest strata of Hittite society and they were often directly or indirectly related to the royal house. Since most scribes, on the other hand, were regarded as craftsmen[26], one wonders why so many high officials wanted that symbol so ubiquitously on their "business card." And, finally, if all these powerful individuals wanted to show off their literate capabilities and literacy was so prestigious, why did not any of the kings use it?[27]

It is also difficult to understand why seal impressions with L.326 are relatively rare outside Hattusa, especially at places where writing is amply attested (e.g., Emar, Ugarit) or where writing is thus far absent or scarcely attested (e.g., Kaman-Kalehöyük[28]). At Emar, the north Syrian Hittite satellite state, on a corpus of 205 documents with seal impressions using Anatolian hieroglyphs, nineteen sealings (for all details see Table 14.2 at the end of this chapter) bear an imprint of L.326, i.e., in just over 9 percent of the total as opposed to the 33 percent in the Hattusa corpora of sealings as edited by Herbordt and Dinçol & Dinçol. In most of the Emar tablets the names of the seal owners are repeated in cuneiform at the end of the text. In general, seal owners and witnesses are identified by filiation ("PN_1, son of PN_2") rather than title. When given, the most common titles are those of priest, diviner, and scribe. The scribe's name often comes at the end after the list of witnesses and was probably the one who indeed wrote the tablet. Out of the nineteen sealings impressed on the tablets with L.326, there are only two where the cuneiform mentions the same individual as scribe (LÚ.DUB.SAR). On A102 (attested on a single document) the seal identifies its owner as *Ta-i(a)* L.326 while the cuneiform has ^{m}*Ta ʾe* LÚ.DUB.SAR; on AuOrS1 ME 77 (likewise attested only here) the hieroglyphs spell *A-pi*$^?$*-u*, the cuneiform text lists at the end an *Abiu* LÚ.DUB.SAR, and within the document we find ^{m}*Abiu ilṭur* "Abiu did the writing." The latter seems to be unique. Only two other instances of such an explicit statement are

24 Herbordt 2005. 25 Dinçol & Dinçol 2008. 26 See Chapter 13.

27 For the alleged example of a Hittite king calling himself "scribe" in the Hieroglyphic inscription BOĞAZKÖY 4 see most recently Peker 2014 and Marazzi 2016b.

28 As correctly observed by Weeden 2011b: 611, on Kaman-Kalehöyük see also Weeden 2018: 69; cf. also the seal found at Troy (Hawkins 1996), the one from the plain of Antioch (Dinçol, Dinçol & Peker 2012: 195 w. Fig. 8a–b) and the BHS 5 sealing from Büklükale (Weeden 2016a: 98–9).

known to me. In both cases two scribes are mentioned in the same document: in one (Emar VI no. 127: 19–20), one of the two scribes is expressly identified as *ša tuppa ilṭuru* "the one who did the writing" while the other tablet (Emar VI 201: 51–53) is described as the joint product of the two scribes. The remarks therefore serve to take away any confusion as to who the actual tablet writer was. Abiu on the other hand, is the only scribe mentioned on the tablet he wrote, and the statement must have had a different purpose: it sounds as if it was a special occasion.

All three documents that bear the sealing A33 list Kapidagan as either diviner (LÚ.ḪAL) or diviner's son (DUMU ḪAL) in cuneiform while his hieroglyphic seal has him as both priest-diviner (SACERDOS) and L.326. The latter is not reflected, it seems, in the cuneiform. A Kapidagan, scribe (LÚ.DUB.SAR l. 21), is mentioned in the cuneiform text that carries the impression C14 but the hieroglyphic sealing with L.326 is for Lala who carries no title (l. 23) in the text; the identity of Kapidagan with only L.326 on his sealing B56 remains unclear because the text seems to be unpublished. B54 has an illegible name in hieroglyphs of an individual accompanied by L.326. The cuneiform mentions nobody as scribe, but we do encounter among the witnesses a certain Zulanna, Chief Scribe (GAL.LÚ.MEŠ.DUB.SAR), whose name is unlikely, however, to be read in the hieroglyphic impression and whose cuneiform seal does not mention his status.[29]

From Ugarit (for details see Table 14.3 at the end of this chapter) we have forty-eight seal impressions with Anatolian hieroglyphs[30] on tablets, four of which show L.326, that is, just over 8 percent. However, it needs to be pointed out that twenty of these are royal seals either from Hattusa or Karkamish that, as I already observed, never have the sign. RS 17.251 records the extradition(?) of a man, "son of the mighty one" (*ḫaštanuri*) to the prefect of Ugarit by two princes, Takisarruma and Tulpisarruma, the former of which has impressed his seal on the tablet. Several witnesses are listed, among whom an interpreter, and at the very end we find the scribe Burqanu who drew up the document but is not identified as witness nor did he impress his seal on the tablet.[31] Yet it is Takisarruma who has L.326 on his seal: he is known from cuneiform sources at Hattusa as a prince, not as scribe.[32] The impression one gets is that Takisarruma and

[29] Similarly, A71 has no hieroglyphic but a cuneiform seal for Madidagan (*ma-dì-*^{d}KUR) without title whereas in the text he is LÚ.GAL.DUB.SAR.MEŠ (l. 19).
[30] As collected by Mora 1987.
[31] Similarly, e.g., RS 17.319 (PRU 4, 184), RS 18.02 (PRU 4, 201), RS 18.20 + 17.371 (PRU 4, 203), RS 17.112? (PRU 4, 234), RS 17.248 (PRU 4, 236).
[32] van den Hout 1995: 132–6.

Tulpisarruma represent the central Hittite authority. Another text, RS 17.109, is one of the very few Hittite language documents from Ugarit concerning a debt involving Hittite officials, among them a judicial officer, Naninzi,[33] who is known from Hattusa in that same function. The seal, if correctly read, identifies him as such, and as L.326. One Hattusa cuneiform text has him as LÚ DUB.SAR.MEŠ but he was almost certainly no simple scribal craftsman (see Chapter 13.7). RS 17.28 has the seal of Layadagan that Laroche used to prove his identification L.326 = SCRIBA (see Fig. 14.2). At the same time, we have RS 17.231 where a certain Taprammi has L.326, PITHOS.VIR.DOMINUS (a leading economic–administrative(?) position of some sort)[34], and EUNUCHUS on his seal. Only the last qualification matches "palace courtier" (LÚ *ŠA RE-ŠI* É.GAL-*LIM*, l. 16) of the cuneiform text.[35] This is the same Taprammi who impressed his seal on the tablet KUB 25.32 discussed in Chapter 12.6.

All in all, the evidence from Emar and Ugarit is confusing and discouraging. We have a total of twenty-three attestations of L.326 on seals, on twenty-eight different texts. In eleven cases, L.326 has no possible title to match in the cuneiform text; in three cases the tablet is too fragmentary to know; three tablets from Emar still seem to be unpublished; in three cases we have a possible match of L.326 and DUB.SAR on the tablet (Emar A102, AuOrS 1 ME 77; Ugarit RS 17.28); in four cases we have L.326 and another cuneiform title (A32 DUMU ḪAL, 33 LÚ.ḪAL/DUMU ḪAL, ETBLM 12 LÚ.ḪAL, RS 17.231 LÚ *ŠA RE-ŠI* É.GAL-*LIM*). Moreover, in A33, RS 17.28, and RS 17.231, the seal shows not only L.326 but also other titles such as priest-diviner (A33: SACERDOS), augur (RS 17.28: AVIS), courtier as well as PITHOS.VIR.DOMINUS (both RS 17.231). To this we can add the observation that within the same material sometimes chief and simple scribes are mentioned in the cuneiform text (B54, RS 17.251) either without a seal (Burqanu RS 17.251) or without mention of it in their seal (Zulanna B54). The evidence from Emar and Ugarit thus hardly suffices to justify an equation L.326 = SCRIBA.

Returning to Hattusa, some more problems crop up. One concerns the hieroglyphic title MAGNUS.L.326 ("MAGNUS.SCRIBA") commonly interpreted as chief scribe. As we have seen in Chapter 13.8, according to the cuneiform sources there was in the thirteenth century BC only a single individual holding that function and title at any one time. We have the names of most chief scribes seamlessly, it seems, following one another over the course of that century but the hieroglyphic sources provide us with

[33] For the reading cf. Singer 1999b.

[34] Hawkins 2002: 225, apud Herbordt 2005: 305–6, Mora 2016: 227–8.

[35] Hawkins 2002.

thirteen more names[36] that are difficult to fit in even if we expand the designation to stand for chief wood-scribe as well. Moreover, none of the thirteen names include the actual chief scribes or chief wood-scribes known from the cuneiform record. The only overlap between cuneiform chief scribes and MAGNUS.326-*la* is a spearhead with Walwazidi's name and this qualification on it.[37] Also, no female scribes are attested in the cuneiform sources. Yet among the seal-bearing women there is probably one, Lara, who identifies herself as L.326.[38] Finally, there is the problem of the several graffiti from Hattusa's temples that show a combination of names and 326 that we already discussed in Chapters 9.4 and 10.11. If L.326 does not mean "scribe" but instead expresses some affiliation with the palace or the government, the graffiti writers proudly display their status as government officials and representatives. Whether the graffiti on the temple walls in Hattusa marked the spots where they held their "office hours" is up for speculation.

With the spearhead just mentioned carrying L.326 we have already segued into the non-glyptic evidence. The most interesting piece is a sickle blade found at Hattusa (Fig. 14.5).[39] If the person who owned the blade intended to mark it as his property, inscribing it with the most frequently attested title only, cannot have been very helpful. But if following the original interpretation of Meriggi and Güterbock the object had to be marked as official state or government-issued property – just as the spearhead found in Anitta's palace saying: "Palace of Anitta" (and not simply "Anitta") – this was a highly efficient way of doing so. After having accepted Laroche's interpretation of L.326 as "scribe" Meriggi recognized this problem and suggested it was not a personal mark but could have developed out of "tablet" to "royal chancellery" and by extension meant "official, of the palace," recalling Güterbock's earlier interpretation of the sign but arriving at it in a new way.[40] In addition, there are a few other instances: a small (< 2 cm) bead-like serpentine stone,[41] four so-called pre-firing pot marks, all from Boğazköy/Hattusa,[42] and a sherd "of a

36 Marizza 2010: 34. Marizza 2010: 39 correctly, in my opinion, assigns the three additional Chief Scribes Madi-Dagan, Masamuwa and Zulanna to the court of Karkamish.

37 van den Hout 1995: 174 w. lit.; other seals for Walwazidi (see ibid., to which should be added Dinçol & Dinçol 2008: 55 (no. 260)) either do not have L.326 or do not have it preserved.

38 Herbordt 2005: no. 203, see also Payne 2015: 138; Herbordt 2005: 104–5, counts forty-nine seal impressions of women, which comes to 4 percent of all sealings in her corpus of non-royal seals; see also Mora 2012: 63.

39 Bittel 1937: 21 w. Abb. 9, Tf. 13.1.

40 Meriggi 1975: 290; see also Bossert 1944: 243.

41 Boehmer 1979: 62 (no. 3842) w. Pl. 38 (I am grateful to Willemijn Waal for alerting me to these pieces).

42 See the table of signs in Glatz 2012: 7 Fig. 2 (Type 15).

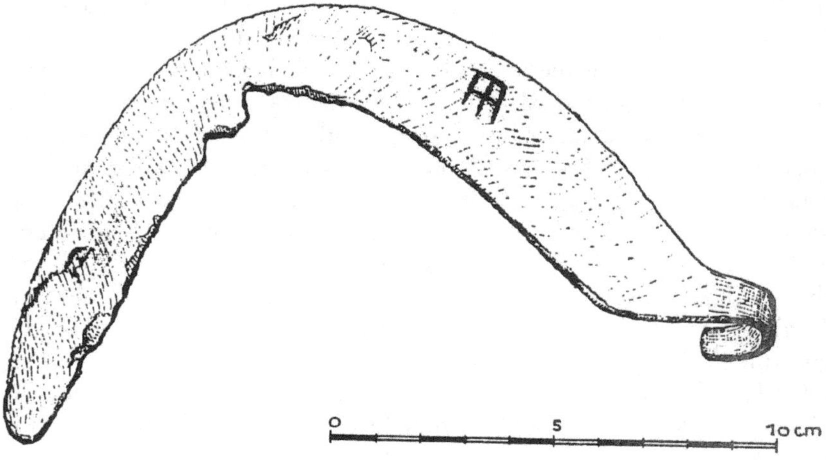

Fig. 14.5 Sickle blade found at Hattusa (from Bittel 1937: Abb. 9; copyright Archive of the Boğazköy Expedition, Deutsches Archäologisches Institut Berlin).

dish (or fruit stand) . . . with a deep red burnished wash inside and out" from western Anatolia (Çivril Höyük).[43] If the four pot marks from Hattusa really were L.326 (SCRIBA) then it would make very little sense and the absence of any other titles on pots would be surprising. A meaning "made for the government (and thus government property)," analogous to the sickle, would be easier to understand. However, as convincingly argued in her fundamental study on pot marks, Claudia Glatz describes them as "devices used by independent potters to distinguish their work from colleagues at a stage of production requiring the use of communal facilities."[44] She correctly dismisses "any overhasty assignment of highly hypothetical functions or meanings on the basis of a generic resemblance to hieroglyphic or other signs."[45] The few similarities with Anatolian hieroglyphs are in all likelihood coincidental.[46] Whether this is also true for the sickle remains to be seen.[47]

[43] Oreshko 2013: 371–73; Oreshko takes this as suggesting "the idea that there existed a class of scribes in west Anatolian society" (and 372). Similar graffiti from the same general area (without L.326) he attributes to "persons of the highest rank." For the description of the sherd see Lloyd & Mellaart 1955: 80.

[44] Glatz 2012: 34. [45] Glatz 2012: 25–9 (quote from p. 26).

[46] A glance at Glatz's Table 7 (Glatz 2012: 29) shows that, for instance, the identification of the alleged sign for king (Type 10: REX %) is weak.

[47] Glatz 2012: 33 briefly discusses "marks on other media" (and mentions the sickle and the bead).

Two of the oldest datable Late Bronze Age non-glyptic attestations come from Aleppo. The stone inscription known as ALEPPO 1 dates to the reign of Mursili II or Muwatalli II (ca. 1300 BC) and mentions a certain *A-ki-*TESSUB*-pa i-tu-wa/i*(URBS) L.326 at the very end of the text. This Akitessub has been taken as the scribe responsible for the inscription, that is, either as the person who composed it and perhaps made the original drawing or even as the stonemason who executed the actual inscription.[48] Such "scribal signatures" or "colophons," as they are sometimes called, are otherwise extremely rare in the ancient world on publicly displayed inscriptions. Indeed, it would seem rather improper for a regular scribe, let alone a stonemason, to draw such visible and prominent attention to himself on a royal monument. As we have seen in Chapter 13, scribal craftsmen usually did not even sign their tablets unless they belonged to the upper strata of Hittite society and worked as scholars rather than tablet writers. One of the rare exceptions to the general anonymous authorship is the statue of Idrimi, king of Alalah in the fifteenth century BC. It has the form of a first-person autobiography with an added third-person statement by a scribe named Sarruwe claiming to have inscribed the text. What we are seeing here is a learned scribe "certainly well established in the higher echelons of the palace bureaucracy" claiming authorship of a memorial for the recently deceased Idrimi,[49] a historical account "very much like a fairy tale"[50] crafted by a high-ranking court official. We will revisit these signatures below when discussing the first-millennium evidence.

In terms of post-Hittite but still second-millennium evidence, I mention here the inscription in the Temple of the Stormgod at Aleppo (ALEPPO 7) dated to the eleventh century BC. It has L.326 twice in very fragmentary context but it shows a *-la* extension and the determinative VIR_2: (VIR_2)L.326*-la-sa* (§§6 and 13). As David Hawkins observes, neither of the two occurrences fits a scribe particularly well: "these clauses do not suggest a usual context for such an inscription."[51] The later Iron Age

48 For the latter position see Gordin 2010: 160, for the former Meriggi 1975: 331.

49 Sasson 1981; Sasson's originally preferred view of the inscription on the statue of Idrimi as a monument erected in the last days of Alalah IB of around 1250 BC, some two centuries after the protagonist, meant to promote "an awareness of Alalah's glorious past" can now be ruled out on chronological grounds, for which see Fink 2007; for the composition as a whole and a discussion of its *Forschungsgeschichte* see von Dassow 2008: 23–45 (I am grateful to my colleague Hervé Reculeau for the references to Fink and von Dassow).

50 von Dassow 2008: 26, on Sarruwe see 31–3; von Dassow also notes that "it is very unusual for the scribe . . . to be named as author."

51 Hawkins 2011b: 50.

material on stone dates in general to the period between the 900 and 700 BC and will be discussed below.[52]

14.1.2 L.326t in the Hittite Kingdom

Finally, we have to consider three occurrences of L.326t with its extended middle vertical or "tail," generally considered a variant of L.326, although quite different in its Bronze Age appearance. The oldest second-millennium attestations for this sign come again from glyptic and non-glyptic material. First, in combination with the "god" sign (DEUS.L.326t), L.326t appears on the KINIK bowl (thirteenth century BC) with its hunting scenes, and the brief inscription ("Taprammi, the [title] and courtier, placed (= dedicated?) this bowl to DEUS.L.326t") in all likelihood indicates the dedicatee (Fig. 14.6)[53].

Expecting a relation between the inscription and the iconography the god in question is likely to have been associated with hunting and game.[54] Secondly, there is a seal from Tarsus, which according to Laroche is to be read *a+ra/i*?-L.326 (Fig. 14.7)[55].

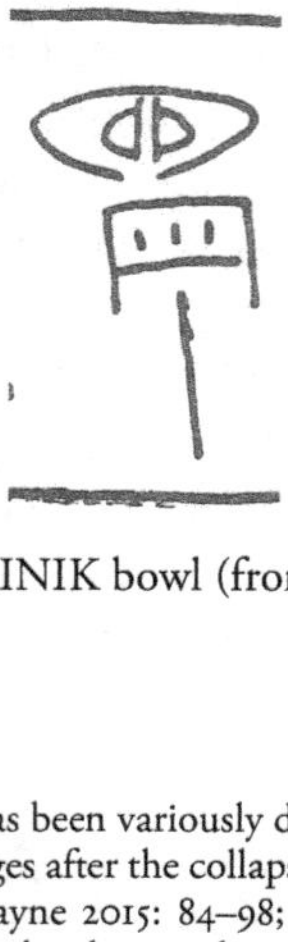

Fig. 14.6 DEUS.L.326t on KINIK bowl (from Hawkins 1993: 715 Fig. 1).

[52] The date of the ANKARA silver bowl has been variously disputed with tentative dates ranging from the fifteenth century BC to the Dark Ages after the collapse of the Hittite kingdom; for an overview of lit. and a detailed discussion see Payne 2015: 84–98; Payne advocates a dating to the twelfth century BC. I will assume a post-Hittite date here and return to it in the next section (§14.2) as well.

[53] *zi/a* CAELUM-*pi* DEUS.L.326t BONUS$_2$.VIR$_2$ EUNUCHUS LEPUS+*RA/I-mi* BONUS$_2$.VIR$_2$ EUNUCHUS PONERE, ed. by Hawkins 1993 and 2006: 50; for the dating see also Schachner 2012: 137 n. 16. This translation here, following Hawkins, assumes an, admittedly, imperfect attempt by the engraver to create a symmetrical and antithetical arrangement of name and titles.

[54] For a possible explanation see footnote 94.

[55] Laroche 1958: 255 (where "G 105" = L.326); for other reading suggestions see Gelb apud Goldman 1956: 249 ("*A+ze*?"-), Mora 1987: 305 (XIIb 1.16; "*Á+ra/í*? (o *Ma+ra/í*?)")) w. lit.

Fig. 14.7 Seal from Tarsus (from Goldman 1956:Pl. 402 [photo], 406 [drawing]).

Third, dated after the fall of the Hittite kingdom but still in the second millennium (twelfth century BC) we have the inscription KARAHÖYÜK §19[56] with L.326t(-)*tà-ha* (or in Hawkins' transliteration SCRIBA(-) CAPERE-*ha*). As Hawkins comments, a writing-related meaning, as proposed by Starke for the KARKAMISH passages "has no obvious appropriateness here."[57] The non-glyptic occurrences for L.326 and L.326t thus do not lend any significant support to the scribal hypothesis.

Summing up, neither iconographically nor contextually does the Ugarit seal impression adduced by Laroche present compelling evidence for L.326 = SCRIBA. In general, the material from Hattusa, Emar, and Ugarit does not support his claim. The early appearance of L.326 from the capital Hattusa is not easily reconcilable with the evidence for the development of writing and literacy in the Old Kingdom. The popularity of the sign in the Empire Period is difficult to explain in view of general notions of literacy in ancient

[56] Hawkins 2000: 290, Pl. 133–4.

[57] Hawkins 2000: 294; differently van Quickelberghe 2013: 256 ("j'ai placé un scribe dans le sanctuaire (de la stèle)").

societies. Why did kings not use the sign if literacy was such a desirable asset and why does it appear as a decorative device unlike all other titles? Why do we encounter it so rarely outside Hattusa, even in places where we know a lively administration (Emar, Ugarit) existed? The individuals allegedly to be identified as chief scribes (MAGNUS.SCRIBA) on sealings from Hattusa cannot be fitted in the list of these officials from the cuneiform sources. And, finally, the non-glyptic evidence for the most part does not support the equation L.326 = SCRIBA either.

14.2 An Alternative Hypothesis

Given the above questions and uncertainties surrounding the second-millennium attestations we are allowed to think in a different direction, and we should do so before considering the later Iron Age use of the sign. I think Piero Meriggi and Hans Güterbock were closer to the original meaning when they suggested notions like "government" or "palace." Especially Meriggi's original idea of a seat or throne explains the shape of the sign much better. Except for the backrest the hieroglyph L.298 interpreted then and now as "throne" (THRONUS) is identical to L.326. It is one of a few signs depicting seats (Fig. 14.8) and can, moreover, be matched with similar renderings in reliefs and other media (Figs. 14.9–10).[58]

The variant without the backrest is attested as a seat or chair a few times in wider ancient Near Eastern iconography[59] and also in Anatolia itself. Compare the so-called Dresden seal (Fig. 14.9)[60].

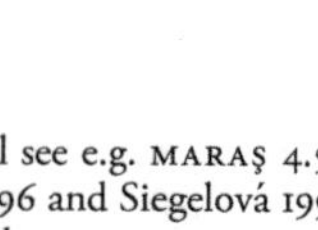

Fig. 14.8 Anatolian hieroglyphic signs depicting thrones (L.298 and 294, respectively).

[58] For L.298 without the middle vertical see e.g. MARAŞ 4.5 (Hawkins 2000: Pl. 109); for Anatolian furniture in general see Symington 1996 and Siegelová 1993–1997b.

[59] Salonen 1963, Pl. XXIII 1j and XXV 4b.

[60] The same seat or a very similar one is known from Kültepe 2 and 1b: see Özgüç 1965: Pl. XVIII no. 55, and Özgüç & Tunca 2001: Pls. 22 (CS 123), 26 (CS 154).

Fig. 14.9 Dresden seal (Boehmer & Güterbock 1987: no. 151 Pl. XVI; copyright Archive of the Boğazköy Expedition, Deutsches Archäologisches Institut Berlin) with L.326 – seat at 11 o'clock.

For the type of seat seen in the KINIK bowl (see Fig. 14.6) compare the Hittite seal (Fig. 14.10)[61].

The idea could be the throne as symbol of kingship and seat of government or that sitting on a chair or stool, especially in the king's presence, was a privilege of the ruling elite. While the seat with the backrest may have been the actual throne, the one without, as depicted in L.326, could have been for others who were allowed to sit in the king's company. That this was important and only permitted to certain persons is clear from documents as old as the Anitta text ("in my presence, he (i.e., the ruler of Purushanda) will sit down on my right"[62]), the Sunassura Treaty from the period of Tuthaliya I ("As soon as he (i.e., Sunassura) comes before His Majesty, the noblemen of His Majesty <will rise> from their seats. No one will remain seated above him"[63]) all the way to the reign of Mursili II ("They will not make Piyassili rise from his seat in His Majesty's presence"[64]). Compare also passages such as:

[61] See also the seat on which the gold woman/goddess at the Metropolitan Museum is sitting in Muscarella 1974: no. 125.

[62] *ap*[(*āš= a*)] *pēram= mit kunnaz ešari* KBo 3.22: 78–79 (CTH 1, OS), ed. by Neu 1974: 14–5 w. dupl. KUB 36.98b rev. 6.

[63] Tr. Beckman 1999: 19; for these texts as indications of protocol at the Hittite court see Bilgin 2018: 413–4. See also the passage from the Festival of Thunder edited by Goedegebuure 2017.

[64] [^{m}*Piyaššilin= ma= k*]*an* [ANA PĀNI ^{d}U] TU-ŠI *lē parkiyanuanzi* KBo 1.28 rev. 2–4 (CTH 57, NS), ed. by Starke 1996: 141 n. 5, CHD P 160, tr. Beckman 1999: 169.

Fig. 14.10 Hittite seal (Boehmer & Güterbock 1987: 48 Abb. 30 c; copyright Archive of the Boğazköy Expedition, Deutsches Archäologisches Institut Berlin) with seat at 12 o'clock.

> As to the brothers of the king who used to sit down in the pres[ence of the father of the k]ing . . . These were his favorite sons.[65]
>
> When the king (and) queen sit in the great assembly and then the Stormgod thunders, they make the princes, princesses, grandees (and) distinguished visitors, who are seated in the presence of the king, stand.[66]

With the additional specification "on my right," the earliest attestation, the Anitta text, shows that the Akkadian phrase (*ANA*) *PĀNI* or Hittite *peran* does not literally mean "before," as in "across from" or "in front of," but "in the presence of."[67] Standing or sitting in royal company – and in what order[68] – said something of one's status in the royal court and one's relation to the king and queen. Therefore, anybody authorized to include that symbol in his or her seal, having it next to their name on an inscription, or handling an object showing L.326 (think of the sickle blade) would identify

[65] *AḪI* LUGAL *ANA P*[*ĀNI ABI* L]UGAL *kuiēš ēškanta* . . . *kī kardiy*[*aš=ša*]*š* DUMU.MEŠ *ešer* KBo 3.34 iii 15, 17 (CTH 8, NS), ed. by Dardano 2006: 58–9.

[66] *mān šallai ašešni* [LU]GAL MUNUS.LUGAL *ašanzi* EGIR-*ann=a* [d]IM-*aš titḫa nu* DUMU.MEŠ LUGAL DUMU.MUNUS.MEŠ LUGAL LÚ.MEŠ DUGUD-*TIM* LÚ.MEŠ *UBARUTIM PĀNI* LUGAL *kuiēš ašanzi n=uš arnuanzi* KBo 34.185 +KBo 20.61 i 1–4 (CTH 631, OS), ed. by Goedegebuure 2017: 105.

[67] Cf. the CHD P s.v. *peran* meaning 2.

[68] Bilgin 2018: 418–9.

themselves as persons of or affiliated with power. In short, the symbol of the chair or stool carried great prestige. In the three instances where we found a match between L.326 and DUB.SAR in Emar we are likely dealing with important officials claiming an affiliation with the central court in Hattusa. There, too, we encounter (Chapter 13.7) some elite scribes. As a Latin transcription one might think of SELLA, as in the Roman *sella curulis*. This stool, identical in shape to the cross-legged folding chair known from the ancient Near East and once the prerogative and symbol of the important office of the *aedilis curulis* in Republican Rome, even became a symbol of the emperor's judicial power in the Roman Empire.[69] Also in other cultures, seating arrangements are often an essential aspect of court protocol.[70]

This interpretation goes well with Carruba's *Palastsiegel* as a description of the anonymous *tabarna*-seal with L.326 in the center used by a lower ranking official on behalf of the king. Just putting a profession in the center of the seal without a name makes much less sense than marking it as a government stamp of approval. A relation with the palace is also something that individuals can be expected to want to show off either by multiple use in the center of their seal or as a decoration surrounding it. It also explains why no king ever uses the sign: if meaning something like "palace" or "government" this would be tautological on a royal seal with the name and title of the king already spelled out. Kings are not affiliated with the royal house, they *are* the royal house. They use the hieroglyph REX (), the others have L.326. All Ugarit examples make sense: Layadagan (RS 17.28), Taprammi (RS 17.231), Takisarruma (RS 17.251), and Naninzi (RS 17.109) act as representatives of the central authority. Except for Layadagan all are known directly from the Hattusa sources while Layadagan acts on behalf of a prince from Karkamish. As we have seen (Chapter 13.13), the latter probably was no ordinary scribe but rather a local scholar at the Karkamish court. It is then understandable that different professionals could act as government representatives whether diviners, courtiers, economic officials, jurists, scholars, or scribes. These important men were not likely to share a title with a group of middle-class scribal craftsmen. Rather L.326 was a prestigious status coming, moreover, in several varieties: regular, MAGNUS, and with markings that look like "one" through "four." Their seal showed their elevated rank wherever they traveled.

69 Alföldi 1970: 140–1 (I am most grateful to my colleague Clifford Ando for the reference).
70 For the Ottoman court see Karateke 2007, esp. 11–4.

In the end, there remains the question of the actual Anatolian second-millennium reading behind SELLA. The individuals who claimed L.326 on their seals should be high-ranking or even the highest-ranking officials of the kingdom. Usually, they are hidden behind Sumerographic titles starting with GAL, UGULA, or EN, or Akkadographic ones like *BĒLUM*. In most cases these persons are heads of units, like "chief of the bodyguards, chief scribe" etc. From a semantic point of view, Hittite *šalli-* "great" and perhaps *ḫantezzi(ya)-* "foremost" come into consideration for these terms, used either as an adjective ("chief scribe") or as a noun ("chief of the bodyguards"). When used as an adjective, GAL sometimes shows an *i*-stem extension (e.g., GAL-*iš/in*), fitting both an underlying *šalli-* or *ḫantezzi-*. For EN/*BĒLUM* we assume the Hittite noun *išḫa-* as the underlying reading. The hieroglyphic title for these unit heads is the sign we transliterate as MAGNUS. But besides the unit heads and chiefs there is also the group of LÚ.MEŠ GAL(.GAL) "grandees." They were the officials who sat down in Tuthaliya I's presence but had to rise when Sunassura entered the audience hall. They were the ones who Suppiluliuma I convened when confronted with the message from the Pharaoh's widow asking for a Hittite prince to marry her. They may also have been the members that made up the *panku*, an advisory council to the king and probably mostly members of the (extended) royal family.[71] The reading of this substantival use of GAL (.GAL) is unknown.[72] The only hint at a possible reading that we have is the frequent complement *-la* appended to L.326. Whereas there is no known *-la*-derivation known from any of the above-mentioned words *ḫantezzi(ya)-* and *šalli-*, whether adjectives or nouns, there is the noun *uralla-*, derived from Luwian *ura-* "great."[73] It is attested in the Palace Chronicles with its usual laconic style (see Chapter 5.6):

> Ispudasinara was a *huprala*-man. Askaliya, the ruler of Hurma, took him and made him governor in the town of Utahzumi. Askaliya wanted to kill him, so he put him in prison. But accusations arose against Askaliya. They sent for Ispudasinara and released him from prison. He confronted Askaliya: "You are depraved! You have really disgraced(?) yourself to the king." The king took Ispudasinara – Suppiuman and Marassa were the chiefs of 1000 charioteers – and he made him their boss (^{LÚ}*urallan*).[74]

[71] Starke 1996: 140–3.

[72] The phonetic complement ($^{\text{LÚ.MEŠ}}$GAL.GAL)-*uš* KBo 3.40 obv. 10 makes it less likely that it was an *i*-stem.

[73] I am grateful to my colleague Petra Goedegebuure for pointing this out to me.

[74] ^{m}*Íšpudašinaraš* ^{LÚ}*ḫupralaš ēšta š= an* ^{m}*Āškaliyaš* LÚ ^{URU}*Ḫurma dāš š= an* INA ^{URU}*Utaḫzumi* ^{LÚ}*maniaḫḫatallan iēt man= an= kan* ^{m}*Āškaliyaš kuienzi š= an* ANA É.EN.NU.UN *daiš* ^{m}*Āškali= ma uddār arāiš* ^{m}*Išpudašinara= ma pier š= an= ašta* IŠTU É.EN.NU.UN *tarner* ^{m}*Āškali= pat tiēt*

There is a lot we do not know but it is clear that Ispudasinara, originally an officer of uncertain rank (a *ḫuprala*-man), was promoted to local administrator or governor by Askaliya who then, possibly afraid that Ispudasinara was becoming too powerful, plotted to assassinate him. The king then saved him and elevated him to an even higher position, that of the highest chief of charioteers. This does not prove in any way that *uralla-* was the reading behind L.326 or GAL but at least it fits the basic semantic ("grandee") and formal (*a*-stem) requirements.

14.2.1 The Iron Age Evidence for L.326: The "Scribal Signatures"

Having established an alternative interpretation for L.326 it is time to review the post-Hittite or first-millennium (Iron Age) evidence. The material for L.326 and L.326t can be divided into four groups, one with the so-called "scribal signatures," a second one with scribal interpretations other than the "signatures," a third one with curse formulae using L.326t, and a fourth with miscellaneous usages. The first group comprises eleven royal inscriptions, ten of them on stone and one engraved on the ANKARA silver bowl. Except for the latter all attestations have the *-la-* suffix albeit without the determinative (VIR$_2$) that we saw in ALEPPO 7 (p. 353). Compare, for instance, the inscription KARABURUN where (§14), strangely separated from and about 0.3 m above the main rock inscription, we find: *wa/i-na-sa* L.326-*la-sá* "Wana, 326."[75] A more informative addendum is found on BOYBEYPINARI, originally a podium for a throne and table for the goddess Kubaba:

> Pedantimuwa, 326-*la-*, and Asatarhunza, the SA$_4$-*nanala*, 'house-descendant' of Suppiluliuma, carved (this)/had (this) carved.[76]

There is little doubt about the notion "to carve" for the hieroglyph SCALPRUM () or for combinations involving the sign (e.g.,  SCALPRUM+CAPERE,  STELE), which probably depicts a stonemason's chisel of some kind.[77] Obviously, "carved" does not necessarily imply here that

maršanza= wa zik LUGAL-*un= wa= z mekki ḫaliḫlatti* $^{d!}$*Išpudašinaran* LUGAL-*uš dāš* ^{m}*Šuppiuman* ^{m}*Maraššann= a* UGULA I! *LI* LÚ.MEŠ.IŠ *ešer apun= a* ^{LÚ}*uralla*(*n*)*= šman iēt* KBo 3.34 ii 15–23 (Palace chronicles, CTH 8, NS), ed. by Dardano 1997: 48–51.

75 Ed. by Hawkins 2000: 481, Pl. 266–7.

76 SCALPRUM+CAPERE-x / ^{m}LOCUS-*tantimuwas* L.326-*las asa*-TONITRUS-*huzas=ha* SA$_4$-*nanalas* PURUS.FONS.MI-*s* DOMUS-*ni*(-)NEPOS-*mīs* BOYBEYPINARI IA §11, ed. by Hawkins 2000: 336, Pl. 165.

77 Payne 2015: 160; see Neve 1992: 29 Abb. 69, for what is probably a real stonemason's chisel (Lat. *scalprum*) found in Boğazköy.

the subject mentioned physically did the work but rather that he *had* it done by a specialist or craftsman. This is the *Caesar pontem fecit* principle ("Caesar built a bridge"): when a king says he has built a palace nobody believes he ever touched a single brick. More important in the last passage is Hawkins' interpretation of DOMUS-*ni*(-)NEPOS-*mīs* as "house-descendant," which places Asatarhunza in the king's family.[78] Intriguing in this context are the two near-duplicating stelae ARSUZ 1 and 2. They were erected in the name of a local king Suppiluliuma, son of Manana. The "scribal signature" at the end of the two texts is by another "Manana, 326-*la*," with L.326 preceded in ARSUZ 1 by BONUS.[79] Within the tradition of papponymy (grandson named after the grandfather) the latter Manana is likely to be the son of Suppiluliuma and grandson of Manana the elder. Two more otherwise unknown individuals take responsibility as BONUS.L.326 for the inscriptions MEHARDE and SHEIZAR[80] in signatures at the end of the text. That individuals who put up such monuments for others did not always call themselves L.326-*la*- is shown by TOPADA §39 and KARKAMISH A4b. The latter says:

> Arnu-L.466, son of Suhi, the ruler, priest of (the goddess) Kubaba, erected this stela.[81]

In the TOPADA signature, separated again from the main inscription, a certain La, "the Great King's [. . .]," professes himself to be the one who "inscribed" the text.[82] With the addition of "the Great King's [. . .]" again a relation to the royal house is given. Two other, unfortunately rather fragmentary examples are IVRIZ fragment 2[83] and the recently published JISR EL HADID 4, a memorial statue dating probably to the eighth century BC, set up by a son for his father.[84] Although no titles are given, the fact that the father gets a statue strongly suggests an elite context. The final and chronologically probably youngest signature comes from Karatepe (KARATEPE 4) from the early seventh century BC, where L.326 does not qualify the two individuals

[78] Hawkins 2000: 338 ("presumably kinship term of some kind"), Giusfredi 2012a: 157 ("potrebbe far supporre un'origine nobiliare").

[79] Dinçol et al. 2015.

[80] For both see Hawkins 2000: 417, w. Pls. 225–8; one of them has the same name (Pedantimuwa) as in BOYBEYPINARI quoted above, the other is *A*-SCALPRUM-*za*. Note that in MEHARDE §2 King Taita is said to have "made" (*izīta*) the stela "for the divine Queen of the land" but that is no more than a topos.

[81] *a=wa=ta za* STELE AVIS-*nu*-L.466 PONERE *Suhis* [?] IUDEX-*ni* (INFANS)*nimuza* (DEUS)*Ku*+AVIS L.355-*s* KARKAMISH A4b §6, ed. by Hawkins 2000: 80 w. Pl. 1.

[82] Hawkins 2000: 454 w. Pls. 250–3.; Hawkins ibid. 460 surmises that there was "perhaps [servant?] at the end."

[83] Hawkins 2000: 530 w. Pl. 304. [84] Dinçol et al. 2014.

Table 14.1 *Elements in the so-called "scribal signatures"*

inscription	1st/3rd person narrative	L.326	evidence for elite membership
ANKARA BOWL	?	+	?
ARSUZ 1&2	1st	+	+
BOYBEYPINARI	1st	+	+
IVRIZ FRAGM. 2	[]	[]	[]
JISR EL HADID 4	3rd	–	+
KARABURUN	3rd	+	?
KARATEPE 4	1st	(+)	?
KARKAMISH A4B	3rd	–	+
MEHARDE	3rd	+	?
SHEIZAR	1st	+	?
TOPADA	1st	–	+

([] means text broken away at this point)

who "carved" the main inscription but serves as the direct object of the carving; for this see the next section.

We thus have eleven expressions of authorship. Table 14.1 puts together the essential features. Is the main body of the text a first-person narrative and thus a pseudo-autobiography by the individual in the signature who always uses the third person? Or is it a third-person narrative throughout? Does the author identify himself as L.326? And, finally, is there evidence for the social status of the proclaimed author?

Although not a "scribal signature" and therefore not included in the above table, it is important to mention here the KULULU 3 inscription, a funerary monument, presenting us with a ruler calling himself L.326-*la*-, this time in the opening sentence of the text as part of the titulature:

> I (am) Ilali, the ruler, 326.[85]

One might object that this goes against the mutual exclusion of "king" and L.326, as observed for the second millennium. However, the Luwian term used by Ilali and rendered here as "ruler" is not "king" (*/handawati-/*, written REX) but *tarwani-* (IUDEX-*ni*-). According to the discussion of Iron Age Luwian titles by Federico Giusfredi *tarwani-* "denoted a non-royal official position" in early Iron Age Karkamish.[86] Later its use widened

[85] EGO *Ilalis* IUDEX-*nis* / 326-*I*[*as*] KULULU 3 §1, ed. by Hawkins 2000: 490 w. Pl. 273.

[86] Giusfredi 2010: 95–6.

geographically and could occur combined with other titles, among them REX. The latter shows that the two titles remained distinct and while Ilali may not have been entitled to calling himself REX he could don himself with L.326 perhaps suggesting other royal connections.

Leaving KULULU 3 aside, all the above texts are added-on notes identifying the person responsible for the inscription. With the explicit evidence of KARKAMISH A4b and TOPADA it is evident that members of a royal family could put up memorials for a king[87] and I therefore expect the same for the four persons for whom we have no such information. A direct parallel for the JISR EL HADID 4 monument where a son erects a statue for his father is the cuneiform document from the reign of Suppiluliuma II, the last known Hittite king, about the statue he put up for his father Tuthaliya IV. Note that L.326 is absent in exactly those inscriptions (KARKAMISH A4b "son of Suhi," TOPADA "the Great King's [...]," JISR EL HADID 4 son for a father) where an explicit link to a ruling dynasty is given. It seems inconceivable to me that all these men were the stonemasons who did the actual stone cutting. Instead they probably were the *auctores intellectuales* or *Urheber* as well as patrons behind each of the inscriptions, they were the ones who composed them and *had* them ultimately carved in stone or metal (in the case of the silver bowl). By identifying themselves as 326(*-la-*), that is, as members of the reigning dynasty, they legitimated the act of commissioning the monuments and at the same time, as patrons, shared in the glory and propaganda such an inscription provided. Finally, it is important to note that there seem to be no parallels for scribal signatures in the contemporaneous northwest Semitic public inscriptions.[88]

14.2.2 The Iron Age Evidence for L.326: The Other "Scribal" Passages

The scribal interpretation has always been used for the passage in KARKAMISH A15b §19 where the ruler of Karkamish, Yariri (ca. 800 BC), allegedly boasts his reading and speaking skills. The relevant forms here are the ablative case endings L.326*-li-ia-ti(-i)*/*-li-ti*, each accompanied by an ethnic adjective. The standard transliteration is, of course, "SCRIBA*-li(ya) ti*" with the derived interpretation "script, writing":

87 Simon 2011b: 228, who also includes the SÜDBURG inscription in Boğazköy. One can certainly add KBo 12.38 ii as reference to a hieroglyphic inscription (ed. by Güterbock 1967) put up by Suppiluliuma II about and for his father Tuthaliya IV.

88 I thank Dennis Pardee and Madadh Richey for discussing this topic with me.

> [. . .] in the City's writing, in the Suraean writing, in the Assyrian writing and in the Taimani writing, and I knew twelve languages. My lord *gathered* every country's son to me by wayfaring concerning language, and he caused me to know every skill.[89]

Unfortunately, the inscription is fragmentary and the sentence with L.326-*li(ya)ti* crucially lacks a verb. The interpretation of the key word is completely based on the traditional understanding of L.326 as "scribe" and, consequently, a lot has been written on what scripts Yariri is exactly referring to.[90] But if we understand the sign as depicting a throne and symbolizing affiliation with a royal house and if we take into account the derivation in *-ya-* (lit. "belonging to (the throne)") we might as well interpret it as "royal representatives":

> [I mingled with/received gifts from *vel sim.*] royal representatives from the City, royal representatives from Tyre(?), royal representatives from Assur, and royal representatives from Taiman . . .

Yariri sought to "raise Carchemish's international profile," as Trevor Bryce puts it[91], but diplomatic relations could be established in many more ways than learning the scripts of foreign states. The "twelve languages" (if thus correctly understood) can still stand as a testament to Yariri's social and diplomatic skills but not automatically linked to any literacy prowess.

The final and latest attestation (ca. 700 BC) for the scribal interpretation comes from KARATEPE 4, a block, separate from but archaeologically clearly associated with the main monument. The text has L.326-*la-li-ia* as the direct object (nom.-acc. pl. neuter) of ("CAPERE+SCALPRUM") REL-*za-ta* "carved, incised":

> these writings Masanis and Masanazamis incised."[92]

Without knowing the exact reading behind L.326-*laliya* it is entirely possible that it refers to the inscription as a royal statement or account ("these royal words" *vel sim.*).

89 Translation Hawkins 2000: 131 (his italics to indicate the uncertainty of the translation); [. . .]URBS-*siyati* 326-*liyati zurawaniti*(URBS) 326-*liyatī asura*(REGIO)-*wanati*(URBS) 326-*liyatī taimaniti=ha* (URBS) 326-*liti* 12=*ha=wa'* "LINGUA"-*latīn* (LITUUS)*uniha wa=mū tanimasin* REGIO-*nisīna'* INFANS-*nin* ("VIA")*harwatahitatī* CUM-*na* ARHA-*sata* DOMINUS-*nanīs amīs* "LINGUA"-*lati* SUPER+*ra' tanimin=ha=wa=mu* (L.273)*warpin* (LITUUS)*unanuta*, ed. by Hawkins 2000: 131, Pl. 36–7, see also the earlier translation of Starke 1997b: 382–3, further Payne 2015: 137.

90 See most recently Younger 2014 w. lit.; I gladly take the interpretation of Zuraean as "Tyraean/from Tyre" from him.

91 Bryce 2012a: 95.

92 Translation Hawkins 2000: 69; *zaya=pa=wa* 326-*laliya* ^{m}DEUS-*nīs* ^{m}DEUS-*na*-(OCULUS)-*azamis=ha* ("CAPERE+SCALPRUM")REL-*zata*, ed. by Hawkins 2000: 69.

14.2.3 The Iron Age Evidence for L.326t: The Curse Formulae

The Iron Age occurrences for L.326t (that is, with the "tail") are usually accompanied by the attached slanted stroke known as the *Dorn* and read as *ra/i* (or *RA/I* in case it is a phonetic indicator rather than a phonetic complement): L.326t+*RA/I*. In a number of cases it is followed by *-da-i* and the combination is usually taken as a verbal stem with a phonetic complement in *-ta-* and the *hi*-conjugation ending *-i*: L.326t+*RA/I-da-i*. All told five similar phrases in the KARKAMISH inscriptions are known. They tell of building projects and the curse formula is each time introduced by a number of sentences painting a picture of the future. The two best preserved ones read:

> (I built a temple for the Stormgod and adorned the gates with orthostats.) I made these *harstani*-structures as living quarters(?) for my beloved wife Anaya and I enthroned (the deity) Atrisuha here in this gate structure with/out of goodness. If in the future it comes to happen that somebody will 326t it/them (i.e., aforementioned structures) and will topple these walls in (these) places or will topple the deity here in (these) places or will erase my name," (then may . . . [curse follows])[93]

> This seat I built for him (i.e., Kamanis, "my lord's child"). If this seat comes (into the possession) of whatever king, if someone 326t it or takes away a stone from these stones or takes away a stela from? the stela or erases my name, (then may . . . [curse follows])[94]

The action expressed by L.326t+*RA/I*(-)*tà-* is the first negative one of a series that involves "toppling" (*san-*) and "erasing" (*ARHA* MALLEUS). Again, following the scribal reading of L.326, several scholars understood the sequence L.326t+*RA/I*(-)*dai* as changing the existing writing on a monument[95] but that is already explicitly addressed in the "erasing of the

[93] *zanzi=pa=wa* (DOMUS)*harasataninzi* ^{f}*Anaya* BONUS-*samī* FEMINA-*tī* DOMUS+SCALA(-)*tawaninzi izīha zan=ha=wa* (DEUS)*Atrisuhan zatianza* PORTA-*nanza* BONUS-*sarati* (SOLIUM)*isanuwaha* POST +*RA/I-wasa<tī?>=pa=wa=ta* REL-*ati* PRAE-*na* CRUS.CRUS-*i wa=ta* L.326t+*RA/I*(-)*dai* REL-*is zanzi= pa=wa=ta* (SCALPRUM)*kutasaranzi* LOCUS-*za* (SA$_4$)*saniti* NEG$_2$=*pa=wa=ta zan* DEUS-*nin* LOCUS-*za'* (SA$_4$)*saniti* NEG$_2$=*pa=wa=ta amanza alamanza'* *ARHA* MALLEUS-*i* (a curse follows), KARKAMISH AII §§19–25 (tenth to early ninth century BC), ed. by Hawkins 2000: 96 w. Pl. 10–1.

[94] *wa=tū zan* (MENSA.SOLIUM)*asan* AEDIFICARE+*MI-ha zas=pa=wa* (MENSA.SOLIUM)*asas* CRUS. CRUS(-)*nizaya* REL-*ati* REL-*tī=ha* REX-*ti* PRAE-*na wa=ara* L.326t+*RA/I*(-)*dai* REL-*sa zīn=pa=wa* SCALPRUM-*suwatī* SCALPRUM-*sun'* NEG$_3$-*i* CUM-*ni* *ARHA* *taya tasan=pa=wa' tasi* NEG$_3$-*i* CUM-*ni* *ARHA* *taya nipawa=ta amanza alamanza* REL-*is* *ARHA* MALLEUS-*la<i>* (a curse follows), KARKAMISH A 6 §§24–29 (end of ninth century BC), ed. by Hawkins 2000: 125 w. Pl. 32–3. Similarly, KARKAMISH AIIb+c §22 (ed. by Hawkins 2000: 104 w. Pl. 16–7; only the tip of the "tail" is visible, rest broken away; tenth to early ninth century BC), A 26c (ed. by Hawkins 2000: 207 w. Pl. 90; date unclear), A 31+ §15 (ed. by Marchetti & Peker 2018: 95, eighth century BC).

[95] Cf. Marazzi 1990: 214–15 ("qualcosa come 'emendare, cambiare, variare lo scritto in oggetto'"), Starke 1990: 464 ("muß . . . etwas mit der weiteren Nutzung der . . . Bauteile zu tun haben. . . .

name." Given the reference in both texts to thrones and seating ((SOLIUM)*isanu-*, (MENSA.SOLIUM)*asa-*) immediately preceding L.326t it seems much more appropriate to think of "un-seating, de-throning, dis-lodging."[96] This is also where the attached "tail" comes in: as convincingly shown by Craig Melchert, the addition of a vertical stroke (MINUS) to a logogram can turn the notion inherent in the sign into its opposite or express a negative action in relation to the logogram.[97] For example, the signs for "house" or "building" (DOMUS, AEDIFICIUM), or "man" (VIR) become "to destroy" (DELERE) or "to die" (MORI) respectively. As SELLA+MINUS the compound sign L.326t thus becomes "to un-seat, overthrow" forming a perfect match both in iconography and context. The reading behind the verb does not have to be linked to a lexeme for "sitting" etc. but can be any verb expressing the notion of "unseating, overthrowing" as shown by Melchert for some of the other signs with MINUS.[98]

14.2.4 *The Iron Age Evidence for L.326 and L.326t: Miscellaneous Attestations*

Some other late inscriptions show L.326 with a clear syllabic value /tu/ transliterated *tù*.[99] Compare KARATEPE 1 where it is attested three times in the Ho-version and corresponds each time in the Hu version with the sign *tu*; for instance, KARATEPE 1 LI Ho 283:

> May the highly blessed Tarhunza give him (*pi-ia-tù* -) . . .[100]

Anbringung neuer Reliefs und/oder Inschriften"), Payne 2010a: 185 ("to take for/as writing surface").

96 Meriggi 1934: 35–6 came close to the meaning proposed here when suggesting "herunter(?) holen" for KARKAMISH A11: "'Herunter' ist gewagt, aber das Ideogramm [L.326: tvdh] spricht dafür: etwa ein Gestell oder Sockel, von dem man etwas herunter holen oder nehmen (. . .) kann."

97 Melchert 1988.

98 Hitt. *dannattaḫḫ-* for AEDIFICIUM+MINUS and *marnu-* for DOMUS+MINUS: see Melchert 1988; Hittite verbs that express the notion of "un-seating, dislodging, overthrowing" are *peššiya-* or *pippa-* (for both see CHD P s.vv.). For the identity of the deity's name on the KINIK bowl (see §14.1.2) this does not help much but note that *peššiya-* "to throw" had a technical meaning in hunting jargon of killing or catching animals (see Neu 1996: 113, Hoffner 2002: 67 ["to bag"]). The sign L.326t on the bowl might thus have been taken to refer to any deity associated with hunting, for which see Hawkins 2006.

99 Hawkins 2000: 33. According to Laroche 1956b: 26–9 (see recently Singer 2003: 345 w. n. 28, 2006b, 243–4 w. lit., and Yakubovich 2017b) it is also present in the compound *tuppalanura-* "Chief (*ura-*) Scribe", attested in Ugarit.

100 Hu: *pi-ia-tu-há-wa/i-tu-u* (DEUS)TONITRUS-*huzas* ARHA *usanuwamis* = Ho: *pi-iá-tù-há-wa/i-tu4-u* (DEUS)TONITRUS-*huzas* ARHA (BONUS)*usanuwamis* KARATEPE 1 LI, ed. by Hawkins 2000: 55–6, cf. Çambel 1999: Pl. 101. The other two attestations are LII 297 and LVI 321.

where the Hu version has *pi-ia-tu-*. It also occurs twice in the TOPADA inscription of the late eighth century BC (§18 *tù-pa-sa*$_6$*-ti* and §20 *wa/i*$_7$*-tù*).[101] The first is probably an ablative case ("I *succeeded*(?) by *battle*(?)"[102]), the second clearly the enclitic personal pronoun in the dative–locative singular ("for/to him/her"). This late sound value /tu/ has often been interpreted as confirmation of the SCRIBA reading of L.326. It seems to match neatly the supposed underlying *tupala-* "scribe", the agent noun derived from *tuppi* "tablet." As some scholars have already indicated, however, this reading is highly uncertain, if not unlikely. The word *tupala-* is attested just once in a fragmentary context that does not contain any hint at scribes, the single *-p-* is unexpected in view of the consistent *-pp-* in *tuppi* and it is unclear how we get to an alleged *a*-stem **tuppala-* "scribe" from an *i*-stem *tuppi*. According to Laroche it is also present in the compound *tuppa* (*la*)*nura-* "Chief (*ura-*) of the Scribes," attested in Ugarit, but some of the same objections apply.[103] Unclear is KULULU 8 (late eighth century BC?), a "graffito-like" inscription on stone: [. . . ?]*walazis* L.326 L.273-*pi*? *ti*.[104]

For L.326t the following unclear attestations are known: ÇALAPVERDI 2 §2? L.326t-*na*-x-*ha* (900–700 BC)[105]; BOYBEYPINARI (ca. 800 BC) III D 2 *awa api* L.326t+*RA/I-wa/i-ma-za* ARHA (PES$_2$)*iha* "and then(?) I went away to 326t"[106]; in KULULU lead strip 1 (750–700 BC), a listing of economic transactions, the sequence L.326t+*RA/I-za* occurs inbetween a town's name, a commodity, and the beneficiary's(?) name.[107] A parallel phrase in the same document is *za+RA/I-wa/i-ia-za* (§7). The only possibility I see is that it refers to a kind of tax: "for town X so many Y (= commodity) as L.326t/*z*.-tax for?/from? Mr. PN."

Only in CEKKE (ca. 750 BC) does L.326t seem to function as a syllabogram. It occurs three times in the name of Kamanis' vizier Sas-L.326t+*RA/I* read as Sastura by Hawkins using the *tu*-value known from KARATEPE and TOPADA.[108] However, since we have seen that L.326t+*RA/I* may have to be kept apart from L.326 with possibly a very different reading, this remains an open question.

[101] Ed. by Hawkins 2000: 453.
[102] Italics Hawkins to express tentative character of his translation.
[103] See Chapter 5 n. 11; for the objections see van den Hout 2010: 266–7, Giusfredi 2012a: 150–1, Giorgieri & Mora 2012: 651–2.
[104] Hawkins 2000: 502, Pl. 284, see also Payne 2015: 88.
[105] Hawkins 2000: 498, Pl. 279.
[106] Hawkins 2000: 337, Pl. 165.
[107] Hawkins 2000: 506 w. Pl. 286 and lit., Giusfredi 2010: 185–207.
[108] Hawkins 2000: 145 w. Pl. 42–43.

14.3 The Shape of L.326 and L.326t

Looking at the different variants both incised and in relief (Figure 14.13) but disregarding the presence or absence of the "tail" there can be little doubt we are dealing with one and the same sign in the post-Hittite period. Compare BOYBEYPINARI IA and KARKAMISH A31+ vs. KULULU lead strip 1 and KARABURUN §14, or KARKAMISH A6 and ALEPPO 7, and finally, within L.326t, compare KINIK and KARKAMISH A11. A comparison, however, of the earlier sign shapes up to and including KARKAMISH A11 for L.326 and 326 t might suggest an initial difference between the two and a later merger. On the other hand, the variation between the ALEPPO 1 type and the KINIK bowl falls well within the iconographic range we find in ancient Near Eastern seats; compare the drawings as depicted by Armas Salonen (Fig. 14.11–12).

Anatolian or Hittite iconography shows a similar variety of forms, as is clear from the hieroglyphic signs (Fig. 14.8) and iconography (Fig. 14.9–10), and each of the basic forms may have had its own name.

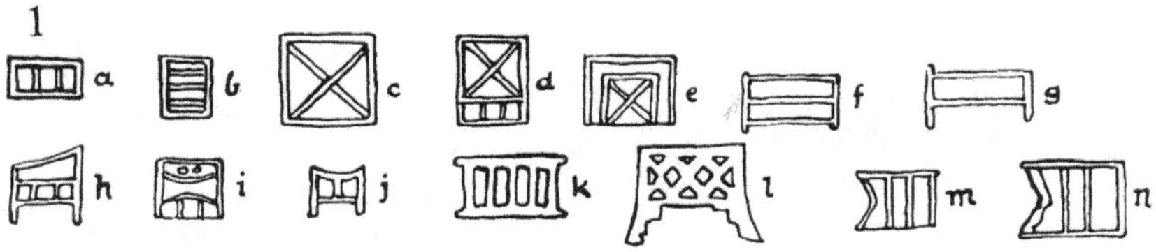

Fig. 14.11 Chairs and seats in Salonen 1963 Pl. 23.

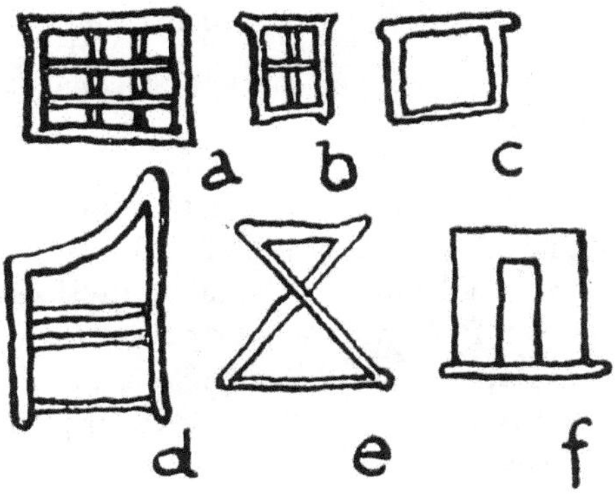

Fig. 14.12 Chairs and seats in Salonen 1963 Pl. 25.

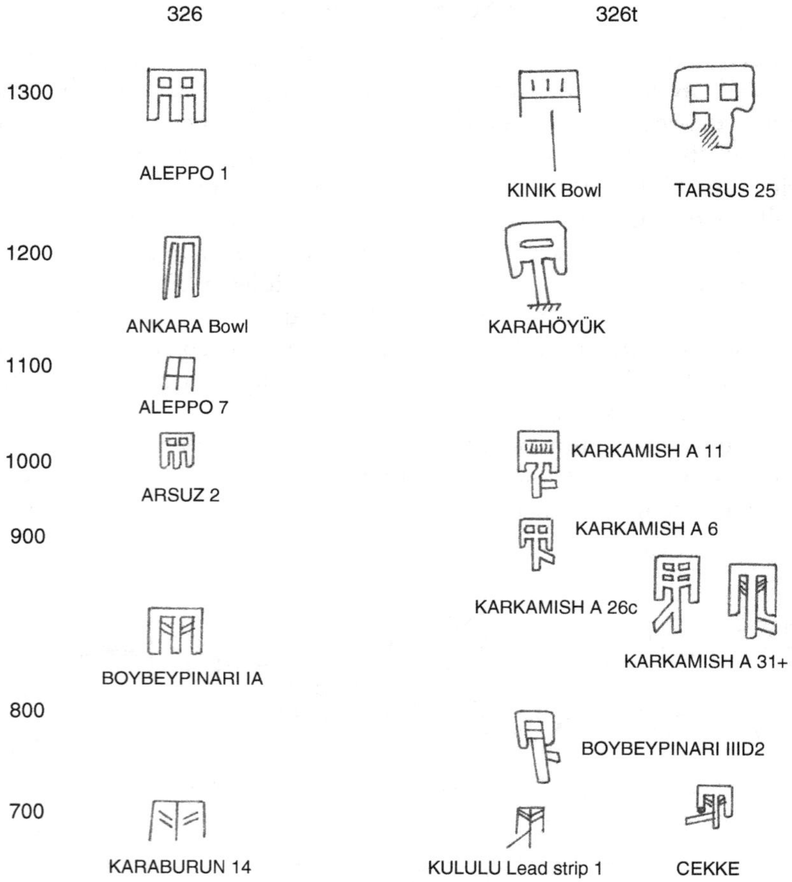

Fig. 14.13 Paleography of L.326 and L.326t (drawing author).

There is no identifiable geographical distribution for the various sign shapes of L.326 but one can see the sign change shape over time. The oldest attestations of 326, both on the numerous seal impressions and outside that corpus (Kinik, Aleppo 1 and 7), have the simple square shape with the open bottom and no slanted lines. The variant without the crossbar as seen on the Ankara bowl is also attested on a silver tripod seal. The classic shape seems to disappear between the eleventh and ninth century when slanted lines on the inside occur for the first time in the ninth century Boybeypinari IA inscription and remain from then on. The

Boybeypinari IIID 2 shape still continues the Karahöyük form.[109] These changes could reflect developments in furniture design but make less sense for tablets of whatever kind.

14.4 Conclusions

The case for L.326 = scriba is problematic in many respects. It is iconographically unlikely, hardly compatible with ancient notions of literacy, and its frequency and distribution on Late Bronze Age sealings remains unexplained both in Hattusa and elsewhere in the Hittite realm. The proposed Hittite reading behind it (**tuppala-*) is weak and faces important objections of spelling and formation. Its shape fits much better the interpretation of a chair or stool, as originally proposed by Piero Meriggi. It seems more appropriate therefore to transcribe it as (Latin) sella, symbolizing the concept of higher office with royal affiliation. This explains the attestations of both the Late Bronze and Iron Age, and particularly the curse formulae in the Karkamish inscriptions seem to find a much easier explanation with this new reading. The so-called "scribal signatures" are not "scribal" but rather dedicatory in nature. Even though we lose an ancient champion of literacy in Yariri, his inscription (Karkamish A15b) still makes sense and he may get to keep his polyglot reputation.

The consequence of all this is, of course, that the attestations for L.326 with all associated names on seal impressions can no longer be used as information on scribes in Hittite society. At first this rejection may seem a major drawback when wanting to find out more about scribes in Hittite society or the spread of literacy in ruling circles. At first, Laroche's identification of the sign back in 1956 vastly expanded the pool of attestations for these professionals and added scores of scribes to those already known from cuneiform sources. On the other hand, that same expansion of the sign L.326 to a general degree of literate schooling also reduced our hopes of learning more about the actual scribes. The uncertainty of who was a professional scribe working in the chancelleries day after day and who was a literate member of the elite brought the core of scribes back again to

[109] This same shape can be seen in the chair of the seated goddess of the gold pendant in the Metropolitan Museum in New York, see Muscarella 1974: nr. 125 (photo on the far left); see already n. 61. The same shape can be seen on the thirteenth century original silver seal published by Dinçol & Dinçol 2010: 88–9.

those identifying themselves as DUB.SAR on the clay tablets with the nagging uncertainty that some might go undetected among the ones boasting the sign L.326 on their seals. Taking the names with L.326 out of the equation may thus deprive us of what seemed a wealth of information, but it solves the uncertainty about who among the ruling class might have served as a real scribe and who did not. At the same time, it puts into sharper focus those who were entitled to the SELLA symbol and thus were able to claim some affiliation to the palace. But since it is no longer tied to questions of literacy it should not concern us here. The reinterpretation of the sign L.326 brings the spread of literacy back to the limited group of actual scribes, the craftsmen who produced the corpus on which we base – together with all non-textual evidence – our knowledge of Hittite history and society.

Below all attestations of the nineteen sealings with L.326 are given along with bibliographic references.[110] The third column indicates whether the seal owner is listed on the tablet with a cuneiform title as well, either the same, a different one, or none (–).

Table 14.2 *Seal impressions with L.326 at Emar*

Seal impression with L.326	*Text*	*Cuneiform title*	*Hieroglyphic name and references*
A7	ME 15	–	*Iapi*-x?-*ia*; Beyer 2001: 52, Arnaud 1991: 54–5, Gonnet apud Arnaud 1991: 200
A15	205, ME 36, 92	–	*Hila*(*ri*?)*zi* ; Beyer 2001: 57, Arnaud 1985–1986: 215–17, 1991: 128–9, 145–6, Gonnet apud Arnaud 1991: 206, 208; the name is not mentioned in the cun., but the seal was used by Burāqu, son of Madukka, without title.
A32	ME 72	DUMU ḪAL	*Kapitaka* (*Kapidāgān*); Beyer 2001: 67, Arnaud 1991: 122–3.

[110] For a similar list see Balza 2009: 99–100; the references in the first column are to Beyer 2001 where one also finds illustrations, descriptions, and discussions of the seals, for the cuneiform texts see Arnaud 1985–1986 (quoted just by number only) and 1991 (number preceded by ME = Moyen-Euphrate).

Table 14.2 (*cont.*)

Seal impression with L.326	*Text*	*Cuneiform title*	*Hieroglyphic name and references*
A33	43, 118, 122	LÚ.ḪAL (43, 122), DUMU ḪAL (118)	*Kapitaka* (*Kapidāgān*); Beyer 2001: 68, Arnaud 1985–1986: 59–60, 125–6, 129–30.
A102	215	LÚ.DUB.SAR	*Tai*(*a*); Beyer 2001: 106, Arnaud 1985–1986: 228–30.
B4	57, 93	–	*Palukarata*; Beyer 2001: 122, Arnaud 1985–1986: 165–6. The shape of L.326 is quite unusual here.
B13	ME 101	(unpublished)	*Takapali*? (*Dagan-bēlu*); Beyer 2001: 125
B21	246	(unpublished)	*Palukarata* (*Bēlu-qarrād*); Beyer 2001: 128, Arnaud 1985–1986: 245; note that the sign L.326 is defective. The tablet itself is only fragmentarily preserved so that it is uncertain whether the name and title were written on the tablet.
B29	86	–	*Zu*(?)*aštarti*; Beyer 2001: 130–1, Arnaud 1985–1986: 96–7.
B48	214	–	*Ipaniya* (*Ibniya*); Beyer 2001: 137, Arnaud 1985–1986: 227–8.
B53	43	–	*Arisarruma*; Beyer 2001: 139; Arnaud 1985–1986: 59–60.
B54	212	–	(illegible); Beyer 2001: 139, Arnaud 1986: 224–5.
B56	ME 116	(unpublished)	*Kapitaka* (*Kāpīdagan*); Beyer 2001: 140
C3	275	–	*Kutumi*(?)*li*(?)*a*?; Beyer 2001: 153–4, Arnaud 1985–1986: 270–1; the cun. text does not list any seals or anyone by the name of Kutumiliya.
C4	93	–	(seal of Imlik-dagan?) hieroglyphs almost illegible; Beyer 2001: 154, Arnaud 1985–1986: 105–6; list of seal owners fragmentary.
C14	ME 34	–	*Lala*; Beyer 2001: 158–9, Arnaud 1991: 100–1.

Table 14.2 (*cont.*)

Seal impression with L.326	*Text*	*Cuneiform title*	*Hieroglyphic name and references*
C15	80	[?]	hieroglyphs of name not preserved (cun. *Madidagan*); Beyer 2001: 159, Arnaud 1985–1986: 87–90.
AuOrS 1	ME 77	LÚ.DUB.SAR	*Apiʾu*; Arnaud 1991: 128–9, Gonnet apud Arnaud 1991: 206–7. Cf. line 23 (cun.) ᵐ*Abiu ilṭur* "Abiu did the writing."
ETBLM	ETBLM 12	LÚ.ḪAL	*Kapita[ka]* (*Kāpīdagan*); Goodnick Westenholz 2000: 33–5 w. Pl. xxxii. Besides L.326 the seal owner also has the title SACERDOS "priest."

Table 14.3 *Seal impressions with L.326 at Ugarit*

Seal impression	*Text*	*Cuneiform title*	*Hieroglyphic name and references*
IV.7.4	RS 17.251/403	[?]	*Takisarrumma*; Schaeffer & Laroche 1956: 37–9, 138–9, Mora 1987: 102, PRU 4.236–7 (for RS 17.251; the text of RS 17.403 is too damaged for interpretation).
IV.9.1	RS 17.231	LÚ ŠA RE-ŠI É.GAL-LIM	*Taprammi*; Schaeffer & Laroche 1956: 50–2, 149–52, Mora 1987: 105, PRU 4, 238.
VII.2.1	RS 17.109	–	*Naninzi*; Schaeffer & Laroche 1956: 54–5, 155, Mora 1987: 173, Laroche 1968: 769–72, Salvini 1995b: 144–6, Singer 1999b: 650–1.
IX.2.2	RS 17.28	ZA A.BA	*Layadagan*; Schaeffer & Laroche 1956: 42–7, 142–7, Laroche 1956b: 26–9, Mora 1987: 221, PRU 4, 109–10.

CHAPTER 15

The End and Looking Back

15.1 The Vanishing of the Hittite Kingdom

How the Hittite kingdom broke up still eludes us.[1] Current archaeological thinking envisions a deliberate abandonment of the capital Hattusa by its elite. Evidence of migrations pushing eastwards from the west, recent interpretations of the Sea People's movements in a similar direction, and the emergence of three Great Kings in Hittite fashion after 1200 in inscriptions from the eastern Konya plain (KIZILDAĞ, KARADAĞ), at KARAHÖYÜK near Elbistan, and several inscriptions from the Malatya area further east may hint at where they went.[2] Did they try to settle down and continue at Tarhuntassa, Karkamish, or elsewhere in that region? Using the fall of Ugarit around 1190 or, as some claim, the end of Emar in the late 1180s as *termini post quos* for the end of the kingdom one might argue for an awareness of a still existing Hittite kingdom into the early twelfth century BC but we do not know whether that was at Hattusa or already elsewhere. The small number of texts[3] and in particular the extremely low number of nine sealings that can be attributed to Suppiluliuma II plead for a rather early breakdown of the system in the capital and subsequent departure well before 1190/1180. If the texts from Ugarit and Emar refer to a Hittite kingdom they still considered existing a decade or so into the twelfth century BC they do not say where it existed.

Whatever happened around 1200 BC and when exactly, in its fall the Hittite state took down the Hittite language and the cuneiform script. What did survive were the Luwian language and its hieroglyphs. The Anatolian hieroglyphs had already been evolving during the early history of the kingdom and their roots can probably be traced back to the days of

[1] See the excellent overview of all relevant arguments in de Martino 2018.

[2] For the inscriptions at KIZILDAĞ, KARADAĞ see Hawkins 1995: 103–7; for the Malatya group see Hawkins 2000: 282–329.

[3] Klinger 2015: 99–100.

the Assyrian trading posts. Their development into a real writing system was a gradual process that according to our current evidence culminated in the fifteenth century BC. At that moment there may have been an urge to speed up the process in order to use the script to communicate with the Anatolian population, not because they already wrote in it – there is no evidence for this – but because it matched their world and environment and its most important pictograms were part of a shared visual language and, perhaps, identity.[4] Because of this, it was a much more ideal medium of communication than the highly abstract cuneiform. Another factor in the survival of the Luwian language is that it had been steadily on the rise since almost the beginning of the kingdom's written record and may have experienced an unintended impetus by the mass deportations of Luwian speakers from western Anatolia under Mursili II. In contrast, by the later thirteenth century BC the Hittite language may not have been much more than the official language of record and the H(igh) variety in a state of diglossia. When the ruling class gave up Hattusa, Hittite may no longer have been anybody's mother tongue for some time already. The cuneiform script being the internal means of written communication and the script's inextricable link to the Hittite language and elite account for its seemingly instant disappearance. With the kingdom, its institutions, and chancelleries gone, the cuneiform script had lost its grounding in Central Anatolia.

The hieroglyphic script, meanwhile, continued and survived, albeit at a considerable distance. After a dip perhaps between 1200 and 1000 BC it became *the* vehicle for the Luwian language in the so-called Neo-Hittite city-states in the southeast corner of Anatolia and along the northern Levantine coast until it, too, disappeared around 700 BC. Both the script and the language had had an already wider following than the cuneiform in the Late Bronze Age, as Hittite kings used the hieroglyphs to address the population at large. The survival of the hieroglyphs perhaps finds its reason in this deeper popularity vis-à-vis the cuneiform script. Also, after 1200 BC the sign shapes still appealed to the Anatolian and northern Syrian population's own visual surroundings, they represented "home," and were in their roots older than the imported cuneiform. To what extent the association of the cuneiform script with an *ancien régime* also worked to its disadvantage is impossible to say but it may have been factor of psychological importance as well.

Finally, right around the time that also the Anatolian hieroglyphs started their decline, we see the western Anatolian languages Lydian, Carian, and

[4] Waal 2012: 305–7.

Lycian, as well as the likewise Indo-European (but more remotely related) Phrygian appear, using alphabets related to those developed by the Phrygians and the Greeks. Under the aegis of the Achaemenids they continued to write but with the coming of Alexander the Great and later the Roman Empire these indigenous alphabets and the Anatolian languages they recorded ceased to be written almost completely. An exception may be the Pisidian tomb inscriptions, that may date to the second and third century AD, but they are written in the Greek alphabet. Then, the curtain definitively falls for the recorded existence of the subgroup of Anatolian languages. Never since the collapse of the Hittite kingdom had there been an again independent Anatolian state of comparable size and prestige that was able to sustain a script, an administration, let alone a literature of its own.

15.2 Looking Back

We are back where we began in the Introduction. The complete and fairly sudden demise of the cuneiform script in Anatolia around 1200 bc confirms its relative invisibility to the population as long as the kingdom was still alive. As we saw earlier, the high degree of stability and lack of variation in the script under Hittite rule suggests that its use was very limited and highly centralized. It functioned within the small circle of scribes and scholars employed by the state but not outside of it. The total absence of any evidence for a wider use outside the ruling class fully accords with this. All texts, as we have them, come from the royal administration and served the dynasty and ruling elite. Virtually all documents, whether short- or long-term (Chapter 12.2), find their place in the Hittite kings' view of what it meant to rule a kingdom of their size. Political, religious, legal, economic, and administrative priorities were all served by the drawing up as well as filing and keeping of all related and relevant records. Even those texts that we may call scholarly rather than administrative (mostly the non-Anatolian imported genres) were likely collected and studied at royal behest. The most personal among them may be the foreign, that is, non-Central Anatolian, rituals if we are correct in assuming that the king ordered their collection because one never knew when they might come in handy. In a way, the most elusive texts in terms of their *Sitz im Leben* are the imported literary works in Hittite translation. Judging by the criteria of the purpose and growth of the collections, as explained and discussed in Chapter 12, the first group (political etc.) rightly deserve the label "archival" while the imported texts could be seen as more library-like in nature.

The probably biggest question confronting anybody trying to describe and explain the Hittite text corpus is the absence of socio-economic records. Seen from a wider ancient Near Eastern perspective and given the preconceptions of ancient literacy based on what we find in Mesopotamia, the lack of adoption records, debt notes, sales contracts, and the like, is nothing less than surprising. As I made clear in the Introduction, the usual explanation that all such documents were written on perishable writing materials is methodologically questionable and raises so many objections as to be unlikely. Instead, we should accept the challenge of seeing the Hittite corpus on its own merits and try to explain it on its own terms. Those terms are mainly economic and ecological. The ecology of Central Anatolia was already briefly described in that same Introduction: a largely mountainous peninsula with very strong natural borders that both defended and isolated this land mass from outside forces and fragmented it within. Add the harsh climate and one gets a country where travel and transportation are often hard and sometimes nearly impossible. It is therefore not easy to unify and control for any power that has the ambition to do so. The obvious and by no means unique solution to this by the Hittite ruling class was decentralization of much of its infrastructure. Our texts attest to considerable religious and legal autonomy for local population groups. The concept of the "1000 Gods" is a clear expression of the former, and we saw written evidence of the condoning of local judicial decisions in Chapter 5.8.

If we take what the Hittites have left us seriously and as a fair reflection of what they committed to writing, the Hittite text corpus and corresponding material situation on the ground suddenly look very different. Instead of an assumed and hypothetical balance between not-preserved secular records and preserved mostly cultic ones, we now have an overwhelming majority of documents preoccupied with the cult and the role of the Hittite king and queen in it. Royal ideology turns out to have been the driving force in the maintenance of power. The royal couple or the king alone traveled the central country in the spring and summer bestowing their riches on local temples and personnel and thereby buying the loyalty of local communities and enforcing the grip on the wealth-based economy. Representatives of Anatolian settlements visited the capital and participated in the staged rites and reported their experiences back home. Carefully orchestrated ceremonies, as exemplified in the cult rituals, helped maintain the mystery surrounding the king and queen. Similar ruling systems are known from elsewhere. Compare the description by Clifford Geertz of nineteenth century AD Bali in Indonesia:

> It was as head of the [land], then, that the king "owned" the realm. Like the gods, and as one, he ensured its prosperity – the productiveness of the land; the fertility of its women; the health of its inhabitants; its freedom from droughts, earthquakes, floods, weevils, or volcanic eruptions; its social tranquility; and even (. . .) its physical beauty. Whether in Water-Opening ceremonies at sacred lakes, first-fruits rites at mountain shrines, demon exorcisms at seashore ones, or royal celebrations at his palace, the king was represented as the prime guardian," "custodian," or "protector," (. . .) of the land and its life, sheltering it as the royal parasol sheltered him and as "the vault of heaven" sheltered them both. (. . .) And the motor (. . .) was state ceremony.[5]

His characterization of kingship on Bali matches almost perfectly not only what our Hittite texts tell us about the role of the king in Late Bronze Age Anatolia but also the focus on his person in Hittite art and iconography.

The role of writing in Hittite society reflects this situation. Until around the turn of the twentieth century BC Anatolian population groups had already successfully existed without any form of writing system for as long as they could remember. Impressions of local symbols on clay, as we know them from Arslantepe or later from Karahöyük near Konya, may have provided as much of manifest checks and balances, as they thought necessary. The Assyrian merchants descending upon the towns and villages of Central Anatolia around 2000 BC with their script and administration did not fundamentally change this. Local trading and bartering continued without the need for written documentation. This may be due as much to the Assyrians' insistence on their own identity in diaspora, as on the Anatolians sticking to their own ways. Nevertheless, over time and through growing relations between the two groups the Anatolians became increasingly exposed to the use of Assyrian cuneiform and it even took hold among Anatolians, albeit in limited quantity. Yet the written language remained Assyrian, and, even if the merchants may not always have been physically involved, the Assyrian context of writing remained the determining factor for script use. How shallow the character of the writing phenomenon in Anatolian society was became clear when the commercial network disappeared. With its demise, writing, not only in Assyrian and in its particular cuneiform writing system, but writing seems to have vanished, period. The adoption and eventual adaptation of a completely different cuneiform variant some two or three generations later shows this clearly.

[5] Geertz 1980: 129.

That seemingly easy disappearance of script usage happened again around 1200 BC when the Hittite kingdom ceased to exist. That is, if ever it continued elsewhere, we don't know it. With the demise of the kingdom both the cuneiform writing and the Anatolian hieroglyphs became extinct in Central Anatolia. The hieroglyphs did survive but only at a considerable remove in time and space.[6] This second vanishing is further confirmation, it seems, of what we have seen throughout this book. The cuneiform script was never much of a prestige item within the Hittite state. Its almost unchanging stability over about four centuries of increasing use, the archaeological contexts, in which the tablets were found, and the clearly defined spread of genres, as we have them, all point to the Hittite state as the sole user of this technology. Also, the development of ways to write local languages like Hattian, Palaic, or Luwian did not lead, as far as we know, to local expressions of literacy in these communities. Seen from the perspective of the local Anatolian population, the low demographic density in the great majority of settlements throughout Central Anatolia[7] made the need for a script for internal purposes on a local community level superfluous. Although prestige may have played a role in the initial decision to adopt the script, because most states to their civilized east had it, the practical advantages of acquiring this technology were probably the Hittites' leading concern. Its diplomatic, ideological, and educational applications were all instrumental to the maintenance of power. All writing, both in cuneiform and hieroglyphs, was practiced by the state and for the state. There is no evidence for diffusion of either script among the population of Anatolia beyond the ruling circles. The choice by the Arzawan king Tarhunaradu for his correspondence with Egypt in the early fourteenth century BC combined with the total absence thus far of any local written documents is telling in this respect. Because of this highly restricted literacy, the 99 percent of the Central Anatolian population remains largely invisible and silent. Writing may have become "essential to the functioning" of the Hittite state and we can therefore call it literate[8] but Late Bronze Age Anatolia was an illiterate society ruled by a literate elite.

[6] See Summers 2017: 258–61 (esp. 259: "Where and in what form the knowledge of hieroglyphic writing of Luwian survived is, therefore, a great mystery").

[7] See above n. 5; for a group size of ca. 150 individuals as the critical threshold where oral communication ("social grooming") is still sufficient to maintain cohesion in a group see Aiello & Dunbar 1993.

[8] Cf. the definition of a literate society by Michael Macdonald as quoted in Chapter 6.4.

Bibliography

Aiello, Leslie & Dunbar, Robin (1993) Neocortex Size, Group Size, and the Evolution of Language, *Current Anthropology* 34, 184–93.

Akdoğan, Rukiye & Hawkins, J. David (2011) The Kırşehir Letter: A new hieroglyphic Luwian text on a lead strip, in A. Süel (ed.) *Uluslararası Hititoloji Kongresi Bildirileri/Acts of the VIIth International Congress of Hittitology 2008* (Ankara: T.C. Çorum Valiliği), 1–16.

Alaura, Silvia (1998) Die Identifizierung der im "Gebaude E" von Büyükkale-Boğazköy gefundenen Tontafelfragmente aus der Grabung von 1933, *Altorientalische Forschungen* 25, 193–214.

(2006) *"Nach Boghasköi!" Zur Vorgeschichte der Ausgrabungen in Boğazköy-Ḫattuša und zu den archäologischen Forschungen bis zum Ersten Weltkrieg* (Münsterschwarzach Abtei: Deutsche Orient-Gesellschaft).

(2011) Aspekte der Gesten–und Gebärdensprache im "Ullikummi-Lied," in M. Hutter & S. Hutter-Braunsar (eds.) *Hethitische Literatur. Überlieferungsprozesse, Textstrukturen, Ausdrucksformen und Nachwirken* (Münster: Ugarit-Verlag), 9–24.

Alföldi, Andreas (1970) *Die monarchische Repräsentation im römischen Kaiserreiche* (Darmstadt: Wissenschaftliche Buchgesellschaft).

Alp, Sedat (1968) *Zylinder–und Stempelsiegel aus Karahöyük bei Konya* (Ankara: Türk Tarih Kurumu Basımevi).

(1991) *Hethitische Briefe aus Maşat-Höyük* (Ankara: Türk Tarih Kurumu Basımevi).

(1997) Die Mehrheit der einheimischen Bevölkerung in der Kārum-Zeit in Kaneš/Neša, *Studi Micenei ed Egeo-Anatolici* 39, 35–48.

Alparslan, Metin & Doğan-Alparslan, Meltem (2018) Handelsrouten und militärische Straßen im hethitischen Anatolien unter besonderer Berücksichtigung der Geographie Anatoliens, in Ü. Yalçın (ed.), *Anatolian Metal VIII. Eliten-Handwerk-Prestigegüter* (Bochum: Deutsches Bergbau Museum), 233–40.

Andrén, Anders (1998) *Between Artifacts and Texts. Historical Archaeology in Global Perspective* (New York & London: Plenum Press).

Archi, Alfonso (1973) L'organizzazione amministrativa ittita e il regime delle offerte cultuali, *Oriens Antiquus* 12, 209–26.

(1979) L'humanité des hittites, in *Florilegium Anatolicum* (Paris: Éditions E. de Boccard), 37–48.

(2005) I modi della memoria, in F. Pecchioli Daddi & M. C. Guidotti (eds.) *Narrare gli eventi* (Roma: Herder), 21–8.

(2010) When did the hittites begin to write in Hittite?, in Y. Cohen, A. Gilan & J. Miller (eds.) *Pax Hethitica. Studies on the Hittites and their Neighbours in Honour of Itamar Singer* (Wiesbaden: Harrassowitz), 37–46.

(2015a) A Royal Seal from Ebla (17th cent. B.C.) with Hittite Hieroglyphic Symbols, *Orientalia* 84, 18–28 w. Tab. I.

(2015b) How the Anitta text reached Hattusa, in A. Müller-Karpe, E. Rieken & W. Sommerfeld (eds.) *Saeculum. Gedenkschrift für Heinrich Otten anlässlich seines 100. Geburtstags* (Wiesbaden: Harrassowitz), 1–13.

Arnaud, Daniel (1985–1986) *Recherches au pays d'Aštata. Emar VI.1–3. Textes sumériens et accadiens* (Paris: Éditions Recherche sur les Civilisations).

(1991) *Textes syriens de l'âge du bronze récent (avec une contribution d'Hatice Gonnet, Sceaux hiéroglyphiques anatoliens de Syrie)* (Barcelona: Editorial AUSA).

Badalì, Enrico & Zinko, Christian (1994) *Der 16. Tag des an.taḫ.šum-Festes* (2nd ed.)(Graz: Scientia).

Bagnall, Roger (2011) *Everyday Writing in the Graeco-Roman East* (Berkeley, Los Angeles & London: University of California Press).

Baines, John (2004) The earliest Egyptian Writing: Development, context, purpose, in St. Houston (ed.) *The First Writing. Script Invention as History and Process* (Cambridge: Cambridge University Press), 150–89.

(2007) *Visual and Written Culture in Ancient Egypt* (Oxford: Oxford University Press).

Balkan, Kemal (1957) *Letter of King Anum-Hirbi of Mama to King Warshama of Kanish* (Ankara: Türk Tarih Kurumu Basımevi).

Balza, Maria Elena (2009) *Sigilli e modalità di sigillatura a Emar nel Tardo Bronzo (XIV-XIII sec. a.C.)* (Pavia: Italian University Press).

(2012) Sealed tablets from Ḫattuša, in M. E. Balza, M. Giorgieri & C. Mora (eds.) *Archivi, depositi, magazzini presso gli Ittiti. Nuovi materiali e nuove ricerche/Archives, Depots and Storehouses in the Hittite World. New Evidence and New Research* (Genova: Italian University Press), 77–110.

Barjamovic, Gojko (2011) *A Historical Geography of Anatolia in the Old Assyrian Colony Period* (Copenhagen: Museum Tusculanum Press).

Barjamovic, Gojko, Hertel, Thomas & Larsen, Mogens (2012) *Ups and Dowens at Kanesh. Chronology, History and Society in the Old Assyrian Period* (Leiden: Nederlands Instituut voor het Nabije Oosten).

Beal, Peter (2008) *A Dictionary of English Manuscript Terminology 1450–2000* (Oxford: Oxford University Press).

Beal, Richard (2003) The predecessors of Ḫattušili I, in G. Beckman, R. H. Beal & G. McMahon (eds.) *Hittite Studies in Honor of Harry A. Hoffner Jr. on the Occasion of His 65th Birthday* (Winona Lake, IN: Eisenbrauns), 13–35.

Beckman, Gary (1982) The Anatolian Myth of Illuyanka, *Journal of the Ancient Near Eastern Society* 14, 11–25.

(1983a) *Hittite Birth Rituals* (Wiesbaden: Harrassowitz).

(1983b) Mesopotamians and Mesopotamian Learning at Ḫattuša, *Journal of Cuneiform Studies* 35, 97–114.
(1995a) The Siege of Uršu Text (*CTH* 7) and Old Hittite Historiography, *Journal of Cuneiform Studies* 47, 23–34.
(1995b) Hittite provincial administration in Anatolia and Syria: The view from Maşat and Emar, in O. Carruba, M. Giorgieri & C. Mora (eds.) *Atti del II Congresso Internazionale di Hittitologia* (Pavia: Gianni Iuculano Editore), 19–37.
(1999) *Hittite Diplomatic Texts* (Atlanta, GA: Society of Biblical Literature).
(2001a) Sargon und Naram-Sin in Ḫatti: Reflections of Mesopotamian antiquity among the Hittites, in D. Kuhn & H. Stahl (eds.) *Die Gegenwart des Altertums. Formen und Funktionen des Altertumsbezugs in den Hochkulturen der Alten Welt* (Heidelberg: Edition Forum), 85–91.
(2001b) The Hittite Gilgamesh, in B. Foster, *The Epic of Gilgamesh* (New York & London: Norton & Company), 157–65.
(2006) Annals of Ḫattušili I, in M. Chavalas (ed.) *The Ancient Near East. Historical Sources in Translation* (Malden, MA: Blackwell), 219–22.
(2009) Hittite literature, in C. S. Ehrlich (ed.) *From an Antique Land. An Introduction to Ancient Near Eastern Literature* (Lanham, MD; Boulder, CO; New York, NY; Toronto & Plymouth: Rowman & Littlefield Publishers), 215–54.
(2013) Under the spell of Babylon: Mesopotamian influence on the religion of the Hittites, in J. Aruz, S. B. Graff & Y. Rakic (eds.) Cultures in Contact. From Mesopotamia to the Mediterranean in the Second Millennium B.C. (New York: Metropolitan Museum of Art), 284–97.
(2016) Birth and motherhood among the Hittites, in S. L. Budin & J. M. Turfa (eds.) *Women in Antiquity. Real women across the Ancient World* (London & New York: Routledge), 319–28.
(2019) Mesopotamians and Mesopotamian learning at Ḫattuša, thirty years on, in P. Avetisyan, R. Dan & Y. Grekyan (eds.) *Over the Mountains and Far Away. Studies in Near Eastern History and Archaeology Presented to Mirjo Salvini on the Occasion of his 80th birthday* (Oxford: Archaeopress Publishing Ltd.), 65–70.
Beckman, Gary, Bryce, Trevor & Cline, Eric (2011) *The Ahhiyawa Texts* (Atlanta GA: Society of Biblical Literature).
Beran, Thomas (1967) *Die hethitische Glyptik von Boğazköy. I. Teil: Die Siegel und Siegelabdrücke der vor- und althethitischen Perioden und die Siegel der hethitischen Grosskönige* (Berlin: Gebr. Mann Verlag).
Berman, Howard (1982) Review of A. Archi, KUB 49 and 50, *Journal of Cuneiform Studies* 34, 118–26.
Beyer, Dominique (2001) *Emar IV. Les sceaux* (Fribourg & Göttingen: Éditions Universitaires & Vandenhoeck & Ruprecht).
Bilgin, Tayfun (2018) *Officials and Administration in the Hittite World* (Berlin & Boston: De Gruyter).
Bittel, Kurt (1937) *Boğazköy. Die Kleinfunde der Grabungen 1906–1912. 1: Funde hethitischer Zeit* (Berlin: Verlag der Akademie der Wissenschaften).

(1950–1951) Bemerkungen zu dem auf Büyükkale (Boğazköy) entdeckten hethitischen Siegeldepot, *Jahrbuch für Kleinasiatische Forschungen* 1, 164–73.

(1976) *Beitrag zur Kenntnis hethitischer Bildkunst* (Heidelberg: Winter Verlag).

(1983) *Hattuscha, Hauptstadt der Hethiter. Geschichte und Kultur einer altorientalischen Großmacht* (Köln: DuMont Buchverlag).

Bittel, Kurt & Güterbock, Hans (1935) *Boğazköy. Neue Untersuchungen in der hethitischen Hauptstadt* (Berlin: Akademie der Wissenschaften).

Bittel, Kurt & Naumann, Rudolf (1952) *Boğazköy-Ḫattuša. Ergebnisse der Ausgrabungen des Deutschen Archäologischen Instituts und der Deutschen Orient-Gesellschaft in den Jahren 1931–1939* (Stuttgart: W. Kohlhammer Verlag).

Bittel, Kurt et al. (1975) *Das hethitische Felsheiligtum Yazılıkaya* (Berlin: Gebr. Mann).

Blair, Ann (2010) *Too Much to Know. Managing Scholarly Information before the Modern Age* (New Haven & London: Yale University Press).

Bodine, Walter (2014) *How Mesopotamian Scribes Learned to Write Legal Documents. A Study of the Sumerian Model Contracts in the Babylonian Collection at Yale University* (Lewiston, NY: The Edwin Mellen Press).

Boehmer, Rainer (1972) *Die Kleinfunde von Boğazköy* (Berlin: Gebr. Mann).

(1979) *Die Kleinfunde aus der Unterstadt von Boğazköy. Grabungskampagnen 1970–1978* (Berlin: Gebr. Mann Verlag).

Boehmer, Rainer & Güterbock, Hans (1987) *Glyptik aus dem Stadtgebiet von Boğazköy. Grabungskampagnen 1931–1939, 1952–1978* (Berlin: Gebr. Mann).

Bolatti-Guzzo, Natalia, Marazzi, Massimiliano & Mora, Clelia (1998) L'inventario dei segni e le modalità di traslitterazione, in M. Marazzi, N. Bolatti-Guzzo & P. Dardano (eds.) *Il Geroglifico Anatolico. Sviluppi della ricerca a venti anni dalla sua "ridecifrazione"* (Napoli: Istituto Universitario Orientale), 3–124.

Bossert, Helmuth (1944) *Ein hethitisches Königssiegel. Neue Beiträge zur Geschichte und Entzifferung der hethitischen Hieroglyphenschrift* (Istanbul: Archäologisches Institut des Deutschen Reiches).

Bryce, Trevor (2002) *Life and Society in the Hittite World* (Oxford: Oxford University Press).

(2003) History, in H. C. Melchert (ed.) *The Luwians* (Brill: Leiden-Boston), 27–127.

(2005) *The Kingdom of the Hittites* (new ed.) (Oxford: Oxford University Press).

(2012a) *The World of the Neo-Hittite Kingdoms. A Political and Military History* (Oxford: Oxford University Press).

(2012b) The Nişantepe Archive and the Hittite Royal Dynasty, *Ancient Near Eastern Studies* 49, 222–35.

Bunčić, Daniel, Lippert, Sandra & Rabus, Achim (eds.) (2016) *Biscriptality. A sociolinguistic typology* (Heidelberg: Winter).

Burgin, James M. (2016) *Aspects of Religious Administration in the Hittite Late New Kingdom*, Dissertation (Chicago: University of Chicago).

Burgin, James & van den Hout, Theo (2016) Weihgabe. B. Bei den Hethitern, *Reallexikon der Assyriologie* 15, 32–5.

Çambel, Halet (1999) *Corpus of Hieroglyphic Luwian Inscriptions. Volume II. Karatepe-Arslantaş. The Inscriptions: Facsimile Edition* (Berlin & New York: Walter de Gruyter).

Cammarosano, Michele (2012a) Hittite Cult Inventories – Part Two: The Dating of the Texts and the Alleged 'Cult Reorganization' of Tudḫaliya IV, *Altorientalische Forschungen* 39, 3–37.

(2012b) Review of J. Klinger, E. Rieken & Chr. Rüster (eds.) Investigationes Anatolicae. Gedenkschrift für Erich Neu, *Bibliotheca Orientalis* 69, 106–13.

(2013) Hittite Cult Inventories – Part One: The Hittite Cult Inventories as Textual Genre, *Welt des Orients* 43, 63–105.

(2018) *Hittite Local Cults* (Atlanta GA: Society of Biblical Literature).

Campbell, Dennis (2016) The Introduction of Hurrian Religion into the Hittite Empire, *Religion Compass*, 2016, 295–306.

Canby, Jean V. (2002) Falconry (Hawking) in Hittite Lands, *Journal of Near Eastern Studies* 61, 161–201.

Cancik, Hubert (1976) *Grundzüge der hethitischen und alttestamentlichen Geschichtsschreibung* (Wiesbaden: Harrassowitz).

Carruba, Onofrio (1966) *Das Beschwörungsritual für die Göttin Wišurijanza* (Wiesbaden: Harrassowitz).

(1970) *Das Palaische: Texte, Grammatik, Lexikon* (Wiesbaden: Harrassowitz).

(1972) *Beiträge zum Palaischen* (Leiden: Nederlands Instituut voor het Nabije Oosten).

(1988) Die Hajasa-Verträge Hattis, in E. Neu & Chr. Rüster (eds.) *Documentum Asiae Minoris. Festschrift für Heinrich Otten zum 75. Geburtstag* (Wiesbaden: Harrassowitz), 59–75.

(1993) Zur Datierung der ältesten Schenkungsurkunden und der anonymen Tabarna-Siegel, *Istanbuler Mitteilungen* 43, 71–85.

(2003) *Anittae Res Gestae* (Pavia: Italian University Press).

Carruthers, Mary (2008 [1990]) *The Book of Memory. A Study of Memory in Medieval Culture* (Cambridge: Cambridge University Press).

Casson, Lionel (2001) *Libraries in the Ancient World* (New Haven & London: Yale University Press).

Catsanicos, Jean (1994) La mise à jour du système de transcription des textes hittites, *Indogermanische Forschungen* 99, 301–35.

Charpin, Dominique (2002) Esquisse d'une diplomatique des documents méso-potamiens, *Bibliothèque de l'École des chartes* 160, 487–511.

(2008) *Lire et écrire à Babylone* (Paris: Presses Universitaires de France).

Christiansen, Birgit (2006) *Die Ritualtradition der Ambazzi. Eine philologische Bearbeitung und entstehungsgeschichtliche Analyse der Ritualtexte CTH 391, CTH 429 und CTH 463* (Wiesbaden: Harrassowitz).

(2008) Review of Dardano 2006, *Zeitschrift für Assyriologie* 98, 302–8.

(2016) Liturgische Agenda, Unterweisungsmaterial und rituelles Traditionsgut. Die hethitischen Festritualtexte in kulturvergleichender Perspektive, in G. Müller (ed.) *Liturgie oder Literatur? Die Kultrituale der Hethiter im transkulturellen Vergleich* (Wiesbaden: Harrassowitz), 31–65.

Clanchy, Michael (1993, 3rd ed.) *From Memory to Written Record. England 1066–1307* (Oxford & Cambridge, MA: Blackwell Publishing).

Cohen, Yoram (2012) The Ugu-mu Fragment from Ḫattuša/Boğazköy KBo 13.2, *Journal of Near Eastern Studies* 71, 1–12.

(2013) *Wisdom from the Late Bronze Age* (Atlanta, GA: Society of Biblical Literature).

(2018) Why 'Wisdom'? Copying, studying, and collecting wisdom literature in the cuneiform world, in T. M. Oshima & S. Kohlhaas (eds.), *Teaching Morality in Antiquity. Wisdom Texts, Oral Traditions, and Images* (Tübingen: Mohr Siebeck), 41–59.

Collins, Billie Jean (1987) §54 of the Hittite Laws and the Old Kingdom Periphery, *Orientalia* 56, 136–41.

Collon, Dominique (1987) *First Impressions. Cylinder Seals in the Ancient Near East* (Chicago: University of Chicago Press).

Cooper, Jerry (2004) Babylonian beginnings: The origin of the cuneiform writing system in comparative perspective, in St. Houston (ed.) *The First Writing. Script Invention as History and Process* (Cambridge: Cambridge University Press), 71–99.

Corti, Carlo (2007) The so-called "Theogony" or "Kingship in Heaven." The name of the Song, *Studi Micenei ed Egeo-Anatolici* 49, 109–21.

Coulmas, Florian (1996) *The Blackwell Encyclopedia of Writing Systems* (Oxford-Malden, MA: Blackwell).

(2013) *Writing and Society. An Introduction* (Cambridge: Cambridge University Press).

Curtius, Ludwig (1950) *Deutsche und Antike Welt. Lebenserinnerungen* (Stuttgart: Deutsche Verlags-Anstalt).

D'Alfonso, Lorenzo & Payne, Annick (2016) The Paleography of Anatolian Hieroglyphic Stone Inscriptions, *Journal of Cuneiform Studies* 68, 107–27.

D'Altroy, Terence & Earle, Timothy (1985) Staple Finance, Wealth Finance, and Storage in the Inka Political Economy, *Current Anthropology* 26, 187–206.

Daniels, Peter (2018) *An Exploration of Writing* (Sheffield, UK & Bristol, CT: Equinox Publishing).

Daniels, Peter & Bright, William (1996) *The World's Writing Systems* (Oxford & New York, NY: Oxford University Press).

Dardano, Paola (1997) *L'aneddoto e il racconto in età antico-hittita: la cosiddetta "Cronaca di Palazzo"* (Roma: Editrice "Il Calamo").

(2006) *Die hethitischen Tontafelkataloge aus Ḫattuša (CTH 276–282)* (Wiesbaden: Harrassowitz).

(2011) Erzählte Vergangenheit und kulturelles Gedächtnis im hethitischen Schrifttum, in M. Hutter & S. Hutter-Braunsar (eds.), *Hethitische Literatur. Überlieferungsprozesse, Textstrukturen, Ausdrucksformen und Nachwirken* (Münster: Ugarit-Verlag), 63–81.

Dehaene, Stanislas (2009) *Reading in the Brain. The Science and Evolution of a Human Invention* (New York: Viking).

del Monte, Giuseppe (1993) *L'annalistica ittita* (Brescia: Paideia Editrice).
(1995) I testi amministrativi da Maşat Höyük/Tapika, *Orientis Antiqui Miscellanea* 2, 89–138.
(2008) *Le gesta di Suppiluliuma. Traslitterazione, traduzione e commento* (Edizioni Plus).
Delnero, Paul (2010) Sumerian Literary Catalogs and the Scribal Curriculum, *Zeitschrift für Assyriologie* 100, 32–55.
(2012) Memorization and the Transmission of Sumerian Literary Compositions, *Journal of Near Eastern Studies* 71, 189–208.
de Martino, Stefano (1999) La cosidetta "Cronaca di Ammuna," in St. de Martino & F. Imparati (eds.) *Studi e testi II* (Firenze: LoGisma editore), 69–82.
(2003) *Annali e res gestae antico ittiti* (Pavia: Italian University Press).
(2005) Hittite Letters from the Time of Tutḫaliya I/II, Arnuwanda I and Tutḫaliya III, *Altorientalische Forschungen* 32, 291–321.
(2013) Hurrian personal names in the kingdom of Ḫatti, in L. Feliu et al. (eds.) *56th Comptes-rendus du Rencontre Assyriologique Internationale, Barcelona* (Winona Lake, IN: Eisenbrauns), 481–6.
(2016) Hittite diplomacy. The royal messengers, in P. Corò, E. Devecchi, N. de Zorzi & M. Maiocchi (eds.) *Libiamo ne' lieti calici. Ancient Near Eastern Studies Presented to Lucio Milano on the Occasion of his 65th Birthday by Pupils, Colleagues and Friends* (Münster: Ugarit-Verlag), 365–75.
(2017) The Hurrian language in Anatolia in the Late Bronze Age, in A. Mouton (ed.) *Hittitology Today: Studies on Hittite and Neo-Hittite Anatolia in Honor of Emmanuel Laroche's 100th Birthday/Hittitologie Aujourd'hui: Études sur l'Anatolie hittite et néo-hittite à l'occasion du centenaire de la naissance d'Emmanuel Laroche* (Istanbul: Institut Français d'Études Anatoliennes Georges-Dumézil), 151–62.
(2018) The Fall of the Hittite Kingdom, *Mesopotamia* 53, 23–48.
Dercksen, Jan Gerrit (2002) Kultureller und wirtschaftlicher Austausch zwischen Assyrern und Anatoliern (Anfang des zweiten Jahrtausends v. Chr.), in H. Blum, B. Faist, P. Pfälzner & A. -M. Wittke (eds.) *Brückenland Anatolien? Ursachen, Extensität und Modi des Kulturaustausches zwischen Anatolien und seinen Nachbarn* (Tübingen: Attempto), 35–44.
(2004) Some elements of old Anatolian society in Kaniš, in J. Dercksen (ed.) *Assyria and Beyond. Studies Presented to Mogens Trolle Larsen* (Leiden: Nederlands Instituut voor het Nabije Oosten), 137–77.
(2007) On Anatolian loanwords in Akkadian texts from Kültepe, *Zeitschrift für Assyriologie* 97, 26–46.
(2010) Anitta and the Man of Purušhanda, in Ş. Dönmez (ed.) *Veysel Donbaz'a Sunulan Yazılar* DUB.SAR É.DUB.BA.A *Studies Presented in Honour of Veysel Donbaz* (İstanbul: Ege Yayınları), 71–5.
de Roos, Johan (2007) *Hittite Votive Texts* (Leiden: Nederlands Instituut voor het Nabije Oosten).
Devecchi, Elena (2005) *Gli annali di Ḫattušili I nella versione accadica* (Pavia: Italian University Press).

(2010) "We are all descendants of Šuppiluliuma, Great King." The Aleppo Treaty Reconsidered, *Welt des Orients* 40, 1–27.

(2012) The Amarna Letters from Ḫatti. A palaeographic analysis, in T. Boiy et al. (eds.) *The Ancient Near East, a Life! Festschrift Karel van Lerberghe* (Leuven-Paris & Walpole MA: Uitgeverij Peeters & Departement Oosterse Studies), 143–53.

de Voogt, Alex (2012) Invention and borrowing in the development and dispersal of writing systems, in A. de Voogt & J. Quack (eds.) (2012) *The Idea of Writing. Writing Across Borders* (Leiden-Boston: Brill), 1–10.

de Voogt, Alex & Döhla, Hans Jörg (2012) Nubian graffiti messages and the history of writing in the Sudanese Nile Basin, in A. de Voogt & J. Quack (eds.) *The Idea of Writing. Writing Across Borders* (Leiden & Boston: Brill), 53–67.

de Vos, An (2013) *Die Lebermodelle aus Boğazköy* (Wiesbaden: Harrassowitz).

Diakonoff, Igor (1967) Die hethitische Gesellschaft, *Mitteilungen des Instituts für Orientforschung* 13, 313–66.

Dietrich, Manfred & Loretz, Oswald (2004) Alalaḫ-Texte der Schicht VII (I). Historische und Juristische Dokumente, *Ugarit-Forschungen* 36, 43–150.

(2005) Alalaḫ-Texte der Schicht VII (II). Schultexte, Vermerke und Sonstiges, *Ugarit-Forschungen* 37, 241–314.

(2006) Alalaḫ-Texte der Schicht VII (III). Die Listen der Gruppen ATaB 40, ATaB 42, ATaB 43 und ATaB 44, *Ugarit-Forschungen* 38, 87–137.

Dinçol, Ali (1989) Mızrakucu Üzerindeki Hieroglif Yazıt/The Hieroglyphic Signs on the Spearhead, in Ç. Anlağan/Ö. Bilgi (eds.) *Protohistorik Çağ Silahları/ Weapons of the Protohistoric Age* (Istanbul: Sadberk Hanım Müzesi), 23, 103–4.

(1998) *The Rock Monument of the Great King Kurunta and its Hieroglyphic Inscription III. Uluslararasi Hititoloji Kongresi Bildirileri, Çorum: Acts of the IIIrd International Congress of Hittitology, Çorum 1996* (Ankara:), 159–66.

Dinçol, Belkıs (2017) A new tablet fragment and a sealed pottery fragment from Alaca Höyük, in A. Mouton (ed.) *Hittitology Today: Studies on Hittite and Neo-Hittite Anatolia in Honor of Emmanuel Laroche's 100th Birthday/ Hittitologie Aujourd'hui: Études sur l'Anatolie hittite et néo-hittite à l'occasion du centenaire de la naissance d'Emmanuel Laroche* (Istanbul: Institut Français d'Études Anatoliennes Georges-Dumézil), 225–8.

Dinçol, Ali & Dinçol, Belkıs (1988) Hieroglyphische Siegel und Siegelabdrücke aus Eskiyapar, in E. Neu & Chr. Rüster (eds.) *Documentum Asiae Minoris. Festschrift für Heinrich Otten zum 75. Geburtstag* (Wiesbaden: Harrassowitz), 87–97.

(2002) Die 'Anzeigen' der öffentlichen Schreiber in Hattuscha, in St. de Martino & F. Pecchioli Daddi (eds.) *Anatolia Antica. Studi in memoria di Fiorella Imparati* (Firenze: LoGisma Editore), 207–15.

(2008) *Die Prinzen- und Beamtensiegel aus der Oberstadt von Boğazköy-Ḫattuša vom 16. Jahrhundert bis zum Ende der Grossreichszeit* (Mainz am Rhein: Verlag Philipp von Zabern).

(2010) Drei hieroglyphische Tripodstempel aus der Perk Sammlung, in Ş. Dönmez (ed.) *Veysel Donbaz'a Sunulan Yazılar* DUB.SAR É.DUB.BA.A *Studies Presented in Honour of Veysel Donbaz* (İstanbul: Ege Yayınları), 87–9.

Dinçol, Ali, Dinçol, Belkıs & Peker, Hasan (2012) New Hittite Hieroglyphic Seals from the Plain of Antioch in the Hatay Museum, *Anatolica* 38, 191–9.

Dinçol, Belkıs, Hawkins, David & Peker, Hasan (2014) A New Hieroglyphic Luwian Inscription from the Hatay, *Anatolica* 40, 61–70.

(2015) Two new inscribed Storm-god stelae from Arsuz (İskenderun): ARSUZ 1 and 2, *Anatolian Studies* 65, 59–77.

Doğan-Alparslan, Meltem (2007) Drei Schreiber, Zwei Könige, *Studi Micenei ed Egeo-Anatolici* 49, 247–57.

Doğan-Alparslan, Meltem & Alparslan, Metin (2011) Wohnsitze und Hauptstädte der hethitischen Könige, *Istanbuler Mitteilungen* 61, 85–103.

Duhoux, Yves (2017) Aides à la lecture à l'âge du bronze: Égée, Chypre et Proche-Orient, in M. -L. Nosch & H. Landenius Enegren (eds.) *Aegean Scripts. Proceedings of the 14th International Colloquium on Mycenaean Studies, Copenhagen, 2–5 September 2015* (Roma: CNR Edizioni), 209–27.

Duranti, Luciana (1998) *Diplomatics. New Uses for an Old Science* (Lanham, MD & London: The Scarecrow Press, Inc.).

Earle, Timothy (2002) *Bronze Age Economics. The Beginnings of Political Economies* (Boulder, CO: Westview Press).

Edel, Elmar (1994) *Die ägyptisch-hethitische Korrespondenz aus Boghazköi in babylonischer und hethitischer Sprache* (Opladen: Westdeutscher Verlag).

Emre, Kutlu & Çınaroğlu, Aykut (1993) A group of metal Hittite vessels from Kınık – Kastamonu, in M. Mellink, E. Porada & T. Özgüç (eds.) *Aspects of Art and Iconography: Anatolia and Its Neighbors. Studies in Honor of Nimet Özgüç* (Ankara: Türk Tarih Kurumu Basımevi), 675–713.

Ertekin, Ahmet & Ediz, Ismet (1993) The unique sword from Boğazköy/Ḫattuša, in M. Mellink, E. Porada & T. Özgüç (eds.) *Aspects of Art and Iconography: Anatolia and Its Neighbors. Studies in Honor of Nimet Özgüç* (Ankara: Türk Tarih Kurumu Basımevi), 719–25.

Ewald, Wilhelm (1914) *Siegelkunde* (München-Berlin: Verlag von R. Oldenbourg).

Everling, János † & Földi, Zsombor (2015) Talmi-Šarruma, an unknown scribe of the ḫišuwa-ritual (CTH 628), *Nouvelles Assyriologiques Brèves et Utilitaires* 2015, 110–13.

Farber-Flügge, Gertrud (1973) *Der Mythos "Inanna und Enki" unter besonderer Berücksichtigung der Liste m e* (Rome: Biblical Institute Press).

Feeney, Denis (2016) *Beyond Greek. The Beginnings of Latin Literature* (Cambridge, MA, London: Harvard University Press).

Fink, Amir (2007) Where Was the Statue of Idrimi Actually Found? The Later Temples of Tell Atchana (Alalakh) Revisited, *Ugarit-Forschungen* 39, 161–245.

Fissore, Gian Giacomo (1994) Conceptual development and organizational techniques in the documents and archives of the earliest Near Eastern civilizations, in P. Ferioli, E. Fiandra, G. Fissore & M. Frangipane (eds.) *Archives before Writing* (Torino: Scriptorium), 339–61.

Forlanini, Massimo (2010) An attempt at reconstructing the branches of the Hittite royal family of the Early Kingdom Period, in Y. Cohen, A. Gilan & J. Miller (eds.) *Pax Hethitica. Studies on the Hittites and their Neighbours in Honour of Itamar Singer* (Wiesbaden: Harrassowitz), 115–35.

Forrer, Emil (1922a) Die Inschriften und Sprachen des Ḫatti-Reiches, *Zeitschrift der Deutschen Morgenländischen Gesellschaft* 76 NF1, 174–269.

(1922b) *Die Boghazköi-Texte in Umschrift. E. Band. Einleitung: Die Keilschrift von Boghazköi* (Leipzig: J. C. Hinrichs'sche Buchhandlung).

Frahm, Eckhart (2004) Royal Hermeneutics: Observations on the Commentaries from Ashurbanipal's Libraries at Nineveh, *Iraq* 66, 45–50.

Francia, Rita (2015) L'archivio di tavolette del complesso B-C-H di Büyükkale e l'organizzazione degli archivi reali ittiti. Considerazioni preliminari, *Vicino Oriente* 19, 247–60.

Frangipane, Marcella et al. (2007) *Arslantepe Cretulae. An Early Centralised Administrative System Before Writing* (Roma: Università di Roma "La Sapienza").

Franklin, Simon (2002) *Writing, Society and Culture in Early Rus, c. 950–1300* (Cambridge: Cambridge University Press).

Fuscagni, Francesco (2007) Hethitische unveröffentlichte Texte aus den Jahren 1906–1912 in der Sekundärliteratur (Wiesbaden: Harrassowitz).

Gamkrelidze, Thomas V. (2008) The Problem of the Origin of the Hittite Cuneiform, *Bulletin of the Georgian National Academy of Sciences* 2/3:169–74.

Gates, Marie-Henriette (2017) Gods, temples, and cult at the service of the early Hittite state, in Y. Heffron, A. Stone & M. Worthington (eds.) *At the Dawn of History. Ancient Near Eastern Studies in Honour of J. N. Postgate* (Winona Lake, IN: Eisenbrauns), 189–210.

Geertz, Clifford (1980) *Negara. The Theatre State in Nineteenth-Century Bali* (Princeton: Princeton University Press).

Gelb, Ignace J. (1935) *Inscriptions from Alishar and Vicinity* (Chicago: Oriental Institute).

Genz, Herrmann (2017) Regional or international? Comments on the origin and development of Hittite weapons and military technology, in A. Schachner (ed.) *Innovation versus Beharrung. Was macht den Unterschied des hethitischen Reiches im Anatolien des 2. Jahrtausends v. Chr.? Internazionaler Workshop zu Ehren von Jürgen Seeher* (Istanbul: Ege Yayınları), 85–103.

Gilan, Amir (2005) Die hethitischen 'Mannestaten' und ihre Adressaten, in A. Süel (ed.) *V. Uluslararası Hititoloji Kongresi Bildirileri/Acts of the Vth International Congress of Hittitology* (Ankara), 359–69.

(2007) Formen der Transaktion im hethitischen 'Staatskult' – Idee und Wirklichkeit, in H. Klinkott, S. Kubisch & R. Müller-Wollermann (eds.) *Geschenke und Steuern, Zölle und Tribute. Antike Abgabenformen in Anspruch und Wirklichkeit* (Leiden & Boston: Brill), 293–322.

(2015) *Formen und Inhalte althethitischer historischer Literatur* (Heidelberg: Winter Verlag).
Giorgieri, Mauro (2000) Schizzo grammaticale della lingua hurrica, *Parola del passato* 55, 171–295.
Giorgieri, Mauro & Mora, Clelia (1996) *Aspetti della regalità ittita nel XIII seculo a. C.* (Como: Biblioteca di Atheneum).
(2012) Luxusgüter als Symbole der Macht: Zur Verwaltung der Luxusgüter im Hethiter-Reich, in G. Wilhelm (ed.) *Organization, Representation, and Symbols of Power in the Ancient Near East. Proceedings of the 54th Rencontre Assyriologique Internationale, Würzburg* (Winona Lake, IN: Eisenbrauns), 647–64.
Giusfredi, Federico (2010) *Sources for a Socio-Economic History of the Neo-Hittite States* (Heidelberg: Winter Verlag).
(2012a) Note di lessico e di cultura "scribale" ittita e luvia, *Centro Mediterraneo Preclassico. Studi e Ricerche* 3, 145–72.
(2012b) The Akkadian Medical Text KUB 37.1, *Altorientalische Forschungen* 39, 49–63.
Glatz, Claudia (2009) Empire as Network: Spheres of Material Interaction in Late Bronze Age Anatolia, *Journal of Anthropological Archaeology* 28, 127–41.
(2012) Bearing the Marks of Control? Reassessing Pot Marks in Late Bronze Age Anatolia, *American Journal of Archaeology*, 116, 5–38.
Goedegebuure, Petra (2002–2003) The Hittite 3rd Person/Distal Demonstrative *aši* (*uni, eni* etc.), *Die Sprache* 43, 1–32.
(2008) Central Anatolian languages and language communities in the Colony Period: A Luwian-Hattian symbiosis and the independent Hittites, in J. G. Dercksen (ed.) *Anatolia and the Jazira during the Old Assyrian Period* (Leiden: Nederlands Instituut voor het Nabije Oosten), 137–80.
(2010) The Luwian adverbs *zanta* "down" and **ānni* "with, for, against," in A. Süel (ed.) *VII. Uluslararası Hititoloji Kongresi Bildirileri/Acts of the VIIth International Congress of Hittitology 2008* (Ankara: T.C. Çorum Valiliği), 299–318.
(2012) Hittite iconoclasm: Disconnecting the icon, disempowering the referent, in N. May (ed.) *Iconoclasm and Text Destruction in the Ancient Near East and Beyond* (Chicago: The Oriental Institute), 407–52.
(2014) *The Hittite Demonstratives. Studies in Deixis, Topic and Focus* (Wiesbaden: Harrassowitz).
(2017) A New Join to a Festival of Thunder: KBo 31.183 + KBo 34.185 + KBo 20.61 (CTH 631), *Nouvelles Assyriologiques Brèves et Utilitaires* 105–7.
Goetze, Albrecht (1925) *Ḫattušiliš. Der Bericht über seine Thronbesteigung nebst den Paralleltexten* (Leipzig: J.C. Hinrichs'sche Buchhandlung).
(1929) Die Pestgebete des Muršiliš, *Kleinasiatische Forschungen* 1, 161–251.
(1933) *Die Annalen des Muršiliš* (Leipzig: J.C. Hinrichs'sche Buchhandlung).
Goldman, Hetty (1956) *Excavations at Gözlü Kule, Tarsus. Volume II: From the Neolithic through the Bronze Age* (Princeton: Princeton University Press).

Goodnick Westenholz, Joan (2000) *Cuneiform Inscriptions in the Collection of the Bible Lands Museum Jerusalem: the Emar Tablets* (Groningen: Styx).
Goody, John (1986) *The Logic of Writing and the Organization of Society* (Cambridge: Cambridge University Press).
Goody, John & Watt, Ian (1963) The Consequences of Literacy, *Comparative Studies in Society History* 5, 304–45.
Gordin, Shai (2010) *Scriptoria* in Late Empire Period Ḫattusa: The case of the É GIŠ.KIN.TI, in Y. Cohen, A. Gilan & J. Miller (eds.) *Pax Hethitica. Studies on the Hittites and Their Neighbours in Honour of Itamar Singer* (Wiesbaden: Harrassowitz), 158–77.
(2011) The Tablet and the Scribe: Between Archival and Scribal Spaces in Late Empire Period Ḫattusa, *Altorientalische Forschungen* 38, 177–98.
(2014) The socio-historical setting of scribal schools of writing as reflected in scribal habits, in S. Gordin (ed.) *Visualizing Knowledge and Creating Meaning in Ancient Writing Systems* (Gladbeck: PeWe-Verlag), 57–79.
(2015) *Hittite Scribal Circles. Scholarly Tradition and Writing Habits* (Wiesbaden: Harrassowitz).
Goren, Yuval, Mommsen, Hans & Klinger, Jörg (2011) Non-destructive Provenance Study of Cuneiform Tablets Using Portable X-Ray Fluorescence (pXRF), *Journal of Archaeological Science* 38, 684–96.
Grélois, Jean-Pierre (1988) Les annales décennales de Mursili II (CTH 61, I), *Hethitica* 9, 17–145.
Groddek, Detlev (2002) *Hethitische Texte in Transkription KUB 55* (Dresden: Verlag der TU Dresden).
Gurney, Oliver (1997) The Annals of Hattusilis III, *Anatolian Studies* 47, 127–39.
Güterbock, Hans Gustav (1937) Schrifturkunden. A. Die Siegel, in K. Bittel, Vorläufiger Bericht über die Ausgrabungen in Boğazköy 1936, *Mitteilungen der Deutschen Orient-Gesellschaft* 75, 1–70.
(1939) Das Siegeln bei den hethitern, in *Symbolae Paulo Koschaker Dedicatae* (Leiden: Brill), 26–36.
(1940) *Siegel aus Boğazköy. Erster Teil: Die Königssiegel der Grabungen bis 1938* (Berlin: Selbstverlag).
(1942) *Siegel aus Boğazköy. Zweiter Teil: Die Königssiegel von 1939 und die übrigen Hieroglyphensiegel* (Berlin: Selbstverlag).
(1944) Zile Yakınında Maşat'tan Gelme Bir Eti Mektubu (Ein hethitischer Brief aus Maşat bei Zile), *Ankara Üniversitesi Dil ve Tarih-Coğrafya Fakültesi Dergisi* II 3, 389–405.
(1956) The Deeds of Suppiluliuma as Told by His Son, Mursili II, *Journal of Cuneiform Studies* 10, 41–130.
(1957) Toward a Definition of the Term Hittite, *Oriens* 10, 233–9.
(1964) A View of Hittite Literature, *Journal of the American Oriental Society* 84, 107–15.
(1967) The Hittite Conquest of Cyprus Reconsidered, *Journal of Near Eastern Studies* 26, 73–81.

(1980) Seals and sealing in Hittite lands, in K. de Vries (ed.) *From Athens to Gordion. The Papers of a Memorial Symposium for Rodney S. Young* (Philadelphia: The University Museum), 51–63.

(1983) Hittite historiography: a survey, in H. Tadmor & M. Weinfeld (eds.) *History, Historiography and Interpretation. Studies in Biblical and Cuneiform Literatures* (Jerusalem & Leiden: Magnes Press & Brill), 21–35.

(1986) A Religious Text from Maşat, *Jahrbuch für Kleinasiatische Forschung* 10, 205–14.

(1997) Erinnerungen an das alte Boğazköy-Archiv und die Landschenkungsurkunde VAT 7436, *Altorientalische Forschungen* 24, 25–30.

(1998) Notes on some Luwian Hieroglyphs, in J. Jasanoff, H. C. Melchert & L. Oliver (eds.), *Mír Curad, Studies in Honour of Calvert Watkins* (Innsbruck: Innsbrucker Beiträge zur Sprachwissenschaft), 201–4.

Güterbock, Hans Gustav & Civil, Miguel (1985) The Series Erim-ḫuš in Boğazköy, *MSL* 17, 97–128.

Güterbock, Hans Gustav & Kendall, Timothy (1995) A Hittite silver vessel in the form of a fist, in J. Carter & S. Morris (eds.) *The Ages of Homer. A Tribute to Emily Townsend Vermeule* (Austin: University of Texas Press), 45–60.

Güterbock, Hans & van den Hout, Theo (1991) *The Hittite Instruction for the Royal Bodyguard* (Chicago: The Oriental Institute).

Haas, Volkert (1970) *Der Kult von Nerik. Ein Beitrag zur hethitischen Religionsgeschichte* (Roma: Pontificium Institutum Biblicum).

(1988a) Das Ritual gegen den Zugriff der Dämonin DDÌM.NUN.ME und die Sammeltafel KUB XLIII 55, *Oriens Antiquus* 27, 85–104.

(1988b) Betrachtungen zur Rekonstruktion des hethitischen Frühjahrsfestes (EZEN *purulliyaš*), *Zeitschrift für Assyriologie* 78, 284–98.

(1994) *Geschichte der hethitischen Religion* (Leiden, New York & Köln: Brill).

(2003) *Materia Magica et Medica Hethitica. Ein Beitrag zur Heilkunde im Alten Orient* (Berlin & New York: Walter de Gruyter).

(2006) *Die hethitische Literatur* (Berlin & New York: De Gruyter).

Haas, Volkert & Wegner, Ilse (1996) Review of KBo 39, *Orientalistische Literaturzeitung* 91, 573–5.

Haas, Volkert & Wilhelm, Gernot (1974) *Hurritische und luwische Riten aus Kizzuwatna. Hurritologische Studien 1* (Kevelaer-Neukirchen-Vluyn: Verlag Butzon & Bercker – Neukirchener Verlag).

Hagenbuchner, Albertine (1989a and 1989b) *Die Korrespondenz der Hethiter. 1. und 2. Teil* (Heidelberg: Winter Verlag).

Hallo, William (1977) Seals lost and found, in M. Gibson & R. Biggs (eds.) *Seals and Sealing in the Ancient Near East* (Malibu: Undena Publications), 55–60.

Hanaway, William (2012) Secretaries, poets, and the literary language, in B. Spooner & W. Hanaway (eds.) *Literacy in the Persianate World. Writing and the Social Order* (Philadelphia: University of Pennsylvania Museum of Archaeology and Anthropology), 95–142.

Hawkins, J. David (1986) Writing in Anatolia: imported and indigenous systems, *World Archaeology* 17, 363–76.

(1992) What does the Hittite Storm-God hold?, in D. J. W. Meijer (ed.) *Natural Phenomena. Their Meaning, Depiction and Description in the Ancient Near East* (Amsterdam, Oxford, New York & Tokyo: Koninklijke Nederlandse Akademie van Wetenschappen), 53–82.

(1993) A bowl epigraph of the official Taprammi, in M. Mellink, E. Porada & T. Özgüç (eds.) *Aspects of Art and Iconography: Anatolia and Its Neighbors. Studies in Honor of Nimet Özgüç* (Ankara: Türk Tarih Kurumu Basımevi), 715–17.

(1995) *The Hieroglyphic Inscription of the Sacred Pool Complex at Hattusa* (SÜDBURG), (Wiesbaden: Harrassowitz).

(1996) A Hieroglyphic Seal from Troia, *Studia Troica* 6, 111–18.

(1996 [1997]) A Hieroglyphic Luwian Inscription on a Silver Bowl in the Museum of Anatolian Civilizations, Ankara, *Anadolu Medeniyetleri Müzesi*, 7–21.

(1998) Tarkasnawa King of Mira: "Tarkondemos", Boğazköy sealings and Karabel *Anatolian Studies* 48, 1–31.

(2000) *Corpus of Hieroglyphic Luwian Inscriptions* (Berlin & New York: Walter de Gruyter).

(2002) Eunuchs among the Hittites, in S. Parpola & R. Whiting (eds.) *Sex and Gender in the Ancient Near East. 47th Rencontre Assyriologique Internationale, Helsinki* (Helsinki: The Neo-Assyrian Text Corpus Project), 217–33.

(2003) Scripts and texts, in H. C. Melchert (ed.) *The Luwians* (Brill: Leiden-Boston), 128–69.

(2006) Tudḫaliya the hunter, in Th. van den Hout & C. van Zoest (eds.) *The Life and Times of Ḫattušili III and Tudḫaliya IV* (Leiden: Nederlands Instituut voor het Nabije Oosten), 49–76.

(2011a) Early recognisable hieroglyphic signs(?) in Anatolia, in F. Kulakoğlu & S. Kangal (eds.) *Anatolia's Prologue, Kültepe Kanesh Karum, Assyrians in Istanbul* (Kayseri: Kayseri Metropolitan Municipality Cultural Publication), 96–7.

(2011b) The Inscriptions of the Aleppo Temple, *Anatolian Studies* 61, 35–54.

Hawkins, David & Easton, Donald (1996) A Hieroglyphic Seal from Troia, *Studia Troica* 6, 111–18.

Hazenbos, Joost (2003) *The Organization of the Anatolian Local Cults During the Thirteenth Century B.C.* (Leiden-Boston: Brill-Styx).

Hecker, Karl (1968) *Grammatik der Kültepe-Texte* (Roma: Pontificium Institutum Biblicum).

Henkelman, Wouter & Folmer, Margaretha (2016) *Your Tally is Full!* On wooden credit records in and after the Achaemenid Empire, in K. Kleber & R. Pirngruber (eds.) *Silver, Money and Credit. A Tribute to Robartus J. van der Spek on the Occasion of His 65th Birthday on 18th September 2014* (Leiden: Nederlands Instituut voor het Nabije Oosten), 133–239.

Herbordt, Suzanne (2002) Hittite seals and sealings from the Nişantepe Archive, Boğazköy: A prosopographical study, in A. Yener, H. Hoffner & S. Dhesi (eds.) *Recent Developments in Hittite Archaeology and History. Papers in Memory of Hans G. Güterbock* (Winona Lake, IN: Eisenbrauns), 53–60.

(2005) *Die Prinzen- und Beamtensiegel der hethitischen Grossreichszeit auf Tonbullen aus dem Nişantepe-Archiv in Hattusa* (Mainz am Rhein: Philipp von Zabern).

Herbordt, Suzanne, et al. (2011) *Die Siegel der Grosskönige und Grossköniginnen auf Tonbullen aus dem Nişantepe-Archiv in Hattusa* (Mainz am Rhein: Philipp von Zabern).

Hill Boone, Elizabeth (2004) Beyond writing, in St. Houston (ed.) *The First Writing. Script Invention as History and Process* (Cambridge: Cambridge University Press), 313–48.

Hirschler, Konrad (2012) *The Written Word in the Medieval Arabic Lands. A Social and Cultural History of Reading Practices* (Edinburgh: Edinburgh University Press).

(2016) *Medieval Damascus. Plurality and Diversity in an Arabic Library. The Ashrafiya Library Catalogue* (Edinburgh: Edinburgh University Press).

Hoffmann, Inge (1984) *Der Erlaß Telipinus* (Heidelberg: Winter Verlag).

Hoffner, Harry A. (1980) Histories and Historians of the Ancient Near East: The Hittites, *Orientalia* 49, 283–332.

(1982) The Milawata Letter Augmented and Reinterpreted, *Archiv für Orientforschung Beiheft* 19, 130–7.

(1995) Hittite laws, in M. Roth, *Law Collections from Mesopotamia and Asia Minor* (Atlanta, GA: Society of Biblical Literature), 213–47.

(1997a) *The Laws of the Hittites. A Critical Edition* (Leiden-New York-Köln: Brill).

(1997b) Hittite canonical compositions. Royal focus. 1. Epic. 2. Historiography, in W. Hallo & K. L. Younger (eds.) *The Context of Scripture. Canonical Compositions from the Biblical World* (Leiden, New York & Köln: Brill), 181–93.

(2001) Some thoughts on merchants and trade in the Hittite kingdom, in Th. Richter, D. Prechel & J. Klinger (eds.) *Kulturgeschichten. Altorientalische Studien für Volkert Haas zum 65. Geburtstag* (Saarbrücken: Saarbrücker Druckerei und Verlag), 179–89.

(2002) The treatment and long-term use of persons captured in battle according to the Maşat texts, in A. Yener & H. Hoffner (eds.) *Recent Developments in Hittite Archaeology and History. Papers in Memory of Hans G. Güterbock* (Winona Lake, IN: Eisenbrauns), 61–72.

(2009) *Letters from the Hittite Kingdom* (Atlanta, GA: Society of Biblical Literature).

Hoffner, Harry & Melchert, Craig (2008) *A Grammar of the Hittite Language* (Winona Lake, IN: Eisenbrauns).

Houston, George (2009) Papyrological evidence for book collections and libraries in the Roman Empire, in W. A. Johnson & H. N. Parker (eds.) *Ancient*

Literacies. The Culture of Reading in Greece and Rome (Oxford & New York: Oxford University Press), 233–67.

Houston, Steven (2004) (ed.) *The First Writing. Script Invention as History and Process* (Cambridge: Cambridge University Press).

Houwink ten Cate, Philo (1967) Muwatallis' Prayer to the Stormgod of Kummanni (KBo XI 1), *Revue Hittite et Asianique* 25/81, 101–27.

(1984) The History of Warfare According to Hittite Sources: The Annals of Hattusilis I (part II), *Anatolica* 11, 47–83.

(1986) Brief comments on the Hittite cult calendar: The outline of the AN.TAḪ.ŠUM Festival, in H. Hoffner & G. Beckman (eds.) *Kaniššuwar. A Tribute to Hans G. Güterbock on his Seventy-Fifth Birthday* (Chicago: Oriental Institute), 95–110.

(1992) The Bronze Tablet of Tudhaliyas IV and its Geographical and Historical Relations, *Zeitschrift für Assyriologie* 82, 233–70.

Hunger, Hermann (1968) *Babylonische und assyrische Kolophone* (Kevelaer-Neukirchen-Vluyn: Butzon & Bercker-Neukirchener Verlag).

Hutter, Manfred (2011) Sammeltafeln – Zufallsprodukt von Schreibern oder Ausdruck von hethitischem Literaturverständnis?, in M. Hutter & S. Hutter-Braunsar (eds.) *Hethitische Literatur. Überlieferungsprozesse, Textstrukturen, Ausdrucksformen und Nachwirken* (Münster: Ugarit-Verlag), 115–28.

Imparati, Fiorella (1974) Una concessione di terre da parte di Tuthaliya IV, *Revue Hittite et Asianique* 32.

Jakob-Rost, Liane (1961) Zu den hethitischen Bildbeschreibungen (I. Teil), *Mitteilungen des Instituts für Orientforschung* 8, 161–217.

Johnson, William (2010) *Readers and Reading Culture in the High Roman Empire. A Study of Elite Communities* (Oxford & New York: Oxford University Press).

Karasu, Cem, Poetto, Massimo & Savaş, Savaş (2000) New Fragments Pertaining to the Hieroglyphic Luwian Inscription of *Yalburt*, *Archivum Anatolicum* 4, 99–112.

Karateke, Hakan (2007) *An Ottoman Protocol Register Containing Ceremonies from 1736 to 1808: Beo Sadaret Defterleri 350 in the Prime Ministry Ottoman State* Archives, *Istanbul* (London & İstanbul: The Royal Asiatic Society/The Ottoman Bank Archive and Research Centre).

Kassian, Alexei (2000) *Two Middle Hittite Rituals Mentioning* [f]*Ziplantawija, Sister of the Hittite King* [m]*Tuthalija II/I* (Moscow: Paleograph).

Kassian, Alexei, Korolëv, Andrej † & Sidel'tsev, Andrej (2002) *Hittite Funerary Ritual šalliš waštaiš* (Münster: Ugarit-Verlag).

Kassian, Alexei & Yakubovich, Ilya (2007) Muršili II's Prayer to Telipinu (CTH 377), in D. Groddek & M. Zorman (eds.) *Tabularia Hethaeorum. Hethitologische Beiträge Silvin Košak zum 65. Geburtstag* (Wiesbaden: Harrassowitz), 423–54.

Kempinski, Aharon (1983) *Syrien und Palästina (Kanaan) in der letzten Phase der Mittelbronze IIB-Zeit* (Wiesbaden: Harrassowitz).

Klengel, Horst (1999) *Geschichte des hethitischen Reiches* (Leiden-Boston-Köln: Brill).

Klinger, Jörg (1996) *Untersuchungen zur Rekonstruktion der hattischen Kultschicht* (Wiesbaden: Harrassowitz).

(1998) "Wer lehrte die Hethiter das Schreiben?" Zur Paläographie früher Texte in akkadischer Sprache aus Boğazköy: Skizze einiger Überlegungen und vorläufiger Ergebnisse, in S. Alp & A. Süel (eds.) *Uluslararası Hititoloji Kongresi Bildirileri/Acts of the IIIrd International Congress of Hittitology* (Ankara: Uyum Ajans), 365–75.

(2001) Historiographie als Paradigma. Die Quellen zur hethitischen Geschichte und ihre Deutung, in G. Wilhelm (ed.) *Akten des IV. Internationalen Kongresses für Hethitologie* (Wiesbaden: Harrassowitz), 272–91.

(2005) Die hethitische Rezeption mesopotamischer Literatur und die Überlieferung des Gilgameš-Epos in Ḫattuša, in D. Prechel (ed.) *Motivation und Mechanismen des Kulturkontaktes in der späten Bronzezeit* (Firenze: LoGisma editore), 103–27.

(2006) Der Beitrag der Textfunde zur Archäologiegeschichte der hethitischen Haupstadt, in D. P. Mielke, U. -D. Schoop & J. Seeher (eds.) *Strukturierung und Datierung in der hethitischen Archäologie/Structuring and Dating in Hittite Archaeology* (Istanbul: Ege Yayınları), 5–17.

(2010) Literarische sumerische Texte aus den hethitischen Archiven aus paläographischer Sicht – Teil II, *Altorientalische Forschungen* 37, 306–40.

(2015) Šuppiluliuma II. und die Spätphase der hethitischen Archive, in A. Müller-Karpe, E. Rieken & W. Sommerfeld (eds.) *Saeculum. Gedenkschrift für Heinrich Otten anlässlich seines 100. Geburtstags* (Wiesbaden: Harrassowitz), 87–111.

Klinger, Jörg & Neu, Erich (2003) Zur Paläographie Akkadischsprachiger Texte aus Ḫattuša, in G. Beckman, R. H. Beal & G. McMahon (eds.) *Hittite Studies in Honor of Harry A. Hoffner, on the Occasion of his 65th Birthday* (Winona Lake, IN: Eisenbrauns), 237–48.

(2012) Literarische sumerische Texte aus den hethitischen Archiven aus überlieferungsgeschichtlicher Sicht. Teil I, in E. Devecchi (ed.) *Palaeography and Scribal Practices in Syro-Palestine and Anatolia in the Late Bronze Age. Papers Read at a Symposium in Leiden, 17–18 December 2009* (Leiden: Nederlands Instituut voor het Nabije Oosten), 79–94.

Kloekhorst, Alwin (2008) *Etymological Dictionary of the Hittite Inherited Lexicon* (Leiden & Boston: Brill).

(2019) *Kanišite Hittite. The earliest Attested Record of Indo-European* (Leiden & Boston: Brill).

Košak, Silvin (1982) *Hittite Inventory Texts (CTH 241–250)* (Heidelberg: Winter Verlag).

(1988) Review of KUB 56, *Zeitschrift für Assyriologie* 78, 145–9.

(1995) The Palace Library 'Building A' on Büyükkale, in J. de Roos & Th. van den Hout (eds.) *Studio Historiae Ardens. Ancient Near Eastern Studies Presented to Philo H.J. Houwink ten Cate on the Occasion of his 65th*

Birthday (Istanbul & Leiden: Nederlands Instituut voor het Nabije Oosten), 173–9.

Kryszat, Guido (2008) The use of writing among the Anatolians, in J. G. Dercksen (ed.) *Anatolia and Jazira during the Old Assyrian Period* (Istanbul & Leiden: Nederlands Instituut voor het Nabije Oosten), 231–8.

Kümmel, Hans Martin (1967) *Ersatzrituale für den hethitischen König* (Wiesbaden: Harrassowitz).

Lacambre, Denis & Nahm, Werner (2015) Pithana, an Anatolian Ruler in the Time of Samsuiluna of Babylon: New Data from Tell Rimah (Iraq), *Revue d'Assyriologie* 109, 17–28.

Lackenbacher, Sylvie (2002) *Textes akkadiens d'Ugarit: textes provenant des vingt-cinq premières campagnes* (Paris: Éditions du Cerf).

Laroche, Emmanuel (1949) La bibliothèque de Ḫattuša, *Archiv Orientální* 17, 7–23.

(1956a) Documents hiéroglyphiques hittites provenant du palais d'Ugarit, *Ugaritica* 3, 97–160.

(1956b) Noms de dignitaires, *Revue hittite et asianique* 58, 26–32.

(1958) Études sur les hiéroglyphes hittites, *Syria* 35, 252–283.

(1960) *Les hiéroglyphes hittites. Première Partie: L'écriture* (Paris: Éditions du Centre National de la Recherche Scientifique).

(1963) Review of H. G. Güterbock & H. Otten, KBo 11 (Berlin 1961), *Orientalistische Literaturzeitung* 58, 245–8.

(1968) Textes de Ras Shamra en langue hittite, *Ugaritica* 5, 769–84.

Larsen, Mogens T. (1988) Introduction: Literacy and social complexity, in J. Gledhill, B. Bender & M. T. Larsen (eds.) *State and Society. The emergence and development of social hierarchy and political centralization* (London & New York: Routledge), 173–91.

(2015) *Ancient Kanesh. A Merchant Colony in Bronze Age Anatolia* (Cambridge: Cambridge University Press).

Lebrun, René (1980) *Hymnes et prières hittites* (Louvain-la-Neuve: Centre d'histoire des religions).

(1985) L'aphasie de Mursili II = CTH 486, *Hethitica* 6, 103–37.

Lenski, Gerhard (1966) *Power & Privilege. A Theory of Social Stratification* (Chapel Hill, NC & London: University of North Carolina Press).

Lloyd, Seton & Mellaart, James (1955) Beycesultan Excavations: First Preliminary Report, *Anatolian Studies* 5, 39–92.

Lombardi, Alessandra (1997) Il culto delle montagne all'epoca de Tuthaliya IV: continuità e innovazione, *Studi Micenei ed Egeo-Anatolici* 39, 85–110.

Lorenz, Jürgen (2013) Kontrastierung und Variation: Zur Verwendung von Logogrammschreibungen und des Zeichens LI besonders in hethitischen Königsnamen, *Journal of Cuneiform Studies* 65, 163–8.

(2014) Der hethitische König: Herr der tausend Feste?, in P. Taracha & M. Kapełuš (eds.) *Proceedings of the Eighth International Congress of Hittitology* (Warsaw: Agade), 470–84.

Lorenz, Jürgen & Rieken, Elisabeth (2010) Überlegungen zur Verwendung mythologischer Texte bei den Hethitern, in J. Fincke (ed.) *Festschrift für Gernot Wilhelm anläßlich seines 65. Geburtstages* (Dresden: Islet Verlag), 217–34.

Lurie, David (2011) *Realms of Literacy. Early Japan and the History of Writing* (Cambridge MA & London: Harvard University Asia Center).

Macdonald, Michael (2005) Literacy in an oral environment, in P. Bienkowski, Chr. Mee & E. Slater (eds.) *Writing and Ancient Near Eastern Society. Papers in Honour of Alan A. Millard* (New York & London: T & T Clark).

Maneuvrier, Christophe & Thébault, Marion (2011) À propos du cartulaire de Mondaye: Les dépôts de sceaux de référence dans les établissements religieux normands au XIIIe siècle, *Annales de Normandie* 61, 109–14.

Marazzi, Massimiliano (1986) *L'Anatolia hittita. Repertori archaeologici ed epigrafici* (Roma: Università di Roma "La Sapienza").

(1990) *Il geroglifico anatolico. Problemi di analisi e prospettive di ricerca* (Roma: Dipartimento di Studi Glottoantropologici, Università "La Sapienza").

(1994) Ma gli hittiti scrivevano veramente su "legno"?, in P. Cipriano, P. Di Giovine & M. Mancini (eds.) *Miscellanea di studi linguistici in onore di Walter Belardi* (Roma: Il Calamo), 131–60.

(2000) Sigilli e tavolette di legno: le fonti letterarie e le testimonianze sfragistiche nell'Anatolia hittita, in M. Perna (ed.) *Administrative Documents in the Aegean and their Near Eastern Counterparts* (Roma: Ministero per i beni e le attività culturali), 79–102.

(2007) Sigilli, sigillature e tavolette di legno: alcune considerazioni alla luce di nuovi dati, in M. Alparslan, M. Doğan-Alparslan & H. Peker (eds.) *Belkıs Dinçol ve Ali Dinçol'a Armağan. VITA/Festschrift in Honor of Belkıs Dinçol and Ali Dinçol* (Istanbul: Ege Yayınları), 465–74.

(2010) Scrittura, percezione e cultura: qualche riflessione sull'Anatolia in età hittita, *Kaskal* 7, 219–55.

(2016a) "Blinding" in Hittite society. Form of punishment or ruling for the control of the labor force? in P. Corò et al. (eds.) *Libiamo ne' lieti calici. Ancient Near Eastern Studies Presented to Luciano Milano on the Occasion of his 65th Birthday by Pupils, Colleagues and Friends* (Münster: Ugarit-Verlag), 307–17.

(2016b) Die sogenannten "eingepunzten" Hieroglypheninschriften von Boğazköy: *Status quaestionis*, in Š. Velhartická (ed.) *Audias fabulas veteres. Anatolian Studies in Honor of Jana Součková-Siegelová* (Leiden, Boston: Brill), 194–209.

Marchetti, Nicolò & Peker, Hasan (2018) The Stele of Kubaba by Kamani and the Kings of Karkemish in the 9th Century BC, *Zeitschrift für Assyriologie und Vorderasiatische Archäologie* 108, 81–99.

Marcuson, Hannah & van den Hout, Theo (2015) Memorization and Hittite Ritual: New Perspectives on the Transmission of Hittite Ritual Texts, *Journal of Ancient Near Eastern Religions* 15, 143–68.

Marizza, Marco (2007) The Office of GAL GEŠTIN in the Hittite Kingdom, *Kaskal* 4, 153–80.

(2010) Le cariche di GAL DUB.SAR^{MEŠ} e GAL DUB.SAR.GIŠ nel regno ittita, *Mesopotamia* 45, 31–45.

Márquez Rowe, Ignacio (2006) *The Royal Deeds of Ugarit. A Study of Ancient Near Eastern Diplomatics* (Münster: Ugarit-Verlag).

Mascheroni, Lorenza (1984) Scribi hurriti a Boğazköy: una verifica prosopografica, *Studi Micenei ed Egeo-Anatolici* 24, 151–73.

Matessi, Alvise (2017) The Making of Hittite Imperial Landscapes: Territoriality and Balance of Power in South-Central Anatolia during the Late Bronze Age, *Journal of Ancient Near Eastern History* 1–46.

Maul, Stefan (2011) Die 'Tontafelbibliothek' einer assyrischen Gelehrtenfamilie des 7. Jahrhunderts v. Chr., in E. Blumenthal & W. Schmitz (eds.) *Bibliotheken im Altertum* (Wiesbaden: Harrassowitz), 9–50.

McKitterick, Rosamond (1989) *The Carolingians and the Written Word* (Cambridge: Cambridge University Press).

McMahon, Gregory (1997) Instructions to commanders of border garrisons (*BEL MADGALTI*), in W. W. Hallo & K. L. Younger (eds.) *The Context of Scripture. Canonical Compositions from the Biblical World, Volume One* (Leiden, New York & Köln: Brill), 221–5.

Melchert, H. Craig (1988) "Thorn" and "Minus" in Hieroglyphic Luvian Orthography, *Anatolian Studies* 38, 29–42.

(2005) The problem of Luvian influence on Hittite, in G. Meiser & O. Hackstein (eds.) *Sprachkontakt und Sprachwandel* (Wiesbaden: Ludwig Reichert Verlag), 445–60.

(2008) Middle Hittite Revisited, *Studi Micenei ed Egeo-Anatolici* 50, 525–31.

(2016) Formal and semantic aspects of Hittite *Gul(aš)ša-* "Fate", in S. Erkut & Ö. Sir Gavaz (eds.) *Studies in Honour of Ahmet Ünal Aramağanı* (Istanbul: Arkeoloji ve Sanat Yayınları), 355–9.

(2018) Review of Payne 2015, *Journal of the American Oriental Society* 138, 591–3.

Meriggi, Piero (1934) *Die längsten Bauinschriften in "hethitischen" Hieroglyphen nebst Glossar zu sämtlichen Texten* (Leipzig: J.C. Hinrichs'sche Buchhandlung).

(1937) Listes des Hieroglyphes Hittites, *Revue hittite et asianique* 27, 69–114.

(1975) *Manuale di eteo geroglifico. Parte II: Testi- 2ª e 3ª serie* (Roma: Edizioni dell'Ateneo).

Metcalf, Christopher (2011) New Parallels in Hittite and Sumerian Praise of the Sun, *Welt des Orients* 41, 168–76.

Michel, Cécile (2010) "Deux textes atypiques découverts à Kültepe", *Journal of Cuneiform Studies* 62, 71–80.

(2011) The Private Archives from Kaniš Belonging to Anatolians, *Altorientalische Forschungen* 38, 94–115.

Mielke, Dirk Paul (2017) From "Anatolian" to "Hittite." The development of pottery in Central Anatolia in the 2nd millennium BC, in A. Schachner (ed.) *Innovation versus Beharrung. Was macht den Unterschied des hethitischen Reiches im Anatolien des 2. Jahrtausends v. Chr.? Internazionaler Workshop zu Ehren von Jürgen Seeher* (Istanbul: Ege Yayınları), 121–44.

Miller, Jared (2004) *Studies in the Origins, Development and Interpretation of the Kizzuwatna Rituals* (Wiesbaden: Harrassowitz).

(2011) Die hethitischen Dienstanweisungen. Zwischen normativer Vorschrift und Traditionsliteratur, in M. Hutter & S. Hutter-Braunsar (eds.) *Hethitische Literatur. Überlieferungsprozesse, Textstrukturen, Ausdrucksformen und Nachwirken* (Münster: Ugarit-Verlag), 193–205.

(2013) *Royal Hittite Instructions and Related Administrative Texts* (Atlanta, GA: Society of Biblical Literature).

(2017) The tablet finds of Temple I from the early excavations at Boğazköy-Hattusa (1906–1912), in M. Doğan-Alparslan, A. Schachner & M. Alparslan (eds.) *The Discovery of an Anatolian Empire/Bir Anadolu İmperatorluğunun Keşfi* (Istanbul: Türk Eskiçağ Bilimleri Enstitüsü), 69–84.

Mora, Clelia (1983) Sul §55 delle leggi ittite, *Oriens Antiquus* 22, 49–51.

(1987) *La glittica anatolica del II millennio a.c.: classificazione tipologica. I. I sigilli a iscrizione geroglifica* (Pavia: Gianni Iuculano Editore).

(1991) Sull'origine della scrittura geroglifica anatolica, *Kadmos* 30, 1–28.

(1994) L'étude de la glyptique anatolienne. Bilan et nouvelles orientations de la recherche, *Syria* 71, 205–15.

(2000) Archivi periferici nell'Anatolia ittita: l'evidenza delle cretule, in M. Perna (ed.) *Administrative Documents in the Aegean and their Near Eastern Counterparts* (Roma: Ministero per i Beni e le Attività Culturali), 63–78.

(2006) Riscossione dei tributi e accumulo dei beni nell'impero ittita, in M. Perna (ed.) *Fiscality in Mycenaean and Near Eastern Archives* (Paris: De Boccard), 133–46.

(2007) I testi ittiti di inventario e gli 'archivi' di cretule. Alcune osservazioni e riflessioni, in D. Groddek & M. Zorman (eds.) *Tabularia Hethaeorum. Hethitologische Beiträge Silvin Košak zum 65. Geburtstag* (Wiesbaden: Harrassowitz), 535–59.

(2012) The enigma of the "Westbau" depot in Ḫattuša's Upper City, in M. E. Balza, M. Giorgieri & C. Mora (eds.) *Archivi, depositi, magazzini presso gli Ittiti. Nuovi materiali e nuove ricerche/Archives, Depots and Storehouses in the Hittite World. New Evidence and New Research* (Genova: Italian University Press), 59–76.

(2016) Activities and roles of court dignitaries towards the end of the hittite empire, in Š. Velhartická (ed.) *Audias fabulas veteres. Anatolian Studies in Honor of Jana Součková-Siegelová* (Leiden & Boston: Brill), 221–32.

Moran, William (1992) *The Amarna Letters* (Baltimore & London: Johns Hopkins University Press).

Morpurgo Davies, Anna (1986) Forms of writing in the ancient mediterranean world, in G. Baumann (ed.) *The Written Word. Literacy in Transition* (Oxford: Clarendon Press), 51–77.

Mouton, Alice (2002) Y a-t-il une relation entre les motifs de la glyptique cappadocienne et les hiéroglyphes anatoliens?, *Studi Micenei ed Egeo-Anatolici* 44, 83–113.

(2016) La fête dite de l'intronisation CTH 659, in Š. Velharticka (ed.) *Audias fabulas veteres. Anatolian Studies in Honor of Jana Součkova-Siegelova* (Leiden & Boston: Brill), 233–56.

Müller-Karpe, Andreas & Müller-Karpe, Vuslat, et al. (2009) Untersuchungen in Kayalıpınar und Umgebung 2006–2009, *Mitteilungen der Deutschen Orient-Gesellschaft* 141, 173–238.

(2017) Untersuchungen in Kayalıpınar 2015, *Mitteilungen der Deutschen Orient-Gesellschaft* 149, 57–84.

Muscarella, Oscar White (ed.) (1974) *Ancient Art. The Norbert Schimmel Collection* (Mainz: Verlag Philipp von Zabern).

Nakamura, Mitsuo (2002) *Das hethitische* nuntarriyašḫa-*Fest* (Leiden: Nederlands Instituut voor het Nabije Oosten).

Neu, Erich (1974) *Der Anitta-Text* (Wiesbaden: Harrassowitz).

(1980) *Althethitische Ritualtexte in Umschrift* (Wiesbaden: Harrassowitz).

(1983) *Glossar zu den althethitischen Ritualtexten* (Wiesbaden: Harrassowitz).

(1996) *Das hurritische Epos der Freilassung I. Untersuchungen zu einem hurritisch-hethitischen Textensemble aus Ḫattuša* (Wiesbaden: Harrassowitz).

Neumann, Günter (1992) *System und Ausbau der hethitischen Hieroglyphenschrift* (Göttingen: Vandenhoeck & Ruprecht).

(1998) La scrittura geroglifica anatolica: comparazioni tipologiche, in M. Marazzi (ed.) *Il geroglifico anatolico. Svilupi della ricerca a venti anni della sua "ridecifrazione". Atti del Coloquio e della Tavola rotonda, Napoli-Procida 1995* (Napoli: Istituto Universitaria Orientale), 127–48.

Neve, Peter (1975) Der grosse Tempel in Bogazköy-Hattusa, in *Le Temple et le Culte, Compte Rendu de la vingtième Rencontre Assyriologique Internationale, Leiden 1972* (Istanbul: Nederlands Historisch-Achaeologisch Instituut), 73–9.

(1982) *Büyükkale. Die Bauwerke. Grabungen 1954–1966* (Berlin: Gebr. Mann).

(1992) *Ḫattuša, Stadt der Götter und Tempel. Neue Ausgrabungen in der Hauptstadt der Hethiter* (Mainz am Rhein: Philipp von Zabern).

(1996) Bemerkungen zu einem neuentdeckten Felsrelief in Sirkeli, *Antike Welt* 1, 19–21.

Nougayrol, Jean (1955) *Le palais royale d'Ugarit: Textes accadiens et hourittes des archives est, oest, et centrales* (Leiden: Brill).

Oettinger, Norbert (1976) *Die militärischen Eide der Hethiter* (Wiesbaden: Harrassowitz).

Ong, Walter J. (1982) *Orality and Literacy* (London & New York: Routledge).

Oppenheim, A. Leo (1960) Assyriology – Why and How?, *Current Anthropology* 1, 409–23.

(1964) *Ancient Mesopotamia. Portrait of a Dead Civilization* (Chicago: University of Chicago Press).

Oreshko, Rostislav (2013) Hieroglyphic inscriptions of western anatolia: Long arm of the empire or vernacular tradition(s)?, in A. Mouton, I. Rutherford & I. Yakubovich (eds.) *Luwian Identities. Culture, Language and Religion Between Anatolia and the Aegean* (Leiden & Boston: Brill), 345–420.

Otranto, Rosa (2000) *Antichi liste di libri su papiro* (Roma: Edizioni di storia e letteratura).
Otten, Heinrich (1942) *Die Überlieferungen des Telipinu-Mythus* (Leipzig: J. C. Hinrichs Verlag).
(1956) Hethitische Schreiber in ihren Briefen, *Mitteilungen des Instituts für Orientforschung* 4, 179–89.
(1958) Keilschrifttexte, *Mitteilungen der Deutschen Orient-Gesellschaft* 91, 73–84.
(1971a) *Ein hethitisches Festritual (KBo XIX 128)* (Wiesbaden: Harrassowitz).
(1971b) Das Siegel des hethitischen Großkönigs Taḫurwaili, *Mitteilungen der Deutschen Orient-Gesellschaft* 103:59–68.
(1973) *Eine althethitische Erzählung um die Stadt Zalpa* (Wiesbaden: Harrassowitz).
(1981) *Die Apologie Hattusilis III. Das Bild der Überlieferung* (Wiesbaden: Harrassowitz).
(1984) Die Tontafelfunde aus Haus 16, apud Peter Neve, Die Ausgrabungen in Boğazköy-Ḫattuša 1983, *Archaologischer Anzeiger* 1983, 372–75.
(1988) *Die Bronzetafel aus Boğazköy. Ein Staatsvertrag Tutḫalijas IV.* (Wiesbaden: Harrassowitz).
(2000) Ein Siegelabdruck Dutḫalijas I. (?), *Archäologischer Anzeiger* 2000, 375–76.
Otten, Heinrich & Siegelová, Jana (1970) Die hethitischen Gulš-Gottheiten und die Erschaffung der Menschen, *Archiv für Orientforschung* 23, 32–8.
Otten, Heinrich & Souček, Vladimír (1965) *Das Gelübde der Königin Puduḫepa an die Göttin Lelwani* (Wiesbaden: Harrassowitz).
Özgüç, Nimet (1965) *Kültepe Mühür Baskılarında Anadolu Grubu/The Anatolian Group of Cylinder Seal Impressions from Kültepe* (Ankara: Türk Tarih Kurumu).
Özgüç, Nimet & Tunca, Önhan (2001) *Kültepe-Kaniš. Mühürlü Ve Yazıtlı Kil Bullalar/Seals and Inscribed Clay Bullae* (Ankara: Türk Tarih Kurumu).
Palaima, Thomas (2001) The Modalities of Economic Control at Pylos, *Ktema* 26, 151–9.
Panagiotopoulos, Diamantis (2014) *Mykenische Siegelpraxis. Funktion, Kontext und administrative Verwendung mykenischer Tonplomben auf dem griechischen Festland und Kreta* (München: Hirmer Verlag).
Papritz, J. (1959) Archive in Altmesopotamien. Theorie und Tatsachen, *Archivalische Zeitschrift* 55, 11–50.
Paroussis, Michel (1985) *Les listes de champs de Pylos et Hattusa et le régime foncier mycénien et hittite* (Paris: Les belles lettres).
Parpola, Simo (1983) Assyrian Library Records, *Journal of Near Eastern Studies* 42, 1–29.
Payne, Annick (2008) Writing systems and identity, in B. Collins, M. Bachvarova & I. Rutherford (eds.) *Anatolian Interfaces. Hittites, Greeks and Their Neighbours* (Oxford: Oxbow Books), 117–122.

(2010a) "Writing" in hieroglyphic Luwian, in I. Singer (ed.) *ipamati kistamati pari tumatimis. Luwian and Hittite Studies Presented to J. David Hawkins on the Occasion of His 70th Birthday* (Tel Aviv: Tel Aviv University), 182–7.

(2010b) *Hieroglyphic Luwian. An Introduction with Original Texts*, 2nd rev. ed (Wiesbaden: Harrassowitz).

(2012) *Iron Age Hieroglyphic Luwian Inscriptions* (Atlanta, GA: Society of Biblical Literature).

(2015) *Schrift und Schriftlichkeit. Die anatolische Hieroglyphenschrift* (Wiesbaden: Harrassowitz).

Payton, Robert (1991) The Ulu Burun Writing-Board Set, *Anatolian Studies* 41, 99–106.

Pecchioli Daddi, Franca (1982) *Mestieri, professioni e dignità nell'Anatolia ittita* (Roma: Edizioni dell'Ateneo).

(2003) *Il vincolo per i governatori di provincia* (Pavia: Italian University Press).

Pecchioli Daddi, Franca & Polvani, Anna Maria (1990) *La mitologia ittita* (Brescia: Paideia Editrice).

Peker, Hasan (2014) BOĞAZKÖY 4, A New Reading and Interpretation, *Nouvelles Assyriologiques Brèves et Utilitaires* 2014 3, 111–12.

Petschow, Herbert (1956) *Neubabylonisches Pfandrecht* (Berlin: Akademie-Verlag).

Poetto, Massimo (1993) *L'iscrizione luvio-geroglifica di Yalburt. Nuove acquisizioni relative alla geografia dell'Anatolia sud-occidentale* (Pavia: Gianni Iuculano Editore).

(2018 [2019]) A Hieroglyphic graffito on a pitcher from Kültepe, *News from the Land of the Hittites* 2, 17–25.

Polvani, Anna Maria (2005) Aspetti della narrativa degli Annali di Muršili II, in F. Pecchioli Daddi & M. Guidotti (eds.) *Narrare gli eventi. Atti del convegno degli egittologi e degli orientalisti italiani in margine alla mostra "La Battaglia di Qadesh"* (Roma: Herder), 279–83.

Ponchia, Simonetta (2009) On the witnessing procedure in neo-assyrian legal documents, in N. Bellotto & S. Ponchia (eds.) *Witnessing in the Ancient Near East/I testimoni nella documentazione del vicino oriente antico* (Padova: S.A.R.G.O.N. Editrice e Libreria), 131–73.

Popko, Maciej (1995) *Religions of Asia Minor* (Warsaw: Dialog).

(2005) Der Zukraši-Text: althethitisch?, *Nouvelles Assyriologiques Brèves et Utilitaires* 2005, 74.

(2005 [2006]) Einige Bemerkungen zum alt-und mittelhethitischen Duktus, *Rocznik Orientalistyczny* 58, 9–13.

(2007) Althethitisch? Zu den Datierungsfragen in der Hethitologie, in D. Groddek & M. Zorman (eds.) *Tabularia Hethaeorum. Hethitologische Beiträge Silvin Košak zum 65. Geburtstag* (Wiesbaden: Harrassowitz), 575–81.

(2008) *Völker und Sprachen Altanatoliens* (Wiesbaden: Harrassowitz).

Popova, Olga (2014) Le /wa/ dans l'écriture hittite: graphie, phonologie, influences extérieures, in P. Taracha & M. Kapełuš (eds.) *Proceedings of the Eighth International Congress of Hittitology* (Warsaw: Agade), 682–95.

Posner, E. (1972) *Archives in the Ancient World* (Cambridge, MA: Harvard University Press).

Postgate, J. Nicholas (1984) Cuneiform Catalysis: The First Information Revolution, *Archaeological Review from Cambridge* 3 2, 4–18.

(1992) *Early Mesopotamia. Society and Economy at the Dawn of History* (London & New York, NY: Routledge).

(2013) *Bronze Age Bureaucracy. Writing and the Practice of Government in Assyria* (Cambridge: Cambridge University Press).

Postgate, Nicholas, Wang, Tao & Wilkinson, Toby (1995) The Evidence for early writing: utilitarian or ceremonial?, *Antiquity* 69, 459–80.

Puchstein, Otto (1912) *Boghasköi. Die Bauwerke* (Leipzig: Hinrich'sche Buchhandlung).

Quinn, Josephine (2018) *In Search of the Phoenicians* (Princeton & Oxford: Princeton University Press).

Radner, Karen (2008) The delegation of power: Neo-Assyrian bureau seals, in P. Briant, W. Henkelman & M. Stolper (eds.) *L'archive des Fortifications de Persépolis. État des questions et perspectives de recherches* (Paris: Éditions de Boccard), 481–515.

Radner, Karen & Robson, Eleanor (eds.) (2011) *The Oxford Handbook of Cuneiform Culture* (Oxford: Oxford University Press).

Rieken, Elisabeth (2000) Die Partikeln *-a*, *-ia*, *-ma* im Althethitischen und das Akkadogramm Ù, in *125 Jahre Indogermanistik in Graz. Festband anläßlich des 125jährigen Bestehens der Forschungsrichtung "Indogermanistik" an der Karl-Franzens-Universität Graz* (Graz: Leykam), 411–19.

(2004) Die hethitische 'Ortsbezugspartikel' *-apa*, in Th. Poschenrieder (ed.) *Die Indogermanistik und ihre Anrainer* (Innsbruck: Innsbrucker Beiträge zur Sprachwissenschaft), 243–58.

(2006) Zum hethitisch-luwischen Sprachkontakt in historischer Zeit, *Altorientalische Forschungen* 33, 271–85.

(2009) Die Tontafelfunde aus Kayalıpınar (mit einem Beitrag von Gernot Wilhelm) in F. Pecchioli Daddi, G. Torri & C. Corti (eds.) *Central-North Anatolia in the Hittite Period. New Perspectives in Light of Recent Research* (Roma: Herder), 119–43.

(2014) Ein Kultinventar für Šamuḫa aus Šamuḫa und andere Texte aus Kayalıpınar, *Mitteilungen der Deutschen Orient-Gesellschaft* 146, 43–54.

(2015) Bemerkungen zum Ursprung einiger Merkmale der anatolischen Hieroglyphenschrift, *Welt des Orients* 45, 216–31.

Riemschneider, Kaspar (1958) Die hethitischen Landschenkungsurkunden, *Mitteilungen des Instituts für Orientforschung* 6, 321–81.

(1962) Hethitische Fragmente historischen Inhalts aus der Zeit Ḫattušili III., *Journal of Cuneiform Studies* 16, 110–21.

(2004) *Die akkadischen und hethitischen Omentexte aus Boğazköy* (Dresden: Verlag der TU Dresden).

Rimon, Ofra (1997) *Medical Instruments from the Roman Period* (Haifa: University of Haifa).

Robson, Eleanor (2013) Reading the libraries of Assyria and Babylonia, in J. König, K. Oikonomopolou & G. Woolf, (eds.) *Ancient Libraries* (Cambridge: Cambridge University Press), 38–56.

Roche-Hawley, Carole & Hawley, Robert (2013) An essay on scribal families, tradition, and innovation in thirteenth-century Ugarit, in B. J. Collins, P. Michalowski (eds.) *Beyond Hatti. A Tribute to Gary Beckman* (Atlanta, GA: Lockwood Press), 241–64.

Rogers, Henry (2005) *Writing Systems. A Linguistic Approach* (Oxford & Malden, MA: Blackwell).

Rojas, Felipe (2019) *The Pasts of Roman Anatolia: Interpreters, Traces, Horizons* (Cambridge: Cambridge University Press).

Roszkowska-Mutschler, Hanna (2002) Zu den Mannestaten der hethitischen Könige und ihrem Sitz im Leben, in P. Taracha (ed.) *Silva Anatolica. Anatolian Studies Presented to Maciej Popko on the Occasion of his 65th Birthday* (Warsaw: Agade), 289–300.

Rüster, Christel (1988) Materialien zu einer Fehlertypologie der hethitischen Texte, in E. Neu & Chr. Rüster (eds.) *Documentum Asiae Minoris. Festschrift für Heinrich Otten zum 75. Geburtstag* (Wiesbaden: Harrassowitz), 295–306.

(1992) Zu einem neuen Fragment des Telipinu-Mythos in H. Otten, E. Akurgal, H. Ertem & A. Süel (eds.) *Hittite and Other Anatolian Studies in Honour of Sedat Alp* (Ankara: Türk Tarih Kurumu Basımevi), 475–81.

(1993) Eine Urkunde Ḫantilis II., *Istanbuler Mitteilungen* 43, 63–70.

Rüster, Christel, Neu, Erich (1989) *Hethitisches Zeichenlexikon. Inventar und Interpretation der Keilschriftzeichen aus den Boğazköytexten* (Wiesbaden: Harrassowitz).

Rüster, Christel & Wilhelm, Gernot (2012) *Landschenkungsurkunden hethitischer Könige* (Wiesbaden: Harrassowitz).

Rutz, Matthew (2012) Mesopotamian Scholarship in Ḫattuša and the *Sammeltafel* KUB 4.53, *Journal of the American Oriental Society* 132, 171–88.

Sagona, Antonio & Zimansky, Paul (2009) *Ancient Turkey* (London & New York: Routledge).

Sallaberger, Walther & Schrakamp, Ingo (eds.) (2015) *History & Philology* (Turnhout: Brepols).

Salomon, Richard (2012) Some principles and patterns of script change, in S. Houston (ed.) *The Shape of Script. How and Why Writing Systems Change* (Santa Fe: School for Advanced Research Press), 119–33.

Salonen, Armas (1963) *Die Möbel des alten Mesopotamien* (Helsinki: Suomalainen Tiedeakatemia).

Salvini, Mirjo (1993) Un documento del re ittita Ammuna, *Studi Micenei ed Egeo-Anatolici* 32, 85–9.

(1994) Una lettera di Ḫattušili I relativa alla spedizione contro Ḫaḫḫum, *Studi Micenei ed Egeo-Anatolici* 34, 61–80.

(1995a) *Geschichte und Kultur der Urartäer* (Darmstadt: Wissenschaftliche Buchgesellschaft).

(1995b) La tablette hittite RS 17.109, *Studi Micenei ed Egeo-Anatolici* 36, 144–6.
Sanders, Seth (2004) What was the Alphabet for? The Rise of Written Vernaculars and the Making of Israelite National Literature, *Maarav* 11, 25–56.
(2009) *The Invention of Hebrew* (Urbana, Chicago & Springfield, IL: University of Illinois Press).
Sasson, Jack (1981) On Idrimi and Šarruwa, the Scribe, *Studies on the Civilization and Culture of Nuzi and the Hurrians* 1, 309–24.
Schachner, Andreas (2009) Das 16. Jahrhundert v. Chr. – eine Zeitenwende im hethitischen Zentralanatolien, *Istanbuler Mitteilungen* 59, 9–34.
(2011a) *Hattuscha. Auf der Suche nach dem sagenhaften Großreich der Hethiter* (München: Beck).
(2011b) Von einer anatolischen Stadt zur Hauptstadt eines Großreichs – Entstehung, Entwicklung und Wandel Hattušas in hethitischer Zeit, *Mesopotamia* 46, 79–101.
(2012) Gedanken zur Datierung, Entwicklung und Funktion der hethitischen Kunst, *Altorientalische Forschungen* 39, 130–66.
(2017) Die Rolle der hethitischen Hauptstadt Hattuša für die Transformation des hethitischen Reiches, in A. Schachner (ed.) *Innovation versus Beharrung. Was macht den Unterschied des hethitischen Reiches im Anatolien des 2. Jahrtausends v. Chr.? Internazionaler Workshop zu Ehren von Jürgen Seeher* (Istanbul: Ege Yayınları), 219–37.
Schachner, Andreas & Seeher, Jürgen (eds.) (2016) *Ausgrabungen und Forschungen in der westlichen Oberstadt von Ḫattuša I* (Berlin & Boston: De Gruyter).
Schaeffer, Claude (1956) *Ugaritica III. Sceaux et cylindres hittites, epée gravée du cartouches de Mineptah, tablettes chypro-minoennes et autres découvertes nouvelles de Ras Shamra* (Paris: Paul Geuthner).
Schirmer, Wulf (1969) *Die Bebauung am unteren Büyükkale-Nordwesthang in Boğazköy. Ergebnisse der Untersuchungen der Grabungscampagnen 1960–1963* (Berlin: Gebr. Mann Verlag).
Schoeler, Gregor (2009) *The genesis of literature in Islam. From the aural to the read*, rev. ed (Edinburgh: Edinburgh University Press).
Schoop, Ulf-Dietrich (2009) Indications of structural change in the Hittite pottery inventory at Boğazköy-Hattuša, in F. Pecchioli Daddi, G. Torri & C. Corti (eds.) *Central-North Anatolia in the Hittite Period. New Perspectives in Light of Recent Research* (Roma: Herder), 145–67.
Schwemer, Daniel (1998) *Akkadische Rituale aus Hattusa: Die Sammeltafel KBo XXXVI 29 und verwandte Fragmente* (Heidelberg: Winter Verlag).
(2005–2006) Lehnbeziehungen zwischen dem Hethitischen und dem Akkadischen, *Archiv für Orientforschung* 51, 220–234.
(2012) Qualitätsmanagement für das Wohlergehen des Landes: die hethitische Festritualtradition, *Würzburger Jahrbücher für die Altertumswissenschaft. Neue Folge* 36, 39–57 (German version of Schwemer 2016).
(2013) Gauging the influence of Babylonian magic. The reception of Mesopotamian traditions in Hittite ritual practice, in E. Cancik-Kirschbaum, J. Klinger & G. Müller (eds.) *Diversity and Standardization.*

Perspectives on social and political norms in the ancient Near East (Berlin: Akademie Verlag), 145–71.

(2016) Quality assurance managers at work. The Hittite Festival tradition, in G. Müller (ed.) *Liturgie oder Literatur? Die Kultrituale der Hethiter im transkulturellen Vergleich* (Wiesbaden: Harrassowitz), 1–29 (English version of Schwemer 2012).

Seeher, Jürgen (2001) Die Tontafelfunde von Büyükkaya und vom Ostteich 2, in *KBo* 42, viii-ix.

(2003) The cuneiform tablet archives and libraries of Hattusha, in *Ancient Libraries in Anatolia. Libraries of Hattusha, Pergamon, Ephesus, Nysa* (Ankara: Middle East Technical University Library), 7–17.

(2009) Der Landschaft sein Siegel aufdrücken – hethitische Felsbilder und Hieroglypheninschriften als Ausdruck des herrscherlichen Macht- und Territorialanspruchs, *Altorientalische Forschungen* 36, 119–39.

(2018) *Büyükkaya II. Bauwerke und Befunde der Grabungskampagnen 1952–1955 und 1993–1998* (Berlin-Boston: De Gruyter).

Sherratt, Susan (2003) Visible Writing: Questions of Script and Identity in Early Iron Age Greece and Cyprus, *Oxford Journal of Archaeology* 22, 225–42.

Siegelová, Jana (1971) *Appu-Märchen und Ḫedammu-Mythus* (Wiesbaden: Harrassowitz).

(1986) *Hethitische Verwaltungspraxis im Lichte der Wirtschafts- und Inventardokumente* (3 vols.) (Prague: Národní Muzeum).

(1993–1997a) Metalle und Metallurgie. A. II. In den heth. Texten, in *RlA* 8, 112–19.

(1993–1997b) Möbel. A. II. Bei den Hethitern, in *RlA* 8, 330–4.

(2002) Blendung als Strafe für den Eidbruch, in St. de Martino & F. Pecchioli Daddi (eds.) *Anatolia Antica. Studi in memoria di Fiorella Imparati* (Firenze: LoGisma Editore), 735–7.

(2015) Die hethitische Königin und die Wirtschaft der Krone, in A. Müller-Karpe, E. Rieken & W. Sommerfeld (eds.) *Saeculum. Gedenkschrift für Heinrich Otten anlässlich seines 100. Geburtstages* (Wiesbaden: Harrassowitz), 239–50.

Simon, Zsolt (2011a) *Vorarbeiten zu einer hethitischen Demographie I. Die Einwohnerzahl des hethitischen Reiches anhand der schriftlichen Quellen* (Budapest: Verano).

(2011b) Hethitische Topoi in der hieroglyphen-luwischen Historiographie. Bemerkungen zur Frage der Kontinuität, in M. Hutter & S. Hutter-Braunsar (eds.) *Hethitische Literatur. Überlieferungsprozesse, Textstrukturen, Ausdrucksformen und Nachwirken* (Münster: Ugarit-Verlag), 227–43.

Singer, Itamar (1983) *The Hittite* KI.LAM *Festival. Part One* (Wiesbaden: Harrassowitz).

(1984a) *The Hittite* KI.LAM *Festival. Part Two* (Wiesbaden: Harrassowitz).

(1984b) The AGRIG in the Hittite Texts, *Anatolian Studies* 34, 97–127.

(1987) Dating the End of the Hittite Empire, *Hethitica* 8, 413–21.

(1995) Some Thoughts on Translated and Original Hittite Literature, *Israel Oriental Studies* 15, 123–8.

(1999a) A new Hittite letter from Emar, in L. Milano, St. de Martino, F. Fales & G. Lanfranchi (eds.) *Landscapes, Territories, Frontiers and Horizons in the Ancient Near East* (Padova: Sargon), 65–72.

(1999b) The Head of the MUBARRÛ-men on Hittite Seals, *Archív Orientální* 67, 649–53.

(2001) review of Hoffner 1997, *Journal of Near Eastern Studies* 60, 286–9.

(2002) *Hittite Prayers* (Atlanta, GA: Society of Biblical Literature).

(2003) The Great Scribe Taki-Šarruma, in G. Beckman, R. H. Beal, G. McMahon (eds.) *Hittite Studies in Honor of Harry A. Hoffner Jr. on the Occasion of his 65th Birthday* (Winona Lake, IN: Eisenbrauns), 341–48.

(2006) The failed reforms of Akhenaten and Muwatalli, *British Museum Studies in Ancient Egypt and Sudan* 6, 37–58.

(2013) The 'Royal Land Registry' in Hattuša and its Seal Impressions, *Bibliotheca Orientalis* 70, 5–16.

Smith, Stuart Tyson (1996) The transmission of an Egyptian administrative system in the second millennium B.C.: Sealing practice in Lower Nubia and at Kerma, in P. Ferioli, E. Fiandra & G. Fissore (eds.) *Administration in Ancient Societies* (Torino: Scriptorium), 67–86.

Sommer, Ferdinand & Falkenstein, Adam (1974) *Die hethitisch-akkadische Bilingue des Ḫattušili I. (Labarna II.)* (Hildesheim: Verlag Dr. H.A. Gerstenberg).

Souček, Vladimir (1959a) Die hethitischen Feldertexte, *Archiv Orientální* 27, 5–43.

(1959b) Die hethitischen Feldertexte (Fortsetzung), *Archiv Orientální* 27, 379–95.

Soysal, Oğuz (2000) "Analysis of a Hittite Oracular Document", *Zeitschrift für Assyriologie* 90, 85–122.

(2004) *Hattischer Wortschatz in hethitischer Überlieferung* (Leiden-Boston: Brill).

(2005) Beiträge zur althethitischen Geschichte (III). Kleine Fragmente historischen Inhalts, *Zeitschrift für Assyriologie* 95, 121–44.

Soysal, Oğuz & Süel, Aygül (2016) The Hattian–Hittite foundation rituals from Ortaköy (II). Fragments to CTH 726 "'Rituel bilingue de fondation d'un temple ou d'un palais", in Š. Velhartická (ed.) *Audias fabulas veteres. Anatolian Studies in Honor of Jana Součková-Siegelová* (Leiden, Boston: Brill), 320–64.

Spooner, Brian & Hanaway, William (2012) (eds.) *Literacy in the Persianate World. Writing and the Social Order* (Philadelphia: University of Pennsylvania Museum of Archaeology and Anthropology).

Starke, Frank (1985) *Die keilschrift-luwischen Texte in Umschrift* (Wiesbaden: Harrassowitz).

(1990) *Untersuchung zur Stammbildung des keilschrift-luwischen Nomens* (Wiesbaden: Harrassowitz).

(1995) Zur urkundlichen Charakterisierung neuassyrischer Treueide anhand einschlägiger hethitischer Texte des 13. Jh., *Zeitschrift für Altorientalische und Biblische Rechtsgeschichte* 1, 70–82.
(1996) Zur "Regierung" des hethitischen Staates, *Zeitschrift für Altorientalische und Biblische Rechtsgeschichte* 2, 140–82.
(1997a) Troia im Kontext des historisch-politischen und sprachlichen Umfeldes Kleinasiens im 2. Jahrtausend, *Studia Troica* 7, 447–87.
(1997b) Sprachen und Schriften in Karkamis, in B. Pongratz-Leisten, H. Kühne & P. Xella (eds.) *Ana šadî Labnāni lū allik. Beiträge zu altorientalischen und mittelmeerischen Kulturen* (Kevelaer and Neukirchen-Vluyn: Verlag Butzon & Bercker and Neukirchener Verlag), 381–95.
Steele, Philippa (2019) *Writing and Society in Ancient Cyprus* (Cambridge: Cambridge University Press).
Stein, Gil (2008) A Theoretical Model for Political Economy and Social Identity in the Old Assyrian Colonies of Anatolia, *Türkiye Bilimler Akademisi Arkeoloji Dergisi/Turkish Academy of Sciences Journal of Archaeology* 11, 25–40.
Steinkeller, Piotr (1977) Seal practice in the Ur III period, in M. Gibson & R. Biggs (eds.) *Seals and Sealing in the Ancient Near East* (Malibu: Undena Publications), 41–53.
Strauß, Rita (2006) *Reinigungsrituale aus Kizzuwatna. Ein Beitrag zur Erforschung hethitischer Ritualtradition und Kulturgeschichte* (Berlin & New York: Walter de Gruyter).
Streck, Michael (2009) review of CAD Vols. 18 and 19, *Zeitschrift für Assyriologie und Vorderasiatische Archäologie* 99, 135–40.
(2010) Großes Fach Altorientalistik: Der Umfang des keilschriflichen Textkorpus, *Mitteilungen der Deutschen Orient-Gesellschaft* 142, 35–58.
Strupler, Néhémie (2012) Reconstitution des vases à reliefs monochromes d'Alaca Höyük et d'Eskiyapar, *Anatolia Antiqua* 20, 1–12.
Süel, Aygül (1992) Ortaköy: Eine hethitische Stadt mit hethitischen und hurritischen Tontafelentdeckungen, in H. Otten, E. Akurgal, H. Ertem & A. Süel (eds.) *Hittite and Other Anatolian Studies in Honour of Sedat Alp* (Ankara: Türk Tarih Kurumu Basımevi), 487–92.
(1994 [1999]) The Hittite Name of Ortaköy, XII. *Türk Tarih Kurumu*, 117–28.
Süel, Aygül & Soysal, Oğuz (2003) A practical vocabulary from Ortaköy, in G. Beckman, R. Beal & G. McMahon (eds.) *Hittite Studies in Honor of Harry A. Hoffner Jr.* (Winona Lake, IN: Eisenbrauns), 349–65.
(2007) The Hattian-Hittite Foundation Rituals from Ortaköy (I). Fragments to CTH 725 "Rituel bilingue de consécration d'un temple", *Anatolica* 33, 1–22.
Summers, Geoffrey (2017) After the collapse, continuities and discontinuities in the Early Iron Age of Central Anatolia, in A. Schachner (ed.) *Innovation versus Beharrung. Was macht den Unterschied des hethitischen Reiches im Anatolien des 2. Jahrtausends v. Chr.? Internazionaler Workshop zu Ehren von Jürgen Seeher* (Istanbul: Ege Yayınları), 257–74.

Sürenhagen, Dietrich (1985) *Paritätische Staatsverträge aus hethitischer Sicht. Zu historischen Aussagen und literarischer Stellung des Textes CTH 379* (Pavia: Gianni Iuculano Editore).

(1998) Verwandtschaftsbeziehungen und Erbrecht im althethitischen Königshaus vor Telipinu – ein erneuter Erklärungsversuch, *Altorientalische Forschungen* 25, 75–94.

Symington, Dorit (1991) Late Bronze Age Writing-Boards and Their Uses: Textual Evidence from Anatolia and Syria, *Anatolian Studies* 41, 111–23.

(1996) Hittite and Neo-Hittite furniture, in G. Herrmann (ed.) *The Furniture of Western Asia Ancient and Traditional* (Mainz: Philipp von Zabern), 111–38 w. Pls. 28–33.

Taggar-Cohen, Ada (2006) *Hittite Priesthood* (Heidelberg: Winter Verlag).

Taracha, Piotr (1990) More About the Hittite *taknaz da* Rituals, *Hethitica* 10, 171–84.

(2000) *Ersetzen und Entsühnen. Das mittelhethitishe Ersatzritual für den Großkönig Tutḫalija (CTH *448.4) und verwandte Texte* (Leiden-Boston-Köln: Brill).

(2003) Is Tutḫaliya's Sword really Aegean? in G. Beckman, R. Beal & G. McMahon (eds.) *Hittite Studies in Honor of Harry A. Hoffner Jr. on the Occasion of His 65th Birthday* (Winona Lake, IN: Eisenbrauns), 367–76.

(2016) Tudhaliya III's queens, Šuppiluliuma's accession and related issues, in *ANTAHŠUM^SAR "Çiğdem". Eski Anadolu Araštırmalarına ve Hititlere Adanmış Bir Hayat. Studies in Honour of Ahmet Ünal Armağanı* (Ankara: Arkeoloji ve Sanat Yayınları) 489–97.

(2017) *Two Festivals Celebrated by a Hittite Prince (CTH 647.I and II-III). New Light on Local Cults in North-Central Anatolia in the Second Millennium* BC (Wiesbaden: Harrassowitz).

Taş, Ilknur & Adalı, Selim (2016) A Hittite view of Lullubum and its world, in Š. Velhartická (ed.) *Audias fabulas veteres. Anatolian Studies in Honor of Jana Součková-Siegelová* (Leiden-Boston: Brill), 374–88.

Taylor, Jon & Cartwright, Caroline (2011) The Making and Re-making of Clay Tablets, *Scienze dell'Antichità* 17, 297–324.

Thomas, Rosalind (1992) *Literacy and Orality in Ancient Greece* (Cambridge: Cambridge University Press).

(2009) Writing, reading, public and private 'literacies.' Functional literacy and democratic literacy in Greece, in W. A. Johnson & H. N. Parker (eds.) *Ancient Literacies. The Culture of Reading in Greece and Rome* (Oxford: Oxford University Press), 13–45.

Tinney, Steve (2011) Tablets of schools and scholars: A portrait of the old Babylonian corpus, in K. Radner & E. Robson (eds.) *The Oxford Handbook of Cuneiform Culture* (Oxford: Oxford University Press), 577–96.

Tjerkstra, Françoise (1992) Review of Paroussis (1985) *Bibliotheca Orientalis* 49, 189–95.

Tognon, Rosanna (2004) Il testo oracolare ittita KUB V 7, *Kaskal* 1, 59–81.

Topçuoğlu, Oya (2016) *Emblems of Power: Ideology and Identity in Late Old Assyrian Glyptic*, Dissertation (Chicago: University of Chicago).

Torri, Giulia (2008) The Scribes of the House on the Slope, *Studi Micenei ed Egeo-Anatolici* 50, 771–82.

(2010a) The *Scribal School* of the Lower City of Hattuša and the beginning of the career of Anuwanza, court dignitary and lord of Nerik, in M. Biga & M. Liverani (eds.) *ana turri gimilli. Studi dedicati al Padre Werner R. Mayer, S.J. da amici e allievi* (Roma: Università degli Studi di Roma "La Sapienza"), 383–96.

(2010b) Hittite scribes at play: the case of the sign AN, in J. Klinger, E. Rieken & Chr. Rüster (eds.) *Investigationes Anatolicae. Gedenkschrift für Erich Neu* (Wiesbaden: Harrassowitz), 317–27.

(2011) The phrase ṬUPPU URU*Ḫatti* in colophons from Ḫattuša and the work of the scribe Ḫanikkuili, *Altorientalische Forschungen* 38, 135–44.

(2012) Hiding Words behind the Signs: The Use of Logograms in Hittite Scribal Praxis, *Orientalia* 81, 124–32.

Ünal, Ahmed (1989) Drawings, graffiti and squiggles on the Hittite tablets: Art in scribal circles, in K. Emre, B. Hrouda, M. Mellink & N. Özgüç (eds.) *Anatolia and the Ancient Near East. Studies in Honor of Tahsin Özgüç* (Ankara: Türk Tarih Kurumu Basımevi), 505–13.

(1993) Boğazköy Kılıcının Üzerindeki Akadca Adak Yazısı Hakkında Yeni Gözlemler, in M. Mellink, E. Porada & T. Özgüç (eds.) *Aspects of Art and Iconography: Anatolia and Its Neighbors. Studies in Honor of Nimet Özgüç* (Ankara: Türk Tarih Kurumu Basımevi), 727–30.

(1998) *Hittite and Hurrian Cuneiform Tablets from Ortaköy (Çorum), Central Turkey* (Istanbul: Simurg).

Urton, Gary (2003) *Signs of the Inka Khipu. Binary Coding in the Andean Knotted-String Records* (Austin, TX: University of Texas Press).

van den Hout, Theo (1984) Kurunta und die Datierung einiger hethitischen Texte, *Revue d'Assyriologie* 78, 89–82.

(1989) A Chronology of the Tarḫuntašša Treaties, *Journal of Cuneiform Studies*, 41, 100–14.

(1991) A Tale of Tiššaruli(ya): A Dramatic Interlude in the Hittite KI.LAM Festival?, *Journal of Near Eastern Studies* 50, 193–202.

(1994) Death as a Privilege. The Hittite Royal Funerary Ritual, in J. M. Bremer, Th. P. J. van den Hout & R. Peters (eds.) *Hidden Futures. Death and Immortality in Ancient Egypt, Anatolia, the Classical, Biblical and Arabic-Islamic World* (Amsterdam: Amsterdam University Press), 37–75.

(1995a) *Der Ulmitešub-Vertrag. Eine prosopographische Untersuchung* (Wiesbaden: Harrassowitz).

(1995b) Tuthalija IV und die Ikonographie hethitischer Grosskönige des 13. Jhs., *Bibliotheca Orientalis* 52, 545–73.

(1998) *The Purity of Kingship. An Edition of CTH 569 and Related Hittite Oracle Inquiries of Tutḫaliya IV* (Leiden, Boston & Köln: Brill).

(2001) Bemerkungen zu älteren hethitischen Orakeltexten, in Th. Richter, D. Prechel & J. Klinger (eds.) *Kulturgeschichten. Altorientalische Studien für Volkert Haas zum 65. Geburtstag* (Saarbrücken: Saarbrücker Druckerei und Verlag), 423–40.
(2002) Another view of Hittite literature, in St. de Martino & F. Pecchioli Daddi (eds.), *Anatolia Antica. Studi in memoria di Fiorella Imparati* (Firenze: LoGisma Editore), 857–78.
(2003) Review of J. Puhvel, Hittite Etymological Dictionary. Vol. 4: Words Beginning with K. (Trends in Linguistics. Documentation 14, Berlin, 1997) and Vol. 5: Words Beginning with L. Indices to Volumes 1–5. (Trends in Linguistics. Documentation 18, Berlin, 2001), *Bibliotheca Orientalis* 60 (2003) 174–77.
(2003–2005a) Omina (Omens). B. Bei den hethitern, *RlA* 10, 88–90.
(2003–2005b) Pirwa, Perwa, *RlA* 10, 575–6.
(2004) Some thoughts on the composition known as Muršili's Aphasia (CTH 486), in M. Mazoyer & O. Casabonne (eds.) *Antiquus Oriens. Mélanges offerts au professeur René Lebrun, Vol. I* (Paris: L'Harmattan), 359–80.
(2005) On the Nature of the Tablet Collections of Ḫattuša, *Studi Micenei ed Egeo-Anatolici* 47, 277–89.
(2006) Administration in the reign of Tutḫaliya IV and the later years of the Hittite Empire, in Th. van den Hout (ed.) *The Life and Times of Hattusili III and Tuthaliya IV* (Leiden: Nederlands Instituut voor het Nabije Oosten), 77–106.
(2007a) Some Observations on the Tablet Collection from Maşat Höyük, *Studi Micenei ed Egeo-Anatolici* 49, 387–98.
(2007b) The prayers in the Haus am Hang, in D. Groddek & M. Zorman (eds.) *Tabularia Hethaeorum. Hethitologische Beiträge Silvin Košak zum 65. Geburtstag* (Wiesbaden: Harrassowitz), 401–9.
(2007c) Institutions, vernaculars, publics: The case of second millennium Anatolia, in Seth Sanders (ed.) *Margins of Writing, Origins of Cultures*, second printing with postscripts and minor corrections of article of 2006 (Chicago: Oriental Institute) 221–62.
(2007d) Seals and Sealing Practices in Hatti-Land: Remarks à propos the Seal Impressions from the *Westbau* in Ḫattuša, *Journal of the American Oriental Society* 127, 339–48.
(2008a) Some Observations on the Tablet Collection from Maşat Höyük, *Studi Micenei ed Egeo-Anatolici* 49, 387–98.
(2008b) A classified past: Classification of knowledge in the Hittite Empire, in R. Biggs, J. Myers & M. Roth (eds.) *Proceedings of the 51st Rencontre Assyriologique Internationale, Chicago 2005* (Chicago: The Oriental Institute of the University of Chicago), 211–19.
(2009a) A Century of Hittite Text Dating and the Origins of the Hittite Cuneiform Script, *Incontri Linguistici* 32, 11–35.
(2009b) Reflections on the origins and development of the Hittite tablet collections in Hattuša and their consequences for the rise of Hittite literacy,

in F. Pecchioli Daddi, G. Torri & C. Corti (eds.) *Central-North Anatolia in the Hittite Period. New Perspectives in Light of Recent Research* (Roma: Herder), 71–96.

(2009–2011a) Schaf. B. Bei den Hethitern. in *RlA* 12, 121–6.

(2009–2011b) Schreiber. D. Bei den Hethitern. in *RlA* 12, 273–80.

(2010) [LÚ]DUB.SAR.GIŠ = 'clerk'?, *Orientalia* 79, 255–67.

(2011) The written legacy of the Hittites, in H. Genz & D.P. Mielke (eds.) *Insights into Hittite History and Archaeology* (Leuven, Paris & Walpole, MA: Peeters), 47–84.

(2012a) The ductus of the Alalaḫ VII Texts and the origin of the Hittite cuneiform, in E. Devecchi (ed.) *Palaeography and Scribal Practices in Syro-Palestine and Anatolia in the Late Bronze Age* (Leiden: Nederlands Instituut voor het Nabije Oosten), 147–70.

(2012b) Review of Herbordt, Suzanne et al. 2011, *Zeitschrift für Assyriologie* 102, 350–3.

(2012c) Administration and writing in Hittite society, in M. E. Balza, M. Giorgieri & C. Mora (eds.) *Archivi, depositi, magazzini presso gli Ittiti. Nuovi materiali e nuove ricerche/Archives, Depots and Storehouses in the Hittite World. New Evidence and New Research* (Genova: Italian University Press), 41–58.

(2015) In Royal Circles: The Nature of Hittite Scholarship, *Journal of Ancient Near Eastern History*, 2015 (2016), 203–27.

(2016a) A brief note on the syntax of writing in Hittite, in Š. Velharticḱa (ed.) *Audias fabulas veteres. Anatolian Studies in Honor of Jana Součková-Siegelová* (Leiden-Boston: Brill), 426–37.

(2016b) Purandamuwa, der Verlorene Sohn Mittannamuwas?, in H. Marquardt, S. Reichmuth & J. V. García Trabazo (eds.) *Anatolica et Indogermanica. Studia linguistica in honorem Johannis Tischler septuagenarii dedicata* (Innsbruck: Innsbrucker Beiträge zur Sprachwissenschaft), 343–8

(2017) Schreiben wie Seeher. The art of writing: Remarks on the when and how of Hittite cuneiform, in A. Schachner (ed.) *Innovation versus Beharrung. Was macht den Unterschied des hethitischen Reiches im Anatolien des 2. Jahrtausends v. Chr.? Internazionaler Workshop zu Ehren von Jürgen Seeher* (Istanbul: Ege Yayınları), 39–47.

(2018) The Silver Stag Vessel: A Royal Gift, *Metropolitan Museum Journal* 53, 114–27.

van der Toorn, Karel (2007) *Scribal Culture and the Making of the Hebrew Bible* (Cambridge, MA & London: Harvard University Press).

van Gessel, Ben (1998) *Onomasticon of the Hittite Pantheon, Part One and Two* (Leiden, Boston & Köln: Brill).

(2001) *Onomasticon of the Hittite Pantheon, Part Three* (Leiden, Boston & Köln: Brill).

van Quickelberghe, Étienne (2013) Réflexions autour de la stèle de Karahöyük (Elbistan), *Le Muséon* 126, 253–63.

Veenhof, Klaas (1982) The Old Assyrian Merchants and Their Relations with the Native Population of Anatolia, *Berliner Beiträge zum Vorderen Orient* 1, 147–60.

(1993) On the identification and implications of some bullae from Acemhöyük and Kültepe, in M. Mellink, E. Porada & T. Özgüç (eds.) *Aspects of Art and Iconography: Anatolia and Its Neighbors. Studies in Honor of Nimet Özgüç* (Ankara: Türk Tarih Kurumu Basımevi), 645–57.

(1995) Old Assyrian *iṣurtum*, Akkadian *eṣērum* and Hittite GIŠ.ḪUR, in Th. van den Hout & J. de Roos (eds.) *Studio Historiae Ardens. Ancient Near Eastern Studies Presented to Philo H.J. Houwink ten Cate on the Occasion of his 65th Birthday* (Leiden: Nederlands Instituut voor het Nabije Oosten), 311–32.

(2003) *The Old Assyrian List of Year Eponyms from Karum Kanish and its Chronological Implications* (Ankara: Türk Tarih Kurumu).

(2008) Some Displaced Tablets from Kārum Kanesh (Kültepe) (kt 86/k 48, kt 86/k 204 and kt 91/k 539), *Altorientalische Forschungen* 35, 10–27.

Veenhof, Klaas & Eidem, Jesper (2008) *The Old Assyrian Period* (Freiburg: Universitätsverlag).

Veldhuis, Niek (2011) Levels of literacy, in K. Radner & E. Robson (eds.) *The Oxford Handbook of Cuneiform Culture* (Oxford: Oxford University Press), 68–89.

(2012) Cuneiform. Changes and developments, in S. D. Houston (ed.) *The Shape of Script. How and Why Writing Systems Change* (Sante Fe, NM: School for Advanced Research Press), 3–23.

(2014) *History of the Cuneiform Lexical Tradition* (Münster: Ugarit-Verlag).

Visicato, Giuseppe (2000) *The Power and the Writing. The Early Scribes of Mesopotamia* (Bethesda, MD: CDL Press).

von Dassow, Eva (2008) *State and Society in Late Bronze Age Alalaḫ under the Mittani Empire* (Bethesda, MD: CDL Press).

(2013) Piecing Together the Song of Release, *Journal of Cuneiform Studies* 65, 127–62.

von Schuler, Einar (1957) *Hethitische Dienstanweisungen für höhere Hof- und Staatsbeamte* (Graz: Archiv für Orientforschung Beiheft 10).

Waal, Willemijn (2011) They Wrote on Wood. The Case for a Hieroglyphic Scribal Tradition on Wooden Writing Boards in Hittite Anatolia, *Anatolian Studies* 61, 21–34.

(2012) Writing in Anatolia: The Origins of the Anatolian Hieroglyphs and the Introductions of the Cuneiform Script, *Altorientalische Forschungen* 39, 287–315.

(2014) Changing fate: Hittite *gulš-*/GUL-*š-*, ᵈ*Gulšeš*/ᵈGUL-*šeš*, cuneiform Luwian *gulzā*(*i*)-/GUL-*zā*(*i*-), hieroglyphic Luwian REL-*za-* and the *Kuwanšeš* deities, in P. Taracha & M. Kapełuš (eds.) *Proceedings of the Eighth International Congress of Hittitology* (Warsaw: Agade), 1016–33.

(2015) *Hittite Diplomatics. Studies in Ancient Document Format and Record Management* (Wiesbaden: Harrassowitz).

(2017) Anatolian hieroglyphs on Hittite clay tablets, in D. Kertai & O. Nieuwenhuyse (eds.) *From the Four Corners of the Earth. Studies in Iconography and Cultures of the Ancient Near East in Honour of F. A. M. Wiggermann* (Münster: Ugarit-Verlag), 297–307.

(2019) Fate Strikes Back: New Evidence for the Identification of the Hittite Fate Deities and its Implications for Hieroglyphic Writing in Anatolia, *Journal of Cuneiform Studies* 71, 121–32.

Wang, Haicheng (2014) *Writing and the Ancient State. Early China in Comparative Perspective* (Cambridge: Cambridge University Press).

Watson, Rita & Horowitz, Wayne (2011) *Writing Science before the Greeks. A Naturalistic Analysis of the Babylonian Astronomical Treatise MUL.APIN* (Leiden-Boston: Brill).

Weeden, Mark (2011a) *Hittite Logograms and Hittite Scholarship* (Wiesbaden: Harrassowitz).

(2011b) Adapting to new contexts: Cuneiform in Anatolia, in K. Radner & E. Robson (eds.) *The Oxford Handbook of Cuneiform Culture* (Oxford: Oxford University Press), 597–617.

(2011c) Hittite Scribal Schools Outside of Hattusa?, *Altorientalische Forschungen* 38, 116–34.

(2013a) A Hittite Tablet from Büklükale, *Anatolian Archaeological Studies* 18, 19–35.

(2013b) A Probable Join to the "Kırşehir Letter", *Anatolian Archaeological Studies* 18, 15–17.

(2014a) State correspondence in the Hittite world, in K. Radner (ed.) *State Correspondence in the Ancient World. From New Kingdom Egypt to the Roman Empire* (Oxford: Oxford University Press), 32–58.

(2014b) Anatolian hieroglyphs: Logogram vs. ideogram, in S. Gordin (ed.) *Visualizing Knowledge and Creating Meaning in Ancient Writing Systems* (Berlin: PeWe-Verlag), 1–20.

(2016a) Hittite Epigraphic Finds from Büklükale 2010–14, *Anatolian Archaeological Studies* 19, 81–104.

(2016b) Hittite scribal culture and Syria. Palaeography and cuneiform transmission, in S. Yamada & D. Shibata (eds.) *Cultures and Societies in the Middle Euphrates and Habur Areas in the Second Millennium BC, I. Scribal Education and Scribal Traditions* (Wiesbaden: Harrassowitz), 157–91.

(2017) The construction of meaning on the cuneiform periphery, in M. Wissa (ed.) *Scribal Practices and the Social Construction of Knowledge in Antiquity, Late Antiquity and Medieval Islam* (Leuven, Paris & Bristol, CT: Peeters), 33–60.

(2018) Hieroglyphic writing on old hittite seals and sealings? Towards a material basis for further research, in S. Ferrara & M. Valério (eds.) *Paths into Script Formation in the Ancient Mediterranean* (Roma: Edizioni Quasar), 51–74.

Wegner, Ilse (2007) *Hurritisch. Eine Einführung (2. überarbeitete Auflage)* (Wiesbaden: Harrassowitz).

Weidner, Ernst (1923) *Politische Dokumente aus Kleinasien. Die Staatsverträge in akkadischer Sprache aus dem Archiv von Boghazköi* (Leipzig: J. C. Hinrichs'sche Buchhandlung).

Werner, Rudolf (1967) *Hethitische Gerichtsprotokolle* (Wiesbaden: Harrassowitz).

Wilcke, Claus (2000) *Wer las und schrieb in Babylonien und Assyrien. Überlegungen zur Literalität im Alten Zweistromland* (München: Verlag der Bayerischen Akademie der Wissenschaften).

Wilhelm, Gernot (1986) Urartu als Region der Keilschrift-Kultur, in V. Haas (ed.) *Das Reich Urartu. Ein altorientalischer Staat im 1. Jahrtausend v. Chr.* (Konstanz: Universitätsverlag Konstanz), 95–113.

(1992) Zur babylonisch-assyrischen Schultradition in Ḫattuša, in *Uluslararası 1. Hititoloji Kongresi Bildirileri* (Çorum: Kültür Bakanlığının), 83–93.

(1994a) Hymnen der Hethiter, in W. Burkert & F. Stolz (eds.) *Hymnen der Alten Welt im Kulturvergleich* (Freiburg-Schweiz, Göttingen: Universitätsverlag Freiburg Schweiz), 59–77.

(1994b) *Medizinische Omina aus Ḫattuša in akkadischer Sprache* (Wiesbaden: Harrassowitz).

(1997) *Kuşaklı-Sarissa Band 1,1. Keilschrifttexte aus Gebäude A* (Rahden, Westf.: Verlag Marie Leidorf).

(2001) D Epische Texte. Das hurritisch-hethitische "Lied der Freilassung", *TUAT Ergänzungsheft*, 82–91.

(2005a) Zur Datierung der älteren hethitischen Landschenkungsurkunden, *Altorientalische Forschungen* 32, 272–9.

(2005b) Eine mittelhethitische topographische Beschreibung aus den Grabungen bei Sarıkale, *Archäologischer Anzeiger* 2005, 77–9.

(2009) Demographic data from the Hittite land donation tablets, in F. Pecchioli Daddi, G. Torri & C. Corti (eds.) *Central-North Anatolia in the Hittite Period. New Perspectives in Light of Recent Research* (Roma: Herder), 223–33.

(2010a) Remarks on the Hittite cuneiform script, in I. Singer (ed.) *ipamati kistamati pari tumatimis. Luwian and Hittite Studies Presented to J. David Hawkins on the Occasion of His 70th Birthday* (Tel Aviv: Tel Aviv University), 256–62.

(2010b) Ein Fragment mit hurritischen Gallenomina und der Beginn der hurritischen Überlieferung in Ḫattuša, in J. Becker, R. Hempelmann & E. Rehm (eds.) *Kulturlandschaft Syrien. Zentrum und Peripherie. Festschrift für Jan-Waalke Meyer* (Münster: Ugarit-Verlag), 623–35.

(2012) Šuppiluliuma I. und die Chronologie der Amarna-Zeit, in R. Hachmann, *Kāmid el-Lōz. 20. Die Keilschriftbriefe und der Horizont von el-Amarna* (Bonn: Dr. Rudolf Habelt), 225–57.

Winckler, Hugo (1907) Vorläufige Nachrichten über die Ausgrabungen in Boghaz-köi im Sommer 1907, *Mitteilungen der Deutschen Orient-Gesellschaft* 35, 1–59.

Withuis, Jolande (2016) *Juliana. Vorstin in een Mannenwereld* (Amsterdam & Antwerpen: De Bezige Bij).

Wittenberg, Hartmut (2017) Capture and management of ground and stratum water in the Hittite empire: Technology and cultural significance, in A. Schachner (ed.) *Innovation versus Beharrung. Was macht den Unterschied des hethitischen Reiches im Anatolien des 2. Jahrtausends v. Chr.? Internazionaler Workshop zu Ehren von Jürgen Seeher* (Istanbul: Ege Yayınları), 163–73.

Wolf, Maryanne (2007) *Proust and the Squid. The Story and Science of the Reading Brain* (New York: HarperCollins Publishers).

(2016) *Tales of Literacy for the 21st Century* (Oxford: Oxford University Press).

Woods, Christopher (2010) Visible language: The earliest writing systems, in Chr. Woods, E. Teeter & G. Emberling (eds.) *Visible Language. Inventions of Writing in the Ancient Middle East and Beyond* (Chicago: The Oriental Institute), 15–25.

Woolf, Greg (2009) Literacy or literacies in Rome?, in W. A. Johnson & H. N. Parker (eds.) *Ancient Literacies. The Culture of Reading in Greece and Rome* (Oxford & New York, NY: Oxford University Press), 46–68.

Yakubovich, Ilya (2008) Hittite–Luvian Bilingualism and the Development of Anatolian Hieroglyphs, *Acta Linguistica Petropolitana*, 4, 9–36.

(2010) *Sociolinguistics of the Luvian Language* (Leiden-Boston: Brill).

(2012) The Reading of Luwian ARHA and Related Problems, *Altorientalische Forschungen* 39, 321–39.

(2013–2014) The Luwian Deity Kwanza, *Aramazd* 8, 282–97.

(2015) Phoenician and Luwian in Early Iron Age Cilicia, *Anatolian Studies* 65, 35–53.

(2017a) The Slavic draughtsman, in B. Simmelkjaer, et al. (eds.) *Etymology and the European Lexicon* (Wiesbaden: Harrassowitz), 529–40.

(2017b) The Luwian title of the Great King, in A. Mouton (ed.) *Hittitology Today: Studies on Hittite and Neo-Hittite Anatolia in Honor of Emmanuel Laroche's 100th Birthday/Hittitologie Aujourd'hui: Études sur l'Anatolie hittite et néo-hittite à l'occasion du centenaire de la naissance d'Emmanuel Laroche* (Istanbul: Institut Français d'Études Anatoliennes Georges-Dumézil), 39–50.

Yalçıklı, Derya (2000) Zwei Bronzegabeln aus Zentralanatolien (mit einem Beitrag von Aygül Süel), *Istanbuler Mitteilungen* 50, 113–30.

Younger, K. Lawson (2014) The Scripts of North Syria in the Early First Millennium: The Inscription of Yariri (KARKAMIŠ A15b) Once Again, *Transeuphratène* 46, 169–83.

Index Locorum

Cuneiform Texts
ABoT 64, 169n.117
ABoT 65, 171n.128
ABoT 65 rev. 8, 319n.145
ABoT 2.292: 6, 204n.85
ATT 41 = 20.06, 61n.13
ATT 882/9 = 43.12, 207n.102
Ax of Ammuna, 60, 68n.37
Bronze Tablet, (Bo 86/299), 306
Bronze Tablet i 78, 296n.40
Bronze Tablet iv 21–25, 64n.21
HKM 12: 4–5, 299n.63
HKM 17 and 18, 298n.51
HKM 18: 22, 299n.60
HKM 21: 20–21, 261n.72
HKM 21: 22–24, 299n.64
HKM 22: 12–16, 261n.72
HKM 27, 298n.51
HKM 52, 299n.63
HKM 55: 36, 299n.57
HKM 56, 298n.51
HKM 56: 2, 299n.62
HKM 56: 7–12, 26–27, 261n.74
HKM 60, 4–8, 191n.24
HKM 62, 298n.51
HKM 71 left edge 1–3, 261n.73
HKM 72, 298
HKM 72: 34, 299n.57
HKM 72: 34–36, 300n.69
HKM 81: 29–32, 261n.70
HKM 116, 171n.128
IBoT 1.31 obv. 2–3, 12–15, 182n.33, 192n.28
IBoT 1.36 iii 1–5, 260n.69
IBoT 1.36 iii 1–11, 152n.39
IBoT 2.1 vi 13, 188n.14
IBoT 2.102 +, 204, 205
IBoT 2.102 rev. 4, 204
IBoT 2.131 obv. 21, 188n.14, 198n.55
IBoT 2.131 rev. 17, 196n.46
IBoT 3.101 obv. 4, 198
KBo 1.6 obv. 3–8, 257n.60
KBo 1.6 rev. 21–22, 314
KBo 1.11 rev.! 14–15, 66n.29
KBo 1.28 rev. 2–4, 357–352n.64
KBo 1.28 rev. 13, 317n.139
KBo 1.44 obv. 11–13, 160n.71
KBo 3.1 ii 15, 57n.1
KBo 3.1+ ii 31 and 33, 76n.23
KBo 3.1+ ii 46–49, 76n.21
KBo 3.3 iv 14, 317n.139
KBo 3.4 i 25–29, 146n.23
KBo 3.4 iii, 74–75, 59n.9
KBo 3.4 iv 44–48, 147n.24
KBo 3.7 i-ii 5–9, 96n.105
KBo 3.22 obv. 33–35, 28n.28
KBo 3.22 rev. 49–51, 27n.21
KBo 3.22 rev. 78–79, 357n.62
KBo 3.34 i 11–23, 86n.73
KBo 3.34 ii 15–23, 361n.74
KBo 3.34 iii 15, 17, 358n.65
KBo 3.38 obv. 25, 73n.11
KBo 3.40 obv. 10, 360n.72
KBo 3.57 iii 1, 75n.17
KBo 3.57 iii 19–20, 74n.16
KBo 3.59: 1–3, 75n.19
KBo 4.2 rev. 41–46, 207n.102, 264n.82
KBo 4.10, 306
KBo 4.10 rev. 21–24, 64n.21
KBo 4.11 rev. 39–41 and 45–46, 153n.48
KBo 4.12 obv. 5–11, 323n.166
KBo 4.14 i 25–26, 207n.102, 209n.111
KBo 5.1 iv 43, 317n.139
KBo 5.6, 246
KBo 5.6 iv 16–18, 147n.25, 246n.33
KBo 5.7, 78n.36
KBo 5.7 rev. 55, 81n.54
KBo 5.8 i 12–14, 147n.26
KBo 5.11, 328n.186
KBo 5.11 iv 27, 330
KBo 6.2 + KBo 22.62 iii 12–22, 88n.87
KBo 6.3 iii 19–25, 88n.87
KBo 6.6 i 19–32, 88n.87

KBo 6.34 + KUB 48.76 i 41–45 ii 1–4, 149n.29
KBo 7.7, 161
KBo 7.14, 45n.10
KBo 7.14 obv. 16, 73n.11
KBo 8.16, 151n.37
KBo 8.32 obv. 9–12, 295n.34
KBo 9.96, 197
KBo 10.1 rev. 14, 73n.13
KBo 10.2 i 15–21, 42n.5
KBo 10.2 iii 21, 73n.12
KBo 10.31 iv 29–34, 295n.37
KBo 10.47 c left edge 1, 317n.139
KBo 11.1 obv. 21, 198
KBo 11.1 obv. 21–22, 200n.62
KBo 11.1 obv. 21–24, 264n.85
KBo 11.1 obv. 41, 198
KBo 11.1 rev. 26, 330
KBo 12.38, 201n.71
KBo 12.38 ii, 364n.87
KBo 12.95 rev. 2–3, 316n.138
KBo 12.128 right col. 6–17, 193n.31
KBo 13.2, 163
KBo 13.18 right col. 4–5, 162n.79
KBo 13.58 ii 21–25, 229n.47
KBo 13.62 rev., 177n.21, 180
KBo 13.106 left edge, 317n.139
KBo 15.25 obv. 30–31, rev. 20–21, 201n.67
KBo 14.12 iv 33–39, 260n.67
KBo 14.86 iv 14–15, 248n.38
KBo 15.10 iv 3, 80
KBo 15.52 vi 39–47, 247n.36, 324n.167
KBo 15.52 vi 46–47, 313n.122
KBo 16.65 iv 5–9, 185n.4
KBo 17.65 +, 204n.85
KBo 17.65 + FHG 10 rev. 45, 204
KBo 18.82 obv. 9, 198, 261
KBo 18.151, 76n.25
KBo 18.179 v 9, 206n.97
KBo 18.181 obv. 15, rev. 30, 207n.102, 209n.112
KBo 19.28, 319n.144
KBo 19.28 obv. 1–7, 296n.44
KBo 19.37: 6, 76n.24
KBo 19.99 Seite b: 1–2, 79n.42
KBo 20.34 obv. 11–12, 201n.67
KBo 22.1: 4–6, 99n.114
KBo 22.1: 16–25, 76n.26, 216n.133
KBo 22.129 rev. 10, 317n.139
KBo 22.214 vi 3, 317n.139, 328n.186, 330
KBo 26.20 ii 39–41, 160n.72
KBo 26.178 iv 2, 3, 8, 330
KBo 26.178 iv 7, 310n.104
KBo 26.181: 2, 296n.41
KBo 26.181: 4, 204
KBo 27.40, 262n.78
KBo 28.51, 246n.28
KBo 28.54, 151n.37
KBo 28.65, 152n.41
KBo 28.82, 152n.41
KBo 28.108, 152n.41
KBo 30.15 iv? 1–7, 194n.35
KBo 31.1++ i, 333n.193
KBo 31.8 + KUB 30.42 iv 21–24, 333n.192
KBo 31.47 rev.? 7, 198
KBo 32.14 ii 42, 44, 201n.73
KBo 34.185 +KBo 20.61 i 1–4, 358n.66
KBo 34.195 rev. 5, 6, 330
KBo 35.200 iv 15, 330
KBo 35.260 left edge 1, 314n.128
KBo 39.43 iv 1, 2, 326 Fig. 13.1, 330
KBo 39.272: 8, 314n.131
KBo 40.345 iv 4, 307n.90
KBo 42.2 iv? 1–2, 313n.123
KBo 42.22 i 7, 305–11
KBo 42.28 vi, 315
KBo 42.28 vi 3–8, 315n.137
KBo 44.7, 152n.41
KBo 45.37 vi 1, 307n.90
KBo 48.273: 8, 198
KBo 59.111: 6, 307n.90
KBo 62.32, 152n.41, 165n.101
KBo 71.81, 27n.19
Kp 14/95 rev. 4–5, 199n.60
Kp 14/95 rev. 4, 198
Kp. 15/8+ i 25, 198
Kt k/k 4, 31n.36, 50n.25
Kt 90/k 360, 31n.36,37, 46n.14
KUB 1.16 iii 56–57, 74n.14
KUB 2.5, 250
KUB 2.5 i-vi, 277 Appendix 1
KUB 2.5 i-iii, 280 Fig. 12.7
KUB 2.5 vi 1–2, 277n.124
KUB 2.6 vi 1–4, 193n.32
KUB 2.9 vi 3–10, 194n.33, 249n.43
KUB 2.13 vi 32–37, 249n.40
KUB 3.1 i 16–17, 8n.14
KUB 4.1 iv 41, 317n.139
KUB 4.38, 331
KUB 4.38: 3, 4, 5, 6, 7, 329 Fig. 13.3, 330
KUB 4.53, 314, 320n.154
KUB 7.1 iv 15–16, 293n.24
KUB 7.20 rev. 6–7, 316n.138
KUB 8.1 iii 15–16, 162n.79
KUB 8.79, 151n.37
KUB 10.45 iii 12–14, 195n.40
KUB 10.96, 328n.186
KUB 10.96: 3, 4, 330
KUB 12.31, 331
KUB 12.31 rev. 19, 21, 207n.102
KUB 12.31 rev. 27, 330
KUB 13.2 i 8–10, 13–14, ii 42–43, 202n.75

KUB 13.2 iii 9–14, 92n.98
KUB 13.2 iii 21–22, 206n.101
KUB 13.2 iv 18–19, 191n.23
KUB 13.3 iii 10, 296n.41
KUB 13.4 ii 32–44, 190n.19
KUB 13.4 ii 51–52, 201n.70
KUB 13.6 ii 23–35, 190n.19
KUB 13.7 iv 3–7, 247n.34, 308n.96
KUB 13.35 iv 28–31, 294n.32
KUB 14.8 obv. 6–12, 263n.81
KUB 14.8 obv. 8–20, 235n.3
KUB 14.10 i 2–5, 245n.27
KUB 14.10 ii 1–14, 235n.3
KUB 14.13 column i end, 247 Fig. 12.1, 327, 328, 331
KUB 14.17 iii 21–23, 147n.27
KUB 15.31 iv 38–40, 244n.23
KUB 15.34 iv 55–57, 207n.102, 208n.105
KUB 15.42, 252n.52
KUB 17.6 i, 96n.105
KUB 17.18 iii 14–18, 193n.30
KUB 17.28 iv 59, 317n.139
KUB 19.37 ii 20–34, 147n.27
KUB 19.37 ii 31–32, 147n.27
KUB 19.55 rev. 38–42 + KUB 48.90: 6–10, 190n.22, 257n.61
KUB 20.24 obv. iii 6–15, 262n.78
KUB 20.59 v 1–6, 262n.77
KUB 20.76, 179
KUB 21.2 + KUB 48.95 i 3–9, 265n.86
KUB 21.5 i 2–6, 265n.86
KUB 21.38 obv. 17–20, 192n.27
KUB 22.60 i 17, 207n.102
KUB 23.92, 150n.35
KUB 23.103, 150n.35
KUB 24.1 + KBo 58.10 i 1–7, 245n.25
KUB 24.1+ iv 18, 245n.26
KUB 24.2 obv. 1–6, 245n.25
KUB 24.8 I 7–12, 115n.44
KUB 24.8 iv 13–18, 115n.45
KUB 25.1, 250
KUB 25.1 ii-vi, 277 Appendix 1
KUB 25.1 i-iii, 278 Fig. 12.6
KUB 25.1 vi 43–48, 277n.123
KUB 25.23 iv 60, 63–64, 309n.104
KUB 25.31 + KBo 55.263 obv. 8–9, 295n.35
KUB 25.32 columns iii-iv, 253 Fig. 12.2, 350
KUB 26.1 iv 49–53, 149n.31
KUB 26.43, 306
KUB 26.43 + rev. 35 and 36, 184n.3
KUB 26.71 obv. 21–24, 75n.19
KUB 26.79 i 15–17, 147n.27
KUB 26.91, 170n.119
KUB 26.92, 151n.37
KUB 27.59 iv 22 + KBo 45.168, 248n.38
KUB 28.4, 178 Fig. 9.2
KUB 29.8 iv 38–39, 244n.24
KUB 30.15+ obv. 21–23, 200n.66
KUB 30.33 iv 14, 308n.98
KUB 30.42+ iv 9–10, 332n.188
KUB 30.42+ iv 11, 332n.189
KUB 30.42+KBo 31.8 iv 9–30, 332n.190
KUB 31.49 left edge, 316n.138
KUB 31.68 obv. 5–6, 191n.24
KUB 31.84 iii 66–67, 202n.75
KUB 31.86 iv 6–7, 206n.101
KUB 32.19 + iv 50(?), 156
KUB 32.133 i 4–10, 294n.33
KUB 32.133 i 6–7, 154n.50
KUB 33.120 + KUB 48.97 + KBo 52.10 iv 30–32, 326n.177, 330
KUB 34.45 + KBo 16.63 obv. 11, 142
KUB 34.89 rev. 2–5, 295n.36
KUB 35.16 i-ii, 254n.53
KUB 35.18 i, 254n.53
KUB 35.133 i 24–30, 201n.68
KUB 36.98a 4–5, 28n.28
KUB 36.98b rev. 6, 357n.62
KUB 36.98b rev. 8–11, 75n.19
KUB 36.98 rev. 10, 188n.14
KUB 37.1, 162
KUB 38.1 i 32–33, 201n.69
KUB 38.1 iii 1, 296n.41
KUB 38.1 iii 2, 195
KUB 38.3, 179
KUB 38.3 ii 8–9, 201n.72
KUB 38.12, 196
KUB 38.12 i 11–18, 297n.46
KUB 38.19 rev. 1–2 + IBoT 2.102: 4–5, 205n.94
KUB 40.77, 150n.35
KUB 41.4 ii 2, 17, 184n.2
KUB 42.11 ii 3, 207n.102, 209n.113
KUB 42.22 rt. col. 13, 206n.96
KUB 42.100 i 17, iii 22, 204
KUB 42.100 i 17–19 + KBo 26.181: 1–3, 205n.90
KUB 42.100 i 19, 198
KUB 42.100 i 22, ii 6, 264n.83
KUB 42.100 iii 26, iv 3, 33, 264n.83
KUB 42.100 iv 10, 204
KUB 42.100 iv 34, 204
KUB 42.103 iii? 13–14, 199n.58
KUB 42.103 iii? 14, 198, 200n.65
KUB 43.50 + KUB 12.27 rev. 28–32, 207n.102,103, 264n.82
KUB 43.55 ii 11–21, 203n.79
KUB 43.55 v 1–6, 208n.107
KUB 43.58, 252n.52
KUB 43.77 rev. 3, 5, 330
KUB 44.24 vi 4–13, 249n.44
KUB 44.61, 328n.186

KUB 44.61 left edge 4, 312n.117, 330
KUB 45.79 rev.? 18–19, 207n.102, 208n.106
KUB 46.34 ii 5, 327 Fig. 13.2, 327, 331
KUB 50.6 iii 12, 198
KUB 50.6 iii 16–21, 199n.61
KUB 50.6 iii 18, 198, 200n.62
KUB 52.68 iii 31, 41, 328n.185
KUB 52.89: 3–4, 188n.14, 190n.21, 198n.55
KUB 55.39 i, 254n.53
KUB 55.48 i 16, 204
KUB 55.48 i 16–17, 205n.91
KUB 55.181: 6, 198
KUB 57.91 i 4, 204n.85
KUB 58.7 ii 22–23, 200n.63
KUB 58.7 ii 23, 198
KUB 58.11 obv. 11, 263n.79
KUB 58.38, 262n.78
KUB 58.43 i, 254n.53
KUB 60.161 ii 36–40, 193n.30
KuSa 1 and 2, 171n.122
RS 16.249, 228n.44
RS 17.28, 343, 344 Fig. 14.2, 350, 359
RS 17.62 + 17.237, 33n.44
RS 17.109, 350, 359
RS 17.231, 350, 359
RS 17.251, 349, 350, 359
Sword of Tuthaliya I, 63, 68n.44, 247
VBoT 24 iv 38, 330
VBoT 114 obv. 3, 207n.102

Unpublished Cuneiform Texts

Bo 2710, 263n.79
Bo 3289: 12’, 204, 205n.93
Bo 3295 iii 7, 204
Bo 3617 i 16–17, 203n.78
Bo 3785 iv 6–7, 314n.127
Bo 7103: 6, 198
Bo 69/200, 152n.41
Bo 86/299, see under Bronze Tablet
Bo 97/9 (+), 275n.113
Bo 2004/1: 31–34, 310n.104
Bo 2006/9, 165n.101
310/b, 274n.110
332/b, 274n.111
383/b, 274n.110
645/c, 274n.111
1253/c, 274n.111
1335/z (+), 275n.113
1523/c, 274n.111
1600/c, 274n.111
39/e, 274n.109
434/e, 274n.111
51/g +, 271n.103
29/k, 45n.10
67/k, 274n.111
3005/k + 132/x, 275n.113
48/l, 220n.5
2015/l +, 275n.113
171/m, 274n.111
234/m, 274n.111
118/n, 274n.111
119/p, 274n.111
228/p, 167n.108
1371/u, 79n.43
797/v: 1–4, 149n.29
896/z +, 275n.113
Kp 14/95 rev. 4, 198
Kp 14/95 rev. 4–5, 199n.60
Kp 15/8 + i 25, 198
OyT 09/1, 166n.105
VAT 13019b iv 19, 20, 330

Anatolian Hieroglyphs

ALEPPO, 176
ALEPPO 1, 128, 175, 176n.8, 353, 361, 369, 370
ALEPPO 7, 353, 361, 369, 370
ANKARA Bowl, 362, 370
ARSUZ 1 and 2, 362, 363
Beran 1967: no. 125, 345 Fig. 14.3
Beran 1967: no. 134, 346n.14
BEYKÖY, 176
BOĞAZKÖY, 176n.7
BOĞAZKÖY 1, 252n.51, 254 Fig. 12.3
BOĞAZKÖY 4, 348n.27
BOYBEYPINARI, 363
BOYBEYPINARI IA §11, 361n.76, 369, 370
BOYBEYPINARI IIID 2, 368, 371
CEKKE, 368
ÇALAPVERDI 2 §2?, 368
ÇIVRIL, 176
Dinçol & Dinçol 2008: nos. 10, 16, 25, 346n.14
Dresden seal, 357 Fig. 14.9, 357
Emar seals, 372
EMIRGAZI I-V, 176n.7
FRAKTIN, 176n.8
Herbordt 2005: no. 382, 347 Fig. 14.4a
Herbordt 2005: no. 476b, 347 Fig. 14.4b
IVRIZ fragment 2, 362, 363
JISR EL HADID 4, 362, 363, 364
KARABEL, LATMOS, 176
KARABURUN, 363
KARABURUN §14, 361, 369
KARADAĞ-KIZILDAĞ, 176
KARAHÖYÜK §19, 355, 371
KARAKUYU, 176n.8
KARATEPE 1 LI, 367n.100, 367
KARATEPE 4, 362, 363, 365
KARKAMIS A4b, 362, 364

KARKAMIS A4b §6, 362n.81, 363
KARKAMIS A 6 §§24–29, 366n.94, 369
KARKAMIS A11 §§19–25, 366n.93, 367n.96, 369
KARKAMIS A11b+c §22, 366n.94, 367n.96
KARKAMIS A15b §19, 364, 371
KARKAMIS A 26 c, 366n.94
KARKAMIS A 31+ §15, 366n.94, 369
KINIK BOWL, 354 Fig. 14.6, 354, 369, 370
KIZILDAĞ, see KARADAĞ
KULULU 3, 363, 364
KULULU 3 §1, 363n.85
KULULU 8, 368
KULULU lead strip 1, 368, 369
MEHARDE and SHEIZAR, 362n.80, 363
NIŞANTAŞ, 176
RS 17.28, 344 Fig. 14.2
SIRKELI, 176n.8
SÜDBURG, 176n.8
SÜDBURG §§1a and 18, 175n.3
Tarsus seal no. 25, 355 Fig. 14.7, 355
TOPADA, 363, 364
TOPADA §§18 and 20, 368
TOPADA §39, 362
YALBURT, 176
YAZILIKAYA, 176
Ras Shamra seals, 374
SBo 1.90, 346n.14
SBo 1.91, 343 Fig. 14.1, 346n.12
SBo 2.130, 213 Fig. 10.4

General Index

/f/-sounds
  in Hattian, Palaic, Hurrian, 107

Acemhöyük, 36
adaptation
  of writing system, 105–10, 259
aide-mémoire, 72, 77, 84, 96, 150, 151, 338
Akkadian
  in the charters, 110–13
  use of, 63–9
Alaca Höyük, 169
Alalah, 169, 353
Alalah (VII), 31, 40–51, 61, 64, 77, 106, 207
Alalah VII, 39
Aleppo. *See* Halpa
Alişar Höyük, 29
Alluwamna, 61, 68, 71, 78
Ammuna, 57, 60, 61, 65, 67, 68, 75, 77, 84, 103, 110, 144, 184
ANA GIŠ.ḪUR=*kan ḫandan*, 249, 251, 276
ANA PĀNI/PĀNI PN, 309, 317
Anitta, 6, 7, 27–37, 38, 40, 67, 100, 126, 184, 351, 357
ankh, 130, 344
Anumherbi, 27, 31
Anuwanza, 249, 293, 306, 307, 310, 311, 312, 315, 316, 330, 331
apprentices. *See* scribes
Appu, 115
archival, 242
archives, 81, 225, 273, 290, 377
  definition, 237
Arnuwanda I, 61, 67, 68, 79, 112, 140, 142, 143, 149
Arnuwanda II, 142, 156
Arnuwanda III, 176, 291, 312
Arslantepe, 36, 133, 225, 379
Arzawa, 39, 130, 140–1, 143, 157, 170, 236, 265, 288
Assyrian. *See* Old Assyrian
audience, 21, 75, 86, 93, 96, 113, 114, 116, 145, 147, 154, 160, 183, 220, 262, 274, 360
Aztecs, 35

bookkeeping, 16, 19, 36, 97–8, 105, 118, 144, 165, 169, 182, 202, 207, 238, 293, 294
boustrophedon. *See* reading direction
Büklükale, 125, 127, 170, 348
bullae, 81, 152, 177, 187, 218–33

charters, 59–69, 71, 77–83, 87, 97, 102, 110–13, 117, 118, 142, 143, 152, 165, 166, 167, 174, 184, 190, 217, 218–30, 239, 243, 268, 269, 274, 314, 346
Chief Scribe. *See* scribes, chief scribes
Chief Wood-Scribe. *See* scribes, chief wood-scribes
colophons, 81, 164, 240, 246, 247, 249, 256, 263, 292, 293, 326, 328, 330, 335, 337
consonants
  short vs. long, 105
contrasigillum, 227
copying, 246–8
correspondence. *See* letters
Cretan. *See* hieroglyphs
cretulae. *See* bullae
cult rituals. *See* festivals
cuneiform
  centralization, 170, 171, 377
  stability, 377, 380
cursivization
  hieroglyphs, 212

depositions, 151, 239, 240, 335
determinatives, 52, 259, 296
^{d}GUL-*šeš*, 202
dictation, 244
diglossia, 181, 376
digraphia, 181
dissemination, 92, 145, 148
dossiers, 83, 205, 223, 260
drama, 96, 157
drawings, 177, 237
ductus, Syrian, 31, 33, 34, 44, 45, 60, 66, 67, 99

ecology, 26, 38, 378
edicts, 148–52, 239
editing, 249–56
Emar, 165, 169, 174, 258, 345, 348, 350, 355, 359, 372, 375
eschatocol, 82, 83
Eskiyapar, 127, 170
exempla, 152, 257, 258

festivals, 152–5, 239, 242, 249, 296, 335, 339
findspots, 265–76
firing. *See* tablets
fraud and forgery. *See* seals

Gilgamesh, 143, 160, 163, 336
GIŠ.ḪUR. *See* tablets
gloss wedges, 259
Glossenkeil. *See* gloss wedges
graffiti, 12, 59, 63, 67, 84, 98, 127, 176, 184, 213, 265, 351, 352
GUL-*š*- "to mark", 214
gulzattar, 197–204
GUL-*zattar*. *See* gulzattar

Halpa, 39, 175, 314
Hanikuili, 79, 83
Hantili II, 61, 62, 68, 79
ḫatiwi(ya)-, 195
Hattian, 6, 7, 8, 12, 26, 51, 96, 103, 107, 116, 117, 118, 134, 142, 153, 164, 171, 173, 182, 239, 332, 380
Hattusa
  changes, 101
Hattusili I, 4, 38–51, 59, 61, 63, 68, 72, 73, 74, 75, 84, 89, 91, 92, 94, 100, 101, 113, 114, 142, 144, 145, 148, 243, 322
Hattusili III, 21, 65, 121, 143, 145, 148, 150, 159, 164, 176, 235, 238, 246, 289, 290, 306, 312, 315, 323, 339, 340
  Annals, 148
  Apology, 145
ḫazziye-, 76, 216
hieroglyphs
  Anatolian, 2, 12, 13, 17, 18, 34, 135, 144, 167, 168, 173–83, 184–217, 221, 252, 291, 302, 303, 305, 375–7, 380
    Egyptian influence, 129
    origins and development, 361–5
  Cretan, 129
  L.326, 213, 341
  origin and development, 120–34
historiography, 144, 239, 245
homophony, 51
Hurrian, 8, 12, 26, 31, 71, 103, 107, 114, 115, 117, 118, 139–41, 142, 143, 159, 160, 163, 171, 182, 238, 239, 242, 266, 296, 320, 321, 325
Huzziya, 39, 57, 63, 68, 79, 87
Huzziya II, 71
hymns. *See* prayers

Idrimi, 353
illiteracy, 31, 34, 49, 72, 101, 228, 347
  illiterate, 3, 4, 30, 34, 35, 65, 100, 260, 261, 324, 380
Illuyanka myth, 95
Inandık, 170
ink, 187, 212
inscriptions
  building, 176
instructions, 87, 102, 117, 143, 148–52, 239, 244, 251, 290, 335
inventories
  cult, 155, 167, 171, 205, 238, 239, 241
  palace storerooms, 166, 239, 240, 296
  tablet, 264
  tablets, 239, 241, 331–7
ištarniyaš appan tarnumaš, 249, 251, 255, 276
iṣurtum, 188, 203

k/gaštarḫait/da, 196
k/kurt/da-, 204
Kaman-Kalehöyük, 132, 233, 348
Kanesh, 7, 15, 18, 24–36, 38, 40, 42, 45, 51, 85, 98, 113, 122, 123, 133, 342
  Kanesh 1a, 25, 38
  Kanesh 1b, 25, 26, 27, 31, 33, 34, 36, 38, 42, 45, 98, 123
Karkamish, 174, 236, 258, 343, 365, 375
Kayalıpınar, 127, 140, 166, 170, 177, 197, 199
Kizzuwatna, 59, 63, 68, 70, 71, 76, 102, 117, 118, 130, 139, 140, 142, 143, 157, 159, 164, 247, 289, 313, 323, 332, 335
Konya-Karahöyük, 36, 123, 124, 133, 342
Korucutepe, 174
Kültepe. *See* Kanesh
Kumarbi, 143, 163
Kuruntiya, 64, 190, 226, 227, 246, 289, 290, 306, 310
Kussar, 27, 38, 40
  Kussara, 7, 31, 32
Kuşsaray, 170

L.326. *See* hieroglyphs
Labarna, 4, 7, 31, 36, 38–51, 58–63, 66, 67, 68, 72, 85, 87, 89–93, 99, 101, 102, 113, 118, 228, 265, 310
labels, 81, 239
Landschenkungsurkunden. *See* charters
laws, 239
  Hittite, 103
Laws, Hittite, 87–94, 103

letters, 150, 170, 171, 238, 240, 242, 245, 258, 259, 299
LĒ'U, 207–9
lexical lists, 14, 84, 97, 143, 159, 163, 171, 238, 239, 292, 324, 335, 336
library, 92, 157, 160, 265, 272, 273, 333, 336, 337, 377
Linear A and B, 129
lists, 166, 168
literacy, 71, 72, 73, 77, 78, 84, 92, 119, 171, 245, 260, 293, 341, 347, 371, 380
literati. *See* scholars
literature
  in the vernacular, 113–16
liver models, 161
logographic reading, 133
Luwian, 2, 6, 7, 8, 12, 18, 26, 30, 51, 103, 116, 118, 121, 127, 130, 134, 144, 153, 162, 172, 173, 175, 179–83, 196, 198, 200, 211, 212, 214, 239, 291, 301, 321, 360, 363, 375, 376, 380, 380

Maşat Höyük, 80, 81, 141, 150, 168, 170, 217, 240, 297, 319
Maya, 35
memorization, 337–40
mirror invariance, 131
Mittani, 140, 143
Mittannamuwa, 235, 287, 289, 308, 311–16, 322, 323, 324, 326, 335
Mixtecs, 35
Mursili I, 4, 21, 38–51, 57, 59, 70, 72, 73, 74, 85, 89, 101, 118, 145, 148, 176
Mursili II, 25, 26, 33, 59, 65, 92, 114, 132, 142, 143, 146–8, 154, 156, 159, 175, 207, 215, 228, 234, 242, 245, 256, 260, 263, 264, 296, 312, 313, 323, 324, 327, 335, 338, 353, 376
Mursili III. *See* Urhitessub
Muwatalli I, 71
Muwatalli II, 21, 65, 143, 175, 176, 200, 256, 264, 265, 287, 288, 312, 315, 322, 353
myth, 171
mythology, 239

oaths, 148–52, 239
Old Akkadian, 40, 160
Old Assyrian, 12, 15, 18, 24–37, 40, 41, 45, 51, 58, 67, 72, 87, 98, 101, 109, 123, 124, 125, 202, 203, 204, 341, 379
Old Babylonian, 31, 40–50, 172, 293, 299, 317, 319, 328
Old Script corpus, 116
omens, 161, 239, 324, 335
oracles, 155, 156, 167, 171, 238, 239, 240, 241, 323, 335
orality, 71, 86, 90, 96–100, 114, 145
Oymaağaç, 166, 170, 206, 241

Palace Chronicles, 84, 85, 86, 87, 88, 89, 90, 91, 93, 97, 99, 100, 142, 143, 360
Palaic, 8, 12, 103, 107, 116, 117, 118, 134, 153, 182, 239, 321, 380
parkui tuppi, 249, 251, 252, 276
parzaki(š), 206
Pithana, 27, 28, 33
Piusti. *See* Wiusti
Political Testament, of Hattusili I, 73, 77, 87
polyphony, 51, 53, 106
polyvalence. *See* polyphony
population size, 175
prayers, 155–7, 239, 242, 245
Proclamation, of Telipinu, 39, 57, 58, 70, 75, 76, 77, 84, 89, 90, 93, 102, 145, 148
Puduhepa, 156, 164, 166, 176, 191, 192, 241, 247, 289, 309, 313, 323, 335
Purushattum, 26, 27

Ramses II, 21, 150, 191, 192, 258, 287, 288, 289, 290, 322
ration lists, 166
reading, 259–63
  out loud, 262
  silent, 261
reading direction
  boustrophedic, 132, 135
  dextroverse, 135
  vertical arrangement, 135
record management, 19, 81, 82, 83, 97, 263
recycling, 81, 97, 167, 168, 226, 273, 275, 276, 320
retroacta, 242, 263
ritual
  royal funerary, 154
rituals, 155, 239, 324, 335
Rus, 35, 172

Sammeltafeln, 83, 151, 208
Samuha, 140
Sapinuwa, 101, 140, 144, 171, 287, 319
Satanduhepa, 127, 129
scholars, 322–40
scholarship, 157–64, 239
scribe(s), 315–19
scribes. *See* copying, editing, reading
  Akkadian names, 300
  apprentices, 248, 313–15, 319
  chief scribes, 311–13
  elite, 305–11
  graffiti, 213–14
  on seals, 301–5, *See* Excursus in Chapter 14
  organization, 315–19

societal status, 297–301
wood-scribes, 187, 195, 210, 263, 294–7, 318
seals, 35, 61, 65, 81, 102, 121–34, 152, 173–4, 181, 211, 218–33, 243, 291, 341, *See* scribes, on seals
fraud and forgery, 227–32
reference collections, 230
tabarna seals, 61, 78
semasiography, 12, 122, 124, 133
Sipazidi, 248, 306, 307, 308, 311, 324
Song of Release, 114, 143
standardization
signs, 106
state archives, 152, 223, 243
stream of tradition, 238
style, 85, 86, 90, 91, 101, 125, 145, 146, 148, 172, 360
undermarking, 86, 93
styli, 5, 76, 177, 211, 216, 261, 342
Suppiluliuma I, 59, 128, 134, 141, 142, 145, 146, 147, 156, 174, 175, 176, 220, 224, 259, 260, 263, 360
Suppiluliuma II, 128, 144, 224, 238, 291, 364, 375

tabarna. *See* Labarna
tablet
wood, 209, 226
tablets
bronze, 147, 216, 226, 246
collections, 246, 258
firing, 184, 222
GIŠ.ḪUR, 204–5, 252
GIŠ.ḪUR*tuppi?*, 206
gold, 226
iron, 226
lead, 144, 167, 168, 169, 179, 368
retrieval of, 81
silver, 226
total number of, 144, 273
wood, 182, 204–5, 210, 320
Tahurwaili, 59, 68, 71
tallying, 202, 203
Talmisarrumma, 256, 314
Tapikka. *See* Maşat Höyük
Taprammi, 252, 350, 354, 359, 374
Tarhunaradu, 170
Tarhunmiya, 261, 298, 299
Tarhuntassa, 287, 288, 375
Tarsus, 169, 174, 354, 355
Tawagalawa-Letter, 32
Tel-el-Amarna, 170
Telipinu, 10, 39, 57, 58, 59, 61, 64, 67, 68, 70–90, 92, 93, 94, 101–3, 117, 118, 127, 133, 139, 141, 142, 145, 146, 148, 224, 245, 286, 332–5, 346
Tell Afis, 169
Tell Kazel, 169
Tell Nebi Mend, 169
texts
cadastral, 168, 176
hippological, 239
monolingual Sumerian and Akkadian, 162
scholarly. *See* scholarship
socio-economic and legal, 97, 165–9
Tikunani, 42, 60, 165
trade diaspora, 30, 31, 34
training
scribal training, 313, 319, 320, 337
training, scribal, 292, 293
treaties, 148–52, 217, 239, 242, 244
Tunip-Tessub, 42, 60, 63, 72, 118
tupala-, 368
tuppi, 184, 191, 368
Tuthaliya I, 21, 59, 60, 61, 63, 65, 68, 71, 79, 80, 84, 118, 126, 127, 129, 139–46, 149, 164, 173, 184, 216, 220, 357, 360
Tuthaliya II, 21, 127, 140, 141, 164
Tuthaliya III, 139, 141, 287, 312
Tuthaliya IV, 64, 65, 143, 150, 176, 184, 226, 227, 228, 231, 238, 246, 251, 257, 290–2, 306, 310, 312, 315, 364

Ugarit, 169, 174, 343, 345, 349, 350, 355, 374, 375
Uhhazidi, 236
Ulmitessub, 64, 246, 306
Ulu Burun, 186
Urartu, 30
Urhitessub, 21, 65, 176, 288, 312, 323
Urshu-Text, 32, 87, 99
Uşaklı Höyük, 170

vidimus, 143, 256, 257, 288, 290
vows, 156, 166, 167, 238, 239, 241

Walmu, 190, 226, 257, 290
Walwazidi, 247, 289, 308, 311–16, 323, 324, 351
Warshama, 27, 31
Wiusti, 27
wooden tablets. *See* tablet, wood
word space, 106, 108, 259

Yassı Höyük, 170

Zalpa, 38, 73, 84–92, 97, 100, 114
Zukrasi Text, 44